HAUS EBERLANZ

THE ROUGH GUIDE TO
NAMIBIA
WITH VICTORIA FALLS

Written and researched by
Sara Humphreys

With additional contributions by
Rob Humphreys

**ROUGH
GUIDES**

Contents

Introduction to

Namibia

A vast land of mesmerizing landscapes, abundant wildlife and an astonishing array of natural wonders, Namibia promises adventure. Its defining feature is the Namib, an ancient desert that runs the entire 1500km of the country's wind-lashed coastline. Encompassing towering dunes, dramatic mountains and lichen-encrusted gravel plains, it's populated by desert-adapted beasts, with flamingos and colonial German architecture bringing splashes of colour to the waterfront. Capital Windhoek has a distinctly European feel, but you won't want to linger too long; from here tempting arterial roads reach out to geological wonders in the south, and the beguiling Kalahari to the east, inhabited by some of Africa's oldest peoples. To the north lie game-rich reserves and the majority of Namibia's elusive population, from where the country's lush panhandle lures you to within touching distance of Victoria Falls.

Arguably the most impressive **natural wonder** in Namibia is the Fish River Canyon, in the far south, which affords breathtaking views across a deep serpentine chasm in the Earth's crust, while in the northeast, the impressive sandstone Waterberg Plateau stands sentinel over the surrounding bushveld. At the very north of Namibia, the species-rich wetlands of the Zambezi Region, a 450km arm of luxuriant subtropical forest that stretches out above Botswana towards Zimbabwe and Victoria Falls, provide a wholly different landscape.

While, traditionally, tourists have been drawn to Namibia for its wilderness terrains, the country is now also attracting attention for its **wildlife**; specifically, the increasing numbers of rare large mammals that are thriving in the semi-arid areas. Beyond the game-heavy confines of Etosha – Namibia's premier national park – the world's largest concentrations of free-roaming cheetah stalk the plains, while desert-adapted elephant and black rhino lumber along the valleys and riverbeds of northwest Namibia. In many cases these beasts

ABOVE COLONY OF CARMINE BEE-EATERS

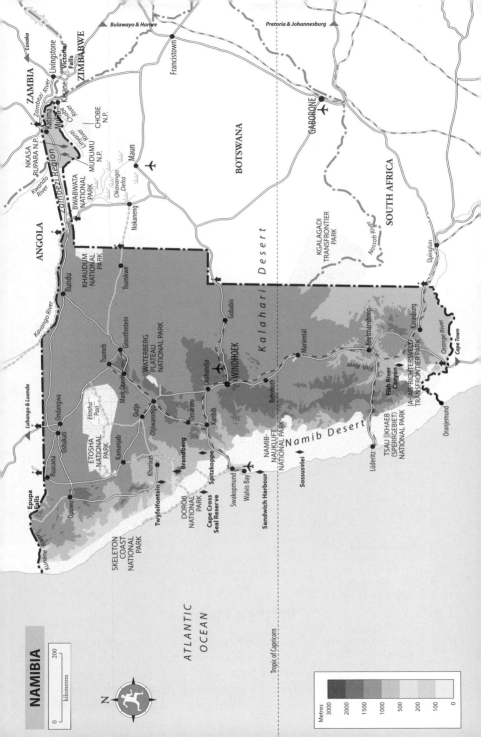

FACT FILE

• Namibia is the second **least densely populated** country in the world after Mongolia, with only 2.68 **inhabitants** per square kilometre.

• **Rugby union** has been played in Namibia since 1916, and the national team has qualified for the last five world cups.

• On account of low population density and low light pollution, the country's glittering **night sky** is one of the world's top **stargazing** destinations.

• Though **social inequalities** are slowly improving, the richest ten percent of the population – including the six percent white minority – receive over half the national income.

• The Kunene Region has the world's greatest concentration of **black rhinos**.

• Over a tenth of the Namibian population – from the Nama, Damara and San peoples – speak a **click language**.

• **Etosha Pan** is Africa's largest **saline pan**, a vast white sheet visible from space.

• Namibia's all-time greatest athlete, **Frankie Fredericks**, held the indoor world 200m record for eighteen years before Usain Bolt broke it in 2014.

are protected by conservationists working hand in hand with local communities – communities that are also beginning to open up to visitors, who can learn more about these cultures and lifestyles.

The Namib also hosts many extraordinary succulent plants and dune-dwelling endemics – especially lizards – that have adapted to the harsh conditions, and which have featured in many a nature documentary. In complete contrast, the lush, subtropical Zambezi Region holds almost three-quarters of the country's bird species and many large mammals not seen elsewhere in the country.

As with most other countries in Africa, Namibia's socio-political landscape has been indelibly shaped by **colonialism**, specifically the regimes of Germany and then South Africa, which resulted in the imposition of **apartheid** and the Namibian **War of Independence** that lasted over twenty years. While the adverse effects were considerable – and some still endure – it's true to say that Namibia's **cuisine** has benefited from its colonial past, from cream-laden German cakes, tasty filled *brötchen* and good coffee, to the dried, cured meats favoured by South Africans. Namibia was one of the last countries in Africa to gain **independence** – in 1990 – and it has taken time for the government to realize the country's tourism potential, just as foreign tourists have been slow to appreciate Namibia's haunting scenery, fascinating wildlife and rich cultural diversity. Now, Namibia is becoming established on the tourist map: high-quality, affordable **lodges and campgrounds** are sprouting up, often in conjunction with local conservancies; rural communities are inviting visitors to learn about their cultures, traditions and modern-day challenges; and new ways of experiencing Namibia are constantly being devised, from skydiving or hot-air ballooning over the desert to tracking rhino or kayaking with crocs.

Where to go

International flights arrive at **Windhoek**, the country's capital and transport hub, conveniently located in the centre of Namibia. A small city, more akin to a provincial town, it's a pleasant spot to wander around for a couple of days, taking in the few modest sights, browsing the shops

RIGHT OWAMBO WOMAN FISHING IN AN OSHANA

and sampling the local cuisine. From here, you need to plot your route carefully; although the tarred and gravel roads are maintained to high standards in Namibia, the distances are vast, which means you can easily end up spending most of your time getting to places. That said, much of Namibia's appeal lies in its vast, uninhabited landscapes, which are best appreciated by driving through them.

Most first-time visitors, and those short of time, travel a circuit round central and northern Namibia, but with a quick detour – by Namibian standards – southwest to the **Sossusvlei** area of the **Namib-Naukluft National Park**, where the towering apricot sand dunes that change colour with the light are truly spectacular. From here many visitors head northwest to enjoy the milder climate and colonial architecture of the country's top coastal resort, **Swakopmund**, which lies almost due west of Windhoek. Though no beach hangout – it's too cold to swim most of the year – it's a fascinating place, surrounded by dunes that you can explore on foot, on horseback or on a quad bike; it's also rapidly emerging as a centre for **adventure sports**, such as skydiving and sand-boarding. A short excursion south takes you to **Walvis Bay**, the country's main port, where you can consort with seals, dolphins and pelicans on the lagoon.

Moving north, organized tours and self-drive travellers often take in the **Cape Cross seal colony** before cutting inland via the desolate, mist-shrouded **Skeleton Coast National Park** to **Damaraland**, where some of the country's most evocative scenery lies. At the southerly limit of this region, the domed **Erongo Mountains** and the pointed **Spitzkoppe** – both composed of giant burnished granite slabs – provide wonderful hiking and

birdwatching opportunities, as well as some examples of San rock paintings. Far better preserved paintings are to be found at the **Brandberg**, Namibia's largest massif, further north, while the continent's oldest rock engravings at **Twyfelfontein** give fascinating insights into the spiritual world of some of Africa's oldest inhabitants. The wonderful lodges in the area make the most of the picturesque scenery and offer the chance to spot desert-adapted elephant and rhino (see box below).

It's a bit of a detour to the mountainous northwest, where the rocky, reddish-brown land and the frontier town of Opuwo are home to the semi-nomadic **Himba**; a further two-hour drive north takes you up to the scenic **Epupa Falls**, on the Kunene River, which marks the border with Angola. Many miss out this area and head straight to **Etosha National Park** – indisputably the top wildlife-watching spot – where they spend a few days before returning to Windhoek, sometimes via the scenic **Waterberg Plateau**. With more time, a journey

THE GIANT DESERT SURVIVORS

Roaming the weathered mountains, gravel plains and broad, mopane-shaded sandy riverbeds of Namibia's arid Kunene Region, some of the planet's most hunted animals are fighting for survival. This inhospitable environment is home to the world's largest numbers of critically endangered **black rhino** – distinguishable from the white rhino on account of its hook-shaped upper lip – as well as swelling numbers of desert-adapted **elephants** and **lions**. While the elephant and rhino roam inland, the lions more often prowl the dunes of the Skeleton Coast. All three majestic beasts share the ability to **go without water** for several days – or weeks, in the case of lions – provided they manage a gemsbok or ostrich kill.

They have also all been brought back from the brink of extinction through the combined efforts of dedicated professional conservationists, committed local communities, government support and – more surprisingly – from **tourism**. Volunteer programmes and sensitive rhino and elephant tracking, often on foot, are being promoted by the various foundations, often in collaboration with private lodges and community conservancies. Community involvement, above all, is critical to conservation success, since they are bearing the brunt of this increase in elephant and lion populations, as they compete for the scarce food and water resources.

For further **information** contact the Save the Rhino Trust (SRT; ⓦsavetherhinotrust.org), Elephant-Human Relations Aid (EHRA; ⓦdesertelephant.org) and Desert Lion Conservation (ⓦdesertlion.info). Wilderness Safaris (ⓦwilderness-safaris.com) a pioneer in this tourism–conservation synergy, offers some of the best tracking experiences in their Desert Rhino, Hoanib Skeleton Coast and Damaraland camps (see p.201, p.203 & p.198) – the last one being almost wholly community-owned and -managed.

Author picks

Our author has driven, hiked and paddled the length and breadth of Namibia, across deserts, over mountains, down rivers and through the bush. These are some of her favourite travel experiences.

Close encounters with wildlife While Etosha deservedly ranks as one of Africa's finest national parks, the Kwando Core Area of the Bwabwata National Park, in the Zambezi Region (p.286), can offer more unexpected encounters with nature and more abundant birdlife – and without the crowds.

Desert panoramas You don't need to scale great heights to be rewarded with mesmerizing desert vistas that stretch to the horizon: clamber up a simple kopjie, take on the Spitzkoppe (p.192) or drive up the Spreeghoogte Pass (p.116).

Kayaking down the Orange River Spend four days paddling through lovely scenery, enjoying campfire dinners and sleeping on the riverbank (p.161).

Scale the Brandberg The slog to the top is not easy, but the rewards are huge: phenomenal views and pristine ancient rock art that few people have seen (p.194).

A braai in the bush The wilderness campsites of the northern Namib-Naukluft (p.324) and Spitzkoppe (p.193) provide perfect locations to enjoy some of the country's game meat – cooked to perfection over a campfire.

Meet the Ju|'hoansi San It's worth spending several days with a San community (p.274), learning from the ancestors of one of the continent's most ancient peoples, and experiencing the stillness of the desert.

Sleep out under the stars Namibia's clear night skies sparkle and amaze in equal measure. Do it in style in one of the lodges around Sossusvlei (p.113), or be truly adventurous and camp out on top of the Brandberg (p.194).

> Our author recommendations don't end here. We've flagged up our favourite places – a perfectly sited hotel, an atmospheric café, a special restaurant – throughout the guide, highlighted with the ★ symbol.

LEFT DESERT-ADAPTED LION **FROM TOP** JU|'HOANSI SAN (P.274); KAYAKING ON THE ORANGE RIVER (P.161); WILDERNESS CAMPSITE AT THE SPITZKOPPE (P.193)

northeast to the verdant **Zambezi Region** in the panhandle reaps many rewards: lush broad-leaved forests, gliding rivers and plentiful wildlife roaming in unfenced reserves. The less-visited far south is also worth the trek for its remarkable geological fault, the **Fish River Canyon**, from where it's a few hours' drive to the quaint historical German town of **Lüderitz** on the coast. A trip to the sinuous **Orange River**, which marks the border with South Africa, provides welcome respite from the relentless heat of the interior: an opportunity to paddle through beautiful scenery and indulge in some gentle birdwatching.

Visitors with more time should consider heading southeast to gaze at the rippling red dunes of the **Kalahari**, even popping over the South African border into the **Kgalagadi Transfrontier Park**, where vast herds of large mammals follow ancient migration routes. Alternatively, round **Tsumkwe**, in the northern reaches of this semi-desert, an increasing number of San communities are opening up to visitors, keen to share their ancient traditions and survival skills.

When to go

A semi-arid country possessing a climate generally characterized by **low rainfall** and **low humidity**, Namibia is a year-round destination, though the searing summer temperatures (Oct–Feb), which can exceed 40 degrees celsius in some areas, deter many European visitors from holidaying at this time.

The **peak tourist season** in Namibia is in winter – **June to September** – which coincides with the **dry season**: there is virtually no rain and no cloud, so you'll witness stunning night skies. It's also easier to spot **wildlife** during these months as vegetation is

sparse and animals are forced to congregate at established waterholes. Days are sunny but average maximum daytime temperatures are more tolerable – 20–30 degrees, depending where you are – though they plummet at night: at the height of winter (June–Aug) they can drop to between 5 and 10 degrees, even dropping below zero in the desert and more mountainous areas. The downside of visiting in the Namibian summer is that lodge prices and visitor numbers are often higher, although, since the country is so vast, only Etosha, Swakopmund and Sossusvlei get really crowded.

Although climate change is making weather patterns less predictable, the **rains** usually start in earnest in late November or early December, transforming the landscape into a pale green carpet – where sufficient rain falls – and tailing off in March or April. Rain is highly localized, and generally occurs in the late afternoon as intense thundery showers, so is unlikely to spoil your trip. The countryside is more scenic at this time; animals are breeding; and the birdlife is at its best, with many migrants present. On the other hand, wildlife-spotting is much more difficult as the vegetation is denser, and, with food more readily available, animal movements are less predictable since they are not restricted to waterholes. After heavy rain, gravel roads can become impassable.

Generally, Namibia is hotter and drier in the **south**, and wetter in the far **north** and across the Zambezi Region. Indeed, the far northeast and the Zambezi Region possess a **subtropical climate**, receiving on average close to 500mm of rain between December and February. In the months of September and October, before the main rains arrive, the humidity and temperatures build and it can be very uncomfortable. In contrast, much of the country receives very little precipitation, even in the rainy season. The nearer the coast you get, the less rainfall there is – under 15mm annually in some places – though a thick morning **fog** hangs in the air for much of the year on the coast itself, which can make it feel unpleasantly cold.

AVERAGE MONTHLY TEMPERATURES AND RAINFALL

	Jan	Feb	March	April	May	June	July	Aug	Sept	Oct	Nov	Dec
WINDHOEK												
Max/min temp (°C)	30/17	28/16	27/15	26/13	23/9	20/7	20/6	23/9	29/11	29/15	30/15	30/16
Rainfall (mm)	77	73	81	38	6	1	1	0	1	12	33	47
WALVIS BAY												
Max/min temp (°C)	23/15	23/16	23/15	24/13	23/11	23/9	21/8	20/8	19/9	19/11	22/11	22/14
Rainfall (mm)	0	5	8	2	2	1	1	3	1	0	0	0
KEETMANSHOOP												
Max/min temp (°C)	35/19	34/19	32/17	28/14	24/10	21/7	21/6	24/8	27/11	30/13	33/16	35/17
Rainfall (mm)	18	30	34	16	6	2	1	1	1	6	11	13
RUNDU												
Max/min temp (°C)	31/19	30/18	31/18	30/15	29/10	27/6	27/6	30/9	33/14	35/17	33/19	32/19
Rainfall (mm)	128	147	96	37	2	0	1	1	1	15	67	83
VICTORIA FALLS												
Max/min temp (°C)	30/18	29/18	30/17	29/14	27/10	25/6	25/6	28/8	32/13	33/17	20/18	30/18
Rainfall (mm)	168	126	70	24	3	1	0	0	2	27	64	174

LEFT HERERO WOMAN MAKING CRAFTS, OPUWO

19

things not to miss

It's not possible to see everything that Namibia has to offer in one trip – and we don't suggest you try. What follows is a selective and subjective taste of the country's highlights, including cultural encounters, spectacular wildlife, unforgettable activities and extraordinary desert landscapes. Each highlight has a page reference to take you straight into the Guide, where you can find out more.

1

2

3

4

7

8

9

10

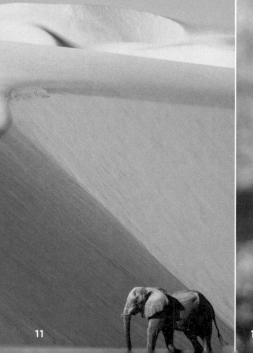

11

12

13

10 SWAKOPMUND
Page 206

Not your average seaside resort, with palm-lined boulevards fronting freezing seas, and some excellent food accompanied by German-style beer.

11 DESERT-ADAPTED WILDLIFE
Pages 24, 34 & 36

Namibia's least hospitable landscape is home to desert-adapted lion, black rhino and elephant.

12 ANCIENT LIFESTYLES
Page 56

Learn about the ancient traditions, and modern-day challenges, of the San or the Himba, by spending time in a rural settlement.

13 HOT-AIR BALLOONING
Page 113

An unforgettable way to appreciate the vastness and beauty of the desert: catch sunrise as you float above the dunes.

14 WILDERNESS LODGES
Page 114

An array of desert lodges, like *Little Kulala* near Sesriem, affords you the chance to get close to nature without sacrificing home comforts.

14

15 A SUNSET CRUISE
Page 283

There's no better way to end the day than with a magical sunset cruise along the Zambezi.

16 QUIVER TREES
Page 149

Southern Namibia's most emblematic and distinctive plant makes a splendid photo – whatever the angle.

17 WINDHOEK
Page 76

Namibia's scenically situated capital offers a chance to unwind in one its many homely guesthouses, restaurants and vibrant bars.

18 WATERBERG
Page 174

Towering above the surrounding plains, this impressive sandstone plateau offers varied, lush vegetation, great birdwatching and superlative views from the top.

19 LÜDERITZ AND KOLMANSKOP
Pages 124 & 132

Thanks to its isolated coastal location, Namibia's best preserved colonial town is relatively tourist free. Don't miss the abandoned mining town of Kolmanskop, partly submerged in sand.

Itineraries

THE GRAND TOUR

The distances are too vast to cover all the country's highlights in one tour, but starting in the capital and finishing in Victoria Falls you could manage most of the well-known sights by road in three weeks – longer if you want to linger.

❶ **Windhoek** Namibia's quaint capital, tucked away in the Central Highlands, is a good place to get your bearings, browse for crafts and sample the local cuisine. **See p.76**

❷ **Fish River Canyon** Peer over the canyon rim, hike along the valley floor or relax in the hot springs of this jaw-dropping geological wonder. **See p.154**

❸ **Lüderitz** Admire the town's well-preserved German colonial architecture, and visit nearby Kolmanskop, where the abandoned diamond-mining buildings are gradually being swallowed by sand. **See p.124**

❹ **Sossusvlei** A photographer's paradise; be sure to catch sunrise or sunset across the dunes and hike over the sand to the ghostly vleis, spotted with skeletal trees. **See p.112**

❺ **Swakopmund** Namibia's main seaside resort offers fascinating desert tours, adrenaline sports on the dunes, and the chance to wine, dine and relax. **See p.206**

❻ **Twyfelfontein** The country's first World Heritage Site contains a vast collection of San rock engravings, with curious geological formations nearby. **See p.195**

❼ **Etosha** Set aside several days to explore Etosha National Park, where a day- or night-time stakeout of a waterhole will get you up close to a host of wildlife. **See p.241**

❽ **Zambezi Region** The lush riverine vegetation makes the perfect backdrop to a sunset river cruise, and a chance to see some stunning birdlife and large animals not present in the rest of the country. **See p.285**

❾ **Victoria Falls** Marvel at these iconic falls, which also play host to a vast range of activities: from bungee-jumping to high tea, white-water rafting to fine dining, canoeing with crocs to breakfast birdwatching. **See p.308**

THE ACTIVITY CIRCUIT

You'd need close to three action-packed weeks to fit in all these activities, longer if you want to do the whole five-day canoe trip down the Orange River.

❶ **Orange River** Float for a day or paddle for five days down the scenic Orange River, camping out on sandbanks under the stars and cooking on campfires. **See p.161**

❷ **Fish River Canyon** Hike this brutal five-day trail in the bowels of the canyon, scrambling over boulders and cooling off in rock pools, before collapsing in the hot springs of |Ai-|Ais. **See p.156**

❸ **Aus Mountains** Rent a bike and hit the trails in the scenic, underexplored Aus Mountains; the truly energetic might consider the annual two-day Klein-Aus Challenge. **See p.123**

❹ **Naukluft Mountains** For an exhilarating bird's-eye view of the desert, balloon over the Namib at dawn, soaring above the rippling dune sea, with the brooding Naukluft Mountains in the distance. **See p.113**

❺ **Swakopmund** Get your blood pumping in Namibia's adventure capital: sand-boarding and quad biking in the dunes, skydiving into the desert or surfing the Atlantic waves. **See p.215**

ABOVE BLUE WILDEBEEST IN THE KGALAGADI TRANSFRONTIER PARK

❻ The Brandberg A strenuous climb up this imposing massif is rewarded with stunning ancient rock art, peerless desert vistas and the chance to sleep under the sparkling stars. **See p.194**

❼ Victoria Falls The adrenaline vortex of Africa offers any number of ways to set your pulse racing: white water rafting down the Zambezi; ziplining across the Batoka Gorge, or peering over the Falls themselves. **See p.305**

WILDLIFE AND CONSERVATION

Bank on three weeks to get round all these sites; if you're short of time, you could omit the Zambezi reserves – and save yourself an extra 1000km driving – though you'd miss out on the country's best birdwatching.

❶ Kgalagadi Transfrontier Park No cross -border vehicle fees prevent you from driving into this vast South African-Botswana park for a couple of days, to catch large herds of migrating wildebeest, hartebeest and eland. **See p.152**

❷ Namib-Naukluft The dunes of the Namib are home to some extraordinary desert creatures, while the spring-fed kloofs of the Naukluft

Mountains nourish some surprisingly lush vegetation, and plenty of birdlife. **See p.106**

❸ Walvis Bay and Sandwich Harbour Spend a glorious morning kayaking on the lagoon, surrounded by dolphins, seals and pelicans, before an exhilarating drive over the dunes to the avian-rich wetlands of Sandwich Harbour. **See p.220 & p.225**

❹ Rhino tracking and desert-adapted elephants Some Damaraland lodges offer unique opportunities to get close to desert-adapted elephants and black rhino. **See p.201**

❺ Etosha Namibia's premier national park, and the place to spot large mammals in abundance, though it boasts a dazzling array of birds and reptiles too. **See p.241**

❻ Zambezi reserves The small reserves of Bwabwata, Mudumu and Nkasa Rupara boast prolific birdlife and large mammals that you won't see elsewhere in Namibia. **See p.287, p.288 & p.289**

❼ Waterberg This striking sandstone table mountain protects rare roan antelope as well as rhino, and is within reach of the educational Cheetah Conservation Fund sanctuary. **See p.174**

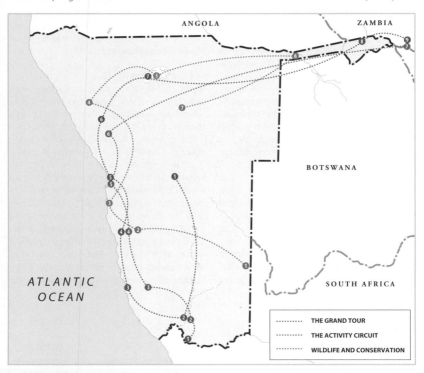

ANGOLA

ZAMBIA

ATLANTIC OCEAN

BOTSWANA

SOUTH AFRICA

········· THE GRAND TOUR
········· THE ACTIVITY CIRCUIT
········· WILDLIFE AND CONSERVATION

Wildlife

While Namibia is unable to compete with vast quantities of megafauna that roam the plains of East Africa, a surprising range of animals manages to survive in the country's harsh arid landscapes, including some extraordinary desert-adapted creatures, both large and small. Namibia boasts around 200 species of terrestrial mammal – 114 of which can be found in Etosha National Park – over 700 birds, and tops the continent for lizard diversity with over 160 varieties.

The photos and accompanying notes in this field guide provide a quick reference to help you identify some of the most common, sought-after or intriguing land mammals in Namibia, alongside a few other desert creatures and a handful of the country's most emblematic birds. The notes give pointers as to where and when you might find these animals.

PRIMATES

Not counting humans, there are three main primates you are likely to encounter in Namibia: the Chacma baboon and the vervet monkey are both highly visible both inside and outside the reserves. Far less visible, but highly engaging, is the nocturnal lesser bushbaby, a relative of the lemurs of Madagascar.

CHACMA BABOON *(Papio ursinus)*
These unmistakable large primates live in large troops – usually between 50–100 – led by a dominant male and are governed by a complex social hierarchy in which gender, precedence, physical strength and kinship determine status. While the female hierarchy is established matrilineally, male dominance is often in flux, and there are often mixed-sex friendships within the chacma baboon troop. Grooming forms part of the social glue and you'll commonly see baboons lolling about while performing this activity. At night baboons take refuge from predators on kopjies, cliff tops, among rocks or up a large tree. Though they prefer fruit, baboons are highly opportunistic omnivores and will just as readily tuck into a scorpion or a newborn antelope. Males can be intimidating and are bold enough to raid vehicles or accommodation in search of food, undeterred by the presence of people. They are particularly widespread in central Namibia, and notorious in Naukluft.

VERVET MONKEY *(Chlorocebus pygerythrus)*
Vervet monkeys need to be near water and prefer savannah woodlands, so are mainly located in the Zambezi Region in the north of Namibia, and round the Orange River in the south, though some populations inhabit the rocky terrain near Tsumeb and Grootfontein. Like baboons, these smaller primates also live in complex social groups, in which grooming each other's silvery-grey coat is a core activity.

Similarly too, the female hierarchy is inherited and male dominance fluctuates, depending on a range of factors including age, physical stature and allies within the troop. Mature males are notable for their bright sky-blue testicles, and both females and males possess cheek pouches in which to store food. Roosting in trees at night, vervets forage for food during the day; their mainly vegetarian diet is supplemented with small invertebrates, birds and rodents, and like their larger relatives, they too are not afraid to raid campground food stores.

LESSER BUSHBABY *(Galago senegalensis)*
The lesser bushbaby is more often heard than seen, being a vocal, nocturnal creature. Arboreal and extremely agile, they can jump great distances between branches. Preferring acacia woodland and riverine forests, their distribution is limited to northern Namibia, from northern Kunene eastwards to Etosha, Waterberg – where they are frequent visitors to the restcamp – and the Zambezi Region. Their diet is mixed as they lick the sap of trees and eat fruit, but they also feed on moths, grasshoppers, beetles and the like. They are attractive creatures, with soft fur, bushy tails, large saucer-like eyes and highly mobile and sensitive outsized ears. Living in small family groups (usually 2–7), they gained their name on account of their frequent nocturnal wailings, which serve to mark territory or communicate within the group, and which resemble the cries of a baby. Females usually give birth to twins, sometimes twice a year.

CATS

Apart from lions, which are the only truly sociable examples, and cheetahs, which often hunt in pairs or small groups, cats are solitary carnivores that generally prefer to move around at night, though they can also be seen at twilight. During the day, they escape the heat of the sun by resting up in, or under, a tree.

LION *(Panthera leo)*

Given that lions tend to top most visitors' wildlife-spotting wish list, it's fortunate that they're relatively easy to spot, being large – the shaggy maned male usually weighs in at 250kg – and lazy, prone to lolling about in the shade of a large tree for much of the day. The only truly gregarious cats, lions can live in prides of up to 30, though more typically are found in groups of 11–13 comprising a handful of related females, their offspring and one or two males. The females do almost all the hunting, generally at night, and are notoriously inefficient, with only around a thirty percent success rate, and only if operating as a group. Males don't hunt at all, if they can help it, but look after the cubs during the pursuit and then tuck in when the prey's been killed, though a large percentage of the lion's diet is scavenged. There are around 600–800 lions in Namibia, mainly in the north; the largest concentration is found in Etosha, with smaller populations in Kunene – including desert-adapted lions (see box, p.8) – Khaudum and the Zambezi Region.

LEOPARD *(Panthera pardus)*

The most numerous, yet elusive, and arguably the most beautiful of Namibia's cats, is the leopard. Usually on the prowl at night, its excellent camouflage – typically a beige, tawny or golden coat dappled with square or round "rosettes" – allows it to creep to within a couple of metres of its prey before lunging and gripping the animal in its vice-like jaw. To safeguard the kill from other predators, the leopard often uses its powerful muscles to drag its meal – which can be well over its body weight – up a large tree, where it also rests up during the day, perfectly hidden among the foliage. Though rarely sighted on account of their camouflage and secretiveness, leopards are widespread across Namibia. They are able to live in a range of habitats, from mountainous areas to low-lying plains, though they prefer plenty of tree cover. Leopards are particularly numerous on farms in central and northern areas, where they are frequently hunted too, on account of their penchant for tucking into livestock. Your best chance of seeing one is in the private reserve of Okonjima, near Otjiwarongo (see p.174), where leopards wear radio collars and can be tracked.

CHEETAH *(Acinonyx jubatus)*

Fabled for being the land's fastest mammal, which can top 70kph for short bursts, the cheetah is built for speed, with a light streamlined body, long legs and a small head. Its lean, spotted form, together with its characteristic tear-like marks down its face, distinguish it from the more muscular leopard, with which it is sometimes confused. Moreover, unlike leopards, cheetahs don't climb trees; they range across open land, hiding in tall grass where possible, and relying on pace to catch their prey, hoping to knock it off balance since they lack the strength of lions and leopards to bring it down by force. Generally hunting alone or in small social groups during the cooler parts of the day, they usually succeed with every second hunt. Namibia is said to host the world's largest cheetah population – an estimated 3500, the vast majority inhabiting commercial and communal farmland – as well as the world's leading cheetah research centre near Otjiwarongo (see box, p.178). In addition to here, and Etosha, cheetahs are most easily sighted in one of the small private reserves, like *Hobatere Lodge* (see p.244).

CARACAL *(Caracal caracal)*

Resembling a small Eurasian lynx with pointed, black-tufted ears, and long canines, the agile, beige-coloured caracal is rarely seen. A supreme nocturnal and solitary hunter, it preys on small antelope – often much heavier than itself – rodents and birds, sometimes snatching them out of the air, as they attempt to take flight. It prefers dry savannah and scrubland, though is occasionally arboreal and occurs everywhere in Namibia except the western coastal desert strip.

SERVAL *(Felis serval)*

Long-legged, small-headed and mainly spotted, the elegant serval bears some resemblance to a cheetah, though it is more diminutive, with some streaking near the head. It also has acute hearing, thanks to its large upright ears that possess distinctive white marks on the back, which help show the way to young kittens through long grass or reeds. A primarily nocturnal yet also crepuscular hunter, it inhabits the moister savannah regions of northeast Namibia, needing water within reach. Its diet is varied; though specializing in rodents, it also feasts on small mammals, frogs and fish, and, like a caracal, it can leap into the air to kill birds in flight.

DOGS AND HYENAS

Namibian members of the canid family include the elusive wild dog, two kinds of fox and two species of jackal. The hyena family, which also includes the aardwolf, is more closely related to dogs than cats.

AFRICAN WILD DOG (*Lycaon pictus*)
Brought to the verge of extinction primarily through hunting, but also disease and their need for a vast territory, the African wild dog remains one of the continent's most threatened predators, though it is making a cautious comeback: the current estimated population is around 6000. Since one of their last strongholds is northern Botswana, African wild dogs occasionally cross the border into the Zambezi Region and Khaudum and Tsumkwe areas; attempts to introduce them into Etosha have so far failed. Also known as painted hunting dogs on account of their colourful blotchy markings, they prefer relatively open areas where they can use their speed to catch antelope. Wild dogs are the most successful of the world's large predators as they hunt intelligently in substantial packs and are able to maintain speeds of around 50kph for some distance. Sociable animals, they live in groups of up to 20, and the entire pack shares the kill as well as parenting duties, regurgitating the food to give to the pups. If you're lucky enough to spot them, it is likely to be during the cooler temperatures of early morning or late afternoon.

BLACK-BACKED JACKAL (*Canis mesomelas*)
Commonly sighted sloping off at dusk and dawn, alone or in pairs, the black-backed jackal is a versatile, opportunistic omnivore that relies heavily on scavenging – look out for them around the rubbish bins in Etosha. The black-backed jackal is widespread throughout Namibia, except for the Zambezi Region, on account of its preference for more arid terrain, including the desert. It is distinguishable from the less common side-striped jackal, which inhabits the lusher parts of the Zambezi Region, by its black saddle flecked with white, to which it owes its name.

BAT-EARED FOX (*Otocyon megalotis*)
The bat-eared fox can easily be distinguished from jackals or the Cape fox (*Vulpes chama*) by its outsized ears, Zorro-like mask and diminutive size. Like other dog relatives, it is an omnivore, eating small rodents, lizards, fruit and insects. However, it favours harvester termites, like the aardwolf, which is where its radar dish-like ears come in handy, helping it to triangulate the position of invertebrates underground, before digging them up with its paws. Though relatively widespread in open scrub and savannah land, they are most commonly seen foraging in a monogamous pair – sometimes accompanied by offspring

– in the southern Kalahari. Mainly nocturnal, they are also active during the day during the cooler months.

SPOTTED HYENA (*Crocuta crocuta*)
Often dismissed as mere scavengers – they can smell a carcass from several kilometres away – spotted hyenas are actually formidable hunters, either alone or in small groups. They are often seen where zebra and medium-sized antelope – their favourite meals – are to be found. The spotted hyena's hunched appearance belies the fact that it is the second-largest predator after lions, and is similarly sociable, living in loose clans led by the larger females. Numbers range from three to five in desert areas to over 20 where food is more plentiful. Possessing exceptionally strong teeth and jaws, spotted hyenas are the most efficient consumers, eating almost every part of their prey including bones and hide. They are most active at night, when their distinctive whooping call counts as one of the eeriest sounds of the bush. Once widely distributed, they are now more common in northern areas, including the Skeleton Coast, though they also inhabit the central Namib.

BROWN HYENA (*Hyaena brunnea*)
The more elusive brown hyena is the dominant predator along the northern coast and drier parts of the Namib, but its range extends to the dry savannah areas inland. Smaller than the spotted hyena, with a shaggy dark brown coat and a beige mantle, the brown hyena also differs in that it scavenges the vast majority of its food, and is a common visitor to the Cape Cross seal colony at dusk. It also lives in generally smaller clans, ranging from a female and her offspring to groups of up to 12, though brown hyenas will generally look for food alone.

AARDWOLF (*Proteles cristata*)
Resembling and related to the striped hyena (not found in Namibia), the otherwise sandy-coloured aardwolf, with a similarly sloping back, bushy tail and dorsal mane, is much smaller. The aardwolf is further distinguished from other hyenas by its insectivorous diet and particular preference for termites, using its broad sticky tongue to lap them up en masse – over 200,000 in one night. Active at night, they rest up during the day in burrows, often ones abandoned by aardvarks. Fairly widely if thinly distributed, aardwolves are absent from the coastal desert strip and the forests of the Zambezi Region. Their timidity means they are rarely sighted.

SMALL CARNIVORES

SMALL-SPOTTED OR COMMON GENET
(Genetta genetta)
Once encountered, never forgotten, the sinuous small-spotted genet has beautiful markings: a spotted body with a long black spine, and a soft, striped tail with a white tip. This distinguishes it from the less prevalent large-spotted genet (*Genetta tigrina*), which flaunts a black-tipped tail. Genets prefer drier woodlands but can be found in riverine habitats too. The small-spotted genet is found throughout Namibia, barring the western desert areas, whereas the larger relation is restricted to the Zambezi Region. An accomplished climber, the small-spotted genet sometimes rests up in a tree during the day, but prefers to unwind in a burrow or rocky crevice, just as it inclines towards hunting on the ground. Though technically a carnivore, whose diet encompasses amphibians, insects, rodents, reptiles and birds, it also takes eggs and fruit and can sometimes be spotted scavenging around game lodges; Okakuejo Camp in Etosha boasts frequent sightings. It is almost exclusively a solitary nocturnal animal, pairing up only for mating.

AFRICAN CIVET *(Civettictis civetta)*
Formerly, African civets were famously hunted, and later kept in captivity, for their anal gland secretions (musk) used in perfumes, which they rub onto trees to mark territory. Almost raccoon-like in appearance, this stubby-legged nocturnal predator boasts a coarse fur covered in blotches and stripes and an impressive erectile dorsal crest that rises to intimidating effect when it's threatened. Mainly carnivorous, the civet also feeds on fruit and carrion and can digest poisonous invertebrates such as millipedes that many other animals avoid. A versatile climber, swimmer and terrestrial hunter, it is rarely observed in the dense savannah, woodland and riverine areas of the Zambezi Region that it inhabits.

HONEY BADGER *(Mellivora capensis)*
Sounding like a character out of *Winnie the Pooh*, the low-slung honey badger gains its name from the eponymous liquid that it steals from bees' nests with the help of its symbiotic partner in crime, the equally aptly named honey guide. This small bird leads the badger to the nest, which the badger then rips open for the two to share the spoils. Despite having a sweet tooth, the honey badger is predominantly a carnivorous forager, using its ferocious claws to dig out food, often shadowed by pale chanting goshawks or black-backed jackals on the lookout for scraps. Mainly nocturnal, it is also nomadic, ranging over a large territory and digging a new den in the ground or in a hollow log or tree stump most nights. It is also highly aggressive: when threatened, it emits a foul smell through its anal glands to deter would-be predators, and has been

known to attack much larger mammals. Widely, if sparsely, distributed across diverse habitats in Namibia – though absent from the Namib – it is a known visitor to the rubbish bins of Halali Camp in Etosha.

BANDED MONGOOSE *(Mungos mungo)*
There are mongooses aplenty in southern Africa in terms of numbers and diversity, and Namibia is no exception, harbouring over a quarter of the world's 34 species – some solitary, some highly sociable. The fairly stocky, dark-brown, banded mongoose is the most frequently observed, living in highly gregarious, chattering groups (generally between 10 and 30). They build warrens in gullies, thickets and rock shelters, but most commonly in abandoned termite mounds in the dry open scrub and grassland across the country. In addition to termites and beetles, they'll feed opportunistically on small rodents, reptiles or amphibians, steal eggs or take fruit – foraging in loose groups, though generally for their own food. Also quite widespread is the smaller, sociable, sandy-coloured yellow mongoose, with a whitish tip on its tail, which co-habits in colonies of up to 20 but generally forages alone. The dwarf mongoose, which, as the name suggests, is the smallest of Africa's mongooses, also favours old termite mounds for its den. It is a similar colour to its banded relative, but without the stripes and only half its size and weight. All three species are diurnal.

MEERKAT OR SURICATE *(Suricata suricatta)*
Popularized and anthropomorphized in television and film, the meerkat – a relative of the mongoose – is renowned for its complex social behaviour. Typically, they live in clans of 10–15, though groups can be much larger; some will be scratching around foraging for food, noisily chattering and squabbling, while others babysit the young ones, groom each other, and, most characteristically, keep guard duty. For this, they stand tall on their hind legs on raised ground, looking out for predators; a sounding of the alarm prompts a mass scarper for cover, into their underground den, if nearby. Although mainly insectivorous, they also eat small rodents, amphibians, reptiles, plants and even scorpions, as they are immune to their venom. Meerkats are distinguishable from the heavier banded mongoose by their silvery-greyish brown coloration and the dark rings round their eyes. Inhabiting Namibia's semi-arid scrubland and savannah, and even the dry riverbeds of the western desert, they are notoriously skittish, which makes them difficult to observe. Your best chance is just after sunrise when they often start the day by stretching up on their hind legs to warm themselves in the sun, and at dusk. *Bagatelle Kalahari Game Ranch* (see p.144) has a clan semi-habituated to humans, and they are prominent in the Kgalagadi Transfrontier Park (see box, p.152).

LARGE ANTELOPE

While travelling through Namibia, antelope are the large mammals you'll most commonly come across. Around twenty types of antelope roam the various landscapes of Namibia, which is just over a quarter of all African antelope species.

ELAND (*Taurotragus oryx*)
Africa's largest antelope, the beige-coloured eland, is built like an ox and moves with the slow deliberation of one, though it is also a superb jumper. Both male and female possess large dewlaps and shortish, spiralling horns. You'll see herds browsing, though they also graze when grass is available. Once fairly widespread, populations are now restricted to Waterberg, Etosha and private reserves in north-central Namibia, and over the border in South Africa (see box, p.152).

KUDU (*Tragelaphus strepsiceros*)
The kudu – or more accurately the greater kudu – is the most commonly observed of the large antelope in Namibia. The male is a magnificent beast: sporting a greyish-brown or tawny coat with vertical white stripes, it possesses a shaggy mane, a white chevron across the nose, and is adorned with spiralling horns that reach 1.5m in length at maturity. The more diminutive female, which is also striped and has large ears, lacks horns. Known for their athleticism, kudu can easily vault over a 2m fence. Males are solitary or move around in small bachelor herds. Females co-exist in larger herds (6–12) with their young, which males join in the breeding season. Kudu prefer savannah woodland, but can also manage more rocky mountainous terrain. They are widely distributed across Namibia, though absent from the Namib.

ORYX OR GEMSBOK (*Oryx gazella*)
Featuring on Namibia's coat of arms, this archetypal desert antelope is unmistakable, with its pale greyish coat, and tall straight horns, combined with striking black and white facial markings and "leggings". Able to go for long periods without water, the oryx is also capable of tolerating extremes of over 40°C; the brain is kept cool by a supply of blood from the nose. When grass and leaves aren't available they'll dig up roots or eat !nara melons. They can be seen lying by the roadsides across the Namib and Kalahari, and they are also an incongruous feature of the centre of Oranjemund.

SABLE ANTELOPE (*Hippotragus niger*)
The majestic jet-black male sable antelope has distinctive white facial markings and underbelly, and fabulous curved horns. Young males start off chestnut brown, like the smaller females, but turn black after three years, when they are expelled from the female herd by the bull. Predominantly diurnal browsers, they range in herds of 10–30 over savannah woodlands and grasslands. In Namibia they are present in pockets of the northeast, with populations in the Zambezi Region, notably in Mahango National Park, and in Waterberg and Khaudum.

ROAN ANTELOPE (*Hippotragus equinus*)
Sometimes confused with a juvenile or female sable antelope, the endangered roan antelope is of a slightly larger build, with smaller horns and a lighter greyish-brown in colour. Grazing on medium and longish grasses, the roan antelope also likes to be near water. Harem herds typically comprise 5–16 females accompanied by a dominant male, which defends them and his territory. In Namibia the roan is rare, existing only in parts of the Zambezi Region, Khaudum, and where it has successfully been reintroduced in Waterberg and western Etosha.

WATERBUCK (*Kobus ellipsiprymnus*)
Instantly recognizable by the white target ring on its rump, the male waterbuck has a shaggy coat and U-shaped horns, which the female lacks. As the name suggests, it needs to be close to water, so in Namibia it is an uncommon sighting, only found in the wetlands of the eastern Zambezi Region, and on farmland in north-central Namibia. Predominantly grazers, they feed mainly in the cool daytime hours. They are sociable animals, gathering in herds of between 6 and 30; the males either lead a territorial herd of females or maintain a territory that is visited by wandering female herds.

RED HARTEBEEST (*Alcelaphus buselaphus*)
A rather awkward-looking creature, the red hartebeest can reach speeds of up to 65kph. Both males and females possess small horns and a smart, gleaming reddish-chestnut coat. You'll find them grazing during the day in semi-arid bush savannah and sometimes open woodland in northern and eastern Namibia. Like gemsbok, they cool the blood to the brain by taking it from their nasal membranes. The red hartebeest is easily confused with the darker and even faster tsessebe (*Damaliscus lunatus*), which can be distinguished by its fawn "socks" and the fact that it only occurs occasionally in the Zambezi Region.

BLUE WILDEBEEST (*Connochaetes taurinus*)
Famed for their migrations in vast herds across the plains of East Africa, blue wildebeest nevertheless congregate in relatively large herds by Namibian standards (20–40). Also known less commonly as the brindled gnu, their heavy heads and shaggy manes are a common sight grazing the savannah plains. They are at their most active during the day but will also graze after dark. Keenly preyed on by lions and hyenas, wildebeest are understandably skittish. Prevalent in northern and eastern Namibia, including Etosha, they prefer to be near water.

SMALL ANTELOPE

IMPALA *(Aepeceros melampus)*
Larger and heavier than the springbok, which it superficially resembles, the elegant and athletic impala is a prodigious jumper; it has been recorded leaping distances of 11m and heights of 3m. Only the male carries the distinctive lyre-shaped horns. Though exceedingly common across southern Africa, its need for water close by and preference for mopane and acacia woodland mean its range is restricted to browsing and grazing the lusher forests of the eastern Zambezi as well as Etosha, where it is quite numerous. Far rarer is the threatened black-faced impala *(Aepeceros melampus petersi)*, an almost identical subspecies found only in southwestern Etosha and northern Kunene; its black facial stripes mark the only visible difference from its more common relative.

SPRINGBOK *(Antidorcas marsupialis)*
Graceful and relatively diminutive, springbok are very common in certain parts of Namibia. In Etosha, in particular, you'll come across them in their thousands, but you'll also encounter large, generally mixed herds in the Kalahari and even in the dunes round Sossusvlei as they have the ability to go for a long time without drinking. Favouring dry open plains and savannah, they can reach speeds of up to 90kph at full throttle. They are also renowned for their extraordinary "pronking", when en masse they arch their backs, straighten their legs, and make multiple leaps into the air as though on a pogo stick; scientists continue to puzzle over what it might mean. Predominantly browsers on succulents and shrubs, and at their most active at dawn and dusk, they can also graze on grass, and feed at other times. They are recognizable by their distinctive white underbelly, accentuated by a horizontal dark patch above, and both sexes possess small, lyre-shaped horns.

COMMON OR GREY DUIKER *(Sylvicapra grimmia)*
The common duiker derives its name from the Afrikaans word "*duik*", meaning "dive", a reference to the fact that, when threatened, after initially freezing, they plunge off into the bush in an erratic zigzagging fashion designed to throw pursuers off balance. Often confused with a steenbok, which is of similar height, the duiker is also heavier, especially the female, and has a greyish rather than brownish coat and a dark blaze down its forehead and nose. It can also be told apart from other antelope by the little black tuft between its small horns. The duiker has a varied diet: beyond herbivorous browsing, it eats small mammals, amphibians, birds and even carrion. Though both diurnal and nocturnal, it tends to feed more at night when close to human settlements, of which it is fairly

tolerant. It is widely distributed throughout Namibia, except in true forest and very open areas, including the Namib.

STEENBOK *(Raphicerus campestris)*
One of the most commonly observed species, the golden-brown steenbok is widely encountered singly or in pairs, selectively grazing and browsing in open woodland and grassland across the country, generally during the day. It likes to take cover in bushes, where it crouches down to avoid detection from predators, once its antenna-like ears have picked up the threat, though it occasionally bolts and may take temporary refuge in other animals' burrows. The single young calf can be born at any time of year, and for the first few weeks the mother takes extra precautions to keep her offspring safe from predation by eating its faeces and drinking its urine in order to reduce the telltale smell.

KLIPSPRINGER *(Oreotragus oreotragus)*
This stocky yet surprisingly agile klipspringer, or dwarf antelope, lives up to its Afrikaans name (meaning "rock hopper") as its raised hooves allow it to climb goat-like up near-sheer cliffs, making it at home on kopjies and in mountainous terrain. Being browsers, and not dependent on pasture, they can often be seen far from water in remote, desolate districts, out and about in the heat of the day. Their thick, coarse hair, which ranges from a brownish to a greyish colour, depending on habitat, helps keep out the cold on winter nights. They are most likely to be seen in the central highlands and the western escarpment; look out for them in the Naukluft Mountains and the Fish River Canyon, for example. Males are horned (though occasionally females are too) and territorial, living with a mate or small family group in quite restricted, often long-term, territories.

DAMARA DIK-DIK *(Madoqua kirkii damarensis)*
Weighing no more than a small turkey and standing only half a metre tall on spindly legs, the tiny, fragile-looking Damara dik-dik is Namibia's smallest antelope, and therefore unlikely to be confused with the larger steenbok, which it otherwise resembles. Despite its name, it is rarely found in Damaraland, more readily frequenting the dense scrub areas of Kunene, Etosha (close to Namutoni) and Waterberg. Dik-diks, which gained their name from their alarm call ("zik-zik"), mate for life; females are larger, whereas the males possess short spiky horns. They are predominantly diurnal browsers, though they will feed at night, and they use their curious prehensile nose to sniff out the best parts of plants, and to help regulate their body temperature.

ZEBRA

Two of Africa's three species of zebra, which are related to horses, live in Namibia. The key to telling them apart is the stripes, though they also inhabit different terrain. Burchell's zebra has thick black stripes and fawn "shadow stripes", both fading out on the legs. In contrast, the thinner, black stripes of Hartmann's mountain zebra continue down the legs. The mountain zebra also has larger ears and a small dewlap, which the Burchell's zebra lacks.

BURCHELL'S ZEBRA *(Equus burchelli)*

Burchell's zebra is by far the more widespread species, numbering 15,000–21,000 in Etosha alone. They are similarly numerous in other reserves and farms across the country. Also dubbed the plains zebra, it ranges across savannah grasslands, often in large herds, grazing alongside wildebeest and other antelope. Diurnal and dependent on water, zebra also like to take dust baths.

HARTMANN'S MOUNTAIN ZEBRA *(Equus zebra hartmannae)*

Closely related to the Cape mountain zebra of South Africa, the Hartmann's mountain zebra is only found in isolated pockets along the western escarpment, including the western area of Etosha, around Dolomite Camp. They live in much smaller family groups of several mares and a stallion, and their slighter frame allows for greater agility in negotiating the rocky terrain.

RHINO

"Hook-lipped" and "square-lipped" are technically more accurate terms distinguishing these two lumbering beasts. "Black" and "white" are probably based on a linguistic misunderstanding; somewhere along the line, the Dutch word "wijd", or Afrikaans "wyd" – both meaning "wide", and referring to the square-lipped's wide mouth – was misheard as "white". The hook-lipped rhino was accordingly named "black" to distinguish it from "white". The truth is that both are a dull grey, though their appearance often depends on the colour of the dust or mud they've been wallowing in. Almost poached to extinction, on account of misplaced beliefs about the potency of their horns, the rhino's cause is not helped by the fact that populations grow very slowly, as the female only gives birth to a single calf every two to three years.

BLACK RHINO *(Diceros bicornis)*

Thanks in no small part to the efforts of the Save the Rhino Trust (see box, p.8), the country now boasts the largest number of free-ranging black rhino in the world, many of which are desert-adapted, able to go several days without water. Namibia's estimated 1700-plus black rhino can be found in the wild and on communal conservancies in the Kunene and Erongo regions, as well as on private reserves and in the national parks of Waterberg and Etosha, where your best chance of spotting them is at one of the floodlit waterholes at night. Unlike the white rhino, the smaller, more cantankerous black rhino is generally solitary, coming together only for mating. It also differs from its relative in being a browser, not a grazer, using its characteristic prehensile upper lip to grasp shoots and leaves.

WHITE RHINO *(Ceratotherium simum)*

Twice as heavy as its black counterpart, the southern white rhino is less aggressive. It is also more sociable, living in small family groups. Its large square muzzle is ideally shaped for grazing short grass on the plains. Often seen at the floodlit waterholes of Etosha – particularly Namutoni – white rhino can also be found in Waterberg. Look out for the smooth "rubbing posts", which are thin tree stumps that have been "polished" by years of rhino scratching themselves after a mud bath to get rid of any parasites.

OTHER LARGE MAMMALS

AFRICAN ELEPHANT (*Loxodonta africana*)
The continent's most emblematic beast, and the world's largest and heaviest land mammal – it can weigh up to 6000kg – the African elephant is a sight to behold. In the flesh, elephants seem even bigger than you would imagine. You'll need little persuasion from the flapping, warning ears of the matriarch to back off if you're too close, but they are at the same time surprisingly graceful, silent animals on their padded, carefully placed feet. In a matter of moments, a large herd can merge into the trees and disappear, their presence betrayed only by the noisy cracking of branches as they strip trees and uproot saplings. Elephants are the most engaging of animals to watch, perhaps because their interactions, behaviour patterns and even individual personalities have so many human parallels. Babies are born after a 22-month gestation, with other cows in close attendance. Calves will suckle for up to three years. The basic family unit is a group of 10–20 related females, tightly protecting their babies and young, and led by a venerable matriarch. Old elephants die in their seventies, when their last set of teeth wears out and they can no longer feed. Grieving elephants pay much attention to the disposal of their dead relatives, often dispersing the bones and spending time near the remains. There are around 2500 elephant in Etosha, and herds also roam freely in Khaudum and across the Zambezi, many drifting over the border from Botswana. Namibia's famous desert-adapted elephant – generally slightly smaller with broader feet – is to be found in the ephemeral riverbeds of the Kunene Region; the camps at Palmwag (see p.201) and the *White Lady Lodge* in Brandberg (p.195) are well known for their sightings.

GIRAFFE (*Giraffa camelopardalis*)
Giraffe are among the easiest animals to spot because their long necks make them visible above the low scrub. The tallest mammals on earth – some males reaching over 5m – with the longest necks, they have a distinctive lolloping gait, and in order to drink, they splay their front legs to lower their mouth to the water. Their unique circulatory system ensures that the blood, which is normally pumped at high pressure up to the head, doesn't cause brain damage once the head is lowered. Giraffe spend their daylight hours browsing on the leaves of acacia trees too high up for other species. Their highly flexible lips and prehensile tongues enable them to select the most nutritious leaves while avoiding deadly sharp thorns. At night they lie down and spend the evening ruminating. If you encounter a bachelor herd, look out for young males testing their strength with neck wrestling, or "necking", as it is known. Of Africa's nine subspecies of giraffe, two are found in Namibia, with the majority of the estimated 12,000 being Angolan giraffes. Healthy populations occur in Etosha, but they also occur in Khaudum and the Zambezi Region, and are common on private reserves, game farms and communal land elsewhere in northern Namibia.

AFRICAN OR CAPE BUFFALO (*Syncerus caffer*)
A powerful ox-like beast, with a rather lugubrious aspect – thanks to its droopy ears – the African or Cape buffalo needs to be near water, and prefers lush savannah, wetlands or even forests. In Namibia, therefore, buffalo are mainly restricted to the Zambezi Region, though they have also been reintroduced to the Waterberg Plateau. The savannah buffalo tends to live in larger herds, and is much bigger and heavier, with adult bulls weighing 500–900kg. The bulls are distinguishable from the cows by their larger horns and more prominent "boss", the part where the two horns fuse. Despite being such large beasts, they are preyed on by lions, though when the herd works together it is often able to repel the attack. Buffalo are prolific grazers that also sometimes browse, feeding both during the day and at night. Lone bulls, especially when wounded, are easily provoked and therefore exceedingly dangerous.

HIPPOPOTAMUS (*Hippopotamus amphibius*)
Hippopotamuses, though highly adaptable, need rivers or lakes that are deep enough for them to submerge, with neighbouring areas of suitable grazing grass. Thus, in Namibia, you'll only see hippos in and around the major rivers of the Zambezi Region, although the private reserves of Mt Etjo and Erindi also have a few. They spend most of the day in water to protect their thin, hairless skin from dehydration, and males are extremely territorial. After dark, they move onto land and spend the whole night grazing, often covering several kilometres in one session. Despite being herbivores, hippos are reckoned to be responsible for more human deaths in Africa than any other large animal (mosquitoes being by far the most deadly). Deaths occur mostly on water, when boats accidentally steer into hippo pods (usually 5–20), but they can be aggressive on land, too, charging and slashing with their fearsomely long incisors, especially if you get between them and water. Their barrel-like bodies and stubby legs belie the fact that they can reach speeds of 30kph if necessary, and have a small turning circle. Although uncertain on land (hence their aggression when cornered), they are supremely adapted to long periods in water. Their nostrils, eyes and ears are in exactly the right places and their clumsy feet become supple paddles. A single calf is born every 2–3 years in water, so it can swim before it can walk.

OTHER SMALL MAMMALS

AARDVARK *(Orycteropus afer)*
One of Africa's – indeed the world's – strangest animals, a solitary mammal weighing up to 70kg. Its name, Afrikaans for "earth pig", is an apt description as it possesses a long tubular snout and holes up during the day in large burrows that are excavated with remarkable speed and energy, using its thick claws. It emerges at night to visit termite mounds within a radius of up to 5km, digging for its main diet before licking up the termites with its long sticky tongue. It's most likely to be found in bush country that's well scattered with tall termite mounds, so it is fairly widely distributed, though rare.

PANGOLIN *(Manis temminckii)*
Sharing the aardvark's penchant for termites and ants, the pangolin – another extraordinary-looking nocturnal creature – has a distinctive "armour plating", made of overlapping keratin scales. This protection is used to good effect since, when threatened, it curls up into a tight ball, an action which gave rise to its name – the Malay "peng-guling" means "roller". It is also known as the scaly anteater, and although it inhabits the central, northern and eastern areas of the country where termite mounds are in evidence, it is rarely observed.

ROCK HYRAX *(Procavia capensis)*
A common sight in rocky terrain, the rock hyrax – also known as a dassie or rock-rabbit – looks like an oversized hamster. Yet, despite being fluffy and small, its closest relative (admittedly from some way back) is the elephant. Like reptiles, hyraxes are poor at regulating their body temperature and rely on taking shelter against both the cold and hot sunlight. They wake up sluggish and seek out rocks to catch the early morning sun – this is one of the best times to look out for them. In the manner of meerkats, one or more adults stand sentry against predators and issue a low-pitched warning cry to the colony in response to a threat. They will browse or graze depending on what's available and are preyed upon by raptors as well as cats.

WARTHOG *(Phacochoerus aethiopicus)*
A ubiquitous and often comical sight, particularly across central and northern Namibia, the warthog is unmistakable with its trademark facial "warts" – more abundant and prominent on the heavier male – upturned tusks and thin covering of dishevelled hair. Diurnal, warthogs are commonly spotted grazing on the verges of the main roads before nonchalantly trotting into the bush, their antenna-like tails erect, to guide their offspring single-file through the undergrowth. They also frequently feed on bended front knees, and enjoy wallowing in mud. At night, warthogs typically take refuge from predators by reversing into disused aardvark burrows, so that they can make a quick escape if necessary. The warthog is unlikely to be confused with its relative, the heavier, hairier and browner bushpig *(Potomochoerus larvatus)* – a rarely observed nocturnal presence in the dense thickets of the Zambezi Region.

CAPE PORCUPINE *(Hystrix africaeaustralis)*
The region's largest rodent, the Cape porcupine, occurs throughout the country, except in the Namib's western coastal strip. Its emblematic banded black-and-white quills provide a prickly defence against predators; the ones at the back are hollow and rattle when shaken to intensify the effect, which is further augmented by erectile coarse hairs that extend from the back of the head to its shoulders. During the day it lies low in one of an assortment of burrows – often made by others – rock crevices or caves, coming out to feed alone or with its monogamous mate at night. Since part of the porcupine's herbivorous diet of roots, bark and tubers consists of crops, farmers often brand it a pest.

BIRDS

Over 700 species of birds have been recorded in Namibia, and many are migratory, arriving when the rains are due (Sept–Nov), and leaving again in March or April. There are also around 16 endemics or near-endemics. Here are just a handful of the more ubiquitous or striking birds that even non-birdwatchers can appreciate.

AFRICAN FISH EAGLE (*Haliaeetus vocifer*)
A handsome and unmistakable sight perched on a treetop, branch or post overlooking fresh water, the African fish eagle is the national bird of Namibia (as well as Zimbabwe and South Sudan), and clearly distinguishable from other large raptors by its white head. Its main diet is fish, though it occasionally eats small waterfowl, amphibians and reptiles; swooping down from a lookout post, the fish eagle grabs the prey in its large barbed talons, then returns to its perch to feast. Fish eagles tend to maintain and reuse several treetop nests, adding extra sticks each year. One to three chicks are usually reared during the dry season, when water levels are low, and fish therefore more concentrated. The larger female does most of the incubation and feeding, handing over care duties to the male only when she flies off to hunt. The easily recognizable haunting cry of the fish eagle is known as the "voice of Africa".

OSTRICH (*Struthio camelus*)
The ostrich is the planet's biggest bird – reaching 2.7m in height and weighing up to 145kg – and lays the biggest egg, twenty times larger than that of a hen. It's also really fast, able to reach speeds of 70kph, aided by its wings, which, though unable to help it fly, make useful stabilizers when it is running. The larger males have smart black feathers and a white tail, whereas females and juveniles are greyish brown and white; both possess long hairy necks. Their large fluffy feathers are also well suited to regulating the bird's body temperature. Preferring open terrain, as their keen eyesight can spot predators from a great distance, they are a common sight around the gravel plains and even on the dunes of the Namib. Living in large nomadic groups of between 10 and 50, female ostriches lay their eggs collectively in a shallow pit in the ground, which may accommodate up to 60 eggs, incubated by both males and females.

HELMETED GUINEAFOWL (*Numida meleagris*)
Clucking, gregarious flocks of helmeted guineafowl are a common sight in much of the Namibian savannah and scrubland, including on farms and close to human habitation. The guineafowl's large body is attractively covered in spotted slate-grey feathers, whereas its tiny, red-and-blue, bald head, topped with a bony "helmet", makes it look rather comical. These gallinaceous birds spend most of the day on the ground scratching around for seeds and insects, covering up to 10km a day, only taking flight with great difficulty.

LILAC-BREASTED ROLLER (*Coracias caudatus*)
It's a dazzling sight when the kaleidoscopic lilac-breasted roller dives off its vantage point – often the top of a bare tree or post – to swoop down on an unsuspecting insect or small lizard. Its green crown, violet breast and patchwork of turquoise, royal- and sky-blue feathers become even more breathtaking when the bird is seen diving, twisting and rolling – hence its name – during its acrobatic aerial courtship display. Living in predominantly monogamous pairs, rollers lay their clutch of 2–4 eggs in a tree hollow, some distance from the ground. Though absent from the coastal strip, they are widespread throughout northern Namibia, including in Etosha, in woodland and savannah land with some tree cover.

GREATER AND LESSER FLAMINGO
(*Phoenicopterus ruber* and *Phoenicopterus minor*)
While it's hard to mistake a flamingo for any other bird – its distinctive pink feathers, long spindly legs and heavy bill being rather a giveaway – it's less easy to tell a greater from a lesser flamingo, both of which inhabit selected coastal areas of Namibia in vast numbers. The greater flamingo is obviously taller, capable of reaching 1.5m in height, and usually paler, though the most notable difference lies in the bill: where the larger bird's is pale with a black tip, the lesser flamingo's is almost entirely black. Flamingos need shallow, saline water, where they filter feed algae, crustaceans and molluscs by holding their shovel-shaped bill upside down, swinging their head from side to side. Pink carpets of thousands of flamingos extend across Namibia's coastal mudflats, notably in Walvis Bay Lagoon – up to 85,000 have been recorded – and Sandwich Harbour, but they also occur in much smaller numbers in Oranjemund and Lüderitz. In seasons of exceptional rain, when Etosha Pan floods – usually March or April – they flock there to breed; otherwise, they migrate further afield.

MONTEIRO'S HORNBILL (*Tockus monteiri*)
Apart from a small corner of southwest Angola, Monteiro's hornbill is endemic to Namibia – one of the country's ten species of hornbill. Inhabiting rugged terrain in the Erongo and Kunene regions, including western parts of Etosha, it is medium-sized with a white underbelly and outer tail feathers, and sports a red bill. It can be distinguished from the red-billed hornbill (*Tockus rufirostris*) by its all-black neck. As with most hornbills, when the time comes to lay eggs, the female holes herself up in a natural tree cavity or rocky crevice and stays there throughout the incubation period, being fed by the male through the small hole that remains.

Cats (DRAWN TO SCALE)

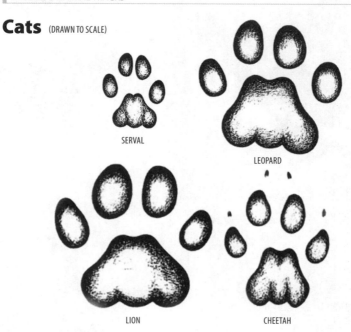

SERVAL

LEOPARD

LION

CHEETAH

Dogs and hyenas (DRAWN TO SCALE)

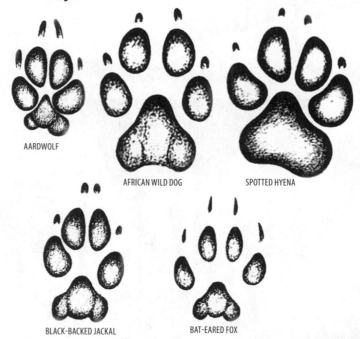

AARDWOLF

AFRICAN WILD DOG

SPOTTED HYENA

BLACK-BACKED JACKAL

BAT-EARED FOX

Large antelope (DRAWN TO SCALE)

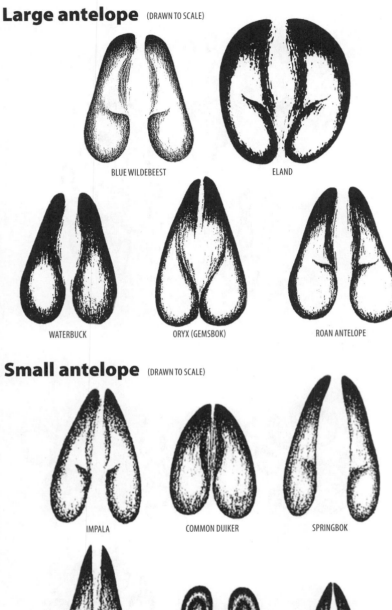

BLUE WILDEBEEST

ELAND

WATERBUCK

ORYX (GEMSBOK)

ROAN ANTELOPE

Small antelope (DRAWN TO SCALE)

IMPALA

COMMON DUIKER

SPRINGBOK

STEENBOK

KLIPSPRINGER

DAMARA DIK-DIK

Primates (DRAWN TO SCALE)

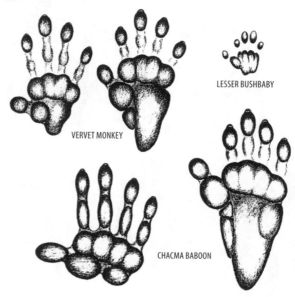

LESSER BUSHBABY

VERVET MONKEY

CHACMA BABOON

Small carnivores (DRAWN TO SCALE)

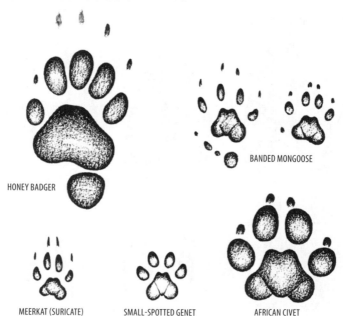

HONEY BADGER

BANDED MONGOOSE

MEERKAT (SURICATE)

SMALL-SPOTTED GENET

AFRICAN CIVET

Other large mammals (NOT DRAWN TO SCALE)

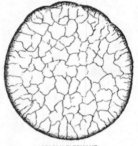

AFRICAN ELEPHANT

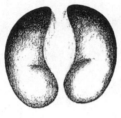

CAPE BUFFALO

GIRAFFE

WHITE RHINOCEROS

BURCHELL'S ZEBRA

HIPPOPOTAMUS

Other small mammals (DRAWN TO SCALE)

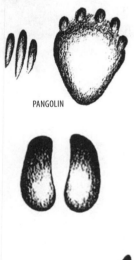

PANGOLIN

PORCUPINE

ROCK HYRAX

WARTHOG

Louis Liebenberg
First Field Guide to Animal Tracks of Southern Africa

LIGHT AIRCRAFT ABOVE THE NAMIB DESERT

Basics

Getting there

Most visitors to Namibia arrive by air, the majority flying via Johannesburg in South Africa, since the only direct flight to Namibia from Europe is from Frankfurt, Germany, and there are no direct flights from either North America or Australasia.

International flights arrive at Windhoek's **Hosea Kutako International Airport** (see p.90), 42km east of the capital. The **Johannesburg route** to Namibia is more popular as you've a greater chance of getting a cheaper last-minute deal to Johannesburg provided you're prepared to shop around online, scour newspaper ads and/ or make more stops on the way. What's more, there are numerous daily connections between Johannesburg and Windhoek. In contrast, the **Frankfurt–Namibia route** is only operated by Air Namibia (✪airnamibia.com), the country's national carrier, and only offers one daily flight. Seats are generally more expensive and more heavily subscribed during the high season (July–Oct), as well as over the Christmas and New Year holiday period. That said, low-season prices are not particularly low. Generally, the further in advance you book, the cheaper the ticket – as with anywhere else in the world. However, you can cut costs by completing the last leg of the journey from South Africa by long-distance bus. It's also possible to reach Namibia by bus from other countries in southern Africa (see box, p.48).

Flights from the UK and Ireland

There are no direct flights from either the UK or Ireland to Namibia. The easiest route is via Johannesburg by one of several carriers from the UK. Virgin (✪virgin-atlantic.com), British Airways (✪ba.com) and South African Airways (✪flysaa .com) offer daily direct overnight flights to Johannesburg, with the latter two offering onward connections via their partner airlines, BA Comair (✪comair.co.za) and South African Express (✪flyexpressaero.com), respectively. Fares from the UK (generally Heathrow) are inevitably pricier in high season, starting from just over £1000. A slightly longer route, but also with only one stop, now operates four times a week with Qatar Airways (✪qatarairways.com) via Doha, at competitive rates. Cheaper options are available if you are prepared to travel more circuitous routes with two stops, on less popular airlines (such as Ethiopian Airlines (✪ethiopianairlines .com) via Addis Ababa), which also involve longer layovers.

Travelling from Ireland, you can either transfer in London or in one of the other major European cities that have carriers operating flights to Johannesburg, such as Air France (✪airfrance.com) in Paris, or KLM (✪klm.com) in Amsterdam. Alternatively, there are cheap flights from Dublin to Frankfurt, where you can connect with the Air Namibia flight to Windhoek.

Flights from the US and Canada

None of the US or Canadian carriers offers direct flights to Namibia, though several US cities, such as New York (just under 15hr) and Atlanta (just over 15hr), have direct flights to Johannesburg, either with US carriers or with South African Airways. Since Canada has no direct flights to South Africa, the best bet is to connect with a US carrier in the States that offers direct flights from there. A return flight to Windhoek from New York costs from around US$2000 in high season, and from US$1600 in low season.

Flights from Australia and New Zealand

The most direct way to reach Namibia from Australia is to take one of the Qantas (✪qantas .com) or SAA nonstop flights to Johannesburg from either Sydney (13hr) or Perth (around 11hr) and change there (AUS$2000–2400). From New Zealand the easiest route is via Sydney.

A BETTER KIND OF TRAVEL

At Rough Guides we are passionately committed to travel. We believe it helps us understand the world we live in and the people we share it with – and of course **tourism** is vital to many developing economies. But the scale of modern tourism has also damaged some places irreparably, and **climate change** is accelerated by most forms of transport, especially flying. All Rough Guides' flights are carbon-offset, and every year we donate money to a variety of environmental charities.

BY BUS FROM SOUTH AFRICA, BOTSWANA AND ZAMBIA

Long-distance **bus travel** to/from Namibia and across southern Africa is synonymous with Intercape Mainliner (⬤intercape.co.za), though there are other, cheaper, less reliable providers. Since distances are vast, the journey times are long, though buses are modern, comfortable, sell hot and cold drinks and, crucially, have air conditioning. Note, however, that on-board entertainment comprises a selection of "wholesome, family-friendly videos promoting the Christian faith". If that is not your cup of tea, bring headphones.

The two main routes from South Africa to Namibia are: **Johannesburg** to Windhoek (changing at Upington, South Africa; 24hr; from ZAR1330 one way); and **Cape Town** to Windhoek (22hr; from ZAR750 one way). Both services operate four days a week and can drop off passengers in Keetmanshoop, Mariental and Rehoboth on the way. From **Livingstone**, Zambia, a short hop from Victoria Falls, a service runs to Windhoek three times a week (20hr; from ZAR600 one way), making a few stops in northern Namibia en route. Tickets tend to be cheaper the further in advance that you book.

Insight Luxury Coaches (☎061 259388, ⬤facebook.com/insightluxurycoaches), a Zambian company, operates twice-weekly transport between Windhoek and **Lusaka** (N$850), via Katima Mulilo (N$400).

In addition, Monnakgotla Transport (⬤monnakgotla.co.bw) and Tok Tokkie Shuttle (⬤shuttlesnamibia.com) both offer a weekly bus service across the Trans Kalahari Highway between **Gaborone**, Botswana, and Windhoek (see p.164).

Flights within southern Africa

There are several daily direct flights to Windhoek **from Johannesburg and Cape Town** with Air Namibia and South African Airways, operated by South African Express (from around ZAR5000 return), as well as with Comair, on behalf of British Airways. SAA and Air Namibia both operate daily flights to Walvis Bay from Johannesburg and from Cape Town (also from around ZAR5000 return). Air Namibia also offers nonstop connections with: Gaborone, Botswana (four times a week, 1hr 20min); Luanda, **Angola** (daily, 1hr 40min); Lusaka, **Zambia** (six days a week, 2hr 15min); and Victoria Falls, **Zimbabwe** (four days a week, 1hr 40min).

Overland by car

The main **entry points** for vehicles **from South Africa** are on the B1 at Noordoewer (the Cape Town route), and at Ariamsvlei on the B3 (the Johannesburg route); both borders are open 24 hours. From **southern Botswana** the Trans Kalahari Highway enters Namibia at Buitepos (7am–midnight), 315km east of Windhoek; travelling from **northern Botswana**, the main border posts are at Ngoma (7am–6pm) and Mohembo (8am–6pm), both in the Zambezi Region. The Wenela Bridge across the Zambezi at Katima Mulilo – usually shortened to Katima – hosts the main border post with **Zambia** (6am–6pm), whereas Oshikango (8am–6pm) is the main entry point from **Angola**. There are several other border crossings into

Namibia, from South Africa and Botswana in particular, often at the end of a dusty road with more limited opening times.

If you're driving to Namibia from one of these neighbouring countries, **border procedures** are fairly straightforward, though if you are not driving a Namibian-registered vehicle you will need to pay road tax (N$159), which allows you to bring your vehicle into the country for a maximum of three months. If coming for business, you'll face additional charges. What's more, if you are driving a rental car, then you'll need to have arranged that with the company beforehand at extra cost, and have the papers handy to prove you have their permission to take it across the border (see p.53).

AGENTS AND OPERATORS

In addition to Namibia-specific holidays, various tour operators offer wildlife-viewing safaris combining Namibia and Botswana, while various overlander trips between Cape Town and Victoria Falls feature Namibia on their itinerary. As well as the small selection of international tour operators listed below, several reliable local operators based in Windhoek (and a couple in Swakopmund) can organize your itinerary (see p.92 & p.213).

African Budget Safaris South Africa ☎ 021 790 1056, ⬤ africanbudgetsafaris.com. Recommended budget operator based in Cape Town, specializing in overlander and other inexpensive trips across southern Africa, including for families.

Exodus UK ☎ 0845 287 7531, US ☎ 1 844 227 9087, Australia ☎ 1 300 131 564, Canada ☎ 1 800 267 3347, New Zealand ☎ 0800 238 368; ⬤ exodus.co.uk, ⬤ exodustravels.com. Experienced adventure travel operator with several offerings in Namibia, including an intriguing combo package with southern Angola.

Expert Africa UK ☎ 020 8232 9777, US ☎ 1 800 242 2434, Australia ☎ 1 800 995 397; Ⓦ expertafrica.com. Extremely experienced and professional outfit that organizes tailor-made trips (generally using mid- to high-end accommodation) for independent travellers in East and southern Africa; also small-group tours, in particular through its newer sibling company, Wild About Africa (Ⓦ wildaboutafrica.com).

Natural Habitat Adventure US & Canada ☎ 1 800 543 8917, Ⓦ nathab.com. Award-winning nature-focused small-group company with top-notch guiding, which offers a couple of Namibia itineraries as well as bespoke tours.

North South Travel UK ☎ 01245 608 291, Ⓦ northsouthtravel .co.uk. Friendly, competitive travel agency, offering discounted fares worldwide. Profits are used to support projects in the developing world, especially the promotion of sustainable tourism.

Responsible Travel UK ☎ 01273 823 700, Ⓦ responsibletravel .com. Leading ethical tourism company offering various tours of Namibia, from cycling to camping or self-drive, some focusing on conservation work. Now with a sibling site in the US (☎ 917 512 2751, Ⓦ responsiblevacation.com).

Safari Drive UK ☎ 01488 71140, Ⓦ safaridrive.com. Specialists in fly-drive safaris to Africa for over 25 years; offers several itineraries in Namibia or can organize bespoke tours for couples, groups and families.

STA Travel UK ☎ 0333 321 00 99, US ☎ 1800 781 4040, Australia ☎ 134 782, New Zealand ☎ 0800 474 400, South Africa ☎ 0861 781 781, Ⓦ statravel.co.uk. Worldwide specialists in independent travel; also student IDs, travel insurance, car rental, rail passes and more. Good discounts for students and under-26s.

Trailfinders UK ☎ 0207 368 1200, Ireland ☎ 021 464 8800 Ⓦ trailfinders.com. One of the best-informed and most efficient agents for independent travellers.

Travel CUTS Canada ☎ 1800 667 2887, US ☎ 1800 592 2887, Ⓦ travelcuts.com. Canadian youth and student travel firm offering discount flights.

Wilderness Safaris South Africa ☎ 011 807 1800, Ⓦ wilderness -safaris.com. Pioneering ecotourism company owning around a dozen exclusive lodges in Sossusvlei and northwest Namibia, often in partnership with local communities. Works through other tour operators rather than accepting direct bookings.

Entry requirements

If you are a visitor from Western Europe, including the UK and Ireland, or from the US, Canada, New Zealand, Australia or South Africa, you do not need a **visa** to enter Namibia. Otherwise you should check with the Namibian diplomatic mission in your country. Even if a visa is not necessary, you do need a **passport** valid for six months after the entry date with at least two blank pages for stamps, and you should be able to show proof of onward travel (by air or bus), though this is unlikely to be requested. On arrival in Namibia your passport will be stamped for up to ninety days; visa extensions can be obtained from the Ministry of Home Affairs and Immigration in Windhoek (☎ 061 2922111; Ⓦ mha.gov.na), on the corner of Kasino Street and Independence Avenue.

FOREIGN EMBASSIES IN NAMIBIA

Australia Australian Honorary Consul, 56 Chaledoon St ☎ 061 300194, ✉ australian.consulate.namibia@gmail.com.

Canada Canadian Consulate, 1st Floor, Office Tower, Maerua Mall, Jan Jonker St ☎ 061 251254.

New Zealand Honorary Consul, 1 Haddy St, Windhoek Central, Windhoek ☎ 061 386600.

Republic of Ireland Contact mission in Zambia Ⓦ embassyofireland.co.zm.

South Africa South African High Commission, Corner of Nelson Mandela Ave and Jan Jonker St ☎ 061 2057111, Ⓦ dirco.gov.za /windhoek.

UK British High Commission, 116 Robert Mugabe Ave, ☎ 061 274800, ✉ general.windhoek@fco.gov.uk.

USA United States Embassy, 14 Lossen St, Ausspanplatz ☎ 061 2958500.

Getting around

While getting around Namibia's relatively few population centres is possible by bus, and even rail in some cases, in order to reach most of the parks, reserves and other places you are most likely to want to visit, you will need to book yourself on a tour or rent a vehicle. Hitchhiking is now banned on some roads in Namibia and in national parks, but in other, more remote, parts of the country it is almost the only way to get around if you are without your own wheels, but be prepared to pay the equivalent of a bus fare.

By bus

Despite the fact that the vast majority of Namibians do not own cars, organized transport is rather scarce outside the main population centres. Intercape Mainliner (Ⓦ intercape.co.za) provides the most reliable **luxury buses** (see box, p.48), running daily services from Windhoek to South Africa, stopping off at Rehoboth, Mariental and Keetmanshoop; it also heads north to Oshakati, Ondangwa and the Angolan border at Oshikango, as well as to Livingstone in Zambia via Rundu and Katima Mulilo, and west to Swakopmund and Walvis Bay. Other private operators also run **shuttles** to specific destinations: Townhoppers (Ⓦnamibiashuttle.com) and Welwitschia Shuttle (Ⓦwelwitschiashuttle.com), both Swakopmund-based firms, operate daily air-conditioned shuttle services between the capital and the coast for N$260. Details are given in the relevant sections. There is also a twice-weekly (Tues & Fri) inexpensive Orange Bus service – also known as the SWAPO bus – operated by Namib Contract Haulage (Ⓣ061 225333, Ⓦkalahariholdings.com) that runs between Soweto Market, Katutura and various towns in the north, including Oshakati (N$225), Outapi and Ruacana (N$255). Most people, however, get around on the less comfortable **minibuses** that don't have a fixed schedule; they leave when full and can be overloaded, and more prone to accidents, but are faster. The 1200km journey between Windhoek and Katima Mulilo costs just under N$400.

By plane

Given the distances involved in Namibia, it's no surprise that there are **internal flights** available, patronized mainly by business folk. In addition to the international airport at Walvis Bay, small airports are scattered across the country at Katima Mulilo, Lüderitz, Ondangwa, Oranjemund and Rundu. Air Namibia (Ⓦairnamibia.com) operates several flights a week on these domestic routes from Hosea Kutako International Airport or from Eros Airport, Windhoek's domestic airport 5km south of the capital, just off the B1 (see p.90). An up-to-date schedule of all their routes can be downloaded from their website. Domestic **fares** range from around N$800 for Windhoek–Walvis Bay one way to around N$1500 for a one-way ticket to fly to Katima Mulilo, at the eastern tip of the Zambezi Region, over 1200km from the capital by road. Additional airstrips serving charter flights are also dotted

	Etosha (Namutoni gate)	Katima Mulilo	Keetmanshoop	Lüderitz	Nordoower	Opuwo
Etosha (Namutoni gate)	-	925	1015	1350	1320	615
Katima Mulilo	925	-	1870	2030	1996	1090
Keetmanshoop	1015	1870	-	335	304	1157
Lüderitz	1350	2030	335	-	609	1490
Nordoower	1320	1996	304	609	-	1460
Opuwo	615	1090	1157	1490	1460	-
Oranjemund	1365	2052	483	394	233	1560
Oshakati	245	1100	1190	1524	1494	320
Otjiwarongo	288	970	727	1060	1030	430
Rundu	415	510	1185	1516	1486	810
Sesriem	852	1530	517	559	820	920
Swakopmund	660	1340	840	730	1144	624
Tsumeb	105	830	932	1118	1230	510
Tsumkwe	445	850	1235	1422	1532	843
Windhoek	533	1210	475	820	786	675

Distances based on the best route by road between towns

around; most of the isolated luxury lodges have their own landing strip. There are several good charter flight operators who regularly fly tourists between lodges, but it is best to ask the lodge(s) you're staying at to advise on flights, since many have agreements with particular charter operators.

By train

Trains have been running in Namibia since 1895, and today, as then, they mainly transport freight, so are exceedingly slow. Most routes on this small network also offer a **passenger service** (both economy and business), and since most departures entail overnight travel you can save a night's accommodation, which may be of interest to budget travellers.

The **routes** of most interest to tourists are: Windhoek–Walvis Bay, via Swakopmund (see p.91), and Windhoek to Keetmanshoop (see p.91); the

opening of the line from there to Lüderitz has been delayed until the authorities find a solution to the dunes blowing onto the tracks.

Fares are inexpensive – N$153 from Windhoek to Walvis Bay, for example, in high season – though it's worth paying the extra N$38 for the fully reclining seats available in business class. Even then, however, the level of comfort is unremarkable – remember to take food with you, and a blanket to ward off the desert chill. Prices are slightly higher at the end of the month and during the December/January holidays. The rail network is owned by the parastatal TransNamib (☎061 2982624, ⓦ transnamib.com .na), and tickets can be booked at the various train stations in advance or on the day, when you should turn up thirty minutes before departure.

At the other end of the scale is the luxurious Desert Express (see box, p.52), a travel experience in its own right rather than as a means of getting from A to B.

Oranjemund	Oshakati	Otjiwarongo	Rundu	Sesriem	Swakopmund	Tsumeb	Tsumkwe	Windhoek
1365	245	288	415	852	660	105	445	533
2052	1100	970	510	1530	1340	830	850	1210
483	1190	727	1185	517	840	932	1235	482
394	1524	1060	1516	559	730	1118	1422	820
233	1494	1030	1486	820	1144	1230	1532	786
1560	320	430	810	920	624	510	843	675
-	1540	1078	1543	642	937	1260	1563	826
1540	-	463	590	992	834	286	618	708
1078	463	-	455	564	370	184	487	245
1543	590	455	-	1020	826	319	338	700
642	992	564	1020	-	297	735	1038	320
937	834	370	826	297	-	554	857	356
1260	286	184	319	735	554	-	340	432
1563	618	487	338	1038	857	340	-	735
826	708	245	700	320	356	432	735	-

THE NAMIBIA DESERT EXPRESS

Somewhat of a misnomer, the luxury **Namibia Desert Express** actually takes 22 hours to cover the 350km from Windhoek to Swakopmund, but that allows you plenty of time to appreciate the train's opulence and gaze at the desert landscape through vast windows, while reclining in soft leather seats. The en-suite sleeping compartments are supremely comfortable; the three-course dinner and extensive breakfast included in the price are delicious; and there's video entertainment and a well-stocked bar to keep you occupied, leaving you little time to actually sleep. The tour also includes a stopover at Okapuka Ranch, north of Windhoek, for some game-viewing activity.

Departures are once a week, leaving Windhoek station on Friday at noon, in winter, or 1pm in summer, and departing from Swakopmund on Saturday at 3pm. Each sleeper compartment accommodates two adults and a child. In addition, if you want to go one way by train and drive back, vehicles can be loaded onto the train for an extra N$1300. At certain times of the year, you can also book a seven-day tour by train that goes up to Etosha as well as Swakopmund and Walvis Bay (N$25,550).

PRACTICALITIES

Contact TransNamib at Windhoek Station for details (☎061 2982600, ✉ desert.express @transnamib.com.na). Note that the Desert Express has had a stop-start history and may not necessarily be functioning for one reason or another, so check well in advance. Rates are N$4123 per person sharing one way, or N$5910 return.

By car

By far the most convenient way to see the country is by having your own wheels; once you've made that decision, the main question is whether to go for a 2WD or 4WD. Many of the main highways are high-quality tarred roads, and the gravel roads necessary for reaching most (though not all) of the main sights are generally navigable in a **2WD** outside the rainy season, though the higher the clearance, the more comfortable the ride. On the other hand, fuel consumption will be much more economical in the 2WD. However, if you do a lot of gravel-road driving you need to be prepared for the greater likelihood of punctures.

Most lodges that demand 4WD access have a safe parking area for saloon cars, and will transfer guests in their own 4WD vehicles, usually at no extra cost. They will similarly be able to take you out on game drives in their vehicles. That said, the majority of self-drive visitors rent a 4WD, though they rarely, if ever, actually use the lower gears.

To reach more remote areas, high-clearance **4WD** is essential, but this needs to be accompanied by the knowledge of how to drive such a vehicle – for example in sand, across riverbeds and over rocks. What's more, if you're going to tackle challenging terrain, off the proverbial beaten track, you will probably need to be in a **convoy** of at least two vehicles, with all the necessary **equipment** (see box, p.61).

Be Local (☎061 305795, ✇be-local.com) in Windhoek runs short **courses** for novice 4WD drivers.

Car rental

Car rental is not prohibitively expensive in Namibia, but it is not as cheap as in South Africa – you're likely to get a better deal with an advance online booking. Besides, in peak holiday season 4WD vehicles can be hard to come by. You certainly can't expect just to turn up and rent a car on the spot. In high season, **rates** generally start from around £170/week for a small, manual 2WD with air conditioning; thereafter the rate comes down slightly. For a mid-size 2WD, bank on paying over £400/week. 4WD vehicles cost from around £700/week and guzzle fuel, though they offer a more comfortable ride on dirt roads and afford you better views of the countryside; moreover, in some parts of the country, and especially during the rains, a high-clearance 4WD is the only form of transport to reach remote areas, especially in northwest Namibia. Local 4WD rental specialists usually also offer rates that include camping equipment from an extra N$100 per day. Otherwise, there are a couple of companies in Windhoek that provide this service (see p.99).

Some of the cheapest deals have a mileage limit, though most offer unlimited mileage, which in such a large country is advisable. However, rental rates can vary quite considerably for the same vehicle, depending on how many kilometres it's clocked up and on the conditions for the collision and theft damage waivers (CDW and TDW); you can often opt to pay a higher daily rental rate in order to reduce the excess payable in case of accident. Damage to tyres, windscreen and headlights (often from gravel on the road) is usually not included in the standard insurance, but you can take out extra cover. Including an **additional driver**, which is highly recommended given the long hours on the road you're likely to face, may not necessarily cost extra. **Dropping off at a different location** can be done, and again charges depend upon the distance from the pick-up point; for example, you'll pay over N$4000 to leave a car in Katima Mulilo that you have rented in Windhoek, unless the company has an office there. Taking the vehicle **across the borders** in most of southern Africa, especially South Africa and Botswana, is fairly easy, but advance notice is necessary to give the rental company time to sort out the relevant papers and insurance, for which you'll be charged extra (around N$500 for a multiple entry permit). In addition, you'll have to pay vehicle entry fees at the border, generally in the relevant local currency (for example P140 for Botswana).

As for **age restrictions**, drivers of 2WD cars generally need to be over 21, and in some cases over 23, though younger drivers may be accepted for an additional charge; for 4WD you generally need to be over 25, and have held a licence for several years. Theoretically, an international driving permit (purchased before you leave home) is required for car rental – to be presented alongside your national driving licence – but if your licence is written in English, or at least in Roman script, it is rarely requested. In addition, you should carry your driving licence with you when on the road to show at police checkpoints.

As well as the usual international car rental companies (Avis, Budget, Hertz, etc), there are several good local operators, often specializing in 4WD rental, based in Windhoek, and some of the local tour operators even have their own fleet of vehicles.

CAR RENTAL AGENCIES

Aloe Car Hire ⓦ aloecarhire-namibia.com. Friendly, efficient, family-run outfit with competitive prices, especially in low season (Jan–June).

Asco Car Hire ⓦ ascocarhire.com. Highly professional outfit specializing in 4WD across southern Africa, with a wide range of vehicles in good condition, and excellent briefings and back-up service; also rents out satellite phones and GPS gear.

Namibia Car Rentals ⓦ namibiacarrentals.com. Broker for the big agencies, with offices across Namibia and good rates, especially for 2WD. **Savanna Car Hire** ⓦ savannacarhire.com.na. Small, family-run business specializing in Toyota 4WD.

Driving tips and regulations

Cars are driven on the left in Namibia, as in most of southern Africa. Although the quality of the roads is high, so is the **accident rate**, especially on gravel roads and for foreign tourists who are unused to the conditions. Losing concentration at the wheel is also a hazard, given the vast distances involved and the monotony of some of the driving, so making regular stops is essential. The **speed limit** is 120kph on tarred roads out of town, 60kph in urban areas, 80kph on gravel roads, and 60kph in most reserves and parks. Note also that **seat belts** are compulsory. Along the coast roads during the morning mist, it's recommended to drive with **headlights** on; drivers also tend to keep them on when there is a lot of dust around. A substantial number of accidents also occur from vehicles hitting pedestrians, or wildlife, more often at night, which is why you should not **drive in the dark** if at all possible, especially on gravel roads or in the north of the country, where there are plenty of domesticated animals loose on the roads to add to the hazards.

Whether you opt for a 2WD or 4WD, there are certain basic provisions you should have with you, and **precautions** you need to take, since getting stranded in the desert is no joke, and can be fatal (see box, p.61).

Petrol stations are located in all the main towns – usually 24 hours – and even in some more remote corners of the country (with more restricted hours). Most only take cash (though the fuel stations in Etosha take cards, when the machine is working) and are not self-service, so you should be prepared

TYRE PRESSURE

Views differ on the optimum tyre pressure for different surfaces; it also depends on various factors such as the type of vehicle, the kind of tyres on it and the load it's carrying. That said, a rule of thumb for the average 4WD is 2–2.2 bar for **tarred roads**, 1.8 bar for **gravel roads** and 1 bar (15psi) for **sand**. For sand, it's really important to deflate the tyres to increase the surface area, so that this can improve the vehicle's traction. Ask your rental agency what they recommend.

to tip the very underpaid pump attendant (N$5–10) if they do a good job. On request they will wash your windscreen and check your tyre pressure, which should be done at regular intervals, especially after a long period on gravel roads.

At the time of writing, unleaded petrol and diesel were both around N$11/litre in Windhoek, more in more remote areas. Remember that using 4WD gears and air conditioning will increase your fuel consumption. 4WD vehicles often have reserve fuel-carrying capacity, but it's worth having spare fuel canisters even in a 2WD so that if you take a wrong turn, which is easily done, you don't run out in the middle of nowhere. For the same reason, fill up whenever you pass a petrol station.

By organized tour

If you don't have your own vehicle, or don't want to spend hours driving, the easiest way to visit places is to go on an **organized tour** or safari. These can be organized via one of the specialist tour operators in your home country (see p.61), or through one of the Windhoek- or Swakopmund-based tour operators. These range from a budget three-day camping trip to Sossusvlei for N$5200/person to bespoke tours for as long and as far as you like to suit a range of budgets (see p.92 & p.213).

By bike

While you'd imagine the hot dusty roads and huge distances between sights would deter most people from pedalling round Namibia, there are a surprising number of **cycling holidays** on offer from specialist tour operators (such as Mountain Bike Namibia, Ⓦ mountainbikenamibia.com; African Bikers, Ⓦ africanbikers.com; and Bike Tours,

Ⓦ biketours.com), as well as more mainstream companies (such as Exodus, Ⓦ exodus.co.uk, and Trailfinders, Ⓦ trailfinders.com); the latter will also organize your flights. The fact that many roads are deserted and the scenery can be spectacular makes Namibia, in some respects, ideal for cycling. However, the extreme heat, dust and isolation mean that **independent cyclists** need to be experienced, fit and totally self-sufficient in case of breakdown, carrying plenty of water and food, with adequate protection for the head and neck from the brutal sun. The BEN network of bike shops offers **bike repairs** (see box below).

Hitchhiking

Although forbidden in national parks and along some routes, such as the Swakopmund–Windhoek road, **hitchhiking** is a common way of getting about in less populated areas, though you'd be wise not to do it alone. You should, however, offer to contribute to fuel costs (generally the price of a bus fare), though if you're lucky your ride may decline to take you up on the offer. On some roads you could be waiting hours for a vehicle to pass, so it's important to have enough food and especially water to sustain you, as well as protection from the sun. Shared rides are sometimes advertised in the backpacker hostels in Windhoek.

Accommodation

Although accommodation can seem expensive compared to many parts of Africa, standards are usually high and the value for money often excellent, especially if you're coming from a country with favourable exchange rates. Moreover, there's a lot of variety to suit a range of budgets, from basic campgrounds to all-inclusive luxury lodges and tented camps, or moderately priced B&Bs and guestfarms on private reserves. Backpacker hostels outside Windhoek are fairly thin on the ground, but staying at community campgrounds is another budget alternative, which helps provide the community with much-needed income. Self-catering options are also widespread. Note that almost all lodges and guesthouses require you to check out by 10am and check in after 3pm.

BICYCLE EMPOWERMENT NETWORK

What grew from a project to supply secondhand bikes and mechanical support for outreach health workers has developed into a successful development enterprise in its own right: a network of over thirty self-supporting community-based **bicycle repair workshops** is now thriving. See the Bicycle Empowerment Network's (BEN) website for the location and contact details of the bike shops (Ⓦ bennamibia.org).

Hotels, B&Bs and guesthouses

Hotels are generally confined to the major urban centres, and by law **hotel** rooms must all be en suite (with a bath or shower and toilet) and have windows. More common – even in Windhoek – however, are family-run **guesthouses** and smaller **B&Bs**, both of which are also sprinkled around the smaller towns in Namibia. They are usually owner-managed, offer more personalized hospitality and on average charge between N$900 and N$1700 for a double room, including breakfast. Some of the guesthouses also provide evening meals and/or packed lunches on request.

Many lodgings still follow the German tradition of preferring **twin beds**, rather than doubles, though the two beds will often be arranged side by side. If having a double bed is important to you, make sure you ascertain the bed configurations before booking.

Lodges and tented camps

Namibia's **lodge** scene has grown substantially over the last fifteen years, particularly at the luxury end of the market, where you can pay over N$10,000 per person sharing per night for an **all-inclusive package**. Although lodges inside the national parks are almost exclusively run by the parastatal Namibia Wildlife Resorts (see p.65), there are many on private concessions that border the parks, catering to a range of budgets. In addition to them is a handful of remote, luxury wilderness camps – often reached by a charter flight – whose isolation and spectacular desert scenery are generally the main attraction. Several tour operators manage a portfolio of lodgings within Namibia. The Gondwana Collection (🌐gondwana-collection.com), for example, owns twenty diverse and distinctive properties and campgrounds right across the country, characterized by efficient, friendly service; a strong emphasis on sustainability; excellent buffet food; and good-quality but affordable accommodation, including upmarket campgrounds. South Africa-based Wilderness Safaris (🌐wilderness-safaris.com), which has ecotourism operations in several African countries owns a dozen exclusive camps (from 6 to 23 units) in Namibia, predominantly in the northwest including the pioneering Damaraland Camp, which is jointly owned, and largely managed, by the local community conservancy.

Guestfarms

Guestfarms are generally run by Namibians of German or white South African heritage; they are large working farms that look to supplement their income to a greater or lesser extent through tourism. They often combine the family-style hospitality of a guesthouse, which includes communal dining with the hosts, with the advantage of being surrounded by nature. A number of guestfarms offer hiking trails round their property, and some include reserves stocked with large mammals, offering good opportunities for **wildlife viewing**; they may also be involved in conservation work; others (though none listed in this Guide) are hunting farms. Other activities provided by guestfarms include farm tours, 4WD trails, stargazing, sundowner excursions and horse riding.

Hostels and budget accommodation

The country's few **backpacker hostels** are concentrated in Windhoek (see p.94) and in the coastal resorts of Swakopmund (see p.214) and Lüderitz (see p.129), with a couple also in Tsumeb (see p.185), charging around N$170–200 for a bed in a dorm, and N$500–650 for a double or twin with shared or private bathroom. Camping is another option for budget travellers, especially at the cheaper community-run campgrounds. **Restcamps**, which by law have to offer at least four types of accommodation, also tend to be good value, usually providing inexpensive self-catering units and camping pitches among other no-frills options.

Camping

Camping is by far the best way to experience Namibia's wilderness scenery, the sounds of the bush and the country's magical sunsets. What's more, it doesn't have to be the unforgiving endurance activity of guide or scout camps. On the contrary, camping can be pretty luxurious in Namibia, and at very little cost. Bank on paying N$110–250 per person per night, though some campgrounds also charge for the vehicle and/or have an additional site charge. Increasingly, campgrounds are offering private ablution blocks and even private food preparation areas and sinks, particularly in the case of lodges that also cater for campers. Hot-water showers are the norm, though in some cases, the water may be heated by a donkey (wood-fired water heater), and you may need to buy the wood and build the fire yourself. Electricity is usually available, except in community or wilderness campsites, as are power points to charge electrical equipment. You'll almost certainly have a private braai stand or pit, but not necessarily a grill, which you can rent (see opposite). Larger places, such as the NWR camps (see p.65), will have communal ablution blocks and a camp shop that sells basic provisions, including "braai packs", which usually comprise a couple of steaks, pork chops or kebabs and a piece of boerwors with which to kick-start your BBQ. These are also often available on guestfarms, where the meat comes straight from their own livestock.

Several places also rent out tents that are already set up and equipped with beds (or mattresses), bedding and electricity for little more than a campground fee.

Wild camping should not be undertaken unless there's no other option – such as a breakdown somewhere; usually there's a community campground, however rudimentary, within reach, in even the remotest areas.

Community-based tourism

Community-based tourism (CBT) in Namibia, especially through the country's progressive conservancy system, has rightly been championed across the world. Though it's not without its share of challenges (see box, p.364), it offers the traveller a way of engaging with rural populations while helping to support communities without threatening their lifestyles, which more conventional tourism does not. That said, it takes various forms: most notably there are a number of excellent **community-run campgrounds** across the country, usually comprising only a handful of pitches, which sometimes lack electricity. The outstanding success story in CBT is the international award-winning **Conservancy Safaris Namibia** (🌐 kcs-namibia.com.na; see also box, p.259), which is almost completely owned by Himba and Herero communities. In existence in the Kunene Region for a number of years, it is starting to expand its operations into the Zambezi Region. Increasingly, conservancies are entering into joint ventures with

---

NAMIBIA'S LIVING MUSEUMS

There are six **"living museums"** across northern Namibia, which aim to preserve and transfer aspects of traditional culture, educating fellow Namibians and foreign tourists, providing opportunities for intercultural exchange and, importantly, creating sources of income for rural communities.

Five different ethnic groups are represented in the living museums (the Ju |'Hoansi-San, Mafwe, Damara, Mbunza and Himba) and are supported by the non-profit organization, The Living Culture Foundation of Namibia (🌐 lcfn.info). By visiting one of these sites you can choose from a menu of **interactive programmes**, ranging from a couple of hours to a whole day, or even an **overnight stay** (which will afford you far greater insight), as you learn about and practise traditional skills, herbal remedies or dances, before sampling traditional food. Provided you manage to avoid arriving when the village is being stage-managed to entertain large tour groups, it is possible to engage in genuine interaction with community members, not only about traditional life, but also about the ways in which the communities are adapting to modern life.

more experienced lodge operators; there are now over thirty such ventures.

Another way some communities are benefiting from tourism, which is not without its critics, is through the "living museum" experience (see box, p.56).

In urban areas, "township tourism" is also taking off; run by local black operators in the former townships of Windhoek (see p.92), Swakopmund (see p.214) and Walvis Bay (see p.224), it's an area where they can outdo the leading (almost exclusively white-owned) tour operators in Namibia. A couple of the more successful companies have now succeeded in branching out into offering more mainstream activities to tourists.

At its best, township tours give tourists insights into the various changing cultures, challenges and everyday lives of people in these areas, and a chance for some intercultural interaction. At its worst, it can be very voyeuristic – hence why it is often referred to as "slum" or "poverty" tourism.

It's definitely not everyone's cup of tea, and much depends on the attitudes and actions of the people doing the tour as well as the way the tour is managed and the interactions that take place. Ambivalence exists among township residents too; recent research in Katutura showed that, while some residents felt happy that visitors valued their lives and what they were doing, others thought they were just coming to gawp at their poverty. The research also showed that the money from the tours did not spread very widely into the community since tours tend to visit the same places and people each time (such as Penduka in Windhoek). If you want to ensure that your tourist dollars are spread more widely, make enquiries beforehand and see where you might go that is off the beaten track.

Eating and drinking

Eating and drinking in Namibia can be a real pleasure, especially for carnivores, as the country has a reputation for excellent meat, and game meat in particular. On the coast too, the Benguela Current ensures an ample selection of fresh fish. Though locally grown vegetables and fruit are harder to come by, the large supermarkets in the main towns stock plenty of imported fruit and vegetables from South Africa.

Traditional dishes

Most visitors will never get to taste the sort of food eaten by the vast majority of the population, which varies according to location, ethnic group and season, but whose staple is usually sorghum or pearl millet made into a thick **porridge** – *oshifima, oshimbombo*, to give just two names. The Herero and Himba in particular often mix sour milk (*omaere*) with the porridge, which in turn may be eaten with wild or dried spinach (*ombidi* or *ekaka*) or other vegetables, and sometimes meat or chicken. Head for Soweto market in Katutura, though, and you'll easily come across the popular street food **kapana** – bite-sized strips of red meat sizzled on the grill then dipped in a chilli, tomato and onion sauce; they go well with the ubiquitous **fat cakes** – deep-fried balls of dough, which are surprisingly tasty if eaten straight from the pan.

For most tourists, though Namibian cuisine is about **venison**, or **game meat**: you're just as likely to see springbok, kudu and oryx laid out on your plate as you are to spot them springing across the road. At the coast, **seafood** is abundant: kabeljou, kingclip, hake, sole and lobster are popular, while Namibian oysters are garnering an international reputation. If staying by the Zambezi and Kavango rivers, you can count on some tasty tigerfish, tilapia and bream. Being the most fertile regions of the country, they also produce more vegetables and fruit than elsewhere in Namibia: check out the market and roadside stalls for monkey orange (*maguni*), Kavango litchi (*makwevo*), bird plum (*eembe*) and *marula* – as used to make the cream liqueur Amarula.

What is most commonly billed as "Namibian cuisine" is usually heavily influenced by **German culinary traditions**. Expect to spot *Wiener schnitzel* and *spätzle* (thick egg noodles) on menus, and rolls (*brötchen*) and calorific cakes laden with cream in coffee shops in Windhoek, Swakopmund and Lüderitz. Similarly, no camping trip to Namibia is complete without that Afrikaaner institution, the braai (it rhymes with

PRICING AND TAXES

Most advertised prices on restaurant menus and for accommodation include the **government taxes**. In all cases, we have included them in the prices given in this Guide.

SEASONAL DELICACIES

Namibia has a few standout seasonal delicacies you should take the opportunity to sample. **Kalahari truffles** – known as ǁnabba or *mafumpula* locally – are dug out of the desert sands of eastern Namibia after the rains in April/May, and used to flavour sauces and soups. **Omajava** – tasty giant wild mushrooms – are plucked from the bases of termite mounds from late January to March, when they are occasionally available from roadside stalls. Swakopmund **asparagus** (Sept–May) is another favourite, possessing a distinctive flavour due to being grown in brackish water.

The culinary rite of passage for many tourists, though, is the chance to tuck into a bowl of **mopane worms** (*omagungu* in Oshiwambo), something you are only likely to want to do once. Harvested across northern Namibia (and indeed in other parts of Africa) from February to April, they are actually the caterpillars of emperor moths that gain their name from the fact they are found in mopane trees. Highly nutritious, they are dried and sold as crispy snacks, or cooked in a variety of ways. Still, no amount of frying in onion and tomato can disguise their bulging heads and prickly legs; nor does the knowledge that they are packed with protein make them any easier for the unpractised to swallow.

"dry"), or BBQ, on which you need to toss a hefty coil of *boerewors* (farmer's sausage), large steaks and *sosaties* (lamb or mutton kebabs), to be washed down with gallons of beer. Potjies (stews cooked in a three-legged metal pot – traditionally over a few coals) are also popular.

Vegetarians will have a tougher time; although there are almost always a couple of vegetarian options on restaurant menus, they rarely stray much beyond a plateful of roasted vegetables or a mushroom risotto.

Drink

Tap water is generally very safe in Namibia, even though the taste varies. It is especially pure when it comes from lodge or farm boreholes. That said, bottled water is widely available, though as an alternative you might consider bringing water **purifying tablets** with you – these days sold with neutralizing tablets to take away the aftertaste – to help alleviate the huge amount of plastic waste generated by getting through multiple bottles of water each day.

Fresh **fruit juice** is really only available in the lusher Zambezi and Kavango regions – seek out, for example, the delicious *sabdariffa* juice, made from wild hibiscus flowers. But cans and cartons of the South African brands of Ceres and Liquifruit, which contain 100 percent fruit juice without additional sugar, are not bad substitutes and are widely stocked in shops, supermarkets and petrol stations. Coke and all the usual fizzy beverages are widespread, though you might try the popular, refreshing, near-enough non-alcoholic **rock shandy**, consisting of half lemonade, half soda water or sparkling water, a slice of lemon and a dash of Angostura bitters.

Namibia's Teutonic heritage has ensured that good **coffee** is widely available in towns and lodges; a cup of **tea** is equally easy to come by, including the popular herbal rooibos (or redbush) tea. You may need to specify cold milk with your tea, as the default way to drink tea in South Africa is with hot milk.

Probably the most widely appreciated German colonial legacy, however, is Namibia's **beer**, made according to Bavarian purity laws, resulting in the excellent Windhoek Lager, Tafel Lager and the premium Windhoek Draught. Namibia Breweries also produces a winter bock beer, Urbock, as well as a number of other beers under licence. Namibia's desert landscape is not ideal for viticulture, yet amazingly the country possesses a few small **wineries**, most notably the Neuras Winery (🌐 neuraswines.com), 80km from Sesriem, which produces several reds, and Kristall Kellerei (see p.189) outside Omaruru, which also produces an award-winning Nappa (Namibian grappa), and a tasty gin from its distillery by Naute Dam near Keetmanshoop. Cheaper and more established South African wines are widely available; you can pick up a drinkable bottle of wine for under N$80. Note that alcohol isn't sold after 1pm on Saturdays in either supermarkets or bottle stores (off licences). Licensing hours are Monday to Friday 9am–7pm, Saturday 8am–1pm. Of course, there are plenty of shebeens selling their own, much cheaper and more potent tipple at any time of day and night: **oshikundu** (made from fermented millet and drunk the same day) or **mataku** (watermelon wine), for example.

Health

Provided you're up to date with vaccinations and take anti-malarials if visiting malarial areas, your main health risks are likely to be dehydration, heatstroke or sunburn due to the intensity of the desert sun, though travellers' diarrhoea is always a possibility. These, however, are easily prevented by taking the simple precautions below.

Should you be unfortunate enough to fall ill, or have an accident, you can take heart from the fact that Namibia generally enjoys high-quality private **medical facilities** – though they are only located in the main towns, which could be some distance away. For this reason, you should make sure your medical cover includes emergency evacuation, especially if you intend to travel to remote parts of the country.

Inoculations

There are no mandatory inoculations for Namibia, although **tetanus, typhoid and hepatitis A** are typically recommended. In addition to checking some of the available online medical resources (see p.60) for further advice, make sure you consult a **travel clinic** six to eight weeks in advance of travel to give you time for any jabs or boosters. Clinics will often suggest considering further injections for hepatitis B and maybe even rabies, but they are only likely to be of relevance if you are intending to spend extended periods of time living among poor rural communities. In the case of rabies, even if you have the vaccinations, you will still need post-exposure treatment – a series of jabs – in the extremely unlikely event of your being bitten by a dog or wild animal. Travellers from countries where yellow fever vaccinations are mandatory must be able to produce a yellow fever inoculation certificate. Similarly, if you have come from a yellow fever-prone country such as Angola, you may be required to show proof of vaccination upon entry.

Sunstroke and sunburn

The danger of **sunstroke** or **heatstroke** posed by Namibia's intense desert sun cannot be overemphasized. Wherever possible you should avoid any exertion during the heat of the day; walk in the shade; wear a wide-brimmed hat; and cover yourself with sunblock. Shoulders, noses, bald heads and feet (especially if wearing sandals) are particularly prone to **sunburn**. Drink plenty of water (see opposite) and other non-alcoholic drinks to avoid dehydration, and keep up your salt intake. It's wise to carry a few rehydration sachets with you on your travels; these are widely available in pharmacies.

Traveller's diarrhoea

That catch-all phrase **traveller's diarrhoea**, which usually results from drinking or eating contaminated food, is not commonly experienced in Namibia, in part because the water most visitors get to drink is of good quality and the amount of street food available in Namibia – usually confined to open markets – is limited. If in doubt, however, follow the tried and tested maxim – if a tad clichéd: peel it, boil it, cook it or forget it. If you do happen to get the runs, dehydration is a more likely risk so you should ensure you drink plenty of water afterwards, with some of it preferably mixed with rehydration salts.

Malaria

Malaria – transmitted by a parasite in the saliva of an infected female anopheles mosquito – can be fatal if left untreated. **Symptoms** – fever, chills, headaches and muscle pains – are easily confused with flu. Thankfully, only the northern strip of Namibia along the perennial rivers is a year-round high-risk area; other areas, broadly covering the northern third of the country, hold some risk during the rains (Nov/Dec–April/May), when periodically there are areas of stagnant water where mosquitoes can breed.

Malaria is most effectively combated through **prevention** – wearing long loose sleeves and trousers for protection at dawn and dusk, when the mosquitoes are at their most active, dousing yourself in repellent, and sleeping under a mosquito net or in screened rooms. Taking a course of appropriate **prophylactics** – consult a travel clinic – is also strongly advised.

Bites, stings and parasites

Snakes and scorpions may feature heavily in films set in deserts, but in reality there's very little chance of your seeing one, let alone getting bitten by one, as most scarper at the mere approach of a human. Moreover, the vast majority of snakes in Namibia are not dangerous. Still, it's wise to take precautions: where there are places for snakes to hide, wear long trousers and closed shoes to minimize the risk of getting bitten; carry a torch when walking at night; and if camping, shake your shoes out before putting them on in the morning. If someone is bitten, above all ensure they don't panic – but don't try to suck or cut out the venom or apply a tourniquet in true Hollywood style; all these measures will do more harm than good. Try to remember what the snake looked like, keep the infected area immobile, tie a bandage (not too tight) a few centimetres above the area, and seek immediate medical attention.

In the areas of sluggish or slow-moving water in the Kavango and Zambezi regions, there's a very low risk of **bilharzia** (schistosomiasis), though you're unlikely to be swimming in the rivers due to the much greater risk of providing a crocodile with a good meal.

MEDICAL RESOURCES

UK AND IRELAND

Fitfortravel Ⓦ fitfortravel.nhs.uk. Excellent NHS (Scotland) public access site with country-specific advice, the latest health bulletins and information on immunizations.

Hospital for Tropical Diseases Travel Clinic ☎ 020 7388 9600 (Travel Clinic), ☎ 020 7950 7799 (24hr Travellers Healthline Advisory Service – see website for additional country-specific information), Ⓦ thehtd.org.

MASTA (Medical Advisory Service for Travellers Abroad) ☎ 0870 606 2782, Ⓦ masta-travel-health.com. List of affiliated travel clinics where you can get vaccinations and detailed country-specific health briefs.

National Travel Health Network and Centre Ⓦ nathnac.org. Excellent website for health professionals and the travelling public, providing fact sheets on various travel health risks and a free database of country-specific health info.

STA Travel Ⓦ statravel.co.uk. List of STA travel clinics in England and vaccination prices; full-time students with student card can get a 10 percent discount.

Tropical Medical Bureau ☎ 1850 487 674, Ⓦ tmb.ie. List of travel clinics in Ireland.

US AND CANADA

Centers for Disease Control and Prevention (CDC) ☎ 800 232 6348 (24hr health helpline), Ⓦ cdc.gov/travel. Official US government travel health site that's laden with info.

Public Health Agency of Canada Ⓦ phac-aspc.gc.ca. Distributes free pamphlets on travel health and provides a comprehensive list of travel clinics in the country.

Travellers' Medical and Vaccination Centre Ⓦ tmvc.com. List of travel health centres in Canada and vaccination costs plus brief travel health tips.

AUSTRALIA, NEW ZEALAND AND SOUTH AFRICA

Travellers' Medical and Vaccination Centre Ⓦ traveldoctor .com.au. User-friendly site listing travel clinics in Australia, New Zealand and South Africa, plus accessible fact sheets on travel health and postings of health alerts worldwide.

Festivals

Namibia hosts a handful of national and regional festivals.

A FESTIVAL CALENDAR

Bank Windhoek Arts Festival Feb–Sept. Windhoek. Annual festival of the visual and performing arts in venues across the capital, which climaxes in September. Includes the national Triennial Visual Arts competition, in which prize-winning works are exhibited.

Enjando Street Festival March. Central Windhoek. Also known as Mbapira, this festival sees a two-day extravaganza of music, dance and colourful costumes, attracting groups from all over Namibia.

Herero Day Sunday closest to Aug 23. Okahandja. Colourful Herero costumes, poetry and military parades remember those who died in the resistance against the German army.

Küste Karneval Aug. Swakopmund. Annual German street carnival involving parades, food stalls and plenty of partying for adults and kids.

Lusata Festival Last week of Sept. Chinchimani Village, 6km from Katima Mulilo. The annual traditional cultural celebration of the Mafwe people that takes place in the village of the tribal chief, Chinchimani Village, and attracts Mafwe from outside Namibia too.

Oruuano of Namibia Arts Festival Sept & Nov. Soweto Market, Katutura. Organized by the Oruuano Namibian Artists' Union, involving lots of dance and music.

Windhoek Show First week of Oct. Windhoek. The country's main agricultural and industrial trade fair, accompanied by funfair entertainment, live music and food stalls.

Oktoberfest Last week of Oct. Windhoek. A German import, the Oktoberfest draws an international crowd, complete with beer-swilling, games, Lederhosen, Dirndl dresses and oompah bands.

Going on safari

Although Namibia isn't a conventional safari destination – Etosha aside – in terms of gazing at herds of wildebeest migrating across the plains, there are several good reasons why it is a top place to head out on safari, especially a self-drive adventure. Roads are generally in good condition, and most are suitable for first-time safari-goers; even in high season there are few crowds – unlike in

STAYING SAFE ON THE ROADS

Though all rental agencies should give you a full briefing about the vehicle and check that all equipment is present and in working order, some don't, especially the international rental agencies when handing over a 2WD in high season and staff are stretched. Ensure that you get fully briefed; stories abound of tourists being given vehicles with no **functioning jack**, or without being advised not to **travel in the dark**. Make sure you're not one of them.

Check the car has a jack and one, or preferably two (which you can pre-book at extra cost), **spare wheels** in good condition before you start out. Most 4WD rentals should also include a **first-aid kit**, a **shovel** to dig yourself out of sand or mud, and a **tow rope** in case the digging fails. A **tyre pressure gauge and pump** are also essential if you're going to remote areas such as the Kaokoveld, or if you'll be needing to deflate (and then reinflate) your tyres after driving through deep sand.

Also make sure you always travel with plenty of **water and snacks**, in case of a long wait for the cavalry to arrive should your vehicle break down.

some of Africa's more renowned wildlife-viewing hotspots; and it's very safe. What's more, it's a great deal of fun. The main drawback is the distances you're likely to cover, and the fuel costs involved.

Planning your trip

There are various decisions to be made before embarking on a safari adventure, regarding whether you drive yourself, or travel as part of a group. Should you book accommodation through a travel agent in your home country, or in Namibia? If money's not a concern, but time is, are you going to fly in and out of some or all of your destinations? It's also possible to arrange a combination tour, with some organized activities, and other self-drive elements, which you can sort out yourself or pay a tour operator to do everything for you.

Three issues you need to be clear on before planning can begin relate to your budget, the length of time available, and the destinations within Namibia you want to cover. This last issue is particularly relevant if you're going to be driving, or be driven everywhere, which in turn has a bearing on the time it will take. Given that lodges and camps have to be vacated by 10am, and check-in is not before 3pm, it makes sense to plan for at least two nights, preferably three per destination – providing you with at least one full day – to allow you to make the most of your surroundings and the activities on offer, otherwise you may feel you're constantly on the road.

Organized tours

Organized tours obviously take any spontaneity out of the equation, but can help reduce the time and stress of planning everything yourself. Larger companies tend to offer set itineraries, generally on specific dates, though they may also arrange bespoke tours, which many of the smaller operators specialize in, and which inevitably cost more. Price primarily relates to the type of accommodation (camping or luxury lodge?) and the associated degree of pampering, as well as the size of the group, though the number and quality of the guides is also an important factor. Group tours can be organized through specialist tour operators in your home country, or ones in Namibia, or even South Africa.

If you book through a **company in your own country**, the trip is likely to be more expensive since agencies are covering overheads and wages higher than those in Namibia (unless you're coming from South Africa). On the other hand, they may also sort your flights, include better insurance deals in case of cancellation, and you may be able to pay using a credit card or Paypal. Many operators in Namibia do not accept credit cards and demand bank transfers in advance of your arrival in Namibia. This is fine if you're transferring from South Africa (within the Common Monetary Area), and no big deal if you're only paying one tour operator – and indeed is a good reason for working through an operator rather than planning your itinerary yourself; otherwise, you'll find yourself having to pay for international bank transfers for every night's accommodation or activity that you book, which can be costly. Some lodgings may accommodate you if you write and explain and will hold your credit card details (though they often ask you to email them!) as insurance until you reach the country and can pay cash (from an ATM or bank withdrawal) directly into a bank account or turn up on their doorstep with the required sum.

National park	Description	Main attractions	Accommodation
|Ai–|Ais/Richtersveld Transfrontier Park N$80, plus N$10/ vehicle for canyon and springs. South African section R210 (see p.154)	Desert mountainscape, Orange River and Fish River Canyon with hot springs at southern end – 2WD. 4WD for South African section, preferably convoy.	Namibia: Fish River Canyon, |Ai–|Ais Hot Springs, hiking. South African Richtersveld: hiking, rock formations, succulents.	Hobas (Fish River Canyon): NWR campsite and chalets; spa and lodges nearby; South African Richtersveld: Sanparks chalets and wilderness camps.
Bwabwata National Park Mahango Core Area N$40, plus N$10/ vehicle (see p.285)	Kavango River, floodplains and grasslands, broad-leaved woodland; eastern area 2WD, western area 4WD.	Riverine environment; birdwatching; hippo, crocs, elephant, roan and sable antelope, tsessebe; Popa Falls; boat trips and game drives.	No park accommodation, but private riverside lodges and camping nearby.
Bwabwata National Park Kwando Core Area N$40, plus N$10/ vehicle (see p.286)	Riverine environment by Kwando River; deciduous woodland on low-lying sand dunes; 4WD necessary.	River setting, boat trips; birdwatching – carmine bee-eaters; elephant, buffalo, hippo and wild dog (rare); game drives.	*Nambwa Lodge and Campsite* inside the park; private lodges and camps across the river.
Dorob National Park N$80, plus N$10/ vehicle (seal colony); otherwise free (see p.226)	Undeveloped, coastal park bridging the Skeleton Coast NP and Namib-Naukluft; 2WD.	Cape Cross seal colony; impressive lichen fields; 4WD trails.	NWR campsites on coast including at Cape Cross; *Cape Cross Lodge,* and lodgings in Henties Bay.
Etosha National Park N$80, plus N$10/ vehicle (see p.241)	Huge park centred on vast salt pan, with mopane woodland; hillier terrain further west; 2WD.	Lion, rhino, elephant, cheetah, giraffe, zebra and antelope; illuminated waterholes; Etosha Pan; game drives.	NWR restcamps and two lodges inside the park; private reserves, lodges and camping outside.
Khaudum National Park N$40, plus N$10/ vehicle (see p.276)	Forested dunes with bush cover and some grassland, ephemeral water courses; minimum 2-vehicle 4WD convoy, food and water for 3 days.	Wilderness camping, 4WD driving; many large mammals: roan and sable antelope, wildebeest, hartebeest, and elephant (dry season), wild dog.	Bush camps due to be renovated. *Nhoma Camp* and *Tsumkwe Lodge* within reach.
Mangetti National Park N$40, plus N$10/ vehicle (see p.277)	Small, community-managed new park with no infrastructure but dense bush and deep sand; 4WD.	Eland, blue wildebeest, sable antelope and wild dog; three waterholes – wildlife difficult to spot.	No accommodation in the park, or nearby.
Mudumu National Park N$40, plus N$10/ vehicle (see p.288)	Riverine forest and floodplain of the Kwando River.	River setting, herds of buffalo and elephant, plus roan, sable antelope and wetland antelope; excellent birdwatching.	NWR campsites, the private *Lianshulu Lodge*; other private lodges outside the park.
Namib-Naukluft National Park N$80, plus N$10/ vehicle at Sesriem; N$40/person, plus N$10/vehicle for other entrances (see p.106)	Namib Desert: dunes, rocky landscapes, gravel plains and inselbergs. Naukluft Mountains: steep cliffs and plateau top; 2WD, but 4WD for some wilderness camps.	Sossusvlei: dunes and wildlife; Naukluft Mountains: hiking trails, Hartmann's mountain zebra and good birdlife. Northern section: welwitschias and lichen, desert walks. Sandwich Harbour: wetland birds and dunes.	Sesriem/Sossusvlei: NWR lodge and campsite. Naukluft Mountains: NWR campsite and chalets. Northern sector: NWR bush camps and lodges. Other options available outside the parks.

National park	Description	Main attractions	Accommodation
Nkasa Rupara National Park N$40, plus N$10/ vehicle (see p.288)	Reed-filled marshland and woodland savannah. 4WD; sometimes flooded and inaccessible.	Prolific birdlife and wetland antelope; large herds of buffalo; lions, elephant, hippo and monitor lizards.	Jackalberry Tented Camp inside park, and *Nkasa Lupala Tented Lodge* and campsite just outside.
Skeleton Coast National Park N$80, plus N$10/ vehicle (see p 229)	Gravel plains, rock desert, transected by dry sandy riverbeds, high dunes in the north; bleak coastline.	Wilderness landscapes; lichen fields, dunes (at the northern end) and shipwrecks; lions, elephant and rhino, especially along the riverbeds.	Fly-in safaris to luxury wilderness tented camps; basic NWR chalets and campsites.
Tsau ‖Khaeb (Sperrgebiet) National Park N$85 (Kolmanskop tour). Other areas on tours from Lüderitz; price covers park fees (see p.131)	Vast area comprising desert rock and dune formations, a rocky and sandy coastline and succulents. Organized tours only.	Kolmanskop, ghost mining town; Sperrgebiet day-trips: dunes, lichen, succulents, abandoned towns and Bogenfels Rock Arch.	No accommodation in the park. Lüderitz offers nearest lodgings.
Waterberg Plateau National Park N$80, plus N$10/ vehicle (see p.174)	Sandstone table mountain with lush vegetation due to springs; thick vegetation impedes visibility; 2WD.	Short trails, birdwatching, including Cape Vultures; game drives on plateau top: rhino, eland, tsessebe, antelope.	NWR chalets and campsites in the park; private lodges and guestfarms nearby.
Kgalagadi Transfrontier Park R304 (South African section) (see p.152)	Vast park – duneveld in this area, two dry riverbeds and saltpans. 2WD; smaller tracks and some camps 4WD.	Large migrating herds and smaller mammals such as meerkats, plus predators, including black-maned lions; red linear dunes.	Range of Sanparks accommodation, mainly self-catering chalets and camping, plus *!Xaus Lodge*.
Victoria Falls National Park Entry to the Victoria Falls US$30 (Zimbabwe) (see p.313)	Small park, mainly mopane woodland, extending along Zambezi.	The Victoria Falls (80 percent) including small "rainforest". Adventure activities, plus river cruises, canoeing, helicopter flights.	No park accommodation but a good range in nearby Victoria Falls Town.
Zambezi National Park US$15, plus US$5–10/ vehicle (Zimbabwe) (see p.315)	Riverine forest extending 40km along Zambezi west of Vic Falls; also mopane woodland and grassland inland. 4WD necessary.	Zambezi River; Big Five plus antelope, zebra, giraffe, crocs and hippo; fishing and birdwatching; kayaking, horseback and bush camping.	National Park accommodation in self-catering chalets, fishing camps and campsites along river, plus luxury tented camp.
Mosi-oa-Tunya National Park US$20 (Victoria Falls; Zambia). US$10, plus US$5/vehicle (game reserve; Zambia) see p.329)	Strip extending 12km up the Zambezi from the falls; riverine forest giving way to mopane and miombo woodland with some grassland. 2WD.	The Victoria Falls (20 percent) including Knife Edge Bridge, Boiling Pot and Livingstone Island. Activities like white-water rafting and zip-lining. Game reserve: white rhino tracking; river cruises, hippo and crocs.	No park accommodation but a good range in nearby Livingstone.

Self-drive

Bespoke tour operators can also organize self-drive safaris for you; they'll make all the bookings for lodgings and sort your transport and any extras you may want (such as renting camping gear), and, if they are in Namibia, they can meet and greet you at the airport. Self-organized self-drive safaris, on the other hand, offer the greatest flexibility, especially if you decide to equip yourself with a tent, though you'll still need to make some advance reservations should you intend to visit during high season, even if camping. Should really remote areas like Kaokoland be on your itinerary but you are unsure of your self-drive skills and/or you're travelling alone, you might consider a guided self-drive safari, which some companies offer.

Once you've made your mind up to drive yourself for at least some of the trip, the next decision concerns whether to rent a 2WD or a 4WD. There are pros and cons for both and these relate to your likely itinerary and budget (see p.67). Also, if you intend to do some camping, you'll need to decide whether you want a roof tent or one that you can leave in a campground while you drive around.

For novice safari self-drivers, Namibia can provide the easiest initiation as long as you stick to the main roads and main sights; even so, there are a few basic rules to follow to ensure you stay safe (see box, p.61).

Wildlife viewing

Namibia's most famous reserve and the best location for spotting big mammals, including four of the "Big Five" – which is what many visitors obsess over – is **Etosha National Park**. Here you stand a good chance of seeing large numbers of animals, especially in the dry season (July–Oct), although herds of elephant and buffalo are beginning to return to the newer reserves in the Zambezi Region. Namibia also hosts the world's largest cheetah population and there are several **cheetah conservation projects** that you can visit if you want a near-guaranteed sighting (see box, p.178). More intriguing, perhaps, and unique to Namibia, are the guided excursions into the Namib Desert from Swakopmund that focus on Namibia's "Small Five" – some of the extraordinary tiny creatures that have adapted to this harsh environment (see p.363).

While seeking out wildlife is likely to be one of your main motivations for visiting Namibia, there may well be times when you need to steer clear, or beat a hasty retreat.

Birdwatching

Boasting over 650 species of birds, including numerous near-endemics, Namibia provides plenty of birdwatching opportunities. Peak times for avian activity are during the **rainy season** (Nov–April), when food is more plentiful and nesting occurs. Migrants from Europe and other parts of Africa generally arrive in October and leave around April. While most of the country is home to desert bird species, **Walvis Bay** hosts southern Africa's most important coastal wetlands, enjoyed by around 250,000 birds during the migration season (see p.220). Though Walvis Bay is synonymous with flamingos, which constitute the bulk of the population, and are visible all year, a host of other waders and seabirds also draw birders and casual visitors alike. The freshwater wetlands and rivers of the **Zambezi Region** also provide a wealth of tropical birdlife, from the iconic fish eagle to rainbow-coloured bee-eaters and the extraordinary-looking spoonbill and hammerhead. Several river lodges here offer birdwatching river trips. Two specialist birding tour operators are based in Swakopmund: Batis Birding Safaris (☎064 404908, ⓦ batisbirding safaris.com) and Safariwise (☎064 405220, ⓦ safari toursnamibia.com) both offer day tours as well as multi-day birding trips all around Namibia and further afield.

National parks

National parks and other reserves comprise almost a fifth of Namibia's vast terrain, managed predominantly by the Ministry of the Environment and Tourism (MET).

While only Etosha National Park in the north can claim to host really large quantities of "big game", Namibia's parks and reserves are famous for their extraordinary **wilderness landscapes**, such as the spectacular sand dunes round Sossusvlei in what is currently the country's largest protected area, the Namib-Naukluft National Park (see p.106), and the inaccessible, eerie coastline of the Skeleton Coast National Park (see p.229), in the northwest. One of the more recent national parks, created in 2009, is the Tsau ||Khaeb – better known as the Sperrgebiet; located in the southwest of the country, it was formerly an out-of-bounds diamond-mining area and can currently only be visited on a guided tour from Lüderitz (see p.124). These three major parks are now linked by the Dorob National Park, a relatively open park, which includes areas round Swakopmund and Walvis Bay, and for which there is no fee. Collectively these four parks form the **Namib-Skeleton Coast National Park**, extending the entire 1500km length of Namibia's coastline.

Other major reserves include the dramatic sandstone cliffs of the **Waterberg Plateau Park**, on the road north from Windhoek, and the |**Ai-|Ais/ Richtersveld Transfrontier Park**, which extends into South Africa on Namibia's southern border and includes the awe-inspiring Fish River Canyon. We have a full summary of the major features and attractions of each park and the types of accommodation available (see box, p.62). Downloadable e-brochures on all the flora, fauna and geography of Namibia's main national parks and government-owned reserves are available from the tourist board website (see Ⓦnamibia tourism.com.na/page/national-parks).

In addition to the state-managed national parks and reserves, Namibia boasts a wealth of **private reserves** – often called guestfarms (see p.55) – and **community-managed conservancies**, aimed at combining nature conservation with poverty alleviation initiatives, including many associated with tourism (see p.56, and box, p.364).

Accommodation and permits

Almost all national park accommodation must be booked through **Namibia Wildlife Resorts** (Ⓦnwr.com.na), either online or in person at one of their offices located in Windhoek (see box, p.94), Swakopmund (see p.213) or in Cape Town, South Africa. Lodgings range from campgrounds (from N$150/person) to chalets that vary in levels of comfort, sophistication and location, with **prices** to match: N$1160–5940 for a double room/chalet including breakfast (usually a buffet). The camp/resort restaurants usually serve à la carte during the day and a fixed-price buffet in the evening (N$230), though the newer, smaller exclusive camps may provide a limited à la carte or set menu.

Chalet prices are significantly cheaper in low season (Nov–June), though camping rates remain the same. Children aged 6–12 sharing chalet accommodation with a full fee-paying adult get a 50 percent discount, and children under 6 stay free. There are reductions for Namibians and residents of countries from the Southern African Development Community (SADC). These prices do not include the park/reserve **entry fees**, which go to MET, and are usually payable on entry and valid for 24 hours. They currently stand at N$80 per person per day for the more popular parks of Etosha, the |Ai-|Ais/Richtersveld Transfrontier Park, the Skeleton Coast, the Sesriem (Sossusvlei) entrance to Namib-Naukluft and Waterberg, and N$40 per person per day for other reserves, plus N$10 per day for each vehicle. However, to visit some places, such as parts of the Skeleton Coast and the restricted areas of Namib-Naukluft, you will also need to obtain in advance a special **permit** from the MET permit office in Windhoek, Swakopmund or Walvis Bay (see p.94, p.213 & p.223). If you are going as part of an organized tour, the tour operator will arrange the permit, which is usually included in the price.

Park **activities** such as wildlife-viewing drives or fishing trips can also be booked through the NWR office, usually from N$550–660 per person. They, like the accommodation, fill up early in high season, so book in advance for these too.

Sports and outdoor activities

Namibia's dramatic landscapes provide the perfect backdrop to a wealth of outdoor activities, from ballooning across the spectacular dunes of Sossusvlei to hiking down the Fish River Canyon or gazing up at the stars from the darkness of the desert. There's also plenty of scope for extreme sports, such as skydiving, kitesurfing or hauling your body through the desert in an ultramarathon.

Hiking

While the harsh desert terrain does not make for ideal hiking conditions, Namibia offers a few classic **multi-day trails**, for which you'll need to be in good physical condition and will usually need to carry your own camping gear, food and water. In addition, several of the private reserves and guest-farms have developed a range of **one-day trails**, some for tourists of more moderate fitness levels.

Justifiably, the most popular hike is the hardcore, five-day, 85km hike along the spectacular **Fish River Canyon** (see p.154), which needs a minimum of three people for safety reasons and cannot be done in the extreme heat of summer. On account of the trail's popularity, bookings need to be made many months in advance. The rocky terrain of **Naukluft** in central Namibia is also favoured by hikers, offering a variety of trails, some of which can be walked in a day, though others need several days (see box, p.117).

Though only established in 2015, the six-day Khomas Hochland hiking trail, which covers 91km across five guestfarms (also with a shorter 53km route over four days) is becoming increasingly popular. It offers fine views of the highlands; what's more, there are ways of easing the endurance pain by slackpacking – having your food, bedding and any other luggage transported from camp to camp for you (🌐 hikenamibia.com; see box, p.103).

The sandstone **Waterberg Plateau** three hours north of Windhoek is also a prime area to explore on foot. At the moment, however, you are restricted to short day-walks around the camp, and up to the plateau ridge, as the multi-day hikes had been suspended indefinitely on account of increased anti-poaching security on the plateau (see p.175).

Other favourite places to explore on foot include the private **NamibRand Reserve**, which abuts the Namib-Naukluft National Park, where you can undertake the interpretive three-day guided Tok Tokkie Trail, which offers a desert experience that includes fine dining and camping out under the stars (see p.119). Alternatively, consider ascending Namibia's **Brandberg massif**, which towers 2km out of the gravel plains of former Damaraland (see p.193); three- to five-day hikes are available, taking in some of the best-preserved San rock art on the continent, and offering spectacular panoramic views.

Adventure sports

Swakopmund is the country's centre for adventure sports, with several operators offering an increasingly diverse array of activities (see p.213). On land, the action centres on the **dunes**: sand-surfing or sand-boarding are possible, along with more established diversions such as quad biking (see box, p.215). Skydiving and paragliding are airborne diversions, while the truly fit and masochistic might consider one of Namibia's ultramarathons and other

---

DESERT ECOLOGY AND RESPONSIBLE TRAVEL

Namibia's desert landscape is a fragile environment, where it's easy to inflict lasting damage through a few careless actions. Careering across seemingly desolate dunes on a quad bike can be exhilarating fun, as can charging down the side of a sand dune, but both actions threaten some of the **desert micro-fauna**, most of which lives less than 10cm below dune surface. The eggs, larvae and young of beetles, spiders and reptiles are especially vulnerable on the dune slipface (the steeper incline on the lee side), where these animals concentrate. In particular, you should keep clear of patches of stabilizing vegetation. Generally, the least damage is caused by walking up and down the crest of the dune.

In Swakopmund and Walvis Bay, most tour operators are responsible and operate within designated areas, aimed at **minimizing the impact on the dunes**, and employing guides who ensure that sand-boarding is carried out only on specific slopes, and that on quad bike tours, everyone follows in the same tracks, on set routes, behind the guide. It is generally individuals who have their own bikes and vehicles driving "off-piste" that cause the most damage.

Several companies (notably in Lüderitz) offer off-road wilderness camping adventures through the Namib, but before embarking on one, you need to satisfy yourself that they are trying to minimize their impact on the environment. It is worth asking: what is the maximum number of vehicles they travel in; whether they always follow the same tracks; what they do with their camping waste; and whether they use stoves rather than making fires. There is a **culture of machismo** among some off-road drivers – evident even in some of the Sandwich Harbour tour drivers – that can lead to a greater environmental footprint than is necessary.

Similarly, when corrugations on some of the gravel roads become uncomfortable it's very tempting to drive onto the adjacent, often harder, desert crust, and make new parallel tracks. As well as leaving unsightly marks that can stain the landscape for years, this poses a **threat to birds' nests**, such as those of the endangered Damara tern, and may also destroy **barely discernible lichen** and other plants that have taken hundreds of years to grow, and which provide vital nutrients or shelter for other wildlife. Penetrating the desert crust by off-road driving also exposes softer sand and soil to wind erosion.

BALLOONING

There are few more magical experiences than **ballooning across the dunes of the Namib** at dawn, topped off by a champagne breakfast in the desert (just under N$6000/person). Although you'll only be in the air around an hour, you'll need to set aside a large chunk of the morning, once pick-ups and preparation time have been factored in. Currently, departures are only from Sossusvlei (see box, p.113).

desert challenges that take place in the Namib and in the Fish River Canyon (see ⓦ marathons.ahotu .com/calendar/namibia/trail).

Watersports

Given the general lack of water in Namibia, **watersports** are inevitably restricted to the perennial rivers at the north and south ends of the country, and to the coast. **Surfing** and **kitesurfing** are both available in Swakopmund and Walvis Bay, though Lüderitz, further south down the coast, has a reputation for **windsurfing** and **kite-boarding** world speed records.

A limited range of **kayaking** opportunities exists. You can paddle about on the Walvis Bay lagoon, where the aim is to get close to the wildlife, in particular the Cape fur seals and the prolific birdlife (see p.223). On the other hand, you can enjoy day- and multi-day kayaking trips through stunning scenery along the Orange River, on the South African border (see box, p.161), while the camps and lodges on the Kunene at Epupa offer seasonal half-day **rafting** trips (see box, p.261).

Horse riding

Travelling by horseback is a great way to get off the beaten track in the desert, without the accompanying hum of a 4WD. The experienced international outfit Hidden Trails (ⓦ hiddentrails .com), which specializes in multi-day high-end **horse safaris** worldwide, offers several all-inclusive itineraries in Namibia for experienced, fit riders. The Namibia Horse Safari Company (ⓦ namibiahorsesafari.com) in Aus, southern Namibia, also organizes all-inclusive ten- to eleven-day horse safaris for fit intermediate and experienced riders through the Namib, along the Fish River Canyon and in Damaraland.

Catering for riders of all abilities and for those who wish to spend less time in the saddle, several lodges for the Namib-Naukluft National Park and adjacent NamibRand Reserve offer popular **sunrise and sunset rides**. Check out Wolwedans (see p.119) and the *Desert Homestead Lodge* ⓦ deserthomesteadlodge.com, for example. In the Eros Mountains, and accessible from Windhoek, Namibia-based Equitrails (ⓦ equitrails.org) caters to riders of all abilities offering a range of less pricey **tours**, from a couple of hours to a couple of days in the saddle, overnighting on a guestfarm. Okakambe Trails (see box, p.214) in Swakopmund also has a varied equestrian menu, from short rides into the Swakop riverbed and the moon landscape, to overnight horse safaris of one to five nights, covering 20–30km per day and sleeping in tented camps.

Stargazing

Thanks to a low population density, low air pollution and virtually non-existent light pollution, the pitch-black sky above Namibia's desert landscape is one of the top places in the world for stargazing, especially in the dry winter months. Though almost anywhere away from the few urban areas can provide you with a glittering night sky and opportunities to marvel at the Milky Way, for prime viewing, head for the **Gamsberg Mountains** around 100km southwest of Windhoek, where the Hakos Guest Farm (ⓦ hakos -astrofarm.com) specializes in astrotourism. Kiripotib Guest Farm is another magnet for astronomers or would-be astronomers, while top of the pile sits the **NamibRand Reserve** – Africa's first **International Dark Sky Reserve**. The most luxurious accommodation here, *Sossusvlei Desert Lodge*, has its own telescope and resident astronomer for guests (see p.119).

Travel essentials

Costs

If you're travelling from Europe or North America, **costs** in Namibia may not seem that high, given the favourable exchange rates. On the other hand, with only limited public transport, vast distances to cover between sights, and only a small number of budget lodgings available, expenses can add up. With a combination of hitchhiking and public transport, staying only in budget hostels, campgrounds and cooking your own meals, you can probably get by on N$600 per person per day; add in an extra N$500–800 per person for an excursion or activity. Staying in mid-range accommodation in a shared room on a dinner, bed and breakfast basis, which is the norm, can mean a daily food and lodgings budget from around N$1000 per person, with park fees, car rental costs and fuel on top. 4WD rental will cost double, and if you fancy the exclusive, high-end accommodation near Sossusvlei or the Skeleton Coast, where you're not necessarily paying for traditional hotel luxury – marble bathrooms, rooftop swimming pools and high thread counts – but for remote wilderness and/or incredible wildlife experiences, you'll be paying around N$6000–10,000 per person per day for full board, activities and park fees.

Crime and personal safety

Namibia is an extremely **safe** country to travel around, even on your own, though **petty crime** is on the increase in Windhoek and some of the larger towns. That said, being street-savvy goes a long way towards avoiding problems: not wearing expensive jewellery or watches, not opening your bag or wallet to get cash out in a public place, and always making sure your **car** is locked, the windows are closed, and your belongings are out of sight when you stop in towns or at petrol stations. If you have to leave your car for a time, and there is no guarded, secure car park available, it pays to park in front of a shop or bank, where there will be a security guard whom you can ask (and tip on your return) to keep an eye on your vehicle. Remember, if you do get robbed, you will need a police report to complete an insurance claim once you get home.

Culture and etiquette

Greetings are key to ensuring good social relations in Namibia, as in many parts of Africa. Before you ask a question or a favour, you should always make sure you greet the person and enquire after their health. If you can manage that in the relevant local language (see box, p.370), then so much the better. Handshakes are the most common form of greeting, especially among men, and always with the right hand. Men will often use the three-part African handshake when greeting other men. Women are more likely to greet each other and men with words, though they may shake hands. If in a more traditional rural setting, a small nod, bow or curtsy may be given by the junior to acknowledge seniority.

Modest **dress** is also important, especially when visiting rural areas, which are generally dominated by Christian conservatism. In the extreme heat it may be tempting to strip off to the bare essentials, but notwithstanding the risk of sunburn, short, skimpy attire is fine for the beach but can give offence in villages. Generally, men wear long trousers and shirts and women wear something that covers their shoulders and knees.

While on the subject of village life, if offered something to **drink or eat**, you should always accept the offer. When eating with your hands, often the case in rural communities, you should eat with your right hand even if left-handed, as the left hand is considered unclean.

Photography is a thorny area, which has been badly handled by many tourists over a number of years, especially with regards to the Himba, Herero and the San, where taking photos tends to dominate interactions to a worrying extent. The crass behaviour of some tourists who snap away without permission of the individuals concerned and with minimal interaction with them has led to difficult relations between some Namibian communities and tourists. Some Himba and Herero women in particular are now demanding payment for having their photo taken. Always ask permission if you wish to take a photo, and only after you have spent time in meaningful interaction with the person or people concerned.

Electricity

Electricity is 220 volts in Namibia, and large three-pin round plugs are used, as in South Africa. You're advised to bring an adaptor with you; for sale in Johannesburg airport and in Windhoek, but hard to come by elsewhere in Namibia.

Insurance

Full insurance for flights, medical emergencies and personal possessions is highly recommended. Make sure it covers any adventure sports you might want to do. If you intend to rent a car, you might also consider taking out a standalone car rental excess insurance policy, since this can work out cheaper than the additional fees charged by car rental firms to reduce the excess payable in case of accident.

Internet

Finding somewhere to access the internet will seldom be a problem in Namibia, even in quite remote areas, though in many parts of the country connections are often slow and the service is unreliable. A few **internet cafés** exist in Windhoek and Swakopmund – expect to pay around N$10/30min – and many hotels and hostels across the country have a PC or two available for guest use. However, in most accommodation, as well as in shopping malls and cafés, **wi-fi** is a more common means of getting online. In lodges, wi-fi is usually confined to the main building, and – understandably – the signal strength is usually fairly weak.

Laundry

In Windhoek and the larger towns you'll find launderettes and dry cleaners. In addition, most hotels, lodges and guesthouses offer a laundry service, though this is obviously more expensive.

LGBTI travellers

Sodomy rather than homosexuality is illegal in Namibia, though the Namibian government tends to interpret this as meaning that homosexuality is illegal. Moreover, its attitude towards LBGTI rights is generally one of intolerance. That said, LGBTI travellers can enjoy a hassle-free holiday in Namibia provided they are discreet about their sexuality. What's more, there are two gay-owned and LBGTI-friendly tour companies in Namibia, as well as lodge owners who are happy to facilitate bookings.

Contact New African Frontiers in Windhoek (☎061 222964, ⓦnewafricanfrontiers.com) or JJ Tours in Kamanjab (☎081 424 1114, ⓦnamibiajjtours.com) for advice.

Maps

A range of **maps**, updated every few years, is widely available in specialist map shops and online in Europe and the US. The bookshops in Windhoek and Swakopmund also stock a selection. The Namibian Tourist Board and most tour operators can supply you with the annually updated **Roads Authority Map of Namibia**, which also has details of many campgrounds, but is not very useful. Better quality, however, is the Reise Know-How map, which is easy to read, includes almost all lodges, guestfarms and registered campgrounds, community or private, as well as marking petrol stations. This map alone is adequate for most self-drive visitors. If you're intending to go off the beaten track, on the other hand, then the downloadable **Tracks4Africa GPS map** – which only works for Garmin GPS – and their new paper map should be high on your shopping list (ⓦtracks4africa.com). You can download in advance or purchase the software in Namibia at somewhere like Radio Electronic (ⓦrec.com.na).

Media

There is generally a high level of press freedom in Namibia, particularly in the print media. The country's top **newspaper**, both in quality and circulation, is the mainly English-language (with some content in Oshiwambo) daily The Namibian (ⓦnamibian.com .na). The New Era is the state-owned daily paper. Several other dailies exist, including ones in Afrikaans and German, as well as several weekly papers and monthly magazines. There are over twenty private and community-owned **radio stations**, as well as the ten channels in different languages operated by the government-owned Namibian Broadcasting Corporation (NBC). Many guesthouses, hotels and lodges pay for the DStv satellite package, which is based in South Africa, and predominantly offers a diet of South African and US channels.

Money

The **Namibian dollar** (N$), often abbreviated to "Nam dollar" in common parlance, has been the official currency since 1993. Coins are produced for 5, 10 and 50 cents, and for 1, 5 and 10 Namibian dollars.

Notes are available in denominations of N$10, 20, 50, 100 and 200. Until 2012, the notes exclusively featured Hendrik Witbooi (see p.344). Then, in 2012, a series of more fraud-secure notes was introduced, featuring the post-independence president, Sam Nujoma, on the ten- and twenty-dollar bills.

To add to the currency confusion, prior to independence the **South African Rand** was the official currency, and since the Namibian dollar is still pegged to the Rand (1:1), it is still accepted as legal tender in the country. If you're withdrawing money near the end of your trip, or travelling on elsewhere, it's better to ask for South African Rands rather than Namibian dollars, as they're easier to exchange in other countries.

It is relatively quick and painless to change money at a bank, except at the end of the month, when queues can be substantial. The main **banks** in Namibia are the South African Nedbank, Standard Bank and First National Bank (FNB), in addition to Namibia's Bank Windhoek, which has 53 branches countrywide. Banking hours are usually Monday to Friday 8.30am–3.30pm, Saturday 8.30am–noon. At the time of writing, the **rates of exchange** were N$16.75 to £1, N$13.35 to US$1 and N$14.42 to €1.

Credit and debit cards are widely used to pay for goods and services in Windhoek and the major towns, especially Visa and MasterCard. American Express is less readily accepted. Credit cards are also generally accepted for mid- and high-end accommodation payments. Nearly all petrol stations, however, only accept cash, though this is beginning to change. Thankfully, petrol stations often have an ATM on the premises.

ATMs, though also widespread in the more remote areas, are sometimes out of order or run out of cash, especially at the end of the month or before public holidays. The daily withdrawal limit is usually N$1500–2000. For larger sums you can withdraw cash against a credit card in a bank on presentation of your passport. In the more rural areas, you will need cash; make sure that you carry some of the smaller denominations. **Travellers' cheques** are gradually being phased out, but can still be exchanged for cash at a bank.

> ### EMERGENCY NUMBERS
>
> **Police emergency** ☎ 10111
> **Namibian Tourist Protection Unit** ☎ 061 2092002

Opening hours and public holidays

Shops usually open at 9am, closing around 5.30pm. They also often close for lunch and on Saturdays shut down for the weekend at 1pm. Large supermarkets tend to open earlier (7–8am) and remain open until 7–8pm Monday to Friday; they may operate reduced trading hours on Saturday and Sunday, though some remain closed on Sunday. **Government offices** are open Monday to Friday 8am–5pm, often taking a lunch hour at 1pm.

Namibia doesn't have many **public holidays**, and if the date falls on a Sunday then the holiday is usually held on the following Monday. During these days most government offices, businesses and shops close. Many businesses and government departments also effectively close from mid-December to mid-January for the summer holidays.

HERERO DAY

On the weekend closest to August 23, **Herero Day** or **Red Flag Heroes' Day** (not to be confused with the national Heroes' Day), Herero gather in their thousands in Okahandja to commemorate their deceased chiefs, and, in particular **Chief Samuel Maharero**, who led the revolt against the German colonial army. The chosen date coincides with the reburial of his remains here, following his death in 1923 in South Africa, where he'd been living in exile (see p.345). Since then, Herero have congregated annually for a three-day gathering, the culmination of which is a **procession** round various grave sites of Herero chiefs, followed by a church service. This homage to the dead, which has since become a symbol of resistance against colonialism, is an impressive sight, with the Herero women decked out in their voluminous crimson missionary-era dresses and "cow-horn" headgear, and the men marching in their military-style uniforms according to their paramilitary regiments. Followers of other flags meet at other times of the year in other locations; for example, the White Flag Herero gather in Omaruru in August (see p.188). The Green Flag Mbanderu (see p.356) also meet in Okahandja on the weekend nearest June 11.

PUBLIC HOLIDAYS

January 1 New Year's Day

March 21 Independence Day

March/April Good Friday and Easter Monday

May 1 Workers Day

May 4 Cassinga Day. Commemorates the attack on a SWAPO base in Angola by the SADF in 1978, which killed 600.

May/June Ascension Day

May 26 Africa Day. Remembers the foundation of the Organisation of African Unity (OAU) in 1963.

August 26 Heroes' Day. Recognized by the UN as Namibia Day, which commemorates the official start of the War of Independence in 1966.

December 10 International Human Rights Day

December 25 Christmas Day

December 26 Family Day

Phones

Since **mobile phones** are increasingly more popular than landlines – and indeed the only form of communication in many rural areas – you may want to bring your mobile phone and purchase a Namibian SIM card (N$7) on arrival. These are available at the international airport and at various locations on Independence Avenue in Windhoek, and you can buy credit with pay-as-you-go cards. Old unlocked mobile phones work best if you just want phone, rather than internet, connectivity. If your phone is locked, you will need to pay a standard charge of N$250 to have it unlocked, a process that usually takes 24 hours. The mobile provider with the greatest coverage is MTC; check the MTC website (🌐 mtc.com.na) for the various packages on offer for smartphones. However, since in many remote areas there is no coverage at all, you might want to rent a satellite phone (around N$85/day plus call charges), which can be done at Be Local (🌐 be-local.com), or through your car-rental agency, with advance notice. Skype is also possible, though the slow wi-fi in many places can make it difficult.

To **call Namibia from abroad**, dial the international access code for the country you're in, followed by the country code 264. Note that mobile phone numbers in Namibia are ten digits, beginning with 081.

Post

Across the country, there are over 130 **post offices**, run by Nampost. Their smart, modern exteriors belie a somewhat less than efficient service: while fairly reliable for non-valuable objects, the system is fairly slow. Hours are generally Monday to Friday 8am–4.30pm, Saturday 8am–noon. A stamp for a 10g letter or postcard to Africa (outside SADC) and Europe costs N$6.60; to other destinations it costs N$7.70. Both Fedex (🌐 fedex.com/na) and DHL (🌐 dhl..com.en/na) have offices in Windhoek, Swakopmund, Walvis Bay and Lüderitz.

Shopping

Shopping for most visitors to Namibia revolves around **crafts and curios**. The main area of production is in the north, so if you are travelling to the Kunene, Kavango and Zambezi regions you might want to wait until then to buy (see boxes, p.289 & p.328), especially since more of the money is likely to go to the artisan. Note that a number of shops sell crafts imported from South Africa and elsewhere; the ubiquitous Namcrafts, for example, which has several outlets in the capital, has "Namcraft" labels on all its products, though they are not necessarily from Namibia. So if the origin is important to you, make sure you make thorough enquiries before making a purchase.

There is no shortage of places to look for crafts, both in the street, where you can bargain, and in shops, where you can't. The main craft shops are to be found in Windhoek and Swakopmund and there are two large craft markets in Okahandja (see p.171). The selections, however, are often quite

---

CALLING HOME FROM NAMIBIA

To make an international call, dial the international access code (in Namibia it's 00), then the destination's country code, before the rest of the number. Note that the initial zero is omitted from the area code when dialling the UK, Ireland, Australia and New Zealand from abroad.

UK international access code + 44

Ireland international access code + 353

US and Canada international access code + 1

Australia international access code + 61

New Zealand international access code + 64

South Africa international access code + 27

samey: soapstone figures and wooden carvings, particularly of animals; jewellery made from seeds, beads and shell; and batik cloth and cushion covers, again with animal designs aplenty. Namibia is also renowned for its semi-precious **stones and crystals** but you'll not find many bargains. Still, the Kristall Galerie in Swakopmund (see p.211) is a good places to garner information, or, if you want to make sure the money is benefiting the local community, try one of the Spitzkoppe roadside stalls, selling uncut gemstones.

Time

Namibia is normally GMT+2hr, but from the first Sunday in April to the first Sunday in September Namibia is GMT+1, known as Daylight Saving Time (DST).

Tipping

Tipping is always a tricky issue, and the best advice is to ask locally. There is no culture of automatic tipping in **restaurants**, although for formal establishments 10 percent of the total bill is the norm if the service is decent. For **porters** at airports or hotels expect to pay N$5 per bag. Similarly, N$5–10 would suffice for the **petrol pump attendant** who fills your vehicle if they clean your windows, check oil, tyres etc, and for anyone you ask to watch over your car for a few hours while you're parked in town.

If staying in a **lodge** for several days, only tip at the end – seek advice once there about what constitutes a fair tip; it will depend to an extent on whether the camp/lodge is budget or high-end and how many people are attached to one guide. Generally, it should not be more than US$10/day per person in a small group. Enquire also about whether there are communal tip boxes for the behind-the-scenes staff, many of whom get paid far less than the more high-profile guide. Many lodges pay very low wages and presume that tips will make up the shortfall. The only way to exert pressure and change this kind of behaviour is to complain to the management and/or give feedback online. That said, many tourists want to tip their guide if they have been particularly helpful and informative.

Bear in mind also that **overtipping** is not helpful: it sets a precedent that other travellers may not be able to live up to; it can create professional jealousy among workers; and it can upset the micro-economy, especially in poor, rural communities.

Tourist information

At the time of writing, the **Windhoek tourist office** was operating out of a portacabin on Independence Avenue, in Windhoek, but was due to relocate to new premises in the new Freedom Plaza (see p.92). It can provide you with basic information about Windhoek and tourist maps for other parts of the country. The national tourist board also operates a moderately useful website (Ⓦnamibia tourism.com.na), though it is not the easiest site to navigate. In other towns, tourist information is provided privately, often by tour operators. Many hostels and guesthouses can help with information and make bookings too.

Travellers with disabilities

Travellers with **visual, hearing or mobility impairment**, including wheelchair users, and "senior travellers", are well catered for by Endeavour

---

USEFUL WEBSITES

Useful websites to help you plan your trip include the following:

The Cardboard Box Travel Shop Ⓦnamibian.org. Well-organized, up-to-date website on all aspects of travel in Namibia, with detailed information on sights and accommodation options.

Expert Africa Ⓦexpertafrica.com/namibia. In addition to promoting the company's tours, the site provides insights on Namibian wildlife and where to find it, plus accommodation information.

Open Africa Ⓦopenafrica.org. Useful site promoting locally owned accommodation, restaurants, shops, attractions and other businesses in nine African countries.

Safari Bookings Ⓦsafaribookings.com/namibia. Site dedicated to safaris in Africa, giving user reviews and opinions of an expert panel of writers on tours, tour operators and national parks.

Travel News Namibia Ⓦtravelnewsnamibia.com. Glossy online magazine consisting of short articles accompanied with lots of impressive photos covering most of the main sights and some more intriguing, less publicized, activities or places.

Safaris (Botswana ☎06860887, ⓦendeavour-safaris .com), a company based in Botswana, offering a range of safaris in Namibia, Botswana and South Africa. UK company 2 by 2 Holidays (UK ☎01582 766122, ⓦ2by2holidays.co.uk) specializes in holidays for wheelchair users and offers a wide variety of safaris to Namibia, ranging from 7 to 16 nights. Independent wheelchair travellers should note that many hotels and lodges, including NWR properties in the national parks, have wheelchair-adapted rooms and bathrooms. A list of wheelchair-accessible accommodation in Namibia's major towns can be found on the website of Disabled Holidays (UK ☎0161 804 9898, ⓦdisabled holidays.com), which also offers a Namibia holiday package.

Travelling with children

Travelling with children is fairly easy in Namibia provided they are able to cope with many hours of travel between sights. Many **lodgings** offer discounts for children under 12, usually giving a 50 percent reduction for youngsters aged 6–12, with children under 6 staying free. Some of the smaller, more exclusive lodges that build their reputation on offering peace and tranquillity do not accept children under 12. **Restaurants** often have kids' menus. When it comes to **activities**, there's plenty to entertain kids, especially on the coast, from kayaking to sand-boarding. Children under a certain age (or height, when it comes to ballooning) are often discouraged from participating in some activities, but with parental consent and supervision this can also be waived.

If you're travelling with a baby, then it obviously makes sense to carry it around in a papoose, rather than a pushchair, given the lack of pavements, or even paved roads outside the main streets of the principal towns, never mind the countryside. Babycare products, such as bottled baby food and disposable nappies, are available in the main towns, but bear in mind that when you're camping in the bush, you'll need to transport the used ones with you until you reach a place where they can be disposed of properly. Breastfeeding in public is socially acceptable in Namibia, though the prevalence of breastfeeding babies in Namibia has decreased in recent years on account of fears of mother-to-child HIV transmission.

Volunteering

Voluntourism is a growing industry, and becoming a preferred way of travelling for those who want to "make a difference". Be aware that this can be fraught with pitfalls, both for the volunteer and – in the case of social development projects – the people being "helped". A good place to start is ⓦethicalvolunteering.org, which has a useful checklist about questions to ask before committing to an organization. Getting feedback from former volunteers is also helpful.

In Namibia, the focus is often on **conservation**, with volunteer programmes concerning cheetah, desert-adapted elephant or rhino conservation – sometimes involving scientific research – and at animal welfare sanctuaries. There is stiff competition for applicants for high-profile organizations such as the Cheetah Conservation Fund (ⓦcheetah.org; see p.178).

Generally, you have to pay for your flight to Namibia, transport to and from the location and board and lodging once there; conversely, if volunteering on a guestfarm or on a private reserve, you might have your board and lodging paid for in return for services. In this case, you need to be assured that you will not be exploited in terms of working hours and time off, nor that you are taking the job a paid local Namibian could be doing if the owner were only willing to spend the money.

Almost invariably, the volunteer gets more out of the experience than the people they are there to help. If you are contemplating becoming involved in community development, consider whether you have the appropriate skills for the job; what Namibia – like other African countries – does not need is unskilled labour constructing buildings or untrained teachers in schools. Also, if you really want to make a difference working with people, then you should think about committing to several months, at least, rather than several weeks, especially if the job involves interacting with vulnerable people, such as young children, for whom a constant relay of changing volunteers can be very disruptive. Several websites list volunteer projects in Namibia, which you should submit to scrutiny. They include: Go Overseas (ⓦgooverseas.com /volunteer-abroad/Namibia), which lists 25 programmes, some of which have been reviewed by former volunteers; the similarly entitled Go Abroad (ⓦgoabroad.com) also provides reviews from former volunteers and advertises over thirty projects; even the Namibian Tourist Board (ⓦnamibiatourism.com.na/page/volunteer -opportunities) has a webpage dedicated to voluntourism programmes.

Windhoek and around

KIOSK IN KATUTURA

1

Windhoek and around

Nestled among rolling hills in a valley created by the sloping Khomas Hochland Plateau to the west and the Auas Mountains to the east, Namibia's capital, Windhoek, is scenically situated. At an altitude of almost 1700m, the city avoids the excessive heat experienced in much of the rest of the country, with daytime temperatures rarely topping 30 degrees in summer, or dipping under 10 degrees in winter. What's more, whether due to meticulous German planning or serendipity, Windhoek lies almost in the centre of the country, which makes it the perfect starting point for any tour of Namibia.

Strolling down Independence Avenue, Windhoek **city centre**'s tree-lined main boulevard, it's easy to feel you're in a provincial town in northern Europe. Its tidy, clean pavements, dotted with German colonial architecture, lack the frenetic and chaotic pace and horn-honking mayhem more readily associated with African capital cities. Yet this is a city striving for modernity, keen to shrug off its small-town image and colonial past: new high-rise buildings now pierce the CBD skyline, and the brash multi-million-dollar post-independence constructions, such as the new State House and Heroes' Acre, dominate the surrounding hillsides.

   Windhoek is somewhat short on sights beyond a few modest museums; however, a wander around the National Botanical Gardens in the **suburbs** and a day's outing **beyond Windhoek** to the attractive surroundings of Daan Viljoen Game Park – Namibia's smallest reserve – will whet your appetite for some of the extraordinary landscapes and wildlife that await. Besides, Windhoek's comfortable guesthouses and a handful of pleasant alfresco dining options make it an agreeable environment to spend a couple of days getting your bearings at the start of a trip – as well as stocking up on supplies – or unwinding at the end of a hectic safari.

Brief history

The five-thousand-year-old archeological remains of elephants and hunting implements found in central Windhoek are evidence that the city's hot springs have played host to hunter-gatherers for many years. However, it was **Kaptein Jonker Afrikaner** of the Oorlam (see p.343) who established the first recorded settlement here in 1840. At that time Windhoek was known as |Ae||Gams – "fire water" in Nama – and Otjomuise – "place of steam" in Otjiherero; both names make reference to the importance of the springs to the future capital's location and development. Yet the origin of the name Windhoek remains more of a mystery, either recalling the Winterhoek Mountains in South Africa, home to Jonker's ancestors, or a corruption of the Afrikaans for "windy corner". Either way, the name stuck, whereas the settlement did not – at least not initially, as the ongoing conflict between the Nama, whom Jonker was leading, and the Herero more or less destroyed the place.

JOE'S BEERHOUSE

Highlights

❶ Parliament Gardens Take a lunchtime stroll in this leafy spot, offering shady lawns, landscaped gardens and even a manicured bowling green. **See p.85**

❷ National Earth Science Museum Fascinating fossils and glistening semi-precious minerals are well displayed in this small but informative museum. **See p.90**

❸ Sundowner with a view Sip a cocktail on a terrace bar as you soak up the sweeping cityscape and surroundings; try the hotels *Heinitzburg* and *Thule*, or *Nimm's*. **See p.94, p.95 & p.98**

❹ Joe's Beerhouse There's bags of vibe, good food and plenty to drink at this Windhoek

institution that draws tourists and Namibians alike. **See p.97**

❺ Warehouse Theatre A buzzing arts venue with something on most nights, from theatre to poetry, live music to stand-up comedy. **See p.98**

❻ Namibia Craft Centre The best place to browse for souvenirs, shop and have lunch – all in one location. **See p.100**

❼ Daan Viljoen Game Park Only a twenty-minute drive from the city centre, amid rolling hills, this peaceful spot is ideal for a gentle hike, birdwatching or a picnic. **See p.101**

HIGHLIGHTS ARE MARKED ON THE MAPS ON P.78, P.81, P.87 & P.89

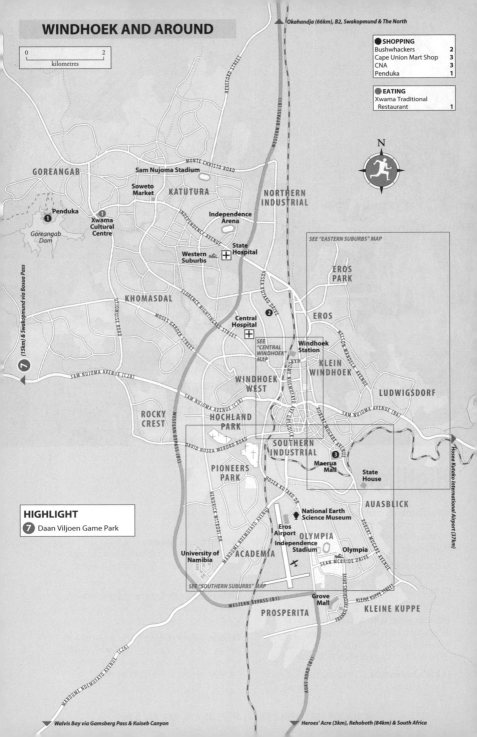

WINDHOEK AND AROUND

0 — 2
kilometres

Okahandja (66km), B2, Swakopmund & The North

N

GOREANGAB

Penduka ①

Goreangab
Dam

Sam Nujoma Stadium

Soweto
Market

KATUTURA

① Xwama
Cultural
Centre

Independence
Arena

NORTHERN
INDUSTRIAL

Western
Suburbs

State
Hospital

MONTE CHRISTO ROAD

HEREFORD STREET

WESTERN BYPASS (B1)

INDEPENDENCE AVENUE

SEE "EASTERN SUBURBS" MAP

EROS
PARK

EROS

KHOMASDAL

Central
Hospital

②

SEE
"CENTRAL
WINDHOEK"
MAP

Windhoek
Station

KLEIN
WINDHOEK

LUDWIGSDORF

FLORENCE NIGHTINGALE STREET

MOSES GAROEB STREET

HOSEA KUTAKO DRIVE

NELSON MANDELA AVENUE

(15km) & Swakopmund via Bosua Pass

OTJIMUISE ROAD

⑦

SAM NUJOMA AVENUE (C28)

SAM NUJOMA AVENUE (C28)

WINDHOEK
WEST

ROCKY
CREST

WESTERN BYPASS (B1)

HOCHLAND
PARK

SAM NUJOMA AVENUE (B6)

ROBERT MUGABE AVENUE

Hosea Kutako International Airport (37km)

SOUTHERN
INDUSTRIAL

③

Maerua
Mall

State
House

AUASBLICK

PIONEERS
PARK

DAVID HOSEA MEROROS ROAD

HENDRICK WITBOOI DR.

HOSEA KUTAKO DR.

MANDUME NDEMUFAYO AVENUE

National Earth
Science Museum

Eros
Airport

Independence
Stadium

OLYMPIA

Olympia

ROBERT MUGABE AVENUE

HIGHLIGHT
⑦ Daan Viljoen Game Park

University of
Namibia

ACADEMIA

SEAN MCBRIDE DRIVE

SEE "SOUTHERN SUBURBS" MAP

WESTERN BYPASS (B1)

Grove
Mall

KLEINE KUPPE

PROSPERITA

KLEINE KUPPE STREET

FRANS INDONGO DRIVE

RUSS ROAD (B1)

MANDUME NDEMUFAYO AVENUE (C26)

Walvis Bay via Gamsberg Pass & Kuiseb Canyon

Heroes' Acre (3km), Rehoboth (84km) & South Africa

German colonial rule

The establishment of modern-day Windhoek came in 1890, six years after German South-West Africa had been claimed as a protectorate, when **Major Curt von François**, leading the German Imperial army, laid the cornerstone of the Alte Feste (Old Fort), establishing it as the HQ for the Schutztruppen (German colonial troops; see p.344). The chosen location served as a strategic buffer between the warring Nama and Herero and was ideal for agriculture on account of the natural springs. After an initially slow start, the influx of German colonists from both Europe and South Africa was given greater impetus when the Swakopmund–Windhoek railway track was completed in 1902, and some of the colony's main buildings, such as the Christuskirche and the Tintenpalast, were erected. Businesses were established and small-scale farming took root, and by 1909, when Windhoek finally became a municipality, the population topped 2700. All the while the indigenous populations were gradually pushed out to the margins, to serve the colonists' interests, or were driven away altogether.

South African rule

German rule came to an abrupt end with defeat in World War I, and the black populations were forced to exchange one colonial power for another as the South African military moved in to rule on behalf of Britain. Periods of growth followed, especially after World War II. The next seismic shift in Windhoek's development occurred in the late 1950s and 60s as South Africa began to impose **apartheid** policies of segregation and surveillance, forcibly removing large swathes of the non-white populations to townships (see box, p.347).

GETTING ORIENTED IN WINDHOEK

Windhoek is more confusing to drive around than it should be given its diminutive size. This is mainly due to its rolling hills and dispersed residential areas – largely a hangover from successive colonial governments' urban planning. On the plus side, however, streets are well signposted, though since most have been renamed since independence, some residents still occasionally refer to the old names. The city's main arteries run broadly parallel from north to south: Namibia's principal highway, the **B1** – which stretches the whole 1500km between the South African and Angolan borders – becomes **Auas Road** as it approaches from the south, passing Eros Airport (the small domestic airport), and then Hosea Kutako Drive as it enters the city. Peeling off to the west, just south of the airport, the aptly named **Western Bypass** circumvents the city, continuing the apartheid-era separation of the former non-white townships of Khomasdal and Katutura from the white areas, before the two main roads rejoin, north of the city. Two other major north/south roads to get a handle on are **Robert Mugabe Avenue**, which undulates along the eastern flank of the city, and **Mandume Ndemufayo Avenue**, which starts in the town centre and heads southwest, through the Southern Industrial Area, where several vehicle rental companies are located, to emerge as the **C26**, the back road to Walvis Bay. The main highway on the east-west axis is **Sam Nujoma Drive**: eastwards it heads out through the Klein Windhoek Valley and on to Hosea Kutako International Airport – where all international flights arrive – Gobabis and the Botswana border, as the **B6**; to the west it skirts Khomasdal and becomes the **C28**, the back road to Swakopmund, passing the Dan Viljoen Game Park.

The **city centre**, however, consists of little more than a kilometre of **Independence Avenue** and a block or two either side, which can easily be explored on foot. Independence Avenue continues northwards all the way to the former black township of **Katutura**, crossing Hosea Kutako Drive and the Western Bypass en route. Most accommodation and restaurants lie in Klein Windhoek – along or just off Sam Nujoma Drive and Nelson Mandela Avenue – and the other eastern suburbs, with a sprinkling of restaurants in the city centre. Some cheaper lodgings are to be found in Windhoek West, and Pioneers Park (also Pionierspark), to the south, beyond Eros Airport.

1

Post-independence

Despite the post-independence dismantlement of the apartheid state in 1990, and the reclassification of the former townships as "suburbs", the racial and socio-economic divisions within the capital still largely persist. In the years since independence, **migration** to the capital has intensified, with bulging informal settlements or "shanty towns" proliferating on the periphery, especially around Katutura. These are stark reminders to the municipality and to central government of the ongoing challenge of addressing the city's swelling population – currently estimated to be around 400,000 – as well as its continuing inequalities.

The city centre

Windhoek's modest sights and tourist attractions are predominantly located in a compact one-kilometre area along or between Independence Avenue, the city's main drag, and Robert Mugabe Avenue, which runs parallel along a ridge to the east. Most can be covered on foot in a day – or two, if you want to take your time and trawl all the disparate sections of the national museum.

Independence Avenue and around

Though not exactly a spectacular street, **Independence Avenue** is pleasant enough, containing a few interesting examples of colonial architecture, an eclectic collection of monuments, and a handful of chic shops and small arcades. The best place to start a walking tour is on the corner of Independence Avenue and John Meinert Street, at the splendid life-size, bronze **kudu monument**, designed by a visiting German sculptor and erected in 1960 to celebrate the kudu's – and other wildlife's – survival of the 1896 *rinderpest* epidemic (see p.345), which all but wiped them out. Halfway along the west side of the busiest section, you'll come across Independence Avenue's most distinctive landmark, namely the domed **clock tower**; it's a replica of one that originally fronted the Deutsche-Afrika Bank. The tower marks the entrance to **Post Street Mall**, a bustling pedestrianized area.

Further south on Independence Avenue, somewhat obscured by the trees and best appreciated from across the road, stand a few **German colonial facades** designed in the early twentieth century. The former Kronprinz Hotel, *Gathemann House*, hosts the renowned restaurant (see p.97), while the most striking, the Erkrath Building – now housing the NWR office – incredibly has a steep sloping roof designed to prevent snow from accumulating.

It's worth making a quick detour to Reverend Michael Scott Street, behind the *Hilton* hotel, to take in the imposing **Supreme Court of Namibia**. It is said to have been inspired by North African architecture, utilizing a hierarchy of space moving from the public to the private domains. Take a peek at the light, airy foyer and colonnaded courtyard, which contains a memorial garden.

Back on Independence Avenue, you pass a **curio market**, where Himba traders garner the greatest interest. A little further on, at the corner of Sam Nujoma Drive, and hidden, ironically, behind a giant-sized recycling bin, stands a bronze **statue of Curt von François**. The cartographer and leader of the German imperial forces is credited – by some, at least – with founding modern-day Windhoek.

Post Street Mall

A short, raised pedestrianized walkway, **Post Street Mall** is probably the city centre's liveliest street, connecting Independence Avenue with Wernhil Park, which harbours the capital's central shopping mall and supermarket. Thronging with activity weekday lunchtimes, it is somewhat overwhelmed by the sprawling displays of street vendors'

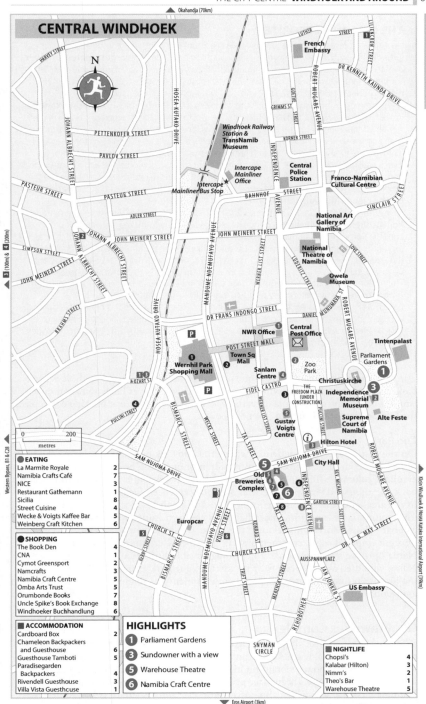

CENTRAL WINDHOEK

▲ Okahandja (70km)

▲ 3 (100m) & 4 (200m)

◀ Western Bypass, B1 & C28

▶ Klein Windhoek & Hosea Kutako International Airport (39km)

▼ Eros Airport (3km)

N

Windhoek Railway Station & TransNamib Museum

Intercape Mainliner Office

Intercape Mainliner Bus Stop

French Embassy

Central Police Station

Franco-Namibian Cultural Centre

National Art Gallery of Namibia

National Theatre of Namibia

Owela Museum

NWR Office

Central Post Office

Tintenpalast

Parliament Gardens

Wernhil Park Shopping Mall

Town Sq Mall

Sanlam Centre

Zoo Park

Christuskirche

Independence Memorial Museum

Alte Feste

Gustav Voigts Centre

THE FREEDOM PLAZA (UNDER CONSTRUCTION)

Supreme Court of Namibia

Hilton Hotel

City Hall

Old Breweries Complex

Europcar

US Embassy

AUSSPANNPLATZ

SNYMAN CIRCLE

Streets labelled on map: HARVEY STREET, LUTHER STREET, LÜTTICHAU STREET, DR KENNETH KAUNDA DRIVE, JOHANN ALBRECHT STREET, PETTENKOFER STREET, HOSEA KUTAKO DRIVE, GOETHE STREET, ROBERT MUGABE AVENUE, GRIMMS ST, PAVLOV STREET, KORNER STREET, INDEPENDENCE AVENUE, PASTEUR STREET, ADLER STREET, BAHNHOF STREET, SINCLAIR STREET, SIMPSON STREET, JOHN MEINERT STREET, JOHANN ALBRECHT STREET, JOHN MEINERT STREET, MANDUME NDEMUFAYO AVENUE, WEBER LIST STREET, LÜDERITZ STREET, LOVE STREET, BRAHMS STREET, DR FRANS INDONGO STREET, DANIEL MUNUMBA ST, ROBERT MUGABE AVENUE, POST STREET MALL, MOZART ST, FIDEL CASTRO, BISMARCK STREET, WECKE STREET, PUCCINI STREET, TAL STREET, SAM NUJOMA DRIVE, SAM NUJOMA DRIVE, REV. MICHAEL SCOTT STREET, GARTEN STREET, CHURCH ST, KERBY STREET, MANDUME NDEMUFAYO AVENUE, VOIGT STREET, KONRAD ST, CHURCH STREET, INDEPENDENCE AVENUE, DR. A. B. MAY STREET, BISMARCK STREET, TRIFT STREET, MEBERSKY STREET, JAN JONKER ST, REHOBOTHER

0 — 200 metres

● EATING
La Marmite Royale	2
Namibia Crafts Café	7
NICE	3
Restaurant Gathemann	1
Sicilia	8
Street Cuisine	4
Wecke & Voigts Kaffee Bar	5
Weinberg Craft Kitchen	6

● SHOPPING
The Book Den	4
CNA	1
Cymot Greensport	2
Namcrafts	3
Namibia Craft Centre	5
Omba Arts Trust	5
Orumbonde Books	7
Uncle Spike's Book Exchange	8
Windhoeker Buchhandlung	6

■ ACCOMMODATION
Cardboard Box	2
Chameleon Backpackers and Guesthouse	6
Guesthouse Tamboti	5
Paradisegarden Backpackers	4
Rivendell Guesthouse	3
Villa Vista Guesthouse	1

HIGHLIGHTS
1 Parliament Gardens
3 Sundowner with a view
5 Warehouse Theatre
6 Namibia Craft Centre

■ NIGHTLIFE
Chopsi's	4
Kalabar (Hilton)	3
Nimm's	2
Theo's Bar	1
Warehouse Theatre	5

1

THE GIBEON METEORITE

No artistic representation, the Gibeon Meteorite Fountain sculpture is comprised of genuine lumps of iron-rich meteorite from what is thought to have been the **largest meteor shower** ever to have hit the planet, some six hundred million years ago. It was named after the place in southern Namibia where the meteors fell, covering an area around 13,000 square kilometres. Although Nama populations had been fashioning tools and weapons out of the extra-terrestrial rocks for many years, it took the "discovery" by a British explorer, **James Alexander**, in 1838, and subsequent tests by a London chemist, to determine the meteoric origin of the samples. More than 25 tonnes and 120 specimens have been recorded over the years, ranging from a tonne to several grams in weight. After being displayed in the Zoo Park for many years, 33 meteorite fragments were put into temporary storage in the Alte Feste in 1975, prior to their installation in Post Street Mall. Two lumps went missing, however, and a third was swiped from the sculpture once in place – their three empty plinths still stand forlornly alongside the other 30 specimens on display. Other pieces of the meteorite are displayed in the **National Earth Science Museum** (see p.90).

Despite the Namibian government's 2004 ban on the removal of any meteorite material from its site, and the threat of a hefty fine, pieces continue to make their way out of the country. Some end up in museums, others in private hands, which is no great surprise as meteorite smuggling is big business. Large chunks of Gibeon meteorite can fetch several thousand dollars, which a quick look at eBay can confirm. In 2016, an 81kg lump was put up for auction at Christie's, in London, with an estimated US$230,000–380,000 price tag. The notion of wearing a bit of outer space on the finger or round the neck has also made Gibeon meteorite jewellery very popular, especially since an attractive lattice-like patterning – known as Widmanstätten – stands out once the stone has been cut, polished and acid etched. One of the more extraordinary Gibeon meteorite products, however, which failed to sell at auction in 2015, is a life-sized sculpted human skull known as "Yorick" (see Ⓦ leedowney.com).

wares: ornate walking sticks, soapstone sculptures, acres of colourful cloth, jewellery, basketry, leatherwork, and carvings of every animal you're ever likely to see on safari. Amid this dizzying cornucopia of crafts it's easy to miss the street's amazing centrepiece, the **Gibeon Meteorite Fountain** (see box above).

Zoo Park

On the east side of Independence Avenue the **Zoo Park** provides a welcome shady retreat and contains a couple of contrasting monuments. The more unusual is the **elephant column**, which marks the spot where elephant bones and early tools dating back five thousand years were found; precious evidence of early human settlement in the area, and now on display in the National Earth Science Museum (see p.90). The column is an intriguing bas-relief of an elephant hunt topped with a sculpted elephant skull. More contentious is the century-old **German war memorial**, crowned by a gilt imperial eagle, commemorating the fallen German soldiers who died in the Nama uprising against colonial rule, though a sibling monument to honour the Nama who died is conspicuous by its absence. The park also hosts the annual **|Ae||Gams Cultural Festival** in September, with plenty of singing, dancing and craft and food stalls.

Old Breweries Complex

While in the city centre, don't forget to check out the **Old Breweries Complex**, one block west of Independence Avenue on Tal Street; the former production site for Windhoek Lager is now a vibrant multifaceted arts, crafts and nightlife venue, notably home to the Warehouse Theatre (see p.98) and its various components, and the Namibia Craft Centre, which also hosts a great café and restaurant (see p.100).

The national museum

As part of the re-visioning of Namibia's history and construction of post-independence identity, the country's **national museum** collections are now dispersed across several sites after being hosted predominantly in the Alte Feste (see below). All are located in the central area, except for the National Earth Science Museum, which shares a building with the Ministry of Mines and Energy, to the south, by Eros Airport.

Owela Museum

4 Robert Mugabe Ave • Mon–Fri 9am–6pm, Sat & Sun 10am–5pm • Free • ☎ 061 276800

The rather musty but worthwhile **Owela Museum**, which takes its name from the Oshiwambo for the popular wooden board-and-bean game you see played under trees across Africa, is primarily concerned with ecology and the **ethnography** of Namibia's indigenous populations. The traditional lives of the Nama, Damara, Herero, Himba, Kavango and San are depicted through dioramas, artefacts and photos, giving insights into their varied cultural practices – from methods of hunting and agriculture to music and puberty rituals – some of which exist in mutated form even today. Highlights include Nama cosmetic powder boxes made of tortoiseshell and embellished with beads, and an oryx-horn trumpet used by the Himba to herd cattle. While the majority of displays adhere to the "pickled-in-aspic" approach to preserving cultural traditions, a more recent display on the San shows greater critical engagement with the complexities of a culture undergoing modernization.

The smaller **ecology** section inevitably involves overdosing on taxidermy, though there are attempts to bring the hapless animals to life by locating them in dioramas of their natural habitat, some in striking action poses: vultures tuck into a zebra carcass, while a caracal snatches at a fleeing guineafowl.

Independence Memorial Museum

Robert Mugabe Ave & Fidel Castro St • Mon–Fri 9am–6pm, Sat & Sun 10am–6pm • Free • ☎ 061 302230

The gleaming gold spaceship that dwarfs the Christuskirche and the Alte Feste on either side is the new **Independence Memorial Museum**, whose aim is to pay homage to those who fought for the establishment of the Namibian state – don't expect too much critical commentary. Fronted by a larger-than-life statue of Sam Nujoma (see p.350) brandishing the constitution, this predominantly **photographic documentation** of the struggle for independence is still lacking background contextual information, which would greatly help visitors unfamiliar with Namibian history. Sadly, the video screens designed to do just that have not been operational since the museum opened in 2014, when some of the early visitors made off with the relevant touch-screen hardware.

The narrative sets off at a gallop on the first floor with a brief idealized portrayal of pre-colonial life as "peaceful co-existence" before speeding through the Scramble for Africa, early resistance against colonialism, Namibia under apartheid and the formation of the People's Liberation Army of Namibia (PLAN), primarily told through labelled photographs but also including some graphic slavery-themed friezes. The second floor documents guerrilla operations from neighbouring states with more photos supplemented with a couple of tanks and some weaponry, while the final floor illustrates some of South-West Africa People's Organisation's (SWAPO) activities in exile (see p.348), and celebrates the resettlement and repatriation of exiles and the final achievement of independence. Don't miss the opportunity to soak up the capital's best view from the museum's fifth-floor bar and restaurant (see p.98).

The Alte Feste

Robert Mugabe Ave near Fidel Castro St • Mon–Fri 9am–6pm, Sat & Sun 10am–5pm • Free • ☎ 061 2934362

Resembling a toy-town fort with its gleaming white exterior, corner turrets and neat crenellations, the **Alte Feste** (Old Fort) is Windhoek's oldest surviving building. Designed as a headquarters for the Schutztruppen, its cornerstone was laid in 1890,

1

THE REITERDENKMAL

The controversy surrounding the siting and status of the **Reiterdenkmal** – equestrian memorial monument of a Schutztruppe (see p.344) – is symptomatic of the tensions within post-independence Namibia as it comes to terms with its colonial history. Designed in Berlin, and erected in Windhoek next to the Christuskirche in 1912 on the birthday of the German Emperor, Kaiser Wilhelm II, the monument commemorates the German soldiers and civilians who lost their lives during the Herero and Nama uprisings against colonial rule, and the Kalahari Expedition of 1908. However, the bronze, armed cavalryman that presided over the city centre for almost a hundred years is, understandably, viewed by black Namibians as a symbol of **colonial oppression**, and a blatant reminder of the genocide of thousands of Nama and Herero by German troops (see p.346). As a result, the Reiterdenkmal has long been on SWAPO's list for removal – it has already been axed from the country's list of historical monuments. But with opposition from the powerful German-speaking minority – on the grounds that for better or worse it is part of Namibia's heritage and its removal would be a breach of their minority rights – it has been a protracted affair. First, in 2009 the monument was shunted sideways from its hillside vantage point – to make way for the new Independence Memorial Museum – to sit outside the Alte Feste. Then, under cover of darkness on Christmas Eve, 2013 – to avoid any possible confrontation – it was taken inside the old fort. Many black Namibians hope this is a prelude to the monument being shipped back to Germany, while some members of the German-Namibian community have threatened to sue the government if such a move is made.

though it wasn't completed in its present design until some 25 years later. Since then, the fort has had a varied history: as well as housing German, and later South African Union, troops, it has also been a hostel for the adjacent Windhoek High School, and up until 2014, it played host to most of the national museum collection. However, beyond a few historical ox-carts by the entrance, and the new Genocide Memorial by its steps, there's now little to see inside while the government debates how best to utilize the space. Even so, it's worth having a peek at the grassy courtyard to get a sense of the place. At the time of writing, this was temporary home to the controversial Reiterdenkmal, a bronze equestrian monument erected to commemorate some of the German soldiers and civilians who died during the colonial era (see box above).

The TransNamib Museum

First floor of Windhoek train station, Bahnhof St • Mon–Fri 8am–1pm & 2–5pm • N\$5 • ☎ 061 2982624

While the specialist **TransNamib Museum** will have railway enthusiasts in raptures, the average visitor will probably be satisfied with having a peer round this museum in Windhoek's quaint historical train station. Built in 1913, the museum is fronted by "Poor Old Joe", a narrow-gauge steam locomotive that used to chug between Swakopmund and Windhoek.

The handful of small rooms are packed with railway memorabilia, but it is rather like poking round someone's attic as potentially interesting finds are often unexplained, and lie cheek by jowl with pieces that would not be out of place in a car-boot sale. However, the train-buff curator will be only too happy to help you make sense of it all. There are even a couple of tiny rooms dedicated to Namibia's aviation and maritime history. Of more general appeal is the re-creation of a first-class train compartment, complete with original washbasin tucked beneath the stow-away table.

National Art Gallery of Namibia

John Meinert St & Robert Mugabe Ave • Mon–Fri 9am–5pm, Sat 9am–2pm • Free • ☎ 061 231160, ⊛ nagn.org.na

The **National Art Gallery of Namibia** possesses a collection of around 270 pieces of contemporary art – an array of paintings, drawings, sculptures, work in mixed and new media and crafts by Namibian artists, including a substantial number of original linocuts by the internationally acclaimed John Muafangejo. The gallery currently lacks the space to display the whole collection, so rotates the works in a string of temporary exhibitions, sometimes alongside art by other regional and international artists.

The gallery also provides the central exhibition space to display the winning entries in the **Bank Windhoek Triennial** (see p.60).

The Christuskirche

Robert Mugabe Ave & Fidel Castro St • Mon–Fri 9am–6pm, Sat & Sun 10am–5pm • Free

Though still a must-see sight on any tour of Windhoek, it is hard to imagine how the pretty gingerbread **Christuskirche** dominated Windhoek's skyline for over a hundred years as one of Namibia's most distinctive landmarks. These days it's encircled by a busy roundabout and physically overshadowed by the adjacent brash Independence Memorial Museum.

A predominantly neo-Romanesque confection, topped with a steeple and neo-Gothic spire, it was designed by German architect and engineer, Gottlieb Redecker – who was also responsible for the Tintenpalast, Namibia's parliament building. Locally quarried quartz sandstone was used to construct the main building but most other elements were imported from Germany: parts of the roof, the three bells, the clock, the organ and the stained-glass windows, which were a gift from Kaiser Wilhelm II. Marble for the altar and portal was procured from Italy. Since the church was conceived by the German colonizers as a symbol of peace in the wake of the Herero and Nama uprisings and subsequent massacres, it is a sad irony that the vast plaque inside that commemorates the fallen German soldiers and settlers is not matched by any such remembrance of the far greater numbers of the indigenous population who lost their lives.

The Tintenpalast

Robert Mugabe Ave, behind the Christuskirche • Visit by guided tour only (book ahead) Mon–Fri 9am, 10am & 3pm • Free • ☎ 061 2885111

Built to house the administration of German South-West Africa in 1912–13, the **Tintenpalast** (Ink Palace) gained its enduring sobriquet through reference to the copious amounts of ink used in bureaucratic paperwork. Successive governments have occupied the two-storey structure, which accommodates both the National Assembly (lower chamber) and the National Council (upper chamber) that make up **Namibia's parliament**.

The restrained, elegant design was the work of Gottlieb Redecker, the same architect-engineer who had earlier planned the Christuskirche, but the parliament building stands out because it was constructed almost entirely out of locally sourced materials. Given its diminutive stature, a new, larger parliament building has been under discussion for a number of years, but the escalating projected costs are stirring up controversy.

Parliament Gardens

Open access • Free

Surrounding the Tintenpalast are the delightful, shady, landscaped **Parliament Gardens**, which definitely merit a stroll. They are particularly popular at lunchtimes and weekends, when students laze on the lawns poring over their books or each other. Don't miss the bougainvillea-lined bowling green and thatched clubhouse to the north of parliament, which are kept in immaculate condition. Post-independence additions to the grounds include three bronze **statues** of liberation heroes that flank the steps up to parliament's main entrance: Kaptein Hendrik Witbooi – not to be confused with the better-known Hendrik Witbooi (see p.344), who graces Namibian currency notes – opponent of Bantu education; Hosea Kutako, the Herero chief who was instrumental in petitioning the UN for Namibian independence (see p.350); and the less frequently championed – and not so easily pronounced – Reverend Theophilus Hamutumbangela, a priest and vociferous independence activist, who was arrested on various occasions and was allegedly poisoned by the South African authorities under apartheid.

1

The suburbs

Outside the Central Business District – also known as Windhoek Central – the capital melts outwards in all directions in a collection of suburbs, which include the former townships of Katutura and Khomasdal (see box, p.88) to the northwest. These, in turn, have spawned an even greater number of informal settlements, which house an estimated third of the city's population, predominantly in collections of aluminium shacks, which lack adequate access to basic services such as clean water, sanitation, medical care and schooling. Although the Namibian government is committed to building affordable low-cost housing, the serried ranks of boxlike structures in the newer suburbs are still beyond the incomes of many black Namibians.

The eastern suburbs

The old, eastern suburbs are synonymous with affluence, and include the former white residential areas of **Klein Windhoek** and **Ludwigsdorf**, which are also home to many of the city's boutique hotels and guesthouses, upmarket restaurants and embassies. Characterized by slick 4WDs and empty roads that weave their way through high-walled, gated properties and leafy gardens, these areas have changed little in terms of their racial make-up since the days of apartheid.

Klein Windhoek, the oldest district, is where Jonker Afrikaner first settled in 1840, on account of the hot springs. It was also the first area to be developed as a residential zone outside the garrison area of Gross Windhoek once the Germans had established themselves half a century later. Notable landmarks, standing sentinel along the ridge that announces the entrance to the Klein Windhoek Valley, are the three whimsical **castles** of Sanderburg, Heinitzburg and Schwerinsburg. Built in the early 1900s by German architect Wilhelm Sander, the last and largest of the castles had an original military watchtower incorporated into the design. Only Heinitzburg, however, is open to visitors as it now houses a luxury hotel (see p.94), though even non-residents can enjoy its splendid terrace views by lingering over a sundowner or a meal there.

National Botanical Gardens

Oban St, signposted off Sam Nujoma Drive • Mon–Fri 8am–5pm and every first Sat of the month at 8am (3hr guided walk; no need to pre-book) • Free; guided walks N$10 • ☎ 061 2022014, ⍟ nbri.org.na/sections/botanic-garden

Despite only covering a small area, the patch of arid land that comprises the **National Botanical Gardens** provides welcome relief from the surrounding concrete. As long as you limit your expectations, you can easily spend a happy hour or two here. Although not landscaped – in part to save water – the "gardens" lay claim to over six hundred indigenous plant species, many of which are labelled, and around 75 bird species. The small desert house gives a taster of what to expect once you get out to the Namib itself, including many protected species that can otherwise only be seen in remote and inaccessible areas, while elsewhere you can find some splendid examples of candelabra euphorbia. Tucked away near the picnic area lies the grave of a Damara chief who was allegedly captured and beheaded by the German authorities after opposing colonial rule.

The reception desk also has maps with plant listings for the **Aloe Trail**, a short, circular walking trail (2km), which affords views over the Klein Windhoek valley. The trail begins close to the entrance, but do it only if you are in a group, as muggings have been known.

Northwestern suburbs

The former townships of Katutura and Khomasdal dominate the northwestern suburbs, surrounded by an ever-increasing sprawl of makeshift shacks, as more and more people migrate from the rural areas in search of a better life in Windhoek. That said, tourists are beginning to venture into Katutura, in search of the "real Africa".

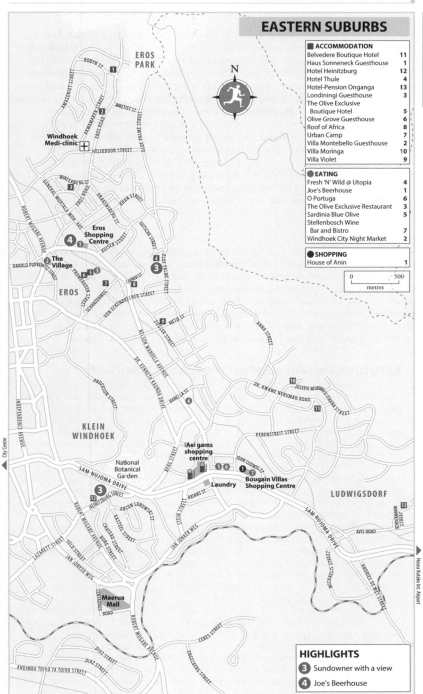

EASTERN SUBURBS

■ ACCOMMODATION

Belvedere Boutique Hotel	11
Haus Sonneneck Guesthouse	1
Hotel Heinitzburg	12
Hotel Thule	4
Hotel-Pension Onganga	13
Londiningi Guesthouse	3
The Olive Exclusive	
Boutique Hotel	5
Olive Grove Guesthouse	6
Roof of Africa	8
Urban Camp	7
Villa Montebello Guesthouse	2
Villa Moringa	10
Villa Violet	9

● EATING

Fresh 'N' Wild @ Utopia	4
Joe's Beerhouse	1
O Portuga	6
The Olive Exclusive Restaurant	3
Sardinia Blue Olive	5
Stellenbosch Wine	
Bar and Bistro	7
Windhoek City Night Market	2

● SHOPPING

House of Anin	1

0   500
metres

HIGHLIGHTS

3 Sundowner with a view

4 Joe's Beerhouse

1

Katutura

Travelling 8km northwest of downtown Windhoek, along Independence Avenue, brings you to **Katutura**, the former apartheid-era black township, which is arguably the city's heartbeat. With an official population of around 43,000 but unofficially housing over four times more if you include the surrounding informal settlements – many in makeshift shanty huts – Katutura is everything that central Windhoek is not: thronging with people, bustling with activity, full of markets, bicycles, running kids and load-carrying guys weaving their way across traffic. To get a greater appreciation of this city within a city, take one of the local operators' "township tours" (see p.92), which will give you the opportunity to visit the small business ventures of Soweto Market, the sizzling kapana grills (see p.57) or the Singles' Quarters meat market – not for the faint-hearted. Then, there's throbbing Eveline Street, "the street that never sleeps", a packed parade of shebeens, hairdressers, mobile phone kiosks and car washers. Tours also often take in the Xwama Cultural Village (see p.98), or Penduka, a successful craft-making women's development project at Goreangab Dam.

Goreangab Dam

The main reason to venture this far, beyond Katutura and through the informal settlement of Goreangab, is to visit **Penduka**, a long-standing women's self-help craft-making development project, scenically situated by Goreangab Dam. Penduka has expanded in recent years to include food and accommodation: the restaurant has a pleasant aspect across the water, and the thatched rondavels are inexpensive and cheery, if somewhat incongruous. If you want to do more than visit their well-stocked craft shop, consider booking yourself on a morning's workshop to learn about basketry and embroidery, or try your hand at drumming, or cooking a *potjiekos* (stew in a

---

KATUTURA AND KHOMASDAL: THE FORMER TOWNSHIPS

Although Namibia's black and mixed-heritage populations had experienced racial segregation and resettlement well before the apartheid era, it was the mass protests of 1959 at the forced removal of the capital's "black" population to the township of **Katutura** – meaning "place where we will not stay/settle" in Otjiherero – that were subsequently identified as the landmark rallying call for independence (see p.348). By 1912, non-whites had been forced to live in two areas of the capital: a segregated area within Klein Windhoek and the Main Location (now called the Old Location), between present-day Hochland Park and Pioneers Park, to the south of the city – in areas that were further subdivided according to ethnicity. When in 1959 the South African regime declared that all blacks had to move to a new township, 8km northwest of central Windhoek, and those who were considered to be of mixed heritage, who were dubbed "coloured", had to move to one called Khomasdal, 5km away, there was a huge outcry. Residents of Katutura would have fewer rights, smaller plots and further to walk to reach the city centre. **Protests** followed, tensions escalated, police brutality increased, and matters came to a head when a march by a group of Herero women and subsequent boycott of municipal services resulted in clashes with police, in what is now known as the **Old Location Uprising**. It resulted in at least 11 dead and 44 injured, while several thousand residents fled from the city for fear of further state reprisals. The dead are buried in the Old Location Cemetery, off Hochland Road, which to this day is the focus for the annual national commemoration of Human Rights Day on December 10.

Though Katutura and Khomasdal have been reclassified as "suburbs", and the apartheid-era stadium-like surveillance lights that deprived residents of a decent night's sleep for many years were torn down long ago, many of their residents, in Katutura in particular, are still very poor. Blacks who can now afford to move out often prefer to live in **Khomasdal**, where there is a similar sense of community, rather than in the eastern suburbs – where houses hide behind high walls, barbed-wire fences and electronic gates – or in other newer developments, which are designed to fit European planning models premised on separate nuclear family units.

three-legged metal pot). Penduka can also organize informative visits to nearby Katutura – including Katutours' bike excursions (see p.92), or to a day-care centre in the informal settlement of Otjimuise. Their tours tend to lack the voyeurism that characterizes some of these sorts of excursions.

Southern and western suburbs

South of the centre is a mixed bag of neighbourhoods separated by the Southern Industrial Area and Eros Airport, on whose access road the National Earth Science Museum is located. Before the airport, just south of Hochland Park, lies the Old Location Cemetery (see box opposite) – signposted off Hosea Kutako Drive. Beyond, to the southwest, Pioneerspark and Academia – appropriately located next to the University of Namibia campus – comprise pleasant middle-class residential areas that are not as wealthy as the eastern suburbs, and where some of Windhoek's less expensive tourist accommodation is situated. More affluent areas lie to the east, however, including the garden suburbs of Suiderhof, Olympia, which hosts an Olympic-sized swimming pool, well worth a plunge in summer (see p.100), the Independence Stadium, as well as Windhoek's newest, glitziest mall (⊕thegrovemall.co.na), which contains a state-of-the-art cinema. The Olympic theme continues in the renaming of one of its main roads: Frankie Fredericks Street, in honour of Namibia's all-time great, multi-Olympic medal-winning track athlete. Presiding over the area from the hillside of Auasblick sprawls the unmissable architectural monstrosity that is the new State House. Designed and predominantly built by North Koreans, and costing some unspecified sum between N$400–600 million, it was completed in 2008. The far more modest old State House, on Robert Mugabe Avenue, a stone's throw from the parliament buildings, is now home to the prime minister.

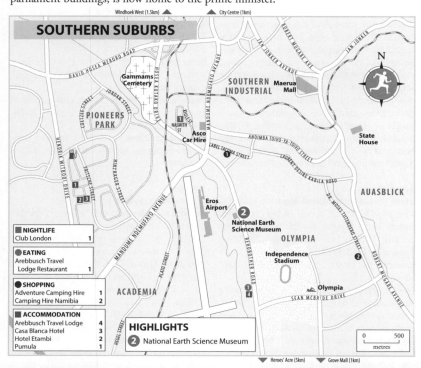

SOUTHERN SUBURBS

NIGHTLIFE
Club London — 1

EATING
Arebbusch Travel
Lodge Restaurant — 1

SHOPPING
Adventure Camping Hire — 1
Camping Hire Namibia — 2

ACCOMMODATION
Arebbusch Travel Lodge — 4
Casa Blanca Hotel — 3
Hotel Etambi — 2
Pumula — 1

HIGHLIGHTS
2 National Earth Science Museum

1

The National Earth Science Museum

Ground floor of the Ministry of Mines and Energy, 1 Aviation Rd, opposite the *Safari Court Hotel* • Mon–Fri 8am–5pm • Free • ☎ 061 2848111 • A taxi from town costs around N\$60

It is well worth making the trek out to Namibia's **National Earth Science Museum**, which boasts small but impressive displays on Namibian palaeontology, minerals and mining. Well-labelled glass cabinets show **fossil collections** from diverse eras, some remarkably preserved, such as the eggs of an ostrich ancestor, the carapace of a giant nineteen-million-year-old tortoise, and the almost-complete, clear fossilized impression of a mesosaurus – a 50cm-long reptile, found on a farm near Keetmanshoop, in southern Namibia (see p.146). Fear not if you're struggling to picture such beasts, since they come alive in the wonderful accompanying illustrations by the late Christine Marais, a South African artist renowned for her portrayals of the Namibian environment.

The museum's **geological section** is a more mixed bag: though the detailed, specialist displays may fail to grip the casual visitor, the collection of sparkling gemstones holds more general appeal – don't miss the cabinet showing UV radiation and fluorescence in minerals, and the exhibits illustrating their household uses in such mundane products as toothpaste and make-up. Namibia's mining industry has sponsored the displays on the country's various mines, so, although informative, they are inevitably laden with PR-speak.

ARRIVAL AND DEPARTURE
WINDHOEK

BY PLANE
INTERNATIONAL

Hosea Kutako International Airport All international flights, including connections with other southern African destinations (see p.48) and some domestic flights, arrive at and depart from Hosea Kutako International Airport, 42km east of the capital. It has a bureau de change, post office, ATM and also a small mobile phone shop, where you can buy a Namibian SIM card and credit. There is no fixed public transport to or from the airport. Many hotels and guesthouses run their own shuttle services to and from the airport (40min), which you can pre-book online. Reliable, independent shuttle services you can pre-book include Windhoek Airport Shuttle (N\$400 for two; ☎ 082 572188, ☎ windhoekairportshuttle .com). Otherwise, the official taxi/shuttle fare, if you engage a driver on the spot outside the terminal, is currently N\$360 for two people. If none is available on your arrival, which is often the case, ask the airport information desk to call one for you, but you'll have to wait until they arrive from Windhoek.

DOMESTIC

Hosea Kutako International Airport In addition to international flights (see above), Air Namibia operates services to the following domestic airports: Lüderitz (3 weekly, 1hr; sometimes via Oranjemund, 2hr 20min); Oranjemund (1–3 flights daily except on Sat, 1hr 15min; sometimes via Lüderitz, 2hr 5min); Walvis Bay (daily; 40min).

Eros Airport Only 5km south of the city centre, just off the B1, the main road south, this tiny domestic airport only services a handful of scheduled flights a day, though more charter plane traffic passes through. Air Namibia operates flights to Katima Mulilo (4 weekly; 1hr 40min); Ondangwa (several daily Mon–Fri, 1 on Sun; 1hr); Rundu (3 weekly;

1hr 5min). There are a few car-rental desks (Avis, Budget, Europcar and Hertz), which are frequently unstaffed. A taxi to/from the airport from/to the city centre costs around N\$60.

AIRLINE OFFICES

Air Namibia Corner of Werner List and Fidel Castro St ☎ 061 225202, ☎ airnamibia.com

British Airways 4 Eadie St, Klein Windhoek ☎ 061 248528, ☎ britishairways.com

Qatar Airways 3rd floor Maerua Mall Office Tower, office no. 37, Jan Jonker Ave ☎ 061 4358325, ☎ qatarairways.com

South African Airways Sanlam Centre, corner of Independence Ave and Fidel Castro St ☎ 061 273340, ☎ flysaa.com

TAAG Angola Airlines Sanlam Centre, shop no. 5, corner of Independence Ave and Fidel Castro St ☎ 061 226625, ☎ taag.com

BY BUS
LUXURY BUS SERVICES

Insight Luxury Buses ☎ +260 975 966742 (Zambia) or ☎ 061 259388 (Namibia), ☎ facebook.com/insight luxurycoaches. Fairly new company based in Lusaka, Zambia, operating a twice-weekly service from Lusaka (Wed & Sat 5am; 26–27hr; N\$850) to Windhoek, via Katima Mulilo (N\$400), returning from Windhoek on Mon & Fri at 2pm (pick-up opposite the Roman Catholic Hospital in the city centre).

Intercape Mainliner Off Bahnhof St, opposite the train station ☎ 061 227846, ☎ intercape.co.za. The comfortable Intercape Mainliner service offers both long-distance services and shorter trips within Namibia (see box, p.48). The ticket office (Mon–Thurs 6am–5/6pm, Fri 6am–8pm, Sat 6am–noon, Sun 9.30am–5.30pm) and bus stop are opposite the train station off Bahnhof St. Prices start at N$200 for the 4hr hop to Swakopmund to N$780 for the 21hr haul to Cape Town.

Destinations Cape Town, South Africa (via Keetmanshoop and Noordoewer; 4 weekly; 21hr); Johannesburg, South Africa (via Upington, 26hr); Keetmanshoop and Noordoewer (4 weekly; 5hr 35min & 9hr 10min); Ondangwa and Oshakati (daily; 10hr 10min & 11hr); Swakopmund (4 weekly; 4hr 15min); Victoria Falls, Zambia border (via Tsumeb, 5hr 30min; Grootfontein, 6hr; Rundu, 9hr 5min; Katima Mulilo, 16hr 50min; and Livingstone, 3 weekly, 21hr 30min); Walvis Bay (4 weekly; 4hr 50min).

Monnakgotla Transport Office 2, Plot 182, Queen's Road, Gaborone **☎**+267 399 5912 (Botswana) or **☎**081 213 5138 (Namibia), **ⓦ**monnakgotla.co.bw. A weekend bus service is offered by this Botswana firm with departures from Gaborone bus station, and from Windhoek outside the *Protea Thuringerhof Hotel*, on the corner of Independence Ave and Bahnhof St (Fri & Sun; 11hr; N$440/ BWP390). Transport is on a 65-seater or a less comfortable 28-seater, depending on demand.

Namib Contract Haulage 161 Nelson Mandela Ave, Klein Windhoek **☎**061 225333, **ⓦ**kalahariholdings .com. The Orange Bus service – also known as the SWAPO bus – operated by Namib Contract Haulage, operates between Soweto Market, Katutura and various towns in the north, including Oshakati (N$225), Outapi and Ruacana (N$255).

Tok Tokkie Shuttle 149C, 4th Floor, Maerua Mall South **☎**061 300743 or **☎**081 127 5285 **ⓦ**shuttles namibia.com. In addition to airport shuttle services, Tok Tokkie Shuttle runs a weekly service (minimum 6 passengers) to Johannesburg, South Africa (Wed; 19hr; N$900), via Gaborone in Botswana (12hr; N$500), in comfortable a/c minibuses with free wi-fi.

COASTAL AND AIRPORT SHUTTLE SERVICES

Two established shuttle services based in Swakopmund, Townhoppers and Welwitschia, run similar daily services in a/c minibuses from Walvis Bay and Swakopmund to Windhoek (5hr & 4hr 30min; N$260), leaving from the coast in the early morning, and returning from Windhoek early afternoon. Both can pick you up at your lodging or organize a transfer to the airport at extra cost.

Tok Tokkie Shuttle **☎** 061 300743 or **☎**081 127 5285, **ⓦ**shuttlesnamibia.com. This slightly cheaper shuttle service is Windhoek-based, leaving at 9am, and returning

from Walvis Bay and Swakopmund in the afternoon (N$210 to Swakopmund).

Town Hoppers Ane Court, Shop no. 2, Otavi St, Swakopmund **☎**064 407223 or **☎**081 210 3062, **ⓦ**namibiashuttle.com. In Windhoek the shuttle departs from the car park by the *Hilton Hotel*.

Welwitschia Shuttle 32 Sam Nujoma Drive, Swakopmund **☎**064 405105 or **☎**081 263 1433, **ⓦ**welwitschiashuttle.com. Offers a daily service similar to Townhoppers' at the same rates, with pick-up from the Christuskirche car park in Windhoek.

MINIBUSES

The majority of the Namibian population travel on minibuses (also known as combis) that often have no fixed schedule but depart when full, and lack a/c. There are two main departure points in the city. Buses that head north to Oshakati, Rundu (8hr) and Katima (11–12hr) depart from the Monte Christo service station just outside Katutura. Transport heading south (to Keetmanshoop (5hr) and Lüderitz (8hr)), and west (to Swakopmund (4hr)) leaves from the Engen service station in Rhino Park, north of the city centre. It's best to get a taxi out to either stop fairly early in the morning if you want to be certain of a ride, especially during holiday periods, and also to ensure you are not arriving at your final destination in the dark, when traffic accidents are more likely. Fares for the above destinations range from about N$150 to N$390.

BY TRAIN

The delightful railway station in Windhoek (see p.84) is the centre of Namibia's railway network, TransNamib (**☎**061 2982032, **ⓦ**transnamib.com.na), which is primarily concerned with transporting goods round the country very slowly. However, it is possible to travel as a passenger on these snail trains, though not in much comfort, even in business class, but it's a good way to meet people and have an adventure of sorts. Since trains take three times as long as cars to reach their destination, few people bother with them. Departures for Swakopmund and Walvis Bay leave weekdays at 7.15pm (peak-season rates from N$115 economy; N$154 business), and are due to arrive at Swakopmund at 5.30am, though they frequently arrive late. A similar schedule (not on Wed or Sat) operates for Keetmanshoop, leaving at 7.40pm and arriving at 7am (peak-season rates from N$115 economy; N$154 business). In either case, you'll need to take food to eat on the way, and for much of the year you'll need a blanket for when the temperature drops at night.

GETTING AROUND

On foot Windhoek city centre is small and most places you are likely to want to visit are within walking distance. That said, though it's safe to wander

around the city during the day, at night you should take a taxi since muggings are becoming more commonplace.

1

By taxi Taxis abound on Independence Ave, and are plentiful outside supermarkets, the Intercape bus stop, and hotels – where they tend to be more expensive – though it is safer to phone for a taxi at night; most accommodation has its own recommended companies, so take a number before you head out if you're anxious about stopping one in the street, or phone Dial-A-Cab (☎ 081 127 055). A short trip anywhere in the town centre is likely to cost around N$60; for places further afield, such as Klein Windhoek or Katutura, a fare of N$80–90 is more usual. Prices are higher at night. Shared taxis broadly follow a set route, from which they will deviate slightly. They are easily flagged down outside the Gustav Voigts building on Independence Ave; the driver will tell you whether your destination is on their route (N$10–12).

By bus A new bus system due to operate in Windhoek from 2016 was suspended due to operational problems, but is due to recommence in 2017, with buses running on fixed schedules fanning out from Wernhil Park in the city centre; check for developments on ⓦ movewindhoek.com.na.

INFORMATION AND TOURS

TOURIST INFORMATION

Windhoek tourist information office (☎ 061 2902596, ⓦ namibiatourism.com.na) currently operates out of a portable cabin on Independence Ave but is due to move into the nearby new FNB building, which was under construction at the time of writing. Staff are helpful and able to answer most questions about Windhoek but are less equipped to deal with questions about places further afield. They can, however, furnish you with city and regional maps, brochures and fliers. You'll also find a wealth of knowledge at the two main backpacker hostels, *Chameleon* and *Cardboard Box*, not least because they both also operate tour companies. Most guesthouses are also pretty knowledgeable and there's plenty of good, up-to-date information online (see box, p.72).

TOUR OPERATORS

There is an increasing number of tour operators in Namibia, most of which work out of Windhoek but do business without an office. The quality of service given by the majority is very high; what follows is only a selection of recommended companies.

ATI Holidays ☎ 061 228717, Toll free (UK) ☎ 0808 234 9378, (US) ☎ 1 888 333 3876. Well-established, professional owner-operated company offering a range of set and bespoke tours – fly-in, fly-drive, camping, the lot – across southern Africa, catering for all purses.

Blue Sky Namibia Tours ☎ 061 229279, ⓦ bluesky namibia.com. This acclaimed family-run business organizes bespoke self-drive or guided tours for small groups of people who already know each other to suit their budget. The owner/qualified guide has many years' experience in wildlife management.

Cardboard Box Travel Shop 15 Bismarck St ☎ 061 256580, ⓦ namibian.org. Over twenty years of experience organizing self-drive and independent travel for individuals and small groups, with an excellent, up-to-date website. Initially focused on the backpackers market, they now arrange tours for clients across the price range.

Chameleon Safaris Namibia 5–7 Voigt St North ☎ 061 247668, ⓦ chameleonsafaris.com. Located at the backpackers of the same name (see p.94), this friendly, professional outfit specializes in short, budget to mid-range tours for individuals or small groups, including several popular day-tours. They often work together with Wild Dog Safaris.

Face 2 Face Tours 231 Virgin Island St, Rocky Crest ☎ 061 265446, ⓦ face2facenamibia.com. Pioneers in Katutura township tours (N$350/person for two or more people), they now also organize other multi-day excursions to Sossusvlei and Etosha.

Katutours Penduka, Goreangab Dam and 105 Eveline St, Katutura ☎ 061 210097 or ☎ 081 303 2856, ⓦ katutours.com. This small enterprise offers informative guided bicycle tours round Katutura for groups of two to fifteen. Half-day morning excursions depart from Penduka (see p.100) or Evelyn St. Ring to reserve the day before. N$450/person.

Mabaruli African Safaris ☎ 061 301563, ⓦ mabaruli .com. Experienced owner-managed operation, which can organize camping or lodge-based tours, family-friendly trips and even cycling safaris.

Namibia JJ Tours Kamanjab, Kunene Region ☎ 081 424 1114, ⓦ namibiajjtours.com. Small owner-operated company that can organize personalized tours and also caters for the LGBTI community.

Nature Travel Namibia ⓦ naturetravelnamibia.com. Highly acclaimed outfit that guides and plans safaris in Namibia, often in conjunction with other countries in southern Africa, though it is based in Namibia. Focuses on cultural tours and wildlife viewing, especially birdwatching.

Wild Dog Safaris 6 Eros Rd, Eros ☎ 061 257642, ⓦ wilddog-safaris.com. Top-notch operators at the budget end of the market, specializing in camping safaris leaving on set dates, with a maximum of fourteen people (minimum of two). Expect inventive bush cuisine and nights round the campfire, as well as quality guiding.

CLOCKWISE FROM TOP INDEPENDENCE MEMORIAL MUSEUM (P.83); WINDHOEK JAZZ FESTIVAL (P.98); HERERO DOLLS, POST STREET MALL (P.80) >

1

VISITING THE NATIONAL PARKS

All bookings for **National Park accommodation** can be made in person at the **Namibia Wildlife Resorts (NWR)** office in the Erkrath Building, 189 Independence Avenue (Mon–Fri 8am–5pm, Sat 8am–1pm; ☎061 2857200, ⓦ nwr.com.na), though you'll need to have made the reservation in advance of your trip if you're hoping to stay at the popular resorts of Etosha and Sossusvlei, and even for the less well-patronized places in high season. Even if you've booked online, though, it's worth popping in to reconfirm your reservation. The office staff can also provide limited information about the parks. In addition to any accommodation booking, you will need to pay daily park entry fees to the Ministry of the Environment and Tourism (MET).

The **MET** permit office, where you can pay park fees is on Robert Mugabe Avenue at Kenneth Kaunda Street (Mon–Fri 8am–5pm; ☎061 2842840). You can buy your **park entry permits** in advance here, though they can usually also be bought at the gate of the respective park. If you're contemplating climbing the Brandberg (see p.194), you need to acquire a permit at the **National Heritage Council** at 54 Robert Mugabe Avenue (Mon–Fri 8am–5pm; ☎061 244375, ⓦ nhc-nam.org), although they are said to be working on a more convenient system that allows for tourists to pick up a permit at the site.

ACCOMMODATION

There is plenty of comfortable accommodation in Windhoek, from inexpensive **backpackers hostels** to family-run **guesthouses**, **self-catering chalets** and modern **hotels**. Guesthouses form the bulk of the properties, with many places only having a handful of rooms, so it pays to book well in advance. Most of the higher-end guesthouses, smaller hotels and restaurants are situated in the leafy eastern suburbs of **Klein Windhoek**, **Ludwigsdorf** and **Eros Park**, though they're little more than a ten-minute drive into the centre of town. Other areas offering generally less expensive lodgings include **Windhoek West**, just west of the city centre, and within walking distance of Independence Avenue, and **Pioneers Park** – good also for self-catering options, a fifteen-minute drive on the main road south, next to the University of Namibia and close to a shopping centre. Within a thirty-minute drive of downtown, accommodation at **Daan Viljoen Game Park** (see p.101) offers a viable alternative. Note that many owner-managed places close down mid-December to mid-January, as people migrate to the coast for the main annual holidays.

CENTRAL WINDHOEK

★**Chameleon Backpackers and Guesthouse** 5–7 Voigt St ☎061 244347, ⓦ chameleonbackpackers.com; map p.81. Head and shoulders above the competition, this superior hostel and adjoining guesthouse boasts clean rooms, friendly and efficient staff, and a pleasant bar and common area set around a splash pool in a shady enclosed garden. The cheaper rooms (N$50 less) share facilities, whereas the pricier, brighter, more cheerfully decorated guesthouse ones are en suite. Other pluses include the DIY continental breakfast, well-equipped kitchen, bar area and secure off-road parking. B&B. Camping per person <u>N$150</u>, dorms <u>N$200</u>, doubles <u>N$550</u>

Guesthouse Tamboti 9 Kerby St ☎061 235515, ⓦ guesthouse-tamboti.com; map p.81. A stalwart of the B&B scene, used by several budget tour operators, this welcoming, central place offers excellent value for its fifteen simple but clean en-suite rooms (single, twin, triple and family). Has a pleasant terrace with city and mountain views and an open-thatch bar-dining area, where you can enjoy a cold buffet breakfast. B&B <u>N$820</u>

Hotel Heinitzburg 22 Heinitzburg St ☎061 249597, ⓦ heinitzburg.com; map p.87. With unmistakable Disneyland-like turrets, this former hilltop German fort offers a mix of colonial-style elegance and modern comfort. The sixteen generous rooms have been individually refurbished with plenty of modern glitz and a fondness for bed canopies and mirrors. Service is courteous and fairly formal, especially at the fine-dining hotel restaurant, but the gardens and pool are relaxing and the delightful terrace affords stellar views across the city. B&B <u>N$3154</u>

★**Villa Vista Guesthouse** 5 Luther St (entrance on Liliencron St) ☎061 222602, ⓦ villavista.com.na; map p.81. Rather goldfish-bowl-like in design – you can peer into your opposite neighbour's room – this two-level guesthouse is super-stylish, laden with original art, and delivers on the vista from a fabulous rooftop terrace, where you can linger over an excellent buffet breakfast. B&B <u>N$1658</u>

WINDHOEK WEST

Cardboard Box 15 Johann Albrecht St ☎061 228994, ⓦ cardboardbox.com.na; map p.81. Classic partying backpackers place with a cheerful if slightly run-down feel, with packed dorms, oversubscribed bathrooms (no en suite) and beer-soaked carpets, all at rock-bottom rates. Don't miss the free pancake breakfast. The action centres on the nice pool and bar area – open until midnight (so don't expect much sleep) – with BYO meat BBQs on Thurs &

Sun. Since non-residents are allowed in to the bar area, it's a great place to meet ordinary Namibians, but the frequent comings and goings mean you'll need to secure your valuables. Camping per person N$110, dorms N$170, doubles N$500

Paradisegarden Backpackers 5 Roentgen St ☎061 303494, ☺paradisegarden.iway.na; map p.81. Popular with long-term residents, this suburban house in a relaxed neighbourhood has been converted into a small, homely backpackers, where you can lounge in a hammock by the large pool or curl up with a book on the terrace. Meals on request. Dorms N$180, doubles N$500

★**Rivendell Guesthouse** 40 Beethoven St ☎061 250006, ☺rivendell-namibia.com; map p.81. This warm, efficient guesthouse offers extremely good value for money, so is often full. Comfortable, simply furnished rooms with en-suite or shared bathrooms (for N$90 less) are supplemented by a communal lounge area with satellite TV, fully equipped kitchen, honesty bar, a pool and patio area. Also has a small self-catering apartment with kitchenette and TV lounge. Generous breakfast included for all accommodation. Doubles N$1000, apartments N$1290

EASTERN SUBURBS

★**Belvedere Boutique Hotel** 76–78 Dr Kwame Nkrumah Rd, Ludwigsdorf ☎061 258867, ☺belvedere -boutiquehotel.com; map p.87. Former guesthouse rebranded as a boutique hotel, but still with the personal touch, with a dozen standard and four superb luxury rooms (N$300 extra), in which you can enjoy scented candles while soaking in the bath, pillows galore on the bed, and a balcony overlooking leafy grounds. The place stands out for its numerous quiet areas, all stylishly and comfortably furnished: a cosy TV lounge; a spacious open-plan kitchen-lounge with fireplace. The jacuzzi, tennis court, superb breakfasts, high-speed wi-fi and efficient, friendly service are other pluses. B&B N$2000

Haus Sonneneck Guesthouse 1 Robyn St, Eros Park ☎061 225020, ☺haussonneneck.com; map p.87. Immaculately kept establishment comprising eight light, spacious, well-appointed rooms, which open out to a private patch of patio with garden chairs and table. The communal grassy front garden and pool area is similarly inviting. B&B N$1322

Hotel Thule 1 Gorges St, Klein Windhoek ☎061 371950, ☺hotelthule.com; map p.87. Illuminated at night on the Windhoek skyline, you'd think the mother ship had landed. In the daylight the place is more down-to-earth, with comfortable if undistinguished carpeted rooms aimed firmly at the business market –workspace, minibar, safe, etc. Fabulous views from the terrace and the restaurant; make sure you order a cocktail as you watch the sun's last rays on the Auas Mountains. B&B N$1785

Hotel-Pension Onganga 11 Schuckmann St, Klein Windhoek ☎061 241701, ☺onganga.com; map p.87. Set on a hillside close to Avis Dam, this cheerfully decorated, modestly priced pension offers ten functional hotel-like rooms, and is a popular pre-flight stopover. It has a Chinese bar-restaurant attached, which is handy if you don't fancy the trek into town. B&B N$1168

Londiningi Guesthouse 11 Winterberg St, Eros Park ☎061 2266201, ☺londiningi.com; map p.87. Set in a lovely tropical garden with small pool, this place offers a variety of rooms, from doubles to a family room for five, with sophisticated African-themed decor and modern amenities. Light lunches and dinner can also be prepared; French–Namibian cuisine, to reflect the ownership. B&B N$1053

★**The Olive Exclusive Boutique Hotel** 22 Promenaden St, Klein Windhoek ☎061 239199, ☺theolive-namibia.com; map p.87. These seven sumptuous suites are in a class of their own in Windhoek in terms of style, comfort and price. The three junior suites and four stunning premier suites – the latter with vast windows and private deck with plunge pool – have each been themed on a different region of Namibia. Laden with antique books and objets d'art, and decorated with paintings and photographic murals, they also contain all modern comforts: sofas you can sink into, vast beds, laptop with wi-fi, Nespresso machine, fireplace and fluffy bathrobes. A swimming pool is set in the olive grove, and dining is top-notch (see p.97). B&B. Junior Suite N$5420, Premier Suite N$6780

Olive Grove Guesthouse 22 Promenaden St, Klein Windhoek ☎061 239199, ☺olivegrove-namibia.com; map p.87. The gloomy contemporary decor (floor-to-ceiling grey cement, including the bedroom and bathroom) of this popular guesthouse – more economical sibling to the adjacent *Olive Exclusive Boutique Hotel* – is an acquired taste, which is partially offset by supremely comfortable beds and superior bed linen. Standard rooms downstairs are noisier, opening onto the kitchen-dining area and car park, whereas the upstairs luxury rooms open onto a shared terrace. Staff are helpful, the breakfasts are excellent, and there's also a three-course à la carte dinner menu (N$300), with the option of fine dining at the exclusive *Olive Restaurant* (see p.97) next door. B&B N$1610

Roof of Africa 124–126 Nelson Mandela Ave, Klein Windhoek ☎061 254708, ☺roofofafrica.com; map p.87. Popular mid-priced business hotel and conference centre with a lively bar area. Though situated on a busy main road, the rather small, modern rooms are sufficiently set back behind a crowded, bamboo-filled courtyard to avoid the noise. B&B N$1424

★**Urban Camp** 2 Schanzen Rd, Klein Windhoek ☎061 244251, ☺urbancamp.net; map p.87. Unlikely, but very

1

welcome, convenient, secure campground in a residential area, within walking distance of a supermarket, ATM and *Joe's Beerhouse*. Offering plenty of natural and artificial shade, clean hot showers, and a pleasant bar area with pool, picnic table and hammocks. Tents equipped with bedding also available. Camping per person N$160, tent provided for two N$500

Villa Montebello Guesthouse 30 Akwamaryn St, Eros ☎ 061 224045 or ☎ 081 245 7744; map p.87. Modern, efficient guesthouse containing eleven spotless rooms with mini-bar, desk, secure parking, and offering a good spread for breakfast. Pleasant walled patio and pool at the back. B&B N$1400

Villa Moringa 111a Joseph Mukwayu Ithana St, Ludwigsdorf ☎ 061 224472, ⓦ villa-moringa.com; map p.87. Nine immaculate, well-appointed and tastefully designed standard doubles (with tea and coffee facilities and minibar), plus five larger and swisher VIP rooms, and a couple for families in this upmarket guesthouse. Lovely airy breakfast area and places to sit out, on the shady dining terrace or the poolside loungers. N$1564

Villa Violet 48 Ziegler St, Klein Windhoek ☎ 061 256141, ⓦ villaviolet.net; map p.87. Newish, upmarket guesthouse with accommodating hosts, comprising five immaculate rooms fitted out in contemporary design. As well as a shady garden and pool with sun-loungers, there's a very comfortable breakfast-lounge area and good coffee and tea available round the clock. Breakfasts are highly recommended. N$1600

SOUTHERN SUBURBS

Arebbusch Travel Lodge Corner of Golf and Auas roads, Olympia ☎ 061 252255, ⓦ arebbusch.com; map p.89. Efficient, modern and clean motel-like property a few kilometres south of town on the main road, with an array of good-value accommodation, from compact self-catering chalets with private patio and braai (no breakfast provided), to standard and superior rooms (some of which are off-site, in the city), or camping – standard or luxury. Book one of the quieter, more private chalets on the Eros Airport runway side, away from the busy main road. Other benefits include a pool and decent restaurant (see p.98), good security and shaded parking. Camping per person N$135, doubles B&B N$1015, self-catering chalets N$1225

Casa Blanca Hotel Corner of Gous St and Fritsche St, Pioneers Park ☎ 061 249623, ⓔ casablanca@afol.com .na; map p.89. German colonial fort meets Spanish hacienda in this whitewashed confection with wrought-iron rail fixtures and some eclectic touches – a tiny gym, jacuzzi, small Moroccan-themed lounge and indigenous plant garden, for starters. Rooms are more conventional: even the standard rooms are spacious and light, with a minibar, DStv, a/c and a lounge area. B&B N$1496

Hotel Etambi Gous St, Pioneers Park ☎ 061 241763, ⓔ etambi@mweb.com.na; map p.89. A dozen rooms and a few self-catering units make up this friendly inexpensive guesthouse. Snug, carpeted rooms possess all the standard business amenities (a/c, minibar, DStv, tea and coffee facilities, phone) without losing their homely feel. B&B doubles N$1100, self-catering units N$1250

Pumula 22 Nissen-Lass St, Pioneers Park ☎ 081 247 8282, ⓦ pumula-accommodation-namibia.com; map p.89. A handful of small, good-value self-catering units (good showers, fan, DStv, well-equipped kitchenettes and braai) and a couple of standard rooms comprise this welcoming place within walking distance of a supermarket. Breakfast (N$50/person) and other meals can also be ordered, and there's a pleasant garden with thatched area, and a splash pool. Though located at the end of a quiet cul-de-sac, morning traffic noise from the nearby bypass can niggle. Doubles N$600, self-catering units N$650

EATING

Culinary offerings in Windhoek are essentially a mix of **European** – with a predictable German bias – and **South African** fare. Meat features strongly whereas **vegetarians** will have fewer menu options to choose from. Most restaurants are located in **Klein Windhoek**, drawing a predominantly white clientele; some offer an alfresco dining experience; others opt for an air-conditioned environment, while some have both. Restaurants in the **city centre** have a more mixed crowd, especially at lunchtime on weekdays. If you want the kind of **Namibian food** that the majority of the population eats, head for the *Xwama Traditional Restaurant* (see p.98) in Katutura, or sample some street food at the market there; other African dishes feature at the Cameroonian-run *La Marmite Royale*, at the Zoo Park (see below).

CENTRAL WINDHOEK

La Marmite Royale (Zoo Café) Independence Ave at the Zoo Park ☎ 081 244 5353; map p.81. The location, overlooking the greenery of the Zoo Park, is reason enough to visit, and the West and Central African menu adds to the draw. Tuck into spicy beef stew with *jollof* rice, or the signature Cameroonian curry (mains N$100–140). Spinach and okra feature strongly, and vegetarians will find other joy in the menu too. The quality can be uneven but it's worth the risk. Daily 8am–11pm.

Namibia Crafts Café Old Breweries, 40 Tal St ☎ 061 249974, ⓦ craftcafe-namibia.com; map p.81. This upstairs terrace is a handy spot for a healthy light bite or an indulgent cake while shopping for crafts. Also does a range of breakfasts. Free wi-fi. Mon–Fri 8am–5.30pm, Sat & Sun 9am–4pm.

★**Restaurant Gathemann** 175 Independence Ave ☎061 223853, ✉gathemann@mweb.com.na; map p.81. The balcony of Windhoek's top dining establishment has presided over the capital's main street and culinary scene for 25 years. Owner-chef, and former Honorary Swiss Consul, Urs Gathemann is renowned for fusing German cooking with local, seasonal ingredients in his dishes. Succulent meat and game with seasonal vegetables feature strongly. Mains start at around N$160, but it's definitely the place to splurge. Leave room for Gathemann's Delight – a delicious triple selection dessert. Mon–Sat noon–10pm.

Sicilia Corner of Independence Ave and Garten St ☎061 225600, ⊛sicilia.com.na; map p.81. This recently revamped Italian restaurant pulls in a mixed crowd for its congenial yet relaxed setting. Decent inexpensive pizza and pasta dishes, finished off with home-made ice cream. Takeaways also possible. Most mains N$120–180. Daily 11am–late.

★**Street Cuisine** Outside the Sanlam Centre, 175 Independence Ave, corner of Fidel Castro St ☎061 223853, ⊛facebook.com/strcuisine; map p.81. A pavement café that's good for breakfast – try the rösti, spinach and poached egg, brunch or a light bite to take away or eat in. The changing daily lunchtime menu is more substantial and good value (from around N$110). Food and service can be variable, but you can't beat the location for people-watching and the Friday cocktail night is catching on. Mon & Tues, 7am–7pm, Wed, Thurs & Sat 7am–8pm, Fri 7am–midnight.

Wecke & Voigts Kaffee Bar Gustav Voigts Centre, Independence Ave ☎061 377000, ⊛weckevoigts .com/kaffee-bar; map p.81. Tucked away in the arcade, Windhoek's leading department store's coffee bar is an ideal spot for breakfast or a light lunch, a cake or a *brötchen* – one with traditional German Roh Hack (minced raw beef, onion and gherkin) is a favourite. Mon–Fri 7am–5.30pm, Sat 7am–1pm, Sun 9am–1pm.

Weinberg Craft Kitchen Old Breweries Complex, 40 Tal St ☎061 236050, ⊛facebook.com/weinbergcraft kitchen.com; map p.81. The vineyard setting has now been swapped for the craft café balcony, but the high-quality fine dining lives on, despite the incongruous setting. Creative mains, such as almond-crusted springbok with *spätzle* and chocolate-chilli sauce, start from around N$130. A tad chilly on winter evenings. Tues–Fri 6–11pm, Sat & Sun 5–10pm.

WINDHOEK WEST

★**NICE** 2 Mozart St, corner of Hosea Kutako Drive ☎061 300710, ⊛nice.com.na; map p.81. As it's a finishing school for chefs and hospitality staff at the Namibia Institute of Culinary Excellence (NICE), generally the staff strive to impress. Expect intimate fine dining in a

dimly lit, sophisticated interior, or in the courtyard by the koi pond. Incorporating organic local produce from their own vegetable garden, dishes are delicious and the menu is varied and creative, such as grilled oryx loin with poached pear and rocket pilaf rice (mains from N$145). Has a vibey bar on site, too (see p.98). Mon–Fri noon–2pm, Sat & Sun noon–2pm & 6–10pm.

EASTERN SUBURBS

Fresh 'N' Wild @ Utopia 64 Nelson Mandela Ave, Klein Windhoek ☎061 402007, ⊛bit.ly/freshnwild; map p.87. Freshly prepared healthy food, using plenty of locally sourced ingredients: breakfasts, snacks and tasty light meals (mains from around N$110) in a pleasant garden setting. Mon–Fri 7am–9.30pm, Sat 7.30am–9.30pm, Sun 7.30am–2.30pm.

★**Joe's Beerhouse** 160 Nelson Mandela Ave, Eros ☎061 232457, ⊛joesbeerhouse.com; map p.87. This renowned, vast watering hole under thatch serves decent, moderately priced pub grub; pork and game meat feature strongly. Try the *sosatie* (kebab) of assorted game meats in mango-chilli sauce with *mealie-pap* croquettes. Often buzzing even midweek, the place can be seething at weekends, with tour groups and locals alike, which inevitably takes its toll on the overworked staff. Reservations recommended. Mon–Thurs 4.30pm until late, Fri–Sun 11am until late.

O Portuga 312 Sam Nujoma Drive, Klein Windhoek ☎061 272900; map p.87. Extremely busy and often noisy restaurant with a buzzing informal atmosphere and TV screens on the walls, drawing a mixed crowd. Portions are large, and the quality consistently good. Unsurprisingly, given that Portuguese dishes dominate, there's a lot of fish and seafood, such as the ever-popular *bacalhau* (dried, salted cod) and potatoes, which will set you back N$230, though most mains are around N$130. Reservations are a must at weekends. Daily noon–11pm.

The Olive Exclusive Restaurant The Olive Exclusive Boutique Hotel, 22 Promenaden St, Klein Windhoek ☎061 239199, ⊛theolive-namibia.com; map p.87. A small, seasonal menu (only three to four starters, mains and desserts) of mouthwatering (though pricey) fusion cuisine in a relaxed but chic mimimalist setting; dine outside on the balcony overlooking the olive grove. Mains from around N$160. Daily 7am–9pm.

Sardinia Blue Olive Schoemann's Building, Sam Nujoma Drive, corner of Nelson Mandela Ave, Klein Windhoek ☎061 258183, ✉sardiniablueolive@gmail .com; map p.87. Authentic Italian food (and more besides) that goes beyond pizzas – though there are plenty – including home-made pasta (mains around N$100). The place is frequently packed, especially at weekends. Daily 9am–10.30pm.

★**Stellenbosch Wine Bar and Bistro** Bougain Villas

1

Shopping Centre, 320 Sam Nujoma Drive, Klein Windhoek ☎061 309141, ⓦ thestellenboschwinebar .com; map p.87. Though the menu features other inventive dishes, this place is all about the beef; various cuts and sizes are served flame-grilled with a choice of sides and sauces (from around N$170) in a delightful colonial-style courtyard setting. Perfect for lingering over a bottle of wine from their extensive and reasonably priced wine list. Reservations essential at weekends. Lunch noon–3pm, dinner 6–10pm; tapas available all day.

Windhoek City Night Market The Village, 18 Liliencron St ⓦ facebook.com/windhoekcitymarket; map p.87. A Friday-night culinary event you shouldn't miss is this extremely popular night market, hosted occasionally in this pleasant leafy courtyard. Shared long benches and tables make for a convivial atmosphere, with stalls of great food and drink to choose from, with accompanying live music. Arrive early to get a seat. Entry from N$25, depending on the event. Twice a month on Fri 4–10pm.

SOUTHERN SUBURBS

Arebbusch Travel Lodge Restaurant Corner of Golf Rd and Auas Rd, Olympia ☎061 252255,

ⓦ arebbusch.com; map p.89. Good value for money – mains start from around N$85 and portions are large. This, combined with friendly, if sometimes slow, service and secure parking, ensures the place draws a good local crowd, as well as guests. There's plenty of seating under the lapa or out in the open air under umbrellas, with the place really humming at weekends, including at the Sunday lunch buffet. Daily 6.30am–10pm.

KATUTURA

Xwama Traditional Restaurant Xwama Cultural Village, corner of Omongo St and Independence Ave, Wanaheda ☎061 210270; map p.78. Rather touristy set-up for some "authentic" African cooking. Be prepared to be taken out of your culinary comfort zone and indulge in some goat's head, donkey meat or mopane worms (see box, p.58); alternatively, there's some more familiar, but tasty, chicken and plenty of spinach, *fufu* and okra to accompany the mains in the twice-weekly African buffet (lunch N$150, dinner N$210), which includes favourites from across the continent. Worth phoning ahead to avoid the tour groups. Village daily 10am–10pm; restaurant Wed noon–9.30pm, Sun 6.30–9.30pm.

NIGHTLIFE

Clubs come and go, and relocate, mainly operating during the latter part of the week and at weekends. **Entry** is usually around N$50, or more for special events. There are now also several nightclubs in **Katutura** that are starting to pull in a more mixed crowd. However, only go with someone who knows the place, and make sure you've transport back fixed up before you hit the nightlife. If you're in Namibia in November, look out for the annual **Windhoek Jazz Festival**, which attracts international artists, such as Letta Mbulu and Caiphus Semenya, as well as talented local acts (ⓦ windhoekjazzfestival.com.na).

Chopsi's Old Breweries Complex, 40 Tal St ☎081 231 3048; map p.81. This indoor and courtyard venue (with benches and tables and basic grill offerings) at the back of the Warehouse Theatre is *the* happening place, where the cocktails are well mixed, the vibe tangible, and the DJ blends hip-hop with house and West African beats. Popular once the karaoke's emptied from the *Boiler Room* on Wednesday nights, and it gets very busy on Fridays and Saturdays, hence the N$40 cover charge for those nights. Daily noon–late.

Club London Nasmith Rd, Southern Industrial ⓦ bit.ly /clublondon1; map p.89. Complete with ceiling drapes, large video screens, laser lights and a range of dance beats from hip-hop to house, kudoro to kizomba, this mainly white venue entices the punters with foam parties, theme nights, drinks specials and occasionally dancing girls. Cheaper entry before 10pm. Wed–Sat 9pm–2am.

Kalabar Hilton Hotel, Rev Michael Scott St ☎061 2962929, ⓦ facebook.com/hilton.windhoek.namibia; map p.81. A fairly bland international hotel bar for most of the time, this place springs to life on Thursday evenings with Jazz etc and Namjams – jazz and other rhythms. Fridays from 7.30pm.

Nimm's Independence Memorial Museum, top floor, Robert Mugabe Ave and Fidel Castro St ⓦ facebook .com/nimms.restaurant; map p.81. The city's top panoramic vista; though you can sink into comfy sofas or prop up the slick bar in air-conditioned comfort, head for the terrace, cocktail in hand, to watch the sun set or to admire the city's glittering lights. The restaurant serves a range of African and European cuisine. Mon–Fri 7am–midnight (happy hour Fri 8.30–9.30pm), Sat & Sun 9am–9pm.

★**Theo's Bar** 2 Mozart St, corner of Hosea Kutako Drive; map p.81. In the same complex as NICE, this chic but relaxed bar has a vibey, cosmopolitan feel, and is a good place just to chat and drink, or you can order from the appetizing bar menu, which includes pizzas and kapana. Mon–Sat 4pm–2am.

★**Warehouse Theatre** Old Breweries Complex, 48 Tal St ☎061 402253, ⓦ warehousetheatre.com.na; map p.81. This former brewery warehouse-turned-theatre is a great, atmospheric venue to experience intimate live music and theatre; there's also a permanent exhibition space and a lively bar, the *Boiler Room*, with something on every evening from live jazz to quiz nights, plus a new rooftop bar, *The Loft*. Mon–Sat 4pm–2am.

ENTERTAINMENT

There's not an overwhelming amount going on in Windhoek when it comes to entertainment. Check out the listings on ⓦ whatsonnamibia.com and keep an eye on the entertainment pages of the local press.

THEATRES

National Theatre of Namibia 12 John Meinert St ☏ 061 374400, ⓦ ntn.org.na. A menu of drama, dance and music, from local amateur performers to international artists. Also hosts the Windhoek Symphony Orchestra.

★**Warehouse Theatre** Old Breweries Complex, 48 Tal St ☏ 061 402253, ⓦ warehousetheatre.com.na. This former brewery warehouse-turned-theatre is a great, atmospheric venue for plays, comedy nights, slam poetry and the like. *The Loft*, its rooftop terrace bar, is great for pre- and post-show drinks with tasty snacks. Mon–Sat 4pm–2am.

CULTURAL CENTRE

Franco-Namibian Cultural Centre 118 Robert Mugabe Ave ☏ 061 260014, ⓦ fncc.org.na. Offers a full programme of European and African films as well as a range of cultural events, from art exhibitions and poetry readings to live music and dance.

CINEMAS

Ster Kinekor The Grove Mall, Frankie Fredericks St, Prosperita ☏ 061 243603, ⓦ sterkinekor.com, ⓦ the grovemallofnamibia.com. A multi-screen cinema, ten-pin bowling alley and games arcade are to be found in Windhoek's newest, largest smart shopping centre in the south of the city.

Ster Kinekor Maerua Mall, Centauraus Rd ☏ 061 215912, ⓦ sterkinekor.com. Just reopened after upgrading to digital, with two 3D screens.

SHOPPING

The main **street markets** are in Post Street Mall and along Independence Avenue by the main car park, where even some Himba have set up a stall. Haggling is expected in both places, though cheaper curios can be found in Okahandja (see p.171). More expensive but often similar offerings are to be found in the **shops** along Independence Avenue, sold at fixed prices. Windhoek's three main **malls** – Wernhil Park, Maerua Park and The Grove – offer much the same diet of South African **chain stores** and **supermarkets**. The first two are centrally located, whereas The Grove is the newest, glitziest and largest addition to the retail scene and lies off the main road south out of the city. The new Freedom Plaza, currently under construction on Independence Avenue next to the *Hilton*, promises to bring more upmarket boutiques.

BOOKS

The Book Den Puccini St at Hosea Kutako ☏ 061 239976; map p.81. The largest privately owned bookshop in Namibia with informed and friendly staff and a good selection of books in English and Afrikaans. Mon–Fri 9am–5pm, Sat 9am–1pm.

CNA Wernhil Park and Maerua Park malls ☏ 061 224090; map p.78 & p.81. South African chain store carrying mainly international bestsellers and magazines. Mon–Fri 9am–6pm, Sat 9am–2pm, Sun 9am–1pm.

Orumbonde Books Old Breweries Complex, 40 Tal St ☏ 081 148 8462; map p.81. A snug shop crammed with books in English, German and Afrikaans, particularly strong on Namibian and southern African culture and history. Mon–Fri 9am–5pm, Sat 9am–2pm.

Uncle Spike's Book Exchange Corner of Garten St and Tal St ☏ 061 226722, ⓦ facebook.com/unclespikes bookexchange; map p.81. Don't be put off by the metal security grill. Just ring the bell, as this place is a real treasure-trove, stuffed full of secondhand books to swap or buy. Mon–Fri 8am–5.30pm, Sat 8am–1pm.

Windhoeker Buchhandlung 69–73 Independence Ave ☏ 061 225216; map p.81. Mainly contains books in German, but with a selection in English, particularly coffee-table books on Namibia. Good selection of calendars and maps too. Mon–Fri 8am–1pm & 2.30–5.30pm, Sat 8am–1pm.

CAMPING EQUIPMENT AND OUTDOOR GEAR

Most local 4WD car rental companies (see p.53) also rent out camping gear, but if you are in need, a couple of Windhoek companies provide a solid service renting out gear; alternatively, you can purchase what you need from one of several outlets.

Adventure Camping Hire 33 Tacoma St, Suiderhof ☏ 061 242478 or ☏ 081 129 9135; map p.89. Rents out individually priced camping items, including satellite phones and GPS for the really remote destinations. Mon–Fri 8am–5pm.

Bushwhackers 32 Rhino St, Rhino Park, Windhoek North ☏ 061 258760, ⓦ nambush.com; map p.78. Just off Hosea Kutako, north of the city centre, this large store is an Aladdin's den of camping, hiking and fishing gear. Mon–Fri 8am–5pm, Sat 8am–1pm.

Cape Union Mart Shop 6 Maerua Mall, corner of Jan Jonker Ave and Centaurus Rd ☏ 061 220424; map p.78. South African chain selling good-quality outdoor clothing, footwear and camping gear – from sleeping bags and rucksacks to cooler boxes and gas stoves. Mon–Fri 9am–5.30pm, Sat 9am–2pm.

Camping Hire Namibia 78 Moses Tjitendero St, Olympia ☏ 061 252995, ⓦ orusovo.com; map p.89. Reliable camping rental outfit. Pre-book a safari package

1

deal (including heavy-duty dome tent, table, chairs and a kitchen box) for N$120/day and pick from a host of individually priced items: from sleeping bags, torches and gas lamps to portable showers and potato peelers. Mon–Fri 8am–4pm, weekends by appointment.

Cymot Greensport 60 Mandume Ndemafayo Ave, ☎ 061 2956000, ⓦ cymot.com.na; map p.81. The place to go for all your camping, fishing and cycling needs – from 4WD accessories to tents and other outdoor gear. Mon–Fri 8am–5pm (closed 1–2pm), Sat 8am–noon.

CRAFTS

House of Anin 19 Bougain Villas Shopping Centre, 78 Sam Nujoma Drive ☎ 061 256410, ⓦ anin.com.na; map p.87. Nama village women's empowerment project has now become a mainstream business, producing distinctive high-quality embroidered bed linen, tablecloths, cushion covers and the like – some done by hand. Mon–Fri 9am–5pm, Sat 9am–1pm.

Namcrafts Shop 2 Carl List Mall, Independence Ave ☎ 061 222614, ⓦ namcrafts.com; map p.81. With various outlets across Windhoek (including in the Old Breweries Complex) and elsewhere in Namibia, it offers a wide choice of crafts; some are made in Namibia, but don't be fooled into thinking the Namcrafts label indicates the

item's origin; there are plenty of imports from South Africa, too. Mon–Fri 9am–5.30pm, Sat & Sun 10am–1pm.

Namibia Craft Centre Old Breweries Complex, 40 Tal St ⓦ namibiacraftcentre.com; map p.81. Great collection of stalls offering an array of handmade crafts from all over Namibia, and sometimes beyond: everything from baskets to stationery, jewellery, wood carvings, textiles, ornaments and paintings. Don't forget to go through to the back courtyard, where there are bigger shops. Mon–Fri 9am–6pm, Sat & Sun 9am–4pm.

Omba Arts Trust Namibia Craft Centre ⓦ omba.org .na; map p.81. It's worth seeking out this particular Fair Trade craft stall, selling exquisite basketry, ostrich-shell jewellery and artwork made by Ju|'Hoansi communities in northeast Namibia. Mon–Fri 9am–5pm, Sat 9am–4pm.

Penduka Goreangab Dam, Katutura ☎ 061 257210, ⓦ penduka.com; map p.78. Although their products are available in various outlets, it's worth getting out to Katutura to see this long-standing women's development project in action (see p.88). The on-site shop sells a range of household products made from embroidered or batik cloth, from tablecloths to sponge bags, cushion covers to oven gloves. Also jewellery from recycled glass. Mon–Sat 8am–5pm.

DIRECTORY

Banks and money Namibia's four main banks all have branches with ATMs on Independence Ave. The city's shopping malls and petrol stations also have ATMs. FNB, Nedbank and Standard Bank have ATMs that always accept Visa and Mastercard. There are also several Bureaux de Change on Independence Ave and at Hosea Kutako International Airport. Novacambios, for example, has several branches in Windhoek, including on Independence Ave and in Maerua Park, The Grove malls and the Gustav Voigts Centre (Mon–Sat 9am–7pm, Sun 9am–5pm).

Hospitals and clinics The two state hospitals are oversubscribed, so you are better off going to one of the private hospitals, which offer 24hr assistance: Rhino Park Private Hospital, Johann Albrecht St, Windhoek West (☎ 061 375000, ⓦ hospital-namibia.co); Medi-clinic, Heliodoor St, Eros (☎ 061 4331000).

Internet Most hotels, hostels and guesthouses offer wi-fi and/or internet access, which is usually free. Connectivity is reasonably reliable but the speed varies. Internet cafés can be found in the main shopping malls.

Laundry Most guesthouses, hostels and hotels provide a laundry service, but will probably need a full day to oblige. If you're short of time, or have filthy camping gear you're too embarrassed to hand over, take them to one of the following, which do both laundry and dry cleaning: Lana Dry Cleaners at Wernhil Park and Maerua Mall (among

other locations), or Laundryland, 339 Sam Nujoma Drive, Klein Windhoek.

Pharmacies There are plenty of well-stocked pharmacists in Windhoek, with knowledgeable staff. In addition to those in medical centres and shopping malls, a couple of useful pharmacies to locate include: Klein Windhoek Pharmacy, 341 Sam Nujoma Drive (Mon–Fri 8.30am–5.30pm, Sat 8.30am–1pm; ☎ 061 227323), and Langerhans Pharmacy, 7 Independence Ave, Ausspannplatz (Mon–Fri 8.30am–5.30pm, Sat 8.30am–1pm; ☎ 061 222581, ⓦ langerhanspharmacy.com).

Police The central police station is on the corner of Independence Ave and Bahnhof St (☎ 061 2093111, emergency ☎ 10111). Of greater use is the 24hr number for the Tourist Protection Unit ☎ 061 2092002.

Post office The main post office is on the corner of Independence Ave and Daniel Munamava St (Mon–Fri 8am–4.30pm, Sat 8am–noon; ☎ 061 2092002).

Swimming There's a fabulous Olympic-size swimming pool and a smaller children's pool on Tennis Rd, Olympia (March–May, Sept & Oct daily 10am–5.45pm; Nov–Feb Mon–Thurs 10am–6.45pm, Fri–Sun 10am–5.45pm; closed June–Aug; N$6; ☎ 061 2903089), set in immaculately kept lawns with thatched shelters and sun-loungers. Since the pools are unheated, they're best enjoyed late afternoon or early evening in the summer, after they've soaked up a day of sun.

Around Windhoek

The nearest escape for city dwellers on hot summer weekends are the rolling hills of **Daan Viljoen Game Park**, a pleasant slice of countryside and a perfect place to picnic a mere thirty-minute drive west of the city centre. On the other hand, if you're prepared to drive an hour or more out of the capital, and fancy a gentle introduction to the Namibian outdoors – as experienced by white Namibians, at least – several **guestfarms** provide the perfect answer, offering hiking or horse-riding opportunities and some hearty farm cooking. On a contrasting note, if you're heading south out of the city on the B1, it's worth swinging by **Heroes' Acre**, which pays homage to those who lost their lives in the independence struggle.

Daan Viljoen Game Park

20km west of Windhoek, signposted off the C28 (an extension of Sam Nujoma Drive) • Daily sunrise to sunset • N$50/person and N$10/vehicle; guided walks N$177/person for two or more people • ☎ 061 232393 • No public transport, though transfers can be arranged

If you have your own transport and fancy escaping the city for a few hours then there's no better place to head for than **Daan Viljoen Game Park**. It's a delightful natural retreat, set among the hills of the Khomas Hochland Plateau, covered in highland shrub vegetation including kudu bush, buffalo thorn and various acacias.

Although the 6km **game drive** is pleasant enough (high-clearance vehicle necessary, 4WD when wet), with some well-sited viewpoints, the absence of predators in the park offers an opportunity to get much closer to the wildlife and really experience the bush by exploring on foot. There are two self-guided walking routes: the 3km – there and back – **"Wag 'n' Bietjie" trail** is a simple stroll from the reception to the Stengel Dam, and is popular with birdwatchers early in the morning; those wanting a more challenging hike should opt for the 9km circular **Rooibos Trail**, which heads uphill from close to the *Boma* restaurant, returning via the Augeigas Dam. If you look carefully enough amid the vegetation, there are still signs of the odd crumbling wall that once demarcated plots of the formerly resident Damara community, which was forcibly relocated by the South African regime in the late 1950s.

Wildlife to look out for includes a variety of antelope: springbok, oryx, kudu and eland, alongside other large mammals such as blue wildebeest and even giraffe; smaller potential sightings are of porcupine, yellow mongoose and rock hyrax, and you can't fail to bump into the ubiquitous warthogs and baboons. Over two hundred **bird species** have been recorded, with plenty of water birds gravitating towards the muddy edges of the dams.

Day visitors are welcome to use the resort's lovely large circular pool and eat at the *Boma*, after making a N$50 deposit, which is redeemable against food and drink purchases.

ACCOMMODATION AND EATING   DAAN VILJOEN GAME PARK

The Boma In the park ☎ 061 232393. The resort restaurant sits under a large thatched roof with indoor and outdoor seating by the pool. Continental buffet breakfast with hot options is available; otherwise meat-heavy à la carte meals are provided with the usual international options, plus a kids' menu. Snacks and light bites can be ordered during the day. Mon dinner only, 6–8.30pm, Tues–Sun 7am–8.30pm.

Sun Karros Daan Viljoen In the park ☎ 061 232393, ⊕ sunkarros.com. Nineteen compact, modern chalets

(most for two people), arranged fairly close together, are tastefully designed with all mod cons, since the place is also a conference venue. Private patios boast a good braai site, with basic crockery and cutlery, comfortable outdoor furniture and pleasant views. A dozen flat and grassy camping pitches look out at the surrounding hills; though not very private, they have all the necessary amenities, including superior ablution blocks with nice ceramic washbasins, arty mirrors and monsoon showers. Camping per person **N$130**, chalets B&B **N$2818**

1

HORSE RIDING IN THE EROS MOUNTAINS

There's no better way to appreciate the rolling countryside surrounding Windhoek than by saddling up for a few hours and **exploring on horseback**. Equitrails (☎ 081 338 0743, ⓦ equitrails.org), a highly experienced and professional outfit with well cared-for horses – riders must not weigh over 90kg, for example – organizes a range of **excursions** to suit riders of all levels of experience, from a couple of hours on the farm (N$650/person for two or more people) to a two-hour ride topped off with a sundowner and a bush braai (N$1100/person), or even a fully inclusive two-night **horse safari**, staying in lodge and guestfarm accommodation (N$5500/person). The stables are based at Elisenheim Guest Farm (ⓦ natron .net/tour/elisenheim/main.html; N$800 B&B) in the Eros Mountains, 15km northeast of Windhoek; hotel transfers from the capital can be arranged for an extra N$100/person.

Heroes' Acre

10km south of Windhoek, signposted off the B1 • Daily 8am–4pm • N$15/person and N$10/vehicle • ☎ 061 2848111

The controversial, vainglorious N$60-million monument that is **Heroes' Acre** is definitely worth a visit, if only to fully appreciate the grandiose monstrosity that is Stalinesque in both conception and scale. Designed and built by a North Korean firm, it was inaugurated in 2002, with the aim of fostering a spirit of patriotism and nationalism to be passed on to the future generations of Namibia. The hillside memorial comprises a vast parade ground and a broad flight of steps, flanked by the tombstones and grave sites of current and future heroes and heroines, that leads up to a towering white marble obelisk, symbolizing a sword. In front stands an 80m bronze **statue of the "unknown soldier"**, who clearly resembles Sam Nujoma (see p.350), depicted carrying a Kalashnikov and brandishing a hand grenade. The strong likeness to the country's first president has fuelled criticism in some quarters that Heroes' Acre is more a glorification of SWAPO than a more general remembrance of Namibians who lost their lives in the struggle, though the vast bronze frieze at the top of the steps is careful to portray the suffering, resistance and ultimate triumph of all black Namibians, irrespective of ethnicity, political allegiance, age or gender. Once you've hauled yourself up the final step, turn round and soak up the stellar view of Windhoek spread out in front of you, before grabbing a cold drink at the on-site **restaurant**.

ACCOMMODATION   AROUND WINDHOEK

Though most people visiting Namibia are itching to head into the desert after finding their bearings in Windhoek, there are a few **guestfarms** and **lodges** within an hour's drive of the capital that are pleasant places to spend a night at either end of a holiday in the country, providing an alternative to spending a first or last night in the city. Some even accept **day visitors**. In general, midweek stays are likely to prove quieter, unless those with conference facilities have them booked out. Serious hikers should note the establishment of a new **multi-day hiking trail** (see box opposite), which takes in several such farms and meanders over the scenic Khomas Hochland, providing a good reason to linger in the area, before clocking up the kilometres on safari.

Auas Safari Lodge Off the D1463, 22km east of the junction with the B1, south of Windhoek ☎ 061 240043 (lodge) or ☎ 061 228104 (reservations), ⓦ auas -safarilodge.com. Well-run thatched lodge with sixteen tidy en-suite rooms (with fan/wall heater and private porch) in the Auas Mountains, 1hr from Windhoek, 45min from the airport. A relaxing place to spend at least a day, it offers massages and manicures, a lapa and restful pool area set in grassy surroundings, from where you can gaze across the savannah. For the more active, there are guided or self-guided walks, hikes and birdwatching. Game drives

(N$400) are popular – the reserve is well stocked with giraffe, wildebeest and antelope, including waterbuck and eland. Quad biking can also be arranged, though it's hard to square that with the wildlife focus. Sunday buffet lunch N$260. DBB **N$2110**

Gästefarm Elisenheim 15km north of Windhoek, signposted east off the B1 ☎ 061 264429, ⓦ natron.net /tour/elisenheim/main.html. Welcoming German–Namibian hospitality and home cooking are the draw here, and it's in a lovely setting, with a shady, grassy pool area to lounge around. Only 15km north of Windhoek, it's also a popular workshop/meeting venue. Carpeted rooms are fairly dowdy though tidy, but the wooden mountain hut built into the rock face is a treat, with indoor and outdoor cooking facilities and sleeping twelve – 4WD needed. There are also five camping pitches. With Equitrails based on the property (see box opposite), this is a great place to saddle up. Camping per person N$110, doubles (B&B) N$800, mountain hut N$2000

Hohewarte Guest Farm East of the C23, 15km south of the junction with the B6 ☎ 081 426 1893, ⊚ hohewarte.com. Former colonial police station, post office, and now working cattle farm, this striking, squat farmhouse provides guests in the seven recently refurbished rooms (some with shared bathroom) with a hospitable service. The lounge is particularly cosy (especially round the fire in winter), if somewhat country-hotel-like in character. Dining is family-style. Though most visitors only stay overnight on the way to or from the airport, you shouldn't leave without a hike up the splendidly named Bismarck Mountain. No internet. DBB rates available. B&B N$2176

Ondekaremba Just north of the B6, 7km west of Hosea Kutako International Airport ☎ 062 540424, ⊚ ondekaremba.com. A perfect layover for those off a late flight, or heading for an early one; airport transfers can be arranged at any hour. This pleasant lodge has a reputation for delicious meals. Fully catered comfortable rooms are available in the main lodge, as well as a handful of self-catering bungalows a 5min walk away, plus three camping pitches. Day visitors are welcome. The lodge sits next to a dry riverbed, boasts a nice pool in tended lawns, and is surrounded by savannah bush, with trails. Camping per person N$160, bungalows N$876, doubles (DBB) N$1930

KHOMAS HOCHLAND HIKING TRAIL

The rolling highveld surrounding Windhoek is often overlooked by visitors in their rush to clap eyes on Namibia's more famous landscapes, but the opening of the new **Khomas Hochland Hiking Trail** (⊚ hikenamibia.com) may soon change that. Covering a **91km circular route over six days** (or 53km over four days), the trail takes you across five farms, hiking through thornbush scrub, along kloofs and across grasslands, scrambling over boulders and even climbing down a rock ladder. It's physically demanding but the rewards are ample: superb views at times, abundant wildlife, and the chance to sleep out under the stars. You'll catch sight of plenty of kudu, oryx, mountain zebra, warthog, klipspringer and baboons, as well as countless small reptiles; the birdlife is prolific too, congregating round the Aretaragas and Otjiseva rivers, farm dams and precious sheltered pools of water in the kloofs, while the ever-elusive leopard keeps out of sight. For the hardcore version of the trail, you need to carry your pack with sleeping bag (one for cold nights), food, extra clothing, utensils, torch or headlamp and all the usual extras – a walking pole is advisable too, as parts of the trail are heavy on the knees. However, if that all sounds like too much hard work for a holiday, worry not, as there's a **slackpacking** option too, in which you take a daypack, with water, snacks, your camera and not much else, while the rest of your gear – food and bedding (including mattresses, or even tents, if you want) – is transported for you from camp shelter to camp shelter.

Though basic, each campground has a toilet, wood- or solar-powered hot shower, braai facilities, a pot and a kettle, with the Monte Christo **treehouse** on the fifth night the standout overnight spot. Rather than confining yourself to light, easy-to-cook meals, you can tuck into a pre-ordered fresh farm meal-pack from each night's host, which includes braai meat and veg as well as freshly baked bread, though you'll need to carry anything you want to spice up the food. It's even possible to request a few cans of beer to enjoy around the campfire. Obviously, this is all at extra cost, but the hike alone is strenuous enough; taking the weight off your back allows you to maximize your enjoyment of the trail.

PRACTICALITIES

The trail starts and finishes at **Dürstenbrook Farm** (☎ 061 232572, ⊚ duerstenbrook.net), located 46km broadly north from Windhoek – 30km along the B1 before turning west. A minimum of three hikers (maximum 12) is required, and the booking can be made online to do the trail between April and September (though experienced hikers are allowed in October and March). The basic costs are N$224 per person per night, if you carry your own pack, and N$370 per night if you go for the slackpacking option, though you'll need to budget for N$800 per day per vehicle to transport your luggage between camps, and for any equipment you want to hire: a mattress, sleeping bag and/or tent (each item N$20–50/night).

The southwest

HOT-AIR BALLOON, SOSSUSVLEI

The southwest

Sandwiched between the cold Atlantic Ocean to the west and the rugged Great Escarpment to the east, southwest Namibia is a land of mountainous dunes, gravel plains and inselbergs. And the weather is just as varied as the landscapes; it's hard to believe, in the scorching midsummer desert heat, that the town of Aus, on the eastern fringes of the Namib, receives occasional winter snowfall. Much of southwest Namibia is inaccessible, but those reachable sights are among the most iconic in the country. The ever-changing Sossusvlei dunes deservedly hog their fair share of the limelight, but the anachronistic mining town of Oranjemund and the ghost mining towns of the Sperrgebiet simmer with intrigue. Lüderitz is also well worth a visit for a colourful glimpse into Namibia's German colonial past.

Much of the Namib, one of the world's oldest deserts, is protected within the boundaries of the largely inaccessible **Namib-Naukluft National Park**, which includes the magical, richly coloured dunes round **Sossusvlei** – one of the country's most visited attractions – and the impressive **Naukluft Mountains**, home to the rare Hartmann's mountain zebra, and a popular hiking destination. Tucked away on the coast at the southwestern limit of the park sits the anachronistic German port town of **Lüderitz**, now an emerging tourist centre and the only point of access to the former diamond mining area that is now the **Tsau ||Khaeb (Sperrgebiet) National Park.**

Down in the far southwest corner of Namibia, right on the South African border, the Orange River empties into an avian-rich estuary at the high-security diamond-mining town of **Oranjemund**, a little-visited, rather off-beat destination. Not far up the road from here, the booming mining settlement of **Rosh Pinah** sparkles with its pristine streets and shopping centre.

Namib-Naukluft National Park

Southern section access points: Sesriem for Sossusvlei and the dunes; 10km southwest of Büllsport on the D854 for the Naukluft Mountains • Open sunrise to sunset • N$80/person and N$10/vehicle per day at Sesriem and Naukluft (see p.112)

The **NAMIB-NAUKLUFT NATIONAL PARK** is one of Africa's largest protected areas. It has increased in size from a small game reserve in 1907 to a vast national park – larger than Switzerland – that now encompasses a huge tranche of the Namib Desert, including former restricted mining areas. Only a fraction of this immense and unique landscape, however, is accessible to the public.

As a tourist destination, the park is renowned above all for the desolate beauty of the vibrantly coloured **dunes** round Sossusvlei, on the eastern edge of a rippling dune sea,

GERMAN COLONIAL ARCHITECTURE, LÜDERITZ

Highlights

❶ Sossusvlei The vibrant changing colours of the Namib's loftiest dunes stand in stark contrast to the ghostly vleis, producing the country's most striking landscape. **See p.112**

❷ Hot-air ballooning Experience sunrise hovering high above the desert, followed by a sumptuous champagne breakfast. **See p.113**

❸ Naukluft Mountains One of the country's most scenic campgrounds provides an excellent base for some challenging hiking in the national park. **See p.117**

❹ The NamibRand Reserve Exclusive tented lodges in some of Namibia's most spectacular scenery, with glittering night skies. **See p.119**

❺ Tiras Mountains The D707, which skirts the muscular Tiras Mountains, is one of the country's most scenic roads. **See p.121**

❻ Lüderitz Home to Namibia's best-preserved German colonial architecture and the fascinating former mining town of Kolmanskop, which lies half buried in the sand. **See p.124**

HIGHLIGHTS ARE MARKED ON THE MAP ON P.108

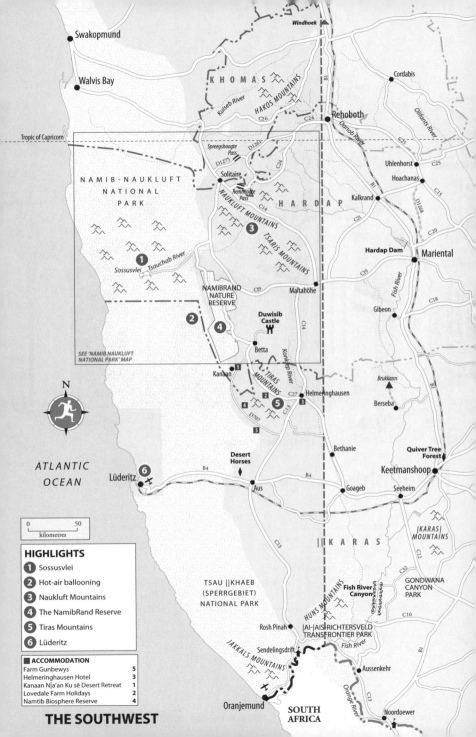

Swakopmund

Walvis Bay

Windhoek

K H O M A S

HAKOS MOUNTAINS

Kuiseb River

C26

C24

Rehoboth

Oanob River

Cordabis

Olifants River

B1

Tropic of Capricorn

Spreetshoogte Pass

D1206

C3

Uhlenhorst

C25

D1275

Solitaire

Hoachanas

C25

NAMIB-NAUKLUFT NATIONAL PARK

Remhoogte Pass

NAUKLUFT MOUNTAINS

C14

3

H A R D A P

Kalkrand

B1

D1268

C15

C21

TSARIS MOUNTAINS

Hardap Dam

Mariental

1

Sossusvlei

Tsauchab River

C9

Maltahöhe

C9

Fish River

C20

C18

NAMIBRAND NATURE RESERVE

Duwisib Castle

C14

Gibeon

2

4

Betta

SEE 'NAMIB-NAUKLUFT NATIONAL PARK' MAP

Kanaan

1

TIRAS MOUNTAINS

Konkiep River

Brukkaros

Berseba

B1

2

5

C27

Helmeringhausen

3

F15

D707

4

5

N

Desert Horses

B4

B4

Bethanie

Quiver Tree Forest

6

Lüderitz

Aus

Goageb

Keetmanshoop

Seeheim

ATLANTIC OCEAN

C13

|KARAS| MOUNTAINS

C12

|| K A R A S

0   50
kilometres

C17

C32

GONDWANA CANYON PARK

HIGHLIGHTS

1 Sossusvlei

2 Hot-air ballooning

3 Naukluft Mountains

4 The NamibRand Reserve

5 Tiras Mountains

6 Lüderitz

TSAU ||KHAEB (SPERRGEBIET) NATIONAL PARK

HUNS MOUNTAINS

Fish River Canyon

|AI-|AIS-RICHTERSVELD TRANSFRONTIER PARK

Fish River

C10

B1

■ **ACCOMMODATION**

Farm Gunbewys	5
Helmeringhausen Hotel	3
Kanaan N|a'an Ku sê Desert Retreat	1
Lovedale Farm Holidays	2
Namtib Biosphere Reserve	4

Rosh Pinah

JAKKALS MOUNTAINS

Sendelingsdrift

Aussenkehr

Orange River

C13

Noordoewer

THE SOUTHWEST

Oranjemund

SOUTH AFRICA

whose relentless progress is eventually halted by the Atlantic Coast to the west, and the Kuiseb River to the north. Yet the **Naukluft Mountains**, which loom out of the gravel plains further east, prove an equally compelling destination for hikers, where the permanent water sources that lurk in the massif's deep ravines (kloofs) support a surprising diversity of **flora and fauna**.

In the northwest corner of the reserve, north of the Kuiseb River, a rockier desert landscape emerges. It is interspersed with pockets of dunes, beyond which extend gravel plains strewn with specimens of the planet's oldest plant, the **welwitschia mirabilis** (see box, p.218). Along the northern section of the park's windswept coastline lie the constantly shifting contours of Sandwich Harbour – a shallow lagoon encircled by majestic dunes, and a major wetland site for resident and migratory birds (see box, p.225). This northern section of the national park is accessed via, or en route to/from, Swakopmund and Walvis Bay, and is covered in Chapter 5 (see p.204). The southern section has two main access points: at Sesriem for the dunescape around Sossusvlei, and southwest of the tiny crossroads and farm at Büllsport, where there is an entrance to the eastern side of the Naukluft Mountains.

2

The dunes

Flaunted in countless holiday brochures, wildlife documentaries and even car ads, the towering **sand dunes** of the Sossusvlei area constitute Namibia's most iconic landscape, epitomizing the country's vast, arid and seemingly uninhabited expanses of wilderness and stark beauty. Yet, despite this overexposure, the dunes rarely disappoint when you finally get to see them for yourself, though at dawn in high season the 65km access road from the Sesriem gate to the Sossusvlei car park can seem like a commuter highway, as a stream of vehicles race to catch the best sunrise shot or beat the crowds to the 325m summit of "Big Daddy", the tallest dune in the area.

The **best time to visit** is early morning, as the rising sun causes the dunes to undergo several dramatic changes in colour, though you'll need several hours to explore the area fully. Late afternoon, towards sunset, is also rewarding, and usually less crowded since only visitors staying inside the park can stay that late. After 10am, with the sun high in the sky, temperatures soar above 40 degrees in summer, and rarely dip much below 30 degrees in winter, although at that time of day you're almost guaranteed to have the place to yourself.

Elim Dune

5km from the Sesriem gate, signposted to the right off the road to Sossusvlei

Given its proximity to the main gate, **Elim Dune** is a popular spot to head for at sunset. Notable for its photogenic tufts of the Namib's endemic stipagrostis grass set against the rich ochre sand, the dune also offers dramatic views across the surrounding gravel plains to the Naukluft Mountains, though it is a deceptively long climb to the top. Possessing relatively abundant vegetation, the dune is interesting to visit at dawn on a calm morning, as you'll see a multitude of criss-crossing tracks made by insects, reptiles and small animals that are supported by the grasses. Watch out for the aggressive Namib dune ant, which has a distinctive black-and-white-striped hairy abdomen and exceedingly long legs, to keep its body well elevated from the hot sand.

Sesriem Canyon

4km inside the park, signposted off to the left as you enter the Sesriem gate

Sesriem Canyon is a narrow, shallow gorge consisting of sandstone and pebble conglomerate whose formation began some 10–20 million years ago when the Tsauchab River, which now only flows every few years after heavy rains, was a much more potent force, carving its way through the landscape. The layers containing larger rocks were formed during periods of strong water flow, whereas those formed of smaller pebbles and

2

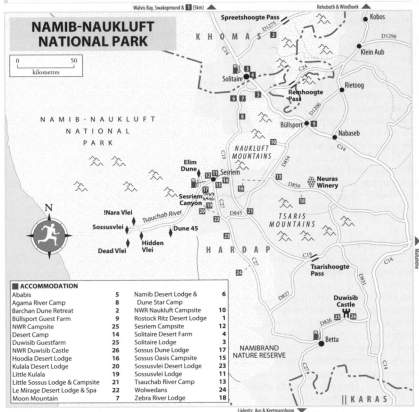

NAMIB-NAUKLUFT NATIONAL PARK

■ ACCOMMODATION			
Ababis	**5**	Namib Desert Lodge &	**6**
Agama River Camp	**8**	Dune Star Camp	
Barchan Dune Retreat	**2**	NWR Naukluft Campsite	**10**
Büllsport Guest Farm	**9**	Rostock Ritz Desert Lodge	**1**
NWR Campsite	**25**	Sesriem Campsite	**12**
Desert Camp	**14**	Solitaire Desert Farm	**4**
Duwisib Guestfarm	**25**	Solitaire Lodge	**3**
NWR Duwisib Castle	**26**	Sossus Dune Lodge	**17**
Hoodia Desert Lodge	**16**	Sossus Oasis Campsite	**15**
Kulala Desert Lodge	**20**	Sossusvlei Desert Lodge	**23**
Little Kulala	**19**	Sossusvlei Lodge	**11**
Little Sossus Lodge & Campsite	**21**	Tsauchab River Camp	**13**
Le Mirage Desert Lodge & Spa	**22**	Wolwedans	**24**
Moon Mountain	**7**	Zebra River Lodge	**18**

higher concentrations of sand were established when the current was less fierce. A continental uplift a mere 2–5 million years ago then set off a process of erosion that continues today. The name Sesriem derives from the *ses* (six) *riems* (leather thongs knotted together) that were needed to draw water up to the gorge rim. You can walk down into the canyon and along its sandy floor; it's only just over a kilometre long, around 30m deep and only a few metres wide in places, flattening out as it heads towards Sossusvlei. In the rainy season, pools of water collect in the canyon's deep hollows.

Dune 45
Signposted left off the access road, 45km after the gate
Probably the area's most photographed dune, **Dune 45** is, believe it or not, 45km from the entrance. Although only 85m in height, this star dune proffers a classic curvaceous spine, with a perfectly situated gnarled camelthorn tree at its base, though it's getting progressively harder to capture a shot of it without vehicles parked in front, or a stream of people toiling up the sand for sunrise.

Hidden Vlei
Follow the trail of posts 2km over the dunes to the left of the 2WD car park
Tucked away behind rust-coloured dunes, **Hidden Vlei**, a ghostly clay pan dotted with dead acacia trees, is less visited than Dead Vlei (see opposite), but just as atmospheric. Look out for the oryx and springbok spoor across the pan.

THE NAMIB SAND SEA

Undoubtedly, for most people desert equals sand, and there are few more spectacular examples of sand desert (erg) than the **Namib dunes**, which stretch for most of Namibia's Atlantic Coast, pushing south into South Africa, and north into Angola. The remarkableness of the 50,000-square-kilometre Namib Dune Sea within the Namib-Naukluft National Park – about the size of Belgium – has now been internationally recognized in its designation as a UNESCO World Heritage Site. Though the Namib boasts some of the highest dunes in the world, at over 300m, it's the ever-changing palette of **colours** that most impresses – from gold to pink, cream to brick-red, apricot to maroon. The coastal dunes are generally paler, consisting of newer sand, much of which originates from sediments washed down the Orange River to be swept northwards by ocean currents and tossed up onto the beaches. The colouration becomes deeper and redder towards the eastern limits of the sand sea, due to the amount of iron oxide present in the predominantly quartz sand and the ways in which the dunes have weathered over time. Even so, the dunes magically alter in hue with the changing light.

Dune morphology, on the other hand, depends principally on the strength and direction of the **wind**; most kinds of sand dunes are longer on the windward side, where the wind pushes the sand up the dune, with a shorter "slip face" in the lee of the wind, where the blown sand tips over. It's here that occasional grasses take root, helping to stabilize the dune, and wind-blown detritus collects, providing food for some of the Namib's extraordinary desert-adapted creatures (see box, p.8). The following main dune formations are present in the Namib:

BARCHAN DUNES

Classic crescent-shaped dunes with two "horns" facing downwind. The most mobile of dunes, forming in strong unidirectional winds; some in the Namib can migrate over 50m per year. They are especially prominent around Lüderitz and Walvis Bay, and up the northern section of the Skeleton Coast. Less common, parabolic dunes are also crescent-shaped but with the horns trailing upwind and the slip face on the inside.

LINEAR (SEIF) DUNES

Converging winds push the sand into long lines or ridges, running parallel to the prevailing wind; some linear dunes in the Namib are over 32km in length.

STAR DUNES

Many examples of these giant dunes are found round Sossusvlei. They are formed when several winds blow from different directions, resulting in three or more steep ridges radiating out from a central peak. Star dunes do not migrate, but continue to grow vertically, and in the Namib form in a south to north direction.

TRANSVERSE DUNES

Long, asymmetrical dunes that form at right angles to the prevailing wind in conditions of abundant sand, such as on the road between Walvis Bay and the airport; with steep slip faces, they appear like giant ripples from the air.

Dead Vlei and "Big Daddy"

To reach Dead Vlei, hike for 3km south across the sand from the Sossusvlei 4WD car park; take plenty of water

Eerily beautiful, **Dead Vlei** was once the end point of the Tsauchab River, until the climate changed and the watercourse became blocked by dunes, leaving the camelthorn trees – some of which are estimated to be nine hundred years old – to wither and die. Their sun-scorched skeletal trunks still remain, due to the aridity of the climate and absence of wood-boring insects; protruding from the parched, white clay-pan floor, they provide a stark contrast to the surrounding golden dunes and cerulean sky. **"Big Daddy"** lies to the south of the vlei, and you'll be rewarded for the hour-long slog to the top by a spectacular panoramic view of the dune sea rippling away into the distance, topped off by a five-minute adrenaline rush as you race down the dune slip face into the pan.

2

Sossusvlei

65km from the Sesriem gate, 4km from the 2WD car park, accessible only by 4WD

The prized destination for most visitors is **Sossusvlei** itself, a large, elliptical-shaped, salt-rich pan surrounded by acacias, grasses and the odd shrub, and enclosed by giant dunes. Look carefully in some of the camelthorn trees, where you may spot the parasitic mistletoe entwined around their branches. Once every five to ten years after exceptionally heavy rains, you may be lucky enough to witness the vlei totally transformed by a flash flood from the ephemeral **Tsauchab River**. The resulting shallow lake remains for weeks, miraculously populated by water lilies and dragonflies, and attracting a flurry of aquatic birdlife.

ARRIVAL AND DEPARTURE

By car There is no public transport to the Sesriem gate, which is the entry point for Sossusvlei. Access from the south or north along the high-quality dirt road C14 is well signposted. Once in the park, you follow a tarred road for 60km to the 2WD car park. Do not drive off the tarmac, whatever the temptation, as your tracks can remain for years. The final 5km to the Sossusvlei car park follows a broad sandy track for which you need to engage 4WD, preferably after letting some air out of your tyres. If you do not have a 4WD vehicle or you are not experienced at driving in sand, it is recommended that you park your

THE DUNES

vehicle in the car park and take the regular Namibia Wildlife Resorts shuttle service to Sossusvlei (N$150), rather than suffer the ignominy of being towed out by the park wardens once stuck – a common occurrence.

On a tour Most tour operators in Windhoek (see p.92) offer short overnight tours to the area. Even if you drive yourself to your accommodation, consider taking one of the local tours offered by various lodgings, as the informative local guides are usually knowledgeable about the dune ecology and can point out some of the extraordinary but often overlooked small wildlife in the area.

INFORMATION AND ACTIVITIES

Park information The NWR park office is at the Sesriem gate (daily sunrise to sunset; ☎063 293252), where you can buy your entry permits (N$80/person per day plus N$10/vehicle). There's also a petrol station and shop. *Sossusvlei Lodge* has an ATM, but don't rely on it.

Activities Sossusvlei Lodge Adventure Centre, by the park gate (☎063 293636, ⓦ sossusvleilodge.com/adventure .html), organizes a range of activities, such as eco-friendly

quad biking, a sundowner drive and even archery, as well as the more usual guided excursions into Sossusvlei and Dead Vlei (N$575/person, for a minimum of four). NWR also runs guided excursions to Sossusvlei and around (N$660/person). The adventure centre can also arrange helicopter rides and hot-air balloon safaris (see box opposite). Tsondab Scenic Flights (☎063 293383, ⓦ tsondab.com), 100km north of Sesriem, offers around

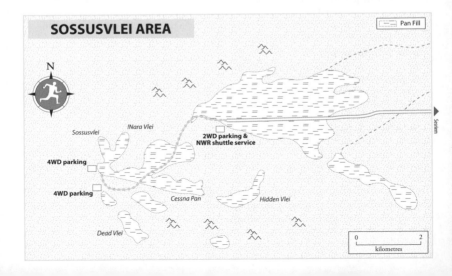

BALLOONING OVER THE DUNES

Of all the ways to comprehend the vastness of the desert and marvel at the play of light on the dunes, it's hard to beat the truly magical experience of witnessing sunrise over the Namib from a **hot-air balloon**. True, it doesn't come cheap, but if you only splurge on one activity during your trip, this should be it. Though you'll only spend around an hour in the air, the whole event lasts several hours, starting with a pick-up around an hour before dawn, followed by a safety briefing, then the balloon envelope is inflated, you clamber aboard and lift off. To the west the dune sea ripples away towards the coast while the Naukluft Mountains stand guard to the east. As you float upwards, you can clearly make out the shapes of the various inselbergs below and track herds of springbok or solitary gemsbok as they trek across the desert. On landing, you can enjoy a sumptuous champagne breakfast before being driven back to your lodgings.

Namib Sky Balloon Safaris 21km south of Sesriem off the C27 ☎ 063 683188, ⓦ balloon-safaris.com. Hot-air balloon rides (N$5,950/person) typically fly over the Namib-Naukluft National Park and NamibRand Reserve, though the precise itinerary depends on the wind. Closed mid-Jan to mid-Feb.

2

1–2hr flights in a six-seater plane on various routes over the desert, including Sossusvlei. Prices are for the whole plane, to be divided by a maximum of five passengers (N$11,350 for 1hr, N$22,700 for 2hr).

ACCOMMODATION

As this is one of Namibia's top tourist areas, places get booked up well in advance for most of the year, and prices are inevitably high, especially for the more exclusive **smaller lodges** that offer a greater wilderness experience. The **larger lodges** with more facilities get to see a lot of tour groups in the busy periods, which inevitably can sometimes detract from the desert feel, not to mention your sleep as many set off pre-dawn to capture the sunrise experience. Note too that the back-to-nature **tented options**, while offering incomparable experiences, can be very chilly at night in the winter months beyond the blanketed warmth of your bed, as temperatures can drop below zero. Another consideration is whether your lodging has air conditioning, a must for some to cool the air, but a noisy intrusion into the stillness of the desert for others. The places listed below are all within an hour's drive of the park entrance.

INSIDE THE PARK

The only options actually inside the park are owned by NWR (ⓦ nwr.com.na), so can be booked online, or through the bookings offices in Windhoek (see box, p.94) or Swakopmund (see p.213). Their chief selling point is that they allow you to set off before sunrise for Sossusvlei and return an hour after sunset.

Sesriem Campsite At the entrance gate ☎ 063 293245 (campground), ☎ 061 2857200 (Windhoek) or ☎ 064 402172 (Swakopmund), ⓦ nwr.com.na; map p.110. A large campground that serves its purpose as an inexpensive base to let you get a head start on the sunrise-chasers at Sossusvlei. With almost forty pitches (plus an overflow area), there's little intimacy about the place, so it's good to get here early to grab a perimeter spot with a wall for shelter from the wind, and away from the noisy staff quarters. Pluses include a pool to cool off in, an adequate bar-restaurant (6.30am–10pm), and most sites offer shade. The overflow site, without electricity or much in the way of facilities, does not offer the same value for money. Per person N$200

★ **Sossus Dune Lodge** 4km inside the entrance gate ☎ 063 293636 (lodge), ☎ 061 2857200 (Windhoek) or ☎ 064 402172 (Swakopmund), ⓦ nwr.com.na; map p.110. Twenty-five desert chalets fashioned out of wood, canvas and thatch, strung out across the sand, with half facing the dunes, and the other half facing the mountains, connected by a wooden walkway. The higher-numbered chalets offer greater seclusion but entail more of a hike to dinner; conversely, you'll not get much sleep in the chalets nearer to the reception, as people traipse past from 4am onwards to catch sunrise in the park. Guided excursions N$660/person. N$5940

SESRIEM AREA

★ **Desert Camp** On the D826, 5km from the entrance gate ☎ 063 683205, ⓦ desertcamp.com; map p.110. This efficiently run camp offers a comfortable self-catering experience, comprising twenty en-suite canvas and adobe camping units, with an extra foldout sofa for young kids. Each has a private open-air kitchenette and BBQ area complete with fridge. Bring your own food, or order a braai pack from reception; booking B&B, and DBB – with meals at the lodge – is also possible. The only incongruity is the big-screen TV at the bar and pool area. N$1759

★ **Hoodia Desert Lodge** On the C19, 22km from the Sesriem gate ☎ 063 683321 (lodge) or ☎ 061 237294 (reservations), ⓦ hoodiadesertlodge.com; map p.110. Relatively new but with a more traditional feel, *Hoodia Desert Lodge* comprises eleven luxury thatched rondavel chalets (with a/c), family-owned and lovingly tended, in a spectacular setting, surrounded by mountains. Expect fine dining and sundowners on the swimming pool deck. All the usual activities can be arranged, and can be included in a good-value two-night special price. DBB **N$5000**

Kulala Desert Lodge Down a dirt road signed off the C27, 15km south of Sesriem, just north of the junction with the D845 ☏(0)11 257 5111 (South Africa), ⊛wilderness.co.za; map p.110. Set in its own private reserve with superb views across to the dune sea, this thoughtfully designed lodge – and its even more exclusive sibling, *Little Kulala* – comprises 23 stylish semi-tented chalets with private rooftop terrace, which are arguably too many for the price tag. It's worth going all-inclusive to take the tour to Sossusvlei, as their vehicles can beat the crowds via their private park entrance (and the guiding's good), whereas self-drive vehicles have to go the long way round. Rates vary considerably depending on the time of year. DBB **N$8180**

Le Mirage Desert Lodge & Spa On the C27, 21km south of the Sesriem gate, just south of Geluk ☏063 683019 (lodge) or ☏061 224712 (reservations), ⊛mirage-lodge.com; map p.110. You'll either love or loathe this extraordinary Hollywood-style Moroccan palace, whose turrets – containing the most sought-after lodgings, with star decks to sleep out on – loom out of the desert. Spacious stone rooms remain cool though dark, with walk-in showers and vast four-poster beds. There's a nice shady pool area, classy dining and the usual trips on offer, as well as popular guided quad bike tours, after which you can soak in the jacuzzi or succumb to a massage in the spa. DBB **N$4120**

Little Kulala Down a dirt road signed off the C27, 15km south of Sesriem, just north of the junction with the D845 ☏081 124 3066, ⊛wilderness.co.za; map p.110. Stylish, minimalist chic reigns in this design-conscious desert retreat, where the decking is dotted with objets d'art and the eleven state-of-the-art, a/c chalets boast gorgeous soft-toned furnishings and come complete with private plunge pool, indoor and outdoor showers, and a candlelit rooftop bed deck. The opulence extends to a library and impressive wine cellar. Rates – which are significantly cheaper in low season – include two activities a day. AI **N$20,750**

Little Sossus Lodge & Campsite At the junction of the C19 with the D854, 35km southeast of Sesriem ☏081 127 9920 (lodge) or ☏081 211 8287 (campground), ⊛littlesossus.com; map p.110. This hospitable homestead has 20 simple, fan-ventilated stone cottages for couples or families. An unpretentious bar-restaurant area spills over into a pleasant garden, where you can enjoy good home cooking if ordered in advance. Superior camping pitches privilege functionality over ambience with a serried rank of car shelters and private kitchen, plus shower blocks with electricity. But they offer views over a couple of waterholes in a well-stocked game reserve. Camping per person **N$120** and **N$100** for the site, cottages B&B **N$1240**

Sossus Oasis Campsite Opposite the entrance gate ☏063 293632, ⊛sossus-oasis.com; map p.110. Also owned by *Sossusvlei Lodge*, this efficient campground is slightly pricier and smarter than the NWR-run one over the road. Has private ablutions, electricity and a braai site, with an adjacent petrol station, internet café and well-stocked shop. Per person **N$180**

Sossusvlei Lodge By the park entrance ☏063 693223, ⊛sossusvleilodge.com; map p.110. Busy lodge with more of a hotel feel, comprising 45 spacious canvas and plaster rooms with tiled floors and a/c. Highlights include bountiful buffet dining, watching wildlife at the floodlit waterhole from the acacia-filled beer garden. The on-site adventure centre is good for arranging activities (see p.112). DBB **N$4620**

Solitaire and around

Just outside the national park boundary, flanked by the Naukluft Mountains to the east, and scanning the flat grasslands to the west, the aptly named **SOLITAIRE** (meaning "isolated" in French) is a classic middle-of-nowhere pit stop, the only source of roadside fuel, food and drink for many miles around. A clump of trees and a collection of rusted-out old vehicles surround this pinprick on a map, which consists of a long-standing general dealer and a petrol station that does efficient tyre repairs and checks. Yet the place has now become a fixture on the tourist circuit; it even has its own website (⊛solitairenamibia.com), due mainly to the widely advertised "Moose" McGregor's Desert Bakery. Though its former larger-than-life patron is no more, his renowned **apple pie**-cum-crumble recipe lives on amid a host of other sweet and savoury goodies, sold at tourist prices, and of variable quality. A number of good lodges and guestfarms lie in the area, several popular with tour groups, as they are within striking distance of Sossusvlei around 80km south. However, they also provide a convenient base to explore the nearby mountain scenery. What's more, Solitaire is a mere 10km from the

turn-off to the **Spreetshoogte Pass**, arguably the most spectacular of the region's several breathtaking mountain roads that cascade off the Great Escarpment (see p.360).

Note also that you can track cats with a resident biologist at the Namib Carnivore Centre, a local **cheetah sanctuary** (see ⓦ solitairenamibia.com; N$350).

ACCOMMODATION

Ababis At the junction of the C14 and the C24, 13km south of Solitaire ☎063 293362, ⓦ ababis-gaestefarm .de; map p.110. Conveniently located midway between the entrances of Sossusvlei and the Naukluft Mountains, this old colonial farmhouse oozes charm and history, packed with antique furniture, paintings, woodcarvings and knick-knacks. Seven spacious double rooms are decorated in earthy tones, plus there's one family room (the only one with a/c). Excellent dining, family-style, is on the long bougainvillea-draped veranda. Enjoy hiking on their reserve, before rewarding yourself with afternoon tea and cake on your return, or soak up sweeping desert vistas on the sundowner drive. Also has a self-catering river house and a more distant mountain retreat. **N$2600**

Agama River Camp On the C19, 34km south of Solitaire, 48km north of Sesriem ☎063 293262, ⓦ agamarivercamp.com; map p.110. Efficient set-up offering block chalets, which blend with the surroundings, each with a/c and a roof deck, which you can arrange to sleep on. Semi-secluded camping pitches are spread along a dry riverbed, where you can rent a tent plus bedding for an extra N$150/person, and cooking utensils if necessary. You can gaze at the starry sky while showering in the communal block, and there's a small pool. Pleasant, open-sided bar-restaurant serving a set menu – for campers meals need to be booked ten days in advance (dinner N$280). Camping per person **N$160**, chalets (DBB) **N$2890**

★**Barchan Dune Retreat** On the D1275, 15km from the junction with the C14 ☎062 682031, ⓦ barchandunes.com; map p.110. Small hospitable guestfarm at the foot of the Spreetshoogte Pass, offering four rooms and three modern bunker-like chalets half-buried in the earth and tastefully designed in stone and wood with vast glass windows to maximize the mesmerizing vistas. The star attraction is Kuangu-Kuangu, a two-person romantic getaway built into the surrounding rock, with outdoor bathroom, kitchenette and private braai, affording stunning views across to the Namib-Naukluft National Park, be it from your bed, or from your private patio. At five minutes' walk from the main lodge, you can choose to eat there if you prefer. Al also available. No credit cards. Doubles and chalets (DBB) **N$1950**, Kuangu-Kuangu **N$1500**

Moon Mountain East off the C19, 32km south of Solitaire ☎067 240975, ⓦ moonmountain.biz; map p.110. Seventeen commodious tented chalets on stilts – including six suites with bidet and lounge – spread over

SOLITAIRE AND AROUND

the mountainside, offering stellar views across the plains to the Namib's petrified dunes from their private decks, each with plunge pool. The common areas include a large restaurant, reading lounge and small cinema/conference room. Guided tours to Sossusvlei and sundowner drives available. DBB. Doubles **N$4000**, suites **N$4420**

Namib Desert Lodge & Dune Star Camp West off the C19, 32km south of Solitaire ☎063 293665 (lodge) or ☎061 427200 (reservations), ⓦ gondwana-collection .com; map p.110. Large lodge booked solid with tour groups in high season. Set at the base of a cliff with 65 cheerfully decorated, comfortable terracotta-tiled rooms (with a/c) of various configurations, and shady patio areas. Plenty of communal seating areas, around the two decent-sized pools set in grassy tree-filled courtyards. Buffet meals served in the cavernous thatched dining area. The more secluded *Dune Star Camp*, a short, guided hike away, is the place to get away from the crowds, comprising nine solar-powered tented chalets atop a dune with great views over yet more richly coloured sand. Camping also available, offering some shade and communal ablution blocks. Don't forget to visit the nearby fossilized dunes while there. Camping per person **N$175**, doubles **N$2442**, dune chalets **N$3256**

Rostock Ritz Desert Lodge 7km east of the C14, 55km north of Solitaire ☎064 694000 (lodge) or ☎081 258 5722 (reservations), ⓦ rostock-ritz-desert-lodge.com; map p.110. Nineteen distinctive stone-and-cement igloos, equipped with mosquito nets and ceiling fans, offer fabulous views through sliding glass doors or from the private patio. À la carte dining is excellent, and draws daytime visitors breaking the journey between Sossusvlei and the coast. Has well-preserved ancient rock paintings on the property, and, after tiring yourself on one of several hiking trails, you can cool off in the pool. Four pitches are available, with superior stone braai sites under shade netting and nice stone ablutions plus a great communal viewing terrace and fire-pit, but the flimsy fence partitioning offers little privacy. Camping per person **N$150**, chalets **N$2544**

★**Solitaire Desert Farm** Signed off by the Solitaire T-junction, 6km down a dirt road ☎062 572024 (guestfarm) or ☎067 240901 (reservations), ⓦ solitairenamibia.com; map p.110. Set in delightfully landscaped desert gardens, which attract plenty of birdlife, this welcoming guestfarm offers 15 comfortable rooms (with a/c) and three deluxe camping pitches. This is a place for pet-lovers, with various rescue animals and a plethora of dogs, rabbits, meerkats and peacocks. Hikes, wildlife drives

and fat-tyre bike rental are on offer, plus there's a great swimming pool and high-quality buffet meals (dinner N$210). Camping per person <u>N$150</u>, doubles <u>N$1840</u>
Solitaire Lodge By the main road and petrol station ☎ 063 293621 (lodge) or ☎ 067 240901 (reservations), ⓦ solitairenamibia.com; map p.110. Bang next to the

frantic daytime comings and goings at the adjacent amenities, the lodge's courtyard desert garden with swimming pool provides a surprising oasis of calm, and is enclosed by 25 spacious, cheerfully decorated rooms (with a/c), each with a small personal patio area and chairs. Dinner is an extra N$235. <u>N$1870</u>

The Naukluft Mountains

2

Entrance on the D854 • Daily park fees N$80/person, plus N$10/vehicle, payable in one of the MET offices in advance or at the park office, at the campground entrance

In the rush to experience what for most people is the "real desert", namely the dunes round Sossusvlei, first-time visitors to Namibia often overlook the **Naukluft Mountains**, an impressive escarpment that falls off the Central Highlands and a rewarding, if challenging, hiking destination. This vast plateau boasts near-vertical cliffs in places, which rise over 1000m from the surrounding gravel plains. Formed 500–600 million years ago, it consists predominantly of porous dolomite and limestone rock, riddled

HIKING IN THE NAUKLUFT MOUNTAINS

There are a couple of fairly demanding circular **day hikes** and an arduous **multi-day trek** that takes eight days, or four days if you arrange a pick-up (or leave a vehicle) halfway. The two day-trails require no prebooking and can be walked year-round, whereas the multi-day hike has to be booked with NWR in advance (see p.112). All three hikes, which are clearly marked with painted footsteps, involve rocky terrain, requiring robust hiking shoes or boots. You'll also need to carry at least two litres of water per day.

OLIVE TRAIL

Probably the most popular trail, this 10km loop (4–5hr) starts from a car park 4km from the park office. It steadily winds its way up onto the plateau past many olive trees before descending via a gradually deepening valley – look out for the quiver trees – where towards the end you will need to use a chain bridge to navigate a canyon wall. The trail eventually joins a 4WD track that leads back to the car park.

WATERKLOOF TRAIL

Starting near the campground, this more strenuous, and arguably more scenic, 17km hike (6–7hr) takes you up a narrow ravine, dotted with pools (in the rainy season), onto an open, exposed plateau and then onto a ridge, which affords superb panoramic views. The trail then descends steeply past further pools and waterfalls (after rains) before meeting the usually dry Naukluft River and then a 4WD track, which you follow back to the start.

MULTI-DAY HIKE

This gruelling, eight-day, 120km trail (with a four-day option that avoids the toughest sections) allows you to experience the full variety of the massif's rocky terrain but is not for the faint-hearted, those afraid of heights, or the inexperienced. Moreover, while some sections of the trail lead you through impressive scenery, others take you along seemingly endless rocky ravines and riverbeds. Averaging around six hours' hiking a day, you'll stay in very basic shelters, offering only water and toilets (no showers), and, with no fires allowed in the park, you'll need to carry a stove. The good news is that it is possible to leave a vehicle with supplies for the last four days at Tsams Ost, the shelter for the fourth night, thereby saving having to carry the extra kilos of food. Those doing the shorter four-day trail will also leave a vehicle here for transport back out of the park.

The Naukluft multi-day hike is only permissible between March 1 and the third Friday in October (Tues, Thurs & Sat); buy a permit in advance from NWR in Windhoek (see box, p.94), for which you need a current medical certificate. The cost is N$135 per person, in addition to park entry fees. A minimum of three people (maximum twelve) is needed to hike the trail.

2

NEURAS WINERY

One of Namibia's many striking curiosities is its desert wineries: one is situated outside Omaruru in the Erongo Region (see p.190), whereas the more visited **Neuras Winery** (☎063 293417, ⓦneuraswines.com) lies only a few kilometres off the D850 – an easy detour and perfect lunch stop if you're travelling between the Naukluft Mountains and Sossusvlei. Since this means it can also be popular with tour groups, it's advisable to phone ahead and time your visit accordingly. While the landscape at first glance would seem too harsh for successful viticulture, a guided tour soon puts you right, explaining the unique microclimate of the spring-fed estate, where the alkaline soil is perfect for planting and the mountainous backdrop protects the vines from the worst ravages of the desert winds. The first wine from Merlot and Shiraz grapes was produced in 2001, resulting in about 3000 bottles. Since then, the estate has expanded, various experimental grapes have been planted, and production is up to 15,000 bottles of red wine and brandy a year. Full tours of the vineyards and cellars take around an hour, culminating in a wine tasting of two reds, accompanied by a platter of cheese (N$285). If you want to skip the tour, you can still sample the wine (at N$20 each), which is surprisingly good, or linger over a light lunch – wraps, salads, pasta, a plate of antipasti and the like (N$45–105) – in their pleasant shady, patio restaurant, and savour a full glass or bottle (from N$245).

with caves, galleries and ravines, sitting atop a solid granite base. Indeed, Naukluft takes its name from a Germanic corruption of the Afrikaans "*nou kloof*", meaning narrow gorge or ravine. Where the underground water spills out in springs and streams in these fissures, crystal-clear pools form that support a surprising variety of **plant and animal life**, including around two hundred bird species. Look out for klipspringer, kudu, steenbok, oryx and Hartmann's mountain zebra, as well as soaring black eagles that nest along the cliffs.

ARRIVAL AND ACTIVITIES

By car The clearly signposted park entrance is located 8km along the D854 road, after the turn-off from the C14, just southeast of Büllsport.

Hiking Three hikes are available (see box, p.117).

Horse riding *Büllsport Guest Farm* (see below) owns a

THE NAUKLUFT MOUNTAINS

large portion of the mountains adjacent to the park, with horse-riding activities too, making it a popular alternative base to the NWR campground for exploring the mountains, charging N$100 for day visitors.

ACCOMMODATION AND EATING

IN THE PARK

NWR Naukluft Campsite 16km along the access road from the D854 ☎061 2857200 (reservations), ⓦnwr.com.na; map p.110. In a lovely setting, hemmed in by rocks and sheltered by thorntrees, this NWR campground boasts six smart "bush chalets" overlooking a stream, 21 camping pitches and a small bar-restaurant. Three-night maximum stay at peak periods. Park fees cost extra. Camping per person N$170, chalets B&B N$1760

OUTSIDE THE PARK

★ **Büllsport Guest Farm** By the junction of the C14 and the D1246, 8km north of the park entrance ☎063 693371, ⓦbuellsport.com; map p.110. Well-established guestfarm, offering five standard rooms and eight newer, design-conscious "luxury rooms", well worth the extra money, boasting heating, walk-in showers, an additional bed and private patio. Campers can choose between a pricier campground for one group

of up to ten, or a shared one, both with a lapa for shade, and simple ablution blocks with donkey-heated hot water (you have to provide the wood). Campers can book meals at the guestfarm too if bored of the braai. Activities include farm tours, self-guided hikes and horse rides, and (long) day-trips to Sossusvlei can be pre-arranged. Camping per person N$230, doubles (DBB) N$3150

★ **Tsauchab River Camp** Signed 500m from the junction between the D850 and the D854 ☎064 464144, ⓦtsauchab.com; map p.110. Wonderful place with six chalets and thirteen camping pitches – some with open-air showers – of varying capacities; all are individually designed and spread over 15km, so there's plenty of privacy for all. There's also a restaurant at reception – a drive away. Sundowner drives, a 4WD trail and self-guided hikes of up to 21km are all available on a property with freshwater pools and a giant fig forest – not forgetting the ever-expanding quirky collection of iron art. Camping per person N$120 plus per site N$160, chalets N$1600

★**Zebra River Lodge** 19km along the D850 from the junction with the D854, then a further 5km down a dirt track ☎ 063 693265, ⓦ zebra-river-lodge.com; map p.110. Looking across to the Tsaris Mountains, this lodge comprises charming, individually designed stone chalets – worth opting for – and some less fancy rooms. A delicious dinner (N$230) is served at the old farmhouse, either inside or on the patio, to the sound of the whistling wind and singing cicadas. The welcome is very warm and there are several good hikes on offer. B&B. Doubles N$1690, chalets N$1855

NamibRand Nature Reserve

2

One of the largest private reserves in Africa, the **NamibRand Nature Reserve** shares a 100km border with the southeastern section of the Namib-Naukluft National Park, thereby creating an important buffer zone. The reserve contains similar scenery to the national park: gravel plains, inselbergs, spectacular dunes and impressive mountains, as well as comparable flora and fauna, attracting over 170 bird species. However, the small handful of exclusive tourist concessions means you won't need to share this beautiful desert wilderness with hundreds of other tourists, as can be the case round Sossusvlei. The reserve is also the first designated **dark sky reserve** in Africa, so it's the perfect spot to indulge in stargazing. The southeastern section of the reserve hosts the only luxury multi-day walking safari in Namibia, the Tok-Tokkie Trail, which provides a unique opportunity to get close to nature for an extended period without sacrificing too many comforts (see box below).

ARRIVAL AND DEPARTURE
NAMIBRAND NATURE RESERVE

By car There are clear signs into the reserve from the C27; the entrance lies 70km south of Sesriem, 40km south of the junction between the C27 and the D845. All accommodation in the park will transfer you from reception to your actual camp.

ACCOMMODATION

Sossusvlei Desert Lodge 4km off the C27, 40km south of Sesriem ☎ (0)11 809 4300 (South Africa), ⓦ andbeyond.com; map p.110. The ultimate in modern desert chic: ten spacious, design-conscious split-level chalets in stone and glass, with sofas, rugs and cushions, all in earthy desert tones. Stargaze through the skylight above the bed or through the lodge telescope, aided by the on-site astronomer, and dine on your private patio, accompanied with fine wines from the extensive cellar; best digested with a loll in the spring-fed circular pool. Only the TV in the lounge seems out of place. The usual desert excursions, plus quad biking and visits to cave paintings, are available. AI N$20,360

WOLDWEDANS COLLECTION
Four of the five exclusive properties in the NamibRand Reserve belong to the Wolwedans Collection, and are located in the northern section of the reserve. In keeping with the ethos of sustainability, the lodges are simple but stylish, blending in with the surroundings, and running off

THE TOK-TOKKIE TRAIL

Taking the nickname of the acrobatic, Tenebrionid beetle (see box, p.363), the **Tok-Tokkie Trail** covers 20km across undulating vegetated sand dunes over one full and two half days of walking. The emphasis is on getting close to nature and learning about desert ecology from a knowledgeable guide, while having encounters with some of the area's more intriguing, less obvious wildlife: from barking geckos to dancing spiders, fairy circles (see box, p.263) to the aforementioned beetle. The two nights are spent out under the stars on camp beds, and guests use hot-water bucket showers. Bear in mind that while the cooler daytime temperatures of the high-season winter months are ideal for hiking, they can make for freezing cold nights, though the bedding will be as warm as possible. The walking is made easier – or as easy as is possible over sand – by only having to carry a light daypack, as a full back-up crew transports the rest of your luggage from camp to camp and provides gourmet alfresco dining, complete with white linen tablecloths. This is serious glamping, though you do need to be reasonably fit to do the trip.

Since group sizes range from two to eight people, you need to make reservations well in advance: ☎ 061 264521, ⓦ toktokkietrails.com; AI N$6520/person).

2

solar-powered hot water but with no a/c or electricity – not even fans – which is why all but the Dunes Lodge are closed during the hottest part of the year. Each tented chalet has a private deck, where you can sleep under the stars if you desire. All the lodges offer excellent guiding, top-notch levels of service and exquisite dining in stunning surroundings – at a price. Walking and vehicle safari activities are included in the rates, but hot-air ballooning, scenic flights, massage and horse riding are extra. Three nights are advised to make the most of the area. Rates also include reserve entrance fees and contributions to the Wolwedans Foundation to help run its conservation and community development programmes. The reception is 20km from the reserve gate, signposted off the C27 70km south of Sesriem (☎ 063 693730 (reception) or ☎ 061 230616 (reservations); ⓦ wolwedans.com; map p.110).

Wolwedans Boulders Camp Small tented camp accommodating only ten people, set on wooden decking nestled among vast granite rocks. The common areas are similarly elegantly furnished, but, as the most remote of the camps, it is impossible to include a visit to Sossusvlei from here. AI N$15,940

Wolwedans Dune Camp A classic desert camp, with half a dozen airy safari tents on private wooden decks, atop a 250m-high dune connected by a walkway to the communal area, which boasts an open kitchen with alfresco fine dining. AI N$13,940

Wolwedans Dunes Lodge Slightly larger and more luxurious than *Dune Camp*, spread across a dune plateau, accommodating twenty in beautifully furnished wooden chalets – also with roll-up canvas walls – and plenty of social areas: a bar-lounge replete with leather sofas, library, two dining rooms and a pool suspended above the sand and surrounded by sun loungers. AI N$12,740

Duwisib Castle

20km off the C27 from the junction with the D826 • Daily 9am–5pm • Entry N$70

One of Namibia's more unlikely sights is the crenellated neo-medieval folly, **Duwisib Castle**, which, incongruously yet proudly, occupies a hilltop off the eastern fringes of the Namib. This sturdy sandstone fortress, erected in the early twentieth century by an eccentric German, "Baron"– as he came to be known locally – **Hans Heinrich von Wolf**, is an anachronistic curiosity that promises more than it delivers. The tale of the mansion's construction and its owners, combined with the novelty value of its semi-desert setting, is of greater interest than the contents per se (see box opposite).

Only a handful of rooms are open to the public, furnished with some of the original antique furniture, though labelling and explanations are scarce. You enter via the Knights' Hall – an early indication of the owner's over-ambition – presided over by a splendid chandelier and bedecked with von Wolf's sword collection, assorted weaponry and numerous pictures with a recurring equine flavour – incongruously sharing wall space with the obligatory portraits of Sam Nujoma and the current president. To the left is the dining room – note the burner to heat the curling tongs – whereas the private rooms lie to the right. Don't forget to pop upstairs and take in the flaking mural and the view outside, before descending into the former wine cellar in the basement. So while the castle does not merit a major detour, if you're in the area, it's worth dropping by, and once you've nosed around, enjoy a slab of cake with afternoon tea in the courtyard café, shaded by two large jacarandas. The main niggle, which undermines the place's otherwise tranquil setting, is the constant daytime hum of the generator; luckily for guests choosing to stay overnight here, the place switches to solar power in the evenings.

ACCOMMODATION
DUWISIB CASTLE

Duwisib Guestfarm 5min walk from the castle ☎ 063 293344 or ☎ 081 354 3619, ⓦ www.farmduwisib.com; map p.110. There's nothing fancy about the rustic accommodation in this working estate's stone farmhouse; solar power means limited electricity – so no a/c or fans (though there's now a pool and renovations are under way). That said, the simple rooms are clean and comfortable and the hospitality is first-class, with excellent meals too in a barnlike dining room. You can also pre-book dinner here if you're staying at the castle. Camping sites are not as scenically located as the NWR ones, but facilities are much better and you can eat at the farm. Two self-catering units also available. Camping per person N$110, self-catering N$770, doubles HB N$1720

NWR campsite map p.110. Just below the castle are ten delightful and well-spaced shady pitches with shared ablutions, and hit-and-miss water. No electricity. Per person N$150

NWR Duwisib Castle ☎ 061 2857200 (Windhoek) or ☎ 064 402172 (Swakopmund), ⓦ nwr.com.na; map

2

NAMIBIA'S DESERT FORTRESS

Duwisib Castle was the fantastical brainchild of **Hans Heinrich von Wolf**, a German from a military background, who had first visited German South-West Africa (as it was then) after volunteering to join the Schutztruppen and help contain the Herero threat. Arriving in 1904, he was so taken by the country that after returning to Germany in 1907, he persuaded his wealthy **American bride**, a Miss Jayta Humphrey, to set up home and live the colonial dream in this improbable desert environment. Having succeeded in buying up several farms, he employed renowned architect Adam Sandler – who had designed Windhoek's three castles (see p.86) – to design his fortified abode. No expense, or pretension was spared: though the solid sandstone blocks were quarried in the area by a local workforce, everything else was sourced in Europe, from the furniture to the fitments and the **lavish furnishings**. These were shipped to Lüderitz and then dragged the 300km across the desert by ox wagon to the site. Here, craftsmen from Italy, Sweden and Ireland set about realizing Heinrich's fanciful 22-room creation. The solid, metre-thick walls, at least, were functional, keeping the desert heat at bay, while providing some insulation again the cold winter nights, aided further by two large fireplaces. There practicality ended, as a lofty "knights' hall," complete with minstrel's gallery, was constructed, as well as a cloistered courtyard with a central fountain, and wine cellar. Amazingly, the whole project took only a couple of years to complete. The farm itself was stocked with high-quality cattle and sheep, though Hans devoted most of his energies to his primary passion: horses. He built up an impressive **stud farm** from imported stock; it is believed that some of the feral Namib horses that cavort around Aus today may have originated from here (see box, p.124).

However, the baron's equine ambitions came to an abrupt end in 1914. He and Jayta were on their way to Britain to purchase yet more horses when World War I broke out; their ship was diverted to South America, where they were briefly interned, though as a US passport holder, Jayta managed to smuggle her husband back to Germany on a boat. Once back in the motherland, Hans rejoined the army, was sent to France and died in the **Battle of the Somme** in 1916. Jayta never returned to Namibia, either to reclaim her inheritance or sell the property.

p.110. The main appeal is the cachet of spending the night in a castle. Five dark en-suite double rooms lead off the courtyard behind saloon-style swing doors, combining old-world charm with modern comforts such as tiled bathrooms. Occasional problems with food deliveries mean dinner offerings at the café can be limited at times, but staff are accommodating. The small courtyard splash pool provides welcome relief in summer. **N$1760**

The Tiras Mountains and around

The rugged, scenic **Tiras Mountains** rarely receive more than a photo stop from most travellers as they skirt their eastern flank, driving up or down the C13, on their way between Aus – and beyond, Lüderitz – and the dunes of Sossusvlei further north. Yet this beguiling range is worth lingering over for a couple of days as it lies at the convergence of several ecological zones, resulting in impressive plant biodiversity and varied landscapes, which transform their colours with the changing light. At the very least, consider a detour round the semicircular gravel D707 – just doable in a 2WD but better in 4WD – one of the most picturesque routes in southern Namibia. It picks its way round the southern and western edges of the mountains – giant rocky outcrops fringed with flaxen grasses, punctuated by hardy succulents – while affording mesmerizing views across to the richly coloured pink and apricot dunes of the Namib to the west.

Helmeringhausen

To the northeast of the Tiras Mountains, where the C13, C14 and C27 converge, stands the small settlement of **Helmeringhausen** – effectively a single farm that has morphed into a quasi-village, with the same owners running a hotel (see p.122) a garage, a shop and a bottle store.

2

ACCOMMODATION

Farm Gunbewys Signposted off the D707, 23km from its junction with the C13, 3km down a sandy track ☎ 063 293013; map p.108. A surprisingly shady oasis, surrounded by desert, within walking distance of pink dunes, and enclosing an old farmhouse with stone floors and lead windows, containing two no-frills twin rooms, a basic self-catering cottage and a couple of rudimentary camping pitches. Electricity and hot water are solar-powered. Camping per person N$100, doubles B&B N$800

Helmeringhausen Hotel Main St, Helmeringhausen ☎ 063 283307, ⓦ helmeringhausennamibia.com; map p.108. A veritable oasis in the desert surroundings, this lovely old stone hotel set in lush tropical grounds provides spacious rooms with stone floors and large windows – cool in summer but freezing in winter. Solar-powered electricity and water means no electricity at the camping pitches, dimly lit rooms and no wi-fi. The dining areas are also dark, and there's no cosy fire to warm you in winter. Dinner N$270. Camping per person N$140, doubles N$1260

Kanaan N|a'an Ku sê Desert Retreat Signposted west off the D707 45km from the junction with the C27 ☎ 063 683119, ⓦ kanaannamibia.com; map p.108. In this private reserve that abuts the Namib-Naukluft National Park, you can soak up the stunning desert vistas encompassing grasslands, dunes and mountains, either from the deck of your simple tented chalet (one of eight), or camping pitch (also one of eight) with private canvas shelter, solar-powered ablutions and windbreak. Join a guided walk, scenic drive or saddle up on horseback. Al available, including one activity per day. Camping per person N$175, chalets (DBB) N$2095

THE TIRAS MOUNTAINS

Lovedale Farm Holidays On the C27, 19km from Helmeringhausen ☎ 081 281 9074 ⓦ lovedale-namibia .com; map p.108. The bleating of sheep and lowing of cattle as you enter the yard tells you this is a serious farm. Specializing in stud farming for swakara sheep, but also with goats, cattle and other sheep, the friendly owners claim that Lovedale is the oldest commercial farm in Namibia still in the same family. Activities are generally farm-related and accommodation is very rustic, but modestly priced, in basic self-catering units (for 2–7 people) with donkey-heated water and solar power. Camping on sandy pitches with hot water, electricity and braai sites. Camping per person N$92, self-catering N$500

★ **Namtib Biosphere Reserve** 47km along the D707 from the junction with the C13, then a further 13km; map p.108. Friendly family-run lodge and camping on a farm focused on sustainability – though strangely no solar power – nestled among boulders at the end of a valley. Five quaint, yellow bungalows and three other rooms are rustically but cheerfully furnished (without a/c or fans), with separate private bathrooms. Homely meals are served family-style (dinner N$220). Don't miss the fabulous sunsets from the sundowner rock terrace, complete with honesty bar. Five camping pitches enjoy similar surroundings, 3km from the lodge – with shade, braai site and donkey-fuelled hot water but no electricity. Campers should be self-sufficient. All can enjoy the self-guided botanical trail, or moderate-length hikes. Guided walks and drives are sometimes available, as well as multi-day horse treks for experienced riders (with advance notice). Camping per person N$130, doubles B&B N$1669

Aus

Around 125 kilometres east of Lüderitz along the B4, a side road drops off into a small valley that shelters the diminutive, yet historically significant, town of **AUS**. As one of the main stations on the railway line between Lüderitz and Keetmanshoop, Aus was of strategic importance to the Germans during the colonial period, prompting them to build fortifications to defend the site, remnants of which are still visible today towards Klein Aus Vista. When, in 1915, the Germans eventually surrendered to the South African Union troops, who took over the town, they were held in a prisoner-of-war camp just east of Aus (see box opposite). As you enter the town, you'll see the recently renovated station just off the main street, and the *Bahnhof Hotel* nearby; the hotel was established at the same time as the railway was completed, in 1906, although the original wooden structure burnt down, and the place was rebuilt in brick. The impoverished local populace are hoping that the eventual reopening of the railway to Lüderitz will lead to jobs and the village's renaissance.

At the moment, Aus receives a steady trickle of people travelling by road who break off for a bite to eat between Keetmanshoop and the coast, though it's worth spending a night or two here to explore the varied flora and fauna in the surrounding **Aus Mountains**. Over 500 plant species have been identified in the area, seven of which are endemic to the immediate vicinity, such as the pretty yellow Aus daisy. This biodiversity is due to the convergence of different biomes: at an altitude of almost

AUS' GERMAN POW CAMP

Signposted off the B4, a few kilometres east of Aus, a track leads northwards to a Commonwealth War Graves **military cemetery**, just beyond the original **prisoner of war camp** that held more than **1500 German soldiers** at one stage. The inadequate tented camp was exposed to the fickle and extreme weather of the area, as captives and captors alike withstood snow, scorching heat, sandstorms and bitterly cold nights. This prompted the industrious Germans – who were already cultivating their own gardens to improve their diet – to start making sun-dried mud bricks to construct accommodation that would afford better protection against the elements. They were soon in more robust lodgings than their South African guards, to whom they even sold their bricks. The Commonwealth cemetery marks the deaths of over **sixty German prisoners of war** and a similar number of their **South African guards** who perished in the camp, not due to any military skirmish, but because they succumbed to a bout of **Spanish influenza** that ripped through the population in 1918.

2

1500m, Aus lies at the western limit of the Nama Karoo of the central plateau, at the eastern edge of the Namib Desert, and at the top end of the Succulent Karoo (see p.154). The place is also affected by different weather patterns, making the weather unpredictable – some years it even receives snow. The rare years of winter rainfall (July–Sept), due to the Cape weather system, trigger a prolific flowering, particularly of succulents and herbaceous annuals, resulting in a multicoloured carpet of colour.

ARRIVAL AND INFORMATION   AUS

By car Aus is signposted off the B4, the main tarred road between Lüderitz (125km west) and Keetmanshoop (215km east).

By minibus Minibuses running between Lüderitz (see p.128) and Keetmanshoop (see p.149) can drop off passengers – and pick up when not full – on the B4 at the entrance/exit to town.

By rail It is hoped that the passenger service, which currently only runs between Keetmanshoop and Aus, will resume between Lüderitz and Keetmanshoop, stopping at Aus.

Tourist information A tourist information centre and café stands at the entrance to the town, full of excellent displays about the area's history and ecology. Sadly, at the time of writing it had closed, due to lack of funding, but there is hope that it will reopen before too long.

ACCOMMODATION

There are a couple of decent enough accommodation options in the town centre, but another excellent option is the Klein-Aus-Vista private reserve, a few kilometres west of Aus.

TOWN CENTRE

Bahnhof Hotel 20 Lüderitz St ☎ 063 258091, ⊛ hotel -aus.com; map p.108. Though rooms have been recently modernized (some have wheelchair access), the hotel has kept its charm: lovely polished wooden floors and high ceilings. It also has a great dining deck overlooking the main street – and a fire-warmed lounge for winter nights – where you can choose from an extensive à la carte menu of light and more substantial dishes. Also offers day-trips into the surrounding area. Restaurant daily 7am–10pm. B&B N$1752

Namib Garage 52 Lüderitz St ☎ 063 258029, ⊛ ausnamibia.co; map p.108. An unlikely spot for good-value if unremarkable (semi-) self-catering – only microwave, kettle and toaster – accommodation, of various configurations, in modern tiled rooms. Breakfast can be arranged. Also six cheap camping pitches with electricity, braai sites and shared water in a sandy

compound over the road. Provisions available at their general store while the garage provides petrol and repairs – truly a one-stop shop. Camping per person N$150, self-catering units N$600

KLEIN-AUS-VISTA

Located on a private reserve that abuts the Sperrgebiet, the distinctive *Klein-Aus-Vista* (South of the B4, 3km west of Aus ☎ 063 258021, ⊛ klein-aus-vista. com; map p.108) offers a variety of well-maintained accommodation in a wonderful natural setting, which you can explore on foot, on a mountain bike (available for rent) or on horseback along trails of varying length and difficulty. Though you'll get tour groups in high season, many independent travellers also stop over, especially in the fabulous stone self-catering chalets. The buffet restaurant food is excellent and there's a cosy lounge-bar (with fireplace for winter) and wraparound

2

THE NAMIB'S WILD HORSES

Travelling along the tarred road between Aus and Lüderitz, you may be lucky enough to catch the incongruous sight of **wild horses** roaming across the desert's gravel plains. Failing that, there is now a strategically positioned viewing hide, just off the main highway, that allows visitors to get a closer look at these resilient animals – possibly the only herd of feral desert horses in the world. Their **origin** is a source of great conjecture, ranging from the view that they escaped from a shipwrecked cargo vessel on the coast to the notion that they belonged to Khoikhoi raiders who came north from South Africa. The ancestry of these athletic, lean-limbed horses would appear to have been of good stock, hence the current prevailing theory that they stem from a mix of stud and cavalry horses from the **German colonial period**. A stud farm was known to have existed nearby, and during World War I a German pilot reportedly dropped a bomb on a South African encampment in the area, probably causing their horses to scatter. These horses may also have been joined later by steeds that were abandoned by the retreating Germans. In the turmoil of war, little effort would have been made to recapture the beasts; even after the conflict, being a diamond mining area, human access was restricted.

Now, a hundred years on, these feral horses are protected within the extended Namib-Naukluft National Park. Their numbers fluctuate between ninety and three hundred depending on climatic conditions, though the establishment of a permanent water trough is likely to guarantee their continued survival, as is the fact that they've become a firm fixture on the tourist trail. The **viewing hide** is situated 100m off the main road, 20km west of Aus (and 90km east of Lüderitz). The dirt track leading to the car park is manageable in an ordinary saloon car. The best time to see the horses is late afternoon, when a few oryx are also likely to be making use of the water trough.

veranda, gift shop and a horseshoe-shaped pool, in keeping with the lodge's equine theme.

Desert Horse Campsite Ten well-spaced camping pitches are scenically situated a couple of kilometres from the lodge, each with solid braai and grill, tap, table with benches (no electricity) and with some shade by a camelthorn tree. Bring your own food or purchase a superior braai pack from the lodge reception. All pitches possess windbreaks. Shared ablutions. Per person N$120

Desert Horse Inn Four rooms in the original lodge building, where communal facilities are located, and ten more double chalets nearby. Fan-ventilated, with hot-water bottles for winter comfort. B&B N$1090

★**Eagle's Nest Chalets** The pick of the accommodation: seven individually designed en-suite stone chalets built into the base of a rock face, offering uninterrupted views across pinkish desert sands to distant mountains – Eagle's View has the best vista. All are self-catering, with kitchenette and braai area, or you can drive the 7km back to the lodge for dinner. Since breakfast is included, you can opt for a take-away pack. B&B N$1485

Geisterschlucht ("Ghost Valley") So-named after a group of diamond thieves who were shot, trying to escape the chasing authorities – their rusted bullet-riddled car still remains in the sand – and who are said to return when the moon is full, in an attempt to reclaim their booty. This rustic, solar-powered, self-catering cabin is tucked away at the end of said valley, and is generally booked by groups or families; it can accommodate up to 18, with bunks and single beds spread over two bedrooms. Minimum booking N$950. Per person N$400

Lüderitz and around

Hemmed in by the wild Atlantic coast and the encroaching dunes of the Namib to the north and south, **LÜDERITZ** is undoubtedly Namibia's most isolated, and for many years forgotten, major town. It's also the country's windiest settlement, with gusts regularly topping 40kmph, especially during the summer months (Nov–Jan), and temperatures rarely top 24 degrees Celsius. Yet, on the mornings when the wind drops and the sun gleams on the pretty, brightly painted colonial buildings that decorate the town's slopes, Lüderitz's charm is clear to see, and its chequered history (see p.126) easy to forget. There's enough to keep the visitor entertained for a few days: taking in the **Jugendstil** (Art Nouveau) **architecture**, making forays into the desert to the abandoned mining communities of **Kolmanskop**, **Pomona** or **Bogenfels**, exploring the lagoon-laden

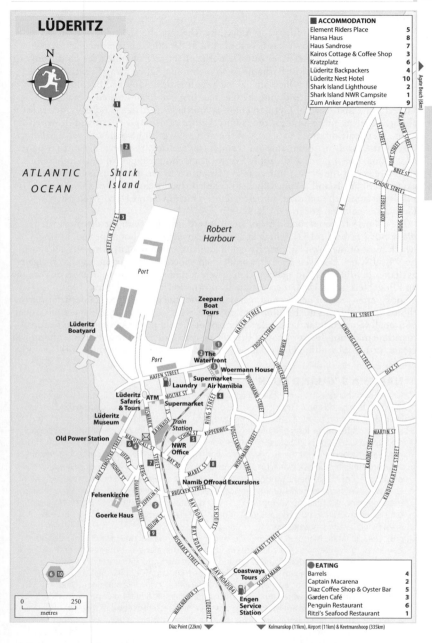

LÜDERITZ

N

ATLANTIC
OCEAN

Shark
Island

Robert
Harbour

Agate Beach (6km)

ACCOMMODATION

Element Riders Place	5
Hansa Haus	8
Haus Sandrose	7
Kairos Cottage & Coffee Shop	3
Kratzplatz	6
Lüderitz Backpackers	4
Lüderitz Nest Hotel	10
Shark Island Lighthouse	2
Shark Island NWR Campsite	1
Zum Anker Apartments	9

Port

Zeepard
Boat
Tours

Lüderitz
Boatyard

Port

The
Waterfront

Woermann House

Supermarket

Laundry   Air Namibia

Lüderitz
Safaris
& Tours

ATM

Supermarket

Lüderitz
Museum

Train
Station

Old Power Station

NWR
Office

Namib Offroad Excursions

Felsenkirche

Goerke Haus

Coastways
Tours

Engen
Service
Station

KREPLIN STREET
HAFEN STREET
HAFEN STREET
TROOST STREET
BREMER
LÜDEGER STREET
WOERMANN STREET
MOLTKE ST
RING STREET
BISMARCK ST
BAHNHOF STREET
SCHINZ ST
KIPPERWEG
VOGELSANG STREET
WOERMANN STREET
NACHTIGALL ST
UFER ST
BAY RD
ROHER ST
BERG ST
DIAMANTBERG STREET
ZEPPELIN ST
MABEL ST
BRÜCKEN STREET
BÜLOW ST
BAY ROAD
STANDER ST
WARET STREET
SCHUCKMANN
BISMARCK STREET
BAY ROAD
WAGENBAUER ST
LÜDERITZ
BAY ROAD
DIAZ STREET SMOLTKE STREET
1ST STREET
KORT STREET
BAY A NOER STREET
BREE ST
SCHOOL STREET
KORT STREET
KORT STREET
HOCH STREET
B4
TAL STREET
KINDERGARTEN STREET
DIAZ ST
MARTIN ST
KAKORO STREET
KINDERGARTEN STREET

0	250

metres

Diaz Point (22km) ▼   ▼ Kolmanskop (11km), Airport (11km) & Keetmanshoop (335km)

● **EATING**

Barrels	4
Captain Macarena	2
Diaz Coffee Shop & Oyster Bar	5
Garden Café	3
Penguin Restaurant	6
Ritzi's Seafood Restaurant	1

rocky peninsula to the south, or seeking out whales, flamingos or penguins on **boat trips** round the bay. The annual wind- and kitesurfing speed challenge (Oct–Nov) and five-day crayfish festival (May–June) – when accommodation prices will be hiked – are also major draws.

2

Brief history

What began life as a trading post buoyed by whaling, the seal trade and guano harvesting (see box below) was first settled in 1883 when an intermediary acting on behalf of German merchant **Adolf Lüderitz** effectively swindled the land from Nama chief Frederick II of Bethanie, who seemingly signed away five times more terrain than he realized. Once official backing for the colony had been granted (including from the British) and the German flag had been hoisted – making Lüderitz the first town of German colonial South-West Africa – Adolf Lüderitz set about acquiring more land for the colony, before vanishing – presumed drowned – on an expedition south in search of the mineral wealth he believed was needed to sustain the newly acquired empire. Despite this setback, the town began to expand as a major transit point and supply line for the Schutztruppen in the conflict with the Herero and the Nama; indeed, slave labour from the infamous concentration camp on Shark Island (see box, p.128) enabled the development of the town's infrastructure – the railroad, in particular – which in turn helped strengthen Germany's colonial grip on the land.

The colony's fortunes took a major step forward in 1908, with the discovery of **diamonds** (see box, p.132), which kick-started an eight-year boom period, during which most of the town's impressive colonial mansions were built. This was cut short by World War I, but even after the conflict had ended, Lüderitz continued to struggle as diamond prices fell and richer pickings were found further south, initially at Pomona and Bogenfels (see p.131), then eventually down at Oranjemund (see p.133).

Today, after years of neglect and marginalization, the prospects for Lüderitz's twenty thousand inhabitants are beginning to improve, with a reviving port, the establishment of a small waterfront, and the redevelopment of the old power station, set to feature a maritime museum. It is also hoped that the revival of the railway to Keetmanshoop will create further jobs; although the line was reopened briefly, the government is currently

---

NAMIBIA'S "GUANO RUSH"

One of Namibia's lesser-known tales of colonial greed played out off the Namibian coast on a clutch of tiny islands near Lüderitz, with the discovery of large deposits of **guano** (bird or bat droppings). A corruption of the Quechua word "*wanu*", guano had been cherished by the Incas as a **natural fertilizer** long before the colonizers in Peru cottoned on to its worth and began shipping it wholesale back to Europe and North America in the early nineteenth century. This may have helped prompt the recollection by a retired British mariner of an old US sea captain's 1828 accounts of islands "covered in birds' manure to the depth of 25 feet (over seven metres)" off the coast of Africa, thereby triggering Namibia's "Guano Rush" some fifteen years later. The cold waters of the Benguela Current provide ideal conditions for the production of the seabird excrement: nutrient-rich upwellings feeding vast quantities of fish, on which large colonies of gannets, cormorants and penguins feast, plus an arid climate that prevents these nutrients from being leached into the sea.

By 1843, Ichaboe Island, some 45km north of Lüderitz, had become a centre of frenzied harvesting of "white gold". Only 15 acres in size – the equivalent of some seven football pitches – Ichaboe was soon home to around 6000 seamen and 350 vessels. Working conditions were appalling and extremely hazardous: constantly damp, squeezed into makeshift accommodation and with no medical facilities, the workers frequently lacked fresh food and drinking water, much of which had to be shipped from Cape Town. What's more, they suffered constant exposure to the stench of excrement and high levels of ammonia. But the financial rewards – for the concession owners, at least – were huge. Within two years, the rush was all but over; the island had been scraped dry, with some 200,000 tonnes removed in two years. The seabirds have now reclaimed the rock, though in depleted numbers, but small-scale sustainable guano harvesting still continues in Namibia today, predominantly on artificial platforms dotted along the coast, most notably at "Bird Island" just north of Walvis Bay (see p.220).

scratching its head over how to combat the constant encroachment by sand on the track, with the latest idea being to build a tunnel through the dunes.

Felsenkirche

End of Kirche St • Mon–Sat: April–Aug 4–5pm, Sept–March 5–6pm • Free

Presiding over Lüderitz, the hundred-year-old Evangelical Lutheran **Felsenkirche** (literally Church of the Rock) is the town's most visible landmark. It is only open an hour a day in the late afternoon in time to catch the sun's last rays, which highlight the building's main attraction: its beautiful **stained-glass windows**. Note the head of Martin Luther in a pane amid the biblical iconography. The other reason to climb up to the church is to soak up the **views** of the town and bay, though some recent additions to the skyline have undermined the panorama somewhat.

Lüderitz Museum

Diaz St • Mon–Fri 3.30–5pm • N$15 • ☎ 063 202532

Eventually to be rehoused in the adjacent power station development, the **Lüderitz Museum** currently consists of a single room crammed with artefacts, photos and dioramas labelled in English and German. While you can take or leave the cabinets of taxidermy, mineral specimens and assortment of whale bones, the museum's real value lies in its extensive **photographic collection**, which gives insight into German colonial fine living in Lüderitz in the diamond-mining heyday of the early twentieth century – gymnastics tournaments, horse racing, shows at the Turnhalle (gymnasium) – in contrast to the brutal working conditions of the several thousand labourers brought down from the north. Contracts were never longer than two years since it was thought that, if they stayed longer, the workers would wise up and start stealing the diamonds.

Goerke Haus

Diamantberg • Mon–Fri 2–4pm, Sat & Sun 2–5pm. Closed public holidays • N$25 • ☎ 063 202532

Built in 1910 for the former soldier turned diamond mining magnate, **Hans Goerke**, this private luxury mansion is the town's most opulent building, appropriately located at the top of Diamantberg (Diamond Hill). Goerke spared no expense in the construction and furnishing of his residence, including importing sand from Germany for the cement. Delightful Art Nouveau features, such as decorative arches and friezes, incorporate local motifs, most notably the flamingos on the stained-glass window on the main staircase – all faithfully restored by Namdeb Diamond Corporation (the current owners) in the 1980s, though modern comforts have been added to accommodate the VIPs the company occasionally lodges here.

Shark Island

A 10–15min walk from the centre of town; turn left at the port entrance below the fountain on Bismarck St, then follow the road to the right

Pick a clear morning to visit **Shark Island**, which is actually a peninsula, and wander round the far tip for splendid sea, harbour and town views, as you watch the oystercatchers flit across the rocks. Then focus on the array of **memorials** that serve as sobering reminders of the island's chequered past (see box, p.128) and of the issues still to be resolved in Namibia's present.

ARRIVAL AND GETTING AROUND   LÜDERITZ AND AROUND

By car Lüderitz is at the western end of the tarred B4, 335km from Keetmanshoop and 125km from the last petrol station at Aus. Note that in the afternoons, when the wind often gets up, the last 30km is dangerous as sand from the dunes often blows onto the road. Avis Car Hire has an office at 25 Bismarck St (☎ 063 203968; Mon–Fri 8am–1pm, 2–5pm).

2

SHARK ISLAND CONCENTRATION CAMP

Taking the idea from the British, who had introduced the concept of the concentration camp in the Anglo-Boer war a few years previously, the Germans set up five **internment centres** for the Herero, and subsequently the Nama, in their attempts to subjugate the local populace. Of these camps, the one at **Shark Island** was the most notorious, dubbed Todesinsel (Island of Death), even by the German troops. Herero prisoners – men, women and children – were initially transported there in 1905, both as a security move to isolate them from other Herero and in order to supply **slave labour** for construction of the railway line to Aus – over 1300 workers were estimated to have died in the process. They were joined the following year by almost 1800 Nama prisoners.

Living conditions were appalling and mortality rates were high; although precise numbers and names were not recorded, there is widespread agreement that the vast majority never survived the incarceration. Malnourished prisoners were squeezed into barely adequate tents with inadequate sanitation on the tiny, windswept peninsula (there was a causeway joining the island to the mainland), which offered no protection from the fierce weather conditions. Disease was rife, as was rape, and prisoners were constantly beaten. On top, the work was dangerous and physically demanding – dynamiting rocks and being forced to work in icy-cold waters to build a new pier and wave-breaker. Most of the dead were given scant burial in shallow graves on the beach, their bodies washing out to sea once the tide came in, and there was a grisly trade in body parts to Europe – including Nama skulls – for medical experiments aimed at validating racist "scientific" assumptions about racial superiority.

By bus Minibuses depart from the former township for Keetmanshoop (N$190) and Windhoek (N$290). Take a taxi (N$10) there from town. Aunt Anna (☎ 081 252 0575) runs a twice-weekly shuttle service to Keetmanshoop and occasional services to Windhoek when there is demand.

By plane Air Namibia flights between Windhoek (Hosea Kutako International Airport) and Lüderitz operate three times a week (1hr), sometimes via Oranjemund (2hr 20min). A taxi to the airport, which is 11km east of town, will cost N$80.

By train At the time of writing there was no train service to Lüderitz, though the service is due to reopen at some stage – but don't hold your breath.

On foot It's easy and safe to get around town on foot. Lüderitz Safaris & Tours will provide you with a town map, which includes an informative walking tour of the many historical buildings.

By taxi If you want transport to Kolmanskop, and don't want to go on a tour, there are plenty of registered taxis available with taxi signs on the roof, hanging round the main street and outside the supermarkets, charging around N$100 there and back, including one hour's wait time.

INFORMATION

Tourist information The de facto information centre is Lüderitz Safaris & Tours on Bismarck St (☎ 063 202719, @ ludsaf@africaonline.com.na), especially since the short-lived municipal office closed down. Very friendly and efficient, they can provide you with maps of the town and peninsula, a list of all accommodation options and current pricing as well as suggestions of what to do. They also issue the NWR passes for access to Kolmanskop, act as an agent for Intercape Mainliner bus tickets, and run a well-stocked souvenir shop. Mon–Fri 8am–5pm, Sat 8.30am–noon, Sun 8.30am–10am.

NWR office At the NWR office on Schinz St (Mon–Fri 8am–5pm; ☎ 063 202752) you can buy a permit for Kolmanskop (N$85) or make last-minute bookings for the Shark Island accommodation, but not for other NWR resorts.

ACTIVITIES AND TOURS

Boat trips Zeepard Catamaran Tours (☎ 081 604 2805, @ zeepaardboattours@gmail.com) organize morning departures (8am; N$400; minimum of six needed) from the waterfront jetty on a motor-driven 2hr trip out of the bay, round Diaz Point to Halifax Island, home to a large colony of African penguins. Likely sightings include Heaviside dolphins, Cape fur seals and a wide variety of seabirds. Take binoculars.

Desert tours An increasing number of guided self-drive, off-road 4WD camping trips are now being led into the Namib from Lüderitz. Ensure you make full enquiries about the company's environmental practices on the tour before signing up (see Basics, p.66).

Windsurfing and watersports Call in at Element Riders Place (see opposite), where they can sort you out with lessons in kitesurfing, windsurfing or paddleboarding, as well as gear rental – though equipment is included in tuition prices – including wetsuits, which are strongly advised. There are also mountain bikes for rent (N$200 for the day).

2

TOURS TO THE SPERRGEBIET

Coastways Tours, on the B4 on the way into town, behind the Engen station (Mon–Fri 8am–5pm; ☏ 063 202002, 🖥 coastways.com.na), specializes in 4WD day- and multi-day trips (see p.131) into the desert. Coastways was the first operator with a licence to enter what is now the Tsau ‖Khaeb National Park, but is better known as the **Sperrgebiet** (meaning "forbidden area" in German – reference to the fact that it is an off-limits diamond-mining area) – and a copy of your passport will need to be submitted well in advance for approval. For its most popular full-day tour (N$3043/person for two people, N$1522/person for four or more people, picnic lunch and park fees included), you'll spend several hours in the back of a 4WD vehicle, but the experience is otherworldly as you cross dune fields studded with lichen and extraordinary succulents, and visit the abandoned mining communities of Pomona and Bogenfels. There are also sobering views of dunescapes wrecked by mining, which you can see before the tour finishes off at the gigantic Bogenfels Rock Arch on the Atlantic coast.

ACCOMMODATION

Element Riders Place Schinz St ☏ 081 206 6562, 🖥 element-riders.com. Lovely old house converted into a small classic backpackers hostel, with basic facilities and shared among seven rooms (doubles and triples), including showers. There's a small, well-equipped kitchen, though common areas are limited. Camping is possible on a patch of grass in the yard. Camping per person N$100, dorms N$100, doubles N$270

★**Hansa Haus** 85 Mabel St ☏ 063 203699 or ☏ 081 128 4336, 🖥 hansahausluderitz.co.za. Glorious hilltop colonial mansion affording commanding views of the town, nicely renovated by the owners, who live on the ground floor. The upstairs rentals, which share self-catering facilities, comprise one two-bedroom family unit with en-suite bathroom, another en-suite double and two doubles with sea views and shared bathroom. The kitchen is fully equipped, with tea/coffee provided, and there are also braai facilities on the balcony. N$700

★**Haus Sandrose** 15 Bismarck St ☏ 063 202630, 🖥 haussandrose.com. Centrally located, these four spotless self-catering units set round a pleasant courtyard with a shared shaded eating area offer excellent value for money. Discounts for multi-night stays. B&B N$830

★**Kairos Cottage & Coffee Shop** Kreplin St, Shark Island ☏ 063 203080, ☏ 081 650 5598, 🖥 kairoscottage .com. Superb value, well-appointed oceanfront B&B, though with some overly twee touches. Only five rooms – all offering sea views through large windows – so you need to book ahead. Be prepared to be serenaded on the piano by your host over breakfast. B&B N$680

Kratzplatz 5 Nachtigall St ☏ 063 202458, 🖥 kratzplatz .info. Friendly, cosy guesthouse with 12 small rooms (each with fridge and TV and some with decorative stone and shell bathrooms) overlooking a tree-filled courtyard. The upstairs rooms that open onto a balcony are nicest. B&B N$790

★**Lüderitz Backpackers** 2 Ring St ☏ 063 202000, 🖂 luderitzbackpackers@hotmail.com. Friendly, warm hostel in an old colonial home with high ceilings, large windows and polished wooden floors. Well-equipped kitchen, shared living room and sheltered outdoor area at the back for the rare occasions when it's warm enough to sit out. For a quieter night's sleep, try to get a room away from the kitchen, and for a unique experience, rent out one of the two converted boat cabins – without a toilet – in the yard. All self-catering. Boat cabins per person N$100, dorms N$140, doubles N$350

Lüderitz Nest Hotel 820 Diaz St ☏ 063 204001, 🖥 nesthotel.com. The town's upmarket modern resort hotel maximizes its location on the bay, with almost all rooms – including some with wheelchair access – overlooking the sea, allowing you to lull yourself to sleep listening to the waves. B&B N$2100

Shark Island Lighthouse Kreplin St, Shark Island ☏ 061 2857200 (Windhoek) or ☏ 064 402172 (Swakopmund), or book at the NWR office in town (see opposite), 🖥 nwr.com.na. The pick of the NWR lodgings is the lighthouse, with two bedrooms, two bathrooms, a kitchen, dining room and TV lounge. True, the paint is peeling, the furniture is dilapidated and the bathroom has grimy grouting, but there are fabulous panoramic views from the roof terrace – and it's cheap. N$660

Shark Island NWR Campsite End of Kreplin St, Shark Island ☏ 061 2857200 (Windhoek), last-minute bookings can be made at the NWR office in town (see opposite), 🖥 nwr.com.na. The campground at the head of the peninsula (with facilities in need of upgrading) offers great sea views but few sheltered spots with shared braai areas, though it's sobering to be camping amid the gravestones. Check in advance that it's still open as there are controversial plans to "upgrade" to chalet accommodation, thereby building on grave sites. Camping per person N$150

2

Zum Anker Apartments Bulow St ☎063 202948, ⓦ zumanker-luderitz.com. Four spotless, well-appointed modern apartments (from one- to four-bedroom properties) offering plenty of home comforts, including washing machines, as well as outdoor BBQ facilities and secure parking. N$850

EATING

Barrels Kratzplatz, 5 Nachtigall St ☎063 202458. Though the streets of Lüderitz are often deserted at night, this cosy, rustic bar-restaurant is frequently packed to the rafters with folk of all ethnicities – locals and visitors alike. The waiting table for pizza, eisenbein and sauerkraut, the house speciality (N$160), and other pub grub can be long. There's occasional live music, and sport on the big screen also brings in the punters. Mon–Sat 6pm until late (food until 9.30pm).

Captain Macarena At the waterfront ☎063 203958. Take-away fish 'n' chips with calamari and kingclip kebabs to enliven the menu. All under N$35. Mon–Fri 9am–6pm, Sat until 1pm.

Diaz Coffee Shop and Oyster Bar Bismarck St ☎081 700 0475. No longer the corner café of old, this place is trying to be all things to all people, with a beer garden out back on its way. That said, the service is friendly, the food inexpensive (mains from around N$80) – though irritatingly each item on the menu is individually priced, from the rice to the sauces for your mains. The fresh oysters are a must. Free wi-fi. Daily 8am–8pm.

★**Garden Café** 17 Hafen St ☎081 124 8317. Enjoy a selection of brötchen (rolls), great cakes – the chocolate cheesecake is seriously heavy duty – and tea from dainty cups in this fabulous café. Relax indoors in the lovingly restored colonial building (if the weather's playing up), or sit outside in a delightful garden overlooking the harbour, on a sunny afternoon. Daily 9am–5pm (Sun until 4pm).

Penguin Restaurant Lüderitz Nest Hotel, 820 Diaz St ☎063 204000. The only place open on a Sunday night, but a decent spot to dine at other times too – bag a table with a sea view for lunch – with a wide-ranging if fairly pricey menu (mains from N$140). Light meals offered at lunchtime but dinner is a full à la carte service. Try the lobster or speciality abalone sea snails. Daily 12.30–2pm & 6.30–10pm.

★**Ritzi's Seafood Restaurant** Upstairs at the waterfront, Hafen St ☎063 202818. With indoor and terrace seating both offering great views across the harbour by day, candlelit dining by night, and arguably the best food in town, Ritzi's is justifiably popular. Though specializing in fish and seafood – with the seafood curry served in a poijke (three-legged pot) a top choice – they also put on chicken and meat dishes, as well as pizzas, and can even knock up a veggie stir-fry. Most mains from N$95. Booking essential Fri & Sat. Mon–Sat 8am–11pm.

The Lüderitz peninsula

On a fine day with your own transport, a tour of the **Lüderitz peninsula** makes for a pleasant morning outing, with a sprinkling of sandy beaches and rocky inlets to explore, as well as several salt pans favoured by flamingos. Most visitors head for the classic, red-and-white-striped lighthouse at **Diaz Point**, 20km by road from Lüderitz – take the B4 2km out of town, then turn right at the sign. Across a rickety wooden bridge there's a replica of the granite cross erected by **Bartolomeu Diaz**, the pioneering Portuguese explorer credited with being the first European to visit the area, in 1487. Continue round the headland, at least as far as **Guano Bay**, where, with a decent pair of binoculars, you can spot the African penguins across the water at **Halifax Island**, though you'll get a better view from a boat (see p.128).

Agate Beach

Though often forbidding and blustery, on a calm, warm weekend, **Agate Beach**, 7km north of town, is a popular destination for a stroll along the sand and a BBQ; a collection of sheltered public braai sites is dotted along the back of the beach. Head out beyond Namdeb and follow the signs past the segregated townships of Nautilus and Benguela – now with more mixed populations and merging with new developments. Consider pausing at the water treatment works, which is a choice location to spot springbok, oryx, and a host of seabirds including flamingos. The beach itself is pleasant but unremarkable, a stretch of tan sand strewn with mussels and other shells and strands of seaweed.

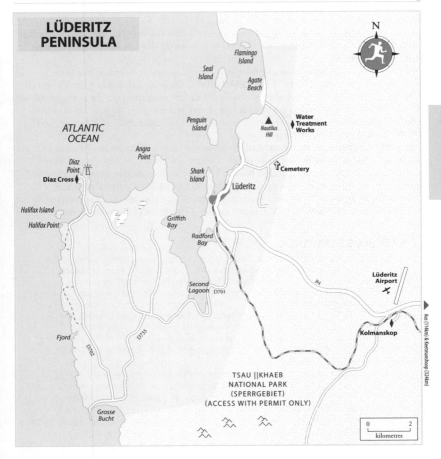

2

The Tsau ||Khaeb (Sperrgebiet) National Park

Despite its designation as a national park in 2008, and renaming to **Tsau ||Khaeb** (meaning "deep, sandy soils" in Nama), the diamond mining **Sperrgebiet** ("Forbidden Area" in German) remains true to its colonial title as it's still pretty much a no-go zone except on a strictly controlled guided tour from Lüderitz (see box, p.129). The park stretches 320km northwards from the important Ramsar-protected wetlands at the mouth of the Orange River, encompassing vast sand sheets and dune areas, mountains, inselbergs and gravel plains, to some 70km north of Lüderitz. From the wild Atlantic coast, whose most photographed feature is the impressive 60m Bogenfels Rock Arch, the park extends 100km inland.

Having been effectively off-limits for over a century, this whole environment has remained pristine, apart from the five percent exploited for mining, where the scars are all too apparent. In particular, the park is renowned for its outstanding **plant biodiversity**, boasting the greatest variety of succulents on the planet. After spring rains they explode in a profusion of colour, enlivening the otherwise stark landscape. And nowhere is the desolation more tangible than at the abandoned mining towns of **Bogenfels** and **Pomona**, where a forlorn graveyard is gradually being engulfed by sand, and the wind speeds regularly top 60kmph in the summer, generating ferocious sandstorms.

2

Kolmanskop

On the B4, 11km from Lüderitz • Mon–Fri 8am–1pm, Sat 8am–noon, Sun 8.30–10am; guided tours Mon–Sat 9.30am & 11.30am, 10am on Sun & public holidays • N\$85, including guided tour; N\$230 for a photo permit to visit out of hours • N\$100 taxi ride from Lüderitz including 1hr wait time

For many, the main attraction of Lüderitz is the chance to poke round the eerie diamond mining "ghost town" of **KOLMANSKOP** – the most accessible part of the Tsau ‖Khaeb National Park – and witness the desert sands reclaiming the decaying buildings of what was once the richest town in Africa. Every few months, diggers are sent into the ruins to excavate some of the sand so that the area's main tourist attraction isn't totally buried beneath the dunes.

In 1908 Kolmanskop was merely an insignificant train station on the line out of Lüderitz, until **diamonds** were discovered, triggering a mining frenzy that in turn fuelled an extravagant construction boom. Within three years, the settlement boasted electricity and a hospital, with the region's first X-ray machine – more to detect diamond smugglers than to serve medical purposes – a ballroom, theatre, casino, swimming pool and bowling alley, plus a wealth of luxurious houses to accommodate

---

NAMIBIA'S DIAMONDS

On April 14, 1908, **Zacharias Lewala**, a black labourer toiling on the railway just outside Lüderitz, discovered a rough **diamond** and showed it to his foreman, **August Stauch**. History doesn't relate what happened to Lewala, who had acquired his keen eye for the mineral while working in Kimberley, but Stauch quietly resigned his position with the railway and set himself up as a diamond prospector, becoming very rich almost overnight. The Germans immediately declared the 320km stretch of coastline (extending 100km inland) from Lüderitz to the Orange River, a Sperrgebiet (Forbidden Area) – which in practice remains in place to this day – so as to control the diamond rush that ensued. Namibia was soon producing 1 million carats (200kg) annually, accounting for 20 percent of world diamond production, and helping German South-West Africa to turn a profit by 1913.

Following German defeat in World War I, the country's diamond mines, mostly along the Orange River, came under the control of Ernest Oppenheimer, founder of Anglo American, and the man behind De Beers, who maintained a monopoly on the Namibian diamond trade right through the apartheid era until the 1990s.

Since 1994, the diamond trade has been controlled by Namdeb, a company set up by De Beers and the Namibian government, who each have a 50 percent stake. Although not found in such quantities as in neighbouring Botswana and South Africa, diamonds continue to be a mainstay of the Namibian economy, with Namdeb, the country's largest taxpayer and biggest foreign exchange generator, contributing a fifth of the country's foreign exchange.

Namibia's diamonds have traditionally been found in alluvial and coastal deposits. Washed downstream over the centuries, into the sea and then back onto the coastline's raised beaches and sand dunes, the diamonds are small but crystal clear, the result of centuries of erosion and weathering which have weeded out the imperfect stones. As a result, some 98 percent are of "gem quality" (the highest proportion in the world) and are highly valued compared to diamonds from the land-based mines of South Africa.

Over the last decade, the biggest challenge for the industry has been the depletion of land diamonds, which are likely to run out completely in the next 15 years, and the increasing reliance on **marine diamonds**, which are now being dredged up from the bottom of the ocean at depths of over 120m. Debmarine, Namdeb's offshore arm, is now its most important asset. The major downside to this marine mining is the obvious negative environmental impact of sucking up the sea bed, sifting it for diamonds and then spewing the remains back into the sea, though the industry argues that such activity is restricted to a relatively small area. The other threat to the diamond market is the arrival of cheaper synthetic diamonds of gem quality – industrial diamonds are nearly all synthetic now, but the gem-quality synthetic diamonds are now so good, it's impossible for experts to tell the difference without the help of expensive technology.

the three hundred white workers and their families resident in the town's heyday. There was even an ice-making factory, to ensure the champagne stayed suitably chilled, though the fresh water needed for the ice still had to be shipped in from Cape Town. After World War I, when diamond prices dropped, and richer deposits were found further south, Kolmanskop's star began to wane, and by 1956, the last remaining families had left, though mining had ceased some time before.

The tours are very informative, but make sure you take time afterwards to look round the exhibits in the **smugglers' room** for tips in case you chance on a diamond. Back in the day, all manner of means were used to spirit the gemstones out of the area; as well as the more predictable methods, such as secreting the stone about the body, hiding it in a shoe or knife handle or sewn up in clothing, diamonds were also fired out over the security fence by crossbow, or attached to a homing pigeon. For this reason homing pigeons are still banned in Oranjemund to this day.

2

Oranjemund and around

Marooned at the far southwestern tip of Namibia, the anachronistic mining town of **ORANJEMUND** lies at the mouth of the Orange River – hence its name, which literally translates from German as "Orange mouth". Although unlikely to be on anyone's holiday hit list any time soon – especially given the security restrictions and the fact that the surrounding desert and the estuary still bear the scars of its mining history – it's an intriguing and incredibly leafy place to visit, full of mature trees, flower-filled gardens and green spaces. Moreover, it has tourism potential since the river delta is a listed RAMSAR wetland site, supporting up to 20,000 birds and over 50 species – when summer migrants pass through – including important populations of southern African endemics such as the Damara tern, Hartlaub's gull, and Cape cormorant. Although so far no bird hides have been established, you can drive down to the river to watch pelicans, flamingos and terns going about their business.

At present, Oranjemund's principal draw is its "forbidden" status; a no-go area for the public for many years, in case they indulged in a little extracurricular prospecting on the beach, security paranoia persists even now that the mining action has moved upriver and out to sea (see box opposite), so a permit is still required to get past two security gates, to visit the town (see box, p.135).

The two extremely modest sights include a museum and a tiny nature reserve. Arguably, however, the star attraction, which features on the town's crest, is the omnipresent oryx: nibbling at residents' herbaceous borders, trimming the parks or the greens at the golf course, lazing around outside the municipal offices or simply strolling around the town centre, window-shopping.

Jaspar House Heritage Centre

Main St • Mon–Fri 11am–2pm, Sat 10am–noon • Free • ☎ 063 234787, ⊕ oranjemundonline.com

Crammed into a few small rooms of the home of the first General Manager of Consolidated Diamond Mines (now Namdeb), the **Jaspar House Heritage Centre**'s focus inevitably is on the town's fascinating diamond mining history, explained through a collection of black-and-white photos and assorted memorabilia. Alas, no diamonds are on display, though a few other semi-precious stones feature, and there's also an interesting section on the area's flora and fauna. Exciting plans are afoot to expand and update the collection by displaying previously unseen – by the public, at least – treasures from a 500-year-old Portuguese trading vessel laden with gold and silver coins, copper ingots, assorted weaponry and the like, which was shipwrecked on Namibian shores, and unearthed in 2008. Until then, however, the museum remains a low-key attraction.

2

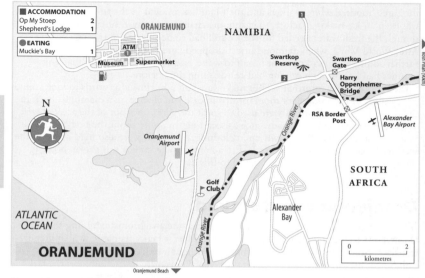

Swartkop Nature Reserve

Swartkop summit, signposted to your immediate right, after the security gate • Open 24hr • Free

Atop the hill of the same name, **Swartkop Nature Reserve** is no more than a patch of earth containing some non-too-apparent rare succulents that is fenced off from the public. That said, it's the perfect spot to soak up fine views across the Orange River estuary and the Oppenheimer Bridge, named after the former gold and diamond magnate and anti-apartheid politician, Harry Oppenheimer.

ARRIVAL AND GETTING AROUND   ORANJEMUND AND AROUND

All visitors need a **permit** to enter Oranjemund (see box opposite), which you'll have to present at the border (6am–10pm): either at the Oppenheimer Bridge from Alexander Bay, if you're coming from South Africa on the other side of the Orange River estuary; at the security gate (6am–10pm) in Namibia, as you turn off the C13 to head towards Oranjemund; or at the airport. In all cases, you'll be given a security pass for your visit, which you return on departure. Note that if you're entering from South Africa and travelling onwards to other parts of Namibia without stopping in Oranjemund, you'll only need to fill in a transit form. For road-users, there is a second security gate, as you enter the town area proper, 7km from the centre, where you'll need to show your pass again.

By car The winding, 80km road from the security gate to Oranjemund is gradually being paved, but even the gravel part is accessible in a saloon car, provided there's not been heavy rain.

By plane Air Namibia flies three times a week from Hosea Kutako Airport, Windhoek, to Oranjemund (1hr 15min), via Lüderitz on two of the flights (2hr 5min). The airport is 6km outside the town.

Getting around The centre of Oranjemund is compact and easy to walk around. However, the town's two lodgings are located close to the security gate, 7km from the town centre, and there's no public transport, though taxis do operate.

TOURIST INFORMATION

Since Oranjemund was only declared a municipality in 2011 and government is still in the process of taking over municipal functions from the mining corporation, Namdeb, there's no tourist information office. Ask at your accommodation.

ACCOMMODATION

Op My Stoep 400m beyond the security gate, on the main road ☎ 063 232874, ⊕ www.opmystoep.com; map p.108. This motel-like property – you park your vehicle outside your room – has 16 functional tiled doubles and several self-catering units. The bar-restaurant, complete with TV and pool table, is a popular social hub for

ORANJEMUND PERMITS

Technically you need to be on official business or be invited by an Oranjemund resident to be eligible for a **permit** to visit the town, but the two guesthouses will "invite" you and do the paperwork, provided that you stay with them. Otherwise, you should contact the permit office directly (☎063 236100; ✉permitsoffice@namdeb.com). You need to send a photocopy of your passport, and indicate whether you'll be coming by air or road, and, if the latter, which of the town's entry points you intend to use: the Oppenheimer Bridge from Alexander Bay, South Africa, or Namibia's one access road from the C13. The permit needs to be secured at least 21 days in advance, and costs N$40. If you get your lodgings to apply on your behalf, they will add the cost to your bill. The permit should be at the security gate when you arrive, where you are given a **security pass**. Make sure that if you're driving a rental car, you have the rental and vehicle documentation with you to show if required. If you have rented the vehicle in South Africa, you'll need to make sure you're displaying a ZA sticker.

2

visitors and locals. Bedecked with baseball caps, car licence plates and assorted mining memorabilia, it serves excellent bar food, though the fact that breakfast ends at 8am tells you that most visitors are here on business. Camping facilities are very rudimentary with no shade or electricity. Camping per person N$90, self-catering N$750, doubles (B&B) N$715

Shepherd's Lodge 1km beyond the security gate, turn right immediately after entering and follow the road over the hill ☎063 232996 or ☎081 283 1481, ✉shepherds@iway.na; map p.108. Tucked away in a shallow north of the Swartkop, this is a peaceful retreat, a tree-filled oasis with water features and appealing birdlife. Rooms are nice, especially the new ones, and the semi-open bar-restaurant is pleasant. Camping on the grass is also possible. Camping per person N$150, doubles N$600

EATING

Muckie's Bay Town centre, next to FNB ☎063 234883. The only place to eat in town is a cosy café-restaurant, nautically themed in blue and white decor. Drop in for breakfast (until noon) or a mid-morning cappuccino, or enjoy a moderately priced meal: from gourmet burgers or salads to the usual range of chicken, pork, steak and fish dishes (N$60–180). Mon–Fri 8am–2pm, 6–9pm; Sat 8am–noon, 6–9pm.

Rosh Pinah

In total contrast to faded Oranjemund, just down the road, the gleaming new centre of the small mining town of **ROSH PINAH** is bristling with confidence and money, boasting freshly painted cream houses with green roofs, neat, clean streets and a sparkling shopping centre. All this is mainly due to the booming Skorpion mine, 25km to the north. After opening in 2000, it has become one of the largest zinc mines in the world, though various rare and valuable minerals have also been found. There's nothing to the town itself, though the setting is attractive – once you turn a blind eye to the slag heaps, which announce your arrival from the south – as it's overlooked by the Huns Mountains to the east and the Swartkloof Mountains that lie to the north and west, straddling the eastern limits of the Sperrgebiet.

The main reason to break your journey here is to use the ATM, get supplies from the well-stocked supermarket in the shopping centre – it's your best bet if you're heading south to camp along the Orange River, or visiting the South African side of the Richtersveld park – and to refuel at the petrol station, as there's nowhere else for 150km in either direction, unless you're bound for Oranjemund. Should you want or need to stay the night, there are a couple of decent guesthouses with restaurants aimed at visiting mining executives.

ACCOMMODATION

ROSH PINAH

Amica Guesthouse 306 Mukarob Close ☎063 274043, ✉amicaguesthouse.wheretostay.na. Comfortable mine-owned property in a quiet residential cul-de-sac. Has ten carpeted rooms with the usual business amenities: mini-fridge, phone, tea/coffee facilities, and a pleasant plant-filled courtyard with a pool, and a two-storey lapa with giant chess set and elevated sundowner deck affording desert views. B&B N$1150

The southern Kalahari and the far south

FISH RIVER CANYON BEFORE SUNRISE

The southern Kalahari and the far south

The vastness of the southern Kalahari and the far south of Namibia is daunting, as is the absence of people: only a fraction of the population lives here. The long, lonely road east out of Windhoek passes through sparse thornveld to the Botswana border, while the road south from the capital stretches for hundreds of kilometres to the South Africa border and the southern Kalahari. But the foray south is well worth the effort. Those who persist with the journey are rewarded with hugely enjoyable canoeing and birdwatching along the Orange River, unrivalled hiking opportunities in the vast Fish River Canyon, and rippling red dunes in the southern Kalahari.

Taking on the main road south from Windhoek promises some of the country's greatest sights and spectacles. The tarred highway speeds through the unremarkable towns of **Rehoboth** – home to one of Namibia's proudest peoples – and **Mariental**, before dividing at **Keetmanshoop**, the region's bustling administrative capital, and a good place to fill up with petrol and stock up with supplies. Northwest of the town, the Brukkaros "false volcano" rewards hikers with wonderful views from the crater rim. And to the northeast of Keetmanshoop, the scenic **Quiver Tree Forest** is well worth the diversion.

   Southern Namibia's great attraction is the spectacular **Fish River Canyon**. A 160km-long serpentine ravine, it hosts a challenging five-day hiking trail that ends in the popular hot-springs resort of |**Ai-|Ais**. The canyon lies within the |**Ai-|Ais/ Richtersveld Transfrontier Park**; extending into South Africa, this remote and rugged area has limited infrastructure but boasts extraordinary plant biodiversity. It's bisected by the scenic **Orange River**, whose meandering progress towards the Atlantic provides great opportunities for birdwatching and canoeing.

   East of the B1, around Mariental, and along the picturesque "back road" from Stampriet to the Mata Mata gate of the **Kgalagadi Transfrontier Park**, the rippling, **red dunes** that gain in height and colour as you move further inland supply the attractive backdrop to a sprinkling of delightful lodges and campgrounds.

   Truth be told, there's not a great deal to lure visitors to the sparse land beyond the Eros Mountains east of Windhoek, unless they're heading for the **Botswana border** or interested in visiting the bat-riddled Arnhem Cave.

The road south

It's a long 500km haul along the B1 between Windhoek, across the Hardap Region to Keetmanshoop, capital of the vast ||Karas Region – the country's largest – the de facto capital of southern Namibia. Once the B1 has wound its way through the Aus

QUIVER TREE FOREST

Highlights

❶ Brukkaros A hike up this false volcano is rewarded by some excellent birdwatching and breathtaking views across an endless, desolate landscape. **See p.145**

❷ Quiver trees Make sure you seek out the "forests" of Namibia's most photogenic plant. **See p.149**

❸ Kalahari Red Dunes The less visited rippling red dunes of Namibia's second desert provide the perfect setting for some rest and relaxation. **See p.150**

❹ The Kgalagadi Transfrontier Park No need to do border formalities; pop over into South Africa for a couple of days and get your fill of vast herds of large mammals following ancient migration routes. **See p.152**

❺ Fish River Canyon Whether you marvel at this gaping chasm from the rim, or take on the gruelling hike along the canyon floor, this is a must-see attraction. **See p.154**

❻ The Orange River A chance to paddle for a day or more through lovely scenery, enjoying campfire dinners and nights sleeping out under the stars. **See p.161**

HIGHLIGHTS ARE MARKED ON THE MAP ON P.140

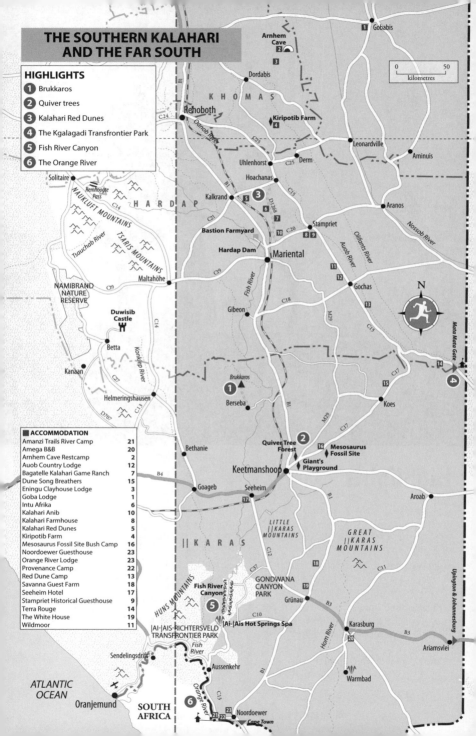

THE SOUTHERN KALAHARI
AND THE FAR SOUTH

HIGHLIGHTS
1. Brukkaros
2. Quiver trees
3. Kalahari Red Dunes
4. The Kgalagadi Transfrontier Park
5. Fish River Canyon
6. The Orange River

0   50
kilometres

ACCOMMODATION
Amanzi Trails River Camp	21
Amega B&B	20
Arnhem Cave Restcamp	2
Auob Country Lodge	12
Bagatelle Kalahari Game Ranch	7
Dune Song Breathers	15
Eningu Clayhouse Lodge	3
Goba Lodge	1
Intu Afrika	6
Kalahari Anib	10
Kalahari Farmhouse	8
Kalahari Red Dunes	5
Kiripotib Farm	4
Mesosaurus Fossil Site Bush Camp	16
Noordoewer Guesthouse	23
Orange River Lodge	23
Provenance Camp	22
Red Dune Camp	13
Savanna Guest Farm	18
Seeheim Hotel	17
Stampriet Historical Guesthouse	9
Terra Rouge	14
The White House	19
Wildmoor	11

Gobabis

Arnhem Cave

Dordabis

KHOMAS

Rehoboth

Kiripotib Farm

Leonardville

Aminuis

Solitaire

Naukluft Mountains
Remhoogte Pass

HARDAP

Uhlenhorst

Derm

Aranos

Nossob River

Tsauchab River

Isaris Mountains

Kalkrand

Hoachanas

Stampriet

Olifants River

Auob River

Bastion Farmyard

Marental

Mata Mata Gate

NAMIBRAND NATURE RESERVE

Maltahöhe

Hardap Dam

Fish River

Gochas

Duwisib Castle

Gibeon

Betta

Kanaan

Konkiep River

Koes

Helmeringshausen

Brukkaros

Berseba

Bethanie

Quiver Tree Forest

Mesosaurus Fossil Site

Keetmanshoop

Giant's Playground

Goageb

Seeheim

Aroab

Upington & Johannesburg

LITTLE KARAS MOUNTAINS

GREAT KARAS MOUNTAINS

||KARAS

HUNS MOUNTAINS

Fish River Canyon

GONDWANA CANYON PARK

Grünau

Karasburg

Ariamsvlei

|AI-|AIS-RICHTERSVELD TRANSFRONTIER PARK

|Ai-|Ais Hot Springs Spa

Fish River

Horn River

Warmbad

Sendelingsdrift

Aussenkehr

ATLANTIC OCEAN

Oranjemund

SOUTH AFRICA

Orange River

Noordoewer

Cape Town

Mountains, and flattened out in the unremarkable yet historically important town of **Rehoboth**, 100km down the road, there's little in the way of engaging scenery to keep your attention as you stare across the roadside fences marking off huge commercial farms at the never-ending flat savannah lands that stretch eastwards into the Kalahari. It's easy to be reduced to ticking off the 10km distance signs as you head towards your destination.

After Rehoboth, the next small town of note is **Mariental**, 180km further south, and then **Keetmanshoop**, another two hours' drive beyond that. To the west, not long after you cross the regional boundary into the ||Karas Region, the impressive massif of the **Brukkaros Mountain** looms out of the surrounding plains, dominating the horizon (see box, p.145).

Rehoboth

Surrounded by acacia woodland, the 30,000-strong town of **REHOBOTH**, situated just north of the Tropic of Capricorn, is of little interest to the casual visitor, though it is home to the fiercely proud Baster people (see box, p.142), whose history is well explained in the local museum. The settlement had already had a couple of names before gaining its current biblical incarnation, thanks to a local missionary in 1844. Drawn by the natural hot springs in the area, a semi-nomadic Damara group that would visit periodically when water was scarce in the Kalahari dubbed the place |Gaollnāus ("Fountain of the Falling Buffalo"). This was later changed to |Anes ("Place of Smoke"), by a group of Nama, making reference to the steam rising from the springs. Even today, there has been an attempt to market Rehoboth as a spa town, though the baths have been closed for some time. Better recreational facilities can be found at the Oanob Dam, 7km outside town (see p.143).

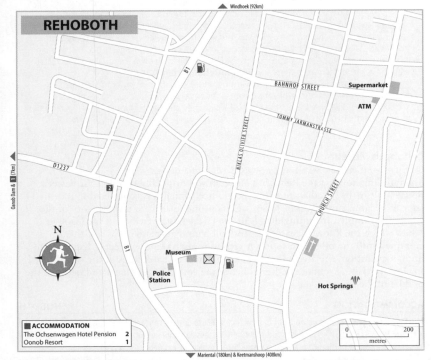

REHOBOTH BASTERS

The **Rehoboth Basters** are one of a number of groups of mixed heritage which emerged in the Dutch Cape Colony in the eighteenth century and were forced by their non-white status to live on the fringes of white colonial society – they were among the many people who were later designated as "Coloureds" in apartheid South Africa and Namibia. They primarily share a mix of black African and European settler heritage that is reflected in the name they proudly bear (which is a corruption of "bastard"). Originally settled in the Northern Cape, the Basters began their great trek north across the Orange River in 1868, when new laws were introduced preventing Coloureds from owning land. Led by their own "Moses", the Basters' first Kaptein, Hermanus van Wyk, some 300 or so Afrikaans-speaking, devoutly Calvinist Basters eventually set up the **Free Republic of Rehoboth**, 100km south of Windhoek, in 1872.

Initially, the Basters were careful to maintain their neutrality in the simmering conflicts of central and southern Namibia. But in 1884, they became the first group to sign a "Treaty of Friendship and Protection" with the Germans and for the next twenty years they threw their lot in with the newly arrived colonial power, even supplying troops and assisting in the genocide of the Nama and Herero during the Namibian War of Resistance (1904–09). With the outbreak of World War I, the Basters reasserted their neutrality, only agreeing to enlist after having been given assurances that they wouldn't be asked to fight their South African neighbours. In April 1915, the Germans ordered the Basters to guard some South African prisoners of war and retreat north away from Rehoboth or be disarmed. Around 300 Basters deserted their posts and, with their families, retreated to Sam Khubis, 80km southeast of Rehoboth. The Germans pursued them, and on May 8, 1915 confronted the Basters in the **Battle of Sam Khubis**. Outgunned all day long, the Basters were left without ammunition by nightfall, but their prayers were answered when the very next day the Germans were ordered to retreat in the face of the advancing South African army. It's a divine miracle that has been celebrated every year since by the Rehoboth Basters.

With the end of the war, the Basters were keen to re-establish their autonomous republic but were thwarted by the new South African rulers of Namibia. In 1924, the Rehoboth Basters revolted, appointing themselves a new Kaptein – the South African response was brutal, sending in troops, bombing the town into submission and arresting over 400 Basters. From that low point, the Basters have been engaged in a long hard struggle to try and reclaim and hold onto their unique status, applying to the UN for help; they even eventually made a deal with the apartheid regime to create a **Rehoboth bantustan** in 1979.

After independence, the Namibian government took control of many of the Basters' communal lands. Since then, they have been fighting an even more desperate rearguard action to try and win back the ancestral land which they originally bought off the local Nama, to preserve their culture (see ⓦ rehobothbasters.org) – a case which looks likely to fail.

Rehoboth Museum

Church St • Mon–Fri 8am–5pm (closed for lunch) • Free • ☎ 062 522954, ⓦ rehobothmuseum.com

The building housing the **Rehoboth Museum** was originally the old postmaster's house built in 1927, adjacent to the post office, which was completed four years later. It became a museum in 1986, and its prime focus is to tell the story of the Baster community, including details of the Great Baster Trek from the Cape in 1868, which the knowledgeable curator will happily expand on. All of this is crammed into the one main room. A second room has more eclectic displays, on human evolution, the area's flora and fauna and even banknotes of the world, used to educate visiting school children – hence the collection of chairs and desks in the middle of the room.

ACCOMMODATION

REHOBOTH

The Ochsenwagen Hotel Pension B1 at the junction with the D1237 ☎ 062 525910, ⓔ info@ochsenwagen .com. If you're heading north and too tired to make the last hour's drive to Windhoek, then this modern, fairly bland roadside establishment fits the bill. There's a sports bar-restaurant, too. Room only N$790

Oonob Resort Oanob Dam off the D1280, 7km west of Rehoboth ☎062 522370, ⓦoanob.com.na. A surprisingly pleasant resort comprising a collection of generous double stone-and-thatch chalets with shared balcony, and freestanding fullye quipped two- or three-bedroom family chalets dotted round the lake, facing the water through shady acacias. The bar-restaurant, which serves decent food, overlooks the dam too – though it's cold in winter as it's lacks a fireplace. A popular getaway for Windhoek families on summer weekends, it's also a first-night stay for tourists who've just arrived in Namibia and are on their way to Sossusvlei. Plenty of campsites with electricity; prices vary according to location and shade. Day visitors also welcome. Camping per person **N$80**, doubles B&B **N$1280**, family chalets (two people) B&B **N$1840**

Mariental

Rather like Rehoboth, to the north, **MARIENTAL**, the low-key administrative centre for the Hardap region, has little to detain the average tourist beyond the usual supermarkets and petrol stations for replenishing supplies and fuel. Indeed, it resembles a glorified industrial estate. That said, the town has several acceptable places to stay if you're in need of a bed for the night, though there are lodges and reserves in the red dunes of the Kalahari (see p.150), only an hour's drive away that are infinitely more preferable if you're looking for recreation.

In classic colonial fashion, Mariental, meaning "Marie's Valley", was named in honour of the wife of the first white settler, a William Brandt, though the notion of a valley was clearly somewhat fanciful. In contrast, the Nama, who had been around for considerably longer, called the place Zara-gaeiba, meaning "dusty", aptly nailing the location's defining characteristic. Indeed, on Sundays, the swirling dust is about the only sign of life in town.

That said, a 15km belt of lush commercial farmland west of Mariental runs parallel to the B1. The Fish River flows through the area from the Hardap Dam northwest of the town, and provides further water for irrigation. The farms focus on sheep, goats, game – especially ostrich – and dairy, as well as the production of alfalfa (more commonly termed lucerne).

Hardap Dam

Signposted west off the B1, 9km north of Mariental, 15km down the road • Daily 6am–11pm • Day visitors $40/person plus N$10/vehicle

Just northwest of town is **Hardap Dam**, Namibia's largest reservoir, which draws its water from the Fish River and hosts an NWR resort (see p.144), which has just reopened after a multi-million Namibian-dollar facelift. Hardap is a Nama name for "nipple" or "wart", which was presumably how the conical hills in the surrounding area appeared to the area's earliest visitors. The nature reserve, comprising the dam and its surrounding dwarf shrub savannah, supports an array of wildlife. Look out for black rhino, as well as Hartmann's mountain zebra, kudu, oryx, eland and red hartebeest. Over 280 bird species have been recorded in the area, with the fish-rich reservoir feeding cormorants, darters, spoonbills, fish eagles and even osprey, in addition to a breeding colony of great white pelican.

ACCOMMODATION   MARIENTAL

Anandi Guesthouse 15 River St ☎063 242220 or ☎081 241 1822, ⓦanandiguesthouse.com. Cheerful lilac buildings and some greenery secure within a lilac walled compound. Staff are friendly and accommodating while rooms are upbeat; some with fans, others with a/c. Gleaming fully tiled bathrooms with fancy modern sinks and some with a jacuzzi-bath. Breakfast is extra (N$75). No dining restaurant. **N$550**

Bastion Farmyard Signposted off the B1, 13km north of Mariental ☎063 240827 or ☎081 274 5574, ⓦbastionfarmyard.com. A relaxing atmosphere, and pleasant surroundings. Five comfortable unfussy rooms with a/c, fans sharing a well-equipped though small kitchen with TV. The farm shop sells braai packs, and passers-by as well as guests can enjoy a slab of cake and a cappuccino on the shady coffee-shop terrace. A top choice for campers, with four superior campsites with every convenience, with private shaded ablutions and kitchen area, and even a luggage rack and washing line. Breakfast N$100. Camping per person **N$120**, doubles **N$550**

MARIENTAL

ACCOMMODATION
Anandi Guesthouse	4
Bastion Farmyard	1
Hardap Dam Resort	2
Tahiti Guesthouse	3

Hardap Dam Resort 22km northwest of Mariental ☎061 2857200 (reservations), ⓦnwr.com.na. A vast and rather soulless resort, in part due to the lack of vegetation, but also the sameness of the spacious, gleaming and tiled 50-plus bungalow-chalets. All have reservoir views, unlike the campsites, which lie in serried ranks behind the chalets. Buffet food is available at the waterside restaurant. Leisure activities were yet to be offered at the time of writing. Camping per person N$120, bush chalets B&B N$900

Tahiti Guesthouse 66 Michael Van Niekerk St ☎063 240636, ⓔtahiti@iway.na. Gloomy but good-value place, with small but clean, motel-like rooms leading off a secure compound/car park, each with a/c, fridge and TV plus firm mattresses mounted on cement slabs. The equally dark but popular restaurant dishes up steaks, grills, pizzas and burgers (mains N$100–160), and has a kids' menu. Good value. Mon–Fri 8am–9pm, Sat 8am–2pm, 5–9pm, Sun 10am–2pm. N$450

Around Mariental

North of Mariental, and east of the B1, several lodges set in private reserves make the most of their surroundings among the picturesque linear red dunes of the Kalahari (see p.150). These dunes, unlike those in the Namib, are generally vegetated, and run northwest to southeast, interspersed with wider inter-dune valleys or "streets" possessing the occasional pan, and studded with acacia trees and shrubs, and shimmering grasses after rain.

ACCOMMODATION   AROUND MARIENTAL

★**Bagatelle Kalahari Game Ranch** On the D1268, 25km north of the junction with the C20 ☎063 240982, ⓦbagatelle-kalahari-gameranch.com; map p.140. A comfortable, converted old farmhouse contains communal areas, with pool and patio, as well as four rooms. An avenue of pricier savannah-facing chalets leads away to the choice, and most expensive, accommodation: a handful of superior tented chalets atop a high red dune, affording fabulous sunset views across a waterhole. Some have private plunge pools. All lodgings have a/c, and the food is high quality. Five

individual campsites have private ablution blocks and provide a pony-and-trap transfer to the lodge if you prefer to eat there. There's lots to do (N$300–750): wildlife-viewing drives at morning, dusk and night – a chance to spot bat-eared foxes, porcupines, aardvarks and other nocturnal creatures; stargazing through a telescope; also watching cheetah feeding, guided walks and horseback safaris. Two-night discounts. Camping per person N$200, doubles DBB N$2900

★**Kalahari Red Dunes** 3km east of the B1, signposted off 5km south of Kalkrand, 70km north of

BRUKKAROS – THE FALSE VOLCANO

Visible over 80km away, as you speed along the B1 north of Keetmanshoop, the forbidding massif of **Brukkaros** looms out of the surrounding flat, parched plains, dwarfing the nearby Nama settlement of Berseba (!Autsawises), one of the oldest villages in Namibia. The original name for the mountain was Geitsigubeb, the Khoekhoen word for a leather apron, which they thought it resembled; this led to the Afrikaans combination of "broek" (trousers) and "karos" (leather apron), which resulted in Brukkaros.

Despite its imposing stature, it is often overlooked by tourists, but is well worth a detour if you like hiking, as it offers commanding views, fascinating rock formations and surprisingly good **birding**. In the colonial era, the Germans used the crater rim as a heliograph station; then in 1926 the National Geographic Society teamed up with the Smithsonian Institute and ran a solar observatory here for a few years.

For a long time it was assumed to be an extinct volcano, suggested by its squat conical shape and existence of a caldera. Yet it's now thought to be the result of an enormous gaseous explosion that occurred around **80 million years** ago: magma pushing upwards encountered groundwater, which then heated, vaporized and expanded, while pressure from the magma continued to build. When the Earth's crust, which had been welling up, could no longer take the strain, it exploded, spewing forth rocks that now form the crater rim. Over time, the central area eroded away, leaving a scree-encircled caldera floor some 350m below the rim. Quiver trees are present, hosting the inevitable sociable weavers' communal nest, and the area generally supports numerous bird species, particularly raptors; look out for black and booted eagles riding the thermals. The mountain also hosts the endemic Brukkaros pygmy rock mouse, though being nocturnal and minute, the chances of spotting one are not high.

HIKING TO THE CRATER

After passing under an unlikely gateway announcing your arrival at Brukkaros, the road bends round a hillock to the former lower campsite and car park; most visitors leave their vehicle here, though it is possible to take a 4WD 2km further up the very rocky track to the upper campsite and parking area, but it's a very bumpy ride. From the upper camping area, a narrow, steep, meandering path takes you up a further 1.5km to the lip of the outflow, marked by a rock waterfall, where you'll only see cascading water after heavy rains. Here you can choose to explore the vegetated caldera, or make a sharp left turn to scramble a further 500m onto the rim itself, and soak up the breathtaking views. The vertigo-hardened might want to navigate a further 4.5km along an increasingly indistinct path round to the northern side of the rim, and nose around the decaying buildings of the abandoned research station, before taking the same route back.

Don't hike on your own since there's no mobile phone coverage and the walk involves a lot of boulder-hopping and rock scrambling, with the real risk of going over on your ankle. Make sure you have robust footwear, plenty of water and protection against the sun, as there's no shelter along the way.

ARRIVAL AND INFORMATION

Access is via the M98, signposted off the B1, 86km north of Keetmanshoop, and just south of Tses, signposted to the village of Berseba (!Autsawises in Nama), which lies 38km down the road, and where there are a couple of basic shops and a fuel station. About a kilometre before the village itself a poorly marked dirt road, the D3904 (accessible in 2WD), leads 10km up to the mountain. Theoretically, a community fee of N$35 is payable upon entry, but there is rarely anyone there to take the money, as the community enterprise – including maintenance of the two campsites – has all but closed down.

Mariental ☎063 264003 (lodge) or ☎061 240020 (reservations), ⓦredduneslodge.com; map p.140. This tastefully designed lodge, run with efficiency and warmth, is not actually set among the dunes, though they feature in the reserve. Rather, the lovely stone-and-thatch chalets (all in the process of being enlarged and upgraded) stand in a vlei, each with uninterrupted views across the Kalahari, through vast windows, or from your private porch, and connected by a series of raised wooden walkways. Lovely central lapa and an excellent range of activities: self-guided and guided (N$290) walks, a mountain-bike trail, wildlife viewing – plains and mountain zebra, nyala, impala, springbok, blesbok, red hartebeest, oryx, kudu and steenbok are around – and sundowner excursions, plus the latest offering: a three-day dune-rambling hike on the reserve, staying in a tented camp en route (N$9900). DBB **N$4310**

INTU AFRIKA RESERVE

Two lodges and one chalet camp share the 100-square-kilometre Intu Afrika reserve, which holds giraffe, oryx, wildebeest, zebra, kudu, springbok and imported blesbok, as well as a host of smaller mammals, including bat-eared foxes. Though the lodges are managed separately, activities are shared. These include a morning walk with a San guide, or a game drive. Strangely, guides also lead quad-bike excursions, which tear round the reserve making a racket, but which they claim does not disturb the wildlife because they've become habituated. The main entrance to Intu Afrika is on the D1268, 35km north of the junction with the C20 (☎ 063 683218 (game reserve) or ☎ 061 237294 (reservations); ⊛ intu-afrika.com; map p.140); the entrance to *Suricate Tented Lodge* is 5km further south.

Camelthorn Kalahari Lodge 5km from the reserve entrance. Good for birdwatching, this place has a lovely snug setting in a dune valley amid plenty of camelthorn, through which oryx and springbok wander at will. Eleven sparsely furnished, stone-and-thatch chalets encircle the pleasant two-storey main lodge with pool and fire-pit. **N$3120**

Suricate Tented Lodge 5km south of the main entrance off the D1268 ☎ 063 240846. Boasting the best views, this row of tented cabins is lined along a dune ridge overlooking a pan. Fan-ventilated tents are compact, with minibar, open-air bathroom and private viewing decks. Dining is family-style in a rather featureless tented dining room, or out on the viewing deck. **N$3880**

Zebra Kalahari Lodge & Spa 5km from the reserve entrance ☎ 063 240855. The main and most luxurious of the three lodges, this hotel-like complex, overlooking a waterhole, comprises eight spacious rooms flanking the main dining-lounge area with pool, and five larger, more private suites, set apart. Accommodation is furnished in ebony, decorated with African masks, and possesses all the usual modern comforts: a/c, fridge, tea/coffee-making facilities, plus additional outside shower. **N$4720**

Keetmanshoop and around

There's little of obvious attraction in **KEETMANSHOOP** – or Keetmans, as many Namibians call it – but it makes for a convenient break in the long haul up or down the B1, and is a good place to pick up supplies if you're heading out into the desert to camp. It's the administrative centre of the vast ||Karas Region, which covers most of southern Namibia, and possesses a population of around 22,000. A former Nama settlement, it was named after Johann Keetman, a German industrialist who donated 1000 gold Marks to construct the first Rhenish Mission Church in 1869. After you've made a pit stop and eaten, you might as well swing by the church's more modern incarnation to check out the museum.

Rhenish Mission Church

Sam Nujoma Drive at 6th Ave • Mon–Fri 7.30am–12.30pm & 1.30–4.30pm • Free; donations appreciated

Dating back to 1895, the **Rhenish Mission Church** is the town's oldest building and houses a small museum collection in the Keetmanshoof Museum. The church is quite striking; made from stone brought by ox-cart from Lüderitz 337km away, it replaced an earlier wooden version that had been swept away in a flash flood in 1890.

Keetmanshoop Museum

The Rhenish Mission Church houses the **Keetmanshoop Museum**, a collection of modest and rather shambolic displays populated mainly by donations – offered, one suspects, by people cleaning out their unwanted junk: Singer sewing machines, coal irons, Bavarian crockery and the like. However, the collection of faded photos is of greater historical interest, documenting in part the War of National Resistance (see p.393) and the awful conditions of the black population during colonial rule. Note the collection of brass passes that indigenous people had to wear round their necks – part of the ruling powers' attempts to control their movements.

3

ACCOMMODATION

Bird's Mansions	2
Bird's Nest Guesthouse	4
Central Lodge	3
Pension Gessert	1

KEETMANSHOOP

B1, Lafenis (4km), B4 & Lüderitz (335km)

Quiver Tree Forest

Gariganus Farm, 14km northeast of Keetmanshoop on the C17, a good-quality dirt road suitable for 2WD · Sunrise to sunset · N$60 · ☏ 063 683421, Ⓦ quivertreeforest.com · Call at the farmhouse first to pay the entrance fee; the Giant's Playground, also included in the price, is 2km further along the road

If you're looking for a worthwhile detour from the seemingly endless slog along the B1, the **Quiver Tree Forest** (Kokerboomwoud in Afrikaans), northeast of Keetmanshoop, is the spot to pick. This farm has an unusually high density of quiver trees, one of Namibia's most emblematic and photogenic plants (see box opposite), which are best appreciated in the early morning or evening light. Enjoy scrambling around the rocks to get a good look at the plants, before driving a couple of kilometres further down the road to the **Giant's Playground**. Another picturesque natural phenomenon, it comprises a vast array of dolerite boulders, weathered over millennia, which resemble piles of giant marbles that have been stacked up by some alien colossus. Camping and chalet accommodation is also available.

Mesosaurus Fossil Site

43km northeast of Keetmanshoop on the C17 · Daily 8am–5pm · N$100 for a 1hr tour · ☏ 063 683641, Ⓦ mesosaurus.com

Less frequented than the Quiver Tree Forest, the **Mesosaurus Fossil Site** is set in similar landscape, full of dolerite boulders, and claims to have the greatest density of **quiver trees** in the country. While this is impossible to verify on a quick visit, there are undoubtedly a great many of them, and enough to satisfy even the most ardent aloe enthusiast. Yet the sight's main attraction is **fossils**, specifically those of the **mesosaurus**, a metre-long reptile with a small skull and long jaws – similar to a small crocodile – that frequented the freshwater habitats of Gondwanaland 290–270 million years ago. The farm owner and guide will show you various partial fossils during the guided tour, though the most complete and impressive specimen is on display in the National Earth

QUIVER TREES

One of the most recognizable sights of southern Namibia, the magnificent **quiver tree** (*Aloe dichotoma*, or kokerboom in Afrikaans) is not a tree at all, but a giant aloe. It gained its name from the Khoisan, who are said to use the hollowed-out branches as quivers to hold their poison-tipped hunting arrows. Perfectly designed to cope with the hot, arid climate, the quiver tree's distinctive crown of thick waxy leaves grows high from the ground – some reach 9m in height – in order to escape the worst of the heat and help reduce water evaporation; the pulpy fibrous tissue of its "trunk" allows it to maximize water storage space, while its branches are coated in a thin white powder, to help reflect the sun's heat; the "scales" on the cracked golden bark are thought to have a cooling effect too when there's a breeze. A slow developer, the kokerboom does not bloom until 20–30 years of age, but its pretty yellow flowers (June and July) attract numerous nectar-feeders, including eye-catching iridescent sunbirds. The succulent is also a popular host of sociable weavers, which construct their haystack-like communal nest amid the rosettes of spiky blue-green leaves to protect the young from the heat and from predators.

3

Science Museum in Windhoek (see 90). There are also a couple of Schutztruppen graves on the farm, and the guide's surprising star turn is to finish off the tour by bashing out a tune on "musical" rocks.

When visiting the site, you have a choice of an unguided walk through the quiver trees, or a guided hike that takes in the fossils and the graves. Visitors staying overnight in the rustic accommodation can also opt to do a self-guided trail (3–10km) on the property, when you can catch the magical morning light on the quiver trees.

ARRIVAL AND INFORMATION

By car Keetmanshoop lies to the west of the B1, 482km south of Windhoek and 304km north of the border with South Africa.

By bus The Intercape Mainliner service between Cape Town and Windhoek stops at Lafenis, 4km south of Keetmanshoop on the B1 at the Engen petrol station and Wimpy (for Windhoek Mon, Wed, Fri & Sat; 4hr 50min; for Cape Town Mon, Wed, Fri & Sun; 14hr 45min). In addition minibuses leave from the Engen petrol station on Fifth Ave for Windhoek (around N$190) and less frequently for Lüderitz (N$190). Opposite, at

JJ Supermarket, is the ticket office for the Intercape Mainliner.

By train There is a nightly overnight train (except Sat) run by TransNamib (Windhoek ☎ 061 2982175; Keetmanshoop ☎ 063 229202) from Windhoek to Keetmanshoop (7.40pm; economy N$161, business N$201), and from Keetmans to Windhoek.

Tourist information A helpful tourist office functions in the Imperial Post Office (Kaiserliches Postampt), 5th Ave (Mon–Fri 7.30am–12.30pm & 1.30–4.30pm; ☎ 063 221266).

KEETMANSHOOP AND AROUND

ACCOMMODATION

Bird's Mansions 6th Ave ☎ 063 221711, ⓦ birdsaccommodation.com. Twenty-three small rooms with rather musty carpets but with good beds and cable TV. The shady, flower-filled beer garden-cum-restaurant is really inviting and the menu is quite extensive, offering the usual pizzas, burgers and salads as well as a variety of beef, pork, poultry, venison and mutton dishes. N$930
Bird's Nest Guesthouse 16 Pastorie St ☎ 063 222906, ⓦ birdsaccommodation.com. Nice secluded environment comprising nine rooms – most newly renovated – with DStv and a fridge, opening onto a tree-filled courtyard, providing secure parking. Breakfast is provided but you'll have to dine elsewhere. B&B N$860
Central Lodge 5th Ave ☎ 063 225850, ⓦ central -lodge.com. A pleasant hotel with a dozen rooms facing in towards a central lawn or the adjoining car park. Rooms are

light, clean and fairly spacious with cable TV, twin beds and telephone – bag one with a jacuzzi for an extra N$70. The onsite restaurant is popular, though the food is variable. B&B N$750
Mesosaurus Fossil Site Bush Camp At the Mesosaurus Fossil Site reception; map p.140. Three rustic stone-and-thatch, twin-bedded self-catering cottages plus one family cottage. All have semi-open kitchen areas. Six campsites are nearby with private water tap and braai site but shared ablutions. Even nicer is the bush camp 3km into the farm, located by a river bed between quiver trees. Camping per person N$120, chalet N$600
Pension Gessert 138 13th St ☎ 063 223892, ⓦ natron .net/gessert/main.html. Seven homely, spotless rooms with a/c opening out onto a shady garden with pool. Breakfast is a veritable feast. B&B N$1000

DESERT OASIS: THE SEEHEIM HOTEL

Tucked away down a rocky ravine some 45km west of Keetmanshoop, the impressive **Seeheim Hotel** (☎063 683643, ⊕seeheimhotel.com; N$1160; map p.140) is an unlikely oasis, flaunting wafting palm trees and a sparkling swimming pool. It dates back to the colonial era when the original stone building first served as a barracks for the Schutztruppen, before being transformed into a hotel in the 1920s, becoming the centrepiece of a thriving town that was a major stop on the Lüderitz–Keetmanshoop railway line. Once road freight took over from the train, Seeheim's star faded and the hotel closed. Fast-forward to the twenty-first century, this magnificent three-tier stone-and-thatch structure manages to retain some of the yesteryear feel, while ensuring more than a modicum of comfort. The hotel also includes a carpentry workshop that produces high-quality, handcrafted furniture – examples of which adorn the hotel's large, cool, fan-ventilated stone rooms.

With a bar and respectable à la carte restaurant, Seeheim is a good place to break the journey between Lüderitz and the Fish River Canyon – a popular lunch stop for tour groups in the season, but also a perfectly pleasant place to overnight. It's well signposted off the C12, just south of the junction with the B4, with a steep rocky descent down to the car park; it's navigable with care in a saloon car when the road is dry, but high clearance is ideal.

The southern Kalahari

Forever in the shadow of the extraordinary Namib, the country's second desert, the Kalahari, is often neglected. Though technically a semi-desert on account of its greater rainfall – some areas receiving over 280mm per year on average – it's difficult to conceive of it as anything other than a desert given that any precipitation immediately drains away through the porous sandy soils. Yet the higher levels of rainfall and the numerous ephemeral rivers that streak the Kalahari inevitably allow it to support more vegetation and more varied wildlife than the Namib. In particular, smaller mammals thrive on the shimmering grasses that follow rain and on the greater availability of even smaller prey: aardwolves, porcupines and honey badgers are all possible sightings, so too scurrying groups of meerkats, mongoose and suricates. Birders will be keen to watch out for the many raptors wheeling above: martial and snake eagles, as well as lappet-faced vultures. Inevitably, snakes and scorpions are common denizens of the desert; keep an eye out for the puff adder and *Panabuthus raudus* – the largest scorpion in southern Africa, which can reach over 12cm, threatening with a particularly impressive tail. Some of the desert's more surprising inhabitants include tortoises and even frogs.

Yet the Kalahari is as much about the stillness and silence of the desert as it is about wildlife, and – in this southern section – the visually stunning **red dunes**, made so by the high iron oxide content in the sand. In contrast to the towering dunes in the Namib, these are rippling vegetated linear dunes, running broadly northwest to southeast. They start just east of the B1 between Kalkrand and Mariental, where several private reserves make the most of this picturesque dunescape, and they cover much of the land between the B1 and the eastern border of Namibia, extending into the South African section of the **Kgalagadi Transfrontier Park**. The park is attracting increasing numbers of self-drive visitors entering via the **Mata Mata gate** on the Namibian border, roughly 200km northeast of Keetmanshoop, as the crow flies. Many take the scenic C15 from the agricultural centre of **Stampriet**, northeast of Mariental, which tracks the relatively lush Auob River valley 230km southeast to the park gate, sometimes stopping of at one of the new campgrounds that are sprouting up along the way.

Stampriet

There's not much to the small settlement of **STAMPRIET** that lies about 55km northeast of Mariental, on the banks of the ephemeral River Auob. Thanks to the area's abundance of artesian water, however, it's a surprising oasis in the Kalahari, complete with wafting palm trees and a gleaming whitewashed hillside church, where cypress trees and topiary hedges thrive. Importantly, it's a major area for fruit and vegetable production, and more recently has become a stopover on the way to the Kgalagadi Transfrontier Park (see p.152). The village has a small supermarket and petrol station, as well as some good, inexpensive accommodation.

ACCOMMODATION   STAMPRIET

Kalahari Anib Signposted north off the C20, 30km west of Stampriet and 21km east of the junction with the B1 ☎063 240529 (lodge) or ☎061 427200 (reservations), ⓦgondwana-collection.com; map p.140. With a hotel-like feel, this 52-room desert lodge, popular with tour groups, is set round a tree-filled grassy central area. Half the rooms look inwards over the pool, the other half face outwards across the bush. The main bar-dining area is an impressive glass-fronted structure with a large fireplace in the bar area, surrounded by red Kalahari sand. Excellent food, worth driving from Mariental to dine here. Three individual campsites too. Walking trails and safari drives on offer. Camping per person N$175, doubles N$2138

Kalahari Farmhouse South off the C20 at Stampriet, close to the stadium ☎063 260259 (lodge) or ☎061 427200 (reservations), ⓦgondwana-collection.com; map p.140. Incongruous oasis with eleven cheerful, rustic stone chalets, complete with wooden shutters set in lush grassy grounds shaded by wafting palm trees. The place is a training school for Gondwana staff and also hosts the company's self-sufficiency centre, which produces vegetables, meats and cheeses to supply Gondwana lodges countrywide, so much of the food here couldn't be fresher. Camping per person N$160, chalets N$2422

★**Stampriet Historical Guesthouse** On the C20, village centre ☎063 260013, ⓦstamprietguesthouse.com; map p.140. Enjoying a pleasant location on a hillside at the village entrance, this guesthouse is surprisingly popular, given its out-of-the way location. Ten basic rooms with private porches are set around a pleasant shady garden, dotted with memorabilia, such as milk churns and an ox cart. The cosy lounge-dining area opens out onto a breezy deck with pool table and more comfy chairs; great for a sundowner. The hospitality is warm and the catering decent, plus the owner is an excellent potter. B&B N$1810

The "back road" to Mata Mata

From Stampriet you can follow the Auob River valley, all 244km down the gravel C15, to the **Mata Mata** gate, which takes you into the Kgalagadi Transfrontier Park. The first 70km between Stampriet and the hilltop village of Gochas – which must surely claim the prize for the largest underused tourist office in the country – is particularly scenic; the road runs parallel to red dunes for a while, before widening into a canyon enclosed by sandstone and shale cliffs. The river's artesian aquifer ensures plenty of greenery, featuring dense thickets of prosopis and a string of farms supporting sheep and cattle. Several places provide simple scenic stopovers.

ACCOMMODATION   THE BACK ROAD TO MATA MATA

Auob Country Lodge On the C15, 6km north of Gochas ☎063 250101; map p.140. Set in its own small reserve harbouring giraffe and various antelope, this 25-room lodge has rather dark and austere communal areas but neat and clean air-conditioned rooms. Adequate for an overnight stay, though it's more popular as a lunch stop with groups doing a scenic tour of the dunes. The food is tasty, the pool in the courtyard pleasant and the rates reasonable. Plenty of camping space too, with electricity. Camping per person N$155, doubles B&B N$1587

★**Dune Song Breathers** Onze Rust Farm, 10km north on the D617 ☎063 252657 or ☎081 122 0175, ⓦdunesong.net; map p.140. A place to enjoy the views and the stars in these three chic, concrete self-catering "bunkers" set atop a red dune, enlivened with some rustic wooden touches. Open-plan design with four single beds, well-equipped kitchen, including fridge-freezer, wood-burning oven – to provide warmth at night – and a large veranda with seating and a braai area. Bush camping also available. 4WD access but the owners will provide transfers from the farm and braai packs if desired. Two-night minimum. Camping per person N$150, chalets N$1000

Red Dune Camp On the C15, 32km south of Gochas ☎063 250164 or ☎081 421 0927, ⓦreddunecamp.com;

3

KGALAGADI TRANSFRONTIER PARK

The **Kgalagadi Transfrontier Park** (Kgalagadi pronounced "ka-la-khadi", the "kh" as in the Scottish "loch") is jointly run by South Africa and Botswana, and stretches over 37,000 square kilometres – an area larger than Belgium. The South African section is bounded by two dry rivers, both of which originate in Namibia: the Auob River marks the park's southwestern boundary until it joins the south-flowing Nossob – delineating South Africa's national boundary with Botswana – at the aptly named Twee Rivieren. No fences exist along this line, allowing wildlife undisturbed access to the ancient migration routes so necessary for survival in the desert, and indeed the park affords great opportunities to watch the seasonal movement of large herbivores such as blue wildebeest, springbok, eland and red hartebeest. It's also renowned for predator watching, with excellent chances of seeing cheetah, leopard, brown and spotted hyena and the Kalahari lion. These commonly have much darker manes than those found in the bushveld, and studies have shown their behavioural and eating patterns to be distinctively well adapted to the semi-desert conditions here. Birdwatchers will be well rewarded with some extravagant **birdlife** including vultures, eagles, bustards and ostrich. There's also a good chance you'll see family groups of **meerkat** striking their characteristic pose of standing on their hind legs, looking round nervously for signs of danger.

The main roads follow the river beds, and this is where the game – and their predators – are most likely to be. Water flows very rarely in the two rivers, but frequent boreholes have been drilled to provide water for the animals. Larger trees such as camelthorn and shepherd's tree offer a degree of shade and nutrition, and desert-adapted plants, including types of melon and cucumber, also provide moisture for the animals. Much of the park is dominated by vegetated linear **red sand dunes**, which, when seen from the air, lie strung out in long, wave-like bands, and offer wonderful photographic opportunities in the changing light.

PARK ENTRY

The park is open from sunrise to sunset. Entry fee is R304/person per day. Get in touch with the park reception in South Africa (☎054 561 2000, ⊛sanparks.org).

WHEN TO VISIT

In a place where ground temperatures in the **summer** can reach a scorching 70°C, timing your visit is everything. The best visiting period is between March and May, when there is still some greenery left from the summer rain and the sun is not so intense. **Winter** can be very cold at night, while **spring**, though dry, is a pleasant time before the searing heat of summer.

ARRIVAL AND DEPARTURE

If you arrive via the Mata Mata gate (daily 8am–4pm) from Namibia and intend to return the same way, there are no border formalities or charges. However, all visitors wanting to exit the park into a different country from the one they entered from should note that all immigration controls must be done at *Twee Rivieren* (daily 7.30am–4pm), which is the largest camp and houses the park headquarters. Also note that a minimum two-night stay in the park is compulsory.

GETTING AROUND

The main park roads are gravel, so an ordinary saloon car can make it, but the higher the clearance the better; entry to the Botswana section of Kgalagadi is 4WD only. Note that you need time to move between camps as the speed limit is 50kph, and the distances considerable: over 100km between *Mata-Mata Restcamp* and *Twee Rivieren* and around 160km between the latter and *Nossob Restcamp*. Fuel is available at these three main camps but is inevitably more expensive within the park than at the petrol stations outside.

map p.140. Assuming the renovations of the wooden shelters are complete when you go, the four sites on a fabulous dune ridge (needing 4WD to access) should have sufficient shade to go with the magnificent sunset views

– two have sundowner decks and one even has a consecrated wooden "chapel" for weddings. Each has a flush toilet, bush shower and fire-pit. Otherwise, you can pitch a tent in their shady grassy garden at the farmhouse,

TOURIST INFORMATION AND ACTIVITIES

The visitor centre at *Twee Rivieren* (one hour after sunrise untill one hour before sunset) is worthwhile, and an informative park guide is for sale at reception at the park office (South Africa ☎ (0)54 5612000; daily 7.30am– sunset). Although most people self-drive round the park, night and day game drives and day walks can be booked on arrival at the main camps. Rates are R250–400/person depending on the activity, numbers and duration.

ACCOMMODATION

It's vital to book park accommodation, even for campsites, as early as you can through South African National Parks in Pretoria (☎ (0)12 428 9111, ⊛ sanparks.org), as places fill up months in advance. The two main types of site are: larger, fenced restcamps at *Twee Rivieren*, *Mata Mata* and *Nossob*, which have electricity (even in some campsites) and creature comforts such as kitchens, fans or a/c, braai areas, pools and shops, with some units wheelchair accessible; and six far more basic and remote unfenced wilderness camps, for which you need to be completely self-sufficient, but which are more appealing if you want to taste the raw flavour of the desert. There is also one community-owned lodge. Camping rates are per site for two people; each additional adult costs R82.

Bitterpan Wilderness Camp A peaceful spot near the centre of the park on a 4WD trail between *Nossob* and *Mata Mata* (access by 4WD only), with four unfenced reed cabins perched on the edge of a saltpan. R1495

Gharagab Wilderness Camp Four log cabins in an unfenced area in the remote far north, a four-hour drive from *Nossob* (access by 4WD only), with elevated views onto a landscape of dunes and thornveld savannah. R1495

Grootkolk Wilderness Camp At the very northern tip of the South African section in prime predator country, so it's booked up months in advance; its four chalets come fully equipped with cooking supplies, linen and fans. R1630

★ **Kalahari Tent Camp** Guarded by an armed guide, this unfenced site has comfortable, fully equipped, self-catering tents built of sandbags and canvas (including one luxurious "honeymoon tent"), all decorated in desert tones with views over the Auob River. There's also a swimming pool. R1665

Kieliekrankie Wilderness Camp Just over 40km northwest of *Twee Rivieren*, it is accessible to ordinary vehicles and consists of unfenced cabins sunk into a red sand dune, providing lovely panoramic views of the desert. R1630

Mata Mata Camp Right by the Namibian border post of the same name. Accommodation is in fully equipped chalets (sleeping two, four or six), including eight brand-new chalets overlooking the Auob River, and a campsite. Other amenities include a waterhole lit up at night, a bird hide, swimming pool, shop and fuel. Camping R305, chalet R945

Nossob Camp The most remote of the three fenced restcamps, on the Botswana border 160km north of *Twee Rivieren* along the Nossob River Rd, has 18 simple chalets for 2–6 people plus a campsite. There's also a supply shop, fuel, plus a predator information centre (the place is famed for nocturnal visits by lions, so night drives are on offer) and a waterhole with hide. Camping R225, chalet R995

Twee Rivieren Camp The first, and most developed, of the three fenced restcamps (the only one with 24hr electricity and mobile phone coverage) right by the South African entrance. Offers over thirty pleasant self-catering chalets with thatched roofs and nice patio areas, a sizeable campsite (with or without electricity), a mediocre restaurant, a pool, fuel, and a shop selling souvenirs and simple foodstuffs. Camping R265, chalet R1100

Urikaruus Wilderness Camp Roughly halfway between *Twee Rivieren* and *Mata Mata*, with an attractive setting among camelthorn trees overlooking the Auob River; the four two-person cabins, all equipped with solar power and kitchen supplies, are built on stilts and connected by a plank walkway. R1630

!Xaus Lodge Signposted north 40km from Mata Mata gate, along a 30km sandy track over 91 dunes (4WD necessary) or transfers from Kamqua picnic site ☎ (0)21 7017860 (South Africa), ⊛ xauslodge .co.za. Owned by San and Mier communities (who also jointly manage the national park), this is the only fully catered lodge in the park: 12 chalets aligned along the ridge of a red dune overlooking a pan and waterhole. Includes cultural engagements with your host communities. DBB with activities R8780

book one of two simple rooms, or stay in their twin-bedded safari tent if you don't have your own. Dune sites (up to four people) N$400, doubles N$500

Terra Rouge On the C15, 45km north of the Mata Mata gate ☎ 063 252031 or ☎ 081 129 0280, ⊛ terrarougefarm.com; map p.140. Working sheep and cattle farm offering three snug, self-catering bungalows with a/c, equipped kitchens, braai areas and private porches. Also five campsites in the Auon riverbed, under large shady camelthorns with braai sites, water and modern ablutions: flush toilets and open-air showers. Braai packs – from their own farm meat – and firewood available. Per person N$100, bungalows N$800

Wildmoor On the C15, 51km south of Stampriet ☎ 063 250222, or ☎ 081 240 8811; map p.140. You can camp in the farmhouse garden, under large shady trees – just keep out of the way of the horns of the "tame" springbok – or in one of the delightful, remote wilderness campsites: one built into the canyon wall, overlooking the valley; the other over the escarpment, deep in the farm. Donkey-fired hot water and open-air shower plus braai site, with firewood included. Camping per person N$150

The Richtersveld and around

At Namibia's southernmost limit, the starkly beautiful, mountainous |Ai-|Ais/ **RICHTERSVELD TRANSFRONTIER PARK** – commonly known as the Richtersveld – straddles the border with South Africa, covering an area around four times the size of Greater London. The park's main attraction is the truly awe-inspiring **Fish River Canyon**, about half of which lies within the park boundaries. The canyon ends at |Ai-|Ais – meaning "burning water" in Nama – Namibia's best-known sulphurous hot springs and a popular tourist attraction in itself. While the Fish River rarely flows, the **Orange River** (!Gariep, in Nama) – which demarcates the border between Namibia and South Africa and bisects the park – is a perennial water source, making it a bird lovers' paradise and a popular place to indulge in a day or more of gentle canoeing or kayaking (see box, p.161).

Importantly, the Richtersveld Park lies within the **Succulent Karoo Biome**, a biodiversity hotspot that has the greatest variety of succulents on the planet, harbouring a third of the world's ten thousand species, 33 of which are endemic to the area. They are at their most impressive between June and October, when – provided there has been sufficient rain – their flowers burst forth in a stunning carpet of colour.

The two succulents most associated with the area are the critically endangered giant or bastard quiver tree (*Aloe pillansii*) – distinguishable from its more common sibling by its towering, pale and statuesque trunk and fewer rosettes – and the more numerous halfmens (meaning "semi-human" in Afrikaans; *Pachypodium namaquanum*). When outlined against the skyline, the spiny tapering trunk has been likened to a human trudging up the mountain, its head inclined slightly – always northwards, for some inexplicable reason – crowned with a single rosette resembling a mop of hair.

The succulents help nourish the animal life in this otherwise barren environment, including the park's fifty species of mammal and just under two hundred bird species, most of which inhabit the terrain close to the river. Lizards and snakes abound, but large mammals such as zebra, klipspringer and springbok are also in evidence, while leopards and other cats remain characteristically shy.

Though most of this vast park lies in Namibia, opportunities for wilderness camping and hiking (excluding the Fish River Canyon) and admiring the succulent-rich landscape are better in the South African section (see box, p.158), which is also home to a handful of **Nama** communities, who jointly manage the park south of the border. Here, they still practise their traditional semi-nomadic lifestyle, moving their livestock according to the season and living in rush-mat domed huts (|haru om).

The Fish River Canyon

The main entrance to the Fish River Canyon is clearly signposted off the C37 along a dirt road • N$80/person per day plus N$10/vehicle, payable at the MET office at the park entrance (also valid for |Ai-|Ais) • ☎ 063 266028

A vast, sinuous chasm, the **Fish River Canyon** is one of Africa's greatest natural wonders, and vies with the Blue Nile Gorge in Ethiopia for the claim to being the Earth's second-largest canyon (after the USA's Grand Canyon). At 160km in length, up to 27km in width and with a depth of 550m in places, its grand scale can best be appreciated by gazing across the canyon rim, or by climbing down the almost sheer rock to the valley floor and undertaking a gruelling five-day hike along the mainly dry river bed (see box, p.156).

Local Nama folklore has it that the deep meanders of the canyon were formed by the death throes of a giant snake killed by their warriors because it had been preying on their livestock. Modern science has a less evocative and more prosaic explanation, and one that stretches over millennia, starting when sediment and volcanic rock deposited around 1.8 billion years ago began to metamorphose under pressure. Around 700 million years ago, doleritic magma forced its way through fissures in the ground, forming the black dolerite dykes you can see today streaking the canyon walls. Periods of tectonic upheaval, the formation of a shallow sea, glaciation and erosion followed, creating much of the dramatic gorge visible today.

It was only around fifty million years ago that the **Fish River** began to flow, further deepening the tortuous ravine. Nowadays, the river only runs for a couple of months a year at the end of the rainy season (assuming sufficient rain); it is soon reduced to a trickle and most months merely consists of pools of water, which feed the occasionally sighted hardy populations of klipspringer, Hartmann's mountain zebra and kudu, as well as the more ubiquitous baboons and rock hyrax. Some of the pools contain sizeable fish. This precious water source in such an arid region was known to Stone Age peoples, as several **archeological sites** have been found in the canyon.

The canyon's main **viewpoint** is 10km west of the park entrance. From here you can drive or walk northwards a couple of kilometres to Hikers' Viewpoint, which marks the start of the five-day trail and offers a different perspective on the canyon. The other two viewpoints involve longer drives southwards (signposted off the main access road) and are only possible in 4WD: the first is to Sulphur Springs (6km), and the second is to Eagle's Rock (another 6km).

|Ai-|Ais Hot Springs Spa

At the southern end of the Fish River Canyon • Sunrise to sunset • N$80/person plus N$10/vehicle (also valid for the Fish River Canyon viewpoint at Hobas) • ☎ 063 262045

Spread out across the valley floor, and hemmed in by steep rock, |Ai-|Ais Hot Springs Spa marks the end of the five-day canyon hike (see box, p.156). As such, it's the perfect place to soak your aching limbs, either in the lovely hot outdoor pool, or in the slightly disappointing indoor whirlpools and jacuzzis, where not all the nozzles work. There's also a massage parlour on site. The outdoor pool, though lacking much shade, is open all night too – a magical place to float on your back as you gaze at the stars. In season, the more energetic can also walk a few kilometres back along the canyon to get a taste of the trail.

FISH RIVER CANYON

[1] Start of the Fish River Hiking Trail
Hiker's Viewpoint
Hell's Bend
Main Viewpoint
MET Office
[3] NWR Office
Sulphur Springs Viewpoint
Sulphur Springs
Table Mountain (845m)
Eagle's Rock
Bushy Corner
Three Sisters
Four Fingers Rock
German Soldier's Grave
Emergency Exit
Kanebis River Track
Fool's Gold Corner
[6] |AI-|AIS-RICHTERSVELD TRANSFRONTIER PARK

■ ACCOMMODATION
NWR |Ai-|Ais Hot Springs Spa	6
Canyon Lodge	5
Canyon Roadhouse	2
Canyon Village	4
Fish River Lodge	1
Hobas Campsite	3

0 — 10 kilometres

N

▼ Orange River (66km)

3

HIKING THE CANYON

For a totally different perspective on this giant chasm in the Earth's crust, you need to **hike into the canyon**. The classic route is a four- to five-day, 85km hike, which has the reputation of being one of southern Africa's most challenging trails. It is not to be embarked upon lightly, as you have to carry all your gear, scramble over boulders, trudge through sand and – at certain times of the year – wade through the river numerous times. Moreover, you only have two emergency exit tracks out of the canyon, once down in the bottom. There are one or two slightly easier ways to experience the valley floor, though none could be classified as a stroll in the park, since even the day-trip hike into the gorge involves a near-sheer descent and ascent, taking several hours, and walking in extreme temperatures for much of the season.

The *Fish River Lodge* offers several day- and multi-day **guided excursions** into the canyon for 2–10 people (W fishriverlodge-namibia.com; N$11,200/person for a four-night hike). Their guided version of the five-day hike (as well as shorter hiking options) also means your luggage is transported along the way and the cooking is done for you. If you just want a taster of the riverbed, they have 4WD access from the western edge of the rim, so you can be driven down to explore the rock pools on foot. Alternatively, you can hike down (and back if you still have the legs for it) in a day (N$1150/person). Gondwana also offers a multi-day hike (mid-April to mid-Sept) along the northern reaches of the canyon (W gondwana-collection.com; N$2000) covering 32km over three days, with four nights camping, including one at base camp. The advantage of the Gondwana and *Fish River Lodge* trails, beyond the fact that your gear is carried for you, is that the meals are far more appetizing: a chef's campfire creations rather than the pot-noodle feasts of the backpacking trail.

PRACTICALITIES

Because of the extreme **temperatures** in the canyon (temperatures can rise into the forties in the summer months), hikes can only be attempted between May 1 and September 15, though at either end of this period temperatures can still be debilitating. NWR **permits** cost N$330 per person, available from the NWR office in Windhoek (W nwr.com.na; see box, p.94) upon presentation of a signed medical certificate (provided by them) that is no older than forty days. **Park fees** (N$80/person per day) are payable at the MET office in Windhoek in advance or at the park entrance. **Hiking groups** must comprise at least three people, and there is a limit of thirty people on the trail per day. Remember to use biodegradable soap, and take water-purifying tablets. A one-way shuttle can take you back to Hobas from |Ai-|Ais at the end of the trail (N$120/person).

ARRIVAL AND INFORMATION

THE FISH RIVER CANYON

By car There is no public transport that goes anywhere near the canyon. In your own vehicle the easiest way to visit is via the park entrance at Hobas, signposted off the C37, the main dirt road that runs down the eastern side of the canyon (accessible in a saloon car in the dry season), around 15–20km from the canyon itself. Hobas has a shop and the MET office, where you can get your park permit. Note that the *Canyon Roadhouse* 13km north of the turn-off to the canyon on the C37 operates a petrol station.

On a tour Several tour companies in Windhoek (see p.92) include the Fish River Canyon on their itinerary. The Gondwana Collection lodges also organize guided excursions to the canyon (see opposite).

Tourist information There is an information centre at the main viewpoint at the canyon rim, which gives details on the geology, flora and fauna, and the human history of the Fish River Canyon.

ACCOMMODATION

Fish River Lodge Western rim of Fish River Canyon ☎ 063 683005 (lodge) or ☎ 061 228104 (reservations), W fishriverlodge-namibia.com. Boasting the ultimate infinity pool on the canyon rim, this thoughtfully designed lodge comprises twenty chalets (including doubles, triples and family rooms) that blend in superbly with their rocky surroundings, maximizing the beauty of the location with private decks overlooking the gorge and lots of light.

Various activities exploring the canyon are on offer, plus there is a masseuse on hand to help soothe aching limbs. 4WD needed to get there. DBB **N$3056**

Hobas Campsite NWR Hobas park entrance, 10km east of the canyon rim ☎ 063 266028 (campground) or ☎ 061 2857200 (reservations), W nwr.com.na. Fifteen pitches located within striking distance of the canyon means this place fills up quickly. You need to be here early to bag one of the nicer, shadier spots by the dry riverbed at the far end of the camp. All sites have the usual braai facilities and electricity, and there's a pool-sized swimming pool – enough to bring the body temperature down in the summer. Simple two-bed bush chalets and a restaurant are currently under construction. The camp shop (daily 7am–7pm) has limited supplies but does stock wood and firelighters, and serves snacks and hot drinks. Camping per person N$170, chalet B&B N$1760

NWR |Ai-|Ais Hot Springs Spa |Ai-|Ais, west end of the C10 ☎ 063 262045 (resort) or ☎ 061 2857200 (reservations), ⊛ nwr.com.na. Doubles are large and comfortable, with huge bathrooms and semi-private balconies opening onto a steep rock face; the slightly pricier river-view rooms have a more pleasant vista across the tree-studded campground (though many of the pitches lack sufficient shade). Even better value are the two-bedroom self-catering bungalows, which come with an enormous kitchen-dining-lounge area with TV and music system as well as a large patio and braai area, plus a private hot-tub. The downside is the catering: the restaurant serves overpriced buffet breakfasts (N$150) and indifferent dinners (N$230); à la carte is only available at lunchtime. Anyone self-catering should get supplies elsewhere if possible, as the shop is often low on stock. Rates exclude park fees. Camping per person N$190, doubles B&B N$1320, bungalows per person N$910

Gondwana Canyon Park

3

Comprising 1300 square kilometres of private reserve, the **Gondwana Canyon Park** is contiguous with the eastern flank of the |Ai-|Ais/Richtersveld Transfrontier Park and therefore provides a great base for exploring the canyon in relative comfort from one of the Gondwana Collection's lodgings. In the twenty years since it was formed from a collection of struggling sheep farms, the land has made a remarkable recovery. There are now small populations of zebra, kudu, springbok, oryx, hartebeest and wildebeest, but it is the wilderness landscape that is truly captivating.

ARRIVAL AND ACTIVITIES

GONDWANA CANYON PARK

By car With no public transport available, you need to have your own vehicle, though 2WD is adequate.
Activities All the accommodation options offer a guided excursion to the Fish River Canyon (3hr; N$750/person). In addition, you can sign up for enjoyable sunrise or sundowner walks, and don't miss the wonderful hike up the escarpment at the back of the *Canyon Village* (guided or self-guided), which affords spectacular views across the distant Huns Mountains.

ACCOMMODATION AND EATING

All accommodation in the park is owned and managed by the Gondwana Collection and is of good quality with excellent customer service, though each option is distinctive in style. Accommodation is around 20km east of the canyon.

★ **Canyon Lodge** 3km along the dirt road, signposted east off the C37, 6km south of the turn-off to the Fish River Canyon ☎ 063 693014 (lodge) or ☎ 061 427200 (reservations), ⊛ gondwana-collection.com; map p.155. The choice accommodation in the area, comprising over thirty chalets nestled among large granite boulders, with lush lawns (using recycled water) dotted with camelthorn trees. Chalets 25 and 28 offer the best views. Behind the old farmhouse, where excellent buffet food is served (dinner N$250), a delightful terrace is shaded by a huge pepper tree. Top of the treats, though, is the infinity pool set apart from the lodge, overlooking the desert plains – an idyllic spot for a sundowner. B&B N$3256

Canyon Roadhouse On the C37, 13km northeast of the turn-off to the Fish River Canyon ☎ 063 683111 (lodge) or ☎ 061 427200 (reservations), ⊛ gondwana -collection.com; map p.155. Wacky place that makes an ideal lunch stop amid the quiver trees and antique cars. Light soups, salads and toasties are just some of the offerings, but the chef's selection for dessert is a must. Tucked round the back are a dozen tidy twin rooms, plus there's a small pool. The campground boasts superior washing facilities, though some sites lack shade. Restaurant 7–9am, 10am–5pm & 6–8.30pm. Camping per person N$175, doubles B&B N$2280

Canyon Village 1.5km along the dirt road, signposted east off the C37, 6km south of the turn-off to the Fish River Canyon ☎ 063 693025 (lodge) or ☎ 061 427200 (reservations), ⊛ gondwana-collection.com; map p.155. Have your luggage delivered to your chalet by horse and cart in this folksy, themed lodge that is popular with German tour groups. Colourful historical murals portray "traditional" Nama life, and the bougainvillea-decorated terrace affords lovely views across a developing indigenous garden to the impressive escarpment beyond – a morning climb is a must, followed by a cool-off in the decent-sized pool. N$2280

To the South African border

South of Keetmanshoop the relentless B1 skirts the forbidding Great ||Karas Mountains to the east for about 100km, while the sibling Little ||Karas Mountains keep their distance, west of the flat, sandy valley that separates the two ranges. A couple of hours' drive south, the road divides at **GRÜNAU**, a small, predominantly Nama and Afrikaner settlement of a few hundred. Of interest to the weary traveller is the roadside petrol station, just north of the junction, which can also provide an injection of caffeine. Despite its seeming insignificance on the ground, Grünau marks an important crossroads: north, the B1 heads towards Windhoek and beyond; west, a gravel road leads to the Fish River Canyon, while south, the B1 continues another 140km to the 24-hour border post with South Africa at Noordoewer, then onwards to Cape Town. Turning west, just before the border, takes you on a very scenic drive along the Orange River – where you can stop off for some gentle kayaking – which meanders a further 250km until it slides into the Atlantic Ocean at Oranjemund (see p.133).

Eastwards from Grünau, the B3 follows the railway for 177km, through **Karasburg**, to the other main border post with South Africa (also 24hr), just beyond Ariamsvlei. This busy crossing serves traffic travelling between Namibia and the Johannesburg area. Karasburg, beyond being a useful refuelling pit stop, is the gateway to the important historical settlement of Warmbad, a forty-minute drive south.

On account of Grünau's strategic location, several hospitable guestfarms lie in the vicinity, providing a convenient stopover for long-distance travellers keen to break their

---

CAMPING AND HIKING IN THE |AI-|AIS/RICHTERSVELD NATIONAL PARK

Though remote and inaccessible, the **|Ai-|Ais/Richtersveld National Park** offers some starkly beautiful, rugged scenery and the opportunity to undertake some challenging wilderness hiking. Names such as Hellskloof, Skeleton Gorge, Devil's Tooth and Gorgon's Head indicate the austerity of the inhospitable brown desert mountainscape, tempered only by a broad range of hardy succulents, mighty rock formations, the magnificence of the light cast at dawn and dusk, and the glittering canopy of stars at night. It's also a place to test your 4WD skills – saloon cars are not admitted into the park – which is another reason why travelling in a convoy of at least two vehicles is advisable.

In summer, the daytime heat can be unbearable – temperatures over 50°C have been recorded – while on winter nights temperatures drop below freezing. For this reason hiking is only permitted between April and September, and only then with a guide. The **best time to visit** is usually August and September, since they are generally the peak months for the succulents to bloom.

The three multi-day hiking trails on offer are pretty tough going and should only be attempted by experienced wilderness hikers. They are: the **Vensterval Trail** (four days, three nights), the **Lelieshoek–Oemsberg Trail** (three days, two nights) and the **Kodaspiek Trail** (two days, one night). Most overnights on the trails are in the Hiking Trails Base Camp in the Ganakouriep Valley within the park, which has bunks, gas stoves, fridges and hot showers. At the time of going to press, the hikes had been suspended due to a shortage of trained guides, but to check the current status and make a reservation, contact South African National Parks (w sanparks.org).

For those less inclined to hike, there are a couple of restful camps with chalet accommodation, as well as camping pitches, and four very rudimentary and remote sites, where you can soak up the stillness and the eerie beauty of your surroundings.

PARK ENTRY

Park hours are daily 7am–6pm. Entry fees are payable in South African Rand (R210/person per day) at the park reception in Sendelingsdrift (South Africa ☎ (0)27 831506; 8am–4pm).

journey, but also worthy of longer stays. Some visitors do a day-trip to the Fish River Canyon (only 100km) from here.

ACCOMMODATION
GRÜNAU

★ Savanna Guest Farm Just off the B1, 40km north of Grünau ☎081 128 0975, ⍇savanna-guestfarm.com; map p.140. Built in the colonial era to billet German troops – the crenellations are a giveaway – this lovely stone-built working sheep farm at the foot of the ‖Karas Mountains offers modestly priced, warm hospitality in self-catering units and large double rooms. Hike round the farm, climb the kopjies, looking out for various antelope, or lounge by the heated pool. Bountiful breakfasts are provided, and hearty home-cooked candlelit dinners (on individual tables) on request. Breakfast N$80 and dinner N$160 – to be ordered in advance. Self-catering and doubles <u>N$700</u>

The White House Just off the B1, 11km north of Grünau ☎063 262061 or ☎081 285 6484, ⍇withuis@iway.na; map p.140. Visible from the B1, this gleaming white colonial farmhouse clamours for attention. Old pine floors, wide verandas and high ceilings (but with a/c) transport you back in time, as do the sagging mattresses and (in winter) heavy blankets. Located in the yard are compact, modern self-catering units and four spaces to camp. Although the pre-order dinner is tasty, it arrives with the next day's breakfast, wrapped in foil, having been prepared in the owners' kitchen 3km down the road. Activities are plentiful: birdwatching in their hides, self-guided walks, day and night farm drives, seeking out succulents, wildlife, plus a visit to a rose quartz mine. Camping per person <u>N$80</u>, self-catering units & doubles <u>N$620</u>

Karasburg

Fifty kilometres from the junction at Grünau the B3 passes through the unremarkable town of **KARASBURG**. With a population of 4000, it's the largest settlement south of Keetmanshoop, and a commercial hub for the surrounding sheep farms, yet there's still

GETTING AROUND

As stated above, ordinary cars are not allowed inside the park; the only way to explore is in a 4WD or a pick-up with a high enough clearance to handle the sandy riverbeds and rough mountain passes between the designated campsites. Pay particular attention along the track linking the Richtersberg and De Hoop campsites, which is covered with thick sand and treacherously jagged rocks.

ACCOMMODATION

It's advisable to pre-book accommodation; reservations should be made through South African National Parks in Pretoria (☎012 428 9111, ⍇sanparks.org). For camping and late bookings, contact reception directly. Camping rates below are for two people on a pitch, plus R82 per additional adult; prices are slightly higher if you want electricity (where available). For the larger chalets the park charges N$240 per extra adult. There is no restaurant in the park, but fuel (only leaded petrol and diesel) and limited supplies (cold drinks and dried and tinned food) are available at the park headquarters at Sendelingsdrift (daily 8am–4pm). Thus, it's advisable to stock up and fill up on the way, in Rosh Pinah (11km north in Namibia; see p.135), and in Alexander Bay (73km west in South Africa).

Gannakouriep Wilderness Camp Seriously remote, these two simple canvas cabins have two single beds, a solar-powered fridge, shower, a stove (no oven) and an outside braai. No power point or drinking water. Cabins <u>R895</u>

Sendelingsdrift Rest Camp By the entry gate at Sendelingsdrift. Ten decent chalets sleeping between two and four people, each equipped with a/c, fridges and stoves. There are views over the Orange River from the front porches, and a swimming pool as well as a campsite. Camping <u>R225</u>, chalets <u>R800</u>

Tatasberg Wilderness Camp Inside the park at Tatasberg, on the border. Picturesque, two-person reed cabins that come with cooking facilities, set among dramatic boulders and enjoying lovely views of the surrounding mountains. Showers are provided, but bring your own drinking water. <u>R895</u>

Wilderness camps At Kokerboomkloof, Potjiespram, Richtersberg and De Hoop. There are four very basic wilderness campgrounds with 8–18 individual sites. All have cold showers except for *Kokerboomkloof* which doesn't have showers. You'll need to bring all drinking water with you, and jerry cans can be filled at Sendelingsdrift. <u>R225</u>

3

3

THE BORDER WITH SOUTH AFRICA

There are four **border posts** with South Africa along the Orange River. By far the most important one is on the B1, 2km south of Noordoewer (signposted to Vioolsdrift, if you're approaching from South Africa). As the major transit point between Cape Town and Windhoek, it is open 24 hours. Two minor border posts lie some distance away either side: 160km due east, reached via the gravel C10 from Karasburg, is the **Velloorsdrift** border (Onseepkans, on the South African side; daily 8am–4.30pm), whereas around 100km due northwest, the border post at **Sendelingsdrift** (daily Sept to March 8am–4.30pm, April to Aug 7am–3.30pm) lies on the western limit of the |Ai-|Ais/Richtersveld Transfrontier Park, and at the only entrance into the park on the South African side. The Sendelingsdrift border is crossed on a pontoon ferry (N$160 single, N$270 return), which does not operate if there are strong winds, or high water levels. It is therefore advisable to ring and check in advance (Namibia ☎ 063 274760; South Africa ☎ (0)27 8312203). The fourth border post straddles the mouth of the river between the two diamond-mining towns of **Alexander Bay** (South Africa) and **Oranjemund** (daily 6am–10pm). Note that visitors arriving from South Africa can continue to spend Rand in Namibia; however, if you're crossing into South Africa, your Namibian dollars will no longer be accepted.

not much to it. Once boasting the busiest railway station in southern Namibia, the town has been struggling since the trains stopped to Upington in the Northern Cape, though with two large supermarkets and several petrol stations, it's an important pit stop for truck drivers travelling to and from South Africa, and handy for travellers too. Town morale was dealt a further blow in 2010, when Karasburg's municipal status was revoked on account of spiralling council debts, epitomized by the headline-grabbing news that they could not afford to buy a ceremonial chain for the mayor.

ACCOMMODATION   **KARASBURG**

Amega B&B 110 7th Ave ☎ 063 270054; map p.140. Three basic, inexpensive fan-ventilated doubles and two family rooms (but no half-price rates for children), with tea/coffee-making facilities and a braai area. Perfect if you've arrived late and need somewhere to lay your head for the night. Doubles B&B N$700

Warmbad

Just under 50km south of Karasburg lies the forlorn, parched settlement of **WARMBAD** (|Aixa-aibes), home to the Nama ‡Gami-!un, more widely referred to as the Bondelswarts. The Nama were already well established, successfully rearing cattle and hunting game, before Jacobus Coetzee rolled up in 1760 and decide to call the place Warmbad. The name in both languages, however, refers to the area's **hot springs**, which, together with the presence of the Hom River, were key to human settlement here. The hot springs, around which spa facilities have recently been built, constitute the area's main attraction. However, the spa has already fallen into disrepair, with the restored sandstone gateway of the old German fort in better condition. Warmbad's only site is a small **museum**; if it's closed, and you can't contact the curator, try the library to find someone to open up and show you round – it's worth the effort. The spa hotel (no number) and restaurant are said to open up periodically, predominantly at weekends. The bottom line is that if you have time on your hands, your own transport, and are interested in history, then it's worth detouring to Warmbad to try your luck; otherwise, wait for better times.

Brief history

A renowned centre of Nama resistance to both German and South African colonizers (see p.343 & p.347), and home to the country's first Christian church in 1806, Warmbad is an important historical site. It lay on a major colonial-era trading route to and from the Cape Colony, but, once by-passed by the road and rail links further north, its star began to fade. These days, the population struggles to survive on subsistence goat farming, pensions, or remittances from other family members, though a nearby tantalite mine provides some formal employment. Attempts by government in 2006 to reinvigorate the economy through tourism have foundered: several million Namibian dollars were spent on establishing a spa round the thermal baths – having brought them back off a private investor – and a country lodge, building tourist bungalows and converting the old German's officers' quarters into a restaurant. But with a rudderless community – they have failed to agree on a kaptein since the previous one passed away several years ago – and a lack of trained personnel, most structures are already falling into disrepair.

The museum

Behind the new library · Mon–Fri 9am–5pm, Sat 9am–1pm · N$10 · ☎ 081 205 7504 (Custodian Loraine Rooi)

The town's small **museum** is housed in the old prison, where many of the Bondelwarts who were arrested after their failed insurgence against the South African regime in 1922 were incarcerated. Indeed, Nama uprisings are the subject of many of the rather musty exhibits – colonial maps, German weaponry, Nama genealogies and even the old telephone exchange – the significance of which only become apparent on a guided tour.

The Orange River

Marking the border with South Africa, the **Orange River** – sometimes referred to by its Nama name, Gariep – carves its way west through ancient rock to the Atlantic. Just before the border post on the B1 (see box opposite), the tarred C13 heads west to Aussenker, 50km downriver. The settlement is surrounded by a vast and ever-expanding emerald carpet of grape farms, which provides a striking contrast to the otherwise desolate but scenic desert hinterland. Many of the reed huts empty at the end of the grape harvest in December, with workers mainly from northern Namibia returning the following June.

In the dry season in particular, it's easy to be put off by the barren landscape, though the verdant ranks of grapes, butternut and peppers hint at the lush riverine

---

CANOEING ON THE ORANGE RIVER

Using inflatable "croc" rafts or two-person Mohawk fibreglass canoes, several outfits offer multi-day **canoe trips** down the Orange River: paddle through dramatic scenery, enjoy excellent campfire cooking and sleep out under the stars. Watch out for the Cape clawless otter cavorting in the water or the aggressive Cape monitor slithering along the riverbank.

The two operators listed below are experienced, with excellent reputations, and can rent out camping equipment. Over the Noordoewer border in South Africa, Bushwhacked Outdoor Adventures (🖳 bushwhacked.co.za) and Umkulu (🖳 orangeriverrafting.com) run similar operations. Since all these companies cater primarily to school groups and South African families, high-season prices coincide with South African school holidays (generally Sept to mid-Oct, mid-Dec to mid-Jan and over Easter), when the camp accommodation (see p.162) is usually booked up, and you'd be well advised to stay clear of the mayhem. You can also organize to go canoeing for a day – usually spending about four hours on the river – at short notice. Prices given below are for high season, per person for two people; the price goes down for larger groups.

Amanzi Trails 15km west of the B1, signposted off the C13 after 11km ☎ 063 297255, 🖳 amanzitrails.co.za. The standard four-day fully inclusive canoe trip costs N$4200/person, but if you're feeling less energetic, a half-day paddle from the bridge at Noordoewer back down to camp will give you a taster (N$350), or you can rent a canoe to

paddle around near the camp.
Felix Unite 10km west of the B1, along the C13 ☎ (0)87 345 0578 (South Africa), 🖳 felixunite.com. Offers half-day excursions (around four hours' paddling, no refreshments included), and four- and six-day camping and canoeing trips on set dates. Half-day trip N$430/person; four-day trip N$4495/person.

environment that lies beyond. Reed-lined banks hide warblers and fluorescent bishops, while kingfishers, fish eagles, cormorants, darters and herons gorge on the fish-rich waters. On the opposite bank, in South Africa, a metamorphic escarpment overlooking the river provides a picturesque backdrop, making it a perfect spot to enjoy a day or more of birdwatching or canoeing (see p.161).

Noordoewer

Blink and you'll miss the ramshackle collection of houses and sandy tracks that constitutes **NOORDOEWER**. Signposted to the west off the C13, it lies nearer to Cape Town than to Windhoek, just under 800km away. This small settlement has grown as Namibians have migrated here from across the country in search of work on the lush fruit and vegetable farms that line this section of the Orange River. Here you'll find a bank, a bottle store and a small supermarket with limited offerings, and very little fresh produce. The *Noordoewer Guesthouse* (see below) also operates a farm shop, where you can stock up on biltong, home-made biscuits and preserves. The overall message, though, is to get supplies elsewhere if you are intending to self-cater here.

ARRIVAL AND DEPARTURE

By car Noordoewer is 2km north of the border with South Africa, just west of the B1 at the junction with the tarred C13. If you're going to the river camps, fill up at the petrol stations on the B1 (both with ATMs), and continue down the C13; the camps are well signposted from the B1/C13 junction and accessible in a 2WD.

THE ORANGE RIVER

By bus The Intercape Mainliner bus (ⓦ intercape.co.za) between Windhoek and Cape Town drops off and picks up passengers at the border (to Cape Town: Mon, Tues, Thurs & Sat; 12hr. To Windhoek: Tues, Thurs, Fri & Sat; 10hr 20min). Both canoe operators (see box, p.161) can arrange a pick-up/drop off at the bus stop for N\$300 per shuttle.

ACCOMMODATION

Even if you don't intend to paddle on the water, it's worth travelling the extra kilometres to the nicer riverside camps. Otherwise, the two places to stay in Noordoewer are perfectly comfortable, though you can hear the intermittent rumbling of trucks on the main road.

IN NOORDOEWER

Noordoewer Guesthouse On the C13, 200m from the junction with the B1, by the Engen garage ☎ 063 297496, ⓦ noordoewerguesthouse.com; map p.140. The restaurant terrace overlooks the vineyard at the back, while the rooms have sliding glass doors that open out onto private porches around an unprepossessing yard. The rooms themselves are well appointed – especially the new ones by the pool below the restaurant terrace – and have a modern, sophisticated feel. N\$990

Orange River Lodge On the B1, by the Shell station, 1km north of the border ☎ 063 297012, ⓦ orlodge .iway.na; map p.140. Light and airy tiled rooms (with a/c) accommodate couples and families and open out onto a small, grassy garden with splash pool. There's a noisy macaw on the terrace and a small bar-restaurant. Breakfast costs an extra N\$50/person. N\$700

ALONG THE ORANGE RIVER

★**Amanzi Trails River Camp** 15km west of the B1, signposted off the C13 after 11km ☎ 063 297255, ⓦ amanzitrails.co.za; map p.140. This quiet riverside spot boasts prolific birdlife and is immaculately kept, with spacious, shady, flat grassy camping pitches, electricity and

sheltered braai sites, protected from the wind by cane divides. There's a bar, where breakfast can be pre-ordered and braai packs purchased, but if you don't want to cook at night you'll need to drive down the road to the restaurant at Felix Unite's *Provenance Camp*. A tent with bedding can be provided if you don't have your own. Camping per person N\$140 and per vehicle N\$50, chalet N\$590

Provenance Camp Felix Unite, 10km west of the B1, along the C13 ☎ 063 297161, ⓦ felixunite.com; map p.140. Popular with overlander groups, this efficient and friendly camp-cum-resort comprises 20 nicely furnished rustic stone-and-thatch chalets with a/c and fan, fridge and tea-making facilities, each with private patio and seating overlooking the river. Chalets 5–9 are the most secluded and have the best views. Highlights include a riverside swimming pool and sun-lounging area plus an open-sided bar area, complete with pool table. Good camping facilities are also available. There's an ATM, camp shop and restaurant (daily 7–10am & noon–10pm), with a small but varied menu, including burgers, salads and pastas (N\$60–90) and a handful of more substantial dishes (around N\$140). Camping per person N\$160, chalets for two (room only) N\$1085, family chalets N\$1825

To the Botswana border

After snaking its way through the Eros Mountains east of Windhoek, past the airport – after which the traffic drops off – the B6 straightens and flattens out, heading for **Gobabis**, Namibia's last sizeable town of note before the Botswana border some 316km away on the western fringes of the Kalahari. The B6 forms part of the Trans Kalahari Highway, the paved road that continues eastwards across the desert to **Gaborone** (around 800km), the capital of Botswana, with onward connections to South Africa. It's a dull slog through dry, dusty and fairly featureless thornveld, unless there's been some seasonal rain to soften the harsh landscape. The only relief comes from the occasional wildlife sighting: a troop of baboons lolloping over the road, a family of warthogs scuttling away from the wide trimmed verges, or a swooping hornbill heading for a tree. On the way, branching off south of the main road, there is a handful of **guestfarms**, as well as Namibia's longest **cave** system.

Arnhem Cave

124km east of Windhoek, off the D1801, on a private farm • Weekends and holiday periods, tours at 9am & 3pm; weekdays by appointment • N$150 (short tour); N$250 (long tour) • ☎ 062 581885 • No public transport • Turn south onto the M51 just after Hosea Kutako International Airport, then after 66km turn left onto the D1506 (10km), and then right onto the D1801, where it is signposted from the road

If exploring subterranean bat-infested chambers appeals, then a visit to **Arnhem Cave** makes for a worthwhile day or overnight excursion from Windhoek, or a diversion en route to Botswana. This system of narrow tunnels and large caverns was formed through solution of dolomitic limestone between layers of quartzite and shale, which then collapsed; the result is the country's longest known cave system, at over 4.5km. While the absence of stalagmites, stalactites and other such interesting features might disappoint casual visitors, bat enthusiasts will be well satisfied. Six species cling to the caves and passageways, including the largest insectivorous chiropteran, the giant leaf-nosed bat (*Hipposidrus vittatus*), which has a wingspan of over 60cm. You're likely to see or feel them whizzing past your face at close quarters, though their honed echo-location skills should ensure no physical encounters. Other smaller residents of the caves include various beetles, spiders, false scorpions and shrews.

Once "discovered" in 1930, the cave was initially heavily mined for guano, and although it is still periodically harvested for use as fertilizer, tonnes of the substance still remain below ground. Tours can last two to three hours, depending on levels of interest; although no crawling on your hands and knees is necessary to explore the underground labyrinth, you should wear old clothes and closed shoes, and perhaps a handkerchief to protect your mouth as it is usually very dusty. Torches can be rented on site.

ACCOMMODATION · ARNHEM CAVE

Arnhem Cave Restcamp On the D1801, 57km south of the B6 ☎ 062 581885, ⓦ facebook.com/arnhem cavelodge. The farm has a pleasant shady restcamp with four neat fan-ventilated thatched chalets with fridges and braai, or camping under camelthorn trees (electricity and hot water). The pleasant pool set in a grassy lawn is kept well trimmed by resident livestock. Tasty farm-cooked meals are available but need to be pre-booked well in advance. Camping per person N$130, chalets N$700

Eningu Clayhouse Lodge 65km southeast of the airport, just south of the junction between the D1471 and the M51 ☎ 062 581880 (lodge) or ☎ 064 464144 (reservations), ⓦ eningulodge.com. Often a stopover at the beginning or end of a tour, this delightfully original lodge is a great spot to unwind for a couple of nights, offering unusual diversions: archery, volleyball and badminton; a visit to a renowned local sculptor; a nature trail and bird hide overlooking an illuminated waterhole, where porcupines are frequent visitors; plus a large-ish sparkling swimming pool. Arnhem Cave is also nearby. Use of clay bricks makes for cool, fan-ventilated rooms, with hand-painted stone floors and various arty touches. Inventive, healthy dining. Airport transfers possible. DBB N$2720

Kiripotib Farm

10km east along the D1448, from the junction with the C15 (M33) · **Shop and workshop** Mon–Sat 8am–4pm · ⓦ kirikara.com

There's a surprising amount of activity at the isolated **Kiripotib Farm**, which as well as offering a pleasant overnight stay is a great place to stop for lunch, if you're heading south into the Kalahari. The main draw is the karakul weaving workshop, where you can watch the workers in action at the spinning wheel or loom, though the rosy-faced lovebirds flitting round the shady trees are also engaging. One of the owners is a goldsmith, and has her atelier on the premises; some of her designs, along with weavings and other high-quality crafts from various parts of Africa, can be found in the craft gallery and shop. Advance notice for visits is preferred, though there's usually someone around if you drop in. There's also an observatory on site, which attracts keen astronomers.

ACCOMMODATION   KIRIPOTIB FARM

Kiripotib Guest Farm ☎ 062 581419, ⓦ kiripotib .com. Comfortable, reasonably priced accommodation is in light airy rooms, with front porch, or slightly more private brick chalets overlooking the flat savannah. The pleasant restaurant sits under a lapa and there's a swimming pool. Guided walks and sundowner drives are possible, or even a day's gliding. B&B Doubles **N$2100**, chalets **N$2650**

Gobabis

Namibia's only sizeable town on the B6 between Windhoek and the Botswana border, **GOBABIS** has an estimated population of about 20,000. It's the administrative centre of the Omaheke Region – a broad expanse of flat sandveld, as the Otjiherero name indicates, which historically has been home to the Mbanderu and the Ju|wa San. The statue of the gleaming white Brahman bull at the town entrance announcing "Cattle Country" alerts you to the main business of Gobabis, which is further reinforced by billboards and signs relating to abattoirs and butcheries, though the nickname "Little Texas" might be stretching matters somewhat. Still, Friday is cattle auction day, when the place is really humming with activity.

Gobabis is thought to be a corruption of a Khoekhoegowab name that means either "elephant's lick" or "place of strife". Certainly, the area has seen plenty of conflict over the years: between Khoikhoi and Mbanderu, then the indigenous populations and the Germans colonists – who made Gobabis a garrison settlement – who, in turn, were later replaced by the South Africans.

As you enter the town, the main road morphs briefly into an attractive tree-lined quasi-boulevard with a surprising number of four-way stops, where the main supermarkets, banks and petrol stations are located. There's also a pretty pink Catholic church at the western edge of the main street. The once bustling information centre, accommodation and restaurant at the Ui Wilderness Centre – also on the main street – has not really recovered from a fire and is only partially functioning. The town's museum has also been closed for a couple of years, and the **Omaheke San Craft Centre**, on Roosevelt St, which is well worth dropping in on, has irregular hours.

ARRIVAL AND INFORMATION   GOBABIS

By car It's an easy two-hour drive along the B6, a good tarred road from Windhoek, or along the Trans Kalahari Highway all the way to/from Gaborone.

By shared taxi Shared taxis (N$120/person) leave when full from the town centre bound for Windhoek when full.

By bus The two long-distance weekly bus services between Windhoek and Gaborone will drop off or pick up passengers in Gobabis en route, but you need to get in touch in advance (Monnakgotla Transport ☎ 081 213 5138, ⓦ monnakgotla.co.bw; Tok Tokkie Shuttle ☎ 061 300743, ⓦ shuttlesnamibia.com).

Tourist information The friendly Ui Wilderness Centre (☎ 062 564743) on the main street has an office and a small café (where you can get a cup of coffee, but not much else). It can provide some information on the area, and can organize a guide to help you explore. Mon–Fri 8am–5pm, Sat 8am–1pm.

CROSSING INTO BOTSWANA

The border post at **Buitepos** lies 316km east of Windhoek, and 111km east of Gobabis. Hours are daily 7am–midnight, though don't forget Namibia's daylight saving – first Sunday in April to the first Sunday in September – makes these times an hour earlier. However, even if the border is open late, it's inadvisable to be travelling onward in the dark on account of the dangers of hitting wildlife, especially in unfenced Botswana. While the Namibian side of the border offers overnight accommodation at the *East Gate Rest Camp* (see below), the nearest place to park up in Botswana is Ghanzi, 210km away, so make sure you fill the tank in Namibia if you're heading that way.

Don't forget that if you're entering Namibia with a car registered outside the country, you'll need to pay approximately N$159 road tax to **import your vehicle** into Namibia. Conversely, if you are entering Botswana with a Namibian-registered vehicle, similar costs will have to be met in Pula (see p.48). In addition, if the vehicle is rented, you'll need to have informed the rental firm in advance and paid the relevant supplement. The Botswana firm Monnakgotla Transport, and the Namibian firm Tok Tokkie Shuttle both run weekly bus services between Windhoek and Gaborone, Botswana (see opposite).

3

ACCOMMODATION

East Gate Rest Camp 400m before the border ☎ 062 560405, 🌐 eastgate-namibia.com. This is the place to crash near the border. A predominantly self-catering restcamp – with grassy campgrounds (or a bush camp) and cabins that share ablutions, and well-equipped bungalows for two or four. It may be short on style, but it is inexpensive and has all the basics you might need: restaurant, shop, fuel station and a pool to wash off the desert dust. They'll even exchange limited amounts of currency. Camping per person N$120, cabins N$200, bungalows N$750

ACCOMMODATION

Goba Lodge Well signposted north off the B6, 1km west of Gobabis ☎ 062 564499, 🌐 goba.iway.na. There's no real reason to stay in Gobabis, but if you do get stuck here, this very pleasant lodge (with cheaper restcamp rooms) on the edge of town has a friendly vibe, and is a good deal. Rooms have all the conveniences, the restaurant is fine, and the place possesses a small pool, plus neat gardens overrun with guinea fowl. N$340

Central-northern Namibia

ROCK ENGRAVINGS AT TWYFELFONTEIN

Central-northern Namibia

Central-northern Namibia, encompassing large chunks of Otjozondjupa, Erongo and Kunene regions, contains some of the country's most compelling natural landscapes, where a range of comfortable lodges and campgrounds makes the most of the dramatic scenery. To the west, gravel roads wend their way through an impressive array of striking geological formations, containing some of the finest examples of ancient rock art, towards remote wilderness areas, where desert-adapted elephant and rhino roam. In contrast, Namibia's main artery, the B1, speeds due north from Windhoek, through more vegetated, flatter terrain. After 250km, on the eastern limit of the Central Highlands, you reach Namibia's very own table mountain, the majestic sandstone Waterberg Plateau, presiding above the savannah plains, which are prime cheetah country.

Heading north from Namibia's capital city, the B1 passes through the historically important town of **Okahandja**, before streaking through endless savannah plains. Several large **private reserves** in this region contain healthy populations of large mammals, though arguably the biggest attraction, some three hours' drive north of Windhoek, is the **Waterberg Plateau**; an impressive sandstone escarpment, and scenic national park, it is a nurturing ground for rare animal species, such as black rhino and sable antelope. The surrounding bush is also cheetah country, with the nearby **Cheetah Conservation Fund centre** a compulsory detour if you're interested in these majestic felines. At **Otjiwarongo**, the regional capital of Otjozondjupa, the road divides: heading northwest along the C38 takes you to the small farming town of **Outjo**, an increasingly popular staging post for forays into Etosha National Park, whereas the B1 veers northeast towards the former mining centres of **Tsumeb**, **Grootfontein** and **Otavi**, otherwise known as the **Triangle**, which possess a handful of low-key attractions, including the world's largest extra-terrestrial rock, the **Hoba Meteorite**, set against the attractive backdrop of the **Otavi Mountains**.

Northwest of Windhoek, the landscape becomes decidedly drier and harsher as you head into flat semi-desert savannah, out of which rise dramatic granite inselbergs produced through volcanic activity millions of years ago: the domed **Erongo Mountains**, the distinctive **Spitzkoppe**, and the vast, brooding **Brandberg**, which shelters thousands of stunning **rock paintings** and boasts impressive biodiversity and endemism. All three areas contain fascinating rock formations and superb **hiking** terrain. Moving further north into southern Kunene, you reach the globally significant collection of San rock engravings at **Twyfelfontein**, located in a hauntingly beautiful landscape. The scenery continues to impress as the road carves its way through the flat-topped basalt plateaus of **northern Damaraland**, though visitors are often drawn more by the prospect of encounters with **free-roaming elephant** and **black rhino** in the area's dry river beds.

SPITZKOPPE CAMPSITE, DAMARALAND

Highlights

❶ Waterberg Plateau This splendid and luxuriant sandstone escarpment, hosting abundant birdlife, offers great savannah views from the plateau top. **See p.174**

❷ Erongo Mountains A sprinkling of rustic campsites, homely guestfarms and comfortable lodges offer the perfect base for exploring these slabs of burnished granite. **See p.190**

❸ Brandberg The country's largest massif, containing the highest peak, looms out of the desert landscape; a challenging hike rewarded

by pristine rock paintings, quiver trees and stunning vistas. **See p.193**

❹ Twyfelfontein Learn the secret meanings of ancient rock engravings on an informative guided tour. **See p.195**

❺ Ugab Terraces Scenically eroded flat-topped pillars and mini table mountains make a great day-trip. **See p.199**

❻ Desert-adapted wildlife Several lodges and wilderness camps in Damaraland offer the chance to get close to desert-adapted rhino and elephant. **See p.201**

HIGHLIGHTS ARE MARKED ON THE MAP ON P.170

The road north

As Windhoek continues to expand northwards, the town of **Okahandja**, 70km away, seems ever nearer, an impression likely to be felt more strongly once the interminable road-widening project between the two urban centres is complete. Once past Okahandja, where the two nearby resorts of **Gross Barmen** and **Von Bach Dam** attract Windhoek's middle classes at weekends, urban life is left behind; the traffic thins out and the land flattens out as the savannah takes over once more. The B1 speeds northwards with scarcely a bend in sight for the next 180km, before

■ ACCOMMODATION		
Aloegrove Safari lodge	7	
Bambatsi Guest Farm	2	
Brandberg Restcamp	18	
Dâureb Isib	20	
Damara Mopane Lodge	1	
Erindi Private Game Reserve	21	
Frans Indongo Lodge	3	
Gross Barmen	24	
iGowati Country Hotel	5	
Khorixas Restcamp	6	
Mount Etjo Safari Lodge	14	
NWR Waterberg Camp	10	
Okonjima	12	
Otjihaenameparero	17	
Ozongwindi	22	
Tungeni Von Bach Resort	23	
Ugab River Camp	13	
Ugab Terrace Lodge	4	
Ugab Wilderness Camp	15	
Vingerklip Lodge	8	
Waterberg Guest Farm	11	
Waterberg Wilderness Lodge	9	
White Lady B&B	19	
White Lady Lodge	16	

HIGHLIGHTS

1 Waterberg Plateau
2 Erongo Mountains
3 Brandberg
4 Twyfelfontein
5 Ugab Terraces
6 Desert-adapted wildlife

CENTRAL-NORTHERN NAMIBIA

eventually arriving at the next main town, and capital of the **Otjozondjupa Region**, **Otjiwarongo**. As you driving north, you'll notice the landscape transitioning into thornbush savannah, with taller shrubs and trees and denser cover than is evident in southern Namibia, due to the relatively higher levels of rainfall and more fertile soil. Termite mounds are visible along this stretch of road too, and families of warthogs are often to be seen at dusk.

Okahandja and around

An hour's drive north of Windhoek, where the main road divides – continuing north as the B1, and veering off west to the coast as the B2 – sits the important historical town of **OKAHANDJA**. Its 24,000-strong population is rapidly expanding, bolstered by growth in light industry, the relocation here of some government offices, and an improving road link with Windhoek, which is making it a commuter town for the capital.

Okahandja has a long history of trade and strategic importance. The Herero were the first to settle here, around 1800, before it later became an important mission station and trading post, as well as a site of conflict between the Herero and Nama, and later, the Germans. Today the town is still the administrative centre of the Herero people, as well as containing the burial sites of many of their former chiefs, notably Samuel Maharero, who led the uprising against the German colonial forces (see p.344), and Hosea Kutako, a pivotal figure in the independence movement (see p.348). These and others are honoured in the annual **Herero Day commemoration** (see box, p.70). Jonker Afrikaner, the Orlaam-Nama leader, is also buried here (see p.343), but these graves are not open to the general public. Nor is the expensive military museum, which has stood behind iron railings on the main street since 2004, but remains off-limits to the public for reasons that are unclear.

However, what the town lacks in tourist sights it makes up for in its fine **craft markets**; two occupy either end of the main road into and out of town. Though basketry, painted gourds, gemstones and the like are on display, the markets are predominantly about **wood**. The array and size of some of the carvings are phenomenal, from beautifully polished masks to sculpted life-size Himba women, giant giraffes and even dugout canoes – not easily stuffed into your luggage. Be prepared to be hassled if the stallholders are short of custom when you arrive.

Less well known to tourists is the town's reputation for high-quality **biltong** – not to be missed, provided you're not vegetarian; head for the Closwa Biltong Factory Shop and Butchery on Vortrekker Street (see *The Waterhole*, p.172). A few kilometres away, two resorts – the hot springs of Gross Barman and the serene Von Bach Dam – have long been favourite weekend getaways for urbanites in need of some R&R.

4

ARRIVAL AND DEPARTURE   OKAHANDJA

By bus Intercape Mainliner services (☎061 227847, ⊕intercape.co.za) from Windhoek to Walvis Bay, Oshakati and Victoria Falls all pass through Okahandja (one daily on Thurs, Sat & Sun; three daily on Mon, Wed & Fri; none on Tues; 1hr). The bus stop is at the Engen and Wimpy garage on the B1. Alternatively, minibuses heading north from Windhoek, and therefore passing through Okahandja, leave from the Monte Christo Service Station in Katutura. The shuttle services between Swakopmund and Windhoek can also drop off and pick up in Okahandja if pre-booked (see p.212).

By train The very slow TransNamib train between Windhoek and Walvis Bay, via Swakopmund, passes through Okahandja every day except Saturday (departure from Windhoek 7.55pm; 2hr).

EATING

Brewed Awakenings Martin Neib Ave, opposite the craft market, by the Shell garage ☎062 500723. This inexpensive café is a handy pit stop – grab a pick-me-up coffee for the road or a full fry-up breakfast (N$80), a light lunch, or an afternoon cuppa with a muffin. Daily 7am–7pm.

Okahandja Country Hotel 2km north of Okahandja on the B1, after the turn to Otjiwarongo ☎062 504299,

Map: OKAHANDJA

EATING
Brewed Awakenings	3
Okahandja Country Hotel	1
The Waterhole	2

okahandjahotel.com. This garden oasis makes the perfect lunch stop with its manicured lawns and bird-filled trees, surrounded by whitewashed stone and thatch. Besides, the food is decent: well prepared and in large portions – the steaks are particularly recommended. Daily 7am–9pm.

★ **The Waterhole** Closwa Biltong Factory Shop, 2456 Vortrekker St ☎ 062 501123, closwa.com. Small café set in the factory outlet for this famous biltong producer, butchery and deli. Sample a biltong *brötchen*, before stocking up on some of their superb cured meat and game for your journey, or fresh cuts for your campfire braai. Also serves surprisingly good hot chocolate. Free wi-fi. Mon–Fri 8am–5.15pm, Sat 8am–1pm.

Gross Barmen

25km southwest of Okahandja, down the D1972 • Daily sunrise to sunset • N$50 day visitors to the picnic area; N$100 for access to the pool and other facilities

Just north of the Swakop River are the sulphurous springs that the Herero – the area's first settlers – called Otjikango, meaning "big fountain". On most tourist maps, however, the place is marked as **Gross Barmen**, a name given to it by Rhenish missionaries, after the small German town where the mission had its headquarters. The reason to visit is to indulge yourself at the NWR-run Gross Barmen **resort**, which boasts two glorious thermal pools fed by the springs: an expansive outdoor one that stays at a pleasant 25°C, and an indoor one that can exceed 40°C, depending on the time of day, and should only be experienced in small doses. Don't be put off by the designer post-apocalyptic cement and rust-effect main building; inside is a **spa** offering a variety of treatments in what look like time capsules, and the resort's location by a reed-fringed dam makes it prime **birdwatching** terrain. After a four-year closure and a multi-million-dollar refurbishment, the place is once again a popular weekend and holiday getaway for Windhoek residents (with chalets and camping available), so aim to visit midweek and off-season.

ACCOMMODATION   GROSS BARMEN

Gross Barmen Resort ☎ 061 2857200, nwr.com .na. A range of lodgings is available, from luxury chalets sharing a jacuzzi, to family self-catering units and regular doubles. They're all rather bland and some are not so well situated, though a handful overlook the dam (chalet 25 has a nice view), as does the grassy outdoor pool area and pleasant restaurant deck: buffet only in peak periods; otherwise à la carte is available. The campground has all the facilities you need, but lacks shade and appeal, especially when the music from the day-visitor picnic area takes over. Camping per person **N$170**, bush chalets **N$2000**

Von Bach Dam

2km along the D2102 from the junction with the B1, 4km south of Okahandja • Daily 6am–7pm (summer), 7am–6pm (winter) • N$40 entry • No public transport

Supplying much of the water for Windhoek and Okahandja, **Von Bach Dam**, which lies on the Swakop River, is also a relaxing recreational resort. Like Gross Barmen, Von Bach is geared up for weekending Windhoekers, keen to picnic or party, enjoy a meal out, or even overnight in the good-value accommodation. The eleven campsites by the water double up as daytime picnic spots with braai sites, shade and ablutions, so if you pick a weekend or holiday period, you'll have the accompanying sounds of a boombox, rather than the bush. Activities include walks, boating and canoe trips, or you can always loll by the pool and admire water-skiers showing off their skills – Namibia's two clubs for the sport are based here. For the average holidaymaker Von Bach will probably only serve as an overnight stop if you are too tired to make it back to Windhoek from a trip up north.

ACCOMMODATION   **VON BACH DAM**

Tungeni Von Bach Resort ☎ 062 500162, 🌐 tungeni .com/tungeni_serenity.html; map p.170. Some 22 stone-and-thatch chalets in two tiers facing the dam: the upper terrace holds two-storey chalets accommodating four, while on the bottom tier smaller two-person chalets reign (numbers 4–19 of these have good views across the water). The pool, though nicely situated, is rather small given the number of weekend guests in the summer. Campsites are in variable condition, and the restaurant serves buffet and à la carte meals. Breakfast 8–10am, lunch noon–2pm, dinner 6–9pm. Camping per person **N$100**, chalets **N$1200**

Between the B1 and the C33

West of the section of the B1 that stretches between Okahandja and Otjiwarongo, and east of the tarred C33 which heads north from Omaruru (see p.188), joining up at Otjiwarongo, there are several major private reserves stocked with large mammals and offering comfortable accommodation that attracts a lot of visitors.

Dinosaur footprints

Otjihaenameparero Farm • Daily sunrise to sunset • N$20

A minor attraction, worth a short detour if you're in the area, are the **Dinosaur footprints**, located on a Otjihaenameparero Farm, midway between the two main roads. Don't expect anything as exciting as Jurassic Park, but they are quite remarkable nevertheless. A larger set and smaller set of around 30 imprints of clawed, three-toed, two-legged dinosaurs – moving in a similar way to a modern-day ostrich – are visible on two separate slabs of sloping red Etjo sandstone; you can follow the larger set of prints for 30m across the rock. It is thought that the imprints were formed around 190 million years ago, in wet sediment, which was then covered by dry wind-blown sand, and compressed, preserving the trace fossils until they were exposed once more several million years later, due to erosion.

ACCOMMODATION   **BETWEEN THE B1 AND THE C3**

Mount Etjo Safari Lodge On the D2843, 40km west of the junction with the B1 ☎ 067 290 0173, 🌐 mount -etjo.com; map p.170. Old-fashioned lodge in a large private reserve set around a lovely lawn overlooking a reed-fringed waterhole, where hippos grunt and flamingos tread delicately. Elsewhere roam elephant, white and black rhino, a host of antelope and smaller creatures. Cavernous stone rooms with outsize bathrooms remain cool, laden with heavy furniture, animal woodcarvings, prints and masks to remind you where you are. Plenty of safari activities, though you might question the keeping of lions and cheetahs in enclosures, and the feeding activities on offer. The *Dinosaur Campsite* (not to be confused with the Dinosaur Footprints – see p.173) lies 6km from the lodge – directions from lodge reception – on old cattle farmland, where six sites are in need of, and currently undergoing, renovations. Campers can use lodge facilities; meals (mainly buffet) need to be pre-booked. Camping per site (up to 4 people) N$480, doubles DBB & afternoon tea N$2865

Otjihaenameparero Signposted off the D2414, 29km from the junction with the C33 at Kalkfeld (not to be confused with signs for the Dinosaur Campsite) ☎ 067 290153, ⓦ dinosaurstracks-guestfarm.com; map p.170. To accompany the dinosaurs' footprints on the property, a small, peaceful campground-cum-picnic area has five simple sites offering limited shade under acacia trees, stone tables and seats, braai pits (but own grill needed) and donkey-fired hot-water showers. A small guesthouse operates – a whitewashed block of three spacious, light guestrooms, with private patio and shared kitchen-lounge. Alternatively, pre-order dinner at the farm. Camping per person N$100, doubles N$840

Ozongwindi 6km south of the D2110, 75km west of the B1, 20km east of the C36 ☎ 062 503990 or ☎ 081 276 8021, ⓦ ozongwindi.com; map p.170. Ten seriously luxurious, thatched chalets (a/c), with private wooden decks overlooking the River Khan, plus self-catering rooms in an old farmhouse. The main lodge has a pool, library, bar-restaurant and satellite TV. Very relaxing place with great birdwatching. Lower rates for two nights or more. Self-catering N$1130, doubles DBB N$3100

ERINDI PRIVATE GAME RESERVE
Set in a vast private reserve (over 700 sq km), and a bit of a conveyor belt, this is canned luxury safari tourism, which you'll either love or hate, where a sometimes-resident group of CwiCwi (San) families also lives. The reserve is full of large mammals, from cats and wild dogs to rhino, hippo and crocs. There are four entrances; 50km north from Okahandja on the B1, turn west onto the D2414 for another 40km (☎ 083 330 1111, ⓦ erindi.com; map p.170).

Camp Elephant 30km from Old Trader's Lodge ☎ 081 621 7027. This budget-minded camp is enormous and somewhat institutional: neatly arranged round a waterhole are 15 two-bedroom self-catering chalets, and 30 luxury campsites, complete with private solar-powered ablutions, food preparation areas, fridge-freezer, picnic table and benches, plus vehicle awning. Self-drive vehicles have to pay a daily fee (N$300). Campers are not allowed to visit the lodge. On-site shop. Camping per pitch (up to six) N$980, self-catering chalets N$2190

Old Trader's Lodge ☎ 081 621 7029. The main accommodation, as the name suggests, harps back to colonial times, with large leather sofas and teak furniture in 47 suites of varying degrees of opulence. There's a vast viewing deck at the long thatched semi-open restaurant (where daylong music can niggle). A vast array of activities (most N$500) ranges from standard game drives to cheetah and leopard conservation project walks. DBB N$4180

OKONJIMA
This private nature reserve is home to the heavily marketed AfriCat Foundation (ⓦ africat.org), which offers many of the activities, such as cheetah or leopard tracking – and more recently wild dogs and spotted hyena – though other wildlife abounds. Game drives and walking tracking activities, which can feel a little staged, cost N$670. 10km west of the B1, 50km south of Otjiwarongo (☎ 067 687032 or ☎ 081 127 6233, ⓦ okonjima.com; map p.170).

Bush Camp An intimate camp, comprising an expansive main lodge overlooking a waterhole, and nine gorgeous open-sided thatched rondavels, decorated in earthy colours. The cuisine is fantastic. AI N$11,880

Omboroko Campsite There are four over-manicured but well-equipped private pitches with shared pool, and a luxury villa. Camping per person N$330

Plains Camp Various accommodations, but the best are fabulous glass-fronted chalets with private porch that allow you to gaze across the savannah and watch antelope graze; dining takes place in a glorified air hangar offering more views, but the high turnover of guests has a factory-like feel. DBB N$3000

Waterberg Plateau National Park
1km off the D2512 • Daily sunrise to sunset • N$80/person and N$10/vehicle per day, guided drives N$550; book at an NWR office in advance or at the camp reception

An impressive table mountain popular with hikers and nature lovers, the extensive **Waterberg Plateau National Park** is located 60km southeast of Otjiwarongo; to the east, it surveys the arid Omaheke Desert – part of the Kalahari – to the west, acacia-covered savannah. The sheer sandstone cliffs that top the plateau glow a glorious deep reddish-orange in the late afternoon sun; they are surrounded by a sloping "skirt" of scree and boulders, with patches of dense vegetation clinging onto the rock face. Water is relatively plentiful, hence the name Waterberg ("water mountain" in Afrikaans). Rain filters through the porous sandstone on top, but upon reaching the impervious lower layers of mudstone and siltstone, it re-emerges as springs through fissures in the southern slopes of the plateau. Unsurprisingly, water, and the resulting abundant wildlife, has attracted human populations for many years. **San rock art** near one of the plateau's waterholes testifies to their having passed through the area for thousands of years. Towards the end of the nineteenth century, the **Herero** settled in the area with their cattle, and it was here, on August 11, 1904, that the decisive **Battle of Omahakari** (or Waterberg) was fought between the Herero, who were defying colonial rule, and the German army (see p.345).

The trails

Waterberg is synonymous with **hiking**; in particular it's renowned for its multi-day trails, which ordinarily are booked through the NWR office in Windhoek (see box, p.94), but for some time all long hikes have been suspended due to an increase in rhino poaching; the park authorities had stepped up security and, at the time of going to press, were still unsure when or whether the trails would reopen. In the meantime, hikers have to make do with the handful of **shorter trails** (maximum 3km) leaving from the camping or chalet areas. The forty-minute hike up to the plateau rim for sunset is well worth the effort, while the Fig Tree Walk is a favourite with birders. Since park visitors are not allowed to drive themselves around the park, the only way to get to know the top of the plateau is by signing up for one of the twice-daily **game drives**, though the ready availability of food and water plus the dense vegetation means that wildlife sightings are often disappointing.

4

ARRIVAL   WATERBERG PLATEAU NATIONAL PARK

By car Around 30km south of Otjiwarongo, take the tarred C22, signposted to Okakara. After 41km, take the gravel D2512 for another 17km to the park entrance. It is accessible in an ordinary saloon car, though parts of the D2512 can be rough after rain. There is petrol (but not diesel) available at the NWR camp.
By bus and hitching There is no scheduled bus service. You may be able to catch some sporadic transport to Okakara from Otjiwarongo – ask at a fuel station – but you would still need to hitch from the junction with the D2512.

ACCOMMODATION

NWR has the monopoly on accommodation in the national park itself, but there are several lodges, with camping facilities too, located in private buffer reserves around the fringes of the plateau.

IN THE PARK
NWR Waterberg Camp ☎061 2857200 (reservations), ⊕nwr.com.na; map p.170. This resort is wonderfully situated, spread out on a vegetated slope below the sandstone cliffs. A shady campground is on flattish land by reception, near the thinly stocked camp shop. Almost sixty chalets and a handful of self-catering units lie higher up the escarpment with simple but

FLORA AND FAUNA OF THE WATERBERG PLATEAU NATIONAL PARK

On account of its inaccessibility, the park is used to reintroduce and breed **rare species**, which are then transferred to other protected areas. These include white and black rhino, eland, tsessebe, roan and sable antelope, and Cape buffalo. They join other **large mammals** present in the park, such as giraffe, wildebeest and kudu. The **birdlife** too is impressive, with over two hundred recorded species, including a number of rarities. Namibia's only breeding colony of Cape vultures inhabits Waterberg's southwestern cliffs, while other notable avian residents include Verreaux's (black) eagles and large numbers of peregrine falcon. But wildlife is not just confined to the mixed wood- and grassland of the plateau top; even around the campground, you'll catch sight of paradise flycatchers flitting around the trees, hoopoes probing the soil and Damara dik-diks picking their way delicately round tents. At dusk, if you're lucky, you might spot the bulging eyes of a lesser bushbaby. Regular visitors you can't miss are the baboons; make sure you keep food stowed away, all chalet and car windows closed, and tents zipped up.

comfortable accommodation for two or four – some with outside braai and seating. Some sit on the cliff edge, offering glimpses of thorntree-covered plains below through the undergrowth; Chalet 57 has a good view. A decent à la carte restaurant and bar, which occupy the former German police station, have terrace seating, with a lovely shallow pool in an adjacent shady area. Camping per site N$130 and per person N$170, doubles N$1320, bush chalets (B&B) N$1620

OUTSIDE THE PARK

Waterberg Guest Farm On the C22, 22km east of the junction with the B1 ☏ 081 751 4866, ⓦ waterberg namibia.com; map p.170. Personalized service and gourmet dining on a cattle and horse stud farm that affords spectacular views of sunrise above the Waterberg Plateau. Four rooms reside in the farmhouse, opening out onto a verandah, but it's worth splashing out on the even nicer, more private "bush bungalows", with rustic exteriors and light, airy contemporary interiors, offering indoor and outdoor showers. Birdwatching is excellent (250 species recorded), plus there's an illuminated waterhole attracting larger fauna, but you need to be a dog-lover as the owner has several that wander freely. Guided or self-guided hikes and spa treatments available. B&B. Doubles N$2014, bush bungalows N$2991

Waterberg Wilderness Lodge 10km beyond the park entrance on the D2512 ☏ 067 687018; map p.170. A former cattle farm turned private reserve that abuts the national park has now been restocked with wildlife. Accommodation ranges from economy canvas chalets to more luxurious rooms in the lively main lodge – a sandstone building set among mature trees and well-tended grounds. Dinner is a set menu, available to campers if there's space. Camping is in two areas, each with a small pool, offering secluded, shady sites with private ablutions in a central block. Camping per person N$170, chalets (DBB) N$1780, doubles (DBB) N$1920

Otjiwarongo

As you enter **OTJIWARONGO**, the road broadens into a dual carriageway, punctuated by traffic lights, leading you to expect a town of some size. But blink and you'll miss the town centre, and find yourself heading back into the bush. That said, Otjiwarongo is the regional capital of the Otjozondjupa Region, and when the jacaranda and flamboyants lining the main street are in bloom, the place exudes a cheery feel.

There are scarcely any attractions in town, though railway buffs should swing by the station to take a look at the splendid retired old German steam locomotive. The only other place that draws visitors is the **crocodile ranch** (Mon–Fri 8am–4pm, Sat & Sun 9am–3pm; N$65; ☏ 067 302121), which gives guided tours of what is effectively a battery crocodile farm providing skin for the European and Asian leather markets – something to consider before paying the entry fee.

For tourists bound for Etosha or Caprivi, Otjiwarongo is a natural pit stop, providing a selection of well-stocked supermarkets and several petrol stations. The town is also within striking distance of the Waterberg Plateau (see p.174), Namibia's premier cheetah research and education centre (see box, p.178) and the AfriCat Foundation at Okonjima (see p.174).

Brief history

As with many places in central-northern Namibia, there are traces of nomadic San and later Damara presence in the area, though the first to settle here and push out any competition were the Herero, whose Chief Kanzambezi eventually allowed a Rhenish mission to be established in 1891. The Herero uprising in 1904 that resulted in their forced "retreat" into the Omaheke Desert and thousands of deaths (see p.345) enabled the Germans to take over the town, establish a garrison and claim much of the land. The town was officially founded in 1906, when the narrow-gauge railway line between Swakopmund and the mines in Otavi and Tsumeb became fully operational, allowing the place to thrive. Otjiwarongo means "place where fat cattle graze" in Otjiherero, which for a cattle-loving society denotes a pleasant location. Cattle are still the mainstay of the town's growing economy, which is aided by its excellent rail links with the coast, as well as road connections with Windhoek, and with Oshakati and Ondangwa, the main population centres in the north. In the last few years the opening of the Otjikoto open-cast gold mine, midway between here and Otavi, has given the

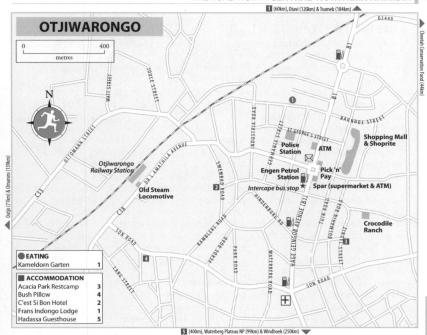

place a further boost, and a new cement factory is being planned. Yet the emergence of new businesses and jobs still cannot keep pace with the influx of rural migrants.

ARRIVAL AND DEPARTURE — OTJIWARONGO

By car Otjiwarongo is right on the B2, 248km from Windhoek, on the road north. Several fuel stations, banks with ATMs and supermarkets lie on the main street.

By bus The Intercape Mainliner bus (☎ 061 227847, ⓦ intercape.co.za) stops at the Engen service station opposite Spar on the main street en route from Windhoek to Oshakati (daily except Sat, 2pm; 7hr 15min; from N$228), and on the Vic Falls bus (Mon, Wed & Fri), departing Windhoek at 6pm, travelling via Rundu and

Katima Mulilo (Mon, Wed & Fri; 16hr 45min; from N$432). The return bus to Windhoek from Oshakati passes Otjiwarongo in the middle of the night (daily except Sun 2.40am; 3hr 30min; from N$252).

By minibus Minibuses leave the Monte Christo service station in Katutura for Otjiwarongo (N$150). For the return journey, catch one from the Engen station opposite Spar on the main street. Minibuses also leave here for Oshakati (N$180).

ACCOMMODATION

Though most visitors prefer to stay out of town, closer to Waterberg, or in one of the private reserves further south, there's some good, inexpensive accommodation in town that would fit the bill for a comfortable one-night stopover.

IN TOWN

Acacia Park Restcamp End of Hindenburg St ☎ 067 303100 or ☎ 081 216 0004, ✉ acaciapark@mweb.com .na. Central but secure spot for those on a shoestring budget: very basic chalets containing a double bed, hot shower and fan, plus a selection of hard campsites with some shade, shared seating, braai facilities and power points, though you may have to share your plot with visiting goats. The ablution block is clean though rather run-down, and you'll get the pounding party music

wafting in at weekends. Camping per person N$80, chalets N$350

Bush Pillow 27 Son Rd ☎ 067 303885, ⓦ bushpillow .hypermart.net. Eco-focused smart guesthouse (run on solar power, emphasizing recycling and supporting environmental projects) aimed at the "discerning tourist" and business clients (hence the offer of an ironing board!). Possesses a handful of bright, elephant-themed rooms, secure parking and a small garden and pool. Also runs multi-day tours. Dinner on request. N$1300

4

CHEETAH CONSERVATION

A third of the world's **cheetahs** – around 3500 – roam the savannah lands of Namibia, predominantly on communal and commercial farms. Africa's most endangered cat is a protected species in Namibia, but there are ongoing conflicts between these powerful hunters and people when livestock is threatened or killed. Loss of habitat and prey is another problem cheetahs face, as the increase in livestock rearing, and subsequent overgrazing, have resulted in bush encroachment. Recent expansion of game fencing has also affected the availability of food.

At the forefront of conservation efforts in Namibia, and the global leader in cheetah research and education, is the **Cheetah Conservation Fund** (daily 8am–5pm; N$200; ☎ 067 306225, ⓦ cheetah.org), 44km east of Otjiwarongo, which is well worth a visit; if driving, turn east off the B1, onto the sandy D2440, just north of Otjiwarongo. The entry fee includes an excellent two-hour **guided walking tour** round the large enclosures, where around fifty rescue cheetahs are kept, though good sightings of these splendid beasts depend on whether they happen to be prowling or lounging close to the perimeter fence. Arriving at feeding time (2pm weekdays, noon at weekends) will increase your chances, as will signing up for the hour-long **cheetah drive** option (N$480, including entry). You'll also be taken to see the veterinary clinic and **livestock dogs**, one of the centre's most successful programmes, in which Kangal and Anatolian Shepherd dogs are trained to live among livestock and bark to scare off predators, thus safeguarding the farmer's livelihood, while saving the cheetah from a likely bullet. Around five hundred dogs now live on farms, with impressive results.

Another highlight is the **Dancing Goat Creamery** – one of several model farms used to help share predator-friendly management practices. Make sure you stock up on some of their superb feta or goat's cheese; they even produce fudge. Then, after trying to absorb all the information in the new interactive **cheetah museum**, you'll probably be ready for a cup of coffee and a bite to eat in the café. If you've not had your fill of cheetahs for the day, you can overnight in the luxurious *Babson House* – another fundraising venture, which can accommodate four in two rooms with four-poster beds, and which overlooks a cheetah pen.

C'est Si Bon Hotel Swembad Rd ☎ 067 301240, ⓦ cestsibonhotel.com. Pleasant, vaguely African-themed thatched hotel with comfortable rooms opening out onto a manicured lawn. The restaurant serves the standard hotel fare, offering a range of poultry, game, meat and seafood dishes (most mains N$90–160), which can be enjoyed inside, or preferably in the garden under a lapa, where you can escape the soporific religious muzak. **N$820**

Hadassa Guesthouse 36 Lang St ☎ 067 307505, ⓦ hadassaguesthouse.com. Upmarket guesthouse catering to business folk and travellers alike, with nine stylishly designed rooms complete with all modern comforts, and a free car wash thrown in. Comfortable common areas and delightful garden with sparkling pool. Rates include afternoon tea. Dinner can be pre-ordered (N$200). B&B **N$880**

NORTH OF TOWN

Frans Indongo Lodge 17km along the D2433, whose turn-off is 43km north of Otjiwarongo ☎ 067 307 9467, ⓦ indongolodge.com. Established by Namibia's most successful black entrepreneur, this well-run lodge pays homage to his roots with an Owambo homestead theme – mopane palisades dividing off the various sections and everyday artefacts as ornaments. The recently renovated thatched chalets (for couples and families), however, are thoroughly modern, with comfortable interiors in earthy tones with all conveniences (a/c, phone, fridge, hairdryer, DStv, kettle). Only two chalets directly face the savannah plains, which can otherwise be enjoyed from the stone-paved pool or viewing deck. Substantial fixed-price lunch (N$115) and dinner (N$270) available. **N$2080**

Outjo

With a small population of about 6000, the ranching town of **OUTJO** – meaning "little hills" in Otjiherero – sits on the pleasantly undulating fringes of the Fransfontein Mountains, just north of the Ugab River. It's a surprisingly leafy town, which has recently taken on a new lease of life as a staging post for tourists trekking up to Etosha, a fact

exemplified by the transformation of the high-street bakery from a small-town shop into a slick two-storey glass-fronted operation with restaurant, large shop and playground.

Beyond stopping for lunch and wandering down the pleasant main street, which boasts a quasi town square, and several tourist shops, there are a couple of German historical monuments worth a cursory glance before moving on, since Outjo was one of the German colonial army's most northerly, and shortlived, outposts; it was established initially to control the *rinderpest* in the areas of white settlement (see p.345), but then to try and win over the Owambo kings. One of the first structures they built was a water tower to pump and supply water to the soldiers, their horses and the hospital. Though the wooden windmill has long gone, the square stone base can still be seen on the east side of town off the northern end of Sonop Street.

Outjo Museum

Corner of Meester St with Tuin St • Mon–Fri 7.30am–1pm, 2.30–5pm • N$10 • ☎ 067 313402

The **Outjo Museum** is an extremely modest affair displayed in Outjo's oldest, and nicely restored, building, known as the **Franke Haus**. It is named after the German commanding officer Major Victor Franke, for whom it was built in 1899 – he also has a tower named after him in Omaruru (see p.188). An exhibition on his exploits, as well as displays of antique artefacts and locally mined gemstones, comprise the museum's collection.

ARRIVAL AND INFORMATION OUTJO

By car Easily reachable on the tarred C38 from Otjiwarongo and with good connections to Etosha, Damaraland and the Kaokoveld.

Tourist information A brand-new, large municipal tourist information centre sits on Sam Nujoma Road (Mon–Fri 8am–4pm, Sat 8am–2pm), which also hosts the *Bistro Kulinarium* (daily 7am–9pm) run by *The Farmhouse*, following the same menu (ⓦ farmhouse-outjo.com; see opposite), and a couple of craft stalls. If the information desk is not staffed (not an uncommon occurrence), enquire at South West Africa Gems (Mon–Fri 9am–5pm, Sat 9–1pm) on Hage Geingob Ave on the square, which has served as the de facto tourist information centre for many years, with knowledgeable and helpful staff; they also sell guides to Etosha and postcards.

ACCOMMODATION

Buschfeld Park Restcamp 2km north of town on the C38 ☎ 067 313665 or ☎ 081 148 2636, ⓦ buschfeldnamibia.com. Six inexpensive and surprisingly pleasant chalets, with braai facilities, set in tree-filled grounds attracting good birdlife. There's a small pool with a bar-restaurant under a lapa. Undergoing renovations at the time of writing, the prices will increase once they've been completed. Eight campsites, not

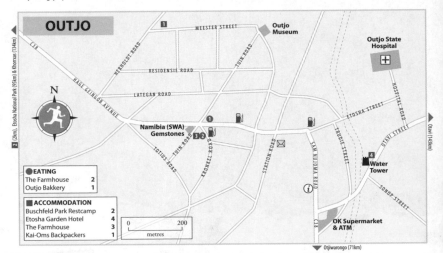

OUTJO

EATING
The Farmhouse 2
Outjo Bakkery 1

ACCOMMODATION
Buschfeld Park Restcamp 2
Etosha Garden Hotel 4
The Farmhouse 3
Kai-Oms Backpackers 1

Otjiwarongo (71km)

especially private, but grassy, agreeably situated, and with electricity. Camping per person N$110, chalet N$760
Etosha Garden Hotel 6 Otavi St ☎ 067 313130, ⓦ etosha-garden-hotel.com. Century-old building set in a luscious tropical garden filled with jacaranda, palm trees and bougainvillea – a good spot for an indulgent lunch. Twenty large rooms (often filled with tour groups) are fairly basic – some with a/c, others with fan & TV – but generally clean and good value for the price. N$770
The Farmhouse Corner of Hage Geingob Ave and Tuin St ☎ 067 313444, ⓦ farmhouse-outjo.com. Above the

restaurant, six light, neat, en-suite rooms of varying sizes and configurations share a TV lounge with DStv. Priced per person, so good for solo travellers. Per person N$880
Kai-Oms Backpackers 2 Meester St ☎ 081 375 0152. Old-style shoestring backpackers: providing basic accommodation: private rooms, dorms and a space to pitch a tent amid the pot plants, quirky ornaments and pond in their courtyard garden, with shared kitchen, braai and outdoor seating (less fun in winter) and with friendly owners. Camping per site (up to four people) N$80, dorms N$180, doubles N$450

EATING

The Farmhouse Corner of Hage Geingob Ave and Tuin St ☎ 067 313444, ⓦ farmhouse-outjo.com. Great for breakfasts and light lunches (from around N$60; from N$100 for more serious steaks) and huge slabs of home-made cakes to devour indoors or in the delightful shady beer garden at the back. Dinner is a bit more hit and miss. Free wi-fi. Daily 6am–9pm.
Outjo Bakkery 9 Hage Geingob Ave ☎ 067 313055,

ⓦ facebook.com/outjobakkery. The hottest spot in town, this expanded bakery is now two-tiered; though still serving up apfelstrudel, doughnuts and home-made bread, a fully fledged restaurant has opened serving pizzas, burgers, pies, steaks and salads (from around N$80), and there's a chill cabinet with canned drinks, as well as biltong and other snacks to go. Free wi-fi. Mon–Fri 6.30am–5pm, Sat 6.30am–2pm.

The "Triangle"

4

Viewed on a map, the roads linking northern towns of **Tsumeb**, **Otavi** and **Grootfontein** form an isosceles **triangle** enclosing the scenic Otavi Mountains, which provide welcome topographic relief to anyone travelling down from the flatlands of the far north. It's one of the most prosperous areas of Namibia, rich both in minerals and agriculture – thanks to fertile soils nurtured by annual rainfall that usually tops 500mm; maize cultivation is particularly widespread, resulting in the sobriquet of the **Golden** or **Maize Triangle**. Located on the way to Etosha's eastern gate as well as the lush game reserves in the Zambezi Region, many visitors pass through these small towns. Of the three, Tsumeb is the most attractive and has the best facilities, followed by Grootfontein; both are good places to withdraw money, stock up on supplies and top up your fuel, with Otavi a rather forlorn third. In terms of sights, the museum in Tsumeb, and the Hoba Meteorite – the world's largest – west of Grootfontein, are worth a brief detour, while a few lodges and guestfarms in the area make the most of their scenic surroundings and offer very pleasant overnight stops.

Otavi

The smallest and most down at heel of the Triangle towns, **OTAVI** seems a forgotten place. Most of the action happens outside town, at the flagship Total petrol station and major truck stop, complete with ATM, neighbouring bar-restaurant and biltong shop, on the main crossroads east of the centre. Here the B1 divides: heading northwest to the population centres of Oshakati and Ondangwa, or northeast along the B8 towards the Trans Caprivi Highway. Note the heavily irrigated areas along this initial stretch of the B8, where the town's original springs – long known to nomadic Hai‖om and Damara groups – are located.

Dominating the skyline as you drive into the nondescript town are the gleaming grain silos of the maize and millet mill, across the railway track. It was the arrival of the railway from Swakopmund in 1906 that marked the town's boom period. The German colonial mining company, the Otavi Minen und Eisenbahngesellschaft (OMEG),

THE TRIANGLE

4

completed what was the longest narrow-gauge track in the world at the time – on the back of slave or enforced labour – in order to transport the copper being mined at Tsumeb and Kombat down to the coast and onto ships bound for Europe. Once the copper deposits were exhausted, the town's fortunes slumped. So far, the new gold mine and cement factory in the area do not seem to have had the economic impact on Otavi that its 4000 inhabitants were anticipating, with Otjiwarongo appearing to benefit more from the mine.

A few kilometres north of town, signposted off the B1, stands the unremarkable **Khorab Memorial**. Of interest only to colonial history buffs, as there's little to see, it marks the site where in World War I, on June 9, 1915, the Schutztruppen, under the ubiquitous Lieutenant-Colonel (by then) Victor Franke, finally surrendered to Louis Botha's South African Union troops, signing the Khorab Peace Treaty six days later.

Otavi Mountains

Even if you do not have time to stay in the area, a drive through the scenic **Otavi Mountains** is a refreshing diversion, especially if you're arriving from the flat arid areas around Etosha. Formed about 700 million years ago, this stratified dolomite and limestone range has numerous **caves**, the most accessible of which is the **Ghaub Cave**, on the guestfarm of the same name (see opposite), where you can arrange to go on a two-hour tour (ⓦghaub-namibia.com; N$350/person). It's 38m deep with 2.5km of chambers and passageways, and although it lacks large stalactites, stalagmites and ancient rock art, there are petrified waterfalls, organ pipes, rock curtains and other interesting crystal growths to interest the casual cave-goer. The place, which is not suitable for the claustrophobic, is dark, slippery and dusty, so dress appropriately.

ARRIVAL AND DEPARTURE   OTAVI

By bus The daily 2pm Intercape Mainliner service from Windhoek (ⓘ 061 227847, ⓦ intercape.co.za) stops at the Total Fourways petrol station in Otavi on the way to Oshakati (daily except Sat; 4hr 45min), returning to Windhoek, and stopping daily except Sun at 1.30am. The Victoria Falls-bound bus from Windhoek stops en route (Mon, Wed & Fri at 6.50pm; 4hr from Windhoek), travelling northwards via Rundu and Katima Mulilo.

By minibus Local minibuses bound for Tsumeb or Grootfontein also leave from here, as do minibuses bound for Windhoek (N$210).

ACCOMMODATION

Otavi Gardens Hotel 6 Park St ☎067 234334. A surprising oasis of cool brick-and-thatch chalets (with a/c and DStv), set in a luscious palm-populated garden. The busy *Grasdak Restaurant* is a social hub for some townsfolk in the evening. N̲$̲7̲5̲0̲

Palmenecke Guesthouse 96 Hertzog Ave ☎067 234199, ⓦpalmenecke.co.za. Rather chintzy but comfortable small guesthouse chock-full of eclectic furnishings and ornaments, with a small terrace overlooking a pleasant garden. Breakfast can be ordered (N$60). N̲$̲5̲5̲0̲

Zum Potjie Restcamp 8km north of Otavi, signposted off the B1 ☎067 234300, ⓦzumpotjie.com. Easy access, and simple, inexpensive lodgings in a friendly farm environment; five neat bungalows with fan, or camping (sites with or without a power point). The farm's crammed full of old artefacts and memorabilia plus the flavoursome potjie stews are not to be missed. Camping per person N̲$̲1̲3̲5̲, bungalow (B&B) N̲$̲1̲0̲0̲0̲

OTAVI MOUNTAINS

★**Ghaub Lodge** 24km along the D3022 from the junction with the B1, 25km north of Outjo ☎067 240188, ⓦghaub-namibia.com. Well-managed and welcoming, this former mission station has twelve airy chalets overlooking expansive lawns; a real treat. So too are the three private luxury campsites with their own stone ablutions, table and braai and superlative views. The main house retains many original features, and the shady terrace garden is an ideal spot to linger over a well-prepared meal. Trips to the Gaub Caves (N$350), farm excursions or guided walks on offer. Camping per person N̲$̲1̲8̲0̲, (DBB & afternoon tea) N̲$̲3̲1̲6̲0̲

Tsumeb

The largest and most populous of the Triangle towns, **TSUMEB** is also the most attractive, its main roads lined with mature trees, including palms, jacarandas and flamboyants – which provide splashes of lilac and red when in bloom, and brightly coloured bougainvillea hedges. There is even a large leafy park, the town's fulcrum, overlooked by several of Tsumeb's main buildings, above which the high street leads. On the park's south side stands the excellent museum (see p.184), next door to the town's oldest existing building; erected in 1913, the striking **Saint Barbara Catholic Church** was aptly named since Barbara is the patron saint of miners. Mining, from the outset, has been the town's *raison d'être*, though the disused mineshaft that dominates the west end of President's Avenue is a reminder of its more recent decline. Nevertheless, Tsumeb is a pleasant enough place to spend a night, with a choice of accommodation, which generally serves up decent food. If you're just passing through en route to Etosha, this is the last stop for groceries, in one of the town's well-stocked supermarkets. At the end of October, the town parties during the annual **Tsumeb Copper Festival**, essentially a trade fair centred on the United Nations Park, but also with the usual food and drink stalls, musical and cultural entertainment.

Brief history

Mining and smelting copper had probably been going on in the area for several thousand years before the London-based South-West Africa Company began prospecting in 1895. The Bergdamara had both mined and smelted copper, whereas the Hai‖om probably dug out the ore and traded with the Owambos for them to smelt. The Hai‖om called the place "Tsomsoub", meaning "to dig a hole in loose ground (that collapses)", which gave rise to the town's modern name Tsumeb. In the second half of the nineteenth century, tensions grew over land ownership and rights in the Triangle as its mineralogical value became increasingly apparent, and there was much wheeling and dealing among different Owambo and Herero groups, European traders and other interested parties, while the Bergdamara and Hai‖om were gradually squeezed out. The first nine tonnes of ore was transported to the coast via ox-cart in 1900, but once the railway line arrived from Swakopmund in 1906, mining production took off in a big way, under the auspices of OMEG initially, and later the Tsumeb Mine Corporation. It created a boom era that lasted decades – with hiatuses during the two world wars – until copper prices sank in the 1990s and the mine was forced to close in 1998. Though more recently small mining operations have started up

4

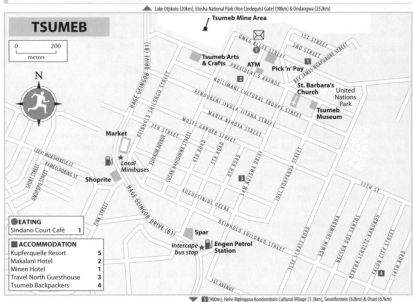

Lake Otjikoto (20km), Etosha National Park (Von Lindequist Gate) (98km) & Ondangwa (252km)

TSUMEB

Tsumeb Mine Area

0   200
metres

N

OMEG ALLEE STREET

1ST STREET

2ND STREET

HAGE GEINGOB DRIVE (B1)

SHILONGO STREET

Tsumeb Arts & Crafts

ATM

PRESIDENT'S AVENUE

Pick 'n' Pay

NGARIBURUBE STREET

St. Barbara's Church

United Nations Park

REV. JAMES

NDILIMANI CULTURAL TROUPE STREET

PENDUKENI IIVULA-IITANA STREET

Tsumeb Museum

REINHOLD SHILONGO STREET

7TH STREET

MARIA NEHOYA STREET

MOSES GAROEB STREET

Market

LEEVI MUASHEKELE ST

KAMEELDOORING ST

ELVERUM AVENUE

SUSAN NAHOLINNA STREET

4TH ROAD

5TH ROAD

6TH ROAD

JOEL KOAPANDA STREET

SPORT STREET

OMURORO STREET

ZINK STREET

Local Minibuses

Shoprite

HAGE GEINGOB DRIVE (B1)

AUGUSTINIUS UEERE

AUGUSTINIUS UEERE

SAM NUJOMA DRIVE

11TH ST

REINHOLD SHILONGO STREET

EATING
Sindano Court Café   1

Spar

Intercape bus stop

Engen Petrol Station

1ST AVENUE

ILSES CRATZ ROAD

EDWIN SHIWEDHA

NELSON DOS SANTOS

BERTHA SCHULTZ-KANUHDU

ELLEN CELE STREET

14TH ROAD

ACCOMMODATION
Kupferquelle Resort   5
Makalani Hotel   2
Minen Hotel   1
Travel North Guesthouse   3
Tsumeb Backpackers   4

5 (900m), Helvi Mpingana Kondombolo Cultural Village (1.3km), Grootfontein (62km) & Otavi (67km)

4

again, they are nowhere near the scale that saw 24.6 million tonnes of ore being extracted. What made the Tsumeb mine stand out, however, was also the variety of minerals it yielded: over 227 recorded, 40 of which were unique to the mine; gemstones such as tourmaline, malachite and dioptase were also an important find.

Tsumeb Museum

President's Ave, opposite the park • Mon–Fri 9am–noon, 2–5pm, Sat 9am–noon • N$30 • ☎ 067 220447

Unlike some provincial museums, the well-curated **Tsumeb Museum** definitely merits a visit, containing a rich collection of well-labelled artefacts, photos and explanatory text in English and German spread over several rooms. After the obligatory ethnography room, looking at the cultural artefacts and traditions of Namibia's various peoples, comes the Khorab Chamber. Here, the star exhibits include some lovingly restored cannons, a machine gun, ammunition wagon and assorted weaponry, from the much larger cache that was hurled into Lake Otjikoto by the Germans in anticipation of losing World War I (see p.346). Other war memorabilia includes a military stretcher, which was discovered up a tree some 65 years later. The third room narrates the town's mining history, with copious examples of rock crystals; don't miss the lump of Hoba Meteorite, or the velvet malachite, which really does look as soft as velour. Ignoring the exhibits resulting from a clear-out of residents' attics, so beloved of Namibian museums – typewriters, camera and crockery – philatelist enthusiasts can linger in the final room, which details the history of Namibia's postal service, complete with an immaculately displayed collection of stamps.

Helvi Mpingana Kondombolo Cultural Village

2km from the town centre on the main road to/from the B1 • Mon–Fri 8am–4pm, Sat 8am–12.30pm • N$35 • ☎ 067 220787

Although it has potential, the **Helvi Mpingana Kondombolo Cultural Village** currently disappoints. The aim is to showcase Namibia's various cultures, and in particular the traditional homesteads, which have been reconstructed with the appropriate materials, dotted around a pleasant patch of bush. However, unless there is an attendant free (rarely the case) who can take you on a guided tour, there is little to be gained from a visit, since information boards, labels and brochures are lacking, though there are plenty of hornbills to enjoy in the surrounding scrubland.

ARRIVAL AND DEPARTURE   TSUMEB

By bus The Intercape Mainliner bus (☎061 227847, ⓦintercape.co.za) from Windhoek (6pm) bound for Oshakati (arriving 5am) stops at the Engen station, at the town entrance (daily, except Sat, at 12.35pm), as well as on the way back south to Windhoek (daily, except Sun; 6am; 5hr 30min; from N$310). In addition, the bus between

Windhoek and Victoria Falls (2pm), via Rundu and Katima Mulilo, stops here three times a week (Mon, Wed & Fri at 7.35pm; 15hr; from N$520). Local minibuses tend to leave from around the market area to Windhoek (N$230), and Grootfontein.

INFORMATION

There is no official tourist office in town, although the *Travel North Guesthouse* is very helpful and has a range of leaflets, while *Tsumeb Backpackers* also offers good advice.

ACCOMMODATION

Kupferquelle Resort 1.5km from the park, on the main road to/from the B1 ☎067 220139, ⓦkupferquelle.com. Large, pricey modern resort just outside town, boasting 40 immaculate, though bland, chalets set in lovely grounds, complete with velvety lawns, an Olympic-sized pool, majestic trees and even a duck pond. The best camping option in town. The restaurant is a *Dros Steakhouse* franchise, with standard menu (steaks from N$120; breakfast N$130), which is decent enough, though service is slow, and with more of a dark evening-time bar vibe, unless you bag a table on the terrace. Daily 6am–10pm. Camping per site (up to six) N$120, chalet N$2600

Makalani Hotel Ndilimani Cultural Troupe St ☎067 221051, ⓦmakalanihotel.com. Great value, this bright yellow hotel exudes cheerfulness and friendly efficiency: well-maintained rooms are arranged on two floors round the poolside courtyard bar-restaurant (so the noise percolates a little) populated by palm trees, though not a makalani in sight. The preferred venue for a meal out for locals as well as hotel residents, with an adjacent sports bar. B&B N$870

Minen Hotel 9 OMEG Allee ☎067 221071, ⓦminen-hotel.com. The original mine hotel for visiting executives

has had a full revamp; though it's lost much of its original charm and character, it is still the top place to stay in town, with a pleasant tree-filled terrace, nice pool, good food – the pepper steak's a solid choice – and smart, business-style rooms. B&B N$990

Travel North Guesthouse Dr San Nujoma Drive (opposite Telecoms) ☎067 220728, ⓦtravelnorthguesthouse.com. Modern, compact guesthouse offering nine neat, comfy en-suite rooms with a pleasant on-site coffee shop and breakfast room, Europcar rental service, skincare and even a hair salon. N$780

Tsumeb Backpackers 1713 13th Rd ☎067 221534 or ☎081 818 4978, ✉lizellegrassow@gmail.com. A 15min walk from the Intercape bus stop (or they'll pick up if arranged in advance) and supermarket, this new backpackers is a small converted house. Only three small twins (which can function as dorms) with shared bathroom, though more rooms are planned. Spacious, well-equipped modern kitchen, pool table and lovely, shady garden with small pool to cool off in. Friendly, laid-back owners. Dorms N$230, doubles N$700

EATING

Sindano Court Café Corner of OMEG Allee and 5th Rd ☎067 222655. Courtyard café in a pleasant plant-filled patio, with a water feature that has seen better days. Good for a beer, a snack, or coffee and cake. The quality of more

substantial meals (from N$70) is less consistent, but it's the only place to eat outside the hotels. Mon–Sat 6am–9pm, Sun 9am–2pm.

Lake Otjikoto

20km north of Tsumeb on the B1 • Daily 8am–5pm • N$40/person and N$10 parking

A rather neglected site right by the main road, **Lake Otjikoto** is interesting more for what you can't see than for what you can. A sinkhole lake formed by the collapse of a vast underground cavern in the dolomite and limestone rocks, it's like an inverted mushroom, with sheer walls that widen out under water, creating overhangs. Measuring 100m in diameter, its depth is less certain, in part because it does not descend vertically. Some believe the lake is actually bottomless and connected via underground passages to the less accessible – as it's on private farmland – nearby sinkhole, **Lake Guinas**. Others claim it's closer to 55m in depth, as colonial-era explorers Galton and Andersson (after whom two of Etosha's gates are named) earlier surmised, while camping here in 1851. When the sun is shining, the lake gleams an attractive deep blue-green colour, but when overcast, the water appears more murky, and it's easy to see why the San dubbed it "Gaisis", meaning "very ugly". Otjikoto, however, is a Herero name, which loosely translates as "too deep for cattle to drink". The lake's main interest lies in its history as the resting place of many of the retreating German army's munitions, which were hastily dumped here in 1915 just before the army's surrender to South African troops, to prevent the arsenal from falling into the enemy's hands. Many items have subsequently been retrieved, over the years, including a couple of cannons, and are on display in the Tsumeb museum (see p.184). Legend has it that a chest of gold bullion is also lurking in the water among the remaining weaponry, which might partly explain why it's the most popular of Namibia's cave diving locations (experienced divers only; Otjikoto Diving Enterprises ☎081 129 5318, ✉sviljoen@mweb.com.na). While the story is highly unlikely, the existence of abundant fish is fact, including the extraordinary dwarf bream (*Pseudocrenolabrus philander dispersus*), whose female protects her eggs and young by carrying them round in her mouth.

Grootfontein

On a sloping hillside at the northern extreme of Namibia's central plateau, **Grootfontein** is really quite attractive in September and October once the jacaranda and flamboyants bloom; even so, it has a slight frontier feel, in part due to the increasing numbers of informal Kavangan street traders in the town centre. Though Grootfontein is set in fertile agricultural land – producing meat, dairy products, sorghum, maize, ground nuts, sunflowers and leather goods – below and to the east stretches the endless Kalahari, while to the north the flat, dry lowlands extend as far as the Okavango River at Rundu, some 250km away. The Otjiherero name for the place, Otjiwandatjongue, meaning "hill of the leopard", was eschewed by the first white colonizers in favour of the earlier Hai‖om and Bergdamara designation, Gei-‖ous, meaning "big spring", giving rise to the Afrikaans name Grootfontein that persists today. There's little to do in the town, except drop by the old German fort that now houses the museum.

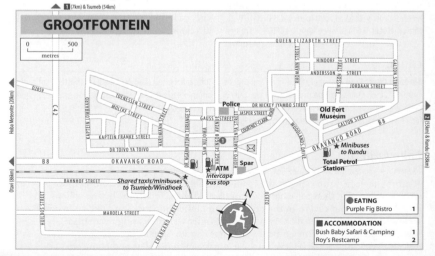

DORSLAND TREKKERS

The **Dorsland Trekkers** were originally granted free land in the area that went on to become Grootfontein by a certain W.W. Jordan, an adventurer and trader, who claimed to have bought a vast tract of land from Ndonga King Kambonde, in exchange for some cash, weaponry and brandy. In 1885, the Dorslanders declared the area the **Republic of Upingtonia** (later Lydensrust), after the prime minister of the Cape Colony at the time, whom they thought would offer support. None was forthcoming, however, leaving them reliant on protection from the Germans. The republic was doomed from the outset, as the Boers were variously challenged by Herero, San and Owambo groups, who disputed their claim to the land, and when Jordan was killed by Owambo King Nehale in 1887, the republic crumbled and was absorbed into German South-West Africa.

Brief history

The area's productive potential in terms of grazing and copper deposits attracted both Owambo and Herero groups to settle here, though the Bergdamara were thought to be the first to introduce copper-smelting to the area. The indigenous populations were soon displaced in 1893, once the South-West Africa Company – initially a British-German enterprise – established its headquarters here. In a short-lived, somewhat bizarre historical episode between 1885 and 1887, a group of Dorsland Trekkers also put down roots here (see box above).

Grootfontein was formally established in 1907, and the railway link was completed a year later. In 1943, the headquarters of the South-West Africa Native Labour organization was established in the town, to recruit workers – primarily Owambo – for the diamond mines in the south but also for the local mines. In the 1970s, the South Africans built a military air base here. Given its history, Grootfontein's 25,000-strong population is unsurprisingly culturally diverse, though most of the farms are still owned by German- or Afrikaans-speaking white Namibians, whereas many of the black population reside in the former township Omulunga, or the informal settlement Blikkiesdorp in far less favourable conditions.

Old Fort Museum

Upingtonia St • Mon–Fri 8.30am–12.30pm, 2–4.30pm (4pm in winter) • N$30 • ☎ 067 242456, ⓦ altefortmuseum.de

The old German fort, which now houses the **Old Fort Museum**, was built in 1896, strategically positioned on a hilltop, with a good view of any impending trouble; the crenellated tower was a later addition. Before its present incarnation in 1975, the building served as a school hostel. It's worth swinging by to have a look at the museum's eclectic collection: standing in the courtyard is a range of colonial-era machinery, including a complete smithy, a steam engine, wood lathes and the obligatory ox-wagon cart – particularly relevant given the town's association with the Dorsland Trekkers, who also feature prominently inside. Add to that displays of German military memorabilia, local gemstones, Kavango basketry and a room dedicated to the Himba, featuring a photo collection and samples of jewellery and apparel, which altogether make the place worth a quick stop.

ARRIVAL AND DEPARTURE   GROOTFONTEIN

By bus The Intercape Mainliner bus (☎ 061 227847, ⓦ intercape.co.za) from Windhoek to Victoria Falls (2pm), via Rundu and Katima Mulilo, stops here three times a week (Mon, Wed & Fri; 8.10pm; 15hr; from N$315). It stops here on the return journey just after midnight (Mon, Thur & Sat; from N$342), arriving in Windhoek at 6am the same day.

By minibus Minibuses leave for Rundu (N$170) from the Total garage north of the town centre, whereas minibuses heading south, to Windhoek (N$230), via Otavi and Otjiwarongo, as well as local buses bound for Tsumeb, leave from the Puma station at the other end of town, close to the junction between the B8 and the C34.

ACCOMMODATION

Bush Baby Safari & Camping Signposted off the C42, 7km from the junction with the B8 ☎ 067 243391 or ☎ 081 829 3711, ⊕ bush-babycamping .com. Rustic lodge in need of a little TLC, but delightful nevertheless. A row of simple stone-and-thatch chalets (number 1 is the nicest), with private patios and exterior ablution blocks, sits atop a high ridge overlooking an illuminated waterhole on the plain below, where a few antelope roam. Meals are limited but served on the lovely main terrace. The shady campground down below by reception also contains smaller bush bungalows, with braai facilities and a couple of basic "luxury" tents, and space to pitch your own. Camping per person **N$90**,

bush bungalows (B&B) **N$1600**, lodge chalets **N$1800**

Roy's Restcamp 55km north of Grootfontein on the B8 ☎ 067 240302, ⊕ roysrestcamp.com. This well-run place is a popular stopover, especially for overlanders and camping groups, with a rustic offbeat vibe reflected in the chalets (though they do have a/c and mosquito nets) and the campground decorations, from wood carvings to rusting vehicles. Sites are fairly close together. Pleasant bar and pool area serving filling meals (dinner N$205); book in advance. The local wildlife can be watched at an illuminated waterhole, and excursions are organized to the Ju|'Hoansi Living Village at Grashoek. Camping per person **N$120**, chalet (B&B) **N$1320**

EATING

Purple Fig Bistro 19 Hage Geingob St ☎ 081 124 2802, ⊕ facebook.com/purplefigbistro. At the back of the private health centre, spa and beauty salon is Grootfontein's only restaurant where you'd want to linger, whether over breakfast, a mid-morning latte and a slice of cake, or at

lunch or dinner. Snacks from N$60, schnitzels, steaks and the like N$90–175, accompanied by mellow jazz in a shady garden or inside. Mon–Fri 6am–10pm, Sat 7am–1pm, 4–10pm.

4 Hoba Meteorite

20km down the D2859, signposted west off the C42, 1km from the junction with the B8 • Daily sunrise to sunset • N$30 entry plus N$10 parking • Note that it's also signposted off the B8 between Grootfontein and Otavi, but this gravel road is much rougher

The most popular attraction in the area is the **Hoba Meteorite**, the planet's largest single known meteorite; measuring just under 3m square, and around 1m deep, it weighs in at approximately 60 tonnes – almost five times heavier than a laden double-decker bus. Though its age is estimated at anything between 190 million and 410 million years old, it can more accurately be said to have fallen to Earth less than 80,000 years ago. This lump of alien rock is primarily made up of iron (82.3 percent and nickel (16.4 percent), with small amounts of other minerals. It was revealed to the outside world in 1920, by Jacobus Hermanus Brits, a farmer who was out hunting on his land when he noticed a strange, black rocky protrusion that stood out from the surrounding pale limestone. He chiselled a chunk off, and took it for analysis, which confirmed its extra-terrestrial nature. After it became clear that Namibia would lose its "fallen star" altogether to enthusiastic vandals who were keen to chip off their own space souvenir, the meteorite was declared a national monument in 1955. Once you've marvelled at the lump, which sits in a sunken stone surround, there's a pleasant picnic area to enjoy and a kiosk selling souvenirs, information leaflets and cold drinks.

Omaruru

Sited at the crossroads between the C33 – the short cut between Swakopmund and Otjiwarongo on the main road north – and the less frequented C36, which leads to the Brandberg, **OMARURU**, a small, somnolent town, makes a good stopover. It's also within easy striking distance of the scenic Erongo Mountains (see p.190). Established in 1868 by Wilhelm Zeraua, the first Herero White Flag chief, it later became a mission town – the old mission house is now a small, rather uninspiring **museum** (Mon–Fri 8am–5pm) – and was repeatedly the focus of battles between the Nama and Herero, then later the Herero and the German army. The distinctive, cylindrical **Franke Tower memorial**, which lies across the Omaruru River in a street parallel to the main

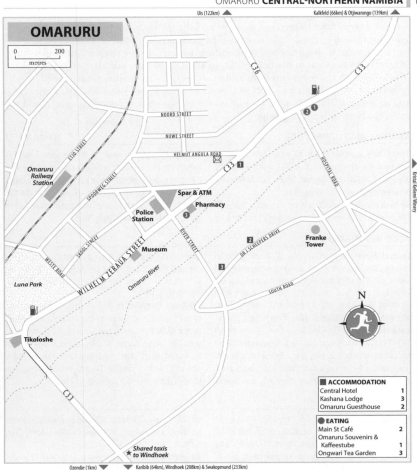

ACCOMMODATION

Central Hotel	1
Kashana Lodge	3
Omaruru Guesthouse	2

EATING

Main St Café	2
Omaruru Souvenirs & Kaffeestube	1
Ongwari Tea Garden	3

drag, is a remnant of the latter. Over the weekend closest to October 10, Herero flock to the former township of Ozondje, to mark **White Flag Day**, in commemoration of those who died fighting colonialism.

These days, Omaruru is garnering a reputation as a centre for arts and crafts – check out the shops on the attractive, shady main street. In particular, don't miss the Tikoloshe workshop and souvenir store (☎064 571215, ⊛tikoloshe.iway.na; daily 9am–4.30pm) at the western end, where you can watch the Kavango root-carving artists at work, and peruse the craft shop, which sells their work, as well as all kinds of crafts from all over Africa. If you're in the area towards the end of September, look out for the increasingly popular annual arts and cultural festival, which involves exhibitions and workshops.

The Kristall Kellerei Winery

4km northeast of Omaruru on the D2328, a dirt road accessible in a saloon car • Mon–Fri 8am–4pm, Sat 8am–12.30pm • Wine-tasting and tour N$60; with cold lunch platter N$120 • ☎ 064 570083 or ☎ 081 127 0954, ⊛ kristallkellerei.com

An unlikely but exceedingly pleasant place to while away a couple of hours is the **Kristall Kellerei Winery**, one of Namibia's rare vineyards, and a real entrepreneurial venture. Have a **tour** (30min) of the vines and the fermentation shed, followed by a generous **tasting** in the delightful, tree-filled garden, full of birdlife. Everything's hand-processed with a great deal of invention, underscored by the need to keep wine temperatures constant in the desert heat. In addition to their popular white and red wines – though the red is currently in short supply while the vines are replanted following a fungal infection – they also produce some knock-out schnapps, a tasty gin, and an award-winning Nappa, Namibia's answer to grappa. It's worth ringing ahead to avoid clashing with a tour group.

ARRIVAL AND DEPARTURE OMARURU

By car Easily accessible on the C33, a good tarred road that runs between Otjiwarongo (see p.176), which lies on the main road north, and Karibib, which lies on the B2, between Windhoek and Swakopmund.

By taxi/minibus Shared transport frequently leaves for Windhoek from the junction between the C33 and the road

leading into Ozondje, south of the Omaruru River. Ask around the Monte Christo Service Station in Katutura for transport to Omaruru; otherwise you might have to take a minibus bound for Swakopmund, getting off at the C36 turn-off north, midway between Okahandja and Karibib on the B2, and hitch the remaining 70km.

ACCOMMODATION

Central Hotel Wilhelm Zeraua St ☎ 064 570030, ⓦ centralhotelomaruru.com. Under new ownership and with a sparkling white coat of paint, this hundred-year-old hotel is a solid bet, possessing spacious rooms with gleaming tiled floors and a decent restaurant and bar, where you can watch football. Mains from N$90. **N$900**

Kashana Lodge Dr Ian Scheepers Drive ☎ 064 571434, ⓦ kashana-namibia.com. A converted casino for Canadian miners is now a good deal for a bed in town, with a decent restaurant under shady trees and a popular, buzzing bar. Offering standard, and slightly

larger, ambitiously named "luxury rooms", there's plenty of space, though bathrooms are small, and rooms come with DStv, a ceiling fan and a/c. Doubles **N$1280**, chalets **N$1580**

Omaruru Guesthouse 305 Dr Ian Scheepers Drive ☎ 064 570035, ⓦ omaruru-guesthouse.com. Larger than it looks, this homely guesthouse has 20 simple fan-ventilated rooms (singles, doubles, triples & family), with faux-wood floors, firm mattresses and the necessary amenities: fridge, satellite TV and tea/coffee. Outside there's a shady verandah and pool. **N$710**

EATING

Main St Café Wilhelm Zeraua St ☎ 064 570544. A bright and cheerful spot serving breakfast, cakes and coffee (though with a great range of speciality teas) or lunch – tasty salads or hot dishes, including the signature meatballs sub, which should lay you out for the afternoon. Most mains cost under N$80, and there's free wi-fi. Tues–Sun 8am–3pm.

Omaruru Souvenirs & Kaffeestube Wilhelm Zeraua St ☎ 064 570230. Food can be served on a pleasant terrace overlooking a garden, or in a circular thatched dining room.

Great for cappuccino and calorific cakes, and it also serves breakfast and lunch. Mon–Sat 7.30am–5pm, Sun 8.30am–5pm.

Ongwari Tea Garden Wilhelm Zeraua St. Pleasant wooden benches and tables on a shady patio at the back of the pharmacy, serving breakfasts, *brötchen*, toasted sandwiches (N$20–30) and smoothies, with a more substantial lunch special on Wed & Fri. Mon–Fri 8am–5pm, Sat 8am–1pm.

The Erongo Mountains

Only a couple of hours' drive northwest of Windhoek, the splendid rounded summits of the **Erongo Mountains** loom out of the landscape, a draw for hikers and those interested in San rock art. The eroded remains of a volcanic magma chamber that collapsed around 110 million years ago, the Erongos comprise vast granite domes – the highest ones in the west topping 2200m – and collections of boulders weathered into fascinating formations, which glow in the late afternoon light. With the Namib Desert to the west, and semi-arid savannah to the east, they lie in an important transition zone and therefore host an impressive diversity of **plant and animal life**, including almost two hundred bird species. In addition to kudu, mountain zebra, klipspringer, steenbok and dik-dik, keep a look out for the rare

ROCK ART IN THE ERONGOS

The Erongos are rich in **San rock paintings**; several of the guestfarms and lodges in the area possess examples on their land and offer guided or self-guided walks to view them. As with most other San rock art, figures include animals and humans, seemingly engaged in hunting or rituals related to fertility and community harmony (see box, p.197). The most celebrated example is **Phillip's Cave**. Located on the land of the *Ameib Guesthouse* – which welcomes day visitors (N$70; see below) – it is known for its giant white elephant with a superimposed red antelope, among other identifiable animals: ostrich, giraffe, rhino and various human figures. The cave, a thirty-minute hike from the parking area, is an impressive overhang, affording extensive views across the desert plains.

black-faced impala and black mongoose as well as the chattering rosy-faced lovebirds or the quieter Rüppell's parrots. Black rhino have also been reintroduced in recent years.

ARRIVAL AND DEPARTURE   THE ERONGO MOUNTAINS

By car The only way to explore the Erongos is with your own vehicle. The main access road, the D2315, runs 60km east–west across the northern edges of the range, where it meets the north–south-running D1395, which gives access to the Erongos from the west, and connects with the B2, the main Windhoek–Swakopmund highway. The turn-off for the D2315, a good-quality gravel road, is on the C33, a couple of kilometres south of Omaruru. Several accommodation options are signposted off the D2315. After about 10km on this road, heading west from Omaruru, you pass through a conservancy gate, where you may need to give your details, but there is no charge.

ACCOMMODATION

Ameib Guesthouse At the end of the gravel D1937, 30km north of Usakos ☎081 857 4639, ⓦameib.com. Remote old farmhouse with nine no-frills doubles, plus a campground – wholly solar-powered – in truly spectacular scenery. There's abundant birdlife in the tree-filled grounds, and a small pool. The fenced campground offers some shade, and shared picnic tables, though each site has a braai. No electricity points. A few basic cement cabins are also available. Camping per person **N$140**, cabins (B&B) **N$850**, doubles **N$1480**

★**Camp Mara** Just off the D2315, 10km west of the conservancy entrance gate ☎064 571190 or ☎081 128 1203, ⓦcampmara.com. Relaxed, informal place, with lots of character, and five individually designed tasteful yet rustic rooms looking out at the thorntrees, where rosy-cheeked lovebirds and Rüppell's parrots flit around, and across to the impressive Erongo Mountains. Camping per person **N$150**, self-catering **N$1100**, double (DBB) **N$1750**

Erongo Plateau Campsite On Guest Farm Eileen ☎061 221567 (reservations). Four pitches – so book ahead – on the edge of a slight plateau offer stunning views across the plains. There's no electricity but good hot showers, which you can take by candlelight, and a braai site and cement "table", sheltered from the sometimes chilly wind. A 5km self-guided trail is available. High-clearance vehicle necessary. Camping per person **N$130**

★**Erongo Wilderness Lodge** Just off the D2315, 10km west of the conservancy entrance gate ☎064 570537 (lodge) or ☎061 239199 (reservations), ⓦerongowilderness-namibia.com. A real gem of a lodge tucked away amid the giant granite boulders, with friendly, professional staff and excellent guiding, though prices have escalated recently. Ten stylish safari tents on polished wooden platforms sit high among the boulders, offering lovely views from their private decks. Bathrooms are semi-open so you can bathe while further soaking up the scenery. There's a lovely intimate dining terrace too, also offering superb vistas, plus a swimming pool carved into the rock with a stone croc at the bottom. Popular with birders. Nature drive N$485. DBB **N$5000**

Guest Farm Eileen Off the D2316, 40km southwest of Omaruru ☎064 570837 or ☎081 277 1668, ⓦerongo .iway.na/eileen. Small, welcoming guestfarm in a scenic setting with five tidy, modest rooms. Meals are eaten communally in the small inside dining area or on the patio overlooking the lovely tree-filled garden, which has a small pool. High-clearance vehicle necessary. DBB **N$1700**

Hohenstein Lodge 25km along the D1935 from the junction with the B2 ☎061 240020, ⓦhohenstein lodge.com. Lovely, simple lodge comprising 14 squat rooms with private patios on which to enjoy superlative views of the Spitzkoppe and the Erongos. Guided hikes, birdwatching and sundowner drives on offer. DBB **N$2900**

★**Omandumba** On the D2315, 40km west of conservancy entrance gate ☎064 571086, ⓦomandumba.de. Spread over two farms, offering a range of accommodation, in a warm, family environment:

4

eight rustic rooms and one self-catering bungalow (for six) are decent enough, but the five camping pitches are the star attraction here. The lovely secluded pitches are spread out across the farm, snuggled in among the boulders, with donkey-fired water, open-air toilet facilities, private braai site but no electricity. Only five spots are available, so book ahead. A San living museum is on the property and open daily. Camping per person N$140, doubles (AI) N$2240

Damaraland

In western Erongo, flattish semi-desert savannah stretches northwards, the horizon interrupted by the distinctive domed peak of the **Spitzkoppe**, much favoured by rock climbers. Beyond is the vast massif of the **Brandberg**, home to the country's finest collection of San rock paintings. This is the area known as **Damaraland** – a colonial and apartheid-era term that has seemingly stuck – which comprises some of the country's most beguiling landscapes, and is still predominantly inhabited by the Damara people, after whom it's named.

As you cross the ephemeral Ugab River – a linear oasis of luxuriant vegetation and a vital source of nourishment for elusive desert-adapted elephants – into **southern Kunene**, the undulating landscape becomes hauntingly beautiful. Expansive grasslands are interspersed with colourful escarpments of layered sediment and endless kopjies of burnished granite, embellished by the occasional dazzling white trunk of the five-lobed sterculia tree clinging onto a boulder. In the middle of all this is one of the continent's largest collections of ancient rock engravings, at **Twyfelfontein**.

4

Spitzkoppe

On the D3176, 11km north from the turn-off from the D1918 • Day-visitors should check in and pay at the campground reception (N$50/person and N$60/vehicle)

One of Namibia's most recognizable landmarks, and a magnet for rock-climbers, the **Spitzkoppe** has featured on the cover of many a holiday brochure. Its distinctive pointed peak – which has earned it the nickname, the Matterhorn of Africa – measures 1728m, and towers around 700m above the surrounding desert plains. This granite bornhardt – a bald, rounded and steep-sided inselberg – was formed around 130 million years ago through volcanic activity and shaped over time as its surroundings were eroded away, resulting in fascinating **rock formations**, including several rock arches. What's more, its giant granite domes and exfoliating boulders positively glow like burnished gold in the late afternoon or early morning light.

Between the Spitzkoppe and the equally impressive neighbouring Pondoks, a fenced area holds a thinly stocked **game reserve** – which you can only visit with a guide – a remnant of when the Hollywood flop *10,000 BC* was filmed here. Of much greater appeal are the **hiking** possibilities and the chance to see some fine examples of **rock art**. Sadly, the most well-known site, Bushman's Paradise, no longer lives up to its name, having been damaged by over-enthusiastic tourists and vandals; however, there are plenty more pristine rock paintings to discover in less accessible spots if you arrange to hike with a guide from the local Damara conservancy (N$50/person for two hours; see below).

ARRIVAL AND TOURS
SPITZKOPPE

By car Turn north off the B2, 23km west of Usakos, onto the gravel D1918 bound for Henties Bay, then north 12km up the D3716.

By bus and hitching The nearest place a bus passes to the Spitzkoppe is the turn-off from the B2, 23km west of Usakos; any of the transport that runs between Windhoek and Swakopmund (see p.91 & p.212) can drop you off, but from there you'd have to hitch, and traffic is sparse.

Guided hikes There are three strenuous guided hikes available (4–8hr), which take in various rock art sites. Guides are all from the local community (and vary in quality) and should be booked at the campground reception. Costs are N$50/person for every two hours of guiding.

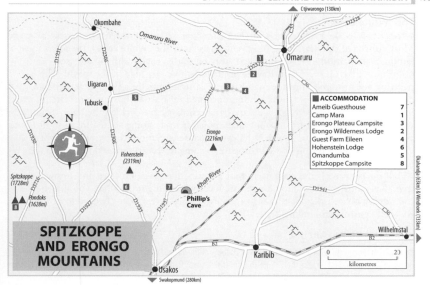

Ctjiwarongo (130km)

Okombahe

Omaruru River

Okahandja (63km) & Windhoek (133km)

Omaruru

Uigaran

Tubusis

N

Erongo (2216m)

Hohenstein (2319m)

Khan River

Spitzkoppe (1728m)

Pondoks (1628m)

Phillip's Cave

D1941

Wilhelmstal

SPITZKOPPE AND ERONGO MOUNTAINS

Usakos

Karibib

0   20

kilometres

Swakopmund (280km)

■ ACCOMMODATION	
Ameib Guesthouse	7
Camp Mara	1
Erongo Plateau Campsite	3
Erongo Wilderness Lodge	2
Guest Farm Eileen	4
Hohenstein Lodge	6
Omandumba	5
Spitzkoppe Campsite	8

ACCOMMODATION

Spitzkoppe Campsite ☎ 064 464144 or ☎ 081 850 2566, ⊛ spitzkoppe.com. This back-to-nature community campground is now a joint venture with a private enterprise, so facilities are gradually being upgraded. Currently there are 31 pre-bookable basic pitches nestled among the boulders, offering varying degrees of seclusion and shade. No electricity, long-drop toilets, no water – fill cans at the tap by the open-air showers, adjacent to the costly bar-restaurant. Here you can book meals and purchase wood and braai packs. Per person N$135

Spitzkoppe tented camp In the Spitzkoppe reserve, 5km beyond the camp entrance ☎ 081 805 3178, ⊛ spitzkoppemountaincamp.com. Newly opened lodge where tented chalets raised on stilts gaze across at the Spitzkoppe itself. Offered on a self-catering (though only braai site and no individual fridges available) or B&B basis. Similar hiking and free-climbing activities to the campsite are on offer, plus mountain bike availability. Also a pool, bar and restaurant on site. N$1280

The Brandberg

Namibia's most magnificent massif, the **Brandberg**, is visible from miles around, towering close on 2km above the surrounding desert plains and shimmering like a pink mirage through the heat haze. Not only a fabulous, and little-explored, **hiking** destination, the Brandberg is also Namibia's pre-eminent site for **rock art**, boasting around nine hundred sites and 43,000 paintings and engravings, many in pristine condition.

Reaching 2573m at one point, the granite massif contains the highest peak in Namibia – **Königstein** – though its mass is equally impressive; formed from the eroded granite remains of a collapsed magma chamber over 130 million years ago, this almost circular inselberg measures nearly 140km round the base. Deep ravines slice through the rock in several places, where precious water collects and vegetation thrives.

The name Brandberg ("Fire Mountain" in German, and Dâures or "Burning Mountain" in Damara) alludes to the glowing effect of the sun on the rock at sunrise and sunset. In contrast, the Otjiherero name – Omukuruvaro – means "Mountain of the Gods", and indeed it is believed to have been a site of spiritual importance for the early San, whose art adorns the numerous overhangs, rock faces and even boulders of the massif. Archeological remains also indicate that groups of migrating San often stayed in the Brandberg's upper reaches, probably drawn by the availability of shelter and water.

The "White Lady"

At the end of the D2359, 20km from the junction with the C35 • Daily 8am–5pm • N$50/person plus N$20/vehicle; entry includes guided walk

Most visitors to the Brandberg only venture as far as the **"White Lady"**, the area's most famous rock painting, which is tucked away beneath a rock overhang an easy 45-minute hike up the Tsisab Ravine on the northwestern side of the massif. The painting got its name from the mainly white central figure in a frieze that seems to depict some kind of procession, whom renowned rock art authority Henri Breuil, back in the 1940s, concluded was a woman. Later scholars have decided the figure is not a woman at all, but probably a young man, possibly undergoing some initiation ritual, or alternatively a traditional healer. Whatever the interpretation, the painting is worth a visit, even if its condition doesn't compare to some of the art secreted higher up the mountain.

Half the pleasure is the **walk** itself, past Brandberg acacias, mustard and ironwood trees. Keen birdwatchers should aim for an early morning start, when you may be rewarded with a display of colour in the form of bee-eaters, rosy-cheeked lovebirds, Rüppell's parrots and bokmakieries.

ARRIVAL AND DEPARTURE   THE BRANDBERG

By car From the south – to access the "White Lady" on the Brandberg's eastern flank – take the C35 north from Uis towards Khorixas; after 13km take the well-signposted turn-off west onto the D2359. From the north, take the C35 south from Khorixas. Access is possible in a saloon car and fuel is available in Uis.

ACTIVITIES AND TOURS

Guides Pay your entry fee to the staff member at the entry kiosk at the "White Lady", who will assign a guide from the Dâureb Mountain Guide Association, one of the country's more successful community-based tourism projects. It is appropriate to tip the guide if they do a good job.

Hiking If you want to do one of the multi-day hikes up the Brandberg, you need to get a permit (N$150) from the National Heritage Council in Windhoek on 53 Robert Mugabe Ave (☎ 061 244375, ⓦ nhc-nam.org), usually giving two days' notice, though there are moves afoot to allow the guiding association the right to sell the permits on the spot. The cost is currently N$300 per person.

ACCOMMODATION

Ugab River Camp End of the D2303, northwest of the Brandberg ☎ 064 403829; email reservations preferred: ⓔ srt@rhino-trust.org.na. Isolated, basic wilderness camp in the dry riverbed, with some sites fenced off with reed partitions. Communal showers and long-drop toilets, plus you need to bring your own firewood and drinking water. Camp fees in aid of the Save the Rhino Trust (ⓦ savetherhino trust.org). Mainly used by 4WD campers exploring the Messum Crater but can be accessed by high-clearance 2WD when dry. Beware of elephants. Camping per person **N$100**

CLIMBING THE MASSIF

Though not a technical ascent – unless you want it to be – **climbing the Brandberg** is not a light undertaking. The heat is intense, you need to carry food and water, and the constant boulder scrambling gets tiring, but it's an unforgettable experience; the chance to sleep out under the stars, peer at some stunningly vivid rock art that few people have seen in modern times, and truly feel on top of the world. However, you need to acquire a **permit** and hire a **guide** from the Heritage Council in Windhoek (see box, p.94) – an attempt by government to regulate visitors and protect the rock art and the area's outstanding biodiversity, which includes a high number of scorpion species. The guiding is generally excellent, undertaken by a member of the highly trained local conservancy guide association (see p.192). The usual trip starts from Uis (see opposite) and lasts three days, and you'll need to carry your food – enough for the guide too – as well as water and a sleeping bag. The first day, the most arduous, you hike and scramble up the mountain (6–8hr); the second day is spent exploring rock art sites and soaking up the jaw-dropping views, before descending again on the third. Ascents of Königstein can also be organized. If you want to avoid the organizational hassle, some of the tour operators in Windhoek and Swakop also organize the trip.

Ugab Wilderness Camp 8km north of the D2359, 6km before the "White Lady". ☏ 081 336 3202. Well-managed community campground that can get busy in high season. Flush toilets and hot-water showers but no running water or electricity. Best of all, a magical location, and a good place to arrange hiking on the Brandberg. Camping per person N$100

★**White Lady Lodge** Signed 27km off the D2359 ☏ 064 684004, ⊚ brandbergwllodge.com. This place is all about location: at the foot of the majestic Brandberg and on the banks of the scenic Ugab River, with a good chance of seeing desert elephants, especially in the dry season. Other than the nicely landscaped grounds, with two pools, everything's pretty rustic, and tired in places: stone rooms and basic campground chalets. But the simple riverside campground (with safari tents if you want) is a nature-lovers' dream, spread out among huge ana trees. Be prepared for elephant visitors. 4WD necessary. DBB or bed-only rates also possible. Camping per person N$100, safari tents N$660, doubles and chalets N$1465

Uis

For several decades **UIS**, 30km southeast of the Brandberg, flourished as a town. The tin-mining industry prospered – the large slag heap that greets you when approaching the town from the south is testament to that – but the dwindling population of around 4000 has struggled since the operation closed down in 1990, and the ultimate insult came in 2010 when the place was downgraded from a village to a settlement. These days there's a down-at-heel feel to the place, yet Uis still sees quite a lot of tourist traffic, stopping to refuel and calling in at the supermarket while travelling between the Spitzkoppe and the Brandberg. Should you wish to break the journey, there are a couple of decent, inexpensive places to overnight here, including the *Brandberg Restcamp*, on the site of the mine's former recreation club.

4

ACCOMMODATION   UIS

Brandberg Restcamp Main road ☏ 064 504038; map p.170. The star attraction of this otherwise no-frills restcamp is the glittering 25m swimming pool in the central courtyard – a leftover from the local tin mine's recreational facilities. Otherwise, there are functional doubles, self-catering (for up to six), dorms or camping facilities to choose from. The bar-restaurant is decent enough and tours can be arranged through reception. Camping per person N$150, dorms N$250, self-catering for two N$700, doubles N$1100

Daureb Isib Corner of 3rd Ave and the golf course ☏ 081 127 0170, ⊚ daurebisib.com; map p.170. Pleasant five-pitch campground (plus one for overlander groups), each with private wood-and-palm shelter, table and chairs, braai site and ablutions, and a shared pool. The *Cactus and Coffee Tea Garden* offers tasty savoury snacks and light bites as well as smoothies, cakes and coffee, and is surrounded by succulents from the on-site tree nursery. Daily 7.30am–5pm.

White Lady B&B 3rd Ave ☏ 064 504102; map p.170. A neat and tidy guesthouse – nothing fancy, but with six simple thatched rooms with mosquito nets and a/c as well as a small sheltered campground (only four sites) set in a high-walled sandy yard. The small pool is a welcome bonus. Camping per person N$130, doubles N$1170

Twyfelfontein and around

At the end of the D3214 • Daily 8am–5pm • N$60/person and N$20/vehicle; entry includes guided tour; N$160 for a guided tour of the petroglyphs, the Zieben Plateau, the Organ Pipes and Burnt Mountain, plus N$60 for parking

At the head of the shallow Huab Valley in southern Kunene, large sandstone slabs that have broken off the flat-topped escarpment lie in jumbled piles, their smooth surfaces covered with one of the continent's greatest concentrations of **rock engravings**. They are collectively referred to as **TWYFELFONTEIN**, meaning "uncertain spring" in Afrikaans, reflecting a farmer's fears about the local water source, though the local Damara name |Ui-||Aes – meaning "place among the rocks" – is now also used, in recognition of the earlier nomadic Damara communities that made seasonal use of the land. Many of the petroglyphs date back to six thousand years ago when San hunter-gatherers inhabited the region, drawn by the availability of water. Note that the name Twyfelfontein is also often used to refer to the general area, which encompasses several other geological curiosities; the **Organ Pipes** and **Burnt Mountain** are worth a quick detour if you've got your own transport and forty minutes to spare.

TWYFELFONTEIN AREA

ACCOMMODATION

Abu Huab Campsite	4
Damaraland Camp	1
Doro !Nawas	2
Granietkop Campsite	6
Madisa Campsite	7
Mowani Mountain Camp	3
Twyfelfontein Country Lodge	5

The rock engravings

In all, an estimated 2500–5000 **rock carvings** were created, as well as a few paintings, though the latter are not for tourist consumption and only a small proportion of the rock engravings can be visited. These predominantly depict humans or animals and animal spoor – including images displaying a mixture of animal and human features – as well as geometric shapes. The choice of **imagery** and the **siting** of the petroglyphs and paintings are now thought to relate to the societies' belief systems, shamanic rituals and the spiritual world that shamans had access to while in a trance, rather than straightforward depictions of the world around them (see box opposite).

As a UNESCO World Heritage Site, the rock engravings of Twyfelfontein are firmly on the tourist trail, attracting around fifty thousand visitors annually, so to miss the crowds and the heat, you should aim for early morning (though some of the rocks are in shadow then), or late afternoon, when the light is at its best. Since there's no shade at the site, avoiding the midday sun, especially in summer, is imperative. To visit, you need to take a **guided tour**: the generally well-informed guides offer three circuits, involving varying degrees of physical exertion, which last thirty, sixty or eighty minutes. There is also an excellent information centre and a small café.

Damara Living Museum

On the D3214 • Daily 8am–5pm • 30min tour N$70; 30min bushwalk N$70; N$140 for both • ⓦ lcfn.info/damara/home

A few kilometres back up the valley is one of Namibia's living museums (see box, p.56): the **Damara Living Museum** gives some insight into traditional Damara skills, crafts and practices, though if a large tour group is visiting, it can make you squirm. The traditional village tour includes talks and demonstrations on blacksmithing, leather tanning, jewellery and other craft-making.

Organ Pipes

On the D3254 • Daily sunrise to sunset • Free • Coming from the rock art site at Twyfelfontein, turn right down the D3254, from where it's a 4km drive. Parking is on the left

The **Organ Pipes**, which, with a little imagination, vaguely resemble the eponymous church instrument, are actually two walls of densely packed polyhedral dolerite pillars at the bottom of a shallow sandy gorge. They make a good subject for photos – mid-morning and mid-afternoon are the best times to catch them. Peer over the edge of the parking area and you'll see the path that leads you down into the ravine.

Burnt Mountain

On the D3254 • Daily sunrise to sunset • Free • Coming from the rock art site at Twyfelfontein, turn right down the D3254, from where it's a 5km drive

A kilometre further along from the Organ Pipes, on the opposite side of the road, the **Burnt Mountain** can often be less impressive: the compacted shale resembles a bleak, black industrial slag heap for much of the day, though the manganese coating gives it a purplish hue in the early morning or late afternoon light, which, together with the golden glow of the neighbouring sandstone, can sometimes make the mountain appear to be on fire.

Petrified Forest

Signposted north off the C39, 45km west of Khorixas • Daily 8am–6pm • N$40/person and N$20/vehicle; entry includes 30–40min guided tour

If you're expecting something akin to a scene from *Lord of the Rings*, you will be disappointed, as the **Petrified Forest** is not a forest per se, but a fascinating collection of some two hundred fossilized tree trunks, some fully exposed, others partly buried in

SAN ROCK ART IN NAMIBIA

When you've climbed, scrambled and sweated your way over endless boulders in the hot afternoon sun and are finally confronted with a crumbling cave wall of barely discernable smudges and shapes, it's easy to wonder why so much fuss is made about **ancient rock art**. But when face to face with some of its more vivid depictions, it's hard not to be moved, especially considering the thousands of years it may have survived the elements.

Of course, being able to **interpret the art** helps to deepen your appreciation, though theories come and go about what it all means and why it was done. More recent thinking, informed by anthropological work with existing San communities about their beliefs and ritual practices, considers most rock art to be related to **San religious cosmology**. Thus, what earlier theorists took to be straightforward representations of hunting scenes, interpreted either as narratives of actual hunts or messages to other San groups about where to find food, are now thought to relate to rainmaking rituals, which involved animals, or to the symbolic association of particular beasts. The oft-represented eland, for example, was frequently led to a hilltop and sacrificed in the belief that rain would fall there; a buffalo may in fact be the "Rain Bull", controller of rain but also of sickness and health and therefore a death deity. A cornerstone of San religious beliefs is the ability of the shaman to enter the spirit world through a **trance dance**, and many of the figures and scenes suggest their trance visions – understood as symbols and metaphors, rather than literal depictions – which are probably linked to San mythology. The high number of paintings that are half-animal and half-human may relate to the widespread San **creation myth** that all animals were once human; alternatively, they may embody the physical transformation the shaman undergoes when entering the spirit world.

Rock art falls into two categories that are rarely found together: **rock paintings** (pictographs), for which the Brandberg is most renowned (see p.193), and **rock engravings** (petroglyphs), found in abundance in Twyfelfontein (see opposite). Increasingly, the **context** of the art is considered to be significant: many paintings or engravings are located near fissures and crevices in the rock, which would serve as entrances to the spirit world; some paintings are situated in dark caves, where shamans were thought to concentrate their energies.

Not all rock art found in Namibia is of San origin: the Apollo 11 Cave, in the inaccessible Huns Mountains west of the Fish River Canyon – and the most ancient known site in Africa, estimated to be over 25,000 years old – is also thought to contain art by the **Khoikhoi**. Their art differed from that of the San, generally displaying more handprints, dots and geometric shapes, and drawn with their fingers rather than with brushes.

4

sandstone – it's the largest collection in southern Africa. Only two are almost full length, at around 45m; the rest are segments but they are incredibly lifelike – you can see the bark and even count the growth rings. The process of petrification began over 200 million years ago, when the trees are thought to have been washed down the valley in a flood and buried in alluvial deposits. Over time, deprived of air and under extreme pressure, rather than decay, the trunks were permeated by aqueous silica, which gradually replaced the organic matter; then, as the water was lost, the wood finally petrified.

On the compulsory **guided tour**, you'll also take in a number of welwitschia specimens (see box, p.218). Note that a few local entrepreneurs have also established their own petrified forest sites in the area, signposted off the C39, but this one has an official sign and operates with trained guides. A craft shop is also on site.

ARRIVAL   TWYFELFONTEIN

By car Twyfelfontein is at the end of the D3214, well signposted off the D2612, 73km west of Khorixas, off the C39. There's no public transport to the area.

Tourist information The information centre at the rock engravings site is the place to direct your enquiries.

ACCOMMODATION

Abu Huab Campsite D3254, 2.6km south of the junction with the D2612 ☎081 396 6064, ✉abahuabreservation@iway.na. Located by the dry river of the same name, a short drive from Twyfelfontein, this community campground is in need of some investment. Apart from the main building, which boasts a bar-restaurant and pool table and one modern shower block, many pitches are rather run-down. Camping per person N$150, tent and bedding per person N$300

Damaraland Camp 5km south of the C39, 2km west of the junction with the D2612 ☎(0)11 257 5111 (South Africa), ⊛wilderness.co.za. Pioneering joint venture with the local conservancy: ten raised chalets – a mix of adobe, thatch and canvas with all the usual wilderness Safari comforts – in a scenic rocky location, with welwitschias down the river bed. N$16,800

Doro !Nawas South Africa ☎(0)11 257 5111, ⊛wilderness.co.za. Looming like a hilltop fort as you approach, the main building of this well-run wilderness camp offers panoramic views of the surrounding mountainscape. As convenient for self-drive visitors as for the more customary all-inclusive package clients, the place comprises 16 spacious stone-and-canvas units under thatch, arranged at the foot of a kopjie, with glass doors and veranda, where you can sleep out under the stars. Activities include a visit to Twyfelfontein – which you could easily do yourself – and tracking desert-adapted elephants. DBB N$9740

★Granietkop Campsite On the D2612, 45km east of Twyfelfontein ☎081 200 6991 or ☎081 727 3163. Four lovely private pitches in this community venture, tucked beside a granite kopjie with wonderful views across the mopane plains, though little shade. Donkey-fired hot water, individual ablutions with nicely made shower and flush toilet, plus a shaded washing-up area. Reception is often unstaffed, but set up camp and someone will turn up eventually. N$150

★Madisa Campsite On the D2612, 50km east of Twyfelfontein ☎081 698 2908, ⊛madisacamp.com. Set among mopane trees, nine individual pitches overlook the Gauntegab River, where desert elephants roam. You'll get the best view from your private, open-air shower-toilet on stilts, powered by a donkey, fired by your substantial braai hearth. Sites 5–9 offer greater privacy and less generator noise (6–9pm), though it's a longer walk to the bar and swimming pool area, nestled among the granite boulders. Meals on request. Also with simple safari tents for rent. Camping per person N$170, safari tents (tent only) N$1430

★Mowani Mountain Camp 3km north of the D2612, 3km east of the junction with the D2354 ☎061 232009, ⊛mowani.com. Blending in with the granite boulders, this tasteful, upmarket eco-lodge with a genuine commitment to community development comprises a dozen canvas-and-thatch rondavels. Comfortably furnished with colonial-style wicker and wood furniture, they also come with viewing decks, some with spectacular vistas. Other attractions include intimate dining, a waterhole and a pool with sundeck built into the rocks. Excursions to Twyfelfontein and guided hikes are on offer. A rustic campground is outside the main gate, without access to lodge facilities; sites have nice private cooking and washing facilities. Camping per person N$250, doubles (DBB) N$5960

Twyfelfontein Country Lodge Huab Valley, 4km from Twyfelfontein ☎021 855 0395, ⊛twyfelfonteinlodge.com. You can't get any closer to the rock engravings than here – in fact the place has its own rock art at the entrance – but you pay for the convenience. Overpriced, rustic, high-ceilinged rooms (with fan) are arranged in blocks under thatch with shared terrace. The big plus is the raised, thatched bar-restaurant, dramatically set against the escarpment with great views, though at lunchtime it can be overrun with tour groups – it's the only place to eat in the area – who pay tourist prices for average food. N$2290

Khorixas

Even when dusty **KHORIXAS** was the administrative centre of Damaraland prior to independence, it was never exactly throbbing with life. Since then, however, regional offices – and with them government jobs – have slowly been moving up to the new capital of the Kunene Region, Opuwo. Now more forlorn than ever, the town's 6000-strong, mainly Damara population suffers from high levels of youth unemployment and its associated social ills. You don't need to stop long before being pestered by some desperate soul trying to flog a sub-standard curio you don't want. On the north side of the main tarred road on the eastern side of town, there's a small square hosting a supermarket, a bank and ATM as well as a petrol station – a busy pit stop for travellers heading north to Etosha, or west to Twyfelfontein.

ARRIVAL KHORIXAS

By minibus Weekend minibuses come from Henties Bay on Friday afternoons, returning on Sunday (N$240). Minibuses also leave for Windhoek when full from the petrol station/supermarket area (N$270).

By car Khorixas lies on the C39, about 110km west of Outjo on a tarred road, and about 80km east of Twyfelfontein on a good gravel road.

Information There is no tourist information office in Khorixas. Your best bet is to make enquiries at reception in the *iGowati Country Hotel.*

ACCOMMODATION AND EATING

Damara Mopane Lodge 20km west of Khorixas signposted off the C39; map p.170. A large lodge comprising concentric semicircles of quaint rustic brick chalets with their own vegetable gardens tended to by folksy metal sculptures – providing for the buffet dinner. Chalets are set around a large mopane-studded pool area. N$2240

iGowati Country Hotel Justus Garoeb Ave ☎067 331592, ✉igowati@afol.com; map p.170. A surprisingly leafy oasis in the centre of town, adequate for an overnight stop: 29 rooms in two semicircular stone-and-thatch buildings overlooking the grassy pool area and semi-open lapa bar-restaurant, which can rustle up a reasonable steak, burger or

pasta dish all day long. Camping sites too, popular with overlander groups. Camping N$150, doubles (B&B) N$480

Khorixas Restcamp 2.5km west of the town, 1km up the D2625 from the turn-off from the C39 ☎067 331111 (restcamp) or ☎061 2857200 (Windhoek), ⊕nwr.com.na; map p.170. Upgraded recently, this sandy place has 20 pleasant and inexpensive bush chalets (with a/c, fridge and kettle) plus two large, well-equipped family chalets with kitchen and TV lounge, and 20 not-especially-shaded camping spots. There's a sometimes-functioning pool and bar-restaurant, where food and service are hit and miss as some of the malaise of the nearby town has begun to permeate. Camping per person N$150, chalets N$1160

Ugab Terraces

Turning off south down the D2743, 52km east of Khorixas, takes you into the spectacular scenery of the **Ugab Terraces**. This broad, flat-bottomed valley, flanked by plateaus rising 160m either side, holds a collection of buttes and mesas – striking, steep-sided, flat-topped pillars of rock, reminiscent of Monument Valley in Arizona; so much so that you half expect John Wayne to appear on horseback at any moment. These harder sandstone conglomerate protrusions have been formed over the last 20 million years or so as the surrounding softer sedimentary deposits of the Ugab River floodplain have gradually been eroded away. While the **Vingerklip** is as far as most people venture along this valley, it's worth completing the 68km semicircular detour along the D2743, which wends its way through picturesque mopane woodland.

Vingerklip

22km along the D2743, from the turn-off from the C49 • N$10; free if you're staying or eating at Vingerklip Lodge • Daily 8am–5pm

The best known of the Ugab Terraces is the 35m-high phallus known as the **Vingerklip** (Finger Rock), whose dramatic presence is enhanced by its location, perched precariously on top of a knoll. The rings on this butte, which has a 44m circumference, tell a geological tale of rising and falling sea levels and the changing force of the Ugab River's flow that helped carve this natural sculpture.

Bambatsi Guest Farm 55km east of Khorixas, signposted north off the C39 (5km track) ☎081 245 8803, ⓦbambatsi.com; map p.170. Old-style guestfarm on a fabulous hilltop, overlooking vast expanses of mopane woodland. Simple, no-frills painted brick bungalows with crazy-paving stone floors. Family-style dining inside or on the delightful plant-filled terrace, where you'll be treated to afternoon tea and cake (dinner N$200). Also two basic campsites – you pay slightly more for the hilltop one. Camping per person $130, doubles N$1720

Ugab Terrace Lodge Signposted off the D2743, 14km south of the turn-off from the C39 ☎081 140 0179, ⓦugabterracelodge.com; map p.170. Crowning one of the terraces, this place has stunning views: from your private chalet terrace (8 offer sunrise view, 8 sunset) or the vast restaurant deck (N$110 for a light lunch; N$200 for dinner) overlooking the Vingerklip, or even the gorgeous pool, set in the rock. For the more active, there are hiking and mountain bike trails (bike not provided) and even a zipline. Three campsites lie amid giant boulders and mopane trees at the escarpment foot. Camping per person N$170, chalets N$2700

★**Vingerklip Lodge** On the D2743, 22km south of the turn-off from the C39 ☎067 290319 (lodge) or ☎061 255344 (reservations), ⓦvingerklip.com.na; map p.170. Delightfully relaxing spot with thatched chalets dotted over a hillside among rock gardens full of succulents. Chalets are cosy: chock-full of furniture and artwork (though overdosing on chrome and with small bathrooms), they afford mesmerizing views from the private stone patios – topped only by the one from the *Eagle's Nest* restaurant, a short hike up the hillside to build up an appetite. For the less mobile or energetic the regular bar-restaurant by reception is popular with day-trippers. For pure indulgence, book the sublime Heaven's Gate luxury chalet on top of a terrace, with surround glass to maximize the panorama, plus private plunge pool. Lodge visitors get to stroll to the Vingerklip for free. DBB N$2490

Kamanjab

Little more than a glorified crossroads, **KAMANJAB** has seen an increase in tourist traffic over the last few years since the Galton Gate on the west side of Etosha was opened up to the public. With two petrol stations and a couple of well-provisioned general stores – not to mention a handy break-down mechanic – it's a place to restock and refuel, before driving north into the national park, or beyond to the Kaokoveld, or west into Damaraland. Note that the ATMs here are unreliable.

Huab Lodge 32km down the D2670, signposted off the C35, midway between Khorixas and Kamanjab ☎067 312070, ⓦhuab.com. Wonderful wilderness spot off the tourist trail, on the banks of the ephemeral Huab River, sometimes frequented by desert elephants. Owner-managed lodge provides eight glorious brick-and-thatch chalets, with private patios. Top-notch guiding, cuisine – dining family-style in the cavernous main lapa – and a hot spring to soak in. Worth staying at least two nights. AI rates also available. DBB N$4860

Oppi Koppi 29 Gemsbok St ☎067 330040 or ☎081 453 0958, ⓦoppi-koppi-kamanjab.com. Basic twin-bed or family-size fan-ventilated rooms with kettle and tea/coffee; for an extra N$420, slightly larger chalets with a/c and fridge. The campsites have electricity and you can buy wood, ice and braai packs on site. Nice à la carte bar-restaurant under a lapa by a welcome pool. Camping per person N$110, chalets (B&B) N$1240

Northern Damaraland

Leaving the Huab Valley of Twyfelfontein, the well-graded C39 heads northwards into what is generally referred to as **NORTHERN DAMARALAND**. The first half of the 82km drive to **Palmwag** is exceedingly scenic, as the road is framed by flat-topped escarpments, shored up by the odd unexpected sand dune. This striking landscape is part of the Etendeka Plateau, one of the planet's largest sheets of ancient lava, which extends as far north as the Hoanib River at **Sesfontein**, and was formed millions of years ago when, following the break-up of Gondwanaland, the South Atlantic opened up and spewed forth volcanic rocks. Different hardness among the basaltic layers has resulted in stepped plateaus, as the surrounding semi-desert plains were eroded down. About halfway to Palmwag, the C39 peels off west to the Skeleton

Coast and the C43 takes up the baton. At Palmwag – essentially a road junction in a fairly featureless patch of semi-desert plain but with a crucial petrol station – the road divides; east takes you over the dramatic Grootberg Pass on the C40, towards Kamanjab some 115km away, whereas the C43 crosses the veterinary fence, travelling a similar distance northwards, to the next sizeable settlement at Sesfontein. On the way, you pass through the sparsely populated communities of **Khowarib** and **Warmquelle**, which offer a few campsites and one very agreeable lodge between them.

Palmwag and around

Just under five hundred square kilometres of the **Palmwag Concession** (pronounced "Palumvag") spreads westwards towards the Skeleton Coast; a stark and at times bleak semi-desert wilderness of reddish-brown rock-strewn earth dotted with euphorbias, and distant plateaus. The southern entrance to the reserve coincides with the veterinary fence, where you can fill up at the adjacent petrol station, and grab a drink at the shop.

ACCOMMODATION   PALMWAG AND AROUND

Desert Rhino Camp 15km southwest of Palmwag ☎ (0)11 257 5111 (South Africa), ⊛ wilderness.co.za. As the name indicates, the draw here is black rhino tracking, (in partnership with the Black Rhino Trust, so you will keep your distance), though birding and guided walks are also on offer, with the usual high standard of service, cuisine and accommodation, in eight classy elevated Meru-style safari tens with decks where you can gaze at the expansive desert vistas. AI N$17,010

★**Etendeka Mountain Camp** 10km north of Palmwag ☎ 061 239199, ⊛ etendeka-namibia.com. Set in the rock-strewn foothills of the Grootberg massif, this award-winning owner-managed eco-camp seeks to minimize its environmental footprint, so you'll need to eschew some comforts: accommodation in ten no-frills,

old-style Meru safari tens with a couple of beds, camp chairs and a solar-heated outdoor bucket shower. The small pool is a more recent concession to "luxury". Expect bush camping over a fire, top-quality guiding about flora and fauna, and stargazing through a telescope. AI N$6310

★**Grootberg Lodge South** Off the C40, 23km east of Palmwag ☎ 067 333212, ⊛ grootberg.com. This community-owned lodge is all about the view, which is breathtaking – though it can be windy – perched on the plateau edge, which plunges into the Klip River valley. 16 pleasant stone-and-thatch chalets are ranged along the precipice, with a communal bar-dining area, which is a tad short of space when full. Steep access road – you can get picked up at the bottom if you're not sure of your driving.

4

> ### WILDLIFE OF NORTHERN DAMARALAND
>
> Though lacking the large numbers of Etosha, further east, **northern Damaraland** nevertheless has plenty of **wildlife** to seek out. Above all, it is associated with the proudly cited statistic of possessing the world's largest number of **free-roaming black rhino** (see box, p.8). Several of the lodges offer whole-day excursions to try and track these magnificent beasts, though you should bear in mind that the emphasis is always on rhino conservation, rather than tourist satisfaction: human interference is kept to a minimum, and so, even assuming your guide manages to locate one, you may not get as close to a rhino as you would in a national park or private reserve. **Desert-adapted elephant** are also sparsely scattered across the area (more visible in the dry season, as they seek out water holes in the dry riverbeds); **giraffe** are also sighted, and, very rarely, a desert-adapted **lion**. More commonly, you'll come across hardy oryx, springbok, Hartmann's mountain zebra, klipspringer, kudu, steenbok and possibly hyena, though in the eastern fringes, nearer Kamanjab, you should keep your eyes peeled for the near-endemic **black-faced impala**. Cheetah and leopard are in evidence, but rarely glimpsed, in the uplands further inland. Bird lovers will be keen to spot Monteiro's hornbill (see p.40), or Rüppell's korhaan strutting across the gravel plains, whereas the rockier hillsides and escarpments are prime raptor territory, featuring imperious Verreaux's (black) eagles.

Various excursions are on offer, including rhino-tracking (N$1925). DBB <u>N$3165</u>

★**Hoada Campsite** 8km south of the C40, 40km east of Palmwag ☎ 067 333212, ⓦ grootberg.com/hoada -campsite. Community campground administered by *Grootberg Lodge*. Fabulous spot amid giant granite boulders and mopane woodland, with a pool carved out of the rock. Each of the eight private sites has its own toilet, and outdoor shower with braai-heated donkey. Also one site for larger groups and recently added tents with bedding for rent. Desert-adapted elephant and rhino are occasionally sighted. Camping per person (own tent) <u>N$190</u>

★**Palmwag** Lodge 6km along the C43 after the junction with the C40 ☎ 081 620 6887, ⓦ palmwaglodge.com. Fabulous oasis by a spring in the Uniab River – where elephants visit – in a rather desolate plain. A popular lunch stop, it can be busy at the pleasant pool-bar restaurant, with green lawn, pool fringed with makalani palms, and decks overlooking the verdant bush. Though recently renovated, the stone chalets are unremarkable, whereas the tented chalets are more appealing. But the guiding is top-notch and you can camp out in the wild for a night or two. Great campsites overlooking the riverbed, with private ablutions, which have access to the pool-bar restaurant (daily 10am–6pm), where you can tuck into toasties, burgers, salads and more filling dishes from around N$120. Camping per person <u>N$205</u>, chalets (DBB) <u>N$3490</u>

Khowarib and Warmquelle

Eleven kilometres apart, along the C43, south of Sesfontein, in the small, predominantly Damara and Herero settlements of **Khowarib** and **Warmquelle**, respectively, you can find some simple community campgrounds and one standout lodge. Both communities lie on the ephemeral Hoanib River, with Khowarib enjoying a more imposing setting at the mouth of the Khowarib Gorge, where the dense aquifer lying close to the surface nurtures large mopane trees, and attracts various large animals, including the local cattle, searching for water. The attraction in Warmquelle, 11km further north, as the name indicates – "Quelle" meaning "spring" in German – is the spring-fed **Ongongo Waterfall**, which tumbles over a rock into an idyllic crystalline pool, a great place to cool off on a really hot day. The local community runs a campground here, but also accepts day visitors (N$20). A small store and a bakery are other points of potential interest on the main road.

ACCOMMODATION

KHOWARIB AND WARMQUELLE

Khowarib Community Campsite Just beyond the Khowarib Lodge ☎ 081 407 9539. Well situated just above the riverbed, with the first plot boasting the best views. Wood-thatch shelters provide shade, and donkeys heat the private showers. Braai sites. Camping per person <u>N$80</u>

Khowarib Lodge 1km east of the C43 at Khowarib ☎ 064 402779 or ☎ 081 219 3291, ⓦ khowarib.com. Delightful location by a spring-fed river towered over by cliffs, with comfortable, rustic tented chalets possessing lovely open stone bathrooms, and private shady decks – great for birdwatching. The main terrace offers atmospheric alfresco dining, a fire-pit with cushions for evening relaxation and a grassed, shady pool area. Service is friendly and efficient, dining good and the place offers worthwhile half- or full-day excursions, from a couple of hours' birding (N$300) to a full day tracking rhino (N$1600), but the place is expensive compared to other similar

lodges. Campers can use the lodge facilities, if the place isn't full. Camping <u>N$150</u>, chalets (DBB) <u>N$4160</u>

Mbakondja River Campsite Signposted off the C43, 50km north of Palmwag. Rudimentary campground down a rocky track, offering little shade but warm hospitality from a Damara–Herero family for whom the campsite is a lifeline. Traditional cow-dung-and-adobe open-air ablutions. Camping per person <u>N$80</u>

Ongongo Waterfall Campsite Warmquelle, 6km off the C43; turn east north of the Independence Bar, past the football pitch and then follow the pipeline ☎ 081 684 3429. Sprawling community campsite with 20-odd pitches, but the nicest, more sheltered ones are down by the luscious reed-encircled spring, which attracts good birdlife. Great when the water's flowing, but less appealing when it's really low. Shared showers and sometimes-flushing toilets. Camping per person <u>N$70</u>

Sesfontein and around

Marking the northernmost limit of Damaraland, and serving as the gateway to the Kaokoveld, **SESFONTEIN** – named after six nearby springs – lies roughly midway between Palmwag and Opuwo, the regional capital of the Kunene Region. This pleasantly relaxed if slightly soporific place, on the banks of the ephemeral Hoanib River, is home to a mix of around seven thousand Herero, Damara, Himba and Owambo people. The main attraction for visitors is the **old German fort**, set among tall wafting palm trees. Following the *rinderpest* epidemic, the Germans set up a series of checkpoints in the north, of which Sesfontein was the most westerly, to control stock movement initially, though they were then used to monitor illegal arms smuggling and poaching. The fort's days as a military station were limited, however, as it was handed over to the police a few years later, and then abandoned altogether in 1914. Its new lease of life came just before independence, when it was faithfully restored to become a hotel. It's an ideal spot to stop off for lunch, and the fuel station at its entrance is the only one for over a 100km.

ACCOMMODATION SESFONTEIN AND AROUND

Camel Top Camping Signposted off the main road 2km west of town. Probably the best camping option, this community-run venture offers six well-spaced, simple, shady sites with electricity and hot water. Open-air rustic showers and braai site (no grill); accessible by 2WD. Camping per person N$80

Fort Sesfontein Lodge Just off the main road as you enter town ☎ 065 685034, ⓦ fort-sesfontein.com. Well-restored hundred-year-old fort with a dozen cool rooms containing wood and rattan furniture, opening onto a shady palm- and bougainvillea-studded courtyard. Dine in the former officers' mess, or on the terrace by the large swimming pool. Half- or full-day tours offered. N$2520

Hoanib Skeleton Coast Camp Border of the Skeleton Coast Park around 75km west-south-west of Sesfontein ☎ (0)11 257 5111 (South Africa), ⓦ wilderness.co.za. Wilderness Safari's latest luxury offering: a stunning, exclusive camp with state-of-the-art, modern safari tents in a unique wilderness environment on the Hoanib River, bordering the Skeleton Coast National Park. Three-day stays include a trip to the coast. Fine dining, efficient service, top-notch guiding and an unforgettable experience, but it doesn't come cheap. AI N$13,055

Zebra Restcamp Main road 1km west of town ☎ 081 614 1410. Four basic, sandy sites under good shade 1km west of town; fire-pit but no grill, and solar-powered showers and toilets that could be better maintained. Camping per person N$75

4

The central coast and hinterland

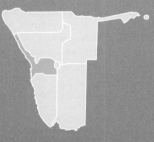

DRIVING TO SANDWICH HARBOUR

5

The central coast and hinterland

It's along Namibia's central coast that visitors can make the most of what the country has to offer, from exploring desert and marine wildlife to visiting former townships and rural communities, and from road trips through dramatic coastal landscapes to a host of adrenaline-pumping adventure sports. All these activities can be enjoyed from the colonial-era towns of Swakopmund and Walvis Bay. Both can be reached from Windhoek in under four hours via the tarred B2 that follows the railway line west, passing through the former mining towns of Karibib and Usakos. Yet far more scenic back routes take you via the dramatic, tortuous Gamsberg or Bosua passes, dropping down onto the flat gravel plains of the Namib, affording opportunities to stop off at a hospitable guestfarm or a wilderness campground along the way.

Around 350km west of Windhoek, the pretty seaside resort of **Swakopmund**, with its German colonial architecture and moderate coastal climate, has long been the holiday playground of Namibia's white population. Boasting comfortable accommodation, excellent cafés and restaurants and a relaxed vibe, it has more recently acquired a reputation as a centre for adventure activities. In contrast, **Walvis Bay**, a thirty-minute drive down the road, is Namibia's main port, home to a vibrant fishing industry, though its wildlife-rich lagoon is now the focus of a burgeoning tourist scene.

Both towns are surrounded by stunning dune scenery – some of which lies within the northern section of the **Namib-Naukluft National Park** and the contiguous, newly formed **Dorob National Park** – which can be explored in any number of ways: on the back of a camel, a horse or a quad bike, or from the air, in a plane, or skydiving out of one. Popular destinations include the fabulously isolated dune-enclosed **Sandwich Harbour**, an avian paradise south of Walvis Bay. Equally appealing is **Welwitschia Drive**, just outside Swakopmund, which takes in a variety of desert landscapes, as well as one of the planet's oldest specimens of the eponymous plant (see box, p.218). Further north, the mythical **Skeleton Coast** stretches 680km to the Angolan border. Most visitors only go as far as Namibia's largest seal colony at **Cape Cross**, 120km north of Swakopmund, but with your own wheels and a permit, you can head inland to the explore the otherworldly **Messum Crater**, or follow the coast road another 200km to experience the desolate desert landscapes of the **Skeleton Coast National Park**.

Swakopmund and around

Wandering along the orderly main streets, past half-timbered colonial-era buildings and pavement cafés, where German is spoken at every turn, it's easy to see how **SWAKOPMUND** – or **Swakop**, to use its more familiar name – is sometimes jokingly referred to as "Germany's most southerly Baltic seaside resort". German-Namibians may only constitute

Highlights

❶ **Colonial architecture** Take a stroll round central Swakopmund and check out the smart colonial-era buildings that still stand proud. **See p.209**

❷ **Adrenaline activity** There are endless ways to set your pulse racing in this unique desert landscape, from sand-boarding to skydiving, quad biking to paragliding. **See p.215**

❸ **Seafood dining with sundowners** Both Walvis Bay and Swakopmund have their share of excellent seafood restaurants; the fresh fish is

best enjoyed with a cocktail in your hand as you watch the sun set. **See p.217 & p.225**

❹ **Explore desert ecology** Head out into the dunes and gravel plains with a knowledgeable guide and learn about Namibia's "Small Five". **See p.219**

❺ **Walvis Bay Lagoon** Get close to nature as you kayak among playful seal pups and marvel at diving pelicans. **See p.223**

❻ **Sandwich Harbour** Towering dunes meet crashing Atlantic waves on this exhilarating trip to an avian wetland paradise. **See p.225**

HIGHLIGHTS ARE MARKED ON THE MAP ON P.208

5

a small percentage of the town's 45,000 population, but German influence is surreally omnipresent in Namibia's only real seaside resort. However, you only need to gaze across the dry Swakop River at the rippling golden dunes, or experience a savage sandstorm on a winter morning, to be brought back to the more defining presence of the **desert**. Indeed, it's the recent exploitation of the desert – and the dunes in particular – as a location for **adventure activities** that is helping attract more foreign tourists and a younger crowd.

Though midweek in winter Swakopmund can seem like a ghost town, the place really comes alive in the **summer holidays** (Dec–Jan), when half of Windhoek decamps here to enjoy the cooler coastal climes, and get some respite from the dry desert interior. The

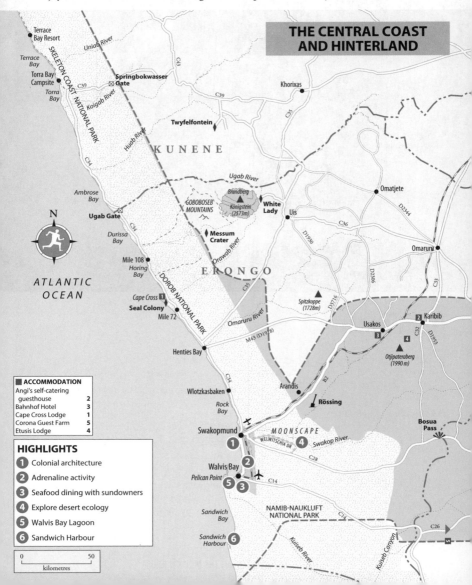

THE CENTRAL COAST AND HINTERLAND

ACCOMMODATION

Angi's self-catering guesthouse	2
Bahnhof Hotel	3
Cape Cross Lodge	1
Corona Guest Farm	5
Etusis Lodge	4

HIGHLIGHTS

1. Colonial architecture
2. Adrenaline activity
3. Seafood dining with sundowners
4. Explore desert ecology
5. Walvis Bay Lagoon
6. Sandwich Harbour

downside of this is that guesthouse rooms and restaurant tables are hard to come by. At other times of the year, the place is less busy, though long weekends can attract crowds too.

Brief history

Swakopmund is a corruption of the Khoekhoen Tsoaxub-ams ("ams" and "mund" both meaning "mouth") – a clear indication that indigenous people had been passing through the area long before the first colonizers put down their roots. Yet it was Germany's desire to establish an alternative port to Lüderitz that gave rise to the establishment of Swakopmund as a permanent settlement. Since the natural harbour of Walvis Bay had already been grabbed by the British, the Germans were forced to look elsewhere for a port, finally opting for a site at the Swakop River mouth – a decision based more on the presence of fresh water than because it afforded any protection to boats. Undeterred, in 1892, a German gunboat, the *Hyäna*, landed and a couple of beacons were erected on the shore, thereby officially founding Swakopmund, though the first arrivals had to dig themselves shelters on the beach until the barracks had been built. The difficult part, which soon became apparent, was to achieve an effective trade link between the coast and German interests in the interior. The impractical hauling of goods by ox-cart across the desert was dealt a final hammer blow by the *rinderpest* epidemic (see p.345), underlining the need to construct a railway between Swakopmund and Windhoek. Fortunately – at least from the German perspective – the loss of livestock due to the *rinderpest* forced many black Namibians from the north to seek waged labour further south, thereby providing the necessary workforce. Within five years, remarkably, the railway was complete, and in 1902 the first train from Swakopmund rolled into Windhoek.

The new port, however, had numerous teething problems: failure to take into account the longshore drift meant that the Mole soon silted up. A wooden jetty was constructed in 1906, a few hundred metres down the shore, but that scarcely lasted any longer, and work on a metal replacement began in 1911, only to be curtailed by the outbreak of World War I. Following German surrender to the South Africans in 1915, the town's fortunes slumped as all maritime trade was transferred to Walvis Bay. The advent of apartheid later led to the creation of the former "black" and "coloured" townships of Mondesa and Tamariskia, respectively. The town had to wait until the 1970s, and the start of operations at the Rössing uranium mine, around 60km inland, before its economic prospects began to improve. Tourism too began to take off in a small way, and is now a major source of income for many.

The town centre

Despite the proliferation of informal settlements and low-cost housing, not to mention smart holiday homes, extending northwards, the **town centre** of Swakopmund remains small. It centres on the main shopping street, **Sam Nujoma Avenue**, and a few blocks either side, and ends at the seafront with the town's delightful ocean promenade, where the evenly spaced palm trees stand to attention. The hub of seafront activity centres on the recently revamped **Mole** – the colonial-era sea wall now topped with a swanky hotel and smart restaurants that protects the only safe, if cold, swimming spot, at Palm Beach. Behind is the **lighthouse**, which was initially built a mere 11m high in 1902, but was given an extra 10m a few years later. The building beside it, constructed at the same time, is the **Kaiserliches Bezirksgericht**; this was originally the district magistrate's court, and now the official residence of the president when visiting. Below, the **craft market** offers a bewildering selection of woodcarvings, whereas a short stroll southwards takes you past the renovated original jetty, and down to the beach overlooking the Swakop River mouth, which marks the southern boundary of the town.

5

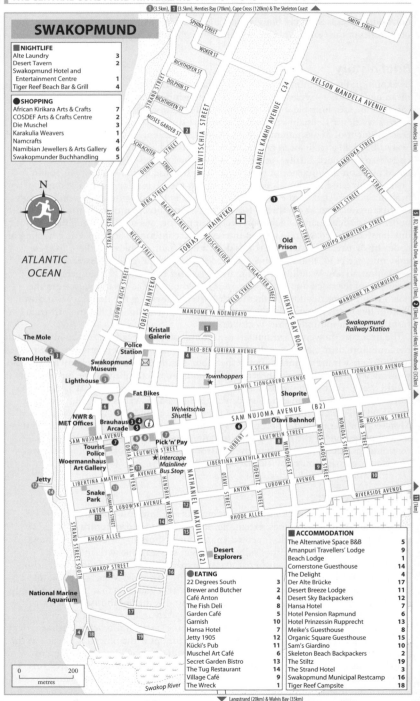

① (3.5km), ① (3.5km), Henties Bay (70km), Cape Cross (120km) & The Skeleton Coast ▲

SWAKOPMUND

■ NIGHTLIFE
Alte Laundry	3
Desert Tavern	2
Swakopmund Hotel and Entertainment Centre	1
Tiger Reef Beach Bar & Grill	4

● SHOPPING
African Kirikara Arts & Crafts	7
COSDEF Arts & Crafts Centre	2
Die Muschel	3
Karakulia Weavers	1
Namcrafts	4
Namibian Jewellers & Arts Gallery	6
Swakopmunder Buchhandling	5

N

ATLANTIC OCEAN

SPHINX STREET
SMITH STREET
WOKER ST
RICHTHOFEN ST
DOLPHIN ST
STRAND STREET
RICHTHOFEN ST
WELWITSCHIA STREET
MOSES GAROEB ST
NELSON MANDELA AVENUE
DANIEL KAMHO AVENUE
C34
SCHLACHTER STREET
DUNEN STREET
BERG STREET
BACKER STREET
NESER STREET
STRAND STREET
TOBIAS HAINYEKO
HEUSCHNEIDER
MC HUGH STREET
HIDIPO HAMUTENYA STREET
WATT STREET
DUSCH STREET
RAKOTOKA STREET

Old Prison

FELD STREET
SCHLACHTER STREET
MANDUME YA NDEMUFAYO
HENTIES BAY ROAD
MANDUME YA NDEMUFAYO

Swakopmund Railway Station

The Mole
Strand Hotel
Kristall Galerie
Police Station
Swakopmund Museum
Lighthouse
THEO-BEN GURIRAB AVENUE
F. STICH
Townhoppers
DANIEL TJONGARERO AVENUE
DANIEL TJONGARERO AVENUE
Shoprite

Fat Bikes
Welwitschia Shuttle
NWR & MET Offices
Brauhaus Arcade
SAM NUJOMA AVENUE (B2)
Otavi Bahnhof
NAMIB ROSSING STREET
NONIDAS STREET
Tourist Police
Woermannhaus Art Gallery
Pick 'n' Pay
LEUTWEIN STREET
WINDHOEK ST
MOSES GAROEB STREET
LUBERT
SAM NUJOMA AVENUE
LEUTWEIN STREET
Jetty
Snake Park
LIBERTINA AMATHILA AVENUE
LIBERTINA AMATHILA
TOBIAS HAINYEKO
BISMARCK STREET
HENDRIK WITBOOI
NATHANIEL MAXUILILI
OTAVI STREET
LÜDERITZ STREET
ANTON STREET
LUBOWSKI AVENUE
RIVERSIDE AVENUE
ANTON LUBOWSKI AVENUE
RHODE ALLEE
RHODE ALLEE
STRAND STREET SOUTH
SWAKOP STREET
(B2)
Desert Explorers
National Marine Aquarium

Swakop River

■ EATING
22 Degrees South	3
Brewer and Butcher	2
Café Anton	4
The Fish Deli	8
Garden Café	5
Garnish	10
Hansa Hotel	7
Jetty 1905	12
Kücki's Pub	11
Muschel Art Café	6
Secret Garden Bistro	13
The Tug Restaurant	14
Village Café	9
The Wreck	1

■ ACCOMMODATION
The Alternative Space B&B	5
Amanpuri Travellers' Lodge	9
Beach Lodge	1
Cornerstone Guesthouse	14
The Delight	4
Der Alte Brücke	17
Desert Breeze Lodge	11
Desert Sky Backpackers	12
Hansa Hotel	7
Hotel Pension Rapmund	6
Hotel Prinzessin Rupprecht	13
Meike's Guesthouse	8
Organic Square Guesthouse	15
Sam's Giardino	10
Skeleton Beach Backpackers	2
The Stiltz	19
The Strand Hotel	3
Swakopmund Municipal Restcamp	16
Tiger Reef Campsite	18

Mondesa (1km)
S3, B2, Welwitschia Drive, Martin Luther (1km), ② (3km), Airport (4km) & Windhoek (352km)

0 200 metres

▼ Langstrand (20km) & Walvis Bay (35km)

5

Swakopmund Museum

Strand St South • Tues–Sun 10am–4pm • N$30 • ☎ 064 402695

Housed in an old customs warehouse, the excellent **Swakopmund Museum** has plenty to keep you busy for at least a couple of hours. As well as the standard museum fare, such as displays of Namibia's mineral wealth, desert flora and fauna – including the inevitable taxidermy specimens – and German military memorabilia, there are more surprising exhibits, such as a vast collection of model cars and a selection of 1930s Shell furniture: so-called because it was crafted from old paraffin and petroleum packing crates – mainly used by impecunious colonial newlyweds. Above all, the artefacts and photographs document **German colonial life**, including a few period rooms, reproducing the interior of a house, an apothecary's and a dental surgery, complete with vicious-looking implements, made all the more scary by the thought that anaesthetic was not available at the time.

To offset the heavy colonial bias of these collections, a new interactive **ethnology wing** focuses on the history and culture of Namibia's main ethnic groups. Among the artefacts, look out for the Kavango sand sledge, the San oracle discs – thrown to determine the direction of a hunt – and the twin horn-and-leather "cosmetic boxes" of the Himba women, containing the necessary ochre and butter fat they mix to produce their body "make-up" (see box, p.256).

Woermannhaus Art Gallery

Bismarck St between Sam Nujoma Ave and Libertina Amathila Ave • Mon–Sat 9am–5pm • Free; donations appreciated

Half the joy of visiting the **Woermannhaus Art Gallery** is the chance to wander round the wood-panelled rooms of Swakopmund's pre-eminent colonial building. Built in 1894 and named after the Woermann Brock trading company, which is still very active in Namibia, its most distinctive feature is the **Damara Tower**, which served as a lookout both for ships and for ox-wagons arriving across the dunes, as well as functioning as a water tower. The **art collection** on the first floor comprises a few rooms, primarily showcasing evocative desert landscapes by immigrant painters; however, there are also a handful of pieces by indigenous artists, including a couple of linocuts by John Muafangejo, Namibia's most internationally renowned artistic talent.

Kristall Galerie

Corner of Tobias Hainyeko St and Theo-Ben Gurirab Ave • Mon–Sat 9am–5pm • N$20 • ☎ 064 406080, ⓦ namibiangemstones.com

Essentially an enticement to purchase gemstones in their shop, the **Kristall Galerie** is nevertheless extremely informative and contains some outstanding samples of Namibia's **quartz** riches, including the largest crystal cluster in the world, which is over 520 million years old, took five years to excavate, and weighs in at over 14,000kg – heavier than a double-decker bus. You peer your way through an exact replica of the mineshaft where the crystal was found, before emerging into the atrium to be confronted by the giant cluster itself. Upstairs, illuminated cabinets display a host of

---

COASTAL FOG

For around half the year, especially in summer, you'll head out of your hotel after breakfast to find Swakopmund or Walvis Bay enveloped in thick **fog**. As the prevailing southwesterly winds are further cooled over the Benguela Current, the air condenses to form cloud and fog. Blown inland, the humid air becomes trapped beneath the less dense hot air, forming an inversion layer. This compact white blanket of low-lying fog is an extraordinary sight as it creeps over the mainland, hovering over the desert, generally reaching around 60km inland (though sometimes twice that distance) until it's dissipated by the strengthening sun. Though responsible for many shipwrecks on the Skeleton Coast, this coastal fog helps maintain the **milder temperatures** at the coast and, crucially, is the lifeblood for much of the Namib Desert's **flora and fauna**, providing five times more water than is provided by rain.

5

precious and semi-precious stones; don't miss the gypsum, resembling crushed rose petals, the green and pink of the aptly named watermelon tourmaline, and the canary-yellow sulphur crystals of pietersite.

Snake Park

5 Libertina Amadhila St • Mon–Fri 9am–5pm; feeding time Sat 10am–1pm • N$100, including tour • ☏ 064 405100

The rather cramped, low-key **Snake Park**, which is substantially enlivened if you get a good guide, boasts over 25 types of Namibian snakes and other reptiles – many well camouflaged in the sand – plus a few larger venomous specimens from elsewhere.

National Marine Aquarium

Strand St South • Tues–Sun 10am–4pm; feeding time 3pm • N$30 • ☏ 064 4101000

The small **National Marine Aquarium** offers insight into the marine life that thrives in the cold Atlantic coast of Namibia. The well-labelled small tanks display a variety of fish, lobsters, sea anemones, starfish and other aquatic life, highlighting some of their more curious features, but the star attraction is a **walk-through tank** affording close-ups of enormous dusky cobs and mean-looking sand sharks. Popular with school groups, it's a place to avoid if you see a school bus parked outside.

Mondesa and the DRC

To the northeast of central Swakopmund lies the suburb, and former apartheid-era black township, of **Mondesa**, where around half of the town's population live. A product of apartheid segregation from the 1950s, there are specific areas demarcated for particular ethnic groups – Owambo, Nama and Herero areas still largely remain intact – although, over time, boundaries have become more blurred. Importantly, the place is far more vibrant than restrained downtown Swakop, with kids playing in the streets, people trading in the market, and neighbours sitting outside chatting and cooking. That said, Mondesa suffers from high unemployment or underemployment – Rössing Mine (see p.220) is the biggest employer; others get casual work in the endless construction boom that has enveloped Namibia's main seaside resort.

On the fringes of Mondesa sprawls the **DRC**, an ever-expanding informal settlement, which some township tours also visit. Taking one of these tours with people who have grown up in the area should enable you to meet and interact with various community members, learn about the area's history and experience its present. You may get to visit a pre-school or development project, browse the open market, sample some local food – mahangu or oshifima most likely – and maybe visit a shebeen. As with any other tour, you should establish the itinerary before signing up and ascertain what is included in the price (see opposite).

ARRIVAL AND DEPARTURE   SWAKOPMUND AND AROUND

BY CAR

Swakopmund lies on the coast, 351km west of Windhoek. Reachable in under four hours by the tarred B2. A slower, more scenic route can be taken along the C28 (see p.232).

BY BUS

Shuttle services Two a/c shuttle services operate the Windhoek–Swakopmund route: Townhoppers (Mon–Fri 8am–4.30pm; ☏ 064 407223, weekends ☏ 081 210 3062; ⓦ namibiashuttle.com) and Welwitschia Shuttle (Mon–Fri 8am–5pm, Sat 8am–1pm; ☏ 064 405105, ⓦ welwitschia shuttle.com). Both have daily early-morning departures from Swakop, with the return trip from Windhoek in the

afternoon (N$260). Connecting transfers to and from Windhoek's international airport can also be booked. Welwitschia also operates a weekday commuter shuttle service to and from Walvis Bay, with two early morning departures from Swakop, returning late afternoon from Walvis Bay. The Welwitschia bus stop in Swakop is Woolworths' car park in the centre of town, and the Windhoek stop is the Christuskirche car park. Townhoppers pick up outside their office on Otavi St in Swakop, and leave from the car park by the *Hilton Hotel* in Windhoek.

Buses The Intercape Mainliner bus (☏ 061 227847, ⓦ intercape.co.za) travels between Windhoek and Swakopmund twice a week (Thurs & Sat, leaving Windhoek

5

THE MARTIN LUTHER

In a rather unprepossessing, brick-and-glass shed 1.5km outside Swakopmund, on the B2, stands one of the town's more curious monuments, the **Martin Luther steam traction engine** (daily 8.30am–4.30pm). It was the country's first such machine, imported from Germany in 1896 to replace the ox wagons that were being used to transport freight, but the venture was doomed from the outset: since the port facilities in Swakop were not up to unloading such a weight, the engine was diverted to Walvis Bay, where it idled in the port for a few months. It then took three more months to struggle the 30km to its destination because it kept sinking into the sand. In 1897, after a few outings, it ground to an inglorious halt in a dune outside Swakop, on the spot where it is currently housed. Its curious nickname came from the apocryphal words of the Protestant reformer Martin Luther, who, when asked to renounce his beliefs or be charged with heresy, responded: "Here I stand; I cannot do otherwise. God help me. Amen."

10am), on the way to or from Walvis Bay. Return buses from Swakop (Fri & Sun, 10.35am; from N$200) pick up on Hendrik Witbooi St, behind *Pick 'N' Pay* supermarket. Tickets available online or at Sure Ritz Travel (☎064 405131) in the Brauhaus Arcade.

Minibuses Minibuses leave the Monte Christo Service Station in Katutura, Windhoek (N$200). Minibuses bound for Windhoek, and other long-distance destinations, leave from the taxi rank in Mondesa.

BY TRAIN

The extremely slow and rather uncomfortable night train from Windhoek to Walvis Bay (weekdays at 7.15pm; peak-season rates from N$115 economy; N$154 business) should arrive at Swakopmund at 5.30am, though they frequently arrive late. The return train to the capital leaves at 8.45pm on the same days.

BY PLANE

Swakopmund airport, 4km along the B2 towards Windhoek, only operates charter flights; scheduled flights leave from Walvis Bay Airport, around a 45min drive from Swakop town centre (see p.209). Welwitschia Shuttle (⊕welwitschiashuttle.com) runs a transfer service there from Swakop (N$200).

INFORMATION

Tourist information There is no longer a municipal tourist office in the town, but Namib I (Mon–Fri 8am–1pm & 2–5pm, Sat 9am–3pm, Sun and public holidays 9am–1pm; ☎064 404327), a private venture on Sam Nujoma Ave, has bags of information and can book activities and tours.

NWR office The NWR office on Bismarck St can book accommodation in all the national parks (Mon–Fri 8am–5pm; ☎064 402172).

MET office The MET permit office is in the same building as the NWR office in Bismarck St, upstairs, where you can purchase your permit for the Namib-Naukluft or Skeleton Coast national parks (Mon–Fri 8am–1pm & 2–5pm, Sat, Sun & public holidays 9am–1pm). Permits cost N$40/person plus N$10/vehicle.

GETTING AROUND

On foot Swakop has a small town centre and most accommodation is within walking distance of sights, shops and restaurants. The centre is also fairly safe to stroll around at night, though the usual precautions apply, such as not walking down dimly lit side streets, or being on your own.

By taxi During the day, taxis can be found hanging around outside supermarkets; if you want a taxi to get home after going out in the evening, get your accommodation or the restaurant to call someone reliable. Most trips around town won't cost more than N$40.

By car Unless you're on a self-drive holiday with your own vehicle (in which case choose accommodation with secure off-road parking), you've a choice when it comes to reaching most out-of-town attractions, such as Welwitschia Drive, Cape Cross seal colony, or popping down the coast to Walvis Bay for the day. You can either go on a tour (see below), or rent a car for the day.

TOURS AND ACTIVITIES

In addition to the **adventure activities** (see box, p.215), for which Swakopmund is justifiably renowned, the town offers a number of half- or full-day **excursions**, many of which take you out into the Namib Desert east of Swakop, to seek out some of the desert-adapted wildlife (see box, p.8). The day tours usually do the above combined with Welwitschia Drive (see p.219). **Cultural tours** to the former township of Mondesa are also gaining in popularity. Some operators also run excursions to Walvis Bay lagoon and/or Sandwich Harbour; more details are given under the Walvis Bay listings (see p.223).

5

Batis Birding ☎064 404908 or ☎081 639 1775, ⓦbatisbirdingsafaris.com. Specializing in birding tours, they also offer other eco-safaris during the day and at night, from inexpensive nature walks in the desert (N$500) to full-day tours to Spitzkoppe, Brandberg or Sandwich Harbour (N$2000). A minimum of four is needed for most excursions.

Camel Farm 12km outside Swakop, signposted off the B2 along the D1901 ☎064 400363, ⓦswakopmund camelfarm.com. Don your keffiyeh (Arab headdress – provided) and live out your Lawrence of Arabia fantasies on a camel. The most common 20min canter will set you back N$150. Mon–Sat 2–5pm.

Charly's Desert Tours Brauhaus Arcade, Sam Nujoma Drive ☎064 404341, ⓦcharlysdeserttours.com. Half-day trips to the desert (N$700) to explore the flora and fauna, as well as full-day tours, which include Welwitschia Drive (N$1250). Also offers short guided tours round Swakopmund, a half-day's tide-dependent outing to explore rock pools and beach life, and excursions down to Sandwich Harbour.

Fat Bike Tours 9 Altona House, Daniel Tjonarero Ave ☎081 395 5813, ⓦswakopfatbiketours.com. The most ecologically sound way to visit the desert, these two-hour tours go up the Swakop riverbed, then onto the dunes, for which you need to be fairly fit (N$380). A less energetic alternative is to do the beach ride at low tide, or rent a bike to explore on your own (daily rates: N$220 town bike, N$450 fat bike). Mon–Fri 8am–5pm, Sat 8am–1pm.

Hata Angu Cultural Tours ☎064 461118 or ☎081 124 6111, ⓦculturalactivities-namibia.com. The name means "Let's get to know one another" in Damara, and they specialize in tours to Mondesa, the former township, and the Democratic Resettlement Community (DRC) informal settlement, both during the day and in the evening, when you can relax into the shebeen experience (N$500). They also offer sand-boarding excursions (N$500).

Mondesa Township Tours ☎081 273 4361 or ☎081 388 6556, ⓦfacebook.com/mondesatownshiptours. As well as the township tours (N$500), during which you'll visit Herero, Owambo and Nama families, and while trying out an Owambo dish, you'll be serenaded by some a cappella singing. Also offers half-day and full-day cycling

tours (N$400/N$700) and the usual day-trips from Swakopmund, such as Cape Cross.

Namibia Tours and Safaris 7c Krohnmeier Courtyard, 37 Sam Nujoma Ave ☎064 406038, ⓦnamibia-tours -safaris.com. Organizes multi-day tours round Namibia and southern Africa, including self-drive and fly-in safaris.

Okakambe Trails ☎064 402799, ⓦokakambe .iway.na. Established stables with well-cared-for horses offering outings of a couple of hours (N$820) or a full day (N$2100), with multi-day camping trips for more experienced riders. Prices assume a minimum of two people. No credit cards.

Pleasure Flights and Safaris ☎081 242 9481, ⓦpleasureflights.com.na. Given the clear skies, spectacular scenery and inaccessibility of much of Namibia, this is one country where it's worth splashing out on a flight. This is an experienced, reputable operator with over twenty years in the business. Prices depend on flight length and number of passengers. Assuming the maximum of four passengers, they range from N$2840/person for a 1hr 30min flight along the coast to N$7040 for a full day's excursion to the Fish River Canyon, via Sandwich Harbour.

Swakop Cycle Tours ☎081 251 5916, ⓦswakop cycletours.com. A great way to visit the former township, Mondesa, is by bike (N$380 for a half day). Shorter tours of Swakop town centre are also offered, as is bike rental (N$255/day).

Tommy's Tours and Safaris ☎064 461038 or ☎081 128 1038, ⓦlivingdeserttours.com.na. The original living desert tour developed in the 1990s. Offers a similar half- or full-day itinerary to Charly's Desert Tours. Cash or bank transfer only. Half day (minimum two people) N$700.

Turnstone Tours ☎064 403123 or ☎081 129 2331, ⓦturnstone-tours.com. At the higher end of the price range, but with superior guiding. Offers full-day excursions to Sandwich Harbour or Cape Cross and Messum Crater (N$1660/person including park fees and lunch). The company also operates acclaimed multi-day camping trips (maximum of four) with a special four-day tour to *Mundulea Bush Camp*, in a private reserve in the Otavi Mountains, which you explore on foot (N$16,600/person, for a group of two to three).

ACCOMMODATION

Swakopmund boasts a wealth of accommodation to suit most budgets; though mid-range **B&Bs** and **guesthouses** predominate, a couple of **backpackers** and **campgrounds** exist for budget travellers. Generally rooms are without air conditioning – it is not usually hot enough – though some have heating for the colder nights. During the main **school holidays** (mid-Dec to mid-Jan), when rates are usually higher, advance booking is a must. During the season for European visitors (late July and August), rooms are also in short supply.

IN TOWN

The Alternative Space B&B 167 Anton Lubowski St ☎064 463348, ⓦthealternativespace.com. This

long-standing anti-establishment art gallery provides a cerebral, aesthetic retreat boasting a handful of whitewashed stone rooms laden with artwork, vintage bathtubs – outside, under a tree in one case – and a secluded courtyard garden. Breakfast is self-service, with the kitchen and BBQ facilities available to prepare other meals. B&B N$900

Amanpuri Travellers' Lodge Corner of Moses Garoeb St and Anton Lubowski St ☎064 405587, ☜amanpuri namibia.com. Motel-like in feel, this place is popular with overlander and tour groups, providing spotless, basic, yet comfortable tiled dorms and doubles. B&B dorms N$200, doubles N$700

Cornerstone Guesthouse Corner of Rhode Allee St and Hendrik Witbooi St ☎064 462468, ☜cornerstone guesthouse.com. Superior B&B with five double and two family rooms, each immaculately kept, with private entrance and patio overlooking the garden. A sumptuous breakfast is served indoors or on the shaded terrace, depending on the weather. Three luxury self-catering apartments with three bedrooms and two bathrooms (sleeping up to six) are also available for rent in town. Doubles (B&B) N$1650, apartments N$1540

★**The Delight** Corner of Theo-Ben Gurirab St and Nathaniel Maxuilili St ☎061 247200 (reservations Windhoek), ☜gondwana-collection.com. A hotel that lives up to its name, flaunting an upbeat modern design with retro touches, in aquamarine and scarlet; enlarged photos of local scenes decorate the walls and nice touches

include an espresso machine with a cookie tin, plus hot-water bottle for winter. The sumptuous champagne breakfast includes fresh oysters. The only niggle is with rooms overlooking the Entertainment Centre; you'll hear them spilling out of the casino in the early hours at weekends. Wi-fi only available in the cosy bar-lobby area and upstairs restaurant. N$1069

★**Der Alte Brücke** Strand St South ☎064 404918, ☜altebrucke.com. What it lacks in character, this resort makes up for in value for money: over thirty modern, well-equipped, fully serviced self-catering units (for two–six) with patios and palm trees, plus deluxe camping pitches. Wind-protected, these have manicured lawns on which to pitch the tent, private ablutions, dining area and a vast braai hearth for a heart-warming blaze on chilly winter nights. Buffet breakfast (except mid-Dec to mid-Jan when closed) and available for campers (N$85). Camping (for two) N$380, self-catering units (B&B) N$1240

Desert Sky Backpackers 35 Anton Lubowski Ave. at the corner with Nathaniel Maxuilili ☎064 402339, ☜desertskylodging.com. This friendly, efficient backpackers makes a great base for campers, backpackers and families on a budget; you can choose from rooms with shared or en-suite facilities and make use of the well-equipped kitchen and braai facilities (breakfast not included). The large walled garden makes a pleasant spot

ADVENTURE ACTIVITIES IN SWAKOP

Swakop is gradually gaining a reputation for **adventure sports**, thanks in particular to the inventive ways of enjoying the dunes, from the more established quad biking to sand-surfing or power-kiting, or – for the ultimate adrenaline rush – skydiving. Below are some of the recommended specialist outfits, which work to minimize their impact on the delicate desert environment (see box, p.66).

Alter Action Sandboarding ☎064 402737 (Amanpuri Travellers' Lodge) or ☎081 128 2737, ☜alter-action.info. A guaranteed morning of action as you build up to speeds of between 60–80kph on your final runs, racing down the dunes. It's good value: N$400 to lie down (for most novices) or N$500 to stand up (if you can surf on water or snow), including transfers, a light lunch and drinks.

Desert Explorers ☎081 124 1386, ☜namibiadesert explorers.com. Focuses on racing round the desert on a quad bike (1hr N$450, 3hr N$900 – min 4 people) but includes combo tours with sand-boarding (N$750), and can book other activities too. Manual or automatic quad bikes are available and helmets are provided.

Element Riders ☎081 666 6599, ☜element -riders.com. Well-regarded outfit specializing in surfing and kitesurfing (in Lüderitz – see p.129). Beginners 2–3hr surf class (N$400–500), including gear rental. Equipment for rent and for sale too.

Ground Rush Adventures Also known as Swakop Skydive; corner of Moses Garoeb and Anton Lubowski St at Amanpuri Traveller's Lodge ☎064 402841 or ☎081 124 5167, ☜skydiveswakop.com. This place offers similar rates to Swakopmund Skydiving with tandem (N$2500) and static line courses (N$1400). Videoing your exploits will cost an additional N$550. Take-off is from the old Swakopmund airport.

Swakopmund Skydiving Club Based at the old Swakopmund airport ☎064 405671 or ☎081 129 1866, ☜skydiveswakopmund.com. Highly experienced outfit offering tandem skydives with an instructor for the novice (N$2500) from 10,000 feet, or solo dives for the more fearless or experienced. The static line course finishes off with a drop from 3000ft (N$1500). Prices include pick-up, training, the plane out and the dive, after which you can return to the bar to watch a DVD of your exploits (for N$1000 extra) over a well-earned beer.

5

for an early evening beer before you hit town. Wi-fi N$30 extra. Camping a little cramped and can be noisy. Camping per person N$160, dorms N$200, doubles N$650

Hansa Hotel 3 Hendrik Witbooi St ☎ 064 414200, ⓦ hansahotel.com.na. From the marble foyer to the Neoclassical columns and heavy drapes, the *Hansa* announces itself as "Namibia's finest and oldest hotel". Rooms are good-sized and comfortably furnished, though nothing special, offering all the services you'd expect from an upmarket business establishment, as well as underfloor heating – particularly welcome in winter. The breakfast buffet is a veritable Teutonic feast, and there's fine dining in the silver service restaurant (see opposite). B&B N$2260

Hotel Pension Rapmund 6–8 Bismarck St ☎ 064 402035, ⓦ hotelpensionrapmund.com. With double and family rooms, this well-established twenty-room hotel is a solid choice, offering reasonable rates in a central location. Bag one of the upstairs rooms with private balcony and don't miss out on the tasty German buffet breakfast. B&B N$1170

Hotel Prinzessin Rupprecht 15 Anton Lubowski Ave ☎ 064 412540, ⓦ en.hotel-prinzessin-rupprecht.com. A former German military hospital, sharing its formal grounds with the neighbouring retirement home; the hundred-year-old building inevitably has long corridors and high ceilings, with most rooms decent-sized, if rather stark, with fridge and kettle. Though recently renovated, it can't quite shake off its austere image but often has space (doubles, triples and family rooms) when others are full, and offers good rates for children. B&B N$1180

Meike's Guesthouse 23 Windhoek St ☎ 064 405863, ⓦ meikes-guesthouse.net. This eco-friendly, solar-powered guesthouse run by experienced hosts offers five recently renovated doubles and two family rooms (sleeping four) with home comforts: TV, fridge, tea- and coffee-making facilities, plus private verandas and walk-in showers. Most rooms are wheelchair accessible. B&B N$1350

Organic Square Guesthouse 29 & 56 Rhode Allee ☎ 064 463979 or ☎ 081 129 0489, ⓦ guesthouse-swakopmund.com. Modern, stylish guesthouse with fifteen rooms spread over two properties: rustic chic reigns in grey and lime green, with modern artwork inside and out. Rooms have DStv, fridge-minibar and spotless bathrooms, and each opens onto private patio-garden space. The healthy organic continental breakfasts are a treat. B&B N$1565

Sam's Giardino 89 Anton Lubowski Ave ☎ 064 403210, ⓦ giardinonamibia.com. The main draw of this Swiss-run oasis is the lovely lush garden, dotted with sun-loungers and sheltered behind high walls. Otherwise, expect comfortable rooms and a guests' lounge where hot drinks, newspapers, books and satellite TV are available. The restaurant serves a five-course set-menu dinner (N$300) at 7.30pm, which is available for non-residents – reservations essential. B&B N$1600

★ **The Stiltz** Strand St South ☎ 064 400771, ⓦ thestiltz.com. Unique accommodation comprising nine raised wood-and-thatch chalets overlooking scrubland, and connected by elevated wooden walkways; number 7 has the standout beach view. Spacious, with large windows and creative use of wood and rustic touches, each chalet has a fully stocked minibar, tea/coffee and a safe. Here you can feel close to nature while being a short hop from town. B&B N$1680

The Strand Hotel The Mole ☎ 064 114000, ⓦ strandhotelswakopmund.com. The new upmarket hotel in town (complete with presidential suite) at upmarket prices, in a top location, on the Mole surrounded by the sea. Apart from the evocative historical photos, the well-appointed rooms (all with sea views) are smart if lacking character. Three distinctive on-site restaurants and a decent spa. B&B N$3584

Swakopmund Municipal Restcamp End of Henrik Witbooi St ☎ 064 410433 or ☎ 081 128 5893, ⓦ swakopmund-restcamp.com. A sound budget choice, this place has been going for years, offering affordable, functional units accommodating from two to six people, all with kitchen and braai sites. The basic Fisherman's cabin with two single beds is the cheapest. Also has an on-site restaurant. N$495

Tiger Reef Campsite Strand St South ☎ 064 400935 or ☎ 081 791 0133, ⓦ facebook.com/tigerreefcampsite. Smallish but secure, private and sheltered camping plots are arranged in a circle round a large expanse of grass. Each pitch comes with thatched lapa and picnic table, braai area, electricity and water, with shared ablutions. You can hear the ocean waves, but can feel the biting ocean wind too, despite the cane shelters. Discounts in low season. Camping per person N$160

OUT OF TOWN CENTRE

Beach Lodge 1 Stint St, Vogelstrand 064 414500, ⓦ beachlodge.com.na. The ship design might have got somewhat lost in translation, but the place lives up to its name, being bang on the beach, 4km north of town. Light and spacious modern rooms boast sea views – through a large porthole in the case of the first-floor accommodation – and come with ceiling fan, heater, satellite TV, fridge and private patio or balcony, from which to admire the sunsets. The family rooms offer the best value (N$3280 for four adults). B&B N$1750

★ **Desert Breeze Lodge** 5min drive east of Swakopmund ☎ 064 406236 or ☎ 081 149 4979, ⓦ desertbreezeswakopmund.com. Perched above the dry Swakop River, these twelve distinctive, luxury studio bungalows (plus villa for six) offer a superb alternative to staying in town: vast windows and private viewing deck maximize the expansive desert vistas, while a cosy wood-burning stove staves off the evening chill. You'll need transport to get into town. B&B N$2250

Skeleton Beach Backpackers 14 Moses Garoeb St ☎ 061 259485 (reservations Windhoek) or ☎ 081 287 0420, ⊛ skeletonbeachbackpackers.com. A stiff 15min hike north of town, this converted house in a quiet residential area is a good deal, if a little cramped when full. Dorms include a shipping container, which is freezing cold in winter. Doubles are en suite with TV (Room 8 even has its own balcony), and other amenities include cable TV in the communal lounge, tea/coffee available all day and a laundry. The shared semi-open kitchen is well equipped and the delightful garden with braai area is a bonus. Cash only. Camping per person <u>N$120</u>, dorms <u>N$170</u>, doubles <u>N$480</u>

EATING

CAFÉS

Café Anton Hotel Schweizerhaus, 1 Bismarck St ☎ 064 400331, ⊛ schweizerhaus.net/cafe_anton.htm. A Swakop institution whose reputation does not always stand up to the test. That said, the patio terrace is perfectly situated and you can't beat the incongruity of biting into a slice of Black Forest gâteau as you gaze at the palm trees. Tasty buffet breakfasts. Daily 6.30am–7pm.

★ **Garden Café** 11 Tobias Hainyeko St ☎ 081 127 0931. This delightful shady oasis in a secluded garden is good for healthy or indulgent breakfasts, brunch, cakes and savoury lunches, including rare treats for vegetarians. (N$50–90). Be prepared to wait. Mon–Fri 8.30am–5pm, Sat & Sun 8.30am–3pm.

Muschel Art Café Brauhaus Arcade ☎ 064 402874. Tucked away in the pedestrian precinct, this sheltered café catches the late afternoon sun, when it's a prime spot to unwind with a coffee and a fresh filled roll or slice of cake. Mon–Sat 8am–6pm, Sun 10.30am–6pm.

Village Café 23 Sam Nujoma Ave ☎ 064 404723, ⊛ villagecafenamibia.com. Quirky café popular with locals and travellers alike. There's well-prepared, inexpensive food, including all-day breakfasts (and grub for visiting dogs), plus good service, with a mellow vibe. Mon–Fri 6.30am–5pm, Sat 6.30am–1.30pm.

RESTAURANTS

22 Degrees South In the lighthouse, Am Leuchtturm St ☎ 064 400380. An intimate place for dinner, yet also family friendly; eat inside and enjoy the cosy, rustic ambience, or outside on the lawn beneath the swaying palms. Italian-based cuisine with some Namibian twists and favourites. Can be slow when busy. Tues–Sun 11am–3pm & 6.30pm until late.

★ **Brewer and Butcher** The Mole ☎ 061 4114512, ⊛ brewer-butcher.com. The pick of *The Strand Hotel*'s three restaurants, with its warming fires, unobtrusive sports screens and buzzing atmosphere, caters for lovers of meat and craft beer – note the two large copper brewhouses on show. Sample the generous tasting tray of three beers, to accompany the house oxtail or any of the succulent steaks or deli-burgers (grills from around N$175) on offer, but leave room for the melt-in-your-mouth chocolate-and-banana Malva pudding. Daily noon–10pm.

★ **The Fish Deli** 29 Sam Nujoma Ave ☎ 064 462979, ⊛ fishdeli-swakopmund.com. A fishmonger's, deli, take-away and restaurant all rolled into one, which is especially busy at lunchtimes, offering the best fresh catch straight from the boat. Try one of their mouthwatering stir-fries: mango, coriander and prawn, or red curry calamari in coconut sauce (around N$110). Mon–Fri 9.30am–9.30pm, Sat 9.30am–1.30pm & 6–9.30pm.

Garnish Corner of Tobias Hainyeko St and Libertina Amadhila St ☎ 064 405401, ⊛ facebook.com/garnishs wakopmund.com. Inevitably pleasing vegetarians, this Indian restaurant is also a popular choice for groups of friends and families to share a number of dishes, though the cost can mount up as sides, rice, naans and rotis are priced separately (mains N$60–80). Also does takeaways. Wed–Mon 11.30am–9.30pm.

Hansa Hotel 3 Hendrik Witbooi St ☎ 064 414200, ⊛ hansahotel.com.na. If you're after refined dining and old-world elegance, this is the place. Sink into your upholstered chair and soak up the white-glove service, damask tablecloths, silver cutlery and crystal decanters – not to mention exquisite cuisine: try impala loin in red wine with Amaretto-flambéed pear. Mains from around N$160. Daily noon–2pm & 7.30–9.30pm.

★ **Jetty 1905** End of the pier ☎ 064 405664, ⊛ facebook.com/jetty1905. Hidden away at the end of Swakop's restored pier, this chic, modern restaurant is all about the view. Surrounded by glass, you can gaze at the ocean from all angles as you tuck into sushi or a plate of baked garlic oysters (a must), or sip your cocktail as the sun sinks over the sea. Most mains N$125–230. Tues–Thurs 5–10pm, Fri & Sat noon–10pm, Sun noon–9pm.

Kücki's Pub 22 Tobias Hainyeko St ☎ 064 402407, ⊛ kuckispub.com. A long-standing culinary institution in Swakop, which has grown in size, but still succeeds in pleasing the palate. Specializing in grilled game meat and seafood – try the seafood platter for two, served with *spätzle, rösti* or fried potatoes – this Bierkeller provides large portions of pub grub at tourist prices, washed down with draught beer and wine by the glass. Upstairs is a louder sports bar, but when packed with tour groups, even downstairs is humming. Daily 5pm until late.

★ **Secret Garden Bistro** Bismarck St ☎ 085 643 8677. Serves up pizzas (around N$150), soups and salad – the small pizza-and-salad combo for around N$110 is good value – plus daily specials. The wood-fired oven pizzas are rightly praised here, while the fairy lights in the garden in summer make for a romantic and intimate setting.

5

Heavy-duty brownies lie in wait for dessert. Mon–Sat 5–9pm, Sun until 8.30pm.

The Tug Restaurant Swakop Jetty ☎064 402356, ⓦthe-tug.com. Iconic, upmarket restaurant spilling out of a beached tugboat, with superlative vistas across the sea from the upstairs "deck". Seafood predominates, including crayfish in season, local oysters and the mountainous Tug Seafood Extravaganza, but vegetarians need not despair as there are several veggie options too. If you can't get a table, a cocktail at sundown will at least let you admire the view. Reservations strongly advised. Mon–Fri 6–10pm, Sat & Sun noon–3pm & 6–10pm.

★**The Wreck** Beach Lodge, 1 Stint St, Vogelstrand (4km north of town centre) ☎064 414500, ⓦthe-wreck.com. Arguably, the top place for fine dining. Imaginative international dishes, such as snails wrapped in blue cheese filo parcels, or grilled kingclip with creamy lentils and slow-roasted tomato, are beautifully presented at this elegant restaurant. The most is made of its second-floor beachside location, as floor-to-ceiling windows and "portholes" afford stunning sea views – best at lunchtime, though the menu is more limited then. Fish mains start at around N\$150, meat from around N\$170. Mon–Sat noon–2pm & 6.30–9.30pm, Sun 6.30–9.30pm.

NIGHTLIFE

★**Alte Laundry** 15 Swakop St ☎064 402135. Swakop's most happening venue, attracting a multiracial crowd most nights. There's a pool table, weekend DJs that get a crowd on the dancefloor, a grill, plus a beer garden hung with fairy lights that hosts occasional live music. The place is open from 10am but doesn't get going until late. N\$30 cover for events. Daily 10am–2am.

Desert Tavern Swakop St ☎064 404204, ⓦdesert-tavern.com. A warm and cosy spot once the fires are blazing at night, with a brick-and-wood interior. It comes alive when there's live music (usually jazz or rock) on a Friday or Saturday evening. Serves large burgers and other pub grub. Mon–Sat 4pm until late.

Swakopmund Hotel and Entertainment Centre 2 Theo-Ben Gurirab Ave ☎064 4105200, ⓦlegacyhotels.co.za. The brashest, glitziest place in town inhabits a conversion of the colonial-era railway station. There's a casino (daily 10am–4am) and the town's only cinema here.

Tiger Reef Beach Bar & Grill End of Strand St South, on the beach ☎064 400935, ⓦfacebook.com/tigerreef. Relaxed, thatched place to kick off your shoes, sink your toes into the sand and watch the sunset, though it can be chilly on windy evenings. Order at the bar, grab a seat on the beach and let the drinks – or the indifferent pub grub (N\$60–120) – be brought to you. Very occasional live music. Tues–Fri noon–midnight, Sat & Sun 11am–midnight.

SHOPPING

Outside Windhoek, Swakopmund is the best place to shop for **souvenirs** in Namibia, and also has a wide choice of supermarkets and deli shops for you to load up with supplies if you're self-catering here or heading back into the desert.

BOOKS

Die Muschel Brauhaus Arcade, Tobias Hainyeko St ☎064 402874, ⓦmuschel.iway.na. A good selection of books in German and English, especially on art, as well as a selection of music and calendars. Mon–Fri 8.30am–6pm, Sat 8.30am–1pm, 4–6pm, Sun 10am–6pm.

Swakopmunder Buchhandling 22 Sam Nujoma Ave ☎064 402613, ⓦfacebook/swakopmunder.buchhandling. A decent enough selection of novels, as well as books on Namibia, in English, plus a wider

---

WELWITSCHIAS

Appearances can sometimes be deceptive: what may look like a mangled giant cabbage run over by a truck is most likely to be Namibia's most remarkable desert survivor, the aptly named **welwitschia mirabilis** – "mirabilis" being Latin for marvellous or wonderful, while "Welwitsch" was the surname of the Austrian botanist who stumbled over some in the mid-nineteenth century. Featuring on Namibia's coat of arms and nicknamed the "living fossil", the welwitschia can live over 1500 years; its most celebrated specimen – rumoured to be one of the oldest and largest – is located inland from Swakopmund and attracts thousands of visitors annually, though the plant's withered and dishevelled appearance can be an initial disappointment.

Welwitschias are endemic to the arid, coastal **gravel plains** that extend 1000km northwards from the Kuiseb River south of Walvis Bay to southern Angola. They survive on very little water and some years get none at all.

Strangely, the welwitschia – a dioecious plant with both female and male specimens – only possesses two grey-green leaves, which shrivel and shred over the years. Though the leaves can reach 2–4m in length, this extraordinary plant rarely grows higher than 1.5m.

selection of books in German, and stationery. Mon–Fri 8.30am–5.30pm, Sat 8.30am–5.30pm, Sun 9.30am–12.30pm.

ARTS & CRAFTS

African Kirikara Arts & Crafts Am Ankerplatz, Sam Nujoma Ave ☎ 064 463146, ⓦ kirikara.com. Swakopmund outlet for Kiripotib Farm karakul weavings and jewellery, alongside other arts and crafts. Mon–Fri 9.30am–1pm, 2.30–6pm, Sat 9am–1pm, 4–6pm, Sun 10am–noon.

COSDEF Arts & Crafts Centre 3km from the town centre, on the B2 ☎ 064 406122, ⓦ facebook.com /cosdefartsandcrafts. Community-based arts and crafts project in a nice new complex: browse for handbags, sandals, cushions or cards, or basketry and jewellery. Also live music on occasions and African drumming sessions. Mon–Fri 8.30am–4.30pm, Sat 8.30am–3pm.

Karakulia Weavers 2 Rakotoka St, NDC Centre ☎ 064 461415, ⓦ facebook.com/karakuliaweavers swakopmund. Successful community development workshop, which produces top-quality karakul rugs and weavings (with made-to-order designs too). Watch the spinning and weaving first-hand or drop in at the smaller outlet in the Brauhaus Arcade in the town centre. Mon–Fri 8am–5pm, Sat 8am–1pm.

Namcrafts Brauhaus Arcade, Tobias Hainyeko St ☎ 064 405910, ⓦ namcrafts.com. Swakopmund outlet of the popular Namibian chain with locally produced crafts as well as South African imports. Mon–Fri 8.30am–6pm, Sat & Sun 9am–1pm.

Namibia Jewellers and Arts Gallery 55 Sam Nujoma Ave ☎ 064 404525, ⓦ namibian.jewellers.online.ms. Original contemporary handcrafted gold and silver jewellery with gemstones, displayed among changing exhibitions of paintings and sculptures in a lovely old colonial-era house. Mon–Fri 8am–1pm, 2.30–5.30pm, Sat 8am–1pm.

DIRECTORY

Banks and money All the major banks, with ATMs, are present in the town centre. There's also a branch of NovaCâmbios (Mon–Fri 8am–5pm, Sat 8am–1pm; ☎ 064 461492, ⓦ novacambios.com) on Hendrik Witbooi St, by Pick 'N' Pay.

Bicycle repairs Cycles 4U on Hidepo Hamutenya Ave sells parts and repairs bicycles (☎ 064 407135; Mon–Fri 9am–5pm, Sat 9am–1pm).

Car rental There are both local and international car rental agencies in Swakop. Avis (ⓦ avis.com.na) and Budget (ⓦ locations.budget.com/sw) share an office in the Swakopmund Hotel and Entertainment Centre on Mandume Ya Ndemufayo St (☎ 064 402527), charging around US$40–50 pay for a small manual saloon car; over double that for a 4WD); Swakopmund Car Hire, 202 Sam Nujoma Ave (☎ 064 400180, ⓦ swakopcarhire .com), is a reliable local outfit, also with an office in Windhoek.

Hospitals and clinics Since the state hospital is always oversubscribed, head for the Mediclinic Swakopmund on Franziska van Neel St for serious matters (☎ 064 412200, ⓦ mediclinic.co.za); to see a doctor, call in at the Bismarck Medical Centre on 17–20 Sam Nujoma Ave (☎ 064 405000).

Laundry Alte Laundry, 15 Swakop St (Mon–Fri 8am–5pm, Sat 8am–1pm; ☎ 064 405618). In the same building as the sometimes functioning nightclub and bar of the same name, so you can enjoy a beer while your clothes wash.

Internet Free wi-fi is available in almost all lodgings and in various cafés, but if you need a PC, try Gogga's Internet Café, on Welwitschia St (Mon–Fri 9am–5pm, Sat 9am–1pm; ☎ 064 403291), which also scans documents and does photocopies.

Pharmacy Try the central, reliable Swakopmunder Apotheke at 26 Sam Nujoma Ave (Mon–Fri 8am–6pm, with reduced hours at weekends and public holidays; ☎ 064 402825, ⓦ swakopmunder.webs.com).

Police The Central Police Station is on Tobias Kanyeko St (☎ 064 402431; emergency ☎ 064 10111).

Post office The post office is next to the police station (☎ 064 402222). Opening hours are Mon–Fri 8am–5pm, Sat 8am–noon.

Vehicle repairs Auto Fix, 43 Schlachter St (☎ 064 400020), does basic repairs.

Welwitschia Drive

As the circuit takes place in the northern section of the Namib-Naukluft National Park you need to purchase a permit from the MET office in Swakopmund (see p.213), which comes with a map of the route

A long-standing favourite excursion from Swakopmund is along **Welwitschia Drive**, a marked interpretive route across the desert that starts a few kilometres from town, and can be done either as a 4WD self-drive (3–4hr) or a half-day tour (see p.213). The route traverses **gravel plains**, where you can stop and peer at **lichen fields** (see box, p.229) and **drought-resistant plants** such as the dollar bush, with its waxy coin-shaped leaves that give it its name. Other highlights include the otherworldly "**moonscape**"

5

– an area of undulating granite mounds that pushed through the Earth's surface around 460 million years ago, and which have been eroded by the wind and the changing course of the Swakop River over time. Last, but not least, you will see **welwitschias** – including Namibia's presumed largest and oldest specimen (see box, p.218).

Rössing Mine

60km northeast of Swakopmund, near Arandis • Half-day tours given the first Fri of every month, leaving at 10am outside Swakopmund Museum • Tickets N$50 available from the museum • No open shoes, and no admittance after you've been drinking; the mine reserves the right to breathalyze you

It's not everyone's idea of a fun day out, but if mineralogy or chemical engineering is your bent then you may fancy a visit to **Rössing Mine** – one of the largest and longest-running open-pit uranium mines in the world. At the very least, you'll be staggered by the scale of the operation: the chasm is currently 3km long and 1.5km wide, and as you peer into the abyss – almost 400m deep – the huge trucks that remove the blasted rocks appear like ants below. Uranium was first identified in the area in 1928, though extraction did not begin until 1976. The mine now looks set to continue until at least 2032. As with any mining behemoth, and especially one involving uranium, there are many questions over its operations. Concerns about environmental degradation, water usage, working conditions of labourers and health effects periodically bubble to the surface. Despite the hard work by Rössing's PR department – including this guided tour – which includes spending millions of Namibian dollars annually on social development projects, many issues remain shrouded in mist and spin.

Swakopmund Salt Works

At Mile 4 – actually around 8km north of Swakopmund by road – off the C34 to Henties Bay, the **Swakopmund Salt Works** provide some great early morning **birdwatching** opportunities. You need to get there before the workers arrive (or after they leave) to increase your chances of being rewarded by sightings of greater and lesser flamingos, a variety of terns, plovers, avocets, oystercatchers, cormorants and pelicans.

Walvis Bay

As a major fishing port possessing a rather dispersed town centre, and lacking the eye-pleasing colonial-era architecture of Swakopmund, **WALVIS BAY**, Namibia's second-largest population centre, attracts few overnight visitors. Tourists that come are usually on a day-trip from Swakopmund to do some activity on the lagoon. However, the town's very ordinariness and down-to-earth nature can actually be quite appealing after the surreal, toy-town nature of Swakop. What's more, tourist-oriented accommodation and decent dining options, clustered round the lagoon and new waterfront, are on the increase, and the town makes a better base for the highly worthwhile excursion to Sandwich Harbour (see box, p.225). Beyond the lagoon, the only sight – and a very modest one at that – is the town's one-room **museum**, in the library basement, which contains some interesting photographs of colonial life in Walvis.

Brief history

Though archeological evidence shows that the semi-nomadic Khoikhoi inhabited central coastal zones from Stone Age times, formal permanent **coastal settlements** did not occur until traders and whalers started to arrive in Sandwich Harbour and **Walvis Bay** ("Whale Bay" in Afrikaans) in the late seventeenth century. The ubiquitous

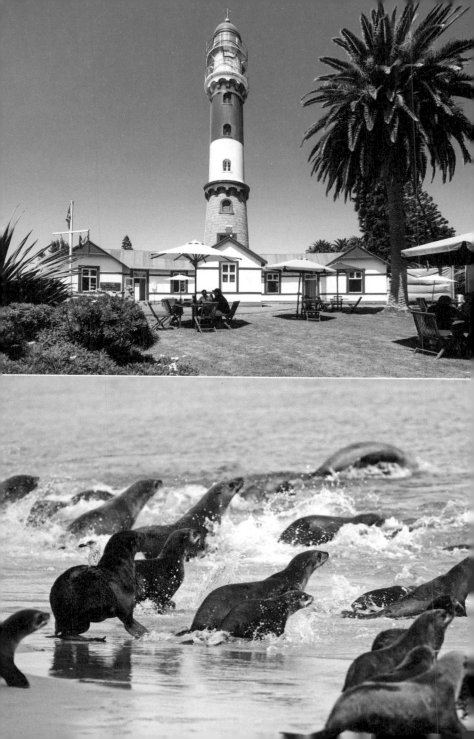

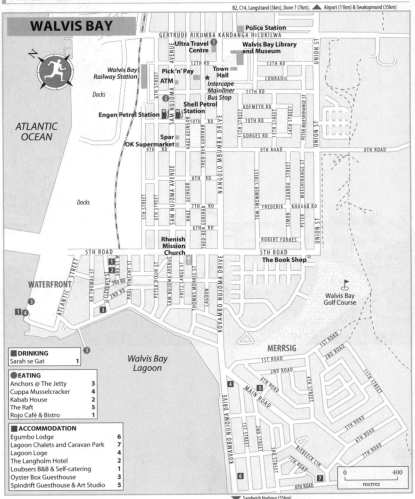

Portuguese explorer Bartolomeu Diaz (see p.342) had earlier drifted into the bay, on his search for a route through to Asia, but it was only later, as the Scramble for Africa (see p.343) gained momentum, that the various competing imperial powers began to recognize Walvis Bay's strategic importance as the only decent-sized natural harbour on the coast. After briefly being bagged by the Dutch in 1793, the port was soon seized by the British – keen to safeguard their ships round the Cape – before eventually being annexed to the Cape Colony in 1878. At the outbreak of World War I, Walvis was briefly overrun by the Germans, before they, in turn, were ousted by South African troops, who eventually took control of the port as part of their League of Nations mandate to govern South-West Africa.

Walvis Bay continued to thrive, especially once its international **fishing industry** took off in the 1950s. Such was the strategic and economic importance of the port, however, that South Africa attempted to cling onto it even after Namibian independence, until they were forced to relinquish sovereignty in 1994, once apartheid had ended in South Africa. However, since the South African authorities had exhausted fish stocks over many years, there followed a major slump in the industry. It is only fairly recently, after enforcing stricter controls, that fishing has enjoyed a resurgence, being the main earner of foreign exchange after mining, and a major contributor to GDP. The industry employs around 8000 people in fishing or fish processing, mostly in Walvis Bay.

The lagoon

As southern Africa's most precious coastal wetlands, **Walvis Bay lagoon**, together with the adjacent tidal mud flats and salt pans, has long been a top destination for keen birders, hosting over one hundred thousand **birds** in summer – notably thousands of flamingos, but also masses of pelicans, terns, plovers, grebes and cormorants – and around fifty thousand in winter. More recently, more casual wildlife lovers have begun to enjoy the lagoon, on **catamaran cruises** or **kayaking tours**, gliding among dolphins and Cape fur seals, which have colonized the sandspit known as Pelican Point that extends a protective arm across the bay, sheltering the lagoon from the wild Atlantic waves beyond. Further out, in season (July–Nov), humpback and southern right whales are regularly sighted from boats, and even the occasional leatherback turtle (Feb–March) or killer whale.

ARRIVAL AND INFORMATION

WALVIS BAY

By car The tarred B2 from Windhoek to Swakopmund continues to Walvis Bay. Alternatively, you can pick the scenic 4WD route that runs parallel to the coastal road and cuts through the desert.

By bus and shuttle Intercape Mainliner (☎ 061 227847, ⊛ intercape.co.za) has two weekly transfers to and from Windhoek. The bus leaves Windhoek (Thur & Sat) at 10am, arriving at 2.50pm, returning at 10.35am (Fri & Sun) from outside the *Spur* restaurant on Theo-Ben Gurirab Ave. Tickets (from N$210) can be bought at the Ultra Travel Centre, 199 Nangolo Mbumba Drive (Mon–Fri 8am–5.30pm, Sat 8.30am–noon; ☎ 064 207997). The Welwitschia Shuttle provides a weekday commuter shuttle service between Swakopmund and Walvis Bay (same stop as Intercape Mainliner), with two early morning departures from Swakopmund (*Woolworths* car park), returning from

Walvis Bay late afternoon. Minibuses leave early morning from Kuisebmund bound for Windhoek (N$200).

By plane Walvis Bay Airport lies 11km outside Walvis Bay. Air Namibia has daily flights to and from Windhoek's Hosea Kutako International Airport (40min), and to and from Cape Town (2hr 10min). South African Express has daily connections with Johannesburg and daily (except Sat) flights to and from Cape Town.

By taxi A shared taxi between Swakopmund and Walvis Bay costs N$40; a private one will set you back around N$200. Taxis can be picked up in the centre of Walvis, in the car park opposite *Spur*.

MET office The MET office, 643 Heinrich Baumann St (Mon–Fri 8am–5pm; ☎ 064 205971), sells permits for the national parks.

GETTING AROUND

By taxi Walvis Bay is quite spread out and it's a stiff 20min hike from the lagoon area to the centre of town along Sam Nujoma Ave, so you might find it easier at times to hop in a taxi, which is perfectly safe during the day and shouldn't cost more than N$20–30. At night you're best

off calling one out, which will cost an extra N$10–20 as most drivers have to come from Kuisebmond, the former township. Other taxi fares include N$100 for a trip out to Dune 7. Ask your accommodation for a recommended driver.

ACTIVITIES AND TOURS

Most activities focus on the **lagoon wildlife**, which you can explore in a kayak (around N$650) or on a catamaran or other motorized vessel. The other main excursion is by 4WD down to **Sandwich Harbour** (see box, p.225). Several "combo" tours visit the lagoon in the morning and tackle the dunes of Sandwich Harbour in the afternoon, which can make for quite an exhausting day. Companies charge much the same rates for the same itinerary and can arrange transfers from Swakopmund, for which some charge an additional fee. Both of these activities need to be booked well in advance if you're intending to visit in late July or August.

KAYAK TOURS

Tours last around 4–5hr and leave early in the morning to make the most of the weather conditions, as the wind

tends to get up in the afternoon. It takes about 45min each way to transfer clients round the bay to Pelican Point; you then spend about 2hr on the water with a guide before

5

enjoying a snack on the beach. Operators take two–twelve clients and offer single and double kayaks. The companies below come highly recommended and can organize a combined excursion with Sandwich Harbour, for which you are picked up en route, rather than having to return to the town in between excursions.

Eco-marine Kayak Tours ☎ 064 203144, ⓦ emkayak .iway.na. N$650.

Namibia Kayak Tours ☎ 081 229 6307, ⓦ namibiakayaktours.com. N$650; N$1000 for the combined kayaking and Sandwich Harbour tour.

Pelican Point Kayaking Jettyshoppe, Waterfront ☎ 081 147 6755, ⓦ pelican-point-kayaking.com. Will take up to sixteen clients but with two guides. Kayak tour N$700, kayak and Sandwich Harbour combo N$2200.

CATAMARAN TOURS

The catamaran tours visit the oyster farms, lighthouse and the wreck at Pelican Point while on the lookout for whales (July–Nov), dolphins (year-round), leatherback turtles and other marine life. They also usually feed a few tame seals and pelicans that come on board, which may not be to everyone's taste. Tours usually last around three hours, and a light buffet, including fresh oysters and sparkling wine, is served on the boat.

Mola-Mola Safaris Waterfront ☎ 064 205511 or ☎ 081 127 2522, ⓦ mola-namibia.com. Well-established company with several speedboat catamarans (and one more leisurely one) offering the usual 3.5hr cruise round the bay (N$620), or a longer one with full lunch. Also offers the half-day Sandwich Harbour tour (N$1200) and the lagoon and Sandwich Harbour combo tour (N$1850).

Ocean Adventures Jetty Kiosk, Swakopmund ☎ 064 402377, ⓦ swakopadventures.com. Three-hour trips for N$550.

Sun Sail Catamaran ☎ 081 124 5045, ⓦ sailnamibia .com. Tries to use the sail as much as possible. Also offers a combo tour with a trip to Sandwich Harbour in the afternoon for N$1900.

TOWNSHIP TOURS

Walvis Bay Tour Guides Wooden office by Mola-Mola, Waterfront ☎ 064 200436, ⓦ walvisbay-eco-tourism .com. The only black-owned operation in town, run by the engaging and experienced Owambo guide, Fried Fredericks; in addition to dolphin and seal cruises in the bay, it also offers its signature cultural tours to Kuisebmund (N$500).

GENERAL TOURS

Kuiseb Delta Adventures Lagoon Chalets, 8th Rd West ☎ 081 128 2580, ⓔ kda@iway.na, ⓦ kuisebonline .com. Highly rated educational quad biking tour over the dunes and a full-day 4WD extravaganza that goes inland to visit a Topnaar (‡Aonin) community and then rides the dunes down to Sandwich Harbour (N$2000).

Sandwich Harbour 4x4 Jettyshoppe, Waterfront ☎ 064 207663, ⓦ sandwich-harbour.com. Full-day tour to Sandwich Harbour (N$1550), or a half-day there combined with a morning boat trip on Walvis Bay lagoon looking at the seals (N$2070).

ACCOMMODATION

Egumbo Lodge Kovambo Nujoma Drive 42 ☎ 064 207700, ⓦ egumbolodge.com. Incongruous yet magnificent, thatched colonial-style lodge set around a pool and small garden. Each of the nine rooms is individually designed and exquisitely furnished in polished teak, with hessian carpets topped with Persian rugs and plenty of storage space. Room 1, with a private balcony overlooking the lagoon, is particularly special. B&B N$1800

Lagoon Chalets and Caravan Park 8th Rd West, Meersig ☎ 064 217900, ⓦ lagoonchaletswb.com. Well-run, secure site four blocks from the lagoon offering a range of accommodation, from dorms to chalets and VIP suites, most with DStv. Units are generally drably painted concrete, and some are a little aged and uninspiring inside, but they're clean, cheap and with the necessary facilities. The good-value campground has sheltered private plots (maximum four people) with their own washing line as well as the usual braai facilities and electricity. The on-site restaurant with wi-fi is a plus. Dorms N$100, camping per pitch (up to four people) N$250, doubles N$300

★**Lagoon Loge** 88 Kovambo Nujoma Drive ☎ 064 200850, ⓦ lagoonloge.com.na. Visible from across the lagoon, this canary-yellow beacon has eight capacious rooms, each amply supplied with eclectic furnishings and artwork. The friendly French owners (hence "loge") help organize tours and activities. There's also a great rooftop sundeck – a prime spot for birdwatching – and a delightfully furnished, comfortable sunlit lounge. B&B N$1860

The Langholm Hotel 18–20 JJ Cleverly St ☎ 064 209230, ⓦ langholmhotel.com. Sparkling green-and-white hotel popular with tourists and business folk, offering reliable service and light, clean rooms with all the usual amenities: fridge, DStv, tea/coffee facilities, safe. There's a pleasant lounge-bar – bedecked with baseball caps – a garden and secure parking. Good value for money. B&B N$1228

Loubser's B&B & Self-catering 11 3rd St West ☎ 064 203034, ⓦ loubseraccommodation.com. Slightly cramped accommodation in a converted house round a yard: three double rooms, two small four-bed dorms with en-suite bathroom and handy kitchenette, and a self-catering unit. The decor is bland, bordering on the chintzy, but you can't beat the price. Shared braai and TV area, with a pool table and darts board. Dorms N$140, doubles N$380

Oyster Box Guesthouse Corner of the Esplanade and 2nd St ☏ 064 202247, ⓦ oysterboxguesthouse.com. This light and airy modern guesthouse makes the most of its lagoon location with vast windows, through which to watch pelicans and flamingos land. Single, twin or triple rooms all have (limited) DStv and a/c (heating) units, but bag one with a sea view (for a little extra) on the first floor to avoid the goldfish-bowl feel of some on the ground floor. B&B N$1608

★ **Spindrift Guesthouse & Art Studio** 22 Main Rd, Meersig ☏ 064 206723 or ☏ 081 129 3940, ⓦ spindrift3 .wixsite.com/spindriftguesthouse. Delightful, homely B&B set in a small tropical garden just a couple of blocks back from the lagoon, with charming hosts. Each of the nine double or family rooms is individually decorated and full of artwork by the owner, but note that emails are rarely answered. B&B N$800

EATING

★ **Anchors @ The Jetty** The Esplanade, Waterfront ☏ 064 205762, ⓦ facebook.com/anchorsatthejetty. This nautically themed restaurant does a brisk trade throughout the day, on account of its location and decor as much as for its moderately priced succulent seafood. The calamari are highly praised, but try out breakfast; this is one of the few places that offers a healthy alternative as well as the usual fry-ups. Tues–Sat 7.30am–10pm, Sun & Mon 7.30am–3pm.

Cuppa Musselcracker The Boardwalk, Waterfront ☏ 081 617 8537. Sprawl on the cushions and admire the sea views in this relaxed café. A top spot for breakfast (only fried; M$40–100), light bites, coffee and indulgent cakes, with the tapas and mains (from N$75) rather hit and miss. Wed–Sat 7.30am–9pm, Sun–Tues 7.30am–5pm.

Kabab House Corner of Sam Nujoma Ave and 11th Rd ☏ 081 476 4962, ⓦ kababhousenamibia.com. An unexpected find in downtown Walvis, this halal Pakistani restaurant, which also offers a spread of Indian dishes, serves up some really tasty meals, with plenty for

vegetarians. There's a pleasant "beer garden" to sit out in – without the beer, which is why you'll find more people taking out than eating in. Meat curries from N$65, with naan, roti and rice sides extra. Most mains N$60–80. Daily 10am–10pm.

★ **The Raft** The Esplanade ☏ 064 204877, ⓦ theraftrestaurant.com. This unmissable large structure on stilts, jutting out into the lagoon, is the ideal spot to laze away an afternoon watching the sea life. Warm wooden interior and winter log fires make for a relaxed ambience. The usual spread of salads, pastas, seafood and flame-grilled meat dishes is on offer, including tasty veggie options. The quality is consistently high and the prices are moderate (mains from N$80). Daily noon–10pm.

Rojo Café & Bistro 199 Nangolo Mbumba Drive ☏ 064 221739. Popular downtown lunchtime spot serving toasties, salads and light bites. Now provides intimate, casual candlelit dining some evenings, serving inexpensive Texmex, pizzas, and the usual fish and meat dishes, nicely presented. Mon & Tues 7am–3pm, Wed–Fri 7am–9pm, Sat 8am–2pm.

DRINKING

Sarah se Gat The Boardwalk ☏ 081 122 0181. Serious drinking den and good sundowner spot, especially in the summer when you can sprawl across the wooden benches and tables on the rooftop terrace and soak up

the panoramic views of the bay. Decent cocktail menu, and live music usually on Fri & Sat evenings from 8pm and Sun afternoons. Mon–Sat 10am–2am, Sun 10am–6pm.

SANDWICH HARBOUR

A long-standing birding hotspot, isolated **Sandwich Harbour**, which lies 55km south of Walvis Bay, has recently begun to attract more casual visitors, drawn by the stunning wilderness scenery, as the rolling golden dunes of the Namib meet the wild Atlantic coast. The "harbour" itself is a lagoon, a mix of fresh and saline water, and an important site for migratory and resident **seabirds and waders**, which also spread over the nearby tidal mud flats. Numbers can top fifty thousand in summer, and twenty thousand in winter. Even non-birders will be amazed at the colourful carpet of huge flocks of flamingos and pelicans, vast numbers of grebes and the immense variety of terns and waders, dramatically enclosed by the dunes.

Though in theory anyone with a high-clearance 4WD can get a permit from the MET office in Swakopmund and drive themselves here, it is not advised, even for experienced 4WD motorists, as the driving conditions are treacherous, and the route constantly shifting with the sand, plus you will only add more eyesore tracks to the sand (see box, p.66). Better to leave your vehicle behind and take one of the **organized day-trips** (see p.223). Even then, research the **tide timetable** thoroughly before booking, as access to the lagoon itself depends on it being low tide so that vehicles can drive along the beach.

5

North of Swakopmund

North of Swakopmund, the increasingly wild and seemingly barren coastline stretches towards the **Kunene River**, which marks the border with Angola about 680km away. Travelling along the compacted salt and gravel coastal road affords you views of endless gravel plains, flat sandy beaches pummelled by the Atlantic waves, and, eventually, pale, distant dunes that creep closer as you drive further north. All of this is punctuated by the occasional flecks of lichen fields, which transform into a colourful tapestry in the early morning mist.

Now, in theory, this whole strip of land (reaching only around 40km inland) is protected, initially by Namibia's most recently formed reserve, the **Dorob National Park** (formerly the West Coast Recreational Area). The park extends southwards to the Kuiseb River Delta, south of Walvis Bay, and northwards to the Ugab River, where the **Skeleton Coast National Park** begins. The ultimate aim is the creation of a coastal megapark that extends the entire length of Namibia's coastline. For the moment, the incipient Dorob National Park is more a paper park, with various excluded areas (where development has already taken place) and no real facilities; as a result, no park fees are charged as yet, except to enter the seal reserve at Cape Cross.

Henties Bay

Once little more than a tiny fishing village, **HENTIES BAY** is expanding: new construction is very much in evidence, and everywhere you look there are road signs to self-catering chalets, guesthouses and B&Bs. Though still primarily geared towards the fishing fraternity, many of whom trek here annually from South Africa, the municipality is keen to attract other tourists, and has invested in a large new tourist centre (see opposite), which can furnish keen walkers with a map of a couple of lengthy unmarked **hikes** (18 or 20km): one goes inland along the Omaruru River – with an unpromising unscenic start through a sand-mining operation – the other heads down the coast to some wetlands. You'd need to set out early in the morning, with plenty of food and water. More popular are the 4WD trails; again the tourist office can provide you with the relevant information, including satellite maps, though having a GPS is

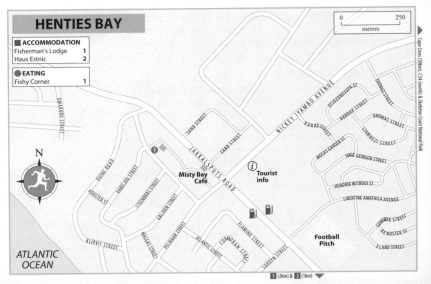

also advisable. Destinations include the impressive Messum Crater (see p.228), a vast natural amphitheatre containing welwitschias and ancient rock art, and the Ugab Menhir – an interesting megalith. Don't miss the impressive lichen fields to the east of the road, 4km north of Henties Bay.

ARRIVAL AND INFORMATION   HENTIES BAY

By car Follow the C34 70km north up the coast from Swakopmund. The compacted salt and gravel road is hard and smooth, for the most part, but can be slippery in the early morning fog and has one or two bumpy moments.

By minibus There are daily minibuses between Henties Bay and Swakopmund (N$55) and weekend departures to Khorixas on Friday, returning to Henties Bay on Sunday (N$240).

Tourist information There is a large municipal tourist office building (☎064 501143, ⌨hentiesbaytourism .com), offering free high-speed wi-fi, with some occasionally open curio stalls and a coffee shop. Here you can get your free MET permits for the 4WD trails and purchase the relevant satellite map; otherwise you need one from the MET office in either Swakopmund (see p.213) or Walvis Bay (see p.223).

ACCOMMODATION

Fisherman's Lodge Auss St 2007 ☎081 303 2694, ⌨huntandfishnamibia.com. Friendly, cheerful fishing-themed guesthouse, primarily catering to fisherfolk, but offering warm hospitality to all, close to the beach. Has 14 tidy, well-kept rooms (Room 4 has a sea view), with twin beds, tea/coffee facilities and TV, plus can provide gourmet meals (host Louis was a former full-time chef). **N$1036**

Haus Estnic 1417 Omatako St ☎064 501902, ⌨hausestnic.weebly.com. Though you might feel overly enclosed, personalized service is guaranteed as this place only has three double rooms – all en suite with fridge, tea/coffee-making facilities and TV. They open out onto a plant-filled patio with shade and a braai hearth to warm you when it's chilly. **N$1050**

EATING

Fishy Corner 19 Benguela St ☎064 501059. Festooned with fishing tackle, and possessing quaint painted wooden furniture, this cosy, friendly place prepares decent-sized portions of fresh fish and other

seafood at modest prices. Choose from hake (N$60), steenbras, calamari, kabeljou or kingklip. Mon–Sat 10am–10pm, Sun 10am–2pm, 6–10pm.

Cape Cross

N$80/person, N$10/vehicle, payable at the MET office (see below)

A pinprick on the map around 120km up the coast from Swakopmund, **Cape Cross** is home to the largest colony of Cape fur seals in the world (see box, p.228). Though the landscape is bare and unremarkable, the seals draw a surprising number of visitors, and the walkway allows you to get close to the action: belligerent bulls tussling for supremacy and mating rights, trying to take chunks out of each other, and female seals and pups, squabbling, playing, dozing off in the sun, or struggling to get out of the surf as it lashes against the rocks.

Nearby is the Cape Cross itself – or rather a replica – which marks the spot where in 1484 Diago Cão, a Portuguese explorer, erected a *padrão*, or stone cross, in an attempt to claim the land for the king of Portugal.

ARRIVAL AND INFORMATION   CAPE CROSS

By car Access is easy even in a saloon car; Cape Cross is accessed via a dirt road signposted off the C34, 48km north of Henties Bay – 70km north of Swakop – which has the only fuel between Swakopmund and the reserve.

On a tour Several tour operators in Swakopmund (see

p.213) include Cape Cross on a half-day or full-day itinerary.

MET office Pay your entrance fee at the MET office (daily 8am–5pm, but opens at 10am during the seal-culling season: July 1–Nov 15; ☎064 694037), 5km from the turn-off to the seal colony; the seals lie a further 3km down the dirt road.

ACCOMMODATION AND EATING

Cape Cross Campsite Halfway between the MET office and the seal colony ☎064 694037. This exposed and

frequently windy site has only minimum facilities: a long-drop latrine and a braai area, but no water or electricity. It's

5

THE CAPE CROSS SEAL COLONY

You're likely to smell it before you see it: the world's largest breeding colony of **Cape fur seals**, which sprawls over the windswept beach at **Cape Cross**. Fur seals (family *Otariidae*), endemic to southern Africa, are commonly known as "eared seals" as they are distinguished from "true seals" (family *Phocidae*) by their visible external ears.

Out in the ocean for much of the year, the vast, blubber-bloated **bulls** heave their 360kg bodies onto shore around mid-October, losing almost half that body weight over the next few weeks as they scrap with other bulls to establish and defend territory and secure a decent-sized harem. The heavily pregnant **cows** arrive a few weeks later but enjoy very little breathing space: no sooner are the pups born (late Nov–early Dec) than the dominant bulls mate with each female in their harem. Development of the fertilized egg is delayed for three months, followed by a nine-month gestation period, which results in females giving birth at the same time each year. **Pups** suckle from their mother for almost a year, though progressively they hunt for longer periods away from home. Just under one in three pups survives – some drown, some are abandoned or lose their mother, or get trampled on by other seals; around a quarter fall prey to brown hyenas and black-backed jackals, which can be spotted at dusk, lurking on the fringes of the colony, awaiting their chance to snatch their prey.

Numbering between eighty thousand and one hundred thousand, the size of the seal colony is kept more or less constant by the extremely controversial **annual culling** that takes place between July and November, during which thousands of seals are slaughtered. The Namibian government maintains that the cull is necessary to protect fish stocks, provide seasonal jobs and as a means of generating income through fur sales; counter-arguments put forward by the increasingly vocal national and international anti-culling protest movement claim fish stocks are not threatened by seals and that more jobs and better revenue could be generated through eco-tourism activities involving seals.

hard to imagine why you'd want to stay here, unless to fish, especially as the campground at *Cape Cross Lodge* down the road offers far better facilities for little extra cost. Closed July 1–Nov 15. Per person N$100

Cape Cross Lodge 4km north of the seal colony, on the coast ☎ 021 8550395, ⓦ capecrosslodge.com. Spacious, comfortably furnished rooms overlooking the desolate coast; upstairs, you get your own balcony, whereas on the ground floor, you can step directly onto the beach. Day visitors are welcome at the reasonably priced restaurant, where you can watch the restless waves. The well-sheltered pitches have high-quality ablutions and braai facilities. Camping per pitch N$400, doubles (DBB) N$2124

Messum Crater

46km northeast of Cape Cross • N$40 permit (plus N$10 for the vehicle) from an MET office in Swakopmund (see p.213), Walvis Bay (see p.223), Windhoek (see p.94) or the NWR office at Sesriem (see p.112); alternatively en route in Henties Bay tourist office (see p.227) • There are three entrances/exits to the Messum Crater that all need 4WD: approaching from the south, a well-graded gravel road is signposted off the C34, 2km north of Cape Cross; another enters/exits the northwest edge of the crater along the Messum River and connects with the C34 at Mile 108; the third exits at the northeast edge of the crater and joins the Messum River, heading eastwards until you join the D2342 that skirts the southern edge of the Brandberg

Straddling the eastern boundary of the Dorob National Park lies the mesmerizing **Messum Crater**, the centre of a collapsed volcano that erupted some 132 to 135 million years ago, and the probable source of much of the basalt that forms the neighbouring Goboboseb Mountains, to the north. The shallow flat caldera, around 20km in diameter, is surrounded by two non-continuous concentric rings of heavily eroded igneous rocks, forming a surreal, eerie wilderness worthy of a science fiction film. The routes to and from the crater also provide opportunities to explore other fascinating natural and human phenomena: lichen fields (see box opposite) and welwitschias lie along the well-graded gravel track from the Skeleton Coast side (see box, p.218); archeological remains, such as stone circles used by ancient nomadic Damara groups, are also visible; and taking the northeastern exit out of the crater, the vast massif of the Brandberg looms as you draw closer, glowing pink and gold when bathed in afternoon sunlight.

Make sure you're well prepared for the drive here. In addition to the satellite map you can purchase from Henties Bay tourist office, a GPS is advisable (and a satellite phone if you're travelling alone and not up to basic breakdown repairs), since it's easy to get lost.

Skeleton Coast National Park

Ugab Gate (main entrance) daily 7.30am–3pm (last entry), last exit 7pm; Springbokwasser Gate (eastern entrance) daily 7.30am–5pm (last entry), last exit 7pm • The MET offices in Windhoek, Swakopmund and Walvis Bay (see p.94, p.2˜3 & p.223) sell entry permits (N$80/ per person plus N$10 for the vehicle per day), or they can be purchased at the Ugab Gate

At the Ugab River the larger-than-life skull and crossbones on the gates herald your entry to the **Skeleton Coast National Park**, evoking images of whalebones strewn along the shoreline, giant rusting hulls of shipwrecked vessels half-buried in the sand, and the twisted skeletons of the hapless crew members who struggled, and failed, to make it out of the desert alive. While some of these images hold true, most shipwrecks have been consumed by either the sand or the sea, and those that remain are to be found in the most northerly section of the park, only accessible on a fly-in safari (or in the equally inaccessible Sperrgebiet), and not the southern section open to self-drive visitors.

As a result, it's easy to be underwhelmed by the Skeleton Coast, especially when driving across never-ending, and seemingly empty, gravel plains in thick coastal fog, flanked by a beach scene that is reminiscent of the North Atlantic in November. There are few actual sights – a couple of small and unimpressive wrecked fishing boats and some abandoned mining equipment. However, if you adjust your expectations, appreciate the stark beauty of the landscape, and take time to stop along the way and seek out some of the smaller pleasures of the desert – the **insect life** and multicoloured carpets of **lichen fields**, which are only apparent when soaking up the morning moisture from the fog (see box, p.211) – then the park will still mesmerize you.

If you persist as far as the last 58km between Torra and Terrace Bay, the dunes reach the road; a 7km **dune drive** affords you a closer exploration. Some 166km after the

---

LICHENS

By the side of the salt road up the Skeleton Coast and en route to the Messum Crater on the Namib's gravel plains lie some of the world's most extensive (foliose) **lichen fields**. One of Namibia's more overlooked treasures – especially since to the uninitiated they resemble shrivelled, dead bits of plant for much of the time – they warrant closer examination. In contrast, on overcast mornings, when there is moisture in the air, they show their true colours, **"blooming"** and producing a kaleidoscope of colour, turning purple, orange, black, green or reddish-brown, only to shrivel up once more as the sun burns more to reduce transpiration. If you happen to miss the show in the morning fog, at any time of day you can stop, sprinkle a little water on a patch, wait a few minutes, and watch the transformation.

Lichens are truly extraordinary: plant-like but not plants, rather **organisms** that are combinations of algae living among the filaments of a fungus in a symbiotic relationship. The alga absorbs light and moisture from the air to photosynthesize and provide food and energy; the fungus also absorbs and stores moisture, draws nutrients from the ground, and usually acts as an anchor. For this reason, lichen are important stabilizers in the Namib, helping prevent erosion, though a relatively common sight is the *Xanthomaculina convoluta*, a free-flowing foliose lichen that blows around and collects in hollows and dry river beds; with a charcoal-grey appearance when sheltering from the sun, it turns green when absorbing moisture.

Of the world's 20,000 known lichen species, the Namib hosts around 120, many endemic to the area. One of the most visually striking is *Teleschistes capensis*, a relatively large bushy specimen, which can grow several centimetres high, and resembles a piece of terrestrial coral the colour of burnished gold when open. Some lichen are thought to be **thousands of years old** – even older than welwitschias (see box, p.218), growing at a glacial pace of only 1mm per year. This also makes them incredibly fragile; a thoughtless bit of off-road driving over seemingly featureless desert can result in the destruction of centuries of growth.

5

Ugab Gate, the fairly bleak collection of exposed cement cabins that comprises **Terrace Bay** marks the end of the road; part of a former mining operation, this isolated outpost is now favoured by fishing fanatics.

ARRIVAL AND DEPARTURE   SKELETON COAST NATIONAL PARK

By car The only way to visit this southern section of the park is in your own vehicle (a saloon car will manage most parts, but 4WD is necessary to reach Terrace Bay), though several overlander tours drive through the bottom corner of the park en route to Damaraland. The main entrance is the Ugab Gate on the C34, at the Ugab River, whereas the eastern entrance/exit, the Springbokwasser Gate, lies on the C39, which eventually leads northeast to Khorixas. The distance between the two gates is around 180km. Visitors to the park are only allowed to drive through the park leaving by the other gate, whereas overnight visitors, who will need to produce their reservation slip on entry, can arrive and leave by the same gate.

On a tour You can only visit the northern section of the national park on a fly-in-safari (see box, p.264).

ACCOMMODATION AND EATING

Terrace Bay Resort ☎ 061 2857200 (Windhoek) or ☎ 064 402172 (Swakopmund), ✇ nwr.com.na. Experience the pounding surf backed by the dune sea in this desolate and frequently windy spot, only really frequented by keen fishermen. The cabins (sleeping six or ten) are basic, though with much-needed hot water and comfy beds. Amazingly, there's a snug bar and excellent restaurant on site, plus a table-tennis table, making the whole visit a surreal experience. Also has a fuel station and small shop. Doubles (DBB) N$2200, cabins N$1880

Torra Bay Campsite ☎ 061 2857200 (Windhoek) or ☎ 064 402172 (Swakopmund), ✇ nwr.com.na. An extremely basic, exposed fishing camp only open seasonally (Dec–Jan). Camping per pitch N$210

The hinterland

The longest yet quickest route to the central coast from Windhoek is via the tarred B2, which peels off the B1 at Okahandja (see p.171), some 66km north of Windhoek, heading west via the small towns of **Karibib** and **Usakos** to complete the remaining 280km to Swakopmund. The journey should take no longer than four hours, though there are diversions that can be made along the way, for example by venturing south into the Otjipatera Mountains south of Karibib, or exploring the bronze boulders and rock art of the Erongo Mountains (see p.190) to the north of Usakos, or even the dramatic Spitzkoppe, slightly further to the west. Try to avoid driving west along this road late Friday afternoon, especially on holiday weekends, as it's prime time for accidents: the traffic is inevitably heavy and travelling fast, yet the dazzling setting sun will be directly in your eyes.

For quieter, more adventurous back roads to both Swakopmund and Walvis Bay, you need to head west and southwest out of Windhoek, along the C28 and C26, respectively – gravel roads that are devoid of shops, petrol stations and, for much of the way, human habitation. Both take you down **scenic passes** as the roads cascade off the central highland plateau, down onto the gravel plains of the central Namib below, across increasingly desolate landscape until you reach the coast.

Karibib

Blink and you can easily miss **KARIBIB** – a small town of around 5000 – as you speed along towards the coast, and although there's little specifically to detain you, it's worth pausing to pick up a cold drink and have a stroll around some of the surviving colonial buildings that bear witness to the small town's former importance that was assured once the first train reached here from Swakopmund in 1900. Much of Karibib's high-grade marble from the local quarry, which started up in the early twentieth century, is exported to Europe. The Karibib Marble and Granite Works still supports around 300 jobs, while a more recently opened gold mine in the vicinity employs a further 400 workers. Other small-scale gemstone mining occurs in the area, the results of which can be seen in the **Henckert Tourist Centre** and craft shop.

ARRIVAL AND INFORMATION
KARIBIB

By bus Intercape Mainliner (☎061 227847, ⓦintercape .co.za) passes through twice a week (Thurs & Sat for Swakopmund, 12.15pm; Fri & Sun for Windhoek, 12.50pm; both from N$180), stopping at the Engen garage.

By shuttle or minibus The daily air-conditioned shuttle services that run between Windhoek and Swakopmund (see p.212) stop to pick up passengers at Henckert's Tourist Centre and charge the same price whichever way you're bound (2hr; N$230). Regular, cheaper minibuses between

the two population centres also pass through.

By train The very slow overnight train between Swakopmund and Windhoek (see p.213) stops off here in the middle of the night, so it's not an especially convenient way to travel.

Tourist information Henckert's Tourist Centre, 38 Hidepo Hamutenya St (Mon–Fri 8am–5pm; ☎064 550700), is both an information centre and a curio shop.

ACCOMMODATION

Angi's Self-catering Guesthouse 315 Fracht St ☎064 550126, ⓔangis@iway.na Perfectly respectable place to bed down for the night; ten functional, mainly twin rooms behind sliding glass doors, with a/c, TV, fridge and kitchenette, plus an on-site bar-restaurant serving pub grub if you don't fancy cooking. B&B N$800

Etusis Lodge Signposted west off the C32, 16km south of Karibib (another 16km to the lodge). Lovely location on a private reserve in the Otjipatera Mountains, surrounded by

fascinating rock formations, best explored on their hiking trails, watching out for kudu, zebra, impala, klipspringer and the like. Alternatively, visit on horseback (N$440 for three hours). Accommodation in large stone-and-thatch bungalows or comfortable, rather than luxury, Meru-style tents, or camping (six sites, each with shade netting) some 20km from the lodge. Hearty home cooking, with local ingredients and dining family-style. Camping per person N$120, safari tent (DBB) N$1860, bungalow (DBB) N$2751

Usakos

Though **USAKOS** has a pleasant aspect, spread across the hillside overlooking the River Khan, with the burnished granite domes of the Erongo Mountains in the background, there's little happening here to disrupt the town's torpor these days. During its heyday as the centre for Namibia's rail network, men were kept busy servicing the engines that came down on the Otavi line from the Tsumeb mine. When the mining tailed off in the 1960s, and with it the railway, Usakos' importance faded too. An old steam locomotive sits forlornly outside the station, as a poignant reminder of better days. Apart from dropping in at the popular farm shop (see p.232), the main reason to stop in Usakos is to stock up with provisions if you're heading off to camp in the Erongo Mountains or the Spitzkoppe. The small supermarket on the main street is your only option. Should you miss the sharp right-angled turn in the high street, if you're heading towards the coast, carry on a block and you'll come across some surprising topiary and a couple of dignified colonial-era buildings.

ARRIVAL AND DEPARTURE
USAKOS

By bus Intercape Mainliner (☎061 227847, ⓦintercape .co.za) passes through twice a week, stopping at the Engen garage in the centre of town, on the main road (Thurs & Sat to Swakopmund at 12.45pm; 1hr 30min, from N$144; Fri & Sun to Windhoek, 2hr 40min, from N$189).

By shuttle and minibus The daily air-conditioned shuttle services that run between Swakopmund and Windhoek drop

off and pick up passengers at the farm shop by the Shell petrol station, 1km west of the town centre (see p.213). Regular, cheaper minibuses also pass through and stop in town.

By train The very slow overnight trains between Swakopmund and Windhoek (see p.213) wait for each other here in the middle of the night to exchange drivers and conductors, before continuing on their way.

ACCOMMODATION AND EATING

Bahnhof Hotel Theo-Ben Gurirab St ☎064 530444. Bang on the main road, with fourteen rooms equipped with the usual basic hotel facilities, plus a bar-restaurant,

beer garden and secure off-street parking. At the time of writing, the hotel was closed for renovations and it was not clear when it would reopen.

5

Namib Oasis Farm Stall & Deli ☎064 530283. A popular place to break the journey on the B2, either to grab a bag of freshly sliced biltong and a take-out coffee, or to order something more substantial from their café: burgers, salads, sandwiches and the like. Camping is also possible N$60/person, though there are much nicer sites in the nearby Erongos (see p.191). Daily 7am–7pm.

Travelling the C28

The 300km-long **C28** takes the back route from Windhoek to Swakopmund, via some delightful scenery, initially across the highland savannah plateau of the Khomas Hochland. Around 45km out of Windhoek, a few kilometres after the turn-off for the D1418, look up through the scrub to your right, to spot the ruins of Curt von Francois' fort, a small squat stone construction on a hilltop, established after the colonial administration had settled in Windhoek, in order to protect the trade route to the coast. It later became a rehab clinic for alcoholic soldiers.

Otjimbingwe

Some 125km west of Windhoek, the D1953 turns north off the C28, arriving, after 46km, in the historical Herero settlement of **OTJIMBINGWE** – worth the detour if you have time. The site of **natural springs**, acknowledged in the Herero name Otjzingue (meaning "refreshing place"), it was the seat of the Herero Royal House of Zerua. It also contains Namibia's **oldest church**, consecrated by the Rhenish

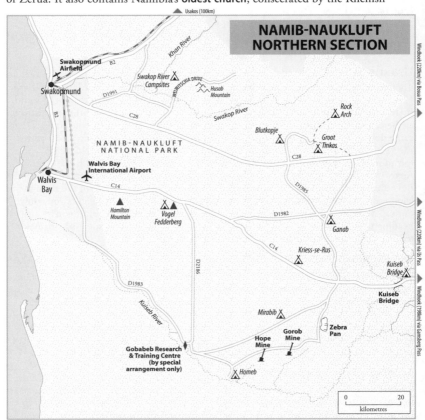

NAMIB-NAUKLUFT NORTHERN SECTION

!NARA MELONS

Across the Namib's dunes and dry riverbeds sprawl the tangled spines of the desert's most valuable food source – the **!nara melon** (*Acanthosicyos horridus*). Several of these spiky green fruits the size of a grapefruit can be found on a single plant, which can live for over a hundred years. Fossil evidence points to its vital role in both human and animal survival for over 40 million years. As well as being a major **source of water and protein**, the !nara's vicious thorn-like leaves – so modified to reduce water loss – afford protection to countless insects, spiders, rodents and reptiles, as well as to its fruit, while the plant's deep and extensive root system is a vital stabilizer of fragile sand dunes. The !nara exists in a symbiotic relationship with the black-backed jackal, which feeds on the pollinated nutrient-rich seeds of the fleshy fruit and then disperses them through its faeces.

The name !nara derives from !na, meaning "more than enough food" in Nama, the language of the **‡Aonin** – more commonly referred to as the Topnaars (see p.354) – who primarily inhabit the Lower Kuiseb River, and whose livelihoods and culture are inextricably entwined with this extraordinarily versatile fruit. Lauded in the ‡Aonin's traditional tales and praise poetry, !nara melons are **harvested** annually from Aug–Sept and Dec–March. Nothing is wasted. The fruit's orangey, proteinous pulp is boiled and eaten as a porridge or then dried and made into !nama cakes (‡hoagaribeb) to store for future consumption, while the seeds, rich in fat and oil, are dried to provide a tasty snack, traded, or used to make natural cosmetics or cooking oil. Even the rind is dried and used as fuel or donkey feed, while its roots are said to have medicinal properties. Traditionally, ‡Aonin families had exclusive harvesting rights to specific !nara plants, though in recent times regulations have been relaxed, which has led to disputes. Like the ‡Aonin, the !nara melon faces major **survival challenges**, in particular decreasing groundwater levels due to increased water usage from dams along the Kuiseb River.

missionaries in 1867 after Chief Zerua had donated 10,000 bricks for it to be built. The church is still quite an impressive structure, with a lofty bell tower – added later – that you can look up into, and a fine wood-panelled ceiling and pews. Otjimbingwe was also the seat of the colonial administration before it was moved to Windhoek.

The Bosua Pass

Around 150km after leaving Windhoek on the C28, you cross into the Erongo Region before the road falls off the escarpment in dramatic fashion at the **Bosua Pass**. The 1:5 gradient and the winding descent are not to be undertaken lightly – check your brakes first – and preferably not driven after heavy rains, as the gravel becomes treacherous, though some of the worst section is paved. Don't forget to pause periodically, however, to take in the breathtaking **views**.

Once the land flattens out, the road streaks away across the more desolate and sparsely vegetated pre-Namib plains towards the Atlantic. As it does, you enter the northern section of the Namib-Naukluft National Park; provided you drive straight through, no park fees are necessary. However, there are a couple of 4WD trails off to various rudimentary **wilderness campsites**; if you want to stop over, you need to organize permits and camping fees in advance in an MET office (see box, p.235).

Travelling the C26

To travel the back way from Windhoek to Walvis Bay, you take the **C26** southeast out of the capital, which eventually swings west, through the **Hakos Mountains** towards the spectacular **Gamsberg Pass** (the "g" is pronounced "ch" as in "loch"). Here, the rugged folds of seemingly endless mountains ripple into the distance; while the daytime views are awe-inspiring, they are equally impressive at night, since the Gamsberg area is one of the world's top sites for stargazing.

5

THE NORTHERN NAMIB-NAUKLUFT WILDERNESS CAMPGROUNDS

While most people confine their camping in the Namib-Naukluft National Park to the popular, **well provisioned sites** at Sesriem (see p.113) and in the Naukluft Mountains (see p.118), lesser-known opportunities for **wilderness camping** exist in the very northern section of the park, in the hinterland behind Swakopmund and Walvis Bay. The settings may not be as dramatic in these isolated spots, but by stopping over at several of these locations, you can get a feel for the desert's variety: shallow and deep watercourses, granite inselbergs, with fantastical stone sculptures due to erosion, flat gravel plains, burnished dunes. What's more, you may not have to share the wilderness with anyone else, except possibly a visiting hyena or jackal and a handful of lizards. Then at night, the sky can appear like a diamond-encrusted black velvet cape.

The most popular route is the one that curves north off the C28, taking in the **Tinkas** and **Bloedkoppie** sites, with **Rock Arch** out on a limb. The other camps are accessed via the C14. The ten campgrounds listed below have only the most rudimentary facilities – some in a poor state of repair, generally only long-drop toilets and the occasional concrete braai site, picnic table or rubbish bin (though you should take all rubbish out with you). You will also need to be totally self-sufficient in terms of fuel, firewood and drinking water. In summer it can be unbearably hot, in winter, very cold at night; the best time is just after the rains, when there should still be enough residual moisture and vegetation to take the harsh edge off the landscape, and the daytime temperatures, though still hot, are more bearable.

AROUND THE C28

Bloedkoppie (Blood Hill) North of the C28. No battle site, the "blood" refers to the rich red colour of this granite outcrop at sunset, less appreciable if you happen to be sitting on top enjoying a sundowner. Saloon car drivers will need to camp on the solid, harder ground on the southern and eastern sides; the shadier sites in the dry riverbed on the northwestern side of the inselberg are only accessible to 4WD.

Ganab Just south of the D9812. Named after ǁGanab, the Nama name for the camelthorn trees that sparsely populate this shallow watercourse and provide some shade in an otherwise exposed area. Look out for the stately Rüppell's korhaan, and possibly a Cape fox at night.

Great Tinkas Between Bloedkoppie and Rock Arch. Several campsites set amid the kopjies and some good hiking trails. There's also an unlikely dam nearby, which, when full following a rare rainfall, attracts a variety of birds and mammals. 4WD only.

Rock arch 30km east of Bloedkoppie. The shade at this campground is provided by its main feature, the eponymous rock arch, like a miniature version of the one at the Spitzkoppe. There is also a short nature walk. Only accessible by 4WD, the track leading here is very rocky.

Once you reach the pass – the tortuous 30km descent requires concentration – but before you plunge off the escarpment and cross the Kuiseb River for the first time, look over to the south, at the Gamsberg itself. Namibia's third-highest peak, at 2347m, is an extraordinary **table mountain**, whose smooth, flat top appears to have been sliced off with a sharp knife. At the bottom of the pass, there are a few nice guestfarms – perfect places to break the journey and make the most of the mountain scenery.

Shortly after the C26 joins the C14 – which leads southwards to Solitaire – you enter the Namib-Naukluft National Park, and find yourself descending into the **Kuiseb Canyon**, a deep incision in the otherwise flat, bleak desert crust, though on a rare stretch of tarred road.

Kuiseb River

The ephemeral **Kuiseb River** rises in the Khomas Hochland, where it begins a 500km journey towards the Atlantic. Like the Tsauchab River at Sossusvlei (see p.112), the Kuiseb fails to reach the ocean – except in the rare years of exceptional rains, when it manages to push through the dunes blocking the way. Rather, it filters away into the sand just south of Walvis Bay. Even after heavy rains, it rarely flows for more than a few weeks, though precious life-giving pools of water remain in more sheltered parts for much longer. The Kuiseb ploughs a deep furrow off the escarpment and then carves its way across the desert. Satellite imagery shows how crucial the river is to halting the northerly progress of the marching Namib sand sea. Nearer the Kuiseb's "delta", ‡Aonin

Swakop River Between the B2 and C28. This most northerly campground is also a popular picnic site on the well-visited Welwitschia Drive trail (see p.219), so may not be as isolated or as clean as you might hope, though the relatively lush riverine vegetation provides good shade.

AROUND THE C14

Homeb 60km south of the C28, at the end of the D2186. Striking camping area for its location by the Kuiseb River, at a point where it separates the dunes to the south from the grey granite folds (reminiscent of the "moonscape" near Swakopmund; see p.219) and gravel plains to the north. The riverine vegetation, which includes ana, wild tamarisk, figs and false ebony, provide excellent shade. It's a good place for spotting raptors, and, if you walk over into the dunes, you may be lucky to spot the elusive dune lark. There is a small ‡Aonin (Topnaar) settlement with assorted livestock nearby.

Kriess-se-Rus 8km west of the turn-off for the D1198. This campground in a dry watercourse just north of the C14 is neither especially attractive nor particularly popular, though the exposed schist rocks provide some shelter.

Kuiseb Bridge Where the C14 crosses the Kuiseb Canyon. What should be one of the most attractive campground, deep in the shady, sandy Kuiseb Canyon, can suffer from the rumble of traffic, especially in high season, as it lies on the Sossusvlei–Swakopmund desert "highway".

Mirabib On the way to the desert research station at Gobabeb, west of the D2186. This isolated inselberg rises out of the desert plains, its weathered granite overhangs providing the only decent shade, which you may share with the bats, with a couple of other sites tucked in among the boulders and rock sculptures.

Vogelfederberg Just south of the C14. A smallish granite inselberg (translating as Bird-feather Mountain) with stunning views from the top. Being around 40km from the ocean, it is susceptible to the Namib's early morning fog.

PRACTICALITIES

Permits need to be purchased in advance from an NWR or MET office (in Sesriem, see p.112; Swakopmund, see p.213; Walvis Bay, see p.223; or Windhoek, see p.94). Permits cost N$40/person per day plus N$10/day for the vehicle, and camping fees are N$120/pitch. These areas are periodically patrolled by park wardens and you will be fined if found driving along one of these minor gravel roads or camping without the relevant permits. When you get your permit you'll be given a rudimentary map of the area; though the roads are generally we l marked and straight-forward, a Tracks4Africa map and GPS are always good backups. Most of the tracks are driveable in a high-clearance saloon car, except where stated, though obviously you should not drive into any riverbeds if you only have a 2WD car. Even with a 4WD, you should always resist the temptation to drive off the marked tracks, and help preserve the fragile desert ecology (see box, p.66).

people, more widely known as Topnaars, a Nama group, inhabit the sandy riverbed, where they are heavily dependent on the !nara melon (see box, p.233) for survival.

The **Kuiseb Canyon**, formed some 20 million years ago, and 200m deep in places, was made famous in the book *The Sheltering Desert*, an account by German geologist Martin Henno of how he and a companion, Hermann Korn, survived there for two years during World War II, to avoid internment (see p.367). The Carp Cliff Viewpoint, signposted off the C14, 1km east of the descent into the ravine, allows you to peer over the edge at one of shelters the Germans used, as well as affording great **all-round views** of the valley and the surrounding otherworldly landscape.

ACCOMMODATION

GAMSBERG

Corona Guest Farm Signposted east off the C26, 16km from the junction with the C14 (another 16km from there – 4WD necessary) ☎ 061 681045 (farm) or ☎ 061 224712 (Windhoek reservations). Heavily themed guest rooms are chock-full of eclectic furnishings and ornaments – many antiques and animal skins from the days when the place was a hunting farm. The place enjoys a lovely garden setting, with superb pool area and dining terrace (food is delicious and beautifully presented), and hiking trails are available. Reduction for more than one night. DBB N$2400

Hakos Guest Farm Signposted 7km north off the C26, just before the Gamsberg Pass ☎ 062 572111, ✆ hakos -astrofarm.com. The country's number one astro-venue enjoys a spectacular setting, imperiously perched on a mountain at the top of the Gamsberg Pass, though the place is rather austere and the 14 single/double rooms feel institutional. But the stargazing is what it's about (at extra cost: N$100–500, depending on equipment) and the area is great for hiking. Camping per person N$120, doubles (DBB) N$1870

Etosha and the far north

BURCHELL'S ZEBRA IN ETOSHA NATIONAL PARK

Etosha and the far north

The far north of Namibia holds some of the country's most-visited and least-explored landscapes. In the former category is the vast expanse of Etosha National Park, which receives over two hundred thousand visitors annually, drawn by almost guaranteed sightings of large numbers of big mammals, as well as abundant birdlife. In contrast, the evocative mountainous wilderness of northern Kunene – lacking in decent roads and largely devoid of people – remains inaccessible to most, though it provides an unforgettable experience for those who make it that far.

6

Centring on a vast salt pan, Etosha National Park is the main reason visitors venture to the north of Namibia, enticed by the prospect of coming face to face with a lion, glimpsing a leopard at dawn, or gazing at herds of zebra and wildebeest sweeping across the savannah. As there is only limited accommodation inside Etosha, many stay in the more comfortable lodges and campgrounds sprinkled just outside the park boundary, often set in **private reserves** that also offer outstanding wildlife-viewing opportunities. North from Etosha, the predominantly flat, sandy scenery extends to the urban and rural developments in the so-called "Four O's" – the small, but densely populated, regions of Oshikoto, Omusati, Ohangwena and Oshana, home predominantly to the **Owambo** peoples. **Oshakati** is the main commercial hub of the chaotic conurbation, a useful pit stop to stock up on supplies, and to witness life outside the tourist bubble. There are a handful of modest cultural attractions in the area, worth taking in if you're passing through: the traditional royal homestead at **Tsandi**, a giant baobab in **Outapi**, or **Lake Oponona**, a large dusty depression for much of the year, which transforms into an avian wetland paradise after good rains.

Heading west into the sparsely populated **northern Kunene** region, the landscape alters dramatically as you enter the **Kaokoveld**, as does the population density – only 1.7 people per square kilometre. From the dramatic **waterfalls** at **Ruacana** and **Epupa** on the Kunene River, striking, reddish-brown stony earth gives way to rugged, mountainous areas, interspersed with desolate valleys at Marienfluss and Hartmann's. Yet further west, the Wilderness Area of the **Skeleton Coast National Park** – only accessible by fly-in safari – eventually melts into rippling dune fields before hitting the Atlantic coast. This remote, starkly beautiful region is home to desert-adapted elephant, black rhino and even lion – and to the semi-nomadic **Himba**, one of Namibia's most recognizable and resilient indigenous peoples. The small, underdeveloped and isolated regional capital of **Opuwo** is the place for independent travellers to start their explorations, though it's not until you spend time in one of their remote settlements that you'll begin to learn more about the people and their environment.

YOUNG HIMBA WOMEN NEAR EPUPA FALLS

Highlights

❶ Etosha National Park The undisputed crown jewel of Namibia's parks in terms of wildlife. Etosha is full of megafauna and has a vast, unworldly, saline pan at its core. **See p.241**

❷ Visiting an open market Feel the buzz in Oshakati, Ondangwa or Ongwediwa, where stalls overflow with pulses, grains, fruits and vegetables you'll struggle to identify, alongside clothing, crafts and household utensils. **See p.252**

❸ Visiting a Himba community With a good guide, and the right sensibility, interacting with Namibia's distinctive semi-nomadic pastoralists is an unforgettable experience. **See p.259**

❹ Epupa Falls Stunning sunsets, basking crocs and glorious cascades of water have helped put this remote outpost firmly on the tourist trail. **See p.260**

❺ Marienfluss If you don't have the necessary vehicle convoy and 4WD experience to drive to this hauntingly beautiful desolate valley, consider a tour with a specialist operator. **See p.261**

❻ Puros Only accessible by 4WD, this gloriously secluded Himba-run campground lies on the banks of the Hoarusib River, whose permanent springs attract desert-adapted elephant, rhino, giraffe – and even lion. **See p.263**

HIGHLIGHTS ARE MARKED ON THE MAP ON P.240

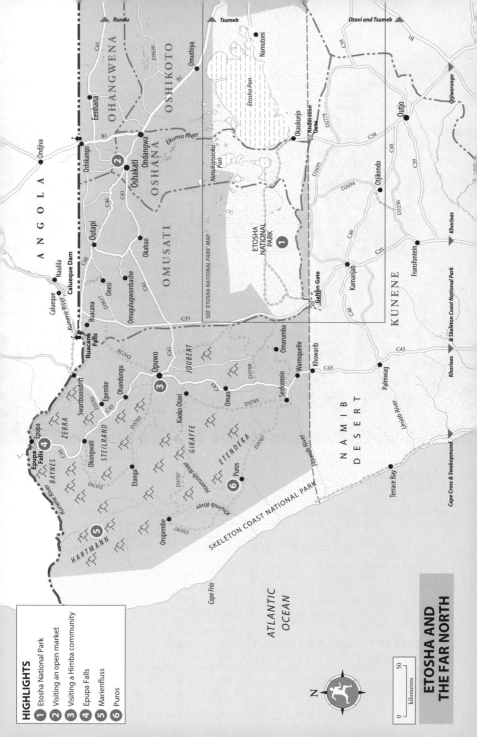

HIGHLIGHTS

1. Etosha National Park
2. Visiting an open market
3. Visiting a Himba community
4. Epupa Falls
5. Marienfluss
6. Puros

ETOSHA AND THE FAR NORTH

N

0   50

kilometres

ANGOLA

OHANGWENA

OSHIKOTO

OSHANA

OMUSATI

KUNENE

NAMIB DESERT

ATLANTIC OCEAN

SKELETON COAST NATIONAL PARK

BAYNES

ZEBRA

STEILRAND

HARTMANN

JOUBERT

GIRAFFE

ETENDEKA

Ondjiva

Rundu

Tsumeb

Otavi and Tsumeb

Ondangwa

Oshikango

Oshakati

Eenhana

Omuthiya

Namutoni

Etosha Pan

Etosha Pan

ETOSHA NATIONAL PARK

SEE ETOSHA NATIONAL PARK MAP

Okaukuejo

Andersson Gate

Galton Gate

Natukanaoka Pan

Ekuma River

Kamanjab

Otjikondo

Outjo

Otjiwarongo

Fransfontein

Khorixas

Khorixas & Skeleton Coast National Park

Outapi

Okahao

Onesi

Omugulugwombashe

Ruacana

Ruacana Falls

Calueque

Naulila

Calueque Dam

Kunene River

Opuwo

Swartbooisdrift

Epembe

Ohandungu

Okongwati

Etanga

Onupembe

Epupa

Epupa Falls

Kunene River

Kaoko Otavi

Omao

Sesfontein

Warmquelle

Khowarib

Omarumba

Palmwag

Puros

Hoarusib River

Khumib River

Hoanib River

Uniab River

Cape Frio

Terrace Bay

Cape Cross & Swakopmund

B1

C45

D3630

C46

C41

C46

C41

C35

D3637

D3720

D3701

C43

D3703

D3707

D3705

D3708

C43

C43

C43

C38

C39

C40

C39

D3236

D2695

D2694

C40

C40

C35

D2773

Etosha National Park

Sunrise to sunset • N$80/person per day (children under 16 free), N$10/vehicle

Located in the far northwest of the country, and covering an expanse of around 22,000 square kilometres, **ETOSHA NATIONAL PARK** is Namibia's premier wildlife-viewing destination, stuffed to zoo-like proportions with a host of large mammals and some spectacular birdlife. In indigenous languages it is variously known as "great white place", "place of mirages" or "lake of a mother's tears", which all refer to the park's defining feature, **Etosha Pan**, a vast saline pan that covers a fifth of its surface area. Around 110km long and more than 50km wide in places, it is Africa's largest salt pan, and is even visible from space. In the dry season it is a seemingly endless expanse of shimmering white, tinged with olive green, which, in years of exceptional rain, briefly morphs into a shallow lake resembling a giant mirror. This transformation harks back to the pan's origins, millions of years ago, when it was probably a much larger, deeper inland lake fed by northern rivers – including the Kunene. When tectonic shifts altered the lie of the land, forcing the rivers to change course, the lake dried up.

Brief history

The establishment of Etosha as a **"game reserve"** by the governor of German South-West Africa in 1907 was as much, if not more, about safeguarding an economic resource for the colony as it was about wildlife conservation. Earlier incursions by European missionaries and traders from the 1950s had opened up trade routes, resulting in a major depletion of wildlife, although after years of conflict, the Owambo chief Nehale Mpingana and his followers had succeeded in driving most settlers away. German troops arrived in 1896, initially to control the *rinderpest* (see p.345). Three years later they built a fort at Namutoni, which was attacked and destroyed by the Owambo but rebuilt the following year – and still stands today. A second outpost was added at Okaukuejo in 1901.

Initially, an area of almost 100,000 square kilometres was envisaged for the park, stretching down to the coast. Over the years the controversial boundaries have been altered and the area reduced to its present size, though inevitably large numbers of people – specifically Hai‖om San, Herero and Owambo – have been dispossessed of their land in the process.

During **German colonial times** the nomadic Hai‖om San population was allowed to stay in the reserve, provided they continued to hunt with bow and arrow, but in 1954, under the South African regime, most were forcibly removed to work on nearby farms; a small percentage have remained as park employees, but they, and other communities, continue to press government for land and greater benefit from the park's income.

WHEN TO VISIT ETOSHA NATIONAL PARK

The best time to visit is during the drier **winter months** (May–Oct), when more animals are concentrated round the waterholes, predominantly scattered around the southern edges of Etosha Pan. Viewing is easier then because the vegetation is sparser, and the lower temperatures make a stakeout at a waterhole a more pleasurable experience. On the other hand, when the wind gets up, the landscape can become enveloped in clouds of dust. Visitor numbers are inevitably higher in winter, especially in the European and Namibian school holidays, though the park is so large and the waterholes so numerous – 86 in all – that it never gets unbearably busy. In the wetter **summer months**, however, the lusher vegetation is much easier on the eye, and the water-filled pans attract an abundance of migratory birdlife, especially between November and April. In the rare years when the rains are really heavy (usually Jan or Feb) and the water lingers, Etosha Pan becomes a vast pink-and-white carpet of pelicans and flamingos, which flock here in their hundreds of thousands to breed.

6

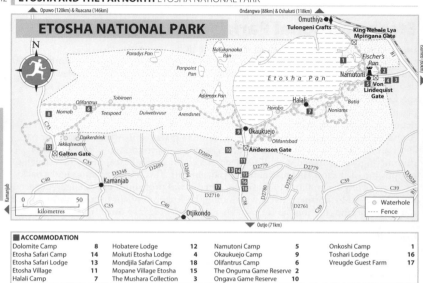

Flora and fauna

Etosha is a wonderful haven for **wildlife**, boasting the continent's largest concentration of black rhino and other large mammals in abundance: elephant, giraffe, lion, leopard, cheetah, wildebeest, kudu, oryx, eland and hartebeest, to name but a few. Round every second corner, you bump into herds of Burchell's zebra, impala and springbok – the park's most numerous antelope. The rarer black-faced impala and Hartmann's mountain zebra are only to be found in the western reaches of the reserve. **Birdlife** too is prolific: 340 species have been recorded in the park. Large bateleurs and martial eagles wheel above, while ostriches, kori bustards and secretary birds stride across the plains; rollers, bee-eaters, sunbirds and orioles provide brilliant flashes of colour; and others fascinate with their extraordinary appearance. Two such birds are the marabou stork, a huge, seemingly bald character with a particularly pendulous gular pouch, and the southern ground hornbill, a turkey-sized creature with distinctive crimson throat and eye patches, whose unearthly booming call can carry for 3km.

Mopane woodland savannah and grassland predominate in the areas surrounding Etosha Pan, with the occasional clump of elegant makalani palms conferring round some of the water sources. Some 30km west of Okaukuejo, however, the ghostly, contorted forms of moringa trees, dubbed the "fairy-tale forest" – overambitiously, given their depleted numbers – form a striking contrast. In the western section of the park, which until recently was closed to the general public, the landscape is markedly different: hillier terrain is covered with a rich reddish brown earth, peppered with rocky dolomite outcrops and covered with smaller mopane shrub.

ARRIVAL AND INFORMATION   ETOSHA NATIONAL PARK

By car There are four points of entry into Etosha, all accessible in an ordinary saloon car via good roads: the Von Lindequist Gate, on the eastern edge, lies 19km west of the B1 between Tsumeb and Ondangwa; the little-used King Nehale Lya Mpingana Gate is on the northern park boundary, only 17km from the B1; the Andersson Gate is on the south side of the park, on the C38, 114km north of Outjo; and the Galton Gate, which only opened to the public in 2014, is tucked away in the southwest corner, on the C35, 59km north of Kamanjab.

Park information The website ⓦ etoshanationalpark .org is a good source of information, and also has detailed maps of the park that can be downloaded. Otherwise, enquire at reception in the restcamps; guides and park staff can advise you on the best places to head for to see particular animals, which change seasonally and from day to day. There is sometimes a visitors' book, in which recent sightings are recorded. NWR also produces a decent booklet, which contains maps and identification charts for some of the more common or sought-after species, and is usually available at the camp shops.

GETTING AROUND

By car The extensive road network consists of good-quality gravel roads, and all camps, except *Onkoshi* (where they can arrange a pick-up from *Namutoni*) are accessible in a saloon car. While the speed limit within the park is 60kph, you really need to be travelling more slowly in most places if you actually want to spot any wildlife and not risk flattening some of it on the road; it's commonplace to go round a bend and find tussling wildebeest or loping giraffes blocking your path You therefore need to plan your route carefully and leave plenty of time, as distances are considerable and the camps are strict about gate closures. Fuel is available at the three main camps and payment by credit card is accepted, provided the machines are working.

ACCOMMODATION

INSIDE THE PARK

All accommodation inside the park is provided by NWR, bookable at their offices in Windhoek (☎ 061 2857200) and Swakopmund (☎ 064 402172), or online (🖥 nwr .com.na), though walk-ins can pay on the spot if there's availability. This is only really an option in the low season (Nov–Feb, excluding the Christmas holiday period). If you are staying in the older "big three" camps (*Okaukuejo*, *Halali* and *Namutoni*) and are self-catering, make sure you stock up on supplies before you arrive since offerings at the camp shops are fairly paltry. Otherwise, dining is à la carte in the smaller camps – high quality but with a limited menu – and a mixture of average buffet and à la carte fare is available at the larger camps. Note that the camps accept credit card payments, provided the machines are working.

★ **Dolomite Camp** Atop a lofty dolomite outcrop, cosy safari tents and private viewing decks are spaced out along the ridge, numbers 1 to 12 facing west for the spectacular sunset views, and 13 to 20 enjoying sunrise. Premium chalet 13 also overlooks a waterhole, and several possess a private plunge pool. The view from the infinity pool is stunning and food is excellent, though the tented dining, lounge and bar areas fail to make the most of the fabulous hilltop location. B&B N$4180
Halali Camp Smaller and more intimate than the other two camps of the "big three". Distinctive for its kopjie with an antenna (yet no mobile phone coverage) and a great sunset-viewing area above the waterhole, where black rhino are regular visitors. Another draw is the pool – long enough to do a few lengths, and adjacent to the restaurant and bar. The a/c rooms are a little cramped, furnished with armchair and fridge. More enticing, pricier bush chalets have a kitchenette, and self-catering family rooms enjoy a

ETOSHA GAME DRIVES

Etosha is predominantly about wildlife viewing, or **game drives**. If not in a tour group, you will inevitably spend some time cruising around the park on your own, taking in waterholes and lookout points. Even if you're driving yourself, however, it is worth considering booking one guided excursion. For a start, the **guides** are knowledgeable about the animals, though it's pot luck what you will see, beyond the ubiquitous springbok and zebra. They also have a better idea of what might be spotted in which areas, and NWR guides can go out into the park before sunrise, ensuring an early stakeout at a waterhole – peak viewing time – and a greater likelihood of catching a lion on the prowl. What's more, the raised seating of the **safari vehicles** provides better vantage points from which to spot and watch wildlife. **Night game drives** are a different, almost ghostly, experience, where the animals' eyes give them away in the vehicle's search lamps.

All game drives organized by NWR within the national park last three hours, leaving at 5.30am, 3pm and 8pm. Daytime drives cost N$550 at the main camps, and N$605 at *Dolomite* and *Onkoshi*; night drives cost N$660 and are only available at *Okaukuejo*, *Halali* and *Namutoni*. You will need to **book a drive in advance**, especially at *Okaukuejo* and *Namutoni* in high season, as spaces are limited.

The private reserves **outside the national park** also offer excursions into Etosha, and sometimes in their own reserves as well. Their rates vary; a half-day tour can cost N$600–700, including park entry fees and cold drinks or just water. Whole-day trips are also organized by some lodges, which may or may not include a picnic lunch (N$1200–1300).

6

private braai hearth to keep you warm in the winter. The campground, with its own bar, offers more shade than *Okaukuejo*; most pitches have stone tables and seating as well as electricity and braai stands. Camping per person N$150, plus per pitch N$250, doubles (B&B) N$2040

Namutoni Camp This camp's 24 large rooms are stylishly furnished, with bathrooms containing a sunken bath and shower, as well as a "bush shower" outside; the twenty bush chalets are larger and plusher, though all rooms show signs of wear. The pick of the NWR campgrounds offers a fair degree of shade. The old fort that constitutes the hub of the resort currently looks as though it's relived the Battle of Namutoni: beyond the gleaming white exterior there are signs of disrepair, though renovations are rumoured. The pool area is not as inviting as at the other two camps, though the recently made-over bar-restaurant area is more appealing. Game drives are good here, as they have access to several restricted waterholes; there's also a shaded viewing area for the waterhole at the camp. Camping per person N$150, plus per pitch N$250, doubles (B&B) N$2160

Okaukuejo Camp The park's administrative hub, and the largest camp, also has a shop and post office; during the day it is always heaving with vehicles coming and going. It's worth splashing out on the premium two-storey waterhole accommodation (chalets W31–35), which have upstairs verandas overlooking the action. The distinctive central tower is another great vantage point (free for all to climb) from which to view the animal goings-on across the pan. Another plus is the pleasant shady pool area, with three pools and a bar. The kiosk offers burgers and toasted sandwiches during the day (9am–5pm); breakfast and dinner are at the main restaurant. The campground could do with an overhaul. Camping per person N$150, plus per pitch N$250, doubles (B&B) N$2620

★**Olifantrus Camp** Opened at the end of 2014, this is a fenced campground on the site of an old abattoir (whose shell remains), used in a controversial elephant-culling operation in the drought of the late 1980s. Ten basic pitches offer very little shade, sandy spots to pitch your tent,

electricity, and cement slabs on which to build a fire. Cooking can also be done in a shared kitchen area. The big draw – shared with day visitors (N$30/person) – is the fabulous two-tier hide overlooking a waterhole, plus the sounds of the bush at night. An on-site kiosk sells drinks and snacks. Camping per person N$280

★**Onkoshi Camp** Fifteen stilted chalets made from canvas, wood and thatch peer over the eastern edge of Etosha Pan, with views extending to the horizon, and fabulous sunsets: gaze out from the comfort of your pillow-piled bed through folding glass doors, or from your private deck. The stylish, rustic design is similar to that of *Sossus Dune Lodge* (see p.113), with indoor and outdoor showers, lovely wooden floors and a raised walkway leading to the chalets. The wildlife viewing from the camp may not be as prolific as elsewhere, but the views more than compensate. Access is by 4WD, or by transfer from Namutoni. B&B N$4620

WEST OF ETOSHA

Hobatere Lodge West of the C35, 5km north of the Galton Gate, 16km down a signposted track ☎ 061 228104, ⓦ hobatere-lodge.com. Set in an 88km private concession, this community-owned lodge has just reopened after closure due to a fire. The friendly and enthusiastic staff make this place a real treat, plus the opportunity to get close to wildlife; there are two waterholes, one with a hide, plus walking safaris as well as game drives on offer. Megafauna such as lion, cheetah, elephant and giraffe are present, but the night safaris offer a chance to spot smaller mammals: bat-eared foxes, aardvarks and genets. The thatched main lodge is new, with plenty of comfortable seating indoors and out, while accommodation is in a row of stone-and-thatch double rooms or half a dozen individual rondavels, some with private veranda. DBB N$2750

SOUTH OF ETOSHA

Etosha Safari Camp C38, 10km south of Andersson Gate ☎ 061 427200, ⓦ gondwana-collection.com.

WHERE TO STAY

The main decision to make when visiting Etosha is whether to stay **inside or outside** the park – assuming you book early enough to have a choice. Ideally, you should try to spend two or more nights inside the park, then a couple of nights outside. There are various advantages to staying **inside the park**: you can be at a waterhole just after sunrise and stay until just before sundown. The main three camps (*Okaukuejo*, *Halali* and *Namutoni*) all overlook waterholes, which attract a host of animals in the dry season, and which are illuminated at night, when they also attract wildlife. These camps also offer night safaris. On the other hand, some of the lodges and campgrounds **outside the park** offer greater levels of comfort, are more intimate, and provide better catering and service than the three main camps. Those within well-stocked private reserves can also offer comparable wildlife-viewing experiences in terms of variety (if not in numbers), though most lodges also run excursions into the national park.

Down the hill from the *Etosha Safari Lodge*, this heavily themed main camp area celebrates the freedom of New South Africa and Namibian independence with quirky decor touches, such as tyre and wheelbarrow seating in the enclosed garden, where the "shebeen" is situated (live music in the evenings). The campground is a refreshing carpet grass, though shade's at a premium. Forty basic but functional brick chalets with a/c are scattered among the thorn trees, and if you don't want to fork out for the buffet dining (N$300), you can braai at the campground. Offers the same excursions as *Etosha Safari Lodge*. Camping per person N$175, chalets (B&B) N$1934

Etosha Safari Lodge C38, 10km south of Andersson Gate ☎061 427200, ⓦgondwana-collection.com. Occupying a prime site on top of a ridge and offering commanding views across to the national park, this large lodge has 65 chalets strung out either side of the elevated main building, but you're never far from one of the three refreshing swimming pools. The a/c chalets are simply but tastefully furnished with French windows that open onto your private patio. However, the vista's even better from the main lodge's extensive terrace, where you can tuck into some of the best buffet food you're ever likely to taste. Half-day (N$800) or full-day (N$1200) safaris into the national park are available. The latter includes a picnic. B&B N$2850

Etosha Village C38, 2km from Andersson Gate ☎067 333413, ⓦetosha-village.com. Well spaced among the thorn trees are distinctive, superior safari tents (with a/c), making intriguing use of stone, metal and branches in their rustic design. Each has an open kitchenette, complete with hob, fridge, kettle, braai and picnic table under shade. Seven shadeless concrete-platform camping pitches have recently been added, with communal braai and dining area, more suited to groups. Breakfasts (N$100) and superior dinners (N$275) are available, and there's a TV at the bar. Run by the Taleni group so the service is friendly and efficient. As well as the usual drives into Etosha you can stargaze through a telescope (N$195). Camping per person N$150, safari tents (DBB) N$2618

★**Mondjila Safari Camp** 3km down a gravel road, 32km south of the Andersson Gate ☎067 333446, ⓦmondjilasafaricamp.com. Affordable, friendly no-frills camp offering excellent value. Set on a rocky ridge, the place makes the most of its location, with lovely sunset views from the main stone-and-thatch lodge – which serves tasty meals (dinner N$280) – and the grassy pool area below, as well as from the private patios of eleven simply furnished, twin-bedded safari tents set on concrete bases. Only a small fan to cool you, but roll up the flaps and let the breeze do the rest. Also with eight grassy camping pitches; each has a power point, and braai stand, with shared ablutions. Inexpensive Etosha game drives (full day

N$650 – min 4 people) is another plus. Camping per person N$140, safari tents (B&B) N$1360

Mopane Village Etosha C38, 14km south of the Andersson Gate ☎081 149 4985, ⓦmopanevillage.com. This no-frills camp has bags of character. The ten tunnel-shaped safari-tents are spacious and fan ventilated, with a nicely designed stone bathroom at the end. Some have braai facilities for self-catering. Otherwise, meals (dinner N$220) are served dinner at a simple, open-sided restaurant or alfresco in a beer-garden-like environment. The four campsites are a good deal, each with shade netting, private shower and toilet facilities, a braai site, sink and electricity. Camping per person N$150, safari tent N$1920

Toshari Lodge Off the C38, 25km south of the Andersson Gate ☎067 333440, ☎081 382 2655, ⓦetoshagateway-toshari.com. It's the communal areas that really make this place: an atmospherically illuminated cavernous lapa for dining, complete with well-stocked bar, and a two-tier swimming pool, both set among well-tended grass and trees. Fanning off a central allée lined with giant white cement urns are freestanding a/c rooms with a contemporary feel. Campers can enjoy three glorious compact pitches on soft grass, under shady mopane trees, with private open-air ablutions, a power point, and braai wood provided, and can enjoy the lodge facilities. Guided day-trips into Etosha on offer (N$700 for a half-day). Good value. Camping per person N$150, doubles (B&B) N$1790

Vreugde Guest Farm 9km down a gravel road, signposted off the C38, 44km from Andersson's Gate ☎081 210 7693, ⓦvreugdeguestfarm.com. Hospitable working sheep and cattle farm with a handful of cool, painted fan-ventilated brick bungalows – some semi-detached, others freestanding, with sliding glass doors opening out onto a lush, well-tended garden that attracts good birdlife. A sparkling, circular pool is well used in the summer. This pleasant, affordable alternative to some of the overpriced lodges round the park offers excursions on the farm, as well as into Etosha, plus birdwatching tours. DBB N$2120

ONGAVA GAME RESERVE

One of Namibia's largest reserves, Ongava Game Reserve (☎083 3303920, ⓦongava.com) covers over 300 square kilometres abutting Etosha's southern perimeter. It has four lodges and is filled with tourist-enticing wildlife: the big cats, including lions, black and white rhino, plains and mountain zebra, black-faced impala, giraffe, elephant and even wild dogs. Activities include game drives, birdwatching, guided walks and rhino tracking.

Andersson's Camp The most affordable – but still pricey – of the Ongava options accommodates 40 people, and, lying closer to the Etosha gate, conducts game drives in the national park rather than on the private reserve.

6

6

An attractive, studied rustic look reigns in the Meru-style tent design, but the big plus is a sunken hide at the waterhole – great for close-up photos of drinking animals. DBB N$6328

Ongava Lodge 10km from the reserve entrance. This luxury venue has a great location atop a kopjie, with a classic safari lodge feel: large open thatched main building with a pool and plenty of deck space, looking down on a waterhole (floodlit at night), and offering great views across the savannah. Fourteen top-notch stone-and-thatch chalets with a/c and fans, comfortable furniture plus plenty of deck space. DBB N$10,178

★**Ongava Tented Lodge** 20km down the gravel drive. Back-to-nature feel in this intimate, luxurious, unfenced bush camp: eight stylish Meru-style tents on wooden decks – a place to keep the tent flaps open, the fan on, and fall asleep to the sounds of lions roaring. Enjoy top-quality dining while watching the floodlit waterhole almost under your nose. Make the most of the guided walks and tracking activities included. The even more exclusive and expensive *Little Ongava* also offers fully inclusive packages. AI N$17,782

EAST OF ETOSHA

Mokuti Etosha Lodge 2km south of the D3028, just outside the Von Lindequist Gate ☎067 229084 (lodge) or ☎061 2075360 (reservations), ⓦmokutietoshalodge.com. With a conference venue, spa and manicured lawns, this is a large (82 rooms) hotel resort-style lodge. Beneath the thatch, rooms are modern with standard hotel facilities: a/c, DStv and hair dryer, with comfortable sofas and armchairs, as well as furniture on the outside porch. Bontebok (imported from South Africa) graze on the grass and the two swimming pools are a decent size. N$2946

THE MUSHARA COLLECTION

The Mushara Collection (south of the D3028, 8km east of the Von Lindequist Gate ☎061 240020 (reservations), ⓦmushara-lodge.com) is made up of three main properties (plus one villa) – with separate entrances off the main road – in a small reserve, though activities are centred on Etosha, with twice-daily game drives (N$580).

Mushara Bush Camp This is a relaxed, family-friendly place with toys and a playground as well as a kiddies' menu and child-minding service. A traditional thatched communal area overlooks a small lawn for dining, enjoying a drink or relaxing. The sixteen light and airy safari tents (four with pull-out couches for families) are nicely kitted out, with a generous, cool stone bathroom, plus a porch looking into the bush, with deckchairs. Book Tent 5 or above, to escape the main lodge noise. Good value. DBB N$2770

Mushara Lodge This smart lodge offers top-of-the-range accommodation in two opulent villas (private plunge pool and fabulous furnishings), but fairly luxurious lodgings in the so-called "standard" chalets: large en-suite rooms are generously furnished and decorated in chic, modern African style. The tasteful designs extend to the ample bar-restaurant area. *Bomas* are held every few nights, even in summer. DBB N$4400

The Mushara Outpost The most exclusive option: eight elegant canvas tents on raised wooden decks boasting modern amenities (minibar, intimate lighting, safe). You can gaze at the sun-baked bush through sliding glass doors from the comfort of your a/c retreat, which also has a cosy fireplace for winter nights. Fine dining takes place in a sophisticated setting, where cushioned sofas are perfect for enjoying a digestif. There's also a nearby waterhole and viewing hide. DBB N$4200

THE ONGUMA GAME RESERVE

The Onguma Game Reserve (7km north of the D3028, signposted just outside the Von Lindequist Gate ☎061 237055, ⓦonguma.com), covering some 340 square kilometres, contains five lodges and two camping areas on the eastern side of Etosha. The reserve borders Fischer's Pan, with lots of plains animals, including recently acquired black rhino. Day and night drives and guided walks are offered on the reserve, as well as excursions into Etosha.

The Fort A forbidding exterior belies an extravagant themed interior, mimicking a Moorish palace, with cascading water features, hanging lanterns, velvet cushions galore and heavy drapes. But the stunning view from the lodge's raised terrace is pure African bush. Alongside, twelve sumptuous mini-suites continue the theme: cavernous stone rooms contain fabulous fireplaces, while each private deck includes a plunge pool and sun loungers. DBB N$7380

Leadwood and Tamboti campgrounds The older, more traditional *Leadwood Camp* is set among shady trees of the same name and surrounded by dense bush. It comprises only a handful of sites on compacted sand. *Tamboti*, a newer, larger venture, offers a more luxurious experience: 25 well-equipped sites, plus a pool and a snack-bar/restaurant overlooking a waterhole (meals should be pre-booked). Camping per person N$220

Onguma Bush Camp The collection's only fenced camp is more modestly priced than the other options, aimed at families – some accommodation comes with a loft room for kids – and groups. Eighteen thatched rondavels and rooms (with fans and a/c) in earthy colours are spread out among well-tended grounds, with a games room, pool and large waterhole. DBB rates also available. B&B N$2340

Onguma Tented Camp An intimate camp comprising seven luxurious tents – a blend of stone, wood and canvas, with a touch of glitz – centred on a waterhole.

Indoor and outdoor showers, fine dining and plenty of space to lounge and chill, watch wildlife or curl up with a book by the infinity pool. Guided walks and night drives are organized on the reserve, as well as game drives into Etosha. Offers the same activities as *Onguma Bush Camp*. DBB N$6220

★**Onguma Tree Top Camp** Not exactly at canopy height, but these five delightful canvas-and-thatch tents on stilts are connected by a raised wooden walkway, and overlook a waterhole. Keep the flaps rolled up at night and listen to the sounds of the bush, or shower outside under the stars. DBB N$4280

The "Four O's"

6

North of Etosha, around forty percent of the population is squeezed into under ten percent of the country's landmass, across four small regions – **Ohangwena**, **Oshana**, **Omusati** and **Oshikoto** – more readily referred to as the "Four O's", or even Owamboland, the former apartheid-era designation for the homeland for the Owambo peoples. It's the SWAPO heartland, where during the 1970s and 80s resistance against South African rule was at its fiercest, resulting in its conversion into a heavily militarized zone (see p.349). Though development and reconstruction money has poured into the region post-independence, the emotional scars will take longer to heal, not helped by high unemployment and poverty – despite some pockets of wealth in evidence – with many people still having to migrate south in search of permanent or seasonal labour.

The urban agglomeration of Ondangwa, Ongwediwa and Oshakati, strung out thirty odd kilometres along the B1 and C46, is the commercial fulcrum of the north's economy. Unprepossessing, flat towns, they contain little to interest the tourist, beyond browsing the open markets, though they are the gateway to a handful of interesting cultural sights in the vicinity. What's more, they are good places to visit a bank and stock up on food supplies and fuel, though you'll need to keep your wits about you and remain streetwise when parking your vehicle and going about your business. Most services are dotted along the dual carriageways in Ondangwa and Oshakati that scythe through the dust, lined with a seemingly endless stream of warehouses, car showrooms, service garages, tyre repair enterprises and cuca shops – shebeens (that also sell basic necessities) named after the Angolan beer that was illegally stocked here in the 1970s and 80s, and with alluring names such as *Hot Stuff Bar*, *Nice Time Shebeen* or *Happy Life Number 2*.

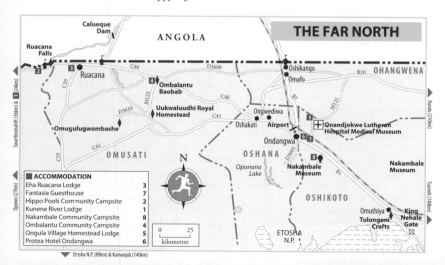

THE FAR NORTH

■ **ACCOMMODATION**

Eha Ruacana Lodge	3
Fantasia Guesthouse	7
Hippo Pools Community Campsite	2
Kunene River Lodge	1
Nakambale Community Campsite	8
Ombalantu Community Campsite	4
Ongula Village Homestead Lodge	5
Protea Hotel Ondangwa	6

6

IISHANA AND OMETALE – NORTHERN NAMIBIA'S VITAL WATER SOURCES

Central to northern Namibia's agro-ecology is the existence of the **Cuvelei-Etosha Basin**, a large water catchment area in the Highlands of Angola, whose perennial rivers filter down across the border into Namibia spreading into 7000 square kilometres of a delta-like network of seasonal watercourses, and shallow pools, known as **iishana** in Oshiwambo (though the anglicized term "oshanas" is commonly used). The **oshana system** is critical to the subsistence crop and livestock farming that sustains the rural populations. This flooding or *efundja*, as it is known, depends on the rainfall in Angola, but occurs most years, and even in seasons when the water inflow is low, local precipitation can fill the *iishana*. In years of exceptional rainfall, the water can even reach as far south as Etosha Pan. Crops are planted in anticipation of the floodwater's arrival, or the first rains, either of which can trigger the emergence of aestivating bullfrogs, crustaceans and other invertebrates. In good years, fish too are washed into the pools, adding welcome protein to the local diet. The grasses and reeds that sprout round the edges are used for basketry, including the basket-fishing nets you'll see women using, as they wade through the shallow pools, alert to trapping the day's meal. Once the water arrives, the landscape is transformed: dotted with bushy marula trees and haughty makalani palms, the pale, dusty, overgrazed flatlands are replaced by mirror-like lakes, where white lilies burst open and a wealth of wetland birds are drawn to feast on this temporary food source. Though the wet season usually runs from November to April, the wettest months are December to February. Many of the more rural communities dig *ometale* (earth dams), which are effectively excavated *iishana*, so that they can retain the water for longer. In good years, despite the high evaporation rates, these communally managed water resources can last much of the dry season, providing a vital lifeline to communities in this challenging environment.

The rural landscape here too is strikingly different; expanses of flat, loamy sands are noticeably lacking in tree cover, beyond the emblematic clumps of makalani palms that stand sentinel, and pockets of mopane, fig and marula trees. Homesteads fill the countryside, though the traditional mopane palisades and conical thatched rondavels are gradually incorporating more aluminium, breezeblock and plastic sheeting in their construction. Hot, dry and dusty for much of the year due in no small part to the insidious downward spiral of overgrazing, land degradation and deforestation, the region's harsh aridity is blunted somewhat once the *iishana* (shallow pools) fill with water and the seasonal rains arrive.

Ondangwa

ONDANGWA is the first sizeable town you encounter after crossing the veterinary cordon fence at Oshivelo, north of Etosha's Von Lindequist Gate. Slightly less frenetic, and less populated than neighbouring Oshakati – it has a population of about 23,000 – it was established in 1890 as a Finnish mission station at the western edge of the Ondonga Kingdom. Following World War I, the British decided to base their administration here; the South African colonial government then followed suit, and from 1918, Ondangwa became the main assemblage point for labourers being recruited to work in the mines and farms in the Police Zone or in South Africa. Once the apartheid regime established Oshakati as the new capital of Owamboland in the mid-1960s, which then became the regional capital post-independence, Ondangwa's political importance faded. However, commerce in the town is still growing, and likely to expand further, given Ondangwa's strong rail and air links, and strategic location on the main transit route between Namibia and Angola – the busy main junction in the town centre sees the B1 turn northwards to Oshikango, Namibia's main border with Angola (see box opposite) 60km away.

Onandjokwe Lutheran Hospital Medical Museum

Along the M121 to Eenhana, a few hundred metres after the bridge over the railway • Mon–Fri 8am–5pm • N$40 • Key kept at the reception of the private ward

The town's one recognized attraction is the well-signposted **Onandjokwe Lutheran Hospital Medical Museum**, located in said hospital, which was the first to be built in northern Namibia, set up by the Finnish Missionary Society in 1911. The gleaming white adobe building draped with bougainvillea is the original clinic, which stands out from the less well-maintained surroundings of the current hospital. And while the exhibition rooms contain some interesting photos of early medical care and of the role of the hospital (and Lutheran Church) during the independence struggle, the insights into the challenges facing present-day healthcare provision that you'll gain from wandering round looking for someone to let you into the museum are likely to leave a more lasting impression.

6

ARRIVAL AND GETTING AROUND
ONDANGWA

By car Ondangwa lies on Namibia's main road, the B1, around 100km north of the King Nehale Gate into Etosha National Park, and 50km south of the Angolan border. It's also 30km southeast of Oshakati.

By bus Intercape Mainliner (☎061 227846, ⓦintercape.co.za) runs an overnight service from Windhoek to Oshakati (daily except Sat, at 6pm; 10hr; from N$320), stopping off in Ondangwa at 4.10am, and a similar overnight service to Windhoek from Oshakati, picking up in Ondangwa at the Engen Olunkono Centre

on the C46 (daily except Sat, at 8.30pm). In addition, minibuses shuttle between the two Engen service stations in Ondangwa and Oshakati. They also leave from the Puma petrol station in Oshakati bound for Windhoek (N$250).

By air The newly renovated airport lies 3.5km along the C46 towards Oshakati after the B1 turn-off to Oshikango. Air Namibia (☎061 225202, ⓦairnamibia.com) operates flights to and from Eros Airport in Windhoek (several daily Mon–Fri, one on Sun; 1hr).

ACCOMMODATION

Fantasia Guesthouse Brian Simita St, Ondangwa ☎065 240528, ⓔfantasia@mweb.com.na. A secure location, with eight spotless en-suite rooms with a/c, TV and kitchenette. The decor's rather chintzy but the place is good value. Eight cramped camping pitches are squeezed

into the yard. Camping per person <u>N$130</u>, doubles (B&B) <u>N$700</u>

Ongula Village Homestead Lodge Eembahu, on the D3670, signposted west off the M121 to Eenhana ☎065 264555 or ☎085 6256551, ⓦongula.com.

CROSSING THE ANGOLAN BORDER

Oshikango, a rather sketchy frontier town, is 60km due north of Ondangwa, and is one of Namibia's five **border crossings with Angola**: the others are at Ruacana (6am–6pm), Omahenene, near Outapi (8am–6pm), Katitwe, some 160km west of Rundu (6am–6pm), and the floating pontoon at Rundu (6am–6pm; see box, p.280). Oshikango's hours are 8am–6pm, but travellers should take note that Namibia's daylight saving between the first Sunday in April and the first Sunday in September means times are an hour earlier then. Oshikango is the busiest Namibian–Angolan border because it connects to the main tarred road to Luanda, so you can look forward to long queues of trucks and lengthy procedures. Make sure you're well acquainted with the latest visa regulations (see ⓦangola.org), as you'll need to get a tourist visa in advance (US$141), for which plenty of supporting documentation and a yellow fever vaccination will be required.

Note that Intercape Mainliner, which provides a regular overnight service between Windhoek and Ondangwa and Oshakati, also connects to Oshikango (☎061 227846, ⓦintercape.co.za; 11hr 30min from N$470). The bus stop in Oshikango is on the main road in front of *Spar*.

The very underused **Ruacana border post** with Angola (daily 8.30am–6.30pm), right by the falls, can only be accessed by 4WD vehicles, since on the Angolan side, the initial road, which leads to the small village of Culueque by the dam, is very rough. A slightly better road continues on to Xongongo, just under 100km further north, where there are tarred connections to Luanda.

A lodge with a difference – five comfortable, cheerily decorated thatched rondavels in a genuine Owambo homestead. In addition to organized excursions to Nakambale Museum or Oshakati markets, you've a chance to join in everyday activities: pounding mahangu (pearl millet), clay-pot-making, or visiting a cuca shop, plus local dishes are served at mealtimes. There is also a new "voluntourism" project (see p.73). DBB **N$2120**

Protea Hotel Ondangwa Main St at the junction between the B1 and the C46 ☎ 065 241900, ⊕ marriott .com. It may not be the four-star establishment it purports to be, but the area's premier business hotel is still surprisingly pleasant, with well-furnished, light carpeted double rooms, acceptable buffet food – though only a limited à la carte menu – a pool and small casino. Feeble wi-fi. B&B **N$1215**

Nakambale Museum

Olukonda village, 14km southeast of Ondangwa • Mon–Fri 8am–1pm, 2–5pm, Sat 8am–1pm, Sun noon–5pm • N$20; N$40 for entry to the museum and the homestead plus N$50 for a tour of the homestead • ☎ 065 245668, ✉ nakambalemuseum@gmail.com • To reach here, take the D3629 signposted west off the B1, about 4km south of Ondangwa

Nakambale is the local name given to Finnish missionary Martti Rautanen, on account of the skullcap he liked to wear that was thought to resemble a basket – *okambale* in Oshindonga. The **Nakambale Museum** is situated in the old mission station – which was also Rautanen's home – established in 1880, and one of the earliest in the north. The modest exhibition has plenty on the missionary's life, including photos, clothing, medical instruments and everyday artefacts. At the same time, there is information on indigenous traditional cultural practices, including a collection of artefacts, such as hunting bows and musical instruments. Next door, an Ndonga homestead has been re-created; while the museum exhibition is fairly self-explanatory, it is worth taking a guided tour of the homestead to make sense of the various partitioned areas and their significance. You can also engage the services of a guide here, to go to Lake Oponona (when it has water) or to the markets in Oshakati and Ondangwa.

ACCOMMODATION   **NAKAMBALE MUSEUM**

Nakambale Community Campsite ☎ 065 245668. There is space to camp by the homestead, with electricity, and shared ablution blocks with hot and cold water, as well as a kitchen and braai area, or if you prefer, you can order a traditional meal in advance (Owambo chicken is a favourite at N$100), or breakfast (N$80). Made-up dome tents with camp beds and linen are available, or you bed down in a small traditional hut. Camping per person **N$50**, huts **N$400**, dome tents **N$200**

Lake Oponona

Broadly at the end of the D3605, approximately 25km southwest of Ondangwa, but it depends on how high the flood levels have risen in any given year

The largest oshana in the Cuvelei Basin, **Lake Oponona** transforms into a glorious wetland in years of *efundja* (see box, p.248), when it increases its surface area several times over and lasts through most of the dry season, thus attracting a wealth of birdlife. This process of expansion gave rise to its name, which means "the one that swallowed up all the water" in Oshindonga. Greater and lesser flamingos, white pelicans, saddle-billed storks, knob-billed ducks – even the critically endangered blue crane – and a host of other migratory birds flock here once other oshanas have dried up.

Oshakati and Ongwediwa

Established in 1966 by the South African colonial administration as the capital of the newly designated Owamboland, **OSHAKATI** means "the place where people meet" or "that which is between" in Oshiwambo – perhaps a reference to its deliberately central location, chosen so that the authorities could further their political and commercial interests. Today, with a population of just under 40,000, Oshakati is Namibia's fourth-largest town; it's the capital of the north and a major commercial centre and transport hub. Along the main dual carriageway, punctuated by traffic lights, and lined

CLOCKWISE FROM TOP BAOBAB AT EPUPA FALLS (P.260); SMOKED MOPANE WORMS (P.58); 4WD ON VAN ZYL'S PASS (P.261) >

OSHAKATI

Outapi (92km) & Ruacana (160km) Oshikango (58km) & Angola

Okahao (73km)

6

Bus Terminal
Observation Tower
Open Market
Yetu Shopping Centre & Shoprite
Cymot
FNB & ATM
Oneshila Engen Service Station, Intercape bus stop & ATM
Police Station
Frans Indongo Shopping Centre
Puma Service Station
Oshakati State Hospital

C46

1 (4km); 2 (6km); Ongwediva (7km); Ondangwa (34km) & B1

KING MANDUME NDEMUFAYO (C45)
C46
ELEAZAR MATALE
DR AGOSTINHO NETO
MALAKIA NAKUUMBA (C41)
LIPUMO SHIKONGO
LEO SHIPALA
ROBERT MUGABE
HAMANEE SHEYO
KWANI MBUMBA ROAD
LEO SHIPALA
PATRICE LUMUMBA STREET

0   750
metres

N

EATING
Oshandira Lodge   2
Rocha's   1

ACCOMMODATION
Cheetah Backpackers   2
Destiny Hotel   1
Oshakati Guesthouse   3

Ompundja (14km)

with the occasional pavement, new supermarkets, warehouses and shopping malls gleam in the sunlight; at the same time, rusted old cars still decorate the waste-ground and the odd herd of goats will slow down the traffic, while battered combis slither on and off the road at will, to pick up or drop off passengers.

Just south of Oshakati, but soon to be sucked into the conurbation, lies the quiet, mainly residential town of **ONGWEDIWA**; established initially to house workers in Oshakati and Ondangwa, the place hosts a faculty of the University of Namibia plus a teachers' education college; more pertinently, it also offers a couple of pleasant places to stay.

Brief history

Oshakati's rapid infrastructural development in the late 1960s was prompted by the immediate militarization of the area as the independence struggle escalated into full-scale war the very year the town was founded (see Contexts, p.349). For much of the 1970s and 1980s, Oshakati was a heavily fortified encampment, with watchtowers, barbed wire, bullet-proof walls and a heavy army and police presence. There soon followed an influx of people from rural areas fleeing poverty and/or the fighting, including large numbers of Angolans, who arrived in the mid-70s, once civil war started north of the border; many such migrants still live in informal or shanty settlements on the town's fringes. In 1970, the population numbered under 3000; by the late 1980s it had swelled to 37,000, more or less matching present-day figures. Since independence much money has been pumped into the place for redevelopment. The biggest project to date is a 23km dyke, built in response to Oshakati's repeated flooding in recent years. You should be able to drive on some of it by the time this guide is published.

Dr Frans Aupu Indongo Open Market

On the corner of the C46 and the C45 • Daily 6am–6pm • Free

If you happen to be passing through Oshakati, take some time to wander round the sparkling new **Dr Frans Aupa Indongo Open Market** – named after the pre-eminent

Namibian entrepreneur – adjacent to the new bus terminal. You'll pass baskets piled high with pulses, grains, fruit, vegetables, dried fish and mopane worms; rails of modern "traditional" Owambo dresses wafting in the breeze while women beaver away on Singer sewing machines; and the sale of all kinds of artefacts and crafts, from fly whisks to carved walking sticks, reed mats to wooden masks and clay pots. Don't forget to visit the stall-holders grilling kapana – sizzling strips of seasoned meat, washed down with some oshikundu (fermented mahangu).

The centrepiece of the N$80-million-dollar market renovation is a twelve-storey observation tower, resembling a spaceship when illuminated at night; the local authorities are still searching for an investor to take it on, but are hoping for a café or restaurant on the top floor.

6

ARRIVAL AND DEPARTURE

By car Oshakati lies 708km north of Windhoek; after turning west off the B1 onto the C46 at Ondangwa, it's a further 30km.

By bus Intercape Mainliner (☎061 227846, ⓦintercape .co.za) operates an overnight service from its terminal in Bahnhof St, Windhoek, to Oshakati (daily except Sat, 6pm; 11hr; N$340) picking up passengers for the return to Windhoek (daily except Sat, at 7.30pm) at the Engen Oneshila service station on the main road in Oshakati. Large buses and minibuses leave on no fixed timetable leave the Monte Christo Service Station in Katutura, Windhoek, bound for Ondangwa and Oshakati (8hr). The inexpensive twice-weekly (Tues & Fri) Orange Bus service, operated by Namib

OSHAKATI AND ONGWEDIWA

Contract Haulage (☎061 225333, ⓦkalahariholdings .com), runs between Soweto Market, Katutura and Oshakati (8am or 5pm; N$225).

By minibus In Oshakati, minibuses (and sometimes shared taxis) fan out to other major centres in the north, such as Opuwo (3hr; N$150) and Rundu (5hr; N$200), as well as shuttling back and forth between the two Engen petrol stations in Oshakati and Ondangwa. Buses usually leave from the new bus terminal adjacent to the open market at the junction between the C46 and the C45, though some transport still uses the more traditional service station – make enquiries at the bus terminal.

By air Oshakati airport only accommodates charter flights.

INFORMATION AND TOURS

There is no official tourist office yet in Oshakati, but the staff of Cheetah Backpackers and Safaris based in the *Shoprite Complex* on the main C46 in Ongwediwa, a few kilometres south of Oshakati, are extremely helpful (Mon–Fri 8am–5pm, Sat 9am–1pm; ☎081 286 1952, ⓦcheetahbackpackers.com). The company runs some interesting, inexpensive day tours, including one round local towns, taking in a market and a cuca shop. Though tours are primarily aimed at the local market, this is a great way to break out of the foreign tourist bubble and meet other Namibians.

ACCOMMODATION

Cheetah Backpackers Reception at the office in the Shoprite Complex on the main C46 in Ongwediwa, ☎065 231530 or ☎081 286 1952, ⓦcheetahbackpackers.com). Located in a residential neighbourhood, a range of functional, inexpensive accommodation options from a well-equipped self-catering unit to dorm beds or regular double rooms, as well as spots to pitch a tent, or you can sleep in a tent already set up. All in a compound with secure parking on a residential street a few blocks east of the main road. Camping per person N$70, tents N$200, dorms N$120, doubles N$1000

Destiny Hotel Turn east off the C46 at Ongwediwa open market, then take the second left and follow signs ☎065 231534, ⓦhoteldestiny.com.na. Welcoming budget business hotel comprising 31 small but spotless tiled rooms, which still manage to pack in all you need: a/c, DStv, phone, hair dryer, desk, tea/coffee-making facilities and, best of all, a monsoon shower. N$940

Oshakati Guesthouse Corner of Sam Nujoma Rd and Leo Shoopla St, Oshakati ☎065 224659, ⊜oshakati guesthouse@iway.na. Efficient, friendly, mid-range business hotel with en-suite tiled rooms and DStv. Bag one of the lighter upstairs rooms. N$1150

EATING

Although the two hotels below have respectable accommodation, their restaurants are the main draw.

Oshandira Lodge Airport Rd ☎065 220443, ⓦoshandira@iway.na. Tucked away in a quiet spot, this is probably the best place to eat in town, so it gets busy at

weekends. Choose from pub-style seating on the veranda or a table under fan-ventilated thatch. The menu has the usual international regulars: schnitzels, pastas, pizzas and steaks, or more local dishes, such as mahangu with Owambo-style chicken, or various potjies – justifiably their most popular orders (most mains from N$100). Daily 11am–9pm.

Rocha's West side of the C46 ☎ 065 222038. A veritable oasis, with wooden tables and benches arranged in a leafy

paved courtyard round a small pool, where you can forget about the dust and noise outside while enjoying some authentic Portuguese cuisine, from prego rolls to their famous bacalhau (cod), or regular burgers, steak and pork dishes with pap or rice. Most mains N$120–145. If you can't take the heat, there's also a tiled dining room with a/c. Daily 6am–11pm.

6 West of Oshakati

West of Oshakati takes you into the heart of the Cuvelei-Etosha basin, and countryside full of oshanas and mahangu plantations (see box, p.248). Most travellers are passing through for Ruacana, Opuwo and the Kaokoveld. However, it's perfectly feasible to plan a circular day-trip from Oshakati all on good tarred roads, which can give you a glimpse of small-town and village life as well as a chance to visit some modest sights of cultural and historical interest. First, you take in the famous **Ombalantu Baobab** in the rapidly growing town of Outapi, and capital of the Omusati Region, some 92km further west along the C46. A half-hour drive south along the little-used M123 then takes you to the small community of Tsandi, where you can stop off to visit the **Uukwaluudhi Royal Homestead**. Those interested in the War of Independence might consider a 20km detour southeast down the D3633 to the monument at **Ongulumbashwe**, though there is not actually much to see. Back on the M123, returning eastwards towards Oshakati, you pass through the small town of **Okahao**, which also possesses a large baobab, before completing the last 70km stretch back to base. Look out on the south side of the road, some 17km outside Oshakati; in the afternoons you will often see women selling large clay pots (left under a cloth if they are absent); though the cooperative they were part of is no more, they still do business on an individual basis, and the pots are definitely worth perusing.

Ombalantu Baobab Heritage Centre
Outapi, behind the open market just after the junction with the M123 to Tsandi • Daily 8am–6pm • N$20 • ☎ 081 438 4705 • N$20

Though not the only such tree in town, the **Ombalantu Baobab** is nevertheless an impressive specimen: it is rumoured to be 800 years old, 28m tall and with a girth, almost as wide, at 26.5m. Its hollowed-out centre has served many purposes over the ages. Initially able to hold 45 people, it was used in the early 1900s as a shelter, to hide and protect the community's women and children whenever they were under attack. In calmer times, it served as a storage facility, and then, in 1940, as Outapi's first post office. Later, it became a church – and indeed it still retains two pews and an altar. After the SADF had established a base in Outapi, the baobab's belly hosted a bar and was also used to detain people who were later interrogated by the police.

The site also has a **craft shop**, selling miniature baobabs, among other items, and is a **community campsite**.

ACCOMMODATION
OMBALANTU BAOBAB HERITAGE CENTRE

Ombalantu Community Campsite By the baobab tree ☎ 081 438 4705. Four simple pitches with braai

facilities and shared ablutions offering warm showers. Camping per person **N$50**

Uukwaluudhi Royal Homestead
On the M123, just opposite the turn-off to Omugulugwombashe • N$40 • Mon–Fri 8am–5pm • ☎ 081 301 2739

In 1978, King Josia Shikongo Taapopi of the Uukwaluudhi – one of the seven Owambo groups – moved out of the traditional mopane-palisaded royal palace (*ombala*) into a modern brick construction with glass windows next door. He then decided to open the old palace up to the public as the **Uukwaluudhi Royal Homestead**. After digesting the writing on the information boards that contextualize the homestead within Uukwaluudhi history and culture, you are then taken on a walk around the labyrinthine complex, a series of fenced-off areas and separate wooden huts, made deliberately confusing to confound enemies and discourage wild animals. To the uninitiated, many of the huts and enclosures look much the same. However, each of the 35 areas has its own purpose, which is carefully explained: places for warriors to gather before battle, or for grain to be stored; royal sleeping quarters, with widely spaced poles to allow for air circulation, or a hut with a calabash in which the milk is churned. In the main forecourt, before entering the palace proper, spreads a magnificent marula tree, where it was customary to wait for an audience with the king. That is theoretically possible for visitors, but he likes to have advance notice.

6

State Cemetery
At the end of the D3633

A fairly innocuous patch of bush hosts the **Omugulugwombashe State Cemetery**, the country's second such cemetery after Heroes' Acre, just outside Windhoek (see p.102), and one which thankfully is a lot less grandiose. Six of the PLAN fighters who lost their lives when their camp here was attacked by the SADF on August 26, 1966, are buried at this site. An evocative bronze sculpture of them strategizing now sits under a tree. There's also a more general monument to those who lost their lives in the struggle, and the compulsory bronze statue of Sam Nujoma, this time waving a rifle.

Ruacana

On the westernmost limit of the Omusati Region lies the near-deserted town of **RUACANA**, which came into being to house workers for the construction of the dam and underground power station on the Kunene River in the 1970s, before hosting an SADF base during the war for independence – the dam and power station were bombed by the Cubans in 1988, just as the South Africans were retreating from Angola (see p.350). Despite its elevation to "town" status in 2010, Ruacana has a population of just three thousand. There's nothing to detain the visitor here, but since there's no fuel for miles around you should fill up at the busy petrol station, which also has a well-stocked shop with **ATM**, though a nearby supermarket offers greater choice. The border post here is underused and suitable for 4WD vehicles only (see p.249).

Ruacana Falls
Well signposted off the C46, 20km west of Ruacana • Daily 8.30am–6.30pm, but dependent on Angolan border post hours • Free • Note that the right-run to the falls, 500m before the access road ends, is not signposted; then you need to go through the Angolan border post into the neutral land – the border guard will point out the dirt road leading to the viewpoint

The **Ruacana Falls** were once a truly spectacular sight, a 600m-wide wall of water, plunging 120m into the gorge below, making it one of the largest falls in Africa. However, a hydroelectric power station and dam built in the late 1970s – now Namibia's main source of power – soon put an end to this natural wonder. Yet, on the rare occasions that heavy rains produce too much water, the sluice gates are opened upriver in Angola (generally Feb–April), and the dramatic aquatic show is resumed, albeit only temporarily. However, even in the dry season the bare, sheer rock face and the impressive gorge below are worth the short detour if you're in the area, provided you ignore the heavily littered viewpoint.

ARRIVAL AND DEPARTURE
RUACANA

By car Easily accessible by good tarred roads from Oshakati, 160km to the east, and from Opuwo, 140km to the southwest. There is also a challenging but scenic track that runs westwards alongside the Kunene, all the way to Epupa Falls (317km), much loved by 4WD fanatics. Much of this is impassable in the rainy season. The first section as far as Swartbooisdrift is fairly straightforward, whereas the longer stretch on through the Zebra Mountains to Epupa requires greater 4WD expertise. There are several basic community campsites along the way, as well as the delightful *Kunene River Lodge* (see p.256).

By minibus Minibuses between Ruacana and Oshakati pull in at the Puma garage.

6

ACCOMMODATION

Eha Ruacana Lodge Ruacana village, on the C46 ☎ 065 271500, ⓦ ruacanaehalodge.com.na. Functional motel-like place with a surprising array of facilities: moderately priced restaurant, bar-lounge area, swimming pool, and even a gym and squash courts. The clean, bland tiled rooms are perfectly adequate if you get stuck for the night, while the campground also contains some small domed budget chalets if you crave a little a/c and a fridge. Camping per person N$144, chalets N$600, doubles N$1236

Hippo Pools (Otjipahuriro) Community Campsite
On the banks of the Kunene, 4km west of the turn-off to the Ruacana. Simple, back-to-basics, shady campground with ten pitches in an idyllic location, affording views across to hilly Angola; here, you can hear the cry of the fish eagle and the grunting of the eponymous hippos in the river below. No electricity; basic washing and long-drop toilet facilities. Guided walks and village visits can be arranged. Camping per person N$90

★ **Kunene River Lodge** 45km west of Ruacana Falls on the D3700 ☎ 065 274300, ⓦ kuneneriverlodge.com. A long-standing favourite, with a relaxed, away-from-it-all feel. The camping pitches take pride of place along the riverbank, under a shady canopy of mature trees, with braai sites, sink, electricity and shared ablution block. Further back, spacious rooms (a/c) and cheaper rustic chalets (fan) overlook a tropical garden, which hides a sheltered pool area. Meals (which need to be pre-ordered) are served on the riverside deck. It's the perfect spot to unwind for a few days, given the wealth of activities: birdwatching (almost three hundred species), canoeing, excursions to a Himba village or to a local gorge, or a chug along the river by boat for a sundowner. 4WD access only. Cheaper for two-night stays. Camping per person N$160, chalets (B&B) N$1440, doubles (B&B) N$1900

Northern Kunene

Occupying the northwest corner of Namibia, **northern Kunene** is a predominantly mountainous wilderness area, accessed by few roads and sparsely populated even by Namibian standards. The **Baynes Mountains**, which overlook the picturesque **Epupa Falls** on the Kunene River, rise to over 2000m. Elsewhere, the land consists of

THE IMPORTANCE OF APPEARANCE IN HIMBA CULTURE

Himba women in traditional attire have graced many a magazine cover and featured in documentaries galore with their distinctive reddish-brown body "paint" and goatskin "miniskirts". And while the Himba's physical appearance often brings out the worst voyeuristic tendencies in tourists (see p.68), appearance is, nevertheless, very important to Himba culture; women spend several hours on their toilette each day. Their body **"paint"** – *otjize* – is actually a mix of ground red ochre and animal butter or fat, scented with resin, and used to cover their skin, hair, clothing and jewellery. It has functional, symbolic and aesthetic value, protecting their skin from the burning sun while keeping insects at bay; its reddish-brown hue evokes both the earth and life-giving blood. Since water is scarce, women often have a smoke "bath", and similarly "wash" their leather clothing by smoking it over incense.

Hair is similarly important: various styles indicate different life stages for both males and females. Toddlers often have shaven heads but as they grow, girls have two plaits, pulled over their face once they hit puberty (to show modesty) while boys maintain one plait at the back, which becomes two at puberty. The style of the plaits indicates the *oruzo*, or patrilineal descent, of the wearer.

Once married, men bundle their hair into a head-wrap, which is only removed for funerals, or when they are widowed. Puberty for young women entails sporting numerous plaits, smeared with *otjize*, and once married, women incorporate a tanned sheep or goatskin headpiece, which is replaced by a different headpiece (*erembe*) after they have been married a year, or given birth to their first child.

Traditionally attired women and men are heavily adorned with a collection of **jewellery** – necklaces, collars, bracelets and anklets, which also serve as a protection against snakebites. The jewellery is fashioned from metal, shell, beads, leather and woven grass, and sometimes weighs several kilos. Inevitably, as westernization encroaches and traditions become eroded, Himba apparel is becoming more hybrid, or abandoned altogether.

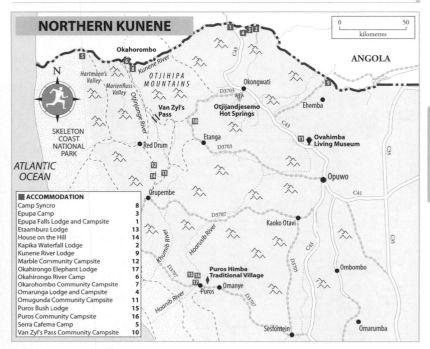

NORTHERN KUNENE

ANGOLA

ATLANTIC OCEAN

SKELETON COAST NATIONAL PARK

OTJIHIPA MOUNTAINS

Hartmann's Valley
Marienfluss Valley
Van Zyl's Pass
Okahorombo
Okongwati
Ehomba
Otjijandjesemo Hot Springs
Etanga
Red Drum
Ovahimba Living Museum
Orupembe
Opuwo
Kaoko Otavi
Ombombo
Puros Himba Traditional Village
Puros
Omanye
Sesfontein
Omarumba

Kunene River
Oljijunge River
Khumib River
Hoarusib River
Hoanib River

■ ACCOMMODATION	
Camp Syncro	8
Epupa Camp	3
Epupa Falls Lodge and Campsite	1
Etaambura Lodge	13
House on the Hill	14
Kapika Waterfall Lodge	2
Kunene River Lodge	9
Marble Community Campsite	12
Okahirongo Elephant Lodge	17
Okahirongo River Camp	6
Okarohombo Community Campsite	7
Omarunga Lodge and Campsite	4
Omugunda Community Campsite	11
Puros Bush Lodge	15
Puros Community Campsite	16
Serra Cafema Camp	5
Van Zyl's Pass Community Campsite	10

6

rock-strewn, reddish earth covered in acacia trees and flat-topped escarpments. Often referred to as **Kaokoland**, the former bantustan name that is still commonly used, or the **Kaokoveld** – designating the geographical area – it is home to the vast majority of the fifty thousand **Himba**, who are very much in evidence in **Opuwo**, the Kunene region's unlikely capital. Stretching from the **Skeleton Coast** in the west a few hundred kilometres inland towards Etosha, northern Kunene is bounded by the perennial Kunene River in the north, which marks the border with Angola, and the dry Hoanib River in the south. It is here, and along the sandy riverbeds of the Huab, Hoarusib and Khumib rivers, that desert-adapted elephants and black rhino wander, seeking out vegetation in the scarce, spring-fed waterholes.

Opuwo

There's a touch of the Wild West about **OPUWO**, a frontier feel that exists nowhere else in Namibia. During the day, there's a purposeful bustle of tourists, NGO workers and the occasional film crew passing through on their way to somewhere else – usually Epupa Falls, lesser-explored parts of the Kaokoveld, or a Himba village – pausing only to stock up with supplies. Indeed, the reason most tourists are drawn to Opuwo – though relatively few ever reach this remote region – is in order to interact with and learn about the Himba.

Only officially declared a town in 2000, Opuwo is now the regional capital of Kunene. For many years after independence it was a neglected backwater, in no small part due to the fact that many Himba and Herero – who are related to the Himba and also fairly well represented in the town – were on the wrong side in the independence struggle (see p.349). Even now, Opuwo's town centre still consists of little more than a couple of paved roads that converge at a T-junction, a collection of government buildings and ever-expanding, informal Himba settlements. Indeed,

6

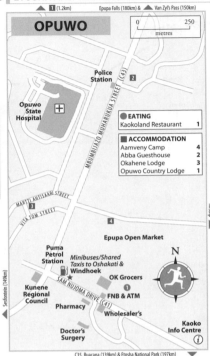

OPUWO

EATING
Kaokoland Restaurant   1

ACCOMMODATION
Aamveny Camp   4
Abba Guesthouse   2
Okahene Lodge   3
Opuwo Country Lodge   1

C35, Ruacana (139km) & Etosha National Park (197km)

when many Himba lost cattle and other livestock in Namibia's worst drought for thirty years, in 2013, they saw little alternative than to migrate to Opuwo in the hope of some relief. These days, pavements are crammed with Himba camping out, the women surrounded by crawling babies, swigging out of large bottles of Fanta, while the older men sit in deckchairs or on makeshift stools, surveying the scene. Himba from remote villages also periodically come into town, to visit the hospital, stock up at the wholesalers, or to sell crafts to tourists.

There are no tourist sights as such, but pick your way through the rubble and rubbish dumped by the roadside and the thriving shebeens to take a wander round the **Himba market** behind the main shopping complex, or seek out the newly opened **Kunene Conservancy** processing plant, **Scents of Africa**, southwest of the T-junction, which manufactures Himba cosmetics made from traditional ingredients, and can offer guided tours with advance notice (☎ 081 214 8448).

ARRIVAL AND DEPARTURE
OPUWO

By car From the south, the quickest route to Opuwo is via the tarred C35 from Kamanjab (237km), turning west onto the signed C48 for the final 56km. Note that, although the road to Opuwo is wholly tarred, you'll come across lots of animals north of the veterinary fence, just north of Kamanjab. There is also no petrol available between the two.

By bus or shared taxi To reach Opuwo from Windhoek,

you need to enquire at the Monte Christo Service Station in Katutura. Alternatively, ring Davi (☎ 081 258 6186) in Opuwo to find out when return transport is heading back north. In Opuwo, to get a ride out of town, ask at the Puma filling station, next to the *OK* supermarket complex; minibuses and shared cars leave regularly for Oshakati (N$120; 3hr) and less frequently for Windhoek, Swakopmund or Walvis Bay (N$200–250; 7–8hr).

INFORMATION

Kaoko Information Centre On the C41, entering town, 500m before the junction ☎ 065 273420, ☎ 081 895 2150 or ☎ 081 691 7378, ✉ kaokoinfocentre @yahoo.com. Run by HIPO (Hizetjitwa Indigenous People's Organisation), this very helpful office can provide you with lots of information about the various Himba, Herero, Zemba and Hakaona communities in the area. They can also

organize a trained local guide to accompany you in your vehicle on day or overnight trips to various villages, including as far as Marienfluss or Hartmann's Valley. Costs vary depending on time and distance but are usually around N$200/person for a day-trip to a settlement, plus food to take to the village, and N$400/person for an overnight excursion; food for you and the guide would be on top.

ACCOMMODATION

Aamveny Camp Formerly Oreness; 50m off Mbumbijazo Muharukua Ave, 300m north of the T-junction ☎ 065 273572 or ☎ 081 275 0156, ✉ westymelchy@yahoo.com. The town's backpacking option is a pleasant, secure and shady spot with

rondavels, twelve basic fan-ventilated twin rooms and grassy pitches, though the town's noise can permeate the place at night. Camping per person **N$80**, doubles (B&B) **N$300**

Abba Guesthouse Mbumbijazo Muharukua Ave,

VISITING HIMBA COMMUNITIES

Activities in Opuwo and northern Kunene generally centre on visiting **Himba communities**. Your first port of call should be the Kaoko Information Centre (see opposite), though visits can also be arranged through English-speaking Himba such as Western, the owner of *Aamveny Camp* (see opposite), or "Queen Elizabeth" (☎081 213 8326), usually found with the other Himba jewellery sellers close to the *OK* supermarket. Alternatively, you can arrange a visit through your accommodation or book with a tour operator. Before deciding, make sure that your visit is likely to involve a small group, be culturally sensitive and benefit the community. Whatever you do, avoid giving tobacco, alcohol or sweets to individuals or communities. Establish what the parameters are in advance. When visiting a village, or even meeting Himba on the way, merely handing over money to adults or sweets to kids is not helpful, as it has already encouraged begging, which is growing among some of the populace along the route to Epupa. Similarly, photo-taking is a sensitive issue; obviously permission should be sought before taking a photo, but better than that is to interact with people in an activity, or on a visit with an interpreter, and maybe after spending time together, you might ask to take a photo of you all together, to share among the group. The snap-for-cash culture that has dominated interactions between Himba women and tourists for some time now is not helping to develop intercultural understanding or positive relations.

Kunene Conservancy Safaris (KCS; ☎064 406136, ☎081 149 0399, ⊛kcs-namibia.com.na) are Namibia's most successful conservancy-based tourism company, with great ethical and environmental credentials, running a range of four- to twelve-day small-group tours led by experts (N$6500/person for a group of up to three; reduced rate for larger groups). All profits go to the five conservancies involved, and some tours include staying at *Etaambura*, the first Himba-owned lodge (see p.262).

Another recent option for travellers who wish to visit independently is to drop in on the newly established Ovahimba Living Museum (call manager John ☎081 838 2556, ⊛lcfn.info /ovahimba), which opened at the end of 2016. It's next door to the community campsite at Omugunda (N$80/person), 42km along the gravel road towards Epupa. As with the other living museums (see box, p.56), each activity is paid for separately in cash. Here you can choose from an hour's bushwalk or body painting (N$100), to a general cultural introduction to the village, or a whole day during which you participate in a whole range of activities with a guide/interpreter on hand (N$500).

500m north of the T-junction, by a school ☎065 273155, ⊛abbaguesthouse.com. Good-value, simple guesthouse with neat and tidy rooms. The budget rooms (with fan) are en suite, but with little more than two beds and a kettle, it's worth splashing out an extra N$400 on the upstairs "luxury" rooms that open out onto a shared balcony, each with a fridge, kitchenette, tea/coffee-making facilities, and even DStv. Secure parking too. The owners are heavily involved in supporting the adjacent church, school and orphanage, towards which a percentage of the guesthouse income goes. Breakfast on request (N$59). **N$360**

Okahene Lodge Mbumbijazo Muharukua Ave, 200m north of the T-junction ☎065 273031, ⊜ohakene@iway.na. Tucked behind the disused Shell petrol station, an unprepossessing exterior belies a pleasant, tropical oasis – a small lawn dotted with palm trees and a tiny pool, around which a dozen tidy tiled rooms (a/c and DStv) are arranged. The small terrace restaurant, which serves nicely cooked,

inexpensive dishes, is open to the public, though they need some warning. Daily 7am–9pm. B&B **N$1030**

Opuwo Country Lodge On the ridge, on the west side of town, signposted off Mbumbijazo Muharukua Ave 500m north of the T-junction ☎065 273461 (lodge) or ☎064 418661 (reservations), ⊛opuwo lodge.com. Surveying Opuwo like the feudal lord, this overpriced hotel is by far the best lodging in town, though is not as good as it thinks it is. The main thatched lodge boasts enviable views across the surrounding countryside from its terrace and infinity pool deck, but only the small "luxury" rooms – crammed with nice furniture – share this view. Even smaller standard rooms sit behind, with shared porch and noisy a/c unit under the tables. 400m away, the campground lacks shade, has rocky and uneven pitches, but it's quiet (unlike in town), and the big plus is access to the lodge's facilities, including its fabulous infinity pool. Camping per person **N$160**, doubles (B&B) **N$1800**

6

THE KUNENE DAM CONTROVERSIES

Since the mid-1990s, when the first feasibility studies were conducted, the Namibian and Angolan governments have been attempting to **dam the Kunene River** and build another hydroelectric power station (in addition to the one at Ruacana), to satisfy the countries' ever-increasing demand for power. The favoured site for the dam, initially, was at **Epupa**, but the Himba, whose ancestral lands would have been flooded and whose way of life was threatened, protested vociferously, supported by national and international human rights and environmental agencies. Bowing to sustained pressure, the Namibian government eventually shelved the plan in 2007, but is now pushing for construction of a dam 40km downstream in the **Baynes Mountains**. Once again, this would flood Himba lands, including gravesites; entail the forced resettlement of some communities; deprive settlements of an important riverine resource, for people and cattle; and lead to the inevitable influx of construction workers and a likely increase in crime, all of which would threaten the Himba way of life. As an alternative, most Himba are in favour of developing **solar power** in the region. In 2012, the Himba took their case to the African Union and the United Nations, followed later by protest marches in Opuwo. This has seemingly pushed the project into abeyance once more, though it is unlikely to be the end of the saga.

EATING

★**Kaokoland Restaurant** Close to the OK supermarket. Recently expanded (though the opening hours have shortened) to include a large, pleasant, thatched lapa alongside a bland, air-conditioned cafeteria with large sports screens, this is the only place to eat in town outside the hotels and market stalls. It does decent breakfast fry-ups, sandwiches, burgers and salads for N$40–80, and more substantial chicken, goat and meat dishes with mealie-pap, rice, chips or salad from around N$60. Has wi-fi. Mon–Sat 8am–5pm, Sat 8am–noon.

Epupa Falls

Before the Kunene River empties into the Atlantic on the Skeleton Coast, it fans out across a broad valley, forming numerous channels that skirt round islands and trip, tumble and cascade over a series of cataracts, before plunging into a chasm. This is **Epupa Falls** – Epupa meaning "falling water" in Otjiherero. The main cataract is a mere 35m and only captures a third of the river's flow, but the whole scene is truly magical: set against the backdrop of the Baynes Mountains, lofty Makalani palms interspersed with majestic jackalberries and sycamore figs fringe the riverbank, while stout baobabs and silvery moringa trees balance precariously on the rocks above the ravines. Though at their fullest and most impressive in April and May, when the water thunders and the spray obscures your view, the falls are picturesque even in the dry season, when expanses of attractive reddish-brown rock and tiny grassy islets are exposed.

Birdlife is abundant – including the localized endemic Cinderella waxbill and rufous-tailed palm thrush – and a walk upriver from the falls is likely to yield sightings of watchful crocs half submerged in the shallows, or lazing on the riverbanks. One of the most delightful places to **camp** in all Namibia, Epupa also attracts visitors whose main aim is to interact with the semi-nomadic **Himba**, one of Africa's most resilient – and most photographed – indigenous peoples (see p.259).

ARRIVAL AND DEPARTURE   EPUPA FALLS

By car Epupa is around a 180km drive northwest of Opuwo (3hr), on a gravel road, which becomes increasingly sinuous as it nears Epupa. Stock up on camping supplies and fuel in Opuwo.

On a tour Lodgings in Opuwo (see p.258) run tours to Epupa, including day-trips, though an overnight stay is preferable to catch the sunrise and sunset, which are often magical.

ACCOMMODATION

★**Epupa Camp** 1km upriver from the falls ☎065 685053 (camp) or ☎061 237294 (reservations), ⓦepupa.com.na. A delightful location, where nine stone-enclosed safari tents are lined along the riverbank; you can watch the water flow from your private porch. Dinner and drinks are served on the deck, where there's a small splash pool to cool off in. Make sure you sway across the new swing bridge to a small island, where you can loll on a swing bed while sipping your sundowner. The adjacent campground lies further upriver, with five quiet, spacious plots boasting private ablutions, though there's less shade than at *Epupa Falls Campsite*. Also has simple dome tents with beds and linen. Camping per person N$160, dome tents N$660, safari tents (DBB) N$3300

★ **Epupa Falls Lodge and Campsite** On the river, at the top of the falls 065 695106 or 081 149 2840, epupafallslodge.com. When the river's full, you can see the spray from this shady camp that has seven camping pitches (five by the river) and five rustic stilted en-suite cabins, which afford great views across the river and are good value. The raised terrace-restaurant deck offers similar vistas. Breakfast is a hefty N$120, dinner N$250. Wi-fi is extra. No electricity. Himba village visits N$750 for a full day, but hiking and birdwatching can also be organized. Camping per person N$125, chalets (DBB) N$2796

Kapika Waterfall Lodge On the ridge, 1km upriver from the falls 065 685111, kapikafalls.com. Perched high on the hillside, affording commanding views of the river from the restaurant deck, this lodge is a prime spot for a sundowner. Ten stone chalets with open-plan bathrooms and semi-private porches are large, though rather bare and bland. Himba village visits N$495/person. B&B N$2400

Omarunga Lodge and Campsite 500m upriver from the falls 064 403096, omarungalodge.com. Nicely maintained, smart riverside lodge offering fourteen safari-tent chalets; numbers 1–5 directly overlook the water. The decent-size pool has a nice shaded area for lounging around, and each of the ten campsites has a light (but no power point), tap and fireplace, with a shared ablution block and kitchen area. Four-hour Himba tour N$630/person. Camping per person N$150, chalets (DBB) N$3490

Marienfluss and Hartmann's Valley

In the far northwestern corner of Kunene, **Marienfluss** and **Hartmann's Valley** constitute one of Namibia's most remote wilderness landscapes, receiving few visitors beyond the semi-nomadic Himba with their cattle and goats, alongside herds of springbok and oryx. Even fewer tourists make it this far, except for a trickle of determined, hardy 4WD adventurers, or a select few who can afford a fly-in safari (see p.264). Tracks are sparse, mobile phone coverage non-existent, and the main reference points are painted oil drums. More self-drive visitors stop in Marienfluss, but if you have the time, the fuel and the water – there's nowhere to replenish stocks en route – then you should try to visit both valleys. Marienfluss is arguably the more beautiful of the two, being lusher – if there's been rain – coated with flaxen grasses, and home to carpets of fairy circles (see box, p.263) along its broad flat sandy floor, flanked by the Otjihipa Mountains to the east and Hartmann's Mountains to the west. What's more, there's a gorgeous riverside campsite to reward the dusty drive, though don't be tempted to jump in the water, as this is prime croc territory. These days there's even a tiny Himba store selling cold beer. Reaching the end of Hartmann's Valley is a rougher ride, 70km of more arid conditions that will take you well over two hours, but its moonscapes have a desolate beauty: vast expanses of flecked cream- or rust-coloured sand, interspersed with endless domes of seemingly barren grey rock; as you approach the Kunene, the huge dunes to the west separate you from the Skeleton Coast, some 50km away.

The best known entrance into Marienfluss is the dramatic descent over the **Van Zyl's Pass**, a precarious, rocky affair, not for those suffering from vertigo or lacking in 4WD experience. You will have to get out and inspect the terrain as you go and move the odd rock, but before focusing your attention on not overturning the vehicle or toppling over the edge, don't forget to pause at the viewpoint and absorb the stunning panorama. However, if you approach the valleys from the comparatively easier route via Red Drum, in the south (which still demands good 4WD experience, GPS, possession of spare parts, some mechanical know-how, a satellite phone and driving in convoy), you will have to return the same way as far as Orupembe, since you are only allowed to cross the Van Zyl's Pass from east to west.

ARRIVAL AND DEPARTURE

By car Van Zyl's Pass is reached via Opuwo along the well-graded C43 road to Epupa, turning off at Okongwati after around 110km, from where it is slow going along a rocky track to Otjitanda. Most people camp here before tackling

MARIENFLUSS AND HARTMANN'S VALLEY

the pass the next day; allow at least three hours for it, and another two to reach camp at the Kunene. From the south, most people access the area via the D3707 from Sesfontein, via Puros (see opposite) and Orupembe.

ACCOMMODATION

There are **community campsites** springing up all the time; some are very rudimentary, but even those that are more developed, with better facilities, may still lack water for one reason or another, especially after several years of drought. Wood may also be hard to come by, so you should bring both water and wood with you, or use a gas stove for cooking. Moreover, if something breaks, it's a long way to go to buy a spare part, so you need to be patient and understanding should facilities not be functioning quite as you might hope.

Camp Syncro Kunene River, Marienfluss ⊖ christinger @campsyncro.com. Recently taken over and renovated by a young Swiss couple, the four lovely riverside campsites have now been augmented by two rustic stone-and-thatch chalets, with outside braai site to cook on. A good place if the community campsite is full. Camping per person N$150 plus per vehicle N$50 (one-off payment), self-catering N$1700

Etaambura Lodge Onjuva, 25km north of Orupembe, in the direction of Marienfluss. Contact Kunene Conservancy Safaris ☎ 064 406136 or ☎ 081 149 7611. Pioneering joint venture between KCS and several Himba communities, this self-catering lodge (though you can pay to have your food cooked for you) boasts spectacular 360° views from five imaginatively designed tent-and-thatch chalets with sliding glass doors to maximize the views. En-suite bathrooms are carved into the marble outcrop. Donkey-heated water and solar power do the rest. Great main lodge made of rock gabions and domed thatch. Opportunities for informal learning about Himba life through organized activities. N$1900

House on the Hill Onjuva, 26km north of Orupembe ☎ 081 124 6826, ⊛ houseonthehillnam.com. Namibian artist working in tandem with the local conservancy has applied his artistic talents to transforming the old marble quarry manager's residence into three solar-powered self-catering units (one for four people, two for two). A good base for forays into Marienfluss or Hartmann's Valley. Great quirky stone-and-wire sculptures around the building. N$900

Marble Community Campsite Onjuva, 26km north

of Orupembe. Close to a disused marble quarry from which it takes its name, this spot is well organized, and has five delightful secluded campsites with private sink and food preparation surface plus braai site, as well as lovely stone ablutions blocks with solar-powered hot water, and when the freezer's working, cold beer is for sale – a real treat. Often full in high season, so get there early. Per person N$100

Okahirongo River Camp Kunene River, Marienfluss ☎ 061 237294, ⊛ okahirongolodge.com. Fairly new, stylish luxury tented chalets hosting up to 14 guests in style – solar-powered but without sacrificing comfort – lots of sofas and cushions to lounge on while watching the crocs in the Kunene doing much the same on the sandbanks, plus a fabulous pool and deck area offering yet more splendid views. Accessible by road or fly-in. N$10,410

Okarohombo Community Campsite Kunene River, Marienfluss ☎ 065 658993. Marienfluss Conservancy office. Five lovely spacious sandy sites under spreading ana trees by the Kunene. Good communal solar-powered hot showers and flush toilets, when working. Per person N$100

Serra Cafema Camp Kunene River, Hartmann's Valley ☎ (0)11 807 1800 (South Africa), ⊛ wilderness-safaris .com. Long-standing wilderness lodge undergoing major renovations at the time of writing, but due to reopen in mid-2017: formerly eight luxury wood-and-canvas thatched chalets amid lush riverine trees, where you can gaze across to Angola from your private deck. It stands in stark contrast to the arid surroundings, which you can explore on a guided quad bike excursion. Himba village

THE NAMIB'S MYSTERIOUS FAIRY CIRCLES

One of the Namib's many curious natural phenomena is that of **"fairy circles"**: from the air they appear like a giant polka-dot pattern across a vast sheet of scorched cloth, along the eastern fringes of the desert. A closer inspection reveals **discs of bare earth**, fringed with lush grasses, which are higher and healthier than the ones between the circles. Measuring between 2–20m in diameter, the larger circles have an average lifespan of between forty to sixty years, as they appear, mature – growing in some cases – and then fade.

To the Himba, they are simply the **footprints** of their deity, Mukuru; scientists, needless to say, have been looking for other explanations, though have so far failed to solve the puzzle. Over the years many **theories** have been put forward – from ostriches taking dust baths, to poisonous underground gases, rival toxic plants, not to mention the inevitable intervention by aliens – but most ideas have eventually been dismissed. The two most persistent explanations relate to sand termites and grasses competing for scarce natural resources. For a long time the **sand-termite** theory held sway, the notion that these busy subterranean insects were eating the roots of grasses and therefore killing them; with no remaining plants to suck up the water, it pools below the surface, allowing the termites to survive the dry season and the grasses on the periphery to thrive. But critics point out that, while termite presence is generally high in fairy circles, termites have not been found in *all* the circles. Moreover, the theory would not seem to explain the regular, almost honeycomb-like spacing of these circles, so clear from aerial surveys, nor the fact that these apparent carpets of bronze coins only occur in a very limited geographical range, in the arid transitional zones between grasslands and true desert.

What really threw the termite theory up into the air was the relatively recent realization among experts that fairy circles, which for years were thought to be unique to Namibia, also exist in the outback of **western Australia**, in similarly arid conditions, but without the number of termites. This would seem to lend greater weight to the notion of grasses in arid conditions "organizing" themselves to maximize scarce water and nutrients. While an even carpet of plants would be unsustainable in such conditions, the argument is that hardier grasses survive, sucking up the water, leaving their neighbours to die; the gap between the vegetation widens and the barren circle of sandy soil is then too hard to take seed, but rather acts as a repository for any moisture, like an oasis, which further nourishes the stronger and healthier plantlife encircling the bare earth. Further evidence that supports this reasoning lies in the fact that the circles seem to grow after dry years and shrink after wet ones. **Self-organization theory** – thanks to maths and computer modelling – has been shown to have explanatory potential for other natural phenomena, such as rock crystal growth, or birds' flocking movements, in which a seemingly unstructured and chaotic group can transform itself into an organized system without any centralized control. The bottom line, however, is that, while this might seem the most plausible theory at the moment, the mystery is far from being unequivocally solved.

6

visits and boat trips on the river also on offer, fortified by fine cuisine. Airstrip nearby for fly-ins, not included in the otherwise fully inclusive rates. N$25,140

Van Zyl's Pass Community Campsite 20km before the pass, near Otjitanda. Three shady sites set along a sandy riverbed, with private ablutions offering a basin and mirror, and donkey-fired hot water. Per person N$100

Puros

Heading south from Orupembe along the D3707 eventually brings you to the mixed Himba and Herero settlement of **PUROS**, some two and a half hours later. It boasts a magnificent setting at the confluence of the Goatum and Hoarusib rivers, surrounded by dark ripples of striated rock, offset by banks of pale sand. The small settlement is aptly named, being a corruption of the Otjiherero word "*omburu*", meaning "fountain". The impressive **Hoarusib River**, with its dramatic cliffs and gorges, has permanent springs that ensure pools of water exist year-round. They are fringed by mature vegetation, a magnet for an abundance of wildlife: desert-adapted elephant, giraffe, zebra and a host of varied antelope are regular visitors to these areas, in turn

6

SKELETON COAST FLY-IN SAFARIS

Hemmed in between the wild Atlantic and the rugged Hartmann Mountains, the remote northern section of the **Skeleton Coast National Park** – the **Wilderness Area** – is the stuff of National Geographic documentaries. Its few visitors are privileged to experience an immense, desolate beauty of unworldly landscapes: a scalloped sea of huge **"roaring" dunes** (sound waves thought to be produced by the friction of sand particles); the **moonscape** and **"clay castles"** – striking sand formations – of the Hoarusib River Valley; and the endless bleak **coastline** pounded by surf and sprinkled with bleached whalebones, rusting shipwrecks and scuttling ghost crabs.

In refreshing contrast stands the avian-rich riverine strip along the **western Kunene River** as it carves its way towards the coast, separating Namibia from Angola. **Fly-in safaris** to the region – the only way to access this isolated wilderness – are not focused on big game; they're about marvelling at the vast and varied desert scenery, seeking out smaller creatures and the extraordinary plants that have adapted to the unforgiving arid environment; and learning about indigenous people – from the Himba, who still inhabit some areas, to the early Khoisan beachcombers, whose ancient ruined shelters and rock art give clues to their way of life. That said, you're still likely to spot the odd loping hyena or black-backed jackal on the scrounge – especially near the Cape Frio seal colony – as well as the perennially hardy oryx, and, with luck, a herd of desert-adapted elephants. Visiting this region is not cheap, but the experience is unforgettable.

TOUR OPERATORS

Skeleton Coast Safaris ☎ 061 224248, ⓦ skeletoncoastsafaris.com. This operation is run by the members of the pioneering Schoemann family, who have been exploring the Skeleton Coast for over forty years, and whose knowledge and guiding skills are legendary. The classic four-day safari – by plane, Land Rover and on foot – flies out of Windhoek and spends a night in each of their three comfortable but basic camps (expect small domed tents, bucket showers and dining under the stars). Groups are of two–eight people. They also run tours that take in Etosha and the Namib round Sossusvlei. AI per person for the whole trip US$7335

Wilderness Safaris South Africa ☎ (0)11 807 1800,

ⓦ wilderness-safaris.com. If you want more luxurious, *Out of Africa*-style accommodation, a higher level of pampering and fine dining, then consider one of Wilderness Safaris' two remote, exclusive tented camps – only accessible by plane. Though both lie just outside the national park boundary, they are effectively "next door", set in similarly awe-inspiring scenery, and they both travel into the park itself. *Serra Cafema* is the more established camp, overlooking the Kunene, while the newer *Hoanib Skeleton Coast Camp* lies in the broad valley of the same name – a prime spot for spotting desert-adapted elephants and rhinos. AI (excluding flights) daily rates: *Cafema* N$25,140; *Hoanib* N$26,110

pursued by the less visible cheetah, hyena and leopard. Even the occasional desert-adapted lion frequents the riverbed. Birdwatchers have the chance to spot the likes of near-endemics such as Monteiro's hornbill, Carp's back tit, and Rüppell's korhaan, but the oasis pools sometimes attract more surprising avian visitors such as hamerkops and Egyptian geese.

This is an excellent area to explore for a couple of days, by engaging one of the trained English-speaking community guides who can take you to the permanent springs in the river, twenty minutes from the campsite, where you're likely to be rewarded by good wildlife sightings in the dry season. The Puros Traditional Village – a conservancy-managed Himba demonstration settlement – is within walking distance of the camp, though you'll need a guide to interpret and help you learn a little about their culture. Crafts are also for sale. Guides can be arranged at the campsite or the bush lodge (see opposite).

ARRIVAL AND DEPARTURE   PUROS

By car 4WD essential. From the south, the D3037 criss-crosses the Goatum River before taking you across the unworldly Giribes Plains to Sesfontein – around a 3hr drive

– where there is fuel (see p.202). From the north, the D3037 carries you the 100km from Orupembe; a straightforward drive, though the corrugations can be bothersome. Experienced 4WD travellers in convoy and with all the necessary gear prefer to take the spectacular

4WD trails down the Khumib and Hoarusib rivers, and even then only in the dry season.

INFORMATION AND ACTIVITIES

Information Enquiries about the area can be made at the campground or the bush lodge reception. Note that mobile phone coverage can be unreliable in this area; you may need to contact the Puros Conservancy Office (☎081 383 6811) on their satellite phone (☎870 762711719). Note that firewood can be purchased at the campground or bush lodge, but should be used sparingly as it's in short supply.

Activities These can be booked at the campground or the

bush lodge: half-day Himba village tour (N$175/person, including the N$50 village entry fee); half-day nature walk (N$175/person, for a group of 2–3); full-day excursion including some hiking (N$300/person – you'll need to take lunch for you and the guide); a half-day's game drive (in your vehicle) down the Puros Canyon in search of elephants (N$225/person, for a group of 2–3). Guiding fees for longer excursions to Marienfluss or Orupembe can also be negotiated.

ACCOMMODATION

Okahirongo Elephant Lodge ☎061 237294 or ☎081 127 4584, ⓦokahirongo.com. The slightly forbidding box-like structures ranged along the hillside belie distinctive, designer-chic interiors, painted in earthy tones to blend into the surroundings. The lodge is laden with expensive African artefacts, and stuffed full of sofas overflowing with cushions. Take in the astounding scenery while lolling in the infinity pool. Discounts for three-night stays. Most guests fly in (see opposite). DBB N$7500

Puros Bush Lodge 2km north of Puros ☎081 758 8461 or ☎870 762711720 (satellite phone). Inexpensive alternative to a night in a tent – but the campground is

nicer; six no-frills brick-and-thatch en-suite chalets, a few hundred metres from the camping, with glass windows, screen-netting but no fan. Outside braai facilities for cooking. N$700

★**Puros Community Campsite** 2km north of Puros ☎081 716 2066 (signal intermittent) or ☎081 383 6811 (Puros Conservancy Office), or contact the Puros Bush Lodge. An absolute treat, offering six secluded, shady, sandy sites (#2 is the most private) spread out among giant ana and camelthorn trees, on the banks of the Hoarusib River. Each has private toilet, hot shower, sink and braai site. Frequented by desert-adapted elephants – so don't leave food lying around. Per person N$110

6

The
northeast

JU|'HOANSI SAN MAN SETTING AN ANIMAL TRAP

The northeast

Namibia's vast size means that most first-time visitors fail to reach the country's northeast corner, encompassing the remote areas of Otjozondjupa, and the Kavango and Zambezi regions – which includes Namibia's idiosyncratic panhandle. In so doing, they miss out on a great deal: a chance to experience the Kalahari through the eyes of the Ju|'hoansi San, and to explore Khaudum, one of the country's most untamed national parks requiring good off-road skills and a sense of adventure; and a chance to immerse themselves in a lush subtropical environment. The five rivers – including the mighty Zambezi – are surrounded by a handful of small national parks, each promising abundant wildlife, including hippos, crocodiles and buffalo – the latter not in Namibia's other parks – unparalleled birdwatching, serene boat trips and glorious sunsets.

7

The vast area between Grootfontein and Rundu, to the east of the B8, is sparsely inhabited, home only to a couple of thousand of **Ju|'hoansi**, scattered across the flat sandveld of the **Kalahari**. Primarily they live in the Nyae-Nyae Conservancy, the 9000-square-kilometre area that was the former apartheid-designated Bushmanland, and is now part of the Otjozondjupa Region. Its isolated centre, Tsumkwe, sits at the end of the area's only road out by the Botswana border. If you're interested in learning more about **San culture**, both past and present, this is the place to do it; approached with sensitivity, it can be an informative and enriching experience.

Back on the B8, heading north, you enter **Kavango East**, though there's still little evidence of human habitation: eighty percent of the region's population live in the 10km strip by the Kavango River, which comes as a welcome relief after so many hours driving through arid landscapes. On a bluff above the river lies **Rundu**, the region's rapidly growing capital, and the gateway to what was previously known as the Caprivi Strip (see box, p.271), but which these days is shared between Kavango East and the Zambezi regions, and traversed by the Trans Zambezi Highway. The few visitors to Namibia who make it this far north, often consider this 500km sliver of land as a place to overnight between Etosha and Victoria Falls. Yet the region merits a much longer sojourn as it is unlike anywhere else in Namibia: verdant, humid and tropical, boasting mature forests, free-flowing rivers and swampland, home to large populations of elephant and buffalo and prolific birdlife.

Moving west to east from Rundu, well-equipped and experienced 4WD adventurers might divert southwards to undeveloped **Khaudum National Park**, where the sense of achievement from getting through the endless deep sand without incident should make up for any shortfall in animal sightings. For most, though, the first port of call is **Popa Falls Reserve**, a picturesque, if not spectacular, series of rapids

Highlights

❶ Visiting a Ju|'hoansi community
Approached with sensitivity and an open mind, a day or two in the company of the Ju|'hoansi San is an unforgettable learning experience. **See p.274**

❷ The Nyae-Nyae Pans in flood A rare sight – only following good rains – makes this experience all the more precious: delightful lilies and waterbirds in the Kalahari bush. **See p.275**

❸ Popa Falls More a series of rapids than a falling torrent of water, Popa Falls are nevertheless extremely picturesque. **See p.283**

❹ Encounters with elephants Wait for long enough at the oxbow lake in the Bwabwata National Park, and you'll be surrounded by herds of elephant. **See p.285**

❺ Relaxing in a riverside lodge Whether overlooking the floodplains of the Chobe or Kavango rivers, the reed-lined Kwando or the sweeping grandeur of the Zambezi, there are lodges to suit all budgets. **See p.287**

❻ Browsing markets and craft stalls
Displayed in roadside stalls, craft centres or town markets, you can find some first-rate crafts in this part of Namibia: from teak woodcarvings to ostrich-shell jewellery and basketry. **See p.289**

❼ Sunset cruise on the Zambezi An evening boat trip on any of the region's rivers is a treat, but a sunset cruise along the Zambezi is truly magical. **See p.292**

HIGHLIGHTS ARE MARKED ON THE MAPS ON P.270, P.284 & P.286

on the Kavango River, which forms the western boundary of the **Bwabwata National Park**, the region's largest and most diverse protected area, which extends right along the strip. Two sections are open to the public, giving access to wonderful wildlife-rich riverine environments: the **Mahango Core Area** and the **Kwando Core Area**, at the park's eastern limit. From here the Kwando River meanders south to the region's southernmost tip, providing opportunities for seeking out antelope and other large mammals and some colourful birds in **Mudumu and Nkasa Rupara national parks**.

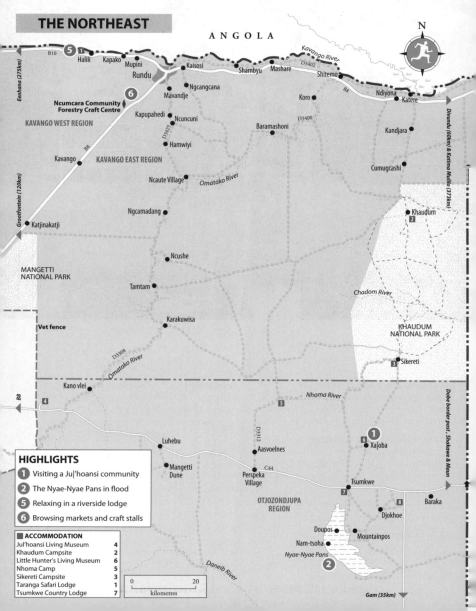

THE NORTHEAST

HIGHLIGHTS

1 Visiting a Ju|'hoansi community
2 The Nyae-Nyae Pans in flood
5 Relaxing in a riverside lodge
6 Browsing markets and craft stalls

ACCOMMODATION

Ju|'hoansi Living Museum	4
Khaudum Campsite	2
Little Hunter's Living Museum	6
Nhoma Camp	5
Sikereti Campsite	3
Taranga Safari Lodge	1
Tsumkwe Country Lodge	7

THE ORIGIN OF NAMIBIA'S PANHANDLE: THE CAPRIVI STRIP

The reason the anomalous **Zambezi Region** or **Caprivi Strip** belongs to Namibia goes back to a **colonial barter** in 1890, in which Germany persuaded Britain to accept the islands of Zanzibar and Heligoland (a small archipelago off northern Germany) in exchange for this sliver of land, which was then part of Bechuanaland (present-day Botswana). Keen to gain access to the Zambezi and create a riverine trade route that would connect with the Indian Ocean, the Germans seemingly overlooked the very substantial obstacle to such a plan: the Victoria Falls. This stumbling block, however, turned out to be irrelevant, since defeat in World War I meant the Germans had scarcely set foot in the area before they were forced to hand it over to **South Africa** – though not before naming the strip of land after the then German Chancellor, General Count Georg Leo von Caprivi di Caprara di Montecuccoli, which was mercifully shortened to Caprivi.

The strip's **strategic potential**, given its location at the confluence of five countries, repeatedly put it at the forefront of a succession of conflicts, and led to the development of the region's eventual capital, Katima Mulilo (see p.289), which soon became a garrison town. In 1964, in opposition to South Africa's apartheid policies, the Caprivi African National Union (CANU) – a movement pushing for Caprivi self-governance (see p.351) – joined forces with SWAPO to fight for Namibian independence with the proviso (so they say) that once it was secured, Caprivi could itself be **independent** – a deal that SWAPO vehemently denies. Discontent about alleged discrimination against Caprivians and repeated calls for Caprivi self-rule simmered throughout the independence struggle and beyond, though matters didn't boil over into full-scale **conflict** until 1999, when an attack on Katima by the **Caprivi Liberation Army** (CLA) – the military wing of the secessionist movement – provoked intervention by the security forces. Several deaths resulted, abuses were committed by both sides, and many civilians were forced to flee. In the end, 121 separatists were arrested and put on trial for treason – a trial that dragged on for around 12 years and which received much criticism from human rights groups. A verdict was finally reached at the end of 2015; the final tally was: 79 not guilty, 30 guilty, while 12 had died in custody. Most of those found guilty have appealed against their sentencing to the Supreme Court, while the Namibian state, in turn, intends to appeal against the acquittals, which is rather ironic given their lack of interest in pursuing similar crimes committed during the independence struggle.

In the meantime, Caprivi has controversially been renamed **Zambezi**, arguably part of the ongoing erasure of colonial names, though opponents of the name change argued that it was another attempt by SWAPO to undermine Caprivi identity and stifle any further secessionist ambitions.

The latter comprises Namibia's main wetland area, and it is here that the Kwando makes a ninety-degree turn eastwards, as the Linyanti, before heading into Botswana, where, as the Chobe River, it eventually flows into the Zambezi. Around 110km west of this confluence lies the bustling capital of the Zambezi Region, **Katima Mulilo**. After a browse round the town's outstanding craft centre, most visitors head eastwards to the secluded riverside lodges and camps tucked along the leafy banks of the Zambezi. Note that malaria is endemic in the region year-round and appropriate preventive measures should be taken (see p.59).

Brief history

Just as the riverine environments of the northern Kavango and Zambezi regions are distinct from the rest of Namibia, so too are the people. What's more, the area's major towns, Rundu and Katima, which were both founded by the South African administration after German colonial rule had been and gone, are both border towns with a more cosmopolitan-African vibe.

The 200,000 Namibians who identify themselves as Kavangans were originally river-dwellers – Kwangali, Mbunza, Shambyu, Gcriku and Mbukushu – Bantu-speaking groups that migrated down from East Africa, settling in the Upper Zambezi before moving southwards to the Kavango at different times between the sixteenth and eighteenth centuries. Scarcely touched by German colonial influence, they were more affected by the arrival of the Portuguese across the river, and then later, by the South Africans, who founded Rundu in 1936 as an administrative base for the Kavangos. At the frontline of SWAPO's lengthy struggle for independence over in southern Angola, Rundu had to accept an SADF base, which led to the town and surrounding villages suffering violence from both sides. This was followed by waves of Angolans – now a large percentage of the town's population – fleeing first from the Namibian conflict and later from their own civil war.

The majority of the people further east towards the Zambezi are **Lozi** and therefore culturally closer to Lozi populations in Zambia, Botswana and Zimbabwe than to most other Namibians. In fact, until the end of the nineteenth century, the area was known as Itenge, or Linyanti, and was part of the Lozi Kingdom of Barotseland, which covered a large chunk of present-day Zambia. The colonial wrangling that followed resulted in the curiously shaped 450km panhandle that stands out on maps of the region today (see box, p.271). More reminiscent of a guitar head than a kitchen utensil, its forested 200km "neck" is only 20km wide, squeezed between Botswana and Angola, while its "headstock" fans out into lush wetlands that border Botswana and Zambia and are within easy striking distance of Zimbabwe.

The northern Kalahari

Namibia's slice of the northern Kalahari is very different to the southern Kalahari east of Mariental and Keetmanshoop (see p.150): there, a series of linear red dunes ripples towards the border, receiving an average annual rainfall of less than 250mm, which results in shorter, scrubbier and sparser vegetation, typically grey camelthorn and shepherd's tree. In contrast, as you move up into central and northern areas of the semi-desert, the duneveld gives way to flatter, paler sandveld, with more savannah grassland and a greater coverage of acacia trees and shrubs. Even further northwards and eastwards, the increase in rainfall – albeit erratic and localized – is aided by a network of *omiramba* (water courses) and a smattering of pans to create a landscape of taller trees and a denser canopy. There are also more broad-leaved species, such as purplepod terminalia, wild teak, wild syringa, mopane or marula. While some visitors are here to tackle this inhospitable environment – usually in convoys of 4WD vehicles armed with GPS, satellite phones and all manner of equipment to get you out of a scrape – most come to interact with the semi-desert's most resilient inhabitants, the Ju|'hoansi San.

Along the C44

Seventy kilometres along the B8, just after the veterinary cordon fence, there's a sign off to the **Ju|'hoansi Living Museum**. The road then dips into the **Omatako Valley**, the region's main *omuramba*, which eventually wends its way northwards to the Kavango River. There is a community campground here, at the Kano junction; at the time of research it was in a state of disrepair, though it may have been renovated by the time you pass. Once the road has climbed back out of the valley, it's almost 90km before the signed turn-off to *Nhoma Camp* (see opposite), and Tsumkwe, another 40km beyond.

ACCOMMODATION   ALONG THE C44

Ju|'hoansi Living Museum 7km north of the C44, along the road to Grashoek, just after the veterinary fence ☏ 081 605 1297, ⊛ lcfn.info/juhoansi. This original living museum receives more visitors than the one at ||Xa||oba, north of Tsumkwe (see box, p.274), which can be a disadvantage if you coincide with a group from *Roy's Restcamp* (see p.188). It also offers a greater range of experiences, from a two-hour bush walk (N$150) to a three-day immersion (N$600). The simple community campground has three sites, each with individual bucket shower, long-drop toilet, fire-pit and tap. Camping per person N$50

Nhoma Camp 185km along the C44, then 40km north along the D3301 ❶ 081 273 4606, ⓦ tsumkwel.iway .na. An opportunity to spend time with members of the N‖hoq'ma community and learn about aspects of traditional culture and current challenges, mediated by Arno Oosthuysen, the camp owner, who has many years' experience with the community. Guests sleep in ten simple Meru-style tents, with partitioned or semi-partitioned bathrooms. Activities also include excursions into Khaudum National Park. Rates fully inclusive for a two-night package. Campers can book activities. Camping per person N$200, safari tents N$5750

Tsumkwe and around

After driving on autopilot along the C44, a seemingly interminable gravel road, for a full 220km, it's easy to drive right through **Tsumkwe** before you even realize you've arrived. You certainly expect the place to be more substantial than the glorified crossroads that it is – enhanced by a short stretch of asphalt – though possibly no less forlorn. It's a place where you do your business as fast as possible, then get out into the far more appealing surroundings. The main reason tourists trek all the way out here is to interact with the Ju|'hoansi (San), though for some it's a stopover on the way to Khaudum National Park. Yet there are also a couple of scenic attractions in the area, too.

The **Nyae-Nyae Conservancy Office**, which should be your first port of call (see p.276), is hidden behind a chain-link fence and a large tree on the right-hand side as you approach the crossroads, the ersatz village centre. Next to the office, **G!hunku Crafts** sells jewellery and artefacts from various settlements, and is worth supporting. Demand for Ju ostrich-shell jewellery is now so great that the conservancy has to import most of its ostrich shells from a farm in South Africa.

Despite having a fluctuating population of 500–800, Tsumkwe possesses a secondary school, which serves the 1500–2000 wider conservancy population, though few of the Ju|'hoansi complete their education. A couple of thinly stocked stores, a petrol station, a courthouse, police station, clinic, a handful of churches and shebeens, and a sprinkling of houses make up the rest of Tsumkwe.

Brief history

Though various San groups have been ranging over southern Africa for 20,000 years or more as nomadic hunter-gatherers (see p.341), over the last couple of centuries their traditional !nores, or hunting grounds, have gradually been eroded, and their lifestyles challenged. However, it was the establishment of Tsumkwe in 1959 by order of the South African apartheid Native Affairs Department that accelerated the process and forced a period of unprecedented change on the Ju|'hoansi, the effects of which are still felt today. A borehole was dug, a gravel road was built, and the Ju|'hoansi were invited to come in from the outlying areas to receive schooling, health care, agricultural training and food handouts. The formal establishment in 1970 of apartheid Bushmanland placed further restrictions on the Ju|'hoansi's land and lifestyles. In the late 1970s and well into the 1980s, as the Namibian War of Independence gathered momentum and the SADF established themselves in Tsumkwe, Ju|'hoansi men were

---

THE BOTSWANA BORDER AT DOBE

Fifty-two kilometres east of Tsumkwe, a small hut constitutes the **Dobe border post** (daily 7am–4.30pm) and since they only see around half a dozen vehicles a day, if that, you'll have their complete attention. After a quick anti-foot-and-mouth spray of the wheels, and maybe getting you to wipe your feet in disinfectant, you can head off towards Nonakeng, 135km away, though the nearest fuel is a lot further. The first 10km are slow going; thereafter it's now a decent enough gravel road.

employed as trackers. Catapulted fully into a cash economy, gripped in a stranglehold of dependency, the Ju|'hoansi became prey to jealousies regarding individual acquisition of wealth – so alien to their culture – exacerbated by the ready availability of alcohol, which often resulted in violence and damaged social relations. Tsumkwe – or Tjum!kui, as the Ju|'hoansi call it, became a rural slum, and has variously been referred to as the "place of death" or "place where problems follow one around".

With the establishment of a farmers' cooperative in the mid-1980s, and then the Nyae-Nyae Conservancy in 1998 (Namibia's first), prospects for the Ju|'hoansi began to look up, and many started to move back to their !nores. Though the wholesale hunter-gatherer lifestyle is now a thing of the past, most communities have members who still forage and hunt to some extent. This is now supplemented by small-scale livestock rearing and crop cultivation, encouraged by the conservancy, though the recent arrival of squatter Herero families, who have moved in from the south with their cattle, poses a new threat. Though the conservancy's biggest money-earner is trophy hunting, ethno- and safari-tourism, including visits by researcher and film crews, is on the increase, providing a steady trickle of cash.

7

Baobab trees

The area possesses some majestic **baobabs**, well worth seeking out, along the main road to the Botswana border, some 15km east of Tsumkwe, and to the south down the sandy track to |Gam. The largest baobab in the area for many years was the aptly, if unimaginatively, named Grootboom (Afrikaans for Big Tree). Though it has

---

VISITING A JU|'HOANSI COMMUNITY

There are several ways to visit a **Ju|'hoansi community** as an independent traveller. A major consideration is language. Within the Nyae-Nyae Conservancy, only three communities currently have English-speaking guides: at Doupos and Mountain Pos, around 8km and 12km south of Tsumkwe, respectively, as well as the *Little Hunter's Living Museum* in ||Xa||oba, 23km north of Tsumkwe (see p.276). The conservancy office can give you directions. In addition, the living museum near Grashoek, off the C44 by the veterinary fence (see p.272), was the first such set-up to be established in Namibia, in 2004, and so is used to receiving visitors. The living museums both have set prices for activities, given on their website, such as N$150 for a bushwalk, or N$200 for a whole four or more hours of mixed activities, which will generally be carried out in traditional animal skin clothing. Activities can include tracking, learning about medicinal plants, setting snares, hunting, making ostrich-shell jewellery, preparing food, storytelling and dancing. You'll get the most out of your visit by being willing to join in and by learning at least a couple of phrases in Ju|'hoan from your hosts. Each museum has a "demonstration village" with the kind of "beehive" grass-covered wooden domed huts the San constructed when they practised a nomadic lifestyle, though if you stay a night or two, you may also be invited to their modern settlement. Be prepared for jeans and T-shirts, and makeshift shelters from sheets of plastic, as well as clay bricks, or breezeblocks and empty Coca-Cola bottles. Each of the living museums has a few nicely located campsites with well-maintained long-drop toilets, a tap, bucket showers and a fireplace. For both these places, you need no prior reservation.

Alternatively, you can stay at *Nhoma Camp*, where the lodge owners have lived and worked among the **N||hoq'ma community** for many years, and the experience is organized much more around the rhythm of the Ju|'Hoansi's daily activities, rather than tourists picking and choosing what to do from a menu. There is no demonstration village and residents wear their normal everyday clothes.

In addition, several villages in the Nyae-Nyae conservancy have established community campsites – a couple under giant baobabs – though some have absolutely no facilities, not even a latrine. On arrival, you should ask permission to camp from one of the community elders. Traditionally the Ju|'Hoansi's non-hierarchical social structure does not entail a headman, though pressure from outsiders wanting to negotiate with leaders has, over time,

now keeled over, it's still impressive, with some parts seemingly still growing. Halboom (Hollow Tree), near the settlement of Djokhoe, is possibly even larger and is commonly visited on local tours. Having collapsed outwards, leaving an empty core, it resembles a shipwrecked galleon. Be careful if you clamber around, since snakes, such as deadly black mambas, may be hiding inside. North of Tsumkwe, on the way to Khaudum, is the so-called Dorsland baobab, which displays some Dorsland Trekker graffiti, carved into the bark in 1891 when they were en route to Angola (see box, p.187).

Aha Hills

Straddling the Botswana border, to the southeast of Tsumkwe, lie the **Aha Hills** – apparently named after the sound of the barking gecko. Though only rising modestly above the surrounding sandveld, these eroded remains of a dolomitic limestone and marble plateau, which formed some 700 million plus years ago, present an agreeable if tricky clamber, rewarded by some fine views. Easily accessible (by 4WD) from the Tsumkwe–|Gam road, they are best explored with a local guide.

7

Nyae-Nyae Pans

A large, interconnected system of saline pans and water, the **Nyae-Nyae Pans** form a large crescent shape that stretches southwards from around 15km south of Tsumkwe. When flooded, they transform into Edenic wetlands – some vegetated, others not – that draw thousands of birds, notably Namibia's largest concentration of wattled

---

pushed some into these leadership positions. Establish what the camping rate is in advance (usually N$60–80/person). Note that wild camping is forbidden. Many of these settlements (which may only consist of around 20–25 people) with campsites are also beginning to invite tourists to join in foraging, hunting, cooking or craft-making activities. Women do the foraging, whereas men hunt. There may not, however, be anyone in the village who speaks English, so unless you have some Afrikaans, which some of the older Ju|'hoansi can speak, you'll be reduced to sign language, though you could make enquires about engaging an interpreter at the conservancy office in Tsumkwe in advance. The conservancy has given the villages general guidelines about payment, which generally relates to fees for groups: N$1000 for a day's activities, N$750 for a half-day.

When **camping** at a community site, make sure you take all rubbish away with you. You should also bring sufficient water, and preferably firewood, with you, as they may not be available, or cook on gas. Where there is a tap, be sparing with the water, and if wood is not available for purchase, you should not collect it from their precious supply. Alcohol is another sensitive issue; be discreet if you're having a beer and do not drink in the presence of your hosts, as alcohol dependency is a problem in many Ju|'hoansi communities. All services and activities currently need to be paid for in cash; that said, bringing some food to share with your hosts, such as nuts, dried or fresh fruit, is welcome. Sweets are not helpful, given the lack of dental care available, though you'll find sugar, tea and tobacco are common purchases in the general store. Excessive tipping is also ill-advised as it disturbs the economic equilibrium within and among communities, creating jealousies and raising expectations that subsequent visitors may not be able to fulfil. Photography is another delicate topic; if you want to take photographs, make sure you ask about the etiquette before you bring out your camera.

A visit to almost any community almost always concludes with an invitation to purchase some **crafts**; these usually have labels with fair, set prices; haggling is not customary. Choose from exquisitely made ostrich-shell necklaces and bracelets, as well as bows, quivers and arrows, small leather pouches decorated with more shells and, best of all, love bows – these miniature blunt arrows are traditionally fired at a young woman's buttocks by an aspiring suitor, and she indicates her response either by picking up the arrow and clasping it to her bosom, or letting it lie in the dust.

cranes and a breeding colony of slaty egrets, but also a host of stilts, rails, crakes, ruffs, grebes, sandpipers and, in exceptional years, flamingos. As the pans start to dry up, and other water sources have already disappeared, elephants, various antelope and other mammals come here to drink.

ARRIVAL AND GETTING AROUND   TSUMKWE

By car To reach Tsumkwe, you turn off the B8, 50km north of Grootfontein; it's then a further 220km along a gravel road. In the dry season it is manageable in a normal saloon car, though there are one or two sandier patches further east. However, once in Tsumkwe, if you intend to visit any of the villages, you will need a 4WD and sand-driving experience to get around. It's a good idea to travel in more than one vehicle, especially in the rainy season, when the deep sand becomes mud, and some roads become impassable. Note that, although there is a petrol station here, it occasionally lacks fuel, and even when available, it is limited to old diesel and leaded petrol.

INFORMATION

Nyae-Nyae Conservancy Office C44 just before the crossroads on the right-hand side ☎ 067 244011. Though it is a community development office, not a tourist office, the staff are very helpful, and can advise you on where to go, and how you might engage a guide, assuming you have not organized anything in advance (see box, p.274). What's more, they will want you to pay your N$30/day conservancy visitors' fee. Mon–Fri 8am–5pm.

ACCOMMODATION

★**Little Hunter's Living Museum** ||Xa||oba, 23km north of Tsumkwe ☎ 081 340 2112, ⊕ lcfn.info /hunters. The best option, as there are fewer groups and everything is well organized and run by the community, with minimal outside interference. The camping facilities are well maintained, and the campsite, a few hundred metres from their village, an idyllic spot. Camping per person N$50

Tsumkwe Country Lodge 1.5km south of the crossroads in Tsumkwe ☎ 067 240901, ⊕ tsumkwe -lodge.com. Unless you're heading out to stay at one of the communities, this is the only place to bed down. Enclosed by an unconvincing low stone wall, ostensibly aimed at keeping elephant out, the lodge comprises 21 simple, small safari tents with chipboard panelling; it's supposedly a training institution for the local Ju|'hoansi community (only a few of whom now work there). The main dining lapa is dark and uninspiring, though the staff try hard to enliven the place. Six campsites, each with light, power point, BBQ and grill, and shared ablutions. Offers expensive village visits (N$1700/person) – though it's unclear how much of the money the village receives – and excursions to Khaudum, or to the pans and baobabs. Camping per person N$130, safari tent (B&B) N$1188

Khaudum National Park

65km north of Tsumkwe and 44km south of Katere on the B8 • Sunrise to sunset • N$40/person and N$10/vehicle

A wild, unruly reserve, undeveloped for tourism, **Khaudum National Park** is probably the least frequented of Namibia's protected areas – outside the Skeleton Coast Wilderness Area – visited more by elephants than people; just the place if you want a real wilderness adventure. Clinging to the Botswana border, this 3,842-square-kilometre expanse of Kalahari sandveld is, for the most part, a dense tangle of tree and shrub savannah, streaked with *omiramba*. These life-giving sandy valleys generally run west to east across the park, feeding into the Okavango in Botswana. It is along the two main *omiramba* that you've the best chance of seeing wildlife, from late August to October – once water has dried up in the clay pans and before the rains have started. There are twelve artificial waterholes and two natural springs, many of which have hides, where you can wait in safety for the animals to show up.

Hosting a wide variety of trees, in addition to the ubiquitous camelthorn and other acacias, Khaudum boasts substantial teak forests, patches of evergreen false mopane, leadwood, wild syringa and the occasional unmistakeable baobab. The thickness of the vegetation, however, makes wildlife-viewing tricky, though the occasional grassy clearing can be particularly rewarding as huge numbers of large mammals – including elephant (with a reputation for aggression) but also the less common roan antelope, eland and tsessebe – inhabit the area. Khaudum is also rich in predators, with plenty of leopard, lion and even wild dogs, though catching sight of them is a wholly different matter.

Birdlife is similarly prolific, with over 320 species: look out for colourful racket-tailed rollers, the russet belly of the African hobby falcon or the extraordinary turkey-size ground hornbill; further brightly coloured delights arrive in summer (Nov–April), including African golden orioles and carmine and blue-cheeked bee-eaters.

Progress through the park is glacially slow, as you have to force your way through deep sand the whole way – or mud if it has rained – probably having to clear away trees that have blown down or been uprooted by elephant. Khaudum is also heavy on fuel. Only if you are experienced at driving in these conditions, and you are fully armed with a GPS (and preferably a *Tracks 4 Africa* map and satellite phone) and are travelling in convoy with plenty of fuel, water and food, should you consider driving here. If all the above seems like too much work, or beyond your skills level or comfort zone, consider visiting on an excursion from *Nhoma Camp* or *Tsumkwe Country Lodge* (see p.273 & opposite).

7

ARRIVAL AND INFORMATION   KHAUDUM NATIONAL PARK

By car There are two entrances to the park, only accessible by 4WD: in the south follow the D3315 65km from Tsumkwe; in the north, turn off the B8 at Katere (there's a sign), and follow the track 44km southwards.

Information Given the wild nature of Khaudum, it's a good idea to contact MET in advance to check on conditions: the regional office (☎ 067 244017), or the park warden in Tsumkwe (☎ 067 244017). Only 4WD vehicles in

a convoy of at least two vehicles are allowed into the park. Wardens will also check that you have food for at least three days per person, and 100 litres of water, and plenty of fuel – 120 litres minimum – before letting you proceed. Since you are not permitted to collect firewood in Khaudum, you should bring any wood with you. You'll also need the skills and the tools to carry out repairs on your vehicles, should disaster strike.

ACCOMMODATION

There are currently two campgrounds in the park, one of which is now managed by a private company (also in the process of building a lodge) in tandem with two conservancies; the other still remains under MET management, and is in a state of disrepair.

Khaudum Campsite Namibia Exclusive ☎ 081 100 6677, ✉ reservations@khaudumcamping.com, ⓦ namibia-exclusive.com.na. Six sites in a nice spot by an *omuramba*, with wooden shaded tables, braai site and private ablutions with warm water, 14km south of the park's northern

entrance. Per person N$330 plus per vehicle N$110

Sikereti Campsite 12km north of the southern park entrance; contact the Sikereti Camp warden ☎ 066 255403. Six free pitches at the south end of the park, in need of repair, with a long-drop toilet and (intermittent) water.

The road from Grootfontein to Rundu

There's little joy to be had from what is effectively a tedious 258km slog along the B8 from Grootfontein to Rundu, where even a stop at the veterinary fence checkpoint, at roughly the halfway point, provides welcome relief. Shortly afterwards, to the east, lies the entrance to **Mangetti National Park** (daily 6am–6pm), which abuts the main road, and sounds much grander than it is. A joint government-community venture, the reserve, which is still used for trophy hunting, was only elevated to national park status in 2014, and needs more infrastructural development before it holds any real appeal. Although it contains over 400 eland and 200 wildebeest, as well as sable antelope and three waterholes, the bush is exceedingly dense, the sand is deep and the tracks are unmarked, so the chances of seeing anything are slim, whereas the chances of getting lost are high.

Along the B8, and with increasing regularity once you near the Kavangan capital, you'll see **woodcarvings** displayed along the roadside. The Kavangans have a reputation for high-quality furniture making and woodcraft, with wild teak, or kiaat, the favoured material, usually taken from sustainably managed community forests in the region. Around 28km south of Rundu, look out for the Ncumcara Community Forestry Craft Centre.

Rundu and around

Sprawling along a bluff above the Kavango River, subtropical **RUNDU**'s rapidly expanding population – an estimated eighty thousand – has doubled over the last fifteen years. With the Trans Caprivi Highway speeding east to Zambia, and improving links with Angola, the town is developing as a commercial and transport hub, prompting the municipal website to declare optimistically that it is "much more than a refuelling stop". Most tourists, however, have yet to be convinced, rarely spending more than a few hours, or a night, here en route to somewhere else. Yet outside the town, along the river, there are several relatively inexpensive lodges where you can unwind for a couple of days, though the setting and wildlife are not as spectacular as that offered by some accommodation further east. Their main appeal is the chance get on the water in a boat, watching the birds flit along the riverbank and soaking up the glorious sunsets. Take note, though, that at the height of the dry season (Sept–Nov), there's rarely enough water in the river to float a rubber duck, never mind a motorboat.

Rundu itself has little in the way of tourist sights, and is trying hard to shrug off its frontier-town feel: hawkers have been banned from flogging their wares along the pavements – though some are defiantly resisting the "clean-up" – and a fairly swanky new shopping mall, with the predictable South African chain stores, has now replaced the older shops on the main street.

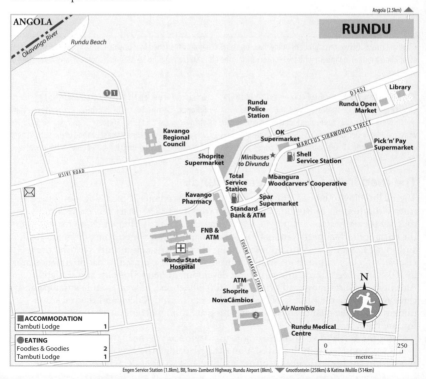

For more local flavour, wander round the **open market**, laden with fruit and vegetables, on Usivi Road. Or call in at the **Mbangura Woodcarvers Cooperative**, next door to the *Spar* supermarket – the Kavango inhabitants of the region are renowned for their woodcarving and here you can see artisans at work. Down at the river, **Rundu Beach** is another community focal point, where folk wash, play in the water, and party to loud music on the sand.

ARRIVAL AND DEPARTURE
RUNDU

By car There's easy access along the tarred B8, 250km northeast of Grootfontein, and 510km west of Katima Mulilo.

By bus Daily minibus services run to Oshakati (N$210), Otjiwarongo (N$190), Katima Mulilo (N$230) and Windhoek (N$250) from the Engen station at the junction of the B8 and the main road into town. Intercape Mainliner (🖥 intercape.co.za) buses also call in at the Engen station on the edge of town on their way to Victoria Falls from Windhoek (Mon, Wed & Fri), and back

from Victoria Falls to Windhoek (Wed, Fri & Sun). The office at the Engen station (Mon–Fri 8am–5pm; ☏ 081 150 8650) sells tickets. Minibuses to Divundu (N$120) leave from beside the *OK* supermarket in the centre of town.

By plane Air Namibia flies between Eros Airport, Windhoek, and Rundu Airport three times a week, sometimes via Katima (Wed, Fri & Sun; 1hr 5min). The Air Namibia office is on Eugene Karakura St (☏ 066 255854; Mon–Fri 8am–5pm).

ACCOMMODATION

IN TOWN

★Tambuti Lodge Above Rundu Beach ☏ 066 255711, 🖥 tambuti.com.na. This delightful lodge, which aims to maintain a low carbon footprint and boasts an excellent restaurant (see p.280), is set on a slope above the river, offering eight light, well-equipped bungalows (a/c, minibar, tea- and coffee-making facilities) sprinkled round a lush tropical garden. Numbers 1 and 8 have wonderful freestanding baths as well as showers. Breakfast is served on a terrace overlooking the river and canoe rental is available. The only downside is the loud music and partying that takes place during holiday periods down at Rundu Beach. B&B <u>N$900</u>

OUT OF TOWN

★Hakusembe Lodge Off the B8, 10km west of Rundu, 5km down a dirt road ☏ 081 886 5788 (lodge) or ☏ 061 427200 (reservations), 🖥 gondwana -collection.com; map p.284. Twenty immaculate African-themed chalets are spread around well-tended, tree-filled grounds that attract abundant birdlife. Though all the same price, the more spacious riverside stone chalets (numbers 2–6) are the most desirable: the older wooden chalets, though completely refurbished, are slightly smaller. Two lovely family-size villas are also available, as well as a rather faded but romantic floating honeymoon chalet. The food is excellent, and service friendly and efficient. The morning coffee brought to

MBUNZA AND MAFWE LIVING MUSEUMS

Two active "living museum" communities (see box, p.56) give insight into some of the past and present practices of Kavango and Mafwe cultures respectively. On the shores of Lake Samsitu, the **Mbunza Living Museum** (daily 8am–5pm; 🖥 lcfn.info/mbunza) offers tours of varying lengths, allowing you to learn about and experience traditional fishing and agricultural techniques, and a whole host of skills, from basketry and mat-weaving to drum-making. Indeed, if crafts are your main interest, you can undertake a craft workshop and focus on making an item to take away with you. The village is located 14km west of Rundu, signposted off the road to *Hakusembe Lodge* (see above).

The **Mafwe Living Museum** (daily 8am–5pm; 🖥 lcfn.info/mafwe), located on a hillside overlooking the scenic Kwando River, offers a similar interactive programme: you can learn how to use an animal trap or weave a fishing net, or go on a bushwalk. The village is signposted north off the B8 just west of Kongola, and is located 19km along the D3509, close to where the Namibian, Angolan and Zambian borders converge.

Tours for both communities cost from N$150/person for a 1hr 30min programme, but you'll get more out of the experience by committing to the full-day programme (actually only four hours) for N$280. You'll also find a range of well-made crafts for sale at both locations.

7

THE BORDER WITH ANGOLA

There is a very makeshift **border crossing into Angola** at the eastern end of Rundu, though the traffic is mainly the other way, with Angolans coming to the Namibian town to shop. To get to the border, take the signed turn-off to *Sarasungu River Lodge* and the 2.5km sandy road will take you to the riverbank, where a couple of tents serve as customs and immigration. There's a passenger ferry (N$10) across the river, as well as a more infrequent car ferry (N$800). While it's an enticing prospect to cross over for the day, you'd still need a visa, which can be a lengthy, frustrating and pricey process lasting several days; the best place to start is at the Angolan Consulate in Rundu (Mon–Fri 9am–3pm; ☎067 255782). There is also a consulate in Oshakati, in Dr Agosthinho Neto St, Oshakati West (Mon–Fri 9am–3pm; ☎065 5221798). Getting a visa for Angola at the embassy in Windhoek is very difficult.

your private porch is a nice touch. Fishing trips and morning or sundowner birdwatching boat cruises are on offer too. B&B N$2850

Kaisosi River Lodge 7km east of Rundu ☎066 267125, ⌨kaisosiriverlodge.com; map p.284. This pleasant lodge set in verdant surroundings has more of a restcamp feel – though with added peacocks and sheep. Camping is good value, if not especially private, on grassy pitches with private ablution blocks and braai sites; the comfortable, modern self-catering units and chalets overlooking the river have a/c and DStv. Champagne breakfast boat cruises are organized for N$210/person. Camping per person N$115, chalets (B&B) N$1080

Mukuku Restcamp 60km east of Rundu on the Kavango River ☎081 245 6633, ⌨facebook.com/mukukucamp; map p.284. Overlooking the Kavango and with bags of shade, this delightful low-key fishing camp – though open to all – has an intimate but mellow vibe. It comprises a collection of small brick or (nicer) all-wood self-catering cabins with a simple but appealing lounge-bar. There is also a pool and a handful of very pleasant grassy campsites. Camping per person N$100, chalets N$900

N'kwazi Lodge 21km east of Rundu on the Kavango River ☎081 242 4897, ⌨nkwazilodge.com; map p.284. A very relaxed, no-frills family-run place committed to local community development. Dark, cool, thatched stone-and-wood chalets fronted with mosquito netting have twin beds and bathroom separated by a saloon door. The sunken lounge-dining area is also dark – cosy round a fire at night in winter, but rather gloomy

at other times – and serves tasty home cooking. The grassy campground has abundant shade and shared ablutions, with some sites more private than others. Restaurant meals can be booked (dinner buffet N$260). Boat trips and guided village tours on offer. Camping per person N$92, chalets (B&B) N$1240

Samsitu Camping Off the B8, 10km west of Rundu, 5km down a dirt road ☎066 257023; map p.284. Also known as "Andy's place", this spot shares the same access road as *Hakusembe Lodge* (bear left at the lodge security gate). It comprises five camping pitches right on the water's edge with a riverside bar and new pool. Note that, while it can be a lovely, chilled spot if you stay in late November and December, you may find yourself partying as it is also used by partying day visitors at weekends, and is popular for year-end functions in Nov and Dec. Boat trips N$190. Per person N$150

Taranga Safari Lodge Halili village, 35km west of Rundu along the B10 ☎066 257236, ⌨taranganamibia.com; map p.270. Lovely setting on a bend in the Kavango, overlooking wetlands that are brimming with birdlife, this stylish tented lodge has eight indulgent tents, set high on stilts, embellished with cream drapes, cooled with fans, and each with fridge and tea and coffee making facilities. Camping too is superior: mature riverine trees ensure constant shade and seclusion for eight grassy sites. The pontoon bar is the perfect spot for a sundowner, and when there's sufficient water you can glide up and down from dawn to dusk, watching the birds and the local lads fishing. Camping per person N$250, tented chalet (DBB) N$3000

EATING

Foodies & Goodies Eugene Kakuru St ☎066 255075. This no-frills hole-in-the-wall joint fits the bill for a quick, inexpensive bite to eat: from breakfasts to a decent cup of mid-morning coffee, rolls and burgers, and changing lunch specials such as curried chicken and rice (N$40). Mon–Fri 7.30am–4pm, Sat

until 1.30pm.

★**Tambuti Lodge** Above Rundu Beach ☎066 255711, ⌨tambuti.com.na. A decent steak and chips can be had here, but you'd be missing out on what this place is about: traditional African cuisine using local produce (most mains N$70–120). The menu offers detailed descriptions of the

dishes' ingredients, origins and nutritional value. Choose from *maafe* (chicken stew in groundnut sauce) with cassava or sorghum and wild spinach, or crocodile or oryx steak, washed down with sorghum beer or hibiscus flower juice, and finish off with marula nut ice cream or mousse. It's a culinary experience not to be missed, but order your meal in advance, and be prepared to wait. Daily noon–9pm.

Between Rundu and Popa Falls

From Rundu, the B8 speeds east 200km to the sizeable village of **Divundu**, which marks the western gateway to Namibia's panhandle. Here, the Kavango River sweeps southwards, tumbling over Popa Falls before heading into the delta in Botswana. The road too divides: the D3430 peels off and shadows the river 32km, passing signs to various lodges and camps, before cutting through a section of the Bwabwata National Park (see p.285) to the Botswana border at Mohembo. Meanwhile, the B8 continues it trajectory, crossing the Kavango, past a police checkpoint, into the narrow corridor that ultimately leads to Katima Mulilo.

As the only place to fill up with fuel and stock up with food for a couple of hundred kilometres in either direction, the Divundu 24-hour Engen service station and adjacent supermarket (Mon–Sat 7am–7pm, Sun 9am–6pm; ☏ 066 259048) and take-away, just west of the junction, are a constant hive of activity. There's even a post office, and the Intercape Mainliner bus stops here. Lodges in the Popa Falls area will provide a transfer (at extra cost) if necessary.

Parallel to the B8, and much closer to the river, the gravel D3403 provides a more interesting but much slower drive between Rundu and Divundu, meandering through a stream of fairly impoverished villages, which bore the brunt of the Angolan civil war spilling over into northern Namibia over a number of years. Subsistence farmers, they live off a mix of livestock and crop farming as well as fishing. The bright blue and red structures resembling oversize post boxes that you'll see along the way are new VIP (ventilated, improved, pit) latrines – part of a government plan to improve sanitation, and provide employment in their installation. Places of mild historical interest en route include the old Catholic mission stations of Nyangana and Andara, in villages of the same name, 100km and 170km east of Rundu, respectively. They can be visited from a couple of the pleasant lodges and camps sprinkled along this stretch of the Kavango. In contrast to the camps round Popa Falls, the only large animals you'll see here are grazing cattle, but the prolific birdlife and relaxing scenery more than compensate.

ACCOMMODATION   BETWEEN RUNDU AND POPA FALLS

★**Mobolo Lodge & Campsite** 33km west of Divundu, signed north off the B8 to Shadikongoro ☏ 081 230 3281, ⓦ mobolo-lodge.com; map p.284. Four tastefully designed, well-equipped, and spotlessly maintained self-catering stone-and-thatch chalets in a scenic spot overlooking an island in the Kavango. Plus inside and outside showers and cooking areas and lovely wooden decks, where a splendid breakfast (N$120) can be served if you fancy being pampered. Six wonderful campsites, set amid immaculate grounds. Offers village visits, game drives or river trips. No credit cards or wi-fi. Reduction for two nights or more. Camping per person N$100, chalets N$1100

★**RiverDance Lodge** 31km west of Divundu, signed north off the B8 to Shadikongoro ☏ 066 258401 or ☏ 081 366 9775, ⓦ riverdancelodge.com.na; map p.284. Classy lodge overlooking the Kavango, with generous use of wood and glass in five cosy, romantic cabins. Lots of private and communal deck areas, to recline and read a book, or watch the river. A telescope for birdwatching too. Four fabulous shady campsites on grassy pitches along a bluff surveying the river, with glorious private ablutions, braai site, but no grill. Camping per person N$150, chalets (DBB) N$2310

Shamvura Camp 110km east of Rundu, signposted north up the D3413 ☏ 066 264007, ⓦ shamvura.com; map p.284. Popular with birders (owner Mark is a renowned ornithologist), this no-frills place offers a great nature-lovers' bush-camping experience (with your own or made-up tents), with secluded pitches offering private or shared facilities in mature woodland. Though the tents don't offer river views, there's a great observation deck overlooking the Angolan floodplains. Small boat rental N$440/hour. B&B or DBB rates also available. Camping per person N$150, safari tents N$940, cottage N$1140

Popa Falls Reserve

West bank of the Kavango River, 5km south of Divundu • Sunrise to sunset • N$20; free if you're staying at Popa Falls Resort

If you've come from Victoria Falls, or even Epupa in northwest Namibia, you're likely to be underwhelmed by the **Popa Falls Reserve** – essentially a series of rapids on the Kavango River that gush over quartzite rocks and scurry their way round banks of reeds and papyrus. Moreover, the reserve is small: it can be explored in under half an hour on foot via raised wooden walkways and viewpoints, unless you book yourself on a river cruise. For all that, Popa Falls is a scenic spot, where the cascading water stretches almost 1km across at its widest, and is set in lush riverine forest frequented by hippos, crocs (see box below) and a host of water birds. It is also a convenient place to break the journey between Rundu and Katima Mulilo, and a popular stopover for travellers heading to or from the Okavango Delta in Botswana. The varied accommodation in and around the falls also makes the area a good base for exploring the nearby, easily accessible Mahango section of the Bwabwata National Park (see p.285).

7

ARRIVAL AND DEPARTURE

By car At Divundu (approximately 200km east of Rundu, and 310km west of Katima Mulilo) take the D3403 southeast off the B8 towards the Botswana border. The reserve lies 5km along this road. There is a fuel station at Divundu.

By bus Minibuses run between Rundu (from the Engen garage) and Divundu (around N$120); transport between Rundu and Katima can also drop you off. After that you'll need to hitch, though some of the lodgings offer transfers.

ACCOMMODATION

The only accommodation inside the Popa Falls Reserve is operated by NWR (ⓦ nwr.com.na). However, there are several lodges and campgrounds close to the reserve, further south along the bank of the Kavango River. All offer two-hour sunset river cruises for around N$200–300/person and guided drives into Bwabwata National Park for around N$450–500/person. Other activities include *mokoro* and fishing trips, or visits to a local village.

Ndhovu Lodge 20km south of Divundu along the D3403 towards the Botswana border ⓞ 061 224712, ⓦ ndhovu.com; map p.284. The location here is the big draw, offering the best views on this stretch of the river, right across into the national park, where in the dry season the wildlife viewing can be superlative. The 2hr boat trips (N$260) are definitely worth doing. The camp itself is simple but pleasing, with ten no-frills Meru-style safari tents with shower cubicles, toilet and shady private decks overlooking the water. The large observation deck at the main lodge allows you to keep an eye on the nearby hippo pool while sipping your sundowner, but communal dining (set menu) takes place in a rather gloomy lapa. The one secluded camping pitch is a treat – pre-booking is essential. Also offers houseboat safaris. Camping per person N$160, safari tents (DBB) N$2660

★**Ngepi Camp** 4km from signed turn-off, 10km south of Divundu on the D3403 ⓞ 066 259903, ⓦ ngepi.com; map p.284. With its trademark quirky open-air bathrooms, this legendary backpacker and overlander stopover with sound eco-credentials (all

---

BEWARE OF THE HIPPOS AND CROCS

Hippos and crocs annually vie for the dubious distinction of being the animal responsible for the largest number of deaths in Africa (the mosquito aside). The bottom line is that both are very dangerous, and are plentiful in the rivers and wetlands of the Zambezi Region. In particular, **hippos** wander freely through many camps at night. Though herbivores, they can be particularly aggressive both in the water and on land when they come out to graze, usually at night. If you happen to encounter one, make sure you are not between them and water. Males on average weigh in at 1.5 tonnes, and they can reach speeds of almost 30kph, so don't try to outrun one. Nile **crocodiles**, on the other hand, are carnivores and see humans as legitimate food. Remain vigilant when walking along riverbanks, giving areas of long grass a wide berth.

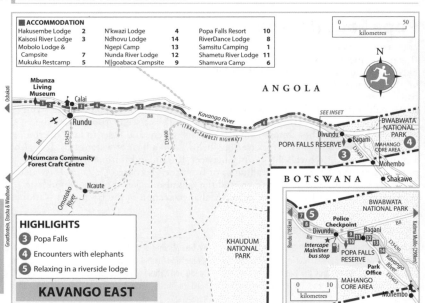

ACCOMMODATION

Hakusembe Lodge	2	N'kwazi Lodge	4	Popa Falls Resort	10
Kaisosi River Lodge	3	Ndhovu Lodge	14	RiverDance Lodge	8
Mobolo Lodge &		Ngepi Camp	13	Samsitu Camping	1
Campsite	7	Nunda River Lodge	12	Shametu River Lodge	11
Mukuku Restcamp	5	N||goabaca Campsite	9	Shamvura Camp	6

HIGHLIGHTS

3 Popa Falls
4 Encounters with elephants
5 Relaxing in a riverside lodge

KAVANGO EAST

solar-powered) actually caters for all sorts of visitors, offering semi-open rustic accommodation that gets you close to nature. The grassy, well-equipped riverside campsites are lovely, and while only two treehouses are actually up trees, the others incorporate the woodland landscape into their design. Thatched bush huts (lacking a river view) are also available. Decent home cooking is available at the bar-restaurant, and there are bags of activities on offer. The occasional generator noise from the park wardens across the river is the only downside, audible from the more southerly accommodation. Camping per person N$150, bush huts (B&B) N$1660, treehouses (B&B) N$1900

N\|\|goabaca Campsite 4km down a sandy track signposted off the D8, 800m east of the bridge ☏ 081 730 7000 or ☏ 081 434 6407; map above. This campground, now a joint community–private venture run by Khwe San, offers four secluded riverside pitches with platforms affording good views across the top section of the falls. Each has private, rustic, semi-open ablutions, with donkey-powered hot water, plus a thatched shelter with sink and food preparation area. There's no electricity and the braai pits are a bit makeshift in some cases, but it's a top spot to camp, and down where the new bar area's being developed you get the best view of the falls in the whole area. Entry to viewpoint per person N$20, camping per person N$120

Nunda River Lodge 9km south of Divundu along the D3403 ☏ 066 259093 or ☏ 081 310 1730, ⓦ nundaonline.com; map above. Possessing a more

manicured feel – thanks in part to the hippos that "mow" the grass at night – than its neighbours, this classic thatched lodge has a comfortably furnished main building and dining area, plus a nice pool. For accommodation choose from chalets (pay the extra N$50 for a slightly larger one on the riverfront), a handful of slightly worn-looking Meru-style tents (avoid numbers 1 and 2, which are close to the kitchen), and some delightfully shady pitches – some on the river – with superior ablution blocks. Camping per person N$120, safari tents (B&B) N$1246, chalets (B&B) N$1424

Popa Falls Resort 5km south of Divundu, down the D3403 ☏ 061 2857200 (Windhoek) or ☏ 064 402172 (Swakopmund), ⓦ nwr.com.na; map above. This recently refurbished resort offers very smart river chalets with chic modern furnishings; large windows open onto a private deck overlooking riverine forest (numbers 5 and 10 offer the best views). To gaze at the falls book one of the four larger luxury units, with vast windows that allow you to fully appreciate the views (opt for Elephant or Rhino). The campground lies at the back of the chalets, and though it has a superior ablution block, the rocky pitches currently lack privacy and shade. The pleasantly situated restaurant is decent enough, but the sundowner bar deck, which offers the best view of the falls, steals the show, though there's often nobody there to serve you. River cruise (N$275) and game drives available (N$330). Camping per person N$150, chalets (B&B) N$2860

THE KAVANGO–ZAMBEZI TRANSFRONTIER CONSERVATION AREA

The recently formed **Kavango-Zambezi Transfrontier Conservation Area** is now the world's largest transboundary reserve, encompassing the Zambezi and Kavango river basins, and spanning **five countries**, namely Angola, Botswana, Namibia. Zambia and Zimbabwe. Incorporating around 36 **protected areas**, including the Okavango Delta, Chobe National Park and Victoria Falls, it aims to open up traditional **wildlife migration routes**. Many fences have already been taken down, allowing the 250,000–300,000 elephants in the region, for example, to wander freely – all the more reason for taking care at dawn and dusk when driving along the Trans Caprivi Highway. Through improved and regionally coordinated conservation efforts and greater community engagement, it is hoped that communities will derive greater benefit from the anticipated increase in tourism opportunities. In the meantime, however, there remain tensions between conservationists and some villages, which are losing increasing numbers of inadequately protected livestock, prompting them to kill the predators responsible (see p.364).

7

Shametu River Lodge 7km south of Divundu along the D3403 towards the Botswana border ☎ 066   259035, ⓦshameturiverlodge.com; map opposite. This fancy new lodge makes the most of its gorgeous setting: the spacious canvas chalets and airy communal areas boast enviable river views – especially the luxury ones (worth the extra N$340), with cuisine and service to back it up. Up the bank, the deluxe camping pitches don't have the same view, nor are they secluded, but they have everything else: grassy pitches, electricity and private ablutions that even have towels. DBB rates available. Camping per person N$130, chalets (B&B) N$1560

Bwabwata National Park

Only re-declared a national park in 2007, following the years of conflict and unrest in the region, the Bwabwata National Park is still in its infancy, with facilities virtually non-existent, yet its scenic riverine environments are wonderful for wildlife viewing. Though the protected area stretches 200km along the entire neck of the Zambezi Region, the only two areas open to tourists lie at either end of the strip: at the western end, the **Mahango Core Area** borders the Kavango River, while at the eastern end, the **Kwando Core Area** borders the river of the same name. Despite being part of the same national park, these two reserves require separate permits. In between these two areas, yet still within the national park boundaries, the tarred B8 – the main artery that traverses the whole region – is punctuated with traditional villages of reed-thatched rondavels, from where cattle and goats occasionally wander onto the highway.

Mahango Core Area

Park entrance on the D3403, 22km south of the turn-off from the B8 at Divundu • Sunrise to sunset • N$40/person and N$10/vehicle; no charge if you are travelling directly to or from Botswana

The main entrance to the **Mahango Core Area** lies on the through gravel road to the Botswana border, which cuts through the park. Visitors to the reserve proper can choose between two circuits. The shorter 15km **river route**, to the east, runs along a decent dirt road (accessible in a saloon car) and is preferred by most visitors, as the more open grasslands, floodplains and stretches of the Kavango River afford more varied scenery – including a couple of giant baobabs – and better wildlife-viewing opportunities, especially in the dry season. Hippos and crocodiles lurk in the river, with elephant and buffalo regular visitors in the heat of the day. You're likely to spot sable and roan antelope grazing alongside the more commonly sighted antelope, while tsessebe and wildebeest are also present. The two "picnic sites," where you are allowed to get out of your vehicle and stretch your legs, lack benches and tables.

The longer 30km meander **west of the main road** is only for 4WD, and takes you through denser broad-leaved woodland, where it's harder to spot animals, though in the dry season, the Thingwerengwere waterhole can attract thirsty visitors. The park is a favourite with bird-lovers, with over 450 species recorded – more than any other park in Namibia.

ARRIVAL AND DEPARTURE	BWABWATA (MAHANGO AREA)

By car The park entrance lies 22km south of Divundu on the D3403. 2WD is possible for the more popular drive east of the road and along the Kavango River. West of the road, 4WD is necessary.

By bus Minibuses run from Rundu and Katima to Divundu (around N$120). Thereafter, you'll have to hitch a ride to the Popa Falls Reserve, or one of the neighbouring camps, which offer guided excursions into the park.

Kwando Core Area

Park entrance on the B8, 1.5km west of the Kwando Bridge • Sunrise to sunset • N$40/person and N$10/vehicle

Unlike its western counterpart (see p.285), this eastern section of Bwabwata National Park, the **Kwando Core Area**, is only accessible by 4WD. It consists of low-lying vegetated sand dunes covered in deciduous woodlands of wild syringa, Zambezi teak and copalwood, as well as areas thick with acacia and combretum species. The main, poorly signed sandy track twists and turns for several kilometres before reaching the **wetland** areas, where your efforts are most likely to be rewarded. And the rewards can be substantial, especially along the banks of the **Kwando River** – where stunning carmine bee-eaters nest (Aug–Nov) – and at **Horseshoe Bend**, an oxbow lake that lies some 10km into the park. Here, resident hippos snort and wiggle their ears while vast herds of elephants can be seen converging on the water in the afternoon, to bathe, drink and play. Buffalo and impala are also present in large concentrations in the reserve, alongside roan and sable antelope, while the elusive sitatunga – a strange swamp-dwelling antelope – can also be spotted. You'd have to be very lucky, though, to encounter **wild dogs**; though the park is one of the last refuges in Namibia for these

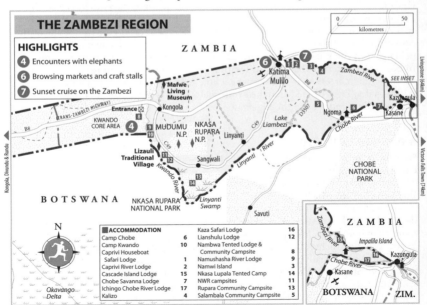

THE ZAMBEZI REGION

HIGHLIGHTS

4 Encounters with elephants

6 Browsing markets and craft stalls

7 Sunset cruise on the Zambezi

ZAMBIA

Katima Mulilo

Zambezi River

SEE INSET

Livingstone (64km)

Kazungula

Kasane

Mafwe Living Museum

Kongola

TRANS-ZAMBEZI HIGHWAY

Entrance

KWANDO CORE AREA

MUDUMU N.P.

NKASA RUPARA N.P.

Linyanti

Lake Liambezi

Ngoma

Chobe River

Lizauli Traditional Village

Sangwali

Linyanti River

CHOBE NATIONAL PARK

Kongola, Divundu & Rundu

Kwando River

BOTSWANA

NKASA RUPARA NATIONAL PARK

Linyanti Swamp

Savuti

Okavango Delta

Kalizo

N

ACCOMMODATION

Camp Chobe	6	Lianshulu Lodge	12
Camp Kwando	10	Nambwa Tented Lodge &	
Caprivi Houseboat		Community Campsite	8
Safari Lodge	1	Namushasha River Lodge	9
Caprivi River Lodge	2	Namwi Island	3
Cascade Island Lodge	15	Nkasa Lupala Tented Camp	14
Chobe Savanna Lodge	7	NWR campsites	11
Ichingo Chobe River Lodge	17	Rupara Community Campsite	13
Kalizo	4	Salambala Community Campsite	5

ZAMBIA

Zambezi River

Impalila Island

Chobe River

Kazungula

Kasane

BOTSWANA   ZIM.

Victoria Falls Town (74km)

THE BOTSWANA BORDER AT MAHANGO

The **Mahango-Mohembe border crossing** (daily 6am–6pm) lies just south of the Mahango Core Area entrance, 35km down the D3403, which turns off the B8 just west of the bridge at Divundu. In addition to the usual form-filling formalities, you'll need to pay Pula 100 (or the Namibian dollar/Rand equivalent) if you're "importing" a **vehicle** into Botswana. Entering Namibia with a foreign vehicle as a tourist you'll need to pay N$149 road tax. The tarred road into Botswana follows the Kavango River into the Okavango Panhandle, to the large village of **Shakawe**, 13km southeast, where vehicles can refuel, and there is onward public transport to **Maun**, the main access point to the Okavango Delta proper.

endangered animals, only a handful are estimated to inhabit the area. You may also catch occasional glimpses of leopard, lion and hyena.

ARRIVAL AND INFORMATION

By car The park entrance is on the B8, 1.5km west of the police checkpoint at the bridge over the Kwando River, and 6.5km west of Kongola. You will be given a makeshift sketch map and information sheet on the park. A 4WD vehicle is essential.

BWABWATA (KWANDO AREA)

ACCOMMODATION

There is an unfenced campground and one new luxury lodge inside the park, which needs 4WD through sand to access, but they'll do transfers from the park entrance; the other accommodation lies on the east bank of the Kwando River, which demarcates the eastern boundary of the national park. All accommodation offers excursions into the national park, either by boat, or on a game drive.

IN THE PARK

★ Nambwa Tented Lodge and Community Campsite 1km from Horseshoe Bend ☎ 081 767 4254 (lodge) or ☎ 061 400510 (reservations), ⊛ nambwalodge.com; map opposite. This long-standing idyllic campground is now rather overshadowed by a top-of-the-range treetop lodge – a new joint venture between a private consortium and the local Mashi Conservancy. It comprises ten well-ventilated, sumptuous safari-tent suites affording wonderful vistas (8, 9 and 10 have the best river views), connected via a raised walkway. The bar-restaurant deck is located to maximize sunset- and wildlife-viewing – above a waterhole, overlooking the savannah. Lots of activities are on offer, from guided bush walks, boat cruises or game drives to village visits (N$380–650). The more adventurous might fancy a night in the new lagoon camp; the Meru tents are not as opulent but the wildlife viewing right next to you is hard to beat. Meals up at the main lodge. Campers can enjoy four lovely spots along a tributary to the Kwando, with clean, private ablutions and hot water but no electricity. Some of the lodge facilities and activities are available to campers. Camping per person N$250 lagoon camp (DBB) N$7800, tent suites (DBB) N$9870

EAST OF THE PARK

Camp Kwando 25km south of Kongola on the C49 (MR125), a dirt road is signposted off to the west; follow it for 3km to the river ☎ 066 686021 or ☎ 081 358 2260, ⊛ campkwando.com; map opposite. This relaxed and low-key place with rustic facilities is in a beautiful location amid the water lilies and papyrus, with tremendous sunsets from the (not especially) private shaded decks of the modest, rustic riverside safari tents. The four marginally more upmarket tents lack the river view. Camping, behind the chalets, is fairly ad hoc, spread around a grassy area with shared braai sites, little reed-and-grass thatched toilets and showers. There is a handful of hammocks and sunloungers, and a small pool for relaxation. Private camping with smarter braai areas and ablutions costs a little more. The three airy lapas of the small main lodge are simply decorated with traditional African artwork. Camping per person N$178, safari tents (B&B) N$1650

Namushasha River Lodge 24km down the C49 (MR125), south of Kongola ☎ 066 686024 (lodge) or ☎ 061 427200 (reservations), ⊛ gondwana-collection .com; map opposite. Popular with groups, this large lodge comprises around thirty simply furnished but comfortable chalets, spaced along a bluff above the Kwando River, with views across the floodplains into Bwabwata National Park. Mature trees shade private balconies, and intimate candlelit dining takes place on the airy bar-restaurant terrace (excellent buffet dinner N$300), high above the water. Nine splendid grassy camping pitches have superior private ablution blocks, plus the usual amenities. With vehicles permanently stationed in the national park, a game drive is only a short water-transfer away. Boat cruises, fishing trips and guided walks are also on offer, and service is good. Camping per person N$170, chalets (B&B) N$2748

Mudumu National Park

Park entrance at Nkatwa Camp, approximately 35km down the C49 (M125) · Sunrise to sunset · N$40/person, N$10/vehicle

The small, flat **Mudumu National Park** covers the eastern riverbank and floodplains of a meandering channel of the Kwando River. Signposting is virtually non-existent and there is only a handful of sandy tracks – some of which peter out into bush – that weave their way through mopane, wild syringa, leadwood and mangosteen, nearly all within the strip of land between the main road and the river itself. That said, you're likely to have the place to yourself – apart from the police, who occupy a small outpost to keep a watchful eye on cross-border activity – especially if you spend the night in one of the three bush camps (see below).

Birdwatching in the park is particularly rewarding; while dawdling along the river, watch out for African skimmers, cranes, storks, jacanas and ibis, while western-banded snake eagles can be sighted wheeling above. The water attracts larger visitors too: elephant and buffalo come to drink in large numbers, and roan and sable antelope and eland are also present. If you're lucky, you might catch sight of a spotted-necked otter in the shallows. Consider also visiting the nearby **Lizauli Traditional Village** – well signposted off the main road to the north of the park – to learn more about Lozi traditional culture; it's also an opportunity to purchase genuine local crafts (see box opposite).

ARRIVAL AND DEPARTURE   MUDUMU NATIONAL PARK

By car The only way to reach and explore this park is in your own vehicle. The park entrance is signposted off the C49 (MR125), approximately 35km south of Kongola. A 4WD vehicle is essential.

ACCOMMODATION

Lianshulu Lodge Just off the C49, at the southern park border ☎ 066 686073 (lodge) or ☎ 061 224420 (reservations), ⓦ caprivicollection.com; map p.286. A rare concession inside a national park, this exclusive camp accommodates a maximum of twenty visitors at a time in ten nicely appointed if rather small – given the price – chalets, each facing a scenic channel of the Kwando River, looking into Botswana. The open, thatched main lodge offers more viewing space and plenty of comfort. Dinner is a set menu, with the occasional braai. Boat trips and game drives into the park are organized, as well as village visits. There's also a more modest bush camp nearby that accommodates group bookings, and more budget-conscious independent travellers. Bush camp (DBB) N$4600, lodge chalets (DBB) N$7470

NWR campsites map p.286. Three unfenced bush campgrounds are located within the reserve, bookable at the park entrance (free). There is currently no charge, since they possess no facilities beyond a pit latrine, though they make for a real wilderness experience.

Nkasa Rupara National Park

Linyanti Swamp, southwest corner of the eastern Zambezi Region, 10km south of Sangwali, off the C49 · Sunrise to sunset · N$40/person, N$10/vehicle

The many channels of water of the Kwando-Linyanti river system comprise Namibia's largest protected wetland, **Nkasa Rupara National Park** (formerly Mamili), a mix of marshland, high reed beds and woodland savannah that collectively offer visitors an area rich in **birdlife**, with over 430 species. Elephant, buffalo – over one thousand – red lechwe, reedbuck and puku wade or jump through the reeds, while huge crocodiles, hippos and water monitor lizards occupy the shallows. Lions are also very much in evidence. The park is mostly inaccessible as many of its "tracks" are filled with water, and much of the area is flooded during the wettest months of the year – usually February and March – and when the floodwaters arrive from the Angolan highlands (which can be weeks later), and so is a true wilderness.

CRAFTS IN THE ZAMBEZI REGION

The Zambezi Region, like the neighbouring Kavango region, is renowned for its **crafts**, especially **woodcarving** and **basketry**. Over the last few years several centres have been established to showcase these skills and sell the fruits of the artisans' labours as souvenirs to tourists. These have been encouraged by government as a means of sustainable development, though with varying degrees of success. However, the overall rise in visitor numbers to Namibia has increased the demand for crafts, resulting in more mass-produced items and fewer genuine, high-quality individually crafted pieces. Indeed, the selection varies little from place to place: walking sticks, wooden animals, baskets, clay pots, soapstone carvings and tie-dye textiles abound, with a smattering of jewellery across the craft shops. Designs often reflect the surrounding environment, also incorporating themes and techniques brought over from Zambia and Zimbabwe, while some items are straight imports from these neighbouring countries.

CRAFT CENTRES

Mashi Crafts Junction of the B8 and the C49 (MR125), Kongola ☎ 066 252800, ⌨ mashicrafts .com. An easy stopover at the intersection, opposite the Engen garage. Plenty of items nicely displayed, including carvings, basketry, pots and jewellery, mainly produced by Zimbabwean and Zambian artisans living in Namibia. There's another smaller, private venture next door. Mon–Fri & Sun 8am–5pm.

Ngoma Crafts On the B8, 2km before the border post ☎ 066 252108. This unmissable, brightly painted thatched rondavel by the main road features particularly attractive baskets, as well as some ceramics. Now with a small café. Mon–Sat 8am–5pm, Sat & Sun 8am–1pm.

Sheshe Crafts Sangwali, just after the turn-off from the C49 towards Nkasa Rupara National Park ☎ 081 238 6366. You'll need to get someone to open up here, to see the rather dusty collection of basketry and woodcarvings. No fixed hours.

Zambezi Arts and Cultural Association Hage Geingob Rd at Hospital Rd, Katima Mulilo ☎ 066 252670. Unequivocally the best regional selection of crafts, chock-full of the customary offerings but with some more unusual items hidden among them. Mon–Fri 8am–5pm, Sat 8am–noon.

ARRIVAL AND DEPARTURE

NKASA RUPARA NATIONAL PARK

By car The park entrance is 10km down the dirt road signposted off the C49 at Sangwali towards *Nkasa Lupala Tented Camp*. A 4WD vehicle is essential, and even then the park is only accessible in the dry season. There is no regular public transport, though you might be able to hitch to Sangwali from Katima.

ACCOMMODATION

★**Nkasa Lupala Tented Camp** 11km south of Sangwali on the park access road signed off the C49 (MR125) ☎ 081 147 7798, ⌨ nkasalupalalodge.com; map p.286. A seriously committed, unfussy eco-lodge with genuine community involvement, comprising ten lovely, simple, fan-ventilated tents on stilts high above the reed bed – unfenced, so you'll get elephants wading through the water right by your private deck and lions prowling around. The birdwatching is superlative, whether from the lodge, on a boat, in a safari vehicle, or even on foot (with an armed guard). 4WD necessary, or arrange for a pick-up in Sangwali. Discount for a stay of two nights or more. DBB N$4000

Rupara Community Campsite Just outside the park boundary, 10km south of Sangwali down the dirt road ☎ 081 367 1677; map p.286. Four pitches scenically located amid the reeds, with private reed-and-thatch ablution blocks and cement braai sites, through no grill or electricity. Pitch 1 has the best waterside location, surrounded by water lilies. Camping per person N$80

Katima Mulilo

Surrounded by lush forest, overlooking the majestic Zambezi, tropical **Katima Mulilo** – usually shortened to Katima, and meaning "to quench the fire" in SiLozi, referring to some nearby rapids – has more in common with towns in Zambia and Zimbabwe than most of Namibia. Indeed, located 1200km away by road from Windhoek, Katima is nearer to the neighbouring capital cities of Lusaka and Harare than to its own, a view soon confirmed by a wander round the vibrant **open market** and the sandy short cuts between buildings, where women in chitenges crouch over makeshift stalls selling fruit, cloth, comics and sweets, and competing Sungura and Zed beat rhythms waft out onto the street.

The **town centre**, such as it is, primarily centres on Hage Geingob Street and its junction with Hospital Road, where there are several large supermarkets, banks and a seemingly never-ending collection of strip malls. While here, be sure to call in at the **Zambezi Arts and Cultural Association** to browse their excellent selection of crafts (see box, p.289).

Should you find yourself anywhere near the suburb, and former township, of **Ngweze**, make sure you seek out the **"toilet tree"** outside the SWAPO office – a giant baobab, which has been hollowed out to accommodate said toilet.

Once the multi-million-dollar **Zambezi Waterfront Park** finally opens, Katima may finally make the most of its lovely waterside setting. For the moment, to fully experience the magic of the Zambezi, you need to head to the *Protea Hotel Zambezi River Lodge*, or stay at one of the lodges out of town.

Brief history

Though the Masubia and Mafwe dominate Katima's urban population, the majority of the people in the Zambezi River area are **Lozi** and therefore culturally closer to Lozi populations in Zambia, Botswana and Zimbabwe than to most other Namibians. In fact, until the end of the nineteenth century, the area was known as Itenge, or Linyanti,

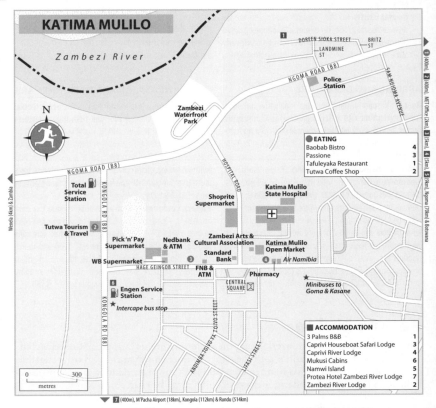

KATIMA MULILO

Zambezi River

Zambezi Waterfront Park

DOREEN SIOKA STREET
LANDMINE ST
BRITZ ST
NGOMA ROAD (B8)
Police Station
SAM NUJOMA AVENUE

● EATING
Baobab Bistro 4
Passione 3
Tafuleyaka Restaurant 1
Tutwa Coffee Shop 2

NGOMA ROAD (B8)
Total Service Station
KONGOLA RD (B8)
Tutwa Tourism & Travel
Pick 'n' Pay Supermarket
Nedbank & ATM
Shoprite Supermarket
Zambezi Arts & Cultural Association
Standard Bank
Katima Mulilo State Hospital
Katima Mulilo Open Market
Air Namibia
WB Supermarket
HAGE GEINGOB STREET
FNB & ATM
Pharmacy
Engen Service Station
CENTRAL SQUARE
Minibuses to Goma & Kasane
Intercape bus stop
KONGOLA RD (B8)
ANDIMBA TOIVO YA TOIVO STREET
LIFASI STREET

0 ———— 300
metres

■ ACCOMMODATION
3 Palms B&B 1
Caprivi Houseboat Safari Lodge 3
Caprivi River Lodge 4
Mukusi Cabins 6
Namwi Island 5
Protea Hotel Zambezi River Lodge 7
Zambezi River Lodge 2

Wenela (4km) & Zambia

● (400m), ● (400m), MET Office (2km) ● (5km), ● (5km), ● (9km), Ngoma (70km) & Botswana

▼ ■7 (400m), M'Pacha Airport (18km), Kongola (112km) & Rundu (514km)

and was part of the Lozi Kingdom of Barotseland, which covered a large chunk of present-day Zambia (see p.358). The colonial wrangling that followed resulted in Germany claiming the curiously shaped 450km panhandle – whose shape is arguably closer to that of a guitar head than a kitchen utensil – that stands out on maps of the region today (see p.271). However, no sooner had the Germans gained this precious fluvial corridor than defeat in World War I forced them to hand it over to the South Africans. The latter are credited – by some, at least – with founding Katima Mulilo in 1935, transferring the Caprivi administration here from Schuckmannsburg (present-day Luhonono) in recognition of its geographically **strategic location**. This turned out to be a double-edged sword, as over the next sixty years Katima was effectively run as a garrison town at the forefront of **conflicts**, with civilians constantly bearing the brunt of the violence, from World War II through apartheid, to the Bush War in Angola and finally the Caprivi secessionist uprising that ignited fully in 1999 (see box, p.271).

Since the **Katima Mulilo Road Bridge** opened in 2004, the Zambezi Region's capital has become increasingly cosmopolitan. Connecting the Zambian Copperbelt and even the distant Democratic Republic of Congo with Namibia's deep-water harbour at Walvis Bay, the re-emergence of this trade corridor has resulted in significant investment and development. Inevitably, as with any busy frontier town, it has fuelled its share of illicit business (including an increase in wildlife trafficking), sprawling shantytowns and accompanying social ills.

7

ARRIVAL AND DEPARTURE
KATIMA MULILO

By car Katima lies 510km east of Rundu along the tarred Trans Caprivi Highway (B8). It is also accessible by car from Botswana, via the Ngoma border (see box, p.293), and from Zambia, across the bridge at Wenela (see box below).

By bus Intercape Mainliner buses (⊚ intercape.co.za) call in at the Engen station on the B8, at Hage Geingob St, on their way to and from Windhoek and Livingstone, Zambia, and as far as the Victoria Falls border with Zimbabwe. Buses leave Windhoek on Mon, Wed & Fri (17hr; from N$580), and leave Katima for Windhoek on Wed, Fri & Sun (15hr). Buses from Katima head for Victoria Falls on Tues, Thurs & Sat (4hr; from N$396). Return buses to Katima from Victoria Falls leave on Wed, Fri & Sun. Ekonolux (⊕ 061 258961, ⊚ ekonolux6.wix. com/ekonolux-transport) operates a less regular, but cheaper, bus service between Windhoek and Katima. Its Katima office is in the Ngweze suburb and former township (⊕ 081 477 5350).

By minibus Minibuses depart from the Engen station on the B8, at Hage Geingob St, for Rundu (N$230),

Oshakati (N$260) and Windhoek (N$290). They also leave around 7am for Kasane in Botswana, via Ngoma (N$70), from the areas of waste ground on Hage Geingob St, east of Lifasi St.

By plane M'Pacha Airport lies 18km southwest of town. Air Namibia (⊚ airnamibia.com) operates four flights per week between Windhoek and Katima, sometimes via Rundu (Mon, Wed, Fri & Sun; 1hr 30min).

By taxi/shuttle Tutwa Tourism and Travel (see p.292) and the *Baobab Bistro* (see p.293) can both organize cross-border transport to Livingstone, Zambia, Victoria Falls, Zimbabwe or Kasane, Botswana. A transfer to Kasane, for example, costs N$1350/person for a minimum of two people – less if more people are travelling; for Victoria Falls the rate is N$2160/person. Tutwa Travel only do private transfers, whereas *Baobab* can arranged shared transport, but they need plenty of advance warning to get several passengers together. *Caprivi Houseboat Safari Lodge* can arrange a taxi driver from Livingstone to provide a transfer to Livingstone or the border for around US$100.

THE ZAMBIA BORDER
Some 4km northwest of Katima, the kilometre-wide bridge at **Wenela** that spans the Zambezi marks the **border between Namibia and Zambia** (daily 7am–6pm). A taxi from Katima to the border costs N$30. If you're driving a private vehicle into Namibia or Zambia, the usual cross-border charges apply (see p.53). To enter Zambia, unless you're from Ireland, you'll need a **visa**, which, from most EU countries, or from the US, Canada or Australia, costs US$50, payable in US dollars – you'll need to change your money before you reach the border. From the border, you can easily hop in a shared taxi to **Sesheke**, a few kilometres away, from where there is reliable onward transport by bus to Livingstone (and **Victoria Falls**) and **Lusaka** (see p.335).

GETTING AROUND

On foot The centre of town is very compact and easy to get around on foot.

Taxis Though there's no need around town, you might need one to get to/from the Zambian border (N$30) or the airport (N$120).

INFORMATION AND TOURS

Tourist information Katima lacks a formal tourist office, but Tutwa Tourism and Travel (Mon–Fri 8am–5pm; ☎066 252793), set back from Kongola Rd, diagonally opposite from the *Pick 'N' Pay* supermarket, has helpful staff and is a good source of local information. They also offer various day-tours to national parks, including Chobe (Botswana), as well as a sundowner cruise on the Zambezi and shuttle services to Livingstone (Zambia), Kasane (Botswana) and Victoria Falls (Zimbabwe), and can book lodge accommodation for you.

MET office Drop by the MET office on Ngoma Rd (☎066 262300) if you want to buy a permit in advance for one of the Zambezi Region national parks, though you can always buy it on the day at the park entrance.

ACCOMMODATION

IN TOWN

3 Palms B&B Doreen Sioka St ☎066 252850, ⓦ3palms.com.na. Superior B&B with immaculate, well-appointed rooms, each with access to private seating in the garden, where you can sip your sundowner overlooking the Zambezi, chill in the lapa or loll in the pool. B&B **N$1400**

Mukusi Cabins On the B8, behind the Engen station ☎066 253255, ⓦmukusi.com. Offering cheap, functional accommodation at the budget end of the scale, ranging from rooms with communal bathroom and standard fan to inexpensive en-suite doubles with a/c and TV. Breakfast N$40/person. **N$560**

Protea Hotel Zambezi River Lodge Kongola Rd ☎066 251500, ⓦproteahotels.com. The premier hotel in town, frequented mainly by business folk and tourists stopping off for the night, but pleasant enough, with decent rooms containing the usual amenities and a good-sized pool set in manicured grounds. Standard international-hotel fare is served at the riverside restaurant. The campground has decent facilities and lovely riverside views. Camping per person **N$150**, doubles (B&B) **N$1520**

OUT OF TOWN

★Caprivi Houseboat Safari Lodge Ngweze, 5km east of town north of the B8 ☎066 252287, ⓦcaprivihouseboatsafaris.com. An informal rustic camp for nature-lovers and dog-lovers – the owner has several large ones – comprising a handful of no-nonsense reed-and-thatch chalets facing the river, with mosquito nets and ceiling fans. One cheaper chalet shares the shower block and kitchenettes with the three camping pitches. The small bar-restaurant, where you need to order meals in advance, has a pleasant veranda overlooking the Zambezi, though the food's indifferent. Two basic camper boats (sleeping up to six in rooftop tents and a bunk bed) can be hired with a guide to explore the rivers and wetlands within striking distance. Camping per person **N$100**, chalets (B&B) **N$1100**

Caprivi River Lodge Ngweze, 5km east of town north of the B8 ☎066 252288, ⓦcapririverlodge.com. This welcoming, well-organized lodge is set in lush grounds brimming with birdlife on the banks of the Zambezi. There are rooms to suit a variety of budgets, from moderately priced river-facing chalets with ceiling fans, to smaller chalets with screened porches, a/c and braai site or tiny budget wooden cabins – resembling garden sheds – also with a screened porch, a/c and braai area, though the lounge-dining lapa overlooking the river is a more pleasant place to hang out. Lots of activities are available, from day-trips to Chobe and Victoria Falls to boat-based fun on the Zambezi. Cabins **N$1177**, chalets **N$1497**, riverfront chalets **N$1862**

★Kalizo 37km east of Katima Mulilo, signposted north off the D3508, 14km south of Katima ☎066 253521, ⓦkalizolodge.com. 4WD necessary but the lodge can do transfers. Relaxed, shady environment under acacias and jackalberrys, overlooking the Zambezi. Modern tent-chalets (some self-catering) with sliding glass doors have fans, mosquito nets, fridge and kettle. Only 7 of the 18 campsites (with braai site and communal ablutions) are on the river, though the viewing deck by the restaurant, which serves nicely prepared food, is open to all. The place is well set up for birding – don't miss the breeding colony of visually stunning carmine bee-eaters (mid-Aug–Nov), with a viewing platform on the bluff, 700m west of the lodge – and fishing, with (long) day excursions to Vic Falls and Chobe too. Camping per person **N$155**, chalets **N$1420**

Namwi Island 9km east of Katima Mulilo ☎066 252243 or ☎081 127 4572, ⓦnamwiisland.com. Despite the fabulous location overlooking a good stretch of the Zambezi, this place feels a bit like a caravan park. Still, the self-catering accommodation's good value if rather gloomy: fully equipped chalets for two (with a/c) or six people (with fan), and budget chalets that share the camping facilities. Campers get solid braai stands and electricity. Camping per person **N$125**, budget chalets **N$425**, chalets **N$938**, family chalets **N$1200**

EATING

Baobab Bistro Hage Geingob Rd. A rather gloomy interior, but the food's decent enough: a range of full fried breakfasts, including the unlikely peanut butter and banana French toast, and hot lunches; home-made burgers are an option. Most mains for around N$55–75. Free wi-fi. Mon–Fri 7am–5pm, Sat 8am–1pm.

Passione Hage Geingob, close to Pick 'N' Pay ☎066 252282, ⓦfacebook.com/passionekm. Probably Katima's best bet for a decent meal, though this upstairs air-conditioned restaurant with TV screens lacks ambience. From the extensive Portuguese-inspired menu, try the pica-pica: strips of beef with chorizo and beans accompanied by rice (mains from N$110). Free wi-fi. Daily 8am–10pm.

Tafuleyaka Restaurant Ngoma Rd ☎066 251500, ⓦproteahotels.com. Several different buffet breakfasts are on offer, while lunch is à la carte. Dinner offers a full buffet (N$180) or you can grab something from the menu – generally grilled meat or game including the standard international fare (steak and chips, club sandwich, pasta; mains from N$80). The bar has a lovely riverside view from which to enjoy a sundowner from the decent cocktail menu. Daily 7am–10am, noon–3pm & 7–10pm.

Tutwa Coffee Shop Kongola Rd/B8. A few tables and umbrellas in a shady garden of sorts provides an unlikely oasis on a dusty main street. Various bacon and egg combos are served for breakfast, and simple lunches are on offer from around N$55: sandwiches, wraps, salads, steak or pie and chips. Mon–Fri 7am–5pm, Sat 8am–noon.

7

Lake Liambezi and Ngoma

From Katima a decent, tarred road heads 70km southeast past a string of tidy, well-swept settlements and wandering cattle to the **Botswana border** (see box below) at the village of **Ngoma**, home primarily to the Masubia, and the location of a cheerfully painted roadside community **craft shop** (see box, p.289). Around 38km from Katima, there's a sign off down the D3507 (around 25km) to **Lake Liambezi**, a curious and constantly changing lake, worth swinging by if you've time. Created in the late 1950s from a major flooding of the Zambezi, it was reduced to a dustbowl for many years in the mid-1980s, possibly due to the large-scale poaching of hippos, which used to keep the water channels open by trampling through them. Heavy rains for several years after 2009 allowed it to replenish, prompting a profitable seasonal fishing industry to mushroom round its edges, with villagers sending off their catch of tilapia, bream and catfish to neighbouring countries and even as far away as the DRC. Hippo and crocs too have now repopulated the lake, which also attracts good birdlife, though at the time of going to press, following several years of drought, the Liambezi was in danger of drying up once more.

ACCOMMODATION   LAKE LIAMBEZI AND NGOMA

★**Camp Chobe** On the Chobe River 2km east of the B8 at Ngoma ☎081 800 0762, ⓦcampchobe.com; map p.286. A proper no-frills solar-powered eco-lodge, overlooking the Chobe floodplains into the national park in Botswana, offering exceptional wildlife viewing – with well over 400 bird species and regular sightings of wild dogs. The 20 simple tented chalets on stilts have glass doors and are solar-powered – the deluxe ones have river

---

THE BOTSWANA BORDER AT NGOMA

The **border with Botswana at Ngoma** (daily 7am–6pm; ☎062 360002) lies around 60km south of Katima Mulilo along a good, tarred road. Across the border, in Botswana, a decent tarred road runs through Chobe National Park to **Kasane**, 70km east, which in turn has onward tarred road connections south to other major towns in Botswana, and east to Victoria Falls, Zimbabwe. If you are transiting the park to Kasane, keeping on the main road, then no park fees are charged. However, if you want to take your time along the more scenic route bordering the Chobe River (4WD necessary), or even strike out southeast towards Savuti and the Okavango Delta, then park fees will apply. The usual cross-border **fees** apply to take a vehicle into Botswana or Namibia (p.53), and note that if you're a motorcyclist, you'll have to find an alternative route as motorcycles are forbidden in national parks in Botswana.

or floodplain views. The main rustic-design lodge is also tented, with similarly impressive viewing decks (plus telescope). Affordable boat, vehicle and walking safaris are available, depending on water levels, and you can even paddle around in a Canadian canoe. The river usually floods March to May, when the road may be inaccessible, necessitating pick-up by boat. The campground, a few hundred metres away, is regularly visited by elephant and has four pitches, with individual facilities, but no power. You can book tours and eat at the lodge (if there's space).

Wi-fi limited and at extra cost. Camping per person N$130, chalets (B&B) N$1500

★**Salambala Community Campsite** Signposted west off the B8, 45km from Katima towards Ngoma ☎081 303 8113; map p.286. Follow the signs 5.5km along a sandy track, for this friendly, community-run camp with four basic pitches set among mopane trees. There's a nearby waterhole, visited by eland, giraffe and wildebeest, and the surrounding pan sometimes floods. Elephant pass through in April/May. Camping per person N$100

Impalila Island and around

At the confluence of the Zambezi and the Chobe rivers, over 100km southeast of Katima, sits **Impalila Island**, which marks the easternmost tip of Namibia. Its unique and enviable position, overlooking both scenic waterways, and within easy striking distance of **Chobe National Park** in Botswana, and **Victoria Falls** in Zimbabwe and Zambia, makes it the perfect spot for high-end **wilderness lodges**. Captivating scenery and glorious sunsets abound, and superlative wildlife safaris can be conducted on water as well as on land – in a motorboat or a *mokoro* (the traditional dugout canoe), or even from the deck of a houseboat.

The island's location, within sight of three of Namibia's neighbouring countries, also justified the island's former strategic importance as a military base for the SADF during the 1980s. Though the base has long gone and the barracks now house a school, the tarred airstrip remains to bring in lodge visitors to Impalila – the only way to access the island without going into Botswana.

The eastern wetlands

Whereas the larger **Zambezi** flows inevitably eastwards towards Victoria Falls and ultimately the Indian Ocean, the **Chobe River** occasionally exhibits a curious phenomenon: on the rare occasions when the upper Zambezi floods, you can witness the Chobe River's flow being temporarily reversed, as it is forced to run westwards, as well as pushing water into Lake Liambezi (see p.293), until the floodwaters recede and it resumes its usual course once more, sliding into the Zambezi.

Between the two rivers, west of Impalila, their swampy **floodplains** extend, laced with deep channels of water lined with high reeds and clumps of papyrus. The area is more populated than you might imagine, with over two thousand **Lozi** making a living from subsistence farming, hunting and fishing, leading a semi-nomadic existence as they move with the rise and fall of the river levels, seeking higher land when the floodwaters swell (generally from March onwards). Significant quantities of large mammals are returning to the region, and the prolific birdlife is a further draw.

ARRIVAL AND DEPARTURE   IMPALILA ISLAND AND AROUND

The lodges listed below, although within Namibia's boundaries, are best accessed either via charter flight (in the case of Impalila Island) or via boat from Kasane in Botswana. Note that citizens from most Commonwealth and European countries, as well as the US, do not need a visa to enter Botswana. Check whether the inclusive rates include the transfer to/from Kasane.

By car and boat If you are self-driving, your accommodation will be able to give advice where you can park up your vehicle safely in Kasane, where a boat will pick you up.

By plane It's possible to take the luxurious option of chartering a plane to Impalila Island or Kasane (Botswana) from Eros Airport, Windhoek. Contact your

accommodation for a recommended charter flight company.
By taxi If you don't charter a plane, and you do not have a vehicle of your own, your best bet is to take a shuttle/taxi from Katima or Victoria Falls to Kasane (see box, p.324), where your accommodation will be able to arrange a pick-up, usually from the Kasane Immigration jetty.

ACCOMMODATION

The location of the lodges, on or near the Chobe River and Chobe National Park in Botswana, which contains one of the largest concentrations of elephants in Africa, virtually guarantees sightings of these magnificent beasts, as well as a host of other large mammals and prolific birdlife. Note that prices for these lodges are in US dollars.

Cascade Island Lodge On an island in the Mombova Rapids in the Zambezi, close to Impalila Island; South Africa ☎ (0)31 762 2424, ⓦ flameofafrica.com/agent -corner/cascade-island-lodge; map p.286. The pinnacle of luxury, this opulent four-suite lodge, with vast windows through which to gaze, provides more comforts than you can think of – plus indoor and outdoor showers, private plunge pool with white sand "beach", intimate fine dining and plenty of opportunities to enjoy the wildlife-rich surroundings, either in a boat or on foot. AI US$1250

Chobe Savanna Lodge Peninsula jutting into the Chobe River, 15km west of Kasane; South Africa ☎ (0)11 394 3873, ⓦ desertdelta.com; map p.286. This sophisticated lodge provides opportunities for some serious armchair wildlife-viewing across the vast floodplains of the Chobe River, be it from the private veranda of one of the twelve stylish brick-and-thatch a/c suites (each with a personal guide for the duration), or from the comfortable open-sided bar area. Guided walks, canoe and boat safaris guarantee further wildlife wonders. Additional comforts include riverside fine dining and a delightful splash pool in a shady garden. AI US$1230

Ichingo Chobe River Lodge Impalila Island; Botswana ☎ (0)71302439 (lodge) or South Africa ☎ (0)21 7152412 (reservations), ⓦ qzcollection.com; map p.286. Highly acclaimed lodge, comprising eight large, well-appointed safari-tent suites (with a/c and new bathrooms), each with private balcony, tucked away in riverine forest and overlooking the Chobe River. Communal meals are served in a high-ceilinged brick-and-thatch dining room, but the real treat is the chance to spend a night or two aboard one of the lodge's contemporary design houseboats, which offer superlative game viewing from the top deck, while dipping your toes in the plunge pool, and sipping a gin and tonic. The boats range from the super-luxurious *Zambezi Queen*, boasting 14 suites and serious pampering, to the smaller *Chobe Princesses*, each with four or five smart cabin suites, also offering plenty of creature comforts. Both the lodge and boats offer two- or three-night all-inclusive itineraries. Safari tents (2-night) US$1200, houseboat (2-night) US$940

Kaza Safari Lodge Formerly Impalila Island Lodge; South Africa ☎ (0)31 762 2424, ⓦ flameofafrica.com /agent-corner/cascade-island-lodge; map p.286. A luxurious lodge overlooking the Zambezi's Mambova Rapids, bang next to a giant baobab, with eight lovely wood-and-thatch chalets on stilts, each with a river view. Other treats include a large infinity pool and a campfire on chilly nights. Fishing, boating and walking safaris are on offer. AI US$736

7

Victoria Falls

VICTORIA FALLS FROM ABOVE

BUNGEE JUMPING AT VICTORIA FALLS

Basics

Arrival and getting around

Most visitors to Victoria Falls arrive by air, generally via Johannesburg, South Africa, since there are no direct international flights from countries outside Africa to either Livingstone (see p.335) or Vic Falls Town (see p.319). Livingstone, however, has slightly more options, offering connections with Cape Town and Nelspruit – the gateway to Kruger National Park – in South Africa, and also with East African hubs of Nairobi (Kenya) and Addis Ababa (Ethiopia), on their respective national airlines. In contrast, Victoria Falls Town is served by Air Namibia, which offers flights four times a week from Windhoek. That said, both airports have recently upgraded their infrastructure and facilities to accommodate larger planes, and, at the time of writing, were busy trying to woo the major airlines to start direct flights.

Alternatively, there are much cheaper, fairly comfortable long-distance buses to Livingstone (see p.335) and Vic Falls (see p.319) from the countries' respective capital cities, and also from South Africa, via Bulawayo or Windhoek. Arriving by train is also an option for those with a sense of adventure and bags of time and patience: from Bulawayo to Vic Falls Town (see p.320), and from Lusaka to Livingstone (see p.335).

Border crossing

There are few more **impressive borders** than the one between Zambia and Zimbabwe (daily 6am–10pm) that spans the dramatic Victoria Falls Bridge, high above the raging Zambezi – the only pity is that scheduled trains no longer ply the route. **Shuttles** run by the various tour operators and lodgings in Vic Falls (see pp.322–326) and Livingstone (see pp.336–338) are allowed to provide cross-border transfers – the cost on a shuttle service between Livingstone Airport and Vic Falls Town, for example, is US$38–40 per person one way, though shuttles usually need a minimum of two people to run. No **taxis** or local **minibuses** are allowed to take customers into the other country, but there are taxis that cover the 1.5km between the two border posts (shared US$1; private US$3).

If travelling to Zimbabwe **from Zambia** (Livingstone), you can take a taxi, hotel shuttle or local minibus (see p.335) to the Zambia border where you'll need to negotiate formalities – which may include paying for a **visa** (see p.300). Then you can either take a shared or private taxi to the Zimbabwe border, or **walk** – pausing on the bridge en route to marvel at the view of the falls and the nerve of the bungee jumpers as they plunge into the void. Once through the Zimbabwe border, you can hike uphill to Vic Falls Town (1.5km) during the day, or grab a taxi (US$5). Don't try walking at dusk or at night (see p.307). Crossing into Zambia **from Zimbabwe** (Vic Falls Town), you'll find taxis to shuttle you between the two border posts (see p.321), and other taxis at the Zambia side of the border to drive you the 10km into Livingstone town (for around US$10 per taxi); alternatively, during the day you can wait for a local minibus (roughly every 20min; US$1), which will drop you off in the centre of town. In the unlikely event that you might contemplate walking, don't: it's not safe (see p.307).

There are also border charges to consider if travelling by **car** (see below).

Car rental and driving

Car rental rates in both Zambia (see p.336) and Zimbabwe (see p.321), including basic insurance cover and limited mileage (usually 200km), are **expensive** – from around US$600–700/week, and over double that for 4WD. Note that driving is **on the left** in both Zimbabwe and Zambia and that if you're intending to cross into any neighbouring country, you will need to inform the rental company in advance, for which there may be an additional charge. What's more, you will be liable for **cross-border fees** to "import" the vehicle into the other country, as well as road tax, insurance etc. These cross-border charges apply to all vehicles that are not registered in the destination country, not just to rental cars. Petrol and diesel are both available at fuel stations in Vic Falls and Livingstone.

Visas

Visa regulations change in this part of the world as often as some people change their socks. At the time of going to press, the convenient **UNIVISA** (or KAZA Visa; see ⓦkazavisa.info), which had been suspended following trialling, had just been

8

reinstated. It allows tourists from around forty countries to pay a one-off US$50 on arrival at particular ports of entry, which affords thirty days of free movement between Zimbabwe and Zambia (across the border at the bridge), and also to make short trips into northern Botswana to visit Chobe National Park (see box, p.324). Visitors at the following ports of entry are allowed to purchase a UNIVISA: the international airports in Livingstone, Harare and Victoria Falls; the Kazungula land border with Botswana into Zimbabwe (not the Kazungula ferry into Zambia), and on the Victoria Falls Bridge between Zimbabwe and Zambia. You cannot, unfortunately, buy a UNIVISA at Namibia's border with Zambia at Katima Mulilo, though there is talk of the agreement extending that far some time in the future. Of course, you are not obliged to buy a UNIVISA, but if you intend to be hopping across the border to see both sides of the falls, it is likely to be the most cost-effective option. If staying in Zimbabwe, however, you can get hold of a day **activity visa** (US$20) at Zambian immigration on the bridge, which allows you to nip over for the day to Zambia from Zimbabwe, but not the other way round.

Of course, depending on your nationality and the visa fees demanded of you, and whether or not you intend to visit both sides of the falls, it may still be preferable to get a regular visa. Most visitors likely to read this book will fall into the category of a country that can buy a visa on arrival; some may even not need a visa at all. Visa **rates** vary considerably depending on your nationality; at the time of going to press, a visa to enter Zimbabwe for a UK/Irish national cost US$55 for single entry, US$30 for a US citizen and US$75 for a Canadian. A double-entry visa for a UK/Irish citizen cost US$70. Visas for entry into Zambia cost US$50, irrespective of country of origin (though with reductions for SADC residents). The bottom line is that you should double-check with the relevant consular section in advance of your trip. In the end, however, what you are charged may depend on the official you encounter since there is often confusion about which visa regulations are in effect.

Accommodation

The big decision to make when visiting the area is where to stay: Zambia, to the north of the falls, or Zimbabwe, to the south. There's a greater choice of accommodation in or around Victoria Falls Town, and most of the activities are organized from this side, but it's possible to book activities from either side; for some you may have to pay for the transfer and an extra visa, depending on the type of visa you have. So which activities (see opposite) you're keen to do might have a bearing on where you choose to stay.

Another important consideration is that the lion's share of the falls – eighty percent – lies in Zimbabwe and is only a ten-minute stroll from the centre. However, in recent years, the town's unbridled commercialism – including incessant hassle from hawkers – and the country's economic and political difficulties have encouraged increasing numbers of visitors to shift over the border to the former Zambian capital, Livingstone (see p.311). One disadvantage of Livingstone is that it is 10km away from the falls, although many lodgings provide free transfers once a day. The town also lacks the compact commercial centre of Vic Falls Town, where everything you need is within a 100m block. On the other hand, Livingstone feels more relaxed, and a more "authentic" place – albeit rather spread out – where, although tourism is increasingly important, people are also going about other business. What's more, there's more of a nightlife scene in Livingstone, and you generally get more

---

ACCOMMODATION PRICES

Most lodgings on both the Zambian and Zimbabwean sides of the falls maintain the same **prices** throughout the year. The few properties that differentiate usually consider high season to run from July to the end of December; some consider high season to end at the end of November, and then charge high-season rates again over the Christmas and New Year period. The prices given here are for the **cheapest double en-suite room in high season (or the year-round price, if consistent)**, which also includes breakfast, unless otherwise stated. Prices are given in the advertised currency for that particular lodging – this is generally the US dollar, although, in practice, most places accept various currencies. Generally, children under 12 are charged half price.

SOME FACTS AND FIGURES

	ZAMBIA	ZIMBABWE
Time zone	GMT + 2hr	GMT + 2hr
Capital	Lusaka	Harare
Country size	752,610 square kilometres	290,760 square kilometres
President	Edgar Lungu	Robert Mugabe
Population	15.2 million (Livingstone: 110,000)	14.6 million (Victoria Falls Town: 34,000)
Main official languages	English, Chibemba and Chinyanja (also known as Chichewa); Silozi and Chitonga are also widely spoken in the Livingstone area	English, Chishona and Isindebele – the last being the main local language in the Vic Falls area
Currency	Zambian kwacha (but some accommodation here is given in and accepts US dollars)	US dollar, South African rand; also officially accepts euros, British pounds, Australian dollars, Botswana pula Chinese yuan, Japanese yen and Indian rupees
Economy	Main industries: mining – copper (85 percent of all exports); agriculture – main export maize; floriculture is a growth industry, as is tourism	Main industries: mining – main exports gold, platinum, diamonds and coal; agriculture – main exports tobacco, cotton and sugar; tourism; manufacturing
Telephone dialling codes	Country +260 / Livingstone 0213	Country +263 / Victoria Falls 013
Mobile phone providers	Airtel, MTN, Zamtel	Econet, Telecel, NetOne
Electricity	220–240V / Plugs: 2 or 3 round pins, or 3 flat pins (as in the UK)	220–240V / Plugs: usually 3 flat pins (as in the UK); sometimes 2 round pins
Water	Tap water usually needs purifying	Tap water usually drinkable

8

for your kwacha than for the US dollar over in Zimbabwe. Note that, in both countries, the backpackers lodgings and less expensive guesthouses or B&Bs are in town, whereas the pricier lodges and hotels are nearer the falls, surrounded by bush, or along the banks of the Zambezi, set in scenic surroundings.

Activities

Beyond ogling the main event, a visit to Vic Falls is all about activities. On both sides of the border, there is an ever-increasing array of ways to get your pulse racing, as well as other more relaxing ways of enjoying the fabulous scenery and teasing out the wildlife. Most activities take place either around the falls, on (and off!) the Victoria Falls Bridge, on the Zambezi, across the Batoka Gorge further downstream, or in the two national parks either side of the Upper Zambezi.

Note that **rates** for activities generally do not include the park fees (usually US$10 for being on the river or air-borne; US$15 for being on land) or visa fees (see opposite) if you are crossing the border for an activity. Additionally, be aware that with some of the half- or full-day excursions you may not spend as much time as you were anticipating doing the actual activity, given time spent on pick-ups, drop-offs, transportation and briefing times. Most pursuits need a minimum of **two people** to run, and some activities are seasonal and dependent on the river level (see box, p.312). With some of the more contrived wildlife encounters, make sure you satisfy yourself in advance that the activity you are engaged in is in the best interests of the animals concerned (see box, p.304).

Getting a good deal

Unsurprisingly, **prices** vary considerably – especially in low season – so it pays to shop around and to have a rough plan of what you want to do before you book anything, since taking **multiple tours** with the same operator usually guarantees reduced rates. The bigger tour operators in Vic Falls Town and Livingstone also offer enticements such as free booze-cruises on the Zambezi if you book two or more activities, and free airport transfers, while "**combo packages**", such as a half-day rafting combined with a bungee jump, can help cut costs. Getting several people together to make a group booking will also result in a better deal per person, and of course bargains are more readily available when business is slack. First, you should compare what the **service providers** themselves are charging – such as the companies in Zimbabwe and Zambia that actually do the whitewater rafting – before comparing rates offered by the various tour operators or booking agents who sell these activities on commission. Of course, if you're not too worried about costs, you're short of time or want the organizational hassle taken out of your hands, then simply let your accommodation's **activity desk** sort everything out for you. The main tour operators are listed under Vic Falls Town (see p.322) and Livingstone (see p.336); what follows is a list of almost all the activities on offer.

An A–Z (almost) of Vic Falls activities

Abseiling

See high-wire activities (see opposite).

Birdwatching

Discover Safaris (see p.433), based in Vic Falls Town, is your best bet on the Zimbabwean side, whereas Savannah Southern Safaris (see p.336) fits the bill on the Zambian side.

Boiling Pot

For yet another perspective on the Smoke that Thunders, hike the 110m down into the gorge, raft across the swirling Boiling Pot and get a first-rate hydro-massage under the falls before hauling yourself back out. Shearwater (see p.322) in Vic Falls Town leads this half-day excursion, for those in reasonable shape, twice a day in the low-water season (late Aug–Dec; US$55). Bundu Adventures

(see p.336) offers a similar, though pricier, experience from the Zambian side (US$74).

Bridge tours

Fun and informative historical tours (US$65) offering insights into the pioneering Victorian engineering skills that resulted in the construction of the Victoria Falls Bridge. This one-and-a half-hour engagement starts with an actor in period costume entertaining you with tales of the times followed by a walk across the gorge along the underside of the bridge. Though you'll be clipped into a safety harness and given a full safety briefing, this is not for anyone suffering from vertigo. As it takes place in "no-mans-land" between the two borders, no extra fees are required.

Bungee jumping

See high-wire activities (see opposite).

Canoeing and kayaking

Both Shearwater (see p.322) and Wild Horizons (see p.322) run full or half-day trips – the latter not really worthwhile – on the Upper Zambezi (US$150 for a full day, plus park fees). With only the occasional bubbling rapid, the water is generally smooth, with lots of reed beds and channels to explore, and abundant birdlife. Frequent pods of hippos will be your main sighting – and concern – plus crocs basking on sandbanks, and possibly elephants. Adventure Zone and Wild Horizons organize overnight and multi-day canoe trips on the Zimbabwean side (see p.322); Bundu Adventures, Safari Par Excellence and Makoro Quest – through Livingstone's Adventures – do the same on the Zambian side (see p.336), charging around US$125 for a full day. Bank on paying around US$385 per person for a two-day canoe safari in Zimbabwe, and a lot less in Zambia (US$285).

Canopy tours

See high-wire activities (see opposite).

Cultural tours

If you're keen to see a bit of rural Zimbabwe and visit a village, the big tour operators and various lodges run cultural tours. They can be rather contrived, especially if you're in a large group, but it depends on the guide, the rapport with the villagers concerned, and the number and sensitivity of the other travellers in the group. Expect it to last a couple of hours, during which you'll be shown round, taking in a market, school and perhaps invited into someone's home to sample a local dish, before usually being shown some local crafts, which you'll be encouraged to buy. In Livingstone, the best way to visit is by bike with Local Cowboy Cycle Tours (see below), though the most popular excursion on the Zambian side is to Mukuni Village (see p.334). The *Gorges Lodge* too (see p.325) offers a chance to visit the community with which they are very involved. Most operators can organize the trip; alternatively, you can pay a taxi driver to take you there, or catch the local minibus heading to the falls, and then change to one leaving opposite the *AVANI resort* bound for Mukuni. Both sides of the border now offer this kind of cultural tour, usually for around US$50. Consider one of the cultural cycle tours, as the groups tend to be much smaller and the service more personalized.

Cycle tours

Bike & Saddle (🌐bikeandsaddle.com) is a Cape Town company that runs fun, though overpriced, three-hour guided cycle tours (US$82) with local guides. The route goes round Zambezi Drive (see p.319), stopping off at the Big Tree, heads through the leafy suburbs and does a circuit of Chinotimba Township, visiting the markets and various community locations there. *Shoestrings Backpackers* (see p.325) also does cycle tours and rents out bikes; *Jollyboys* in Livingstone also rents out bikes. Also in Livingstone, Local Cowboy Cycle Tours (☎0977 747837; US$25) which has a Facebook page, is a good-value, locally owned outfit, which comes highly recommended; its tours are a great way to get off the tourist trail for a half-day, taking in local neighbourhoods, a market and a village, enabling you to get much more of a sense of everyday life in Zambia.

Flights

Take to the air by helicopter or microlight – most awe-inspiring when the falls are in full flow and you can fly through the "smoke". When visitor numbers are really high, though, it can feel as though you're in a production line. The Shearwater-owned (see p.322) Zambezi Helicopter Company (☎013 43569, 🌐zambezihelicopters .com) offers two trips: the more popular is the "Flight of the Angels" – a 12–13min wow-factor spin in a helicopter over the falls and the gorges (US$150). For double the time and nigh on double the price (US$284), you also get to whizz over wildlife in the Zambezi National Park on an airborne safari. Make sure you don't get the middle berth at the back of the helicopter, or else

you might feel short-changed. On the Zambian side, United Air Charters (🌐uaczam.com), which flies from Baobab Ridge, just south of Livingstone, does the same two itineraries, only hovering above Mosi-oa-Tunya National Park, and charging a lot more for the experience. Zambia-based Batoka Sky (☎021 3323589, 🌐seasonsinafrica .com) offers an exhilarating microlight experience (the only operator to do this), exposed to the elements as you soar over the falls with a private pilot. A 15min ride will set you back US$155; a 30min one, which takes in the gorges, costs US$310. Note that cameras are prohibited, in case you drop yours and kill someone, but they will sell you pics of your flight at a vastly inflated price.

High-wire activities

Located midway across the bridge, Victoria Falls Bungee – owned by Shearwater (see p.322) – is the only operator (Zambia ☎0213 324231, Zimbabwe ☎0712 406945, 🌐shearwaterbungee .com) that offers you the chance to throw yourself headfirst 111m towards the Zambezi rapids below (US$160). Single or tandem bridge swings (US$160/240), meanwhile, allow you to look at the falls after you've jumped feet first and begun to swing, and you can also do a solo or tandem zipline (US$40/65). For an orgy of adrenaline, you can do all three for US$210. Note that you'll need your passport to go on the bridge. Wild Horizons (see p.322) offers a similar package of activities downriver across the Batoka Gorge, including relatively sedate abseiling (US$42), the "flying fox", and a foofie swing (US$69), which is a zipline at a sharp angle that you zoom down at speed. There's also the truly terrifying gorge swing (US$95), while the newer Canopy Tour is a more conventional treetop glide along nine ziplines, finishing off with a slide across the gorge for good measure (US$53). You can do a combo of three activities for US$137. The best value, though, is from Zambezi Eco Adventures (see p.336), which provides a whole day of unlimited vertigo-inducing fun in the Batoka Gorge followed by the Devil's Pool Tour for only US$195. The rates for individual thrills are more on a par with their competitors.

Horseback safaris

Zambezi Horse Trails (🌐zambezihorsetrails.com), an established owner-operated stables with horses to suit all levels of experience, offers rides in the Victoria Falls National Park. Those who've scarcely saddled up before can do a two-hour ride (US$100 plus park fees), while experienced riders can choose

8

from a half-, full- or multi-day horse safari (US$160 for a full day). A cheaper option is the Zambia-based Victoria Falls Horse Safaris – now part of Livingstone's Adventure (see p.336) – which does a two-hour trail from the Falls Resort (US$80) or a half-day one, including a light lunch back at the stables, in the national park (US$115).

Livingstone Island and Devil's Pool

Zambia-based Tongabezi (☎0213 327450 or ☎0979 312766, ⓦtongabezi.com) is the only operator for this activity, which offers you the chance to re-create the moment the good doctor peered over the edge and "discovered" the falls. Next, you jump into Devil's Pool (see p.331) at the lip of the chasm – the ultimate infinity pool. This is followed by a breakfast, lunch or high-tea picnic on the island, surrounded by plummeting water and wonderful rainbows; it's a treat, though definitely not for anyone suffering from vertigo. Numbers are limited to sixteen, and the tour is only possible when water levels are low (generally July till end of Feb; late Aug–Dec/Jan for the pool swim). The whole experience runs from US$98–158.

Quad biking and segways

On the Zambian side of the falls, the Livingstone Quad Company, as part of Livingstone's Adventures (☎0213 323589, ⓦseasonsinsafrica.com), operates two quad-bike routes: an hour-long "eco-trail" that blasts through the bush (US$80), promising views across the Batoka Gorge and wildlife sightings, though you'd think the wildlife would scarper at the din; and a more popular two-and-a-half-hour village tour (US$140; minimum four people), that takes in several villages. Helmets are provided and the minimum age is 12. If your kids are too young to clamber onto a quad, you may be able to persuade them to do a more sedate one-hour guided segway tour (minimum age 7) of the footpaths around Zambia's *AVANI Victoria Falls Resort* area.

River cruises

A cruise is one of the finest ways to experience the serenity of the Zambezi after the buzz of the falls – while keeping the hippos at arm's length. Boats of all sizes offer you the chance to have breakfast (the best time for birdwatching), lunch or dinner while gliding smoothly along the Zambezi. Alternatively, do the classic sundowner booze cruise, when the river can be chock-a-block with boats. Costs depend on the type of craft, the length of the cruise and the food and drink offered, but on the whole passengers on the less expensive boats tend to feel they have had better value for money. Excursions tend not to include the park fees. The most exclusive option is the *Ra-Ikane* (ⓦilalalodge.com/activities; US$85–90;

THE ETHICS OF ANIMAL ENCOUNTERS

There is a constantly expanding repertoire of **animal encounters** in the Vic Falls area, from tracking rhinos to walking with and petting lions, elephant-back safaris or cage diving with crocs. All these activities, to differing degrees, raise questions about the **ethics** of these types of interaction with wildlife, to which there are often no simple answers. The operators themselves often argue that they are supporting conservation efforts to protect the animal in question and are rescuing and rehabilitating injured animals that would otherwise have died; some point to the educational value of such interactions, though opponents would argue that since they are wild animals, they would be studied more effectively in the wild. Further justification is the provision of local employment, or the fact that the animals appear to be healthy and happy. Some of these conservation projects are making large sums of money, in part through enthusiastic volunteers, who pay to come and help, but questions remain about the percentage of the profits that are ploughed back into conservation and education initiatives. **Critics** of these animal encounters are also concerned about the low percentage of animals that are actually reintroduced back into the wild and the destiny of those that become old and surplus to requirements; there have been claims about some animals – lions in particular – being sold off for "canned" hunting, as well as cases of animal mistreatment.

In order to satisfy yourself that an activity is in the interests of the animal(s) concerned, you should consider these issues, as well as consulting the wealth of articles and personal testimonies on the internet – some a little disturbing – which include several specifically on Vic Falls.

RAFTING THE WORLD'S BEST WHITE WATER

Since the mid-1980s Vic Falls has been synonymous with **whitewater rafting**, as the churning and tumbling rapids of the Zambezi squeeze through the dramatic cliffs of the Batoka Gorge, providing some of the world's finest, and scariest, white water. Boasting the highest concentration of **Grade V rapids** in the world, the Zambezi provides a roller-coaster ride of huge waves, steep drops, holes and whirlpools, yet the absence of large rocks protruding from the river makes this safer than it might otherwise be. Welcome to Stairway to Heaven, Terminator (I and II), Oblivion and the Gnashing Jaws of Death – the rapids' names are enough to remind you that, while the rafting can be truly exhilarating, it can also be terrifying and dangerous – while thousands make the descent every season without incident, there is the occasional accident, near miss, or, very rarely, a fatality. Not that you should be put off, as the outfits that run the rafting are highly professional and take **safety** seriously: you'll get a full briefing, be armed with a state-of-the-art helmet and high-flotation life-jacket, and accompanied by safety kayakers with radio contact, who periodically help reunite tourists who've flown overboard with their dinghy – something you're likely to experience at least once. Besides, you should grab this opportunity while the rapids are still here; the long-standing, controversial plan to flood much of the gorge and build a hydro-electric power facility has recently been resuscitated and construction companies have already been invited to tender bids.

Once you've decided to take the plunge, there are various decisions to make. One choice to be made ahead of time is when to raft; the preferred **low-water season** generally runs from August to December (see p.312). During this season most rafting companies start at the Boiling Pot below the falls and run rapids 1 to 18 or 19 – though the dinghies are carried round Rapid 9, the Grade 6 Commercial Suicide. The Zimbabwean companies charge around US$150 for a full day, plus US$10 park fee; a half-day of rafting is also possible with some companies, for not much less. In the **high-water season** (usually Jan–June, with a closed season usually at some point in April), which is not as hair-raising, though it's exciting enough for many, rafts are usually taken down rapids 11–23 or 24 at a lower cost of US$140, plus park fees. The next decision is whether you want to paddle yourself or be rowed. Most choose to **paddle themselves**, under instruction from the guide; here you're more involved in the action, but some people prefer the guide to row them down, using giant oars, leaving them to concentrate full-time on staying in the dinghy. The next decision is whether to go with a Zambian firm or a Zimbabwean one. The main difference is that the Zambian outfits charge more (usually around US$160–170 for a full day, though they often offer discounts for online booking) because their prices include a lift out of the gorge on a cable car; this saves the weary rafter from having to haul themselves up a near-vertical cliff to get out of the ravine, which can take up to an hour.

Four **companies** operate from the Zimbabwean side (Adventure Zone, Shearwater, Shockwave and Wild Horizons; see p.322) and three from the Zambian side (Bundu Adventures, Safari Par Excellence and Zambezi Rafting; see p.336), usually offering more or less the same rates as their competitors on the same side of the falls, though the smaller and/or less well-known companies may more readily negotiate a discount if business is slack or you are in a group.

twelve passengers max), which offers the full-on colonial experience: polished teak panelling, club chairs, and superior canapés and cocktails. A further plus is that you can get closer to the action than in the bigger boats, but your view is more restricted for being lower in the water. At the other end of the scale, the *Zambezi Explorer* (☎013 42475, ☻zambeziexplorer.com; US$55 for a sunset cruise) caters for 150 people, spread over three decks; it's worth paying the extra US$25 to sprawl on the sofas of the "signature" top deck.

Wild Horizons (see p.322) and Shearwater (see p.322) have their own mid-sized boats, as do several of the hotels and lodges. On the Zambian side, the triple-decker *African Queen* (see p.336) – without Humphrey Bogart at the helm – and the smaller *African Princess* take you round the Kalai and Siloka islands (US$70). The sleekest boat on this stretch of the river is the *Lady Livingstone* (☻davidlivingstonesafarilodge.com; US$75–80), which resembles a spaceship when illuminated. Backpackers tend to opt for the colourful thatched party boat run by Taonga Safaris (☎0213 322508 or ☎0977 878065, ⊕taonga-safaris.com), which accommodates thirty, has an on-deck BBQ and plenty of atmosphere (US$65). Another good-value small boat is the *Mambushi* (⊕safpar.com; US$50–55), which has lots of comfort food on board and tends to escape the crowds by cruising downstream towards the falls.

Safaris

Classic game drives in open-topped safari vehicles are available in the Zambezi National Park (see p.315) for around US$70, plus park fees, or in the two main, big game-rich, private reserves off the road to Bulawayo: the Victoria Falls Private Game Reserve – which promises a very precise 97 percent chance of spotting a rhino – and the slightly smaller Stanley and Livingstone Private Game Reserve, which also hosts the Bear Grylls Survival Academy (⊕bear gryllssurvivalacademy.com). The main attraction of these private reserves is the existence of rhino, the greater concentration of big game, and the more interactive – and controversial (see box, p.304) – animal encounters, such as walking with lions. Game drives are US$100, inclusive of entrance fee, and can only be done through a tour operator. To really experience the sounds and smells of the African bush, though, you can't beat a walking safari with a knowledgeable – and armed – guide. Most operators and the main lodges and hotels offer a range of safaris in various locations, either in a vehicle or on foot. Discover Safaris (see p.322) does a highly recommended all-day safari, involving both walking and driving, in the Zambezi National Park (see p.315) for US$140. Zambian tour operators take visitors into the Mosi-oa-Tunya National Park for around US$65. Here there are white rhino, which you can track as part of a walking safari. Contact Livingstone Rhino Walking Safaris (☎0213 322267, ⊕livingstonerhinosafaris .com; US$80) or Savannah Southern Safaris (see p.336).

Steam train

Another highly indulgent evening out from the Zambian side of the falls is to dine in style on the Royal Livingstone Express (⊕royal-livingstone -express.com), a beautifully restored 1920s steam train, complete with polished wooden panelling and damask tablecloths, but with modern comforts, such as a/c and a glass observation coach, and large sparkling windows to maximize

---

PUBLIC HOLIDAYS

HOLIDAYS IN ZAMBIA AND ZIMBABWE
New Year's Day January 1
Good Friday and Easter Monday March/April
Labour Day May 1
Africa Day May 25
Christmas Day December 25
Boxing Day December 26

HOLIDAYS IN ZAMBIA
Youth Day March 12
Heroes' Day First Monday of July
Unity Day First Tuesday after Heroes' Day
Farmers' Day First Monday in August
Independence Day October 24

HOLIDAYS IN ZIMBABWE
Independence Day April 18
Heroes' Day Second Monday in August
Defence Forces' Day Second Tuesday in August
Unity Day December 22

---

viewing opportunities. Two trips are offered: the more popular is to the Victoria Falls Bridge – in time for a sundowner, before moving on to enjoy a five-course meal – while the other is to Mosi-oa-Tunya National Park. Departures are Wednesday and Saturday and when there's demand. From the Zimbabwean side of the falls, the slightly less opulent Bushtracks Express does a shorter rail journey offering a similar package. Both cost N$190.

Whitewater rafting and bodyboarding

Rafting (see box, p.305), by both Zimbabwean and Zambian companies, is the adrenaline activity that put Vic Falls on the map as an adventure sports destination and remains as popular as ever. Bodyboarding can only be done on certain rapids so you'll raft down the others, making it a combo trip and so more expensive (around US$190). If you want to get the adrenaline thrills and have a chance to experience the spectacular scenery, then consider one of the multi-day rafting trips, which entail sleeping out on the sandbanks under the stars. As the pace of the river slows, you'll have the close company of crocs and hippos to keep your pulse rate up. A five- or six-day trip costs around US$900–1000.

Health and safety

Malaria is the main health risk in Vic Falls, alongside dehydration and sunburn, especially if you're spending a lot of time on the river, where the sun will be reflected off the water. For further information, see the Basics section of the Guide (see p.56).

The centres of Victoria Falls Town and Livingstone are pretty **safe** places to walk around during the daytime, although, as elsewhere in the world, you should avoid wandering into backstreets and poor neighbourhoods at night. **Moneychangers** are also best avoided if possible; with so many currencies floating about, tourists are easy prey for simple deceptions; go to a bank, exchange bureau or an ATM. **Hawkers** and some stall holders are the main two-legged nuisance in Vic Falls Town during the day – especially when there are few tourists around – as they can be aggressive, partly as a result of the

desperate financial circumstances many of them face. Local businesses now fund the **tourist police**, usually fairly conspicuous in their lime-green bibs, who are there to help visitors and protect them from harassment. In Livingstone, hawkers are less widespread and less insistent, but you should not walk or cycle any of the 10km to the falls on your own, as the occasional **mugging** has occurred. On the Zimbabwe side, its inadvisable to go to or from the town and the falls or the border on foot at night for the same reason. An unwelcome **wildlife** encounter, however, is possibly a greater danger – especially with elephants – at dawn, dusk and at night. The short cut down from Vic Falls Town to the bridge is a prime site for encountering elephants, as is Zambezi Drive. If staying at any of the lodges along the Zambezi, be it in Zambia or Zimbabwe, you should think twice about ambling off along the riverbank, in case you run into a grazing hippo – quite likely at dawn or dusk – or trip over a lounging croc.

8

Victoria Falls

Along with Mount Everest and the Grand Canyon, Victoria Falls – or Mosi-oa-Tunya ("the smoke that thunders") – ranks as one of the world's seven natural wonders. No matter how many pictures you've seen beforehand, nothing can prepare you for the awe-inspiring sight and deafening sound of the falls. The world's widest curtain of water crashes down a huge precipice, producing clouds of spray visible from afar, before squeezing into a zigzag of sheer-sided gorges as a torrent of turbulent rapids, carving its way to the Indian Ocean, well over a thousand kilometres away. Straddling the Zambezi between Zimbabwe and Zambia, the falls are only a few hours' drive from Katima Mulilo, at the northeastern tip of Namibia. Boasting regular bus and air connections with Windhoek and Johannesburg too, they provide a fitting finale to a holiday in southern Africa.

Their dramatic setting on the **Zambezi River** has also made Victoria Falls the undisputed **adventure capital of Africa**. There's an array of adrenaline-fuelled activities on offer, from whitewater rafting and bungee jumping to zip-lining and bodyboarding, or simply the chance to pick your way along the edge of the precipice to bathe and peer over into the abyss. Less touted are the **stunning wildlife viewing** opportunities Victoria Falls affords: the **national parks** that line the serene banks of the Upper Zambezi are home to large mammals, such as elephant, lion, buffalo, giraffe and leopard, as well as a variety of antelope and over 410 bird species. This abundance of wildlife can be observed on foot, from a safari vehicle or canoe, or while on a sunset cruise. Unsurprisingly, given its diversity of attractions, this iconic destination draws visitors from all over the world – partying backpackers, sedate sightseers, thrill-seekers or nature-lovers can all find lodgings that suit their lifestyle and budget in or around the small town of Victoria Falls in Zimbabwe, or its Zambian counterpart, Livingstone.

When to go

Vic Falls is a **year-round destination**, but inevitably some months are better than others depending on what you want to do, how much you want to spend, and how hot you are prepared to be. Taking **cost** first, most hotels and lodgings maintain the same prices for the whole year (see p.300). On the other hand, air tickets and hotel rooms are harder to come by and can be more expensive over Christmas and New Year, Easter, and the main summer holiday period for Europeans and North Americans (July–Aug).

The region's **winter** occurs between May and October, in the generally slightly cooler dry season; **summer** runs from November to April, which coincides with the rainy

SUNSET CRUISE ON THE UPPER ZAMBEZI

Highlights

❶ **Whitewater rafting** Exhilarating and nerve-wracking in equal measure, of the many adrenaline activities on offer, rafting the turbulent rapids of the Zambezi is the highlight. **See p.305**

❷ **The Victoria Falls** Soak up the spray, while marvelling at one of the world's most spectacular waterfalls. **See p.312 & p.313**

❸ **Victoria Falls Bridge** You may not fancy bungee jumping off it, but make sure you seek a vantage point to take in this outstanding feat of imperialist engineering. **See p.315**

❹ **Camping and canoeing** Spend an unforgettable night under canvas before witnessing sunrise over the Zambezi, and paddling right up to the wildlife. **See p.317**

❺ **Walking safari** The only way to really experience the sights, sounds and smells of the African bush is on foot: consider tracking rhinos, or birdwatching at dawn. **See p.322 & p.336**

❻ **Sunset cruise** Glide past lazing crocs and grunting hippos on the Upper Zambezi as you sip your gin and tonic and watch the sun slip below the horizon. **See p.322**

❼ **High tea at the Victoria Falls Hotel** A chance to transport yourself back in time, and indulge in dainty sandwiches, cream scones and tea out of china cups while enjoying the view from the splendid Stanley's Terrace. **See p.325**

HIGHLIGHTS ARE MARKED ON THE MAP ON P.310

season. At the height of winter (May–Aug), daytime temperatures are also more pleasant, remaining in the mid- to late twenties, though you'll need to bring something warm for the cold nights. As the land continues to heat up after the rains stop, the temperatures rise, sometimes exceeding 35°C in October and November, until the arrival of the rains helps cool the place, albeit only very slightly; with the advent of rain, though, humidity levels rise and tropical thunderstorms are common.

The Zambezi's **water levels**, which vary throughout the year, are crucial to your experience of **viewing the falls** (see box, p.312) and other activities such as **whitewater rafting**. Low water levels (generally Aug–Dec) see the rapids at their most hair-raising, whereas when the river is swollen (usually Feb–May or June) some of the rapids get washed out in the surge of water, or are too dangerous to raft down. The summer rains in Vic Falls (Dec–April, usually peaking Dec–Feb) may be insignificant to water levels in the Zambezi, but they affect the vegetation and conditions for **wildlife viewing**. The latter is much easier towards the back end of the drier winter months (July/Aug–Nov), when animals are forced to migrate to the river or congregate at well-established water holes to drink.

Brief history

Archeological evidence indicates that people have lived close to the Zambezi for at least three million years, with particularly high concentrations of human artefacts discovered

AROUND VICTORIA FALLS

▲ Lusaka

N

Kazungula and Botswana, Sesheke and Namibia

M10

Zambezi River

④

⑥

⑤

ZIMBABWE

MOSI-OA-TUNYA NATIONAL PARK

SEE 'VICTORIA FALLS' MAP

Siloka Island

ZAMBIA

Livingstone

Kazungula & Botswana

ZAMBEZI NATIONAL PARK

Elephant Hills Resort Golf Course

Victoria Falls

②

③

◄ KAZUNGULA ROAD

Victoria Falls

⑦

Zambezi River

VICTORIA FALLS NP

A8

①

0   3
kilometres

Victoria Falls International Airport, ▼ Bulawayo & Harare

HIGHLIGHTS

① Whitewater rafting
② The Victoria Falls
③ Victoria Falls Bridge
④ Camping and canoeing
⑤ Walking safari
⑥ Sunset cruise
⑦ High tea at the Victoria Falls Hotel

from the Middle and Late **Stone Ages** in and around the falls, especially where Livingstone is now located. Arguably, the first people to settle permanently in the area, around the seventeenth century, were the **Leya** (or Baleya, or Toka-Leya), as they call themselves now – though at the time, when ethnic identities were more fluid, some people also identified themselves as Toka (Batoka) or Tonga (Batonga). Two of the more prominent Leya chiefs presiding over these small, decentralized communities, which made a living from subsistence agriculture, cattle-herding and fishing, were Mukuni and Sekute (see box, p.329). They originally lived on Siloka Island (sometimes referred to as Lwanda or Long Island) and Kalai Island, respectively. Though initially at war with each other, they eventually found peace through marriage but were squeezed between the more powerful **warrior kingdoms** of the Lozi (Silozi) – to whom they paid tribute – and Kololo (Makololo) north of the Zambezi, and the Ndebele (or Matabele) to the south. With their detailed knowledge of the river, the Leya found themselves indispensible to these more powerful neighbours, helping them to cross the dangerous waterway to carry out raids on each other, though Leya assistance in such matters sometimes resulted in reprisals. Considered inferior to these peoples, the Leya were inevitably left out of the wars, negotiations, treaty-making and trickery that the **British** engaged in with the Lozi and Ndebele elites, as they pushed for imperial dominance in the region during the latter part of the nineteenth century.

The colonial period

Britain's imperial and colonial ambitions in southern Africa were facilitated by the arrival of the railway from Bulawayo and the construction of the Victoria Falls Bridge in 1905, masterminded by arch imperialist **Cecil Rhodes**, head of the British South Africa Company. While the railway was instrumental in kick-starting foreign tourism in the region, its main aims were to serve the development of settler communities and facilitate mineral extraction.

By the early nineteenth century Britain had consolidated its grip on the land by forming the Protectorate of Northwest Rhodesia in 1891, north of the river, before amalgamating it with Northeast Rhodesia in 1911 to establish **Northern Rhodesia** (modern-day Zambia); at the same time present-day Zimbabwe became **Southern Rhodesia** in 1923, and the Zambezi was declared as the boundary between the two. The Leya, and other riverine populations round the falls, became split between the two areas. Though the Lozi royalty still maintained some status in and around Livingstone, and Lozi were generally favoured for jobs in the colonial administration, the **black populations** became increasingly marginalized physically, economically and politically. They faced onerous taxes, restricted access to the river – as game reserves and parks were formed to create a white playground – and eventually **forced evictions** from their lands as they were moved into reserves.

8

VIEWING THE FALLS

Your experience of **viewing the falls** depends very much on the amount of water tumbling over the precipice: you could be gazing at a lengthy, bare rock face with scarcely a trickle of water; alternatively, you may be drenched in thick spray, unable to see a thing. All this depends not on the rain in Vic Falls, but rather on the arrival of the water that has fallen as rain in the Zambezi headwaters in the hills of Zambia and Angola. This usually peaks in late March to early May. When in **full flow**, the "thunder" is deafening, aerial views of the spray are at their most dramatic, and rainbows abound. On the other hand, you will be constantly soaked with spray, visibility will be severely reduced, and photography – unless you have a fully waterproof camera – will be impossible. Conversely, from the end of October to December, as the **river level drops**, many of the falls dry up, exposing vast sheets of bare basalt; at this time of year, you get a much better view of the reddish cliffs, and a greater appreciation of the depth of the gorge, and the falls' geological formation. Thus, arguably the **prime viewing times** are January and February and July to September, when there is usually sufficient water for the falls to impress, but not so much that the thick cloak of spray totally obscures the falls themselves.

Though both protectorates developed different trajectories in the years between annexation by the British and independence, the common thread was one of **white privilege** in every sphere – land tenure, political rights and economic advantage – sustained through force if necessary, punctuated by periodic civil unrest, labour strikes and political protests by some of the black African majority.

8

Struggle for independence

In Northern Rhodesia, the colonial government more readily recognized the "winds of change" in Africa and, despite the usual period of jailing, persecuting and intimidating opposition leaders, the transition to **independence** was relatively smooth – the Republic of Zambia was established in 1964 – compared to the years of bloodshed that occurred across the Zambezi in Southern Rhodesia. Here, inspired by Zambia's independence, two rival factions – the military wing of the Shona-dominated Zimbabwe African National Union (ZANU), led by **Robert Mugabe**, and the Ndebele-dominated Zimbabwe African People's Union (ZAPU), led by **Joshua Nkomo** – took on the Rhodesian white-minority government, which was led by **Ian Smith** and backed by the apartheid South African government. The ensuing Liberation War (often referred to as the **Second Chimurenga**) lasted on and off for fourteen years. It was a brutal civil conflict involving periods of martial law, international sanctions, dirty-tricks campaigns and covert assassinations, and resulted in the loss of around 30,000 lives, before independence was finally achieved in **1980** and Robert Mugabe – the current president – was elected prime minister.

Post-independence

From the late 1960s and throughout the 1970s, **tourism** in the Vic Falls area suffered on both sides of the Zambezi, on account of the conflict in Southern Rhodesia and the growing unrest in South Africa, since most tourists were from those two countries. Once Zimbabwe gained independence and the political situation had stabilized somewhat, visitors began to flock back to Vic Falls and new hotels were built. However, tourism on the Zambian side remained neglected since the government was more concerned with exploiting the country's **mineral wealth** – copper in particular – than promoting tourism. By the mid-1990s, Vic Falls Town was full to capacity while the Zambian side of the falls remained in the doldrums. Once copper prices had plummeted, however, the Zambian government began to promote tourism in the country – highlighting **Livingstone** in particular – as a means of diversifying the economy. Livingstone's emergence as a tourist destination was then aided by the political and economic crisis that was unfolding across the border. Though the Zimbabwean economy was already struggling, it was dealt a further blow by the violence that erupted in 2000 due to the mismanaged fast-track **land reform programme**, which stipulated that white-owned farms should immediately be handed over to black citizens. Land grabs by war veterans (both genuine and bogus) resulted in further political violence, ultimately spiralling into financial chaos and soaring unemployment, sending an already ailing economy into free fall, and pitching many Zimbabweans into yet greater poverty. Visitors and even some businesses fled across the border to Livingstone, whose fortunes were further boosted by two huge hotel investments. Despite all these setbacks, following the hosting of the **UN World Tourism Organization** general assembly in Vic Falls in 2013, Mosi-oa-Tunya is very much back on the global tourism map and flourishing on both sides of the Zambezi.

Zimbabwe

Victoria Falls National Park

Entrance on Livingstone Way, just before the bridge • Daily sunrise–sunset • US$30; US$40 for a lunar viewing for three nights round the full moon • Vic Falls park office ☎ 013 42294 • A 10–15min downhill walk from Vic Falls Town, or a US$5 taxi ride

People from all over the world flock to this corner of Zimbabwe for the fabulous **Victoria Falls**; although also shared with Zambia, eighty percent of the river cascades into the gorge on the Zimbabwean side. When in full flow, more than 500 million litres of water tumble over this 1.7km-wide precipice every minute, providing a full-frontal assault on the senses. But whether you witness this phenomenal spectacle at its peak or are confronted – when water levels are at their lowest (see box opposite) – by a bare, 100m-high sheet of rock, laced only with a few dramatic cascades, the sight is breathtaking. If you want to **avoid the crowds**, as well as the heat of the day, then arrive when the gates open at 6am; this is also the best time to stand a chance of glimpsing some of the park's shy **wildlife**. Rainbows can be seen at any time of the day when there's enough spray, though lunar rainbows are a different matter (see box, p.314). Since your entry ticket is valid for the whole day you could do both. All in all, it'll take you a good couple of hours to meander round the various viewpoints. Be prepared for the **spray** to drench you – and anything you may be carrying – when water levels are high; ponchos

8

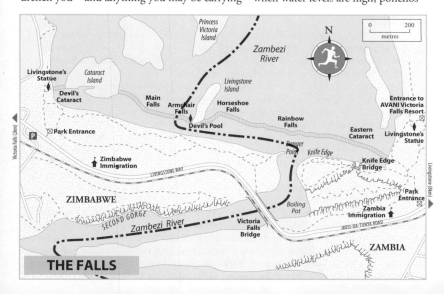

LUNAR RAINBOWS

The falls are famous for their rainbows – some are even double or full-circle – which are at their most magnificent when water levels are high (see box, p.312) and more spray is produced. If your visit happens to coincide with a full moon on a clear night, you might even be treated to a **lunar rainbow**. Also known as a moonbow or white rainbow, the colours appear faded to the naked eye, though they will show up on a photo if taken with a long exposure. Provided the weather is favourable, the park stays open after sunset the night of the full moon (plus a night either side). Bring a torch along, take the usual precautions regarding getting wet, and **organize transport** to and from the falls, which can be easily done via your accommodation. Do not try to walk there or back at that hour since it is unsafe.

---

can be rented at the entrance (US$3), but since they are not made of breathable material, you're likely to get just as wet from sweat on the inside.

Brief history

An aerial view of the present-day falls reveals that their current location is possibly their **eighth incarnation**, 8km upstream from where they were first located, as years of erosion by the powerful Zambezi have been forcing them to retreat.

The geological process that led to the falls' formation in the first place began in the **Jurassic period**, over 150 million years ago, following the breakup of the supercontinent Gondwanaland. In this tectonic upheaval, cracks in the Earth's crust allowed molten lava – basalt – to spew out onto the surface, filling in these cracks, and leaving a thin layer on top. As the hard basalt cooled, it contracted, revealing further fissures, which over time were filled and overlaid with softer sedimentary deposits.

When the Zambezi River, which millions of years ago followed a different course, was eventually forced to settle on its current route, the **erosion process** at the falls that is visible today started in earnest, probably several hundred thousand years ago. Over time, as the Zambezi's force has carved its way through the softer rock in the wide cracks in the basalt – predominantly east-west and west-east, with some narrower ones running north-south – the falls have shifted. Today, the beginnings of a **new falls** are already evident at the far western end, as a ravine is being worn at the lower-lying Devil's Cataract.

The falls

Although plenty of operators offer guided tours of the falls, they are easy to get to and visit **on your own**. Armed with the annotated map given on entry, you are perfectly equipped to start your circuit of the sixteen viewpoints, where you are protected from the cliff edge by the flimsiest of wooden fences, if at all.

At the entrance, head left, past the **statue of David Livingstone** (see box, p.330) – in explorer rather than missionary attire – over to the **Devil's Cataract**, which funnel the greatest volume of water in a year-round raging torrent. Make sure you descend the 56 steps, known as the chain walk, to get an even closer, eye-level, view. Moving east, viewpoints 3–6 give you further perspectives on the Devil's Cataract, before you reach **Main Falls**, an 800m-wide curtain of water that roars when in full flow, throwing up vast plumes of spray that drench the visitor and nourish the surrounding "**rainforest**". Though not rainforest in the true sense, the microclimate produced by constant spray and sunshine nourishes some impressive ebony, fig and mahogany trees as well as a tangle of vines.

A couple of hundred metres further along the path, the vegetation falls away as you look across to **Livingstone Island** (viewpoints 9–10), where the intrepid explorer peered over the edge into the void "to find out where the vast body of water went; it seemed to lose itself in the Earth." These days, in the dry season, look out for tourists doing much the same thing while bobbing in the Devil's Pool (see p.331), to the west of the island. To the east of Livingstone Island, **Horseshoe Falls**, so-named because of their shape,

THE VICTORIA FALLS BRIDGE

Variously condemned as an act of "engineering vandalism", a "hideous monument to Victorian vanity", and a stain on the natural beauty of the landscape, the **Victoria Falls Bridge** has become almost as big a tourist attraction as the falls themselves. Moreover, its construction was instrumental in bringing foreign visitors to Vic Falls in the early twentieth century (see p.311), paving the way for the place to become the major international tourist destination it is today. The motivating force behind the bridge was **Cecil Rhodes** (see p.311), who wanted a bridge across the Zambezi to fulfil his expansionist dream of a Cape-to-Cairo railway. Various locations for its construction were considered, yet Rhodes – who died before ever seeing Mosi-oa-Tunya, and before work on the bridge had even started – was adamant that it should span the gorge below the falls, "**where the trains, as they pass, will catch the spray.**" Designed by consultant engineer George Hobson, the structure's various components were built and assembled in sections in northern England, at a cost of £72,000. After being shipped over 13,000km to Mozambique, they were brought by rail to Vic Falls, where they were reassembled on site in a matter of weeks by a team of engineers and several hundred African labourers, most of whom were paid little more than US$1 per month. The official opening took place on **September 12, 1905**, amid much imperial pomp and fanfare. Remarkably, the project had taken less than a year and a half to complete, resulting in the world's highest bridge at the time, its signature parabolic arch – the world's widest then at 157m – suspended 128m above the Zambezi.

and **Rainbow Falls**, the highest at 108m, cascade into the ravine. Further east along the path, the bare unprotected ledge of rock that forms the aptly named **Danger Point** looks across to the Zambian side of the falls, taking in the **Eastern Cataract** and the rocky **Knife Edge** promontory. If you've got the stomach for it, you can peer over into the **Boiling Pot**, below, where the churning water heads down into the second gorge and under the **Victoria Falls Bridge**. Watch the bungee jumpers (see p.303) plummeting off the bridge before heading back to the exit, where there is a good café and craft shop.

Zambezi National Park

Main entrance on Parkway Drive • Daily 6am–6pm • US$15/person; US$5 for a Zimbabwe-registered vehicle or US$10 for a foreign vehicle

A small but scenic reserve, the **Zambezi National Park** may not compete with the likes of Chobe or Hwange (see box, p.324) for either quantity or variety of large mammals but it is, nevertheless, a beguiling setting. The landscape, comprising a 40km stretch of the majestic Upper Zambezi, is lined with patches of riverine forest, becoming mopane woodland, scrub and open **savannah** further inland. There's enough wildlife in the park to keep you interested too – provided you're not obsessed with seeing large herds of big game. Moreover, with the main entrance only a few kilometres outside Vic Falls Town, it makes an easy half- or full-day outing.

The park is recovering from years of **neglect**, and the underfunded park authorities, aided by local conservation groups, are struggling to deal with the increasing threat from poachers – yet wildlife numbers are improving. Substantial herds of **elephant** can be seen drinking and bathing in the river, especially in the dry season; other large mammals you might see include giraffe, zebra, buffalo and wildebeest; antelope are fairly common – sable, impala, eland, kudu, waterbuck and bushbuck are all present. So too are lion, leopard and even wild dog, though in small numbers and they are seldom spotted. Pods of snorting hippos and watchful crocs, however, are almost guaranteed sightings in the river.

The reserve certainly offers excellent **birdwatching** – over 410 species have been recorded in the area – especially in the early morning as the mist lifts from the reed beds and sandbanks. Keep a lookout for African skimmers on the surface of the river, the shy African finfoot hiding under overhanging vegetation, or the western banded snake eagle on the lookout for prey.

8

ZAMBEZI NATIONAL PARK ACCOMMODATION

If total immersion in nature is what you want, then it's worth spending a night or two within **Zambezi National Park**. Dotted along the banks of the great river in picturesque spots, the various accommodation options are surrounded by bush that is brimming with birdlife and home to plenty of other animals. What's more, the twenty **self-catering "lodges"** (recently refurbished but basic two-bedroom chalets really), which each sleep four, are within reach of Vic Falls Town, only 6km away, at the end of a tarred road. The four unfenced bush **campsites** and three **fishing camps** – which have shelters, but are rather run-down – lie some distance away (up to 46km from the main entrance) and are even more rudimentary, possessing little more than a braai stand (BBQ) and a long-drop toilet (no water). Whichever you choose, you're guaranteed a great wilderness experience. Note that you may well have visitors to your camp – including hippo, buffalo and elephant – especially during the dry season.

PRACTICALITIES

The main disadvantage of staying in the park is the hassle of booking the accommodation. The online system that the national parks office (⊛zimparks.org) has been promising for some time is yet to function, and emails (𝐁bookings@zimparks.co.zw) often go unanswered. You can try phoning central reservations in Harare (☏04 706077). The Victoria Falls and Zambezi National Parks office on Victoria Falls Road (Mon–Fri 8am–4.30pm, ☏013 42294 or ☏013 44566) will accept booking on the day only, or just turn up at the park entrance (☏013 42294) where, if there is availability, you can pay on the spot. Lodges cost $120, campsites $15 per person.

8

Various **tour operators** lead walking or driving safaris into the park (see p.322), but two of the nicest ways to explore the area are to glide down the Zambezi in a canoe (see p.302) or to saddle up on a horseback safari (see p.303). If you decide to **drive** yourself (see p.299), note that 4WD is necessary, and after very heavy rains the park roads may be closed altogether.

PRACTICALITIES   ZAMBEZI NATIONAL PARK

The reserve is bisected by the main road to the border with Botswana, dividing the park into **two distinct areas**. The much more visited area north of the road is accessed via the **main park entrance** on Parkway Drive, 5km from Vic Falls Town. From here the Zambezi River Game Drive leads you towards the river before following it upstream, with the occasional loop road off it. Dotted with riverside picnic sites, it's a popular weekend retreat for local families, but you can have the place to yourself midweek. The **southern section** is accessed along the 25km Chamabondo Game Drive, whose entrance lies off the road to Bulawayo. Initially taking you through teak forest, the road then leads onto open grasslands, punctuated by the occasional waterhole.

Victoria Falls Town

Given that Vic Falls is one of Africa's top tourist destinations, **VICTORIA FALLS TOWN** is surprisingly low-key in many respects. That's not to say it lacks touristy hustle and bustle – and it's certainly not short of hawkers – but the legacy of what was essentially an apartheid development policy in Zimbabwe means that most of the town's black population carry on their day-to-day lives in outlying "suburbs". In **high season**, however, there's an unmistakable buzz about the place – and plenty of toing and froing – as tourists hike to and from the falls or the bridge, nervous about their impending bungee jump, exhilarated and soaked by the spray from the falls, or flying high after a day's rafting. The town centre, moreover, comes alive in the early evening as folk compare tales about the day's events – but just as quickly, it quietens down: bars and restaurants close relatively early, with people returning to their lodgings to carry on partying there, or to have an early night in preparation for the next day's early-morning activities. The exception to all this is three days of hedonistic excess round New Year that is the **Victoria Falls Carnival** (⊛vicfallscarnival.com), which draws a big crowd, and centres on a music festival that attracts big-name DJs and music artists from around southern Africa; at the same time major discounts are offered on the usual adventure activities.

VICTORIA FALLS: A FLUID NAME

Note that Victoria Falls, or "**Vic Falls**", to use the common abbreviation, can refer to the actual falls, the nearby Zimbabwean resort town, and the whole area surrounding the falls, which takes in the Zambian town of Livingstone too.

The **town centre** is little more than a glorified T-junction, where Parkway Drive – the road that leads to the Zambezi National Park and many of the nicer lodges out of town – meets the main highway from Bulawayo, which becomes Livingstone Way as it enters the urban area. At the junction there's an assortment of quaint, old-fashioned **shopping arcades**, fronted by painted signs and stuffed with tour operators, curio (craft) shops and the occasional café or restaurant. Most major **services** are also located in this area. If you head steeply downhill from the junction, across the old railway line, and a kilometre further on, you'll reach the entrance to the **falls**, where the deafening roar beyond the gate will set your pulse racing in anticipation. Beyond lies the Zimbabwe **border post** just before the Victoria Falls Bridge.

Behind the central shopping area, west of Livingstone Way, sprawls a leafy, **middle-class neighbourhood**, home to Vic Falls' white and wealthier black residents, and where the backpackers accommodation, B&Bs and smaller, less expensive lodges are located. On the other side of Livingstone Way, and further out, south of the road to Kazungula, lie the high-density poorer **townships** of Chinotimba and Mkhosana, home to most of Vic Falls' 60,000 black population.

In between these various locations, and at the fringes of the developments, the **bush** encroaches on the town; so too do its inhabitants, as monkeys are often seen scampering across the road, while baboons lope nonchalantly and elephants frequently roam about at night. You are quite likely to encounter some such wildlife, and more besides, if you take an early-morning wander round the 4km **Zambezi Drive loop** (see box, p.319), one of the few free attractions of Vic Falls Town.

Brief history

There were permanent settlements in the Victoria Falls area from around the **seventh century** – and humans have inhabited the place for a great deal longer (see p.341) – but Vic Falls as a **resort town** only came about after the building of the bridge and the arrival of the railway from Cape Town in 1905 (see box, p.315). Even then, it lagged behind development across the Zambezi in Livingstone. The first shop – Clark's Curios – was opened in 1903 by one of the early north-bank settlers, **Percy Clark**. An enterprising man, he soon expanded his business to include photography, tours of the falls, and even excursions upriver in Canadian canoes. By 1911, he had introduced the first motorized launch on the Upper Zambezi, taking the genteel guests from the *Victoria Falls Hotel* (see p.325) – which had opened in 1904 – to sip their G&Ts on deck while watching the sunset. As the falls' fame spread, tourist numbers increased in the 1920s and 30s with the completion of a new **tarred road** from Bulawayo and interest from cruise-ship visitors to Cape Town. However, it wasn't until the era of relatively cheap air travel and the opening of the **airport** in 1967 that mass tourism really began to take off.

Vic Falls remained relatively unaffected in the early stages of the Liberation War of the late 1960s and early 70s (see p.312), but by the middle of the decade, tourism had more or less come to a standstill, until **Zimbabwean independence** in 1980 brought stability to the country.

Tourists soon flocked back to Vic Falls and numbers were increasing until the political and economic troubles from around the year 2000 (see p.312). Add to that the negative press President **Mugabe** and Zimbabwe in general were getting, and tourism collapsed once more. Vic Falls was the last place to feel the effects and it appears to be the first to be getting back on its feet as tourist numbers are on the up once more, though Zimbabwe's economy more generally is still tottering.

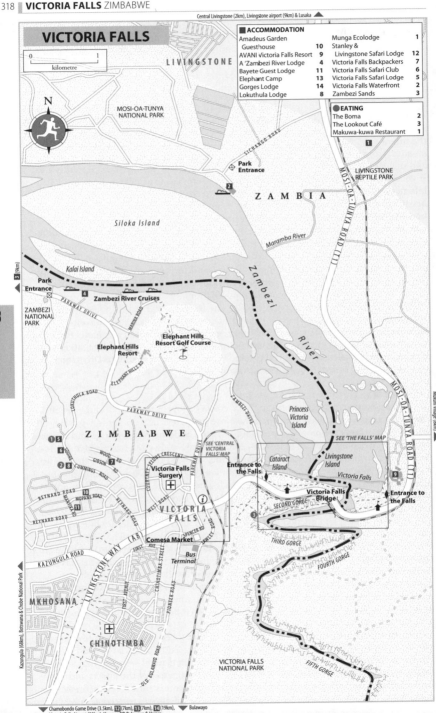

VICTORIA FALLS

■ ACCOMMODATION		
Amadeus Garden		Munga Ecolodge 1
Guesthouse	10	Stanley &
AVANI Victoria Falls Resort	9	Livingstone Safari Lodge 12
A 'Zambezi River Lodge	4	Victoria Falls Backpackers 7
Bayete Guest Lodge	11	Victoria Falls Safari Club 6
Elephant Camp	13	Victoria Falls Safari Lodge 5
Gorges Lodge	14	Victoria Falls Waterfront 2
Lokuthula Lodge	8	Zambezi Sands 3

● EATING	
The Boma	2
The Lookout Café	3
Makuwa-kuwa Restaurant	1

0 ————— 1
kilometre

N

LIVINGSTONE

MOSI-OA-TUNYA
NATIONAL PARK

SICHANGO ROAD

Park
Entrance

ZAMBIA

LIVINGSTONE
REPTILE PARK

Siloka Island

Maramba River

MOSI-OA-TUNYA ROAD (T1)

Kalai Island

Park
Entrance

PARKWAY DRIVE

MADUMA ROAD

Zambezi River Cruises

Z a m b e z i   R i v e r

ZAMBEZI
NATIONAL
PARK

Elephant Hills
Resort Golf Course

Elephant Hills
Resort

ELEPHANT HILLS RD

LOKUTHULA ROAD

PARKWAY DRIVE

ZAMBEZI DRIVE

Princess
Victoria
Island

SEE 'THE FALLS' MAP

Mukuni Village (8km) ▶

Z I M B A B W E

WOOD...RD

GIBSON RD

CUMMINGS ROAD

REYNARD ROAD

MAINWAY RD

MOPANE ROAD

REYNARD ROAD

COURTNEY SELLOUS CRESCENT

WEST ROAD

PARKWAY DRIVE

SEE 'CENTRAL
VICTORIA
FALLS' MAP

Cataract
Island

Livingstone
Island

Victoria Falls

SEE 'THE FALLS' MAP

Victoria Falls
Surgery

Entrance to
the Falls

Victoria Falls
Bridge

Entrance to
the Falls

MOSI-OA-TUNYA ROAD (T1)

V I C T O R I A
F A L L S

SPENCER RD

SWEET RD

SECOND GORGE

Comesa Market

Bus
Terminal

FIRST AVE

CHINOTIMBA STREET

PIONEER ROAD

LIVINGSTONE WAY (A8)

THIRD GORGE

KAZUNGULA ROAD

M K H O S A N A

FIRST AVENUE

FOURTH GORGE

Kazungula (68km), Botswana & Chobe National Park ◀

C H I N O T I M B A

OLD BULAWAYO ROAD

VICTORIA FALLS
NATIONAL PARK

FIFTH GORGE

8

3 (9km)

33 (9km)

THE ZAMBEZI DRIVE LOOP

A pleasant itinerary for a morning stroll is the 4km **Zambezi Drive loop**, which runs parallel to the Zambezi for a couple of kilometres before doubling back to join Parkway Drive and ultimately returning to town again. Along the way, you'll get glimpses of the quickening river as it slides unknowingly towards the falls, while the walk also makes for good **birdwatching**. At around the halfway point, you'll come across the "**Big Tree**", a giant baobab with a sizeable girth (though by no means the largest around) whose main claim to fame is that it once served as the meeting point and shelter for early travellers planning to cross the Zambezi to "Old Drift", the area's original European settlement over the river in present-day Zambia (see p.332). If you are doing the loop in the drier months (and especially in the early morning or at dusk), beware of **elephant** and **buffalo** making their way down to the water.

Jafuta Heritage Centre

Elephant's Walk Mall • Daily 9am–5pm • Free

Tucked away among the shops of the Elephant's Walk Mall is one of the town's few real "sights": the **Jafuta Heritage Centre**, a gem of a small private collection of cultural artefacts – tools, weapons, musical instruments, adornments and pieces of art from the Shona, Ndebele, Lozi and Tonga peoples, all beautifully displayed and accompanied by informative text. The museum's curator, Ephraim, who is often on hand to share his knowledge, is also a practising traditional healer.

ARRIVAL AND DEPARTURE VICTORIA FALLS TOWN

BY PLANE

VICTORIA FALLS AIRPORT

International flights arrive at the recently expanded and upgraded Victoria Falls International Airport (VFA), 23km south of town. Facilities in the new international terminal include an ATM but no money exchange, an Econet desk, where you can purchase a SIM card and airtime, and desks for several car rental firms (see p.321).

Getting into town There is no bus service from the airport into Vic Falls. Most lodgings, however, provide a shuttle, usually at extra cost and for much the same US$14–16/person charged by various tour companies. Otherwise, a private taxi costs US$30, though they may do a cheaper deal if you agree to return to the airport with the same driver.

Flights and airlines There are no direct flights from Europe, North America or Australasia to Victoria Falls. Most international visitors fly in via Oliver Tambo International Airport, Johannesburg, from where there are daily connections to Vic Falls with British Airways on Comair (w britishairways.com) and South African Airways (w flysaa.com). Air Zimbabwe (Mon–Fri 8am–4.30pm, Sat 8am–11.30am; ☎ 013 43168, w www.airzimbabwe .aero), which has an office on Livingstone Way, opposite the Total petrol station, has been an on-off enterprise for a number of years: even when functioning, flights are often cancelled; theoretically, however, it is currently operating daily domestic flights to and from Harare, Bulawayo and Kariba, as well as between Johannesburg and Vic Falls. Air Namibia (w airnamibia.com.na) flies to Vic Falls from Windhoek, Namibia (direct Fri & Sun; via Maun, Botswana, on Mon & Wed; 1hr 40min for the direct flight), returning

directly to Windhoek from Vic Falls on Mon and Wed (and via Maun Fri & Sun). Return flights from Johannesburg to Vic Falls cost from around R4800, but better deals may be had by flying into Livingstone, over the border in Zambia (see p.335) – so check before booking. You would then need to budget for a shuttle transfer on top, and possibly the cost of an extra visa (see p.300).

BY BUS

Intercape Mainliner (w intercape.co.za) offers a reliable bus service three times a week from Windhoek to Livingstone and the Zimbabwean border (Mon, Wed & Fri; 20hr 30min; from R600), from where it is a short hop across the bridge into Zimbabwe (see p.335). The return bus to Windhoek from the Zambian side of the Vic Falls border leaves on Wed, Fri & Sun, with onward connections to Cape Town, South Africa. Intercape also operates services four times a week from Bulawayo to Vic Falls, and from Vic Falls (*The Kingdom Hotel*; see p.324) to Bulawayo (both Mon, Wed, Fri & Sun: 5hr 30min; R214) with onward connections from Bulawayo to Harare and north to Malawi, or south to Pretoria and Johannesburg. Two other companies also offer long-distance bus services between Pretoria and Johannesburg and Bulawayo: Greyhound (w greyhound.co.za) and Intercity (w intercityxpress.co.za); Greyhound offers a slightly quicker, more expensive service (about 14hr; R480).

BY MINIBUS

Minibuses bound for Bulawayo (US$15) and Harare (US$30) leave from the main bus station in Chinotimba township, east of Livingstone Way, as you enter town along the main

8

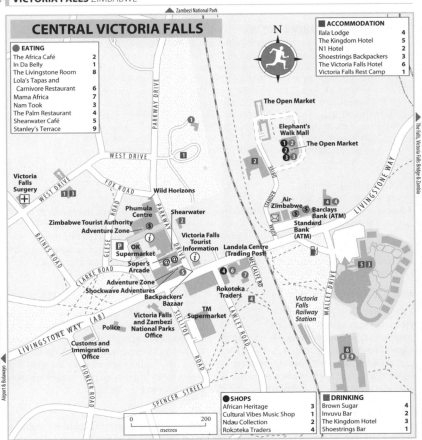

CENTRAL VICTORIA FALLS

▲ Zambezi National Park

N

● EATING

The Africa Café	2
In Da Belly	1
The Livingstone Room	8
Lola's Tapas and Carnivore Restaurant	6
Mama Africa	7
Nam Took	3
The Palm Restaurant	4
Shearwater Café	5
Stanley's Terrace	9

■ ACCOMMODATION

Ilala Lodge	4
The Kingdom Hotel	5
N1 Hotel	2
Shoestrings Backpackers	3
The Victoria Falls Hotel	6
Victoria Falls Rest Camp	1

● SHOPS

African Heritage	3
Cultural Vibes Music Shop	1
Ndau Collection	2
Rokoteka Traders	4

■ DRINKING

Brown Sugar	4
Invuvu Bar	2
The Kingdom Hotel	3
Shoestrings Bar	1

0 — 200 metres

▼ Bus Terminal

road from Bulawayo and the airport. Larger buses usually leave early in the morning or late at night, with minibuses setting off throughout the day when full – or overfull – with music blaring. The minibuses are faster, but the driving is prone to being more reckless and more uncomfortable.

BY SHARED TAXI

Although there's no official transport between Vic Falls and Kasane, Botswana, shared taxis (US$7) leave when full from the turn-off to Kazungula, a few kilometres outside town.

BY TRAIN

A daily overnight service runs between Bulawayo and Vic Falls. Cabins are available for three or six people in second class (US$12), or two or four people in first class (US$15). Trains are in desperate need of refurbishment – including some wonderful 1950s wood-panelled carriages – so it's worth paying the extra for a first-class ticket to ensure a modicum of comfort – but don't raise your expectations

too high; bedding, for example, is no longer provided. Trains depart from Bulawayo at 7.30pm, arriving around 9am in Vic Falls. From Vic Falls trains leave at 7pm, arriving in Bulawayo at 9am. Both trains have a dining car, but the food can be limited so it's advisable to take supplies too. Note, however, that safety is a concern, as robberies have periodically been reported, so enquire about the current security situation before jumping aboard.

Tickets Tickets can be purchased at the Vic Falls station ticket office only on the day of travel (☎ 013 443902; Mon–Fri 7–10am & 2.30–6.45pm; Sat & Sun 9–10am & 4.30–6.45pm; or at Bulawayo train station (☎ 09 362284; Mon–Fri 8am–7.30pm, Sat & Sun 4–7.30pm).

BY CAR

Note that at all these borders you will need to present the vehicle's papers, and be liable for cross-border vehicle charges.

Within Zimbabwe Vic Falls is accessed via a fast, tarred

MONEY MATTERS

Since 2016 the Zimbabwe government has officially recognized **nine currencies** in the country – from yen to euros, pounds to pula. In practice, the US dollar is the most useful currency for day-to-day living, with the fading South African rand more current near the South African border. In Vic Falls Town, where all activities are priced in **US dollars** and the ATM dispenses dollar bills, this currency is king and others, though accepted, tend to get less favourable rates. If the **ATMs** in Vic Falls Town are not working, the banks (see p.328) should **advance** you money on your credit card (provided it is Visa or Mastercard) on presentation of your passport. **Travellers' cheques** are no longer of use, but **credit cards** (Visa and, to a lesser extent, Mastercard) are now accepted by most of the major lodges and tour operators. Even so, it's still a good idea to arrive with some US dollars **in cash**, including some small denominations. At the opposite end of the scale, you're bound to encounter young lads in the street trying to flog you an old Zimbabwean trillion-dollar note as a souvenir.

road from Bulawayo, which lies 440km southeast (around a 5hr drive).

From/to Zambia The town is also easily accessible by good roads from Zambia, via Livingstone, 10km across the border on the Victoria Falls Bridge (daily 6am–10pm; see box, p.315).

From/to Botswana The Kazungula road border with Botswana (daily 6am–6pm) lies only 70km west of Vic Falls on a good tarred road, with good road connections on the Botswana side of the border.

From/to Namibia The two access routes from Namibia both entail travelling via Katima Mulilo: one uses the Ngoma border with Botswana (daily 6am–6pm), through Chobe National Park, crossing into Zimbabwe at the Kazungula road border west of Vic Falls (see p.335); the other involves crossing into Zambia via the Katima Mulilo Bridge over the Zambezi (daily 6am–6pm), driving to Livingstone and then on to the border post at the falls. Note that the 6am opening time is Namibian time, which is one hour behind the time in Zambia, Zimbabwe, Botswana and South Africa for some of the year (see Basics, p.72).

From/to South Africa Depending where you are travelling from in South Africa and where you want to stay en route, you can drive on good roads to Vic Falls through Botswana or Namibia, or cross the border into Zimbabwe at Beitbridge/Mzingwane, 320km southeast of Bulawayo, which is the route most transport from the Johannesburg/Pretoria area takes.

8

GETTING AROUND

BY TAXI

Taxis are plentiful but generally expensive. The standard rate from the Zambian border or the falls (which are within 100m of each other) to town is US$3–5, depending on your negotiating skills and how brisk business is. It's around US$5 for anywhere around town. Rates are a little higher after dark. For the lodges several kilometres out of town, bank on paying nearer US$10 from the border, the falls or from town. A journey to or from the airport costs US$30.

BY SHUTTLE BUS

Outlying lodges and hotels provide courtesy shuttles that will drop you off and pick you up in town. The service, which ranges from hourly to daily, deposits people in town, then goes down to the falls, dropping off or picking up passengers at the entrance, before returning back through town, stopping outside Soper's Arcade, or the main Wild Horizons office (see p.322), to whisk guests back to their accommodation. For most activities hotel transfers are included in the rates.

ON FOOT

Since "downtown" Vic Falls essentially consists of two roads and a couple of small shopping arcades, you can get everywhere easily on foot. The entrance to the falls too is a mere 10–15min walk downhill from the central T-junction, though the lengthier return slog uphill in the heat of the day might persuade you to succumb to a taxi. Although it is perfectly safe to walk during the day, you should take a taxi in the evening.

BY CAR

Car rental is very expensive in Vic Falls (see p.299), but there's no real need (unless you're planning onward travel to other parts of Zimbabwe and southern Africa): you can get around easily, and more cheaply, with a combination of courtesy shuttle services, taxis, tours and walking.

Rental companies Avis, Budget and Europcar have offices at the airport: Avis (T 013 43506, W avis.co.zw); Budget (T 013 2243, W budget.com); Europcar (T 013 43466, W europcarzimbabwe.com). Hertz (T 013 47012, W hertz.co.za) is on Parkway in the Batoka Safaris office; Khanondo (T 013 44884, W khanondosafaris.com), which specializes in 4WD and more high-end vehicles, is in the Bata Building on Livingstone Way.

INFORMATION

There is no municipal tourist service, but two private tourist information offices can both provide you with plenty of information on activities. However, advice on which company to go with may not necessarily be totally disinterested since they receive commission from the operators whose tours they sell.

Backpackers Bazaar Shop 5, Bata Building ☎013 45828 or ☎0712 404 960, ⓦbackpackersbazaarvicfalls .com. Run by *Shoestrings Backpackers* (see p.325), this operator has bags of information, leaflets, can book activities, and also operates a book exchange, for which you make a dollar contribution to the anti-poaching fund. Mon–Fri 8am–5pm, Sat & Sun 9am–4pm.

Victoria Falls Tourist Information Centre Parkway

Drive, at the corner with Livingstone Way ☎013 44202. Managed by the aptly named Knowledge, this place can get good deals on activities, has some fliers, and can sell you maps of the falls (the same one that is included in the falls entry fee), Vic Falls and Zimbabwe. If you want to experience more of "real" Zimbabwe, he can also arrange a half-day visit to the nearby village of Mpisi. Daily 8am–6pm.

TOUR OPERATORS

The biggest **tour operator** in Vic Falls is Wild Horizons, which also runs several lodges, followed by Shearwater, which is the longest-established rafting company. These outfits operate most of the **activities** (see p.301) they offer themselves, though they will also book **third-party** activities for you. Both advertise a wide range of attractions, including excursions to Chobe and Hwange national parks (see box, p.324). Other operators are **specialists** in just one activity, or are general operators that book on behalf of the specialists. The operators below generally keep much the same office hours: daily 6/7am–7pm.

Adventure Zone Shop 4, Phumala Centre ☎013 44424 or ☎0712 210798, ⓦadventurezonevicfalls.com. This operator is mainly about adrenaline sports – and is one of the four rafting operators – though they also offer a village tour and airport transfers.

Backpackers' Bazaar Shop 5, Bata Building ☎013 45828 or ☎0712 404960, ⓦbackpackersbazaarvicfalls .com. *Shoestrings Backpackers* (see p.325) tour company which, along with the usual range of adrenaline, scenic and wildlife-viewing activities, organizes one- to three-night budget camping trips to Chobe and Hwange national parks (see box, p.324), and even to Namibia. A two-day safari to Chobe, for example, costs US\$360 per person.

Discover Safaris ☎013 45821 or ☎0772 177324, ⓦdiscovervictoriafalls.com. Owner-operator Charles Brightman is an excellent professional guide, renowned conservationist and founder of the Victoria Falls anti-poaching unit. He leads private birding or wildlife drives and walking safaris to the Zambezi National Park and further afield. US\$75 for a morning doing any of these activities, or through *Victoria Falls Safari Lodge* (see p.326).

Shearwater Parkway Drive ☎013 44471, ⓦshearwatervictoriafalls.com. Highly professional, experienced operator. As well as being the rafting pioneers,

they can book all manner of tours and activities, and offer combination packages. They also run transfers within Zimbabwe and to Zambia and Botswana, and own several restaurants.

Shockwave Adventures Shop 6, Bata Building Parkway Drive ☎013 43002 or ☎0772 814545, ⓦshockwavevicfalls.com. A rafting outfit known for its personalized customer service and multi-day tours, such as the five-day trip down to the Matestsi River (US\$1138). Also offers good deals on combo packages with other adventure activities, and does transfers. Daily 8am–5pm.

Victoria Falls Guide ☎0776 779932 or ☎013 46213, ⓦvictoriafalls-guide.net. This experienced Zimbabwean husband-and-wife team offers a personalized service and can organize everything from accommodation to tours and car rental. Mon–Fri 8am–5pm.

Wild Horizons 310 Parkway Drive ☎013 44571 or ☎0712 213721, ⓦwildhorizons.co.za. The glitziest office for the biggest tour company, which can organize every aspect of your trip, if you want, from accommodation to transfers, to activities. This major rafting operator offers various combo packages, and owns its own boat which runs highly acclaimed cruises on the Zambezi. Also runs day-trips to Chobe from Zambia.

ACCOMMODATION

There are plenty of options in Vic Falls Town itself, from the historic *Victoria Falls Hotel* to a range of inexpensive accommodation including campsites and backpackers places. Several hotels and lodges are situated a few kilometres outside the town, off Parkway Drive that runs broadly parallel to the Upper Zambezi, and there's a growing number of small lodges, guesthouses and B&Bs sprouting up round Raynard Road, in a quiet suburb about a 40min walk (or a US\$5 taxi ride) from town.

TRIPS TO CHOBE AND HWANGE NATIONAL PARKS

Two of the main excursions outside the Vic Falls area are to these nearby national parks. The most popular destination is **Chobe National Park**, just 70km away over the border in northern Botswana. Chobe is renowned for its vast quantities of large mammals (it has the world's greatest concentration of elephant), likely sightings of predators – including wild dogs – and fabulous river cruises. Those heading for Chobe generally do a **day-trip** (around US$160–170), but this can be a tiring disappointment: you can spend three to four hours on hotel pick-ups and drop-offs, travel, border and other formalities, and you're likely to miss the best times of the day for wildlife viewing – dawn and dusk. What's more, you'll not experience the magical sunsets frequently witnessed on a cruise along the **Chobe River**. A much better option is the acclaimed overnight or two-night basic **camping trip** that can be arranged through *Backpackers' Bazaar* (see p.322) in Vic Falls, or *Livingstone Backpackers* and *Jollyboys* in Livingstone (see p.337), which is usually cheaper. They all generally work with Kalahari Tours in Kasane (ⓦkalaharichobe.com). An overnight stay including a day and a half of activities will set you back US$300–360, and usually includes a game drive or two and a river cruise. Visa fees are not included but park fees are.

Potentially even more rewarding is an excursion to less well-known and less-visited **Hwange National Park**, Zimbabwe's largest reserve (US$20 international park fee), a two-hour drive away (but minus the border hassles). Yet it too has a large elephant population and over four hundred bird species. What's more, you can really enjoy the **wilderness experience** of being largely alone in the bush, whereas Chobe in the dry season can be jam-packed with safari vehicles queuing up to see a lion kill. The big operators will only put on a trip to Hwange if you have a group of at least four together; other operators, such as Khanondo Safaris (ⓦkhanondosafaris .com) in Vic Falls, run a full-day tour with picnic for US$170 (minimum two people), excluding park fees. With your own vehicle, it's an easy drive and there is plenty of private and government accommodation (see ⓦzimparks.org) in or around the park should you wish to spend the night here. As with Chobe, an overnight sojourn is likely to result in a more rewarding experience.

Rates and reservations Most places are overpriced, though you can often bargain a better rate in low season (see p.300), when a lot of package deals are available. Even the inexpensive options are not as cheap as elsewhere in Zimbabwe. However, the number of places to stay does not match the demand in high season when it's essential to book in advance. If you stay out of town, where some of the more luxurious accommodation is located, you will need to budget for taxis in the evening if you want to eat anywhere other than at your lodge. For the all-inclusive rates offered by some lodges, check carefully what is included before committing.

IN TOWN

Amadeus Garden Guesthouse 538 Reynard Rd ☎013 42261, ⓦamadeusgarden.com; map p.318. Well-established, German-run B&B comprising eleven spotless, fan-ventilated rooms (without TV), simply furnished in Zimbabwe teak. Six of the rooms open onto a pool area with sun loungers, the other five outward-facing rooms provide greater privacy. Enjoy a beer in the pleasant, thatched bar-dining area, where you can order from a simple menu if you don't feel like venturing out in the evening. B&B US$160

★**Bayete Guest Lodge** 584 Manyika Rd, off Reynard Rd ☎013 42275, ⓦbayeteguestlodge.com; map p.318. Really stylish thatched lodge set in luscious gardens,

boasting 25 nicely decorated, spacious rooms, leading into similarly design-conscious walk-in bathrooms with monsoon showers (and stand-alone Victorian-style baths in the executive rooms). Lovely pool area with sun-loungers and a pleasant semi-open dining room. Set dinner on request; otherwise it's a US$5 taxi ride into town. B&B US$210

★**Ilala Lodge** 411 Livingstone Way ☎013 44737, ⓦilalalodge.com; map p.320. Superbly located – central yet secluded, and a stone's throw from the falls, which you can hear from the lovely patio – this elegant, welcoming hotel provides 34 spacious, carpeted rooms tastefully done out in reclaimed teak. The gorgeous suites are under the thatch, with a balcony overlooking woodland. Superb food and efficient, friendly service – only the pond-like pool disappoints. B&B US$426

The Kingdom Hotel 1 Mallett Drive ☎013 44275 (hotel) or ☎04 700521 (reservations), ⓦafrican sunhotels.com; map p.320. More in tune with Vegas and Sun City, this Great Zimbabwe-themed hotel and entertainment centre hosts a casino, food court and a health spa. Beyond the ostentatious lobby lie surprisingly pleasant enclosed grounds, including ornamental ponds with reed beds, bridges, manicured lawns and a nice pool area. Smart, if bland, business-style rooms, most with a patio or balcony that overlooks the grounds. Family rooms for four include bunk beds. B&B US$260

★**N1 Hotel** 266 Adam Stander Drive ☎013 45040, ⊕n1hotel.co.zw; map p.320. The cheapest hotel in town is excellent value so it's often full. It offers compact, modern rooms with a/c and TV, plus tea- and coffee-making facilities. Make sure you bag one of the newly renovated second-floor rooms. The secure grassy campsite at the back is the best place to pitch a tent in town, with braai stands, a pleasant pool area with sun loungers, plenty of shade and a bar. Breakfast US$5 extra. Camping per person US$12, doubles US$59

Shoestrings Backpackers 12 West Drive ☎013 40167 or ☎0713 800731, ⊕shoestringsvicfalls.com; map p.320. A classic party backpackers place – so sleep will be limited – with a renowned lively bar serving decent pub grub, and a shady garden with pool and hammocks. Small, brightly painted rooms offer a good range of budget lodgings, with fan or a/c (US$5 extra). Organizes activities through its budget tour operator (see p.322). Camping per person US$8, dorms US$15, doubles US$55

Victoria Falls Backpackers 357 Gibson Rd ☎013 42209 or ☎0712 443333, ⊕victoriafallsbackpackers .com; map p.318. Relaxed, friendly backpackers in a quiet residential area a 15–20min walk from town. Plenty of Zimbabwean art in the leafy garden, plus a giant chess set, pool and nightly campfire. Accommodation is varied, but space is at a premium – the large dorm in particular is rather cramped. New self-drive camping plots available. Meals available at their on-site café. High-speed wi-fi US$3/day. Camping per person US$10, dorms US$18, safari tents US$40, doubles US$60

The Victoria Falls Hotel 2 Mallett Drive ☎013 44751, ⊕victoriafallshotel.com; map p.320. A relic of a bygone era, the *Victoria Falls Hotel* exudes faded colonial splendour, from the framed historical photos and prints that adorn the walls to the original brass taps in the rooms and the chandelier-lit, carpeted corridors. That said, rooms are small, except the new, much pricier, stables rooms, and while these look towards the falls, the grounds' huge trees can obscure the view. B&B US$455

Victoria Falls Rest Camp Parkway Drive at the corner with West Drive ☎013 40509, ⊕vicfallsrestcamp.com; map p.320. Secure, central cheap and with lots of room – though the campground is sloping and rocky – this restcamp attracts lots of overlander groups and end-of-year school parties (in Dec). Inexpensive domed tents with two small beds, table and light are available; so too are very basic chalets in need of renovation, containing little beyond two single beds of varying quality. Both share the spotless camping ablution blocks. The self-catering chalets (two–four guests) are similarly basic and in need of a facelift. The big plus is the lovely pool area with plenty of shade, picnic tables, sun loungers and a good bar-restaurant (see p.326). Camping per person US$16, dome tents US$40, chalets US$46, self-catering US$127

OUT OF TOWN

A 'Zambezi River Lodge 308 Parkway Drive ☎00 800 7297 2900 (toll free from the UK) or ☎1 888 790 5264 (toll free from the USA), or ☎013 44561, ⊕azambezi riverlodge.com; map p.318. With an enviable location on the banks of the eponymous river (though marred slightly by the many boats moored there), the *A 'Zambezi* provides good value for money. More hotel-like than lodge in feel, it comprises two large, semicircular, two-floor thatched buildings containing small, modern en-suite rooms, with a/c, minibar and TV, which open out onto a long shared patio or balcony. Sit and gaze over the nicely maintained grounds – frequented by warthogs – which slope down to the water. À la carte and buffet dining available. B&B US$360

Elephant Camp 10km from Vic Falls Town in the Victoria Falls National Park, off the road to Bulawayo ☎013 44571 or ☎0712 213721, ⊕theelephantcamp .com; map p.318. A luxurious safari experience, with twelve tents that offer fabulous views. Gaze across the bush to the spray from Batoka Gorge from your bed, bath or deck (including private plunge pool and outdoor shower). Top-notch cuisine, service and facilities ensure that you'll want for nothing. AI US$1134

★**Gorges Lodge** Batoka Gorge, 22km from Vic Falls, signposted off the Bulawayo Rd ☎09 252232 or ☎0783 568632, ⊕imvelosafarilodges.com/gorges -lodge.html; map p.318. In a stunning location, peering over a cliff 220m above the Zambezi, and set in butterfly-filled grounds, ten breezy stone-and-thatch chalets with private patios offer spectacular views over the rapids – as does the main lodge. Adjacent is the smaller luxury tented *Little Gorges* camp (same contact details), with its separate bar-dining area. A joint private-community venture, activities include school and village visits, as well as seeking out the resident black eagles. AI US$700

Stanley & Livingstone Safari Lodge Victoria Falls Private Game Reserve, 7km south of Vic Falls Town, off the A8 ☎013 41003, ⊕stanleyandlivingstone.com; map p.318. This colonial-style, thatched lodge comprises sixteen sumptuous suites that combine faux-antique furniture with modern comforts, plus private patios overlooking the manicured grounds or the bush. Located in a well-stocked private game reserve, which is home to the Big Five, its safari drives are a major attraction, as is the busy waterhole overlooked by the terrace. B&B US$672

★**Zambezi Sands** Zambezi National Park, 1hr drive upriver from Vic Falls ☎09 252232, ⊕imvelosafarlodges .com; map p.318. Comprising eight vast, opulent, tented suites in an idyllic location overlooking the Zambezi: each has a private deck with plunge pool, indoor and outdoor ablutions, and is exquisitely furnished. The birdwatching is excellent, and as well as the usual game drives and river cruises, you can go whitewater canoeing, or opt for a more sedate paddle. AI US$1156

8

VICTORIA FALLS SAFARI LODGE ESTATE

Spread over a hillside within a private reserve, abutting the Zambezi National Park, the *Victoria Falls Safari Lodge Estate* (471 Squire Cummings Rd, 3km from Vic Falls; ☎013 43211, ⓦafricaalbidatourism.com; map p.318) contains several outstanding properties, all served by a regular shuttle service from town.

★**Lokuthula Lodge** ☎013 44714. These superior, thatched, self-catering chalets (two- or three-bedroom) are extremely well kitted out (though don't expect a TV), exuding tasteful design yet a homely appeal, and are surrounded by bush. The multi-level pool is a treat, and if you tire of cooking for yourself, stroll over to *The Boma* (see below) or the safari lodge for dinner. B&B package also possible. Two-bedroomed chalets US$280

Victoria Falls Safari Club At the most exclusive end of the scale, these twenty plush residences (sixteen rooms, four suites) include butler service and plenty of treats – afternoon teas, canapés and cocktails – in the rates. Has its own guest lounge overlooking a waterhole, but you can join the masses at the main safari lodge next door if all the pampering palls. B&B. Doubles US$550, suites US$660

★**Victoria Falls Safari Lodge** High on a hill, presiding over the Zambezi National Park, this flagship lodge is a large, multi-tiered, thatched construction boasting panoramic vistas across the bush, and a prime view of the waterhole below; perch at the bar, slouch in the lounge, or sprawl by the pool deck with a drink and enjoy nonstop wildlife viewing. Well-appointed rooms, award-winning restaurants and exceptional service make this lodge a top choice that is consistently voted as one of the best places to stay in the country. If you're here for lunch, don't miss the daily vulture feed at 1pm. US$494

EATING

Beyond the hotels and lodges, which predominantly offer buffet spreads or fine dining, there is a small but varied selection of restaurants in town plus a handful of popular fast-food joints. Restaurants, like everything else in Vic Falls, tend to be expensive, and are often overpriced for what you get. There are a couple of options for self-caterers.

★**The Africa Café** Elephant's Walk Mall; map p.320. Serving breakfast all day (US$7–8), this is the place to go for an inexpensive bowl of yoghurt, fruit and muesli. It also serves tasty light lunches and snacks. Relax among the cheerful sofas to a mix of mellow African music, and don't miss the chef's signature baobab fruit cheesecake. Daily 8am–5pm.

The Boma Lokuthula Lodge (see above), 471 Squire Cummings Rd ☎013 44714, ⓦvictoria-falls-safari -lodge.com; map p.318. The hottest evening ticket in Vic Falls is a high-quality, interactive, touristy affair, which allows you to sample some traditional Zimbabwean cuisine: expect sadza (thick porridge), mopane worms (actually caterpillars) and warthog, amid more familiar dishes. Dinner is a belly-filling BBQ buffet with good veggie options (US$46, excluding drinks), served under a cavernous, semi-open thatch building. Be prepared to don a *chitenge* (traditional sarong), have your face painted, try out some drumming, and be wowed by Ndebele dancers. Daily 7.30pm for 8pm.

In Da Belly Victoria Falls Rest Camp, corner of Parkway Drive and West Drive; map p.320. Open-sided thatched restaurant in a relaxed poolside setting, with a couple of sports screens to entertain during the day and Ndebele singing at night. The drinks are cheaper than in most places, and meals are reasonably priced: try a filling bunny chow (hollowed-out loaf stuffed with curry) for US$8–10, or a full fry-up breakfast (US$9). Service is polite and efficient. Daily 7am–10pm.

The Livingstone Room Victoria Falls Hotel, 2 Mallett Drive ☎013 44751, ⓦlhw.com; map p.320. Formal splendour served up on damask tablecloths, decked with crystal glasses and candles, accompanying exquisite, inventive cuisine. Get the whole table to order the seven-course tasting menu (US$45/person), comprising the restaurant's signature dishes. Mains start around US$25; leave room for the chocolate tart with white chocolate mousse and salted caramel sauce (US$12). Daily 7–10pm.

Lola's Tapas and Carnivore Restaurant Trading Post complex ☎013 42994, ⓦfacebook.com/lolastapas andcarnivore; map p.320. Tucked away in the shopping precinct, this is a nice venue with indoor and outdoor seating and a water feature to enliven surroundings. Popular with tour groups at lunchtime, it serves hot and cold tapas (US$6 a dish), including a range of game meat, and more substantial meals too, including daily specials (mains around US$22; breakfasts US$15). High quality but overpriced. Accompanied by lunchtime marimbas and evening cappella singing. Daily 8am–9pm.

★**The Lookout Café** Top of Batoka Gorge, 400m downriver from the bridge ☎013 42013, ⓦwildhorizons .co.za; map p.318. You can't beat the setting, perched on a clifftop overlooking the Zambezi rapids; install yourself at a table under semi-open thatch or at a table in the garden, and feast on the spectacular view. As it's owned by *Wild Horizons*, you can watch the adjacent zipline action as you tuck into a breakfast platter (US$10) or some freshly prepared comfort food for lunch: steak, ribs, kebabs, wraps or salads (US$13–15) Daily 8am–7pm (kitchen closes at 4pm).

Makuwa-kuwa Restaurant Victoria Falls Safari Lodge, 3km from Vic Falls, 471 Squire Cummings Rd ☎013 43211, ⓦvictoria-falls-safari-lodge.com; map p.318. You can't beat this hillside location: glorious sunsets and (if you reserve early enough) a table overlooking the waterhole so you can watch the elephants guzzle as you tuck into your succulent warthog fillet or Zambezi bream – two of the house specialities (mains from around US$18). The sounds of the bush, however, are likely to play second fiddle to some a cappella singing. Daily 7–10am, 12.30pm–2pm & 7–10pm.

Mama Africa Back of the Trading Post complex ☎013 41725, ⓦmamaafricaeatinghouse.com; map p.320. Popular restaurant where you'll need to book if you want a table on the buzzy, candlelit terrace. Choose from a range of salads and grilled meats (US$18) or plump for one of the house-speciality hot pots (US$15): try the *sadza ndiurae* (literally "sadza kill me"), a Shona stew of spiced, mixed vegetables and steak, served in a three-legged pot (*potjie*), accompanied with sadza or groundnut rice. Be prepared to wait when it's busy and to endure a local group, whose nightly numbers range from African tunes to Elvis and the ubiquitous Bob Marley. Daily 10am–10pm.

Nam Took Elephant's Walk Mall, upstairs, 273 Adam Stander Drive ☎013 46709, ⓦnamtook.co.zw; map p.320. Thai restaurant (with Chinese options too) serving an extensive menu of tasty curries, stir-fries, salads and soups on an upstairs terrace under thatch, decorated with colourful paper lanterns and parasols. Vegetarian options aplenty. Most mains with rice or noodles US$14. Daily noon–3pm & 6–9pm.

★**The Palm Restaurant** Ilala Lodge, 411 Livingstone Way ☎013 44737, ⓦilalalodge.com; map p.320. Enjoy lunch on the terrace to the sound of marimbas, or a more formal candlelit dinner under their giant acacia, listening to the thunder of the falls. Delectable fine dining, with ostrich, kudu, warthog and crocodile served in creative ways, and offering more inventive vegetarian cuisine than most places. Mains around US$24. Daily noon–2pm (light lunches until 4pm) & 7–9.30pm.

★**Shearwater Café** Corner of Parkway Drive and Livingstone Way ☎013 46789; map p.320. This corner terrace (prime people-watching territory) is a popular mid-morning pit stop for a latte and a cake. Breakfasts are great too, if a little pricey (US$8–14): try the eggs Benedict or waffles. In the evening, oil lamps and sophisticated lighting under the umbrellas make it an atmospheric place for a delicious dinner – choose from a wide-ranging menu including the usual international favourites and local dishes, all nicely prepared. Mains US$16–22. Daily 8am–10pm.

★**Stanley's Terrace** The Victoria Falls Hotel ☎013 44751, ⓦlhw.com; map p.320. This is a must for high tea (US$15) or a cocktail sundowner. As you bite into dainty sandwiches, cakes and scones and sip tea out of fine bone china, you can gaze across the manicured lawn and soak up views of the falls, the bridge and the bungee jumping. Then linger in the hotel's fabulous, sofa-filled main lounge on the way out, and admire the beautiful, framed pressed flowers. Daily 11am–9pm (high tea daily 3–5.30pm; no reservation necessary).

DRINKING

Brown Sugar At the back of the Trading Post complex; map p.320. The current happening place where tourists and locals converge. It's a sprawling makeshift venue with a pool table, fire-pit and BBQ (where you can get cheap chicken and sadza on occasions), enlivened by a DJ at weekends. Though open from midday, the place doesn't really get going until 11pm once the many hotel and restaurant staff knock off. Noon till late.

Invuvu Bar Parkway Drive, opposite Soper's Arcade; map p.320. A popular watering hole in the centre of town – especially when there's a big football match on TV – on account of the cheap beer (US$1.50) and food. You'll pay just US$2–3 for a plate of sadza and chicken or bargain game meat such as buffalo or kudu. The game, procured from the park wardens (part of the regulated game culling), is often cooked up late afternoon and runs out fast. Be prepared to eat with your hands. Daily 11.30am–11.30pm.

The Kingdom Hotel 1 Mallett Drive ☎013 44275, ⓦafricansunhotels.com; map p.320. The preferred venue for big-name acts, *The Kingdom Hotel*'s Great Enclosure – a modern parody of its namesake in the ruined city of Great Zimbabwe – has temporarily lost its main casino to a more lucrative conference centre. A scaled-down casino (with slot machines) was due to reopen at the time of going to press, but the bar and food court live on.

Shoestrings Bar Shoestrings Backpackers, 12 West Drive ☎013 40167 or ☎0713 800731, ⓦshoestrings vicfalls.com; map p.320. A really popular bar to kick off the night, hosting occasional DJs, live bands, interactive drumming and theme parties, as well as the Wednesday open mic and cocktail night. The good-value pizzas help soak up the alcohol. Cover charge for events for non-residents. Daily 10am–midnight.

NIGHTLIFE

Most mid-range and high-end hotels and lodges provide nightly entertainment, as do most restaurants. This usually entails one or more of the following: Ndebele a cappella singers, dancers and/or drummers dressed up in traditional ostrich-feather finery, or mellow marimba music. Nightlife is otherwise quite low-key.

SHOPPING

Most tourists are directed towards the ever-expanding Open Market (daily 8am–6pm), which boasts a vast number of stalls selling mass-produced (whatever the stall-holder might tell you) soapstone or wooden crafts. Don't forget to check

8

CRAFTS GALORE

Zimbabwe is renowned for its **crafts** and you can shop till you drop for them in Vic Falls: the place abounds with gift shops (see below) and curio stalls – especially outside the entrance to the falls – and there's an ever-expanding craft market too, named the **Open Market**, at the end of Adam Stander Drive, where you'll find a bewildering array of stalls, many offering much the same wares. **Woodcarvings** – from hardwoods such as olive, teak, ebony or mahogany – are ubiquitous; sculpted animals – everything from large elephants and hippos to small frogs and dung beetles – are the most common. Beyond the wildlife, you can find wooden bowls, masks, carved walking sticks and salad servers. **Shona sculpture** is internationally famous and there's plenty on display, commonly made from soapstone and serpentine, with the "*ukama*", or family sculptures, portraying couples or groups of figures, particularly popular. Equally renowned is Zimbabwe's distinctive **sadza batik cloth**. The women use sadza – just like the porridge you may have tasted on your plate – in much the same way as wax is used in other traditions of batik-making, to prevent colour from entering parts of the cloth. Look out also for the colourful Ndebele beadwork and their brightly painted **geometric designs** on everything from mugs to picture frames and cloth as well as the distinctive, finely woven baskets of the Tonga women from the remote region of Binga. Many of the items on sale these days are mass-produced – don't be fooled by the ubiquitous assertion: "I made it myself" – though you can still pick up the odd original curio.

out the women's cooperative stalls, specializing in basketry and cloth, in the rather gloomy sheds to the left. Most mainstream gift shops are located in the Trading Post Complex on Livingstone Way; also worth checking out is Elephant's Walk Mall (🖥 elephantswalk.com; daily 9am–5pm), which hosts a collection of more varied, upmarket (and expensive) craft stores. For a less touristy market, try the Comesa flea market (daily 8am–5pm), offering cloth, cheap goods and bags of local colour. For fresh fruit and veg, head for the Old Market in Chinotimba.

8

African Heritage Elephant's Walk Mall ☎0772254552; map p.320. Superior gift shop with prices to match stocking quality goods from Zimbabwe and other parts of Africa, and with a fine collection of masks in particular. Daily 9am–5pm.
Cultural Vibes Music Shop Elephant's Walk Mall ☎0772984586, 🖥 cultural-vibes.com; map p.320. The place to come for Zimbabwean CDs; the enthusiastic and knowledgeable owner lets you sample the sounds and can guide you in your selection. Daily 9am–5pm.
Ndau Collection Elephant's Walk Mall 🖥ndau

collection.com; map p.320. Stunning, award-winning, hand-made designer jewellery and accessories, inspired by nature, from dung-beetle earrings to rhino-tusk bangles. Prices range from US$100 to several thousand. Daily 9am–5pm.
Rokoteka Traders Trading Post Complex ☎013 42805; map p.320. Amid the usual sadza-dyed cloth, ceramics, T-shirts and woodcarvings, you'll find many intricately carved items in animal bone – all responsibly sourced. Daily 9am–6pm.

DIRECTORY

Banks and money Barclays Bank (☎013 3375, 🖥zw .barclays.com) is set back from Livingstone Way, opposite the petrol station. So too is Standard Chartered (☎013 44248, 🖥 sc.com/zw). Both have ATMs which take Visa (US$5 charge). Banking hours are Mon–Fri 8am–3pm & Sat 8am–11.30am.
Hospital/clinic The Victoria Falls District Hospital, Chinotimba, is always overstretched, so you are better off going to the THB Private Hospital, 95 West Drive (☎013 46634, 📧 vicfalls@thehealthbridge.org), a state-of-the-art private hospital aimed at tourists, which provides medical and dental care.
Internet Wi-fi is readily available in most restaurants and accommodation and usually free, though it may only be available in the main lodge area, and it's often slow. Otherwise, there are a couple of run-down internet cafés upstairs in Soper's Arcade; charges US$1/hour.
Pharmacy Victoria Falls Pharmacy, Phumala Centre,

Parkway Drive (☎013 44403; Mon–Fri 8am–5pm, Sat 8.30am–1pm & Sun 9am–noon).
Police Livingstone Way (☎013 42206). You are more likely to have contact with the tourist police, recognizable by their lime-green vests.
Post office Livingstone Way, opposite the Total garage (Mon–Fri 8am–4pm & Sat 8–11.30am).
Supermarkets OK Grocers, the main supermarket, is at the back of the Phumala Centre on Clark Drive (Mon–Sat 8am–8pm & Sun 8am–5pm); the small 7–11 store in the same centre is, as the name indicates, open daily 7am–11pm. Across Livingstone Way on Sillitoe Road, T&M is another large supermarket.
Telephones SIM cards are easily purchased from one of the mobile phone service providers' shops on Parkway Drive for around US$0.50. It should cost around US$30 for a phone to be unlocked, more for a smartphone.

Zambia

Mosi-oa-Tunya National Park

Entrance to the falls is on Mosi-oa-Tunya Rd, 10km south of the town centre, just before the Victoria Falls Bridge and Zimbabwe; entrance to the game reserve is on Sichango Drive, signposted off Mosi-oa-Tunya Rd, 3km south of the town centre • Both daily 6am–6pm • US$20/ person for the falls; US$10/person and US$5/vehicle for the game reserve

Encompassing both the Zambian side of the falls and a slender strip of protected land that extends about 12km upriver along the northern bank of the Zambezi, **Mosi-oa-Tunya National Park** is much smaller than the combined area of Victoria Falls National Park and the almost contiguous Zambezi National Park on the Zimbabwean side. But the view of the falls from here is special, and definitely worth the outlay, even if you have seen them from the Zimbabwean side. In contrast, although the Mosi-oa-Tunya game reserve does not boast as much in the way of **large mammals** as the Zambezi National Park across the river – there are usually no elephants, for example – the birdlife and river views alone make for a pleasant drive.

The falls

Although more people flock to the Zimbabwean side of the falls (see p.313), where most of the water thunders into the chasm, you really should try to visit **both sides**: the Zambian section affords completely different perspectives on the spectacle and, moreover, guarantees a quickening of the pulse as you cross **Knife Edge Bridge**, which connects the area surrounding the reserve entrance to the rocky peninsula known as Knife Edge Island. This **circular trail** affords fabulous views across the ravine to the **Eastern Cataract** – though when the water's tumbling at full throttle you may only experience its deafening noise as you become lost – and drenched – in a thick fog of swirling spray. Arguably the most spectacular vista is saved for **Knife Edge Point**, at the far western end of the rocky promontory. From this vantage point, you can gaze in awe down the entire length of the falls gorge (the **First Gorge**): depending on the time of year, you will be treated either to pounding torrents of water and clouds of spray or

8

SYUUNGWE NA MUTITIMA – THE HEAVY MIST THAT RESOUNDS

Mosi-oa-Tunya ("the smoke that thunders"), the Kololo and Lozi word for the falls, is widely promoted as its **indigenous name** – thanks in no small part to the fact that the guides who led David Livingstone (see box, p.330) were Kololo – yet it is by no means the only one. The Mukuni Leya, who claim to be the original river settlers in the area, refer to it as *syuungwe na mutitima*, meaning "**the heavy mist that resounds**", though *syuungwe* also implies a place of rainbows. Legend has it that the resounding in question comes from a drum: it is said that in a battle between Leya chiefs Sekute and Mukuni, Sekute's drum – a potent symbol of his power – fell over the edge of the falls to become wedged at their base, and is now permanently pounded by the falling water. Mukuni Leya also refer to the falls as *syuungwe mufu* ("**mist of the dead**"), since the area possesses important sites associated with the worship of ancestral spirits. One such place is the *katolauseka* ("make offerings cheerfully") – known by tourists as the **Boiling Pot** – into which valuable items were hurled as offerings to placate the ancestral spirits. Another ritual site is *sambadwazi* ("**cleanse disease**"), a pool by the lip of the Eastern Cataract. Ill or diseased people would bathe here and toss their clothes into the water, which would then be washed over the falls, taking the bathers' sickness away with them. A third place of significance is *chipusya*, a spot along the river still known to only a select few, where water would be drawn for rainmaking and other rituals. More generally, the falls are associated with the mythology of **Bedyango**, the original female Leya leader with presumed powers over land, rain and fertility, who is said to have agreed to rule the Leya jointly with the initial Chief Mukuni when he first arrived on the scene. Both the present-day chief and the current Bedyango – a title bestowed on one of the chief's female relatives – live in Mukuni Village outside Livingstone, which can be visited on a **cultural tour** (see p.334).

LIVINGSTONE: FROM FAILED MISSIONARY TO SUPERSTAR EXPLORER

It's easy to see why the Scottish missionary **David Livingstone** became one of the most popular national heroes back in Victorian Britain: his was a rags-to-riches story, combining strong Christian beliefs with a career as a glamorous explorer of "Darkest Africa". Born in Blantyre in 1813 to a teetotal Sunday School teacher, Livingstone worked fourteen-hour shifts in the local cotton mill from the age of 10, followed by several hours' schooling in evening classes. He went on to study medicine and signed up with the **London Missionary Society** (LMS) to go to China, but the First Opium War broke out and he was offered the West Indies instead. In the end, though, Livingstone opted for a post at the LMS mission station in Kuruman, South Africa, inspired by the idea of destroying the **African slave trade**.

It is fair to say that Livingstone was more or less a failure as a missionary, briefly converting just one man, Sechele, leader of the Kwêna people of Botswana. He did, however, succeed in marrying Mary Moffat, the daughter of the head of the mission. In 1849, disillusioned with missionary work, Livingstone gave up his post with the LMS and concentrated all his efforts into combating slavery, which he hoped to do t-hrough encouraging legitimate commercial trade. He believed in the three great Cs – "**Christianity, Commerce and Civilization**" – and was convinced that the key to unlocking trade in central Africa was the Zambezi River, which he believed was as yet unexplored by Europeans.

As an **explorer**, Livingstone was much more successful. Despite losing the use of his left arm after an early encounter with a lion, he was dogged and could endure the most terrible physical conditions. He was also adept at allaying the fears of Africans he met by travelling relatively lightly, and without the usual team of armed soldiers. His first **Zambezi expedition** (1852–56) was his most successful, as he laid claim – possibly erroneously – to being the first European to cross southern Africa from coast to coast, most famously "discovering" Mosi-oa-Tunya, which he renamed the **Victoria Falls** after Queen Victoria.

Returning to Britain the following year, Livingstone published *Missionary Travels in South Africa* in 1857, a bestseller that sealed his status as a national hero. It also enabled him to get government backing for his second Zambezi expedition (1858–64), which proved something of a disaster: most of his team deserted him; he was accused of incompetence; and his uncomplaining wife, Mary, who had borne him six children, died of malaria shortly after joining him in 1862. On the other hand, he declared himself the first European to reach **Lake Malawi**, and uttered his most famous words, "I am prepared to go anywhere, provided it be forward", while at the same time failing to establish a navigable route across the continent.

Livingstone's third and final expedition (1866–73) – partly funded by the Royal Geographical Society (RGS) – was an attempt to find the source of the **River Nile**, which he wrongly believed had so far been incorrectly identified. Once again, the expedition was plagued by disaster, with all but a few of his helpers deserting h m or dying en route, and Livingstone falling so ill that he had to be saved on several occasions by the very **Arab slave traders** he was trying to oppose. Suffering from pneumonia, cholera and tropical ulcers, Livingstone found himself stranded in Bambarre, in eastern Congo, in 1869, just as the wet season began, and was forced to eat his meals in public for the entertainment of the locals, in return for food.

Yet Livingstone's posthumous fame was assured when Gordon Bennett, publisher of the *New York Herald*, decided in 1869 to send the journalist **Henry Morton Stanley** out to Africa to seek out the explorer, who had been out of contact with the outside world for several years. After two years of searching, Stanley finally tracked him down to Ujiji – an Arab slave station on Lake Tanganyika in modern-day Tanzania – where, seeing the only white man for many kilometres around, he uttered the famous words, "**Dr Livingstone, I presume**" – or so the story goes.

Although Livingstone was very ill at this point, he refused to be persuaded to leave Africa, soldiering on until May 1, 1873, when he died in the village of Chitambo in present-day Zambia. His heart and internal organs were buried in a tin box under a mpundu tree by Susi and Chuma, his long-suffering servants. They then **embalmed his corpse**, using salt and brandy, sun-dried it and wrapped it in calico, and spent the next nine months transporting it 1600km to the Tanzanian coast. From there, the body was sent back to London, where it **lay in state** at No. 1 Savile Row, headquarters of the Royal Geographical Society at the time, before being buried in the centre of the nave of Westminster Abbey.

– when water is low (see p.312) – to the sight of the vast, deep sheet of exposed basalt rock; you can also peer into the gaping chasm below at the churning waters of the **Boiling Pot** as they jostle their way downriver through the Second Gorge, and under the **Victoria Falls Bridge**. If you like to get your adrenaline rush by proxy, wait to catch sight of one of the **bungee jumpers** – you get a great view of them plummeting from the bridge from here. For a closer look at the Boiling Pot and a chance to marvel at the falls from below, head back towards the entrance and follow the signs down the **Palm Grove Trail**, an easy, though sometimes slippery, descent; note that it's a hard slog to climb the 100m back out again in the heat of the day. You can also take a **tour** that ferries you across the Boiling Pot in an inflatable to stand under the falls (see p.336), when water levels permit. The Zambian **whitewater rafters** also start at this point (see box, p.305). A more sedate stroll along the reserve's **Photographic Trail** provides yet more perspectives on this natural wonder and takes you parallel to the main road to within touching distance of the Victoria Falls Bridge. Don't forget to pass by the **statue of David Livingstone** standing proud close to the entrance/exit.

Livingstone Island

Stuck in the middle of the falls on the brink of the precipice, with water pouring over the edge either side for most of the year, is **Livingstone Island** – so named because it was where the failed missionary first set eyes on Mosi-oa-Tunya by peering into the abyss. Here, he is also supposed to have carved his name on a **tree**, in a fit of overexcited vandalism, and planted some fruit seeds, though evidence of either activity is absent today. The only way to visit the island is on a tour with Tongabezi (see p.338), generally **on foot**, picking your way precariously across the exposed rocks from the Zambian side, when the water is low, to get the ultimate thrill of jumping – or sliding tentatively – into the island's **Devil's Pool**, where the river is prevented from sweeping you over the edge by a rocky lip beneath the surface – dubbed the **Devil's Armchair**. Peek over the 100m sheer drop if you dare; you'll feel as if you're peering into the bowels of the Earth.

8

The game reserve

Above the falls, the **game reserve** section of the national park comprises tall riverine forest along the Zambezi and, further inland, a mix of grassland, mopane and miombo woodland – miombo trees shed their leaves to reduce moisture loss in the dry season and grow new ones just before the onset of the rains. Although a relatively small protected area of around only 66 square kilometres, the reserve nevertheless hosts abundant **birdlife**, especially along the riverbanks. Unfortunately, the numbers of **large mammals** have dropped in recent years following a series of droughts, which can make a game drive here rather disappointing. Even so, keep a lookout for antelope (including sable, eland and impala), giraffe, buffalo, zebra and warthog. When river levels are low, elephant wade across the river from the Zimbabwean side. For Big Five fanatics, there is the chance to glimpse Zambia's few remaining **white rhino**; there are eight individuals at the current count, and they are heavily guarded, but it's even possible to track them on foot (see p.336). If you adjust your expectations and focus on the tantalizing views of the Zambezi through the trees, you can enjoy a relaxing drive here, although a **river cruise** through the park is often more satisfying.

Livingstone

In contrast to Vic Falls, **LIVINGSTONE** seems like a real town; as you enter from the south, Mosi-oa-Tunya Road becomes a broad, main boulevard lined with lilac jacaranda and flaming flamboyants at certain times of the year. The high street stretches north for a couple of kilometres, hauling itself uphill, away from the falls. The **Livingstone Museum**, on the west side of the road, heralds the start of the town centre and Livingstone's **business district**: a strip of banks, pharmacies, the post office and shops, which gives way

to the well-ordered line of stalls that constitute the **curio market** (Mon–Sat 8am–6pm), where you'll be far less hassled than at Vic Falls. If you head a block east of the high street at the museum and walk northwards, parallel to the museum, you'll come across taxi ranks and **bus stations**, interspersed with **market stalls** where women sell mounds of fruit, vegetables and pulses alongside blankets, cheap shoes and toasted sweetcorn. As you walk around, keep your eye out for a few flashes of faded Edwardian **colonial architecture**.

Brief history

The area round Livingstone – as with Victoria Falls Town – has a long history of **African settlement** (see p.341), peopled by groups identifying themselves variously as Leya, Toka, Tonga and Kololo, while the eastern end of the pre-eminent Lozi Kingdom of Barotseland once also stretched this far. In about 1897, the first Europeans started to settle at **Old Drift**, a place 10km upstream from the falls where the Zambezi was at its narrowest, and which therefore provided the best crossing point. The river-dwelling **Leya** constantly navigated and ferried people across the river here. However, the swampy, malaria-infested area was later abandoned by the colonizers in favour of higher ground on **Constitution Hill**. This new settlement was named **Livingstone** after the good doctor, though it did not really take off until the arrival of the railroad in 1905. Then, in 1911, once the British colonizers had strengthened their grip on the land, it became the capital of the **British Protectorate of Northwest Rhodesia** – and therefore a major administrative centre – until the capital was transferred to Lusaka in 1935. It was during this early colonial period that the **indigenous populations** were gradually pushed out to the margins; even the Lozi royalty, who initially enjoyed a relatively privileged relationship with the colonial administration, found their authority gradually eroded over the years.

In the 1970s, Livingstone thrived as a base for **textile production**, and a vehicle manufacturing plant was also established here. But by the mid-1990s, following the nosedive in the Zambian economy due to the crash in copper prices (see p.312), cars were no longer being made and all but two of the textile factories had closed down. It wasn't until the late 1990s, when the Zambian government started to recognize the potential of **tourism** to contribute to economic development, that Livingstone started to experience renewed growth, especially following the establishment in 2001 of the huge **Sun International resort complexes** (now the AVANI) at the gates of the falls. Other smaller hotels, backpackers and guesthouses have followed, and tourism is gradually expanding. At the same time, completion of the **Katima Mulilo Road Bridge** between Namibia and Zambia in 2004 – which provides Pacific port access to landlocked Zambia as part of the Trans Caprivi or Walvis Bay Corridor – has also helped improve tourist infrastructure, and the newly expanded airport looks set to attract more international flights.

8

The Livingstone Museum

Mosi-oa-Tunya Rd • Daily 9am–4.30pm • US$5 • ☎ 0213 324281, ⓦ museumszambia.org

While the much-vaunted **Livingstone Museum** is Zambia's largest and oldest, it is certainly not going to set your pulse racing. Still, it is worth delving into, not just to learn more about the famed explorer (see box, p.330) – the reason most foreign tourists go – but also for what it has to say about the area's history and people. First established in 1935, the museum has occupied its current, rather ugly, building since the 1950s, and is organized into five sections. Things kick off in the **archeology room**, in which there is a plaster cast of the Broken Hill skull – the original having been spirited away to the British Museum – which was unearthed in 1921 and dates back some 200,000 years. Next up is **ethnography**, in which idealized rural life is pitted against the "mirage" of urban development. Aspects of traditional life are explained through the important life stages of birth, puberty, marriage and death through photos and artefacts; note the rather gruesome objects on witchcraft such as the *ndile*, used to exhume corpses. A large taxidermy collection follows in the **natural history** section with animals set in their various habitats, but don't miss the impressive display of insects, featuring a giant bush locust. A cardboard cutout of Henry Morton Stanley then announces the more recent **Livingstone wing**, which includes some extraordinary memorabilia, including a cast of his humerus, his remarkably well-preserved umbrella and his coat. The objects he collected on his travels were equally eclectic: look out for a portion of hippo jaw, a Nyasaland fishing net and a letter stand. A room detailing the various **peoples** of Zambia follows, tracing their migrations, the advent of colonialism, the subsequent struggle for independence, and post-independence politics, with these last two periods explored mostly through photos and news clippings.

The Railway Museum and The Gateway Jewish Museum

Chishimba Falls Rd • Daily 9am–4pm • US$15, including guided tour • ☎ 0213 324281

Located on the site of the one-time sawmill of the Zambezi Sawmills Railways – for over fifty years, the longest private railway line in the world – Livingstone's **railway museum** is a rather neglected affair. Although ongoing renovations of the old stationmaster's house and a new exhibition room signal a potential revival, the hefty entrance fee is likely to deter all but keen railway buffs.

The railway took off in 1925, as a cheaper way of transporting timber, which had previously been moved by oxen, then by barge along the Zambezi. The trains soon took to taking passengers as well, who initially made the journey perched precariously on piles of logs – photos of which are on display. However, the heart of the museum lies in the fourteen rusting engines and a handful of carriages in varying stages of decay spread around the grounds, which have literally been put out to grass; one dilapidated specimen even has a papaya tree growing inside. The hulking brutes on display are secondhand steam engines manufactured in cities such as Manchester and Glasgow that were then shipped out to Africa. The oldest engine dates from 1892. Don't miss out on the plush, wood-panelled and leather-seated general manager's carriage – a reminder of the lucrativeness of the timber industry.

A more recent, and arguably more compelling, on-site attraction is the fascinating, one-room **Gateway Jewish Museum**, which documents the early Jewish immigrant pioneers at the end of the 1800s, whose participation in the economic and political development of Zambia is closely entwined with the development of the railway.

Livingstone Reptile Park

Signposted east of Mosi-oa-Tunya Rd, 2km south of Livingstone • Daily 9am–4pm • US$15, including guided tour • ☎ 0213 324281, Ⓦ gwembesafaris.com/reptile-park • Take the falls minibus from town and alight at the reptile park sign and walk five minutes, or take a taxi US$5

A guided tour of the **reptile park** takes place along a raised walkway at a safe distance from the menacing crocodiles that are its star inhabitants. The reptiles are primarily nuisance crocs that have been threatening villages along the Zambezi and would otherwise have been killed, though unless you time your visit to coincide with feeding time (check in advance), their general lethargy would mislead you into thinking otherwise. More recently, the park has been asked to take in some venomous snakes – also safely ensconced behind glass.

Around Livingstone

Tourists who have "done" the falls, had their fix of adrenaline-fuelled activities and satisfied their wildlife-viewing ambitions are increasingly turning to culture-oriented excursions. Around Livingstone there are several **villages**, such as Mukuni Village, that welcome visitors and are willing to afford them glimpses of modern-day village life for a fee. While several operators offer tours, you can miss the crowds and increase your chances of having a less contrived experience by getting there under your own steam and arranging a private tour; better still, go on a bike tour to a less visited village with Local Cowboy Bike Tours (see p.303).

Mukuni Village

15km from Livingstone, signposted off the main road just north of the falls • Daily 9am–4pm • US$5, including guided tour; US$50 tour operator package • ☎ 0213 324281 • Take a minibus bound for the falls from the town centre, then transfer to a minibus bound for Mukuni, across the road from the entrance to the AVANI; be prepared to wait, as buses only leave when full

About 10km southeast of Livingstone as the crow flies lies **Mukuni Village**, where Chief Mukuni, head of the six thousand Leya, holds court, when he's not travelling. Forget any thought of seeing a "traditional village", since its proximity to the falls and inevitably the influx of so many tour groups has left its mark. Even so, tours (1–2hr, depending on interest) are informative, and will include the palace, provided the chief's not around, and the giant acacia tree outside, where Livingstone first met Chief Mukuni. The chief refused to greet the explorer in the palace since he was convinced that Livingstone's white skin meant that he was a ghost or spirit. Since then, so the story goes, village gatherings have always been held under the tree.

ARRIVAL AND DEPARTURE

BY PLANE
International flights arrive at the Harry Mwanga Nkumbula International Airport (☎0213 3211153, ⓦnacl.co.zm) 6km northwest of the town centre. Formerly known as Livingstone Airport, but renamed after the Zambian liberation ANC leader, the recently renovated airport now has a second terminal. Facilities include a money exchange, a post office and an ATM, as well as desks for several car rental firms (see p.336). There is free wi-fi throughout.

Getting into town There is no regular bus service from the airport into Livingstone, but shuttles from many lodgings in town provide a free pick-up service. Otherwise, a private taxi costs K50–100 (US$5–10) depending on your negotiating skills and whether you're going into town or to accommodation closer to the Zimbabwe border.

FLIGHTS AND AIRLINES
International flights There are no direct flights from Europe, North America or Australasia to Livingstone. Most international visitors fly in via Oliver Tambo International Airport, Johannesburg, from where there are daily connections to Livingstone with British Airways on Comair (☎0213 322827, ⓦbritishairways.com) and South African Airways (☎0213 323031, ⓦflysaa.com). These flights take 1hr 45min and cost around R4800 return. Airlink (ⓦflyairlink.com), an independent South African airline that primarily flies domestic routes within South Africa, and which is allied to South African Airways, operates a flight from Nelspruit, just outside Kruger National Park, to Livingstone five times a week (1hr 40min) from around R5000 one way, as well as flights from Johannesburg. It is also possible to reach Livingstone from European destinations by flying via East African hubs such as Addis Ababa (Ethiopia) and Nairobi (Kenya), to Lusaka, from where you can take an onward flight, which is usually cheaper than flights via Johannesburg.

Domestic flights Proflight (☎0211 252452, ⓦproflight-zambia.com), Zambia's main airline, flies between Lusaka and Livingstone several times a day (1hr 10min) from around US$270 one way.

BY BUS
From/to Lusaka The reliable Mazhandu Family Bus Service (☎0975 805064) runs several daily services, including an overnight bus, between Lusaka and Livingstone (7hr; K120). The Shalom Bus Service also operates buses between Lusaka and Livingstone on a similar timetable. Both bus companies have offices by the

LIVINGSTONE
market on the corner of Chimwemwe and Zambezi Sts in Livingstone, where their buses depart from.

From/to Namibia and Botswana Shalom and Mazhandu Family Bus Service (☎0977 805064) have 2–3 daily departures from Sesheke, a couple of kilometres from the Namibia border near Katima Mulilo, to Livingstone (3hr; K80). The bus travels via Kazungula, the border with Botswana (from the Namibia border: 2hr; K40). There are taxis that connect with Kasane, the gateway to Chobe National Park, from the Botswana side of the Kazungula border. Intercape Mainliner (ⓦintercape.co.za) offers a reliable bus service three times a week from Windhoek to Livingstone (Mon, Wed & Fri; 20hr 30min; from R700), and then on to the Zimbabwe border at the Victoria Falls Bridge (see box, p.315). The return Intercape bus to Windhoek leaves Livingstone bus station on Wed, Fri and Sun, picking up at the border first if pre-booked – with onward connections to Cape Town, South Africa.

From/to Zimbabwe Access from and to Zimbabwe is via the border on the Victoria Falls Bridge (see box, p.315), a few hundred metres downhill from Vic Falls Town, from where there is onward transport to Bulawayo and Harare, and beyond to South Africa.

BY CAR
Relatively good tarred roads lead to Livingstone from Lusaka (480km; 6hr), and from Sesheke (186km; 3hr), 4km from the border with Namibia at Katima Mulilo (daily 7am–6pm). The route from Sesheke goes via the Botswana border at Kazungula (daily 6am–6pm), which lies 63km from Livingstone. This border crossing is via a large ferry, so often entails a lengthy wait, though a road bridge is under construction. The roads are good from Bulawayo and Zimbabwe too, although fuel is expensive. Note, however, that you will be liable for cross-border vehicle charges and will need to present the vehicle's papers if you bring in a vehicle from another country (see p.299).

BY TRAIN
There are two passenger train services a week between Livingstone and Lusaka, which take forever – 16hr plus – and are notoriously unreliable, but if you fancy an adventure, and a chance to chat to people, this is one way to do it. Economy (K70), Standard, Business and Sleeper (K125) services are available, and there is a buffet car – but take extra supplies just in case. Departures from Lusaka are on Tues and Sat at 7am, and from Livingstone on Mon & Fri at 8pm. Enquire at the relevant train station (Livingstone: ☎0213 321001; Lusaka: ☎0211 228023).

GETTING AROUND

By taxi Taxis are plentiful but can be expensive. The standard rate from the Zimbabwe border or the falls (which are within 100m of each other) to town, which is 10km away, is US$9–10 per taxi, depending on your negotiating skills and how brisk business is. It's around K10–20 for anywhere around town. Rates are a little higher after dark.

A journey between the town centre and the airport costs around K60 or US$5–6 (again, depending on your bartering skills and the exchange rate).

By minibus Minibuses for the border (around every 20min; K10 or US$1) leave from the bus station on Mokambo Rd at the junction with Kapondo St.

On foot It's perfectly possible and safe to wander around central Livingstone on foot during the day. At night the well-lit areas of the main street are fine; otherwise take a taxi.

By bike *Fawlty Towers* (see opposite) and *Jollyboys* (see opposite) both do bike rental, as does Local Cowboy Cycle Tours (☎ 0977 747837; see p.303).

By car Europcar is based at the airport (☎ 0213 322753, 0978 778991, ⊚ europcarzambia.com). Hemingways (☎ 0213 323097 or ☎ 0977 866492, ⊚ hemingwayszambia .com) specializes in 4WD rental and vehicles for people with physical disabilities. Note that if you intend to take your rental car over the border into Botswana (for example), you will be liable for charges (see p.299).

INFORMATION

Livingstone Tourist Centre Mosi-oa-Tunya Rd ☎ 0213 321404, ⊚ zambiatourism.com. Good for a burst of a/c, a friendly face and a glossy brochure that includes a street map – but you'll probably find your accommodation's activities desk has all the information you need. Mon–Fri 8am–5pm.

ACTIVITIES

Unlike in Vic Falls Town, where most of the tour operators are concentrated in a block of a few hundred metres, the ones in Livingstone are far more strung out, often operating out of a lodge or hotel, or otherwise without a physical address. Although most accommodation will usually book activities for you, you might prefer to deal directly with one of the operators listed below to get a combo deal.

Bundu Adventures Maramba River Lodge ☎ 0213 324406, ⊚ bunduadventures.com. Primarily a rafting company, specializing in single- and multi-day rafting trips, as well as the rafting and body-boarding combo. To do all the rapids (1–25) costs US$178, including a ride out of the gorge on the funicular; a helicopter airlift out is extra. For US$1270 you can get the most out of the Zambezi with a six-day trip to Lake Kariba. Also does the swim under the falls (US$75).

Livingstone's Adventure ☎ 0213 323589, ⊚ seasons inafrica.com/adventure-activities-zambia/victoria-falls -activities. A group of diverse specialist activity operators now operate under this umbrella organization, which can offer a river cruise on the *African Queen* or a flight with Batoka Sky microlights (see p.303). They also lay on canoeing with paddling specialists Makoro Quest (see p.302), as well as quad biking, fishing or horse riding.

Safari Par Excellence Victoria Falls Waterfront Hotel, Sichango Drive ☎ 0213 320606, ⊚ safpar.com. Quality operator with its own experienced rafting team (US$160 for a full day, including cable car ride out of the gorge); also does acclaimed overnight canoeing trips. In addition to offering game drives, they have several river cruise vessels of different sizes and can organize transfers both sides of the border.

Savannah Southern Safaris Olga's, 20 Makambo Rd ☎ 0978 169567, ⊚ savannah-southern-safaris.com. Small, community-focused outfit providing knowledgeable, personalized service for private tours: birdwatching, nature walks and rhino tracking in the national park (all US$70/ person, for 2–8 people for three hours). Also does community visits, including to development projects they are involved with (US$60/person for a half-day).

Zambezi Eco Adventures Fawlty Towers ☎ 0213 321188, ⊚ zambezieco adventures.com. The high-wire specialists this side of the Zambezi, who'll pick up clients from Zimbabwe at the border, and include the day visa in the price. On the menu are abseiling, sliding (US$55), or swinging alone or in tandem (US$95/140) high above the Batoka Gorge. A full day of unlimited fun that finishes off with a trip to Devil's Pool and high tea on Livingstone Island is undoubtedly the best value going at US$195.

Zambezi Rafting 22 Mambo Way ☎ 0213 324024, ⊚ zambezirafting.com. If you think being jostled in a raft with half a dozen other people is too tame, then tackle half the rapids (11–25) on your own in an inflatable kayak – though with support. Full-day tour; no more than four kayakers per guide. US$195.

ACCOMMODATION

There is a good range of accommodation around – from backpackers places and guesthouses in **central Livingstone** to high-end lodges and hotels south of town, **near the falls**, and lodges, self-catering and campgrounds further upriver along the Zambezi, **west of town**. Most will do free airport pick-ups, and the backpackers lodgings nearly all do a free daily run to the falls and will pick up anyone hovering at the border for the return, though you may have to pay if you're not booked in with them. While hideaways west of Livingstone along the Zambezi are delightfully free of the whirring of helicopters, **transfers** to do activities at the falls can rack up. Note that most accommodation keeps the same prices all year round, but a few lodges have **peak season** rates (see box, p.300).

IN TOWN

Chapa Classic Lodge 66 Nehru Way ☎0977796710, ⓦchapaclassiclodge.com; map p.332. Really pleasant and excellent value, this non-touristy hotel is spread around tree-filled grounds that feature an attractive pool area. The 27 tiled rooms are clean and cool (with a/c), though the decor's a little chintzy in some. Most have a vast TV screen, fridge, tea/coffee facilities and mosquito nets. Enjoy the hearty full English breakfast. US$60

★**Fawlty Towers** 216 Mosi-oa-Tunya Rd ☎0213 23432, ⓦadventure-africa.com; map p.332. The large leafy garden of this backpackers-cum-guesthouse is the real draw – plenty of space to find your own quiet spot away from the lively poolside bar if you want. Its range of accommodation, all with mosquito nets, includes quality doubles (with a/c), twins, family rooms and dorms that cater for a range of visitors. The usual backpacker facilities include: kitchen, laundry, free afternoon pancakes and a bar. Daily free shuttle to the falls and an excellent activities desk. Dorms US$12, doubles US$50

Gloria's B&B 19 Ghandi Ave ☎0213 22332, ⓦglorias bedandbreakfast.com; map p.332. Located in a quiet residential area a 10–15min walk from town (though it's wise to take a taxi at night), this well-maintained guesthouse has a handful of simply furnished rooms (with a/c and fridge), with kitchen available, and a couple of small bungalows. There's a small pool in the garden. Cash only. US$65

Jollyboys Backpackers 34 Kanyanta Rd, behind the museum ☎0213 324229, ⓦbackpackzambia.com; map p.332. Classic friendly backpackers with an extremely efficient activities desk, and plenty of things to keep you entertained in their fruit tree-filled grounds: have a game of table tennis or pool or grab a paperback from the book exchange and sprawl on the fabulous sunken communal bed. The rooms are a little on the small side: choose from dark, thatched, fan-ventilated A-frames with shared bathroom (US$20 less) or en-suite doubles with a/c. Not to be confused with their sibling *Jollyboys Camp*, further out, geared towards families and travellers on an even tighter budget. Dorms US$15, doubles US$45

Livingstone Backpackers 559 Mokambo Rd ☎0213 324730, ⓦlivingstonebackpackers.com; map p.332. The newest backpackers joint, this place has friendly staff and pleasant chill-out areas, plus a climbing wall. On the downside, the mattresses in the rooms are variable and some of the fans are tiny in the cheaper rooms with shared bathroom. You can squeeze in a tent here or they'll lend you one (for free). Camping per person US$8, dorms US$12, doubles US$65

Olga's 20 Makambo Rd ☎0213 324160, ⓦolgasproject .com; map p.332. Heavily involved in community development, *Olga's* is a worthy as well as a pleasant place to stay. Comprising nine no-frills, spacious thatched rooms with ceiling fan and private bathroom, plus comfortable

beds. The cons are the traffic noise, the sporadically loud church bells and the lack of a really comfortable communal area. Rates vary depending on the season. US$55

Tabonina Guesthouse 3 Maisoko Rd ☎0213 320274 or ☎0979465288, ⓦtaboninaguesthouse.com; map p.332. Owned by a French-Zambian couple, this homely place is set round a delightful flower-filled garden, with a small pool. There's a pleasant social area under thatch with bar, pool table and darts board plus a small TV lounge. Spotless, compact double and family rooms with a/c have good mattresses and small bathrooms – some a little old. For the budget-conscious a shared bathroom is possible, and they have an annexe down the street, offering cheaper fan-ventilated accommodation. US$45

Zigzag Plot 239 Industrial Rd ☎0213 22814, ⓦzigzagzambia.com; map p.332. Ignore the unpromising street address, this welcoming guesthouse is on a quiet road just off the main drag, a 15min walk south of town. The real draw is the lovely shady garden filled with mango trees (where you can eat your lunch) and a pool and children's play area. Rooms are well maintained if rather small, dated and dark, but the a/c works well and you can drink water fresh from their borehole. US$75

SOUTH OF TOWN

AVANI Victoria Falls Resort Formerly the Zambezi Sun; 393 Mosi-oa-Tunya Rd ☎0213 321122, South Africa ☎11 7807810, ⓦavanihotels.com/victoria-falls; map p.318. A sprawling behemoth of a hotel with 212 smart business hotel-style rooms and suites with the usual amenities: a/c, wi-fi, satellite TV, phone, safe, tea- and coffee-making facilities and vast beds. Despite the slightly sterile feel of the rooms, the resort's large-scale fantasy African decor and architectural touches remind you where you are. You've plenty of dining options too, with two restaurants (one serving a huge buffet breakfast), two cafés and a bar beside a lagoon-sized pool. But the real plus is that it's bang next to the falls, with unlimited free access to the Smoke that Thunders. Doubles US$348

Munga Ecolodge Signposted east off Mosi-oa-Tunya Rd, 3.5km south of the town centre ☎0213 327211, ⓦmungaecolodge.com; map p.318. Surrounded by bush, this eco-lodge uses some solar power, and has a naturally filtered swimming pool surrounded by reeds, bulrushes and waterlilies as the centrepiece. Five stone-and-thatch chalets are painted in earthy tones and have a private sun-bathing courtyard at the back, where you can sleep under the stars as the whim takes you. Full board also possible. Reductions in low season. US$242

The Stanley Safari Lodge Off the road to Mukuni Village ☎(+265) 179 4491 (Malawi), ⓦrobinpope safaris.net; map p.318. Three kilometres from the falls as the fish eagle flies, this elegant lodge is all about indulgence. When the Zambezi is in full flow, you can loll in

8

the glorious infinity pool, sipping your cocktail and watching the distant clouds of spray. Choose from ten lovely stone suites and cottages. Eschew the comfort of the a/c for the open-sided accommodation that lets in the sounds of the bush. Al US$1020

Victoria Falls Waterfront (formerly the Zambezi Waterfront) Sichango Drive, 8km by road from the falls ☎0213 320606 or ☎0986 320606, ⓦthevictoriafalls waterfront.com; map p.318. Known affectionately as "the Waterfront", this is the most affordable riverside option in the area, offering camping (in your own or in one of their tents) as well as chalet accommodation, spread out in luscious grounds on the banks of the great river. A-frame chalets comprising three en-suite doubles are comfortable but simple; you pay for the location, in which case it's worth forking out the extra US$40 for the riverside view. Their two-bed domed tents have a light, a padlock and a small fan but can still get very hot. Though camping rates are good, the bar-restaurant, which offers great sunset views and can get lively to rowdy, still charges tourist rates. As the hotel is located in the park, you have to pay an extra US$10 park fee per night. Camping per person US$13, dome tents US$45, doubles US$225

WEST OF TOWN

★**Toka Leya Camp** Parks Rd, Mosi-oa-Tunya National Park, 5km from Livingstone, off the M10. South Africa ☎11 8071800, ⓦwilderness-safaris.com; map p.332. Twelve lovely, luxurious safari tents set back slightly from

the Zambezi – surprisingly with a/c – with inside and outside showers and private decks, though the best views are from the fabulous communal areas and infinity pool, which are bang on the river. There's even a gym overlooking the rapids, and a small spa. Top-notch service and dining. Al US$1540

TONGABEZI

★**Sindabezi Island** ☎0213 327450, ⓦtongabezi .com; map p.332. Brimming with romance, and a short boat ride downriver from *Tongabezi Lodge* (same ownership), this private island hosts five idyllic open-sided thatched chalets on raised wooden decks; you can watch the water glide past without getting out of bed. Fine dining is by lamplight, as you push your toes into the white sand. US$1190

★**Tongabezi Lodge** On the Zambezi, 15km west of Livingstone, off the M10 ☎0213 327450, ⓦtongabezi .com; map p.332. A stunning setting for a collection of sumptuous, individually decorated cottages and houses, featuring fabulous African furnishings and artefacts; each has a private viewing deck overlooking the river, and personal concierge. Service and organic cuisine are top-notch, and the place oozes relaxed indulgence: private dining – even on a sampan on the river – outdoor baths, personal plunge pools. Then there's the *Lookout* – a delightful over-the-water lounge – which is perfect for sundowners and wildlife viewing. Al US$1550

EATING

There aren't too many places to eat out in Livingstone, but the quality of what's available is good and the food is varied, though prices are on the high side.

★**Café Zambezi** 217 Mosi-oa-Tunya Rd ☎0978 978578. Expect a varied menu of African and Caribbean dishes – plus good music – in this vibey rear courtyard, where seating is at picnic tables that are candlelit at night. Choose from the likes of *jollof* rice, groundnut or goat stew or jerk chicken with *nshima* (like porridge), or excellent chips and veg for only K55–65. Pizzas and burgers also feature. Daily 8am–midnight.

Da Canton Mosi-oa-Tunya Rd ☎0953 709666. The Italian owner orchestrates pizzas and home-made pasta dishes from around K50, though also offers a little goat or fish with *nshima* (K40) on the side. Pass through the unpromising-looking bar to a thatched barn-like structure laden with local artwork. Pick up an authentic home-made gelato on the way out. Live music on Saturday night. Daily noon–10pm.

The Golden Leaf 1174 Mosi-oa-Tunya Rd ☎0213 321266. A very popular Indian restaurant with the usual naan and roti accompaniments, and a good spread of vegetarian options. There's both indoor and outdoor seating on a nice

breezy terrace. Mains K80–110. Tues–Sun 12.30–10pm.

★**Kubu Café** Mosi-oa-Tunya Square ☎0213 324093. Under a leafy trellis just outside Shoprite, this is the place for a lingering breakfast: add hash browns, avocado and onion to the usual eggs, bacon and sausage fry-up; alternatively, indulge in eggs Benedict or a healthy yoghurt, fruit and muesli mix (K45–85). Lunchtime offerings include wraps, gourmet burgers and salads, while succulent flame-grilled meats and lamb vindaloo are evening highlights (K50–100). Mon–Sat 8.30am–9.30pm, Sun 8.30am–2pm.

Munali Café 357 Mosi-oa-Tunya Rd ⓦwbake.com. Centrally located, this basic cafeteria and bakery serving cheap food pulls in a steady flow of locals throughout the day. In addition to full fried breakfasts (K30) and pastries, it has a surprisingly good variety of coffees, including espresso. Daily 7am–8/9pm.

Ocean Basket Mosi-oa-Tunya Rd ☎0213 321274. Set back from the road, with a pleasant patio and indoor seating, this South African franchise offers succulent seafood dishes: calamari, prawns, kingklip, or the full

seafood works for a hefty price (most main K120 and above). You can pick up a tasty morsel of Zambezi bream for a mere K75, however. Da ly noon–10pm.
Olga's 20 Mokambo Rd ☎ 0213 324160, ⌨ olgasproject.com. With profits going to support the Youth Community

Training Centre, it's hard to resist the delicious, home-made pasta dishes and tasty thin-crust pizzas (K30–48) – try the crocodile one – or naughty breakfasts, such as chocolate crêpe with ice cream, all served under fan-ventilated thatch. Daily 7am–9/10pm.

DRINKING

Fez Bar 123 Mosi-oa-Tunya Rd ☎ 095 6774215. This no-frills drinking den serves inexpensive booze and cheap eats to help soak it all up – the likes of village chicken and crocodile curry go for just K50. A ping-pong table and sports screens enliven the bar area, while plain wooden dining tables deck out the rest of the place, which comes alive on Friday and Saturday nights after 10pm, with a DJ enticing people onto the dance floor. Daily 11am until late.

Limpo's Pub & Grill Mosi-oa-Tunya Rd ☎ 097 7499663, ⌨ facebook.com/limpospubandgrilllivingstone. Semi-open venue, with a buzzing bar with beer on tap and a pool table under thatch, where you can get a Mosi or Castle for under a dollar. There are sports screens, a stage for live music or DJ and live music from Wednesday to Saturday. There's even a barber's and car wash on site. Daily noon–late.

NIGHTLIFE

Most nightlife doesn't really get going until the weekend, hotting up on Thursday and letting rip on Friday and Saturday. Though places are often open during the day, you'll need to wait until at least 10pm for much sign of life.

Club Fairmount New Fairmount Hotel, Mosi-oa-Tunya Rd. This rather staid-looking hotel hosts the town's most enduring nightclub, with a laser and plasma-screen-filled disco and lounge bar drawing a clientele of varying ages and offering a bit of everything from *kwassa kwassa*, through classic disco hits to hip-hop. DJs Friday and Saturday. K20 from 8pm, though the entry price increases as the night wears on! Thurs–Sat 8pm–late.

East Point Plot 196 Mwela St ☎ 0977 730730. Part of a Lusaka club franchise, this is the most popular venue to party in town. There's a laser-lit dance floor and a couple of bars, but the real action happens outside, in the back yard, where live acts from Lusaka perform at weekends, while punters gyrate until dawn fuelled by chicken from the BBQ. Cover charge for events. Mon–Sat 6pm–4am.

SHOPPING

For **souvenirs**, head for the line of Mukuni Crafts stalls, at the northern end of Mosioa Tunya Road, by Mukuni Park. Most offerings are bought in bulk from Mukuni Village (see p.334), where you'll inevitably get a cheaper deal. The other place to pick up a curio is down by the falls; traders at the **curio market** by the entrance also source most of their goods from Mukuni Village, though some come from further afield, including from outside Zambia. Alternatively, browse the **shops** in some of the smarter hotels, which usually charge more but generally stock goods of more consistent quality. For a taste of market life, head for **Maramba market** down the road of the same name.

DIRECTORY

Banks and money Several of the big banks, including Barclays and Standard Chartered, are in the central area of Mosi-oa-Tunya Rd, just north of the museum. They have ATMs, will advance you money against a Visa or Mastercard credit card, and can change currency. Banking hours are usually Mon–Fri 8.15am–3.30pm, Sat 8.15–11.30am.
Hospitals/clinics Livingstone General Hospital, Akapelwa St ☎ 0213 321475; Dr Shafik's Hospital Katete Ave ☎ 0213 321130.
Internet Free wi-fi is widely available in accommodation, though it's not necessarily very fast. The main internet café in town is Zulunet, 116 Mosi-oa-Tunya Rd (Mon–Fri 8.30am–6pm, Sat 8.30am–1pm; ☎ 0123 322985).
Pharmacy Link Pharmacy (Mon–Sat 9am–7pm, Sun 9am–1pm; ☎ 0213 324222), on Mosi-oa-Tunya Square next to the *Kubu Café*, is well stocked.

Police The police station (☎ 0213 323575) is on Maramba Rd by Davidson Ave.
Post office Mosi-oa-Tunya Rd; Mon–Fri 8am–6pm, Sat 8am–2pm.
Supermarkets Shoprite in Mosi-oa-Tunya Square, opposite *Fawlty Towers*, is the main supermarket. For fresh fruit and vegetables head for the market stalls along Mokambo Rd and round the bus station on Chimwemwe Rd.
Telephones Public phones are few and far between and rarely used, with mobiles much more common. If you have a locked mobile phone, find an MTN shop on the main street and they will unlock it for free, if they can; otherwise, they will refer you to a specialist for around K150–200 (more for smartphones). Zambian SIM cards are readily available for around K5.

8

HEROES' ACRE

Contexts

History

Namibia's pre-colonial history is bound up with its geography, dominated by its arid landscape across which humans have migrated for thousands of years. Gradually, the central and southern regions became home to semi-nomadic foragers and pastoralists, while the more fertile north was characterized by small kingdoms based on agriculture and cattle-farming. The opening up of trade in the mid- to late-eighteenth century and the arrival of Christianity had a profound effect on the country, but it was only with the "Scramble for Africa" in the late 1880s that the modern borders of Namibia were drawn up. Ruled over with brutality first by Germany, and then by neighbouring South Africa, Namibia's independence only came, after a bitter and long struggle, on March 21, 1990. Since then it has enjoyed a relatively stable democratic political system, though widening inequalities in terms of access to land and to employment, exacerbated by increasing drought, coupled with unaired grievances related to the independence struggle, may threaten this stability in the future.

The early settlers

The oldest evidence of human settlement in Namibia (and in the whole of southern Africa) is the **rock art** of southern Namibia, with the decorated slabs of the Apollo 11 Cave dating back more than 25,000 years. The original **Stone Age** inhabitants who arrived here after the last Ice Age (which peaked around 18,000 years ago) are assumed to have been nomadic hunter-gatherers, referred to as either **San** or Bushmen, who spoke languages from the Khoisan language group characterized by the use of click consonants (see box, p.370). The oldest examples of rock art from this period are the paintings and engravings in **Twyfelfontein (|Ui-|Ais)**, which date back at least six thousand years. Around 2000 to 2500 years ago, it's thought that **Khoikhoi** pastoralists (ancestors of today's Nama, known pejoratively in colonial times as Hottentots) migrated from present-day Botswana and settled in the area, bringing with them pottery and their sheep and cattle. The Khoikhoi produced the later rock art at Twyfelfontein. After the ninth century AD the **Damara** people are known to have settled in the grasslands of central Namibia, although their origins are unknown.

In the north, in the rich agricultural land along the Kunene River, the **Owambo** and other Bantu-speaking groups gradually established centralized (mostly matrilineal) monarchies by at least the seventeenth century, but remained outside of colonial control until 1909. Other Bantu-speaking groups, such as the **Herero**, only reached northern and central Namibia in the mid-sixteenth century. They kept cattle and were

Over 25,000 years ago	Over 6000 years ago	1486
The earliest signs of human settlement in Apollo 11 Cave	Post-Ice Age, Khoisan-speakers are the first to arrive: the San/Bushmen, followed by the Khoikhoi, then the Nama	Portuguese explorer Diago Cão, the first European in Namibia, lands at Cape Cross

organized in decentralized clans, each under a leader, whose power was heavily circumscribed by the other clan leaders. It was only when groups such as the **Oorlam** migrated northwards into Namibia from the Cape from the early nineteenth century that stronger single leaders emerged. But by this point, the impact of colonialism, and the trade in slaves, ivory and cattle, not to mention arms and alcohol, was already beginning to cause tensions within southwest South-West Africa.

Early European contact

The coastline of Namibia first became known to Portuguese explorers in the 1480s. First **Diago Cão** landed north of Walvis Bay, in 1486, and erected a limestone cross at Cape Cross (see p.227), then **Bartolomeu Diaz** anchored at Walvis Bay and at Angra Pequeña (Lüderitz). However, Namibia's famously bleak coastline successfully deterred Europeans from attempting to settle (or even trade) until the second half of the eighteenth century. "So inhospitable and so barren a country is not to be equalled except in the Deserts of Arabia" was the opinion of the captain of HMS *Nautilus* in 1786, while scouting the coastline for a suitable place for a penal colony. It wasn't until 1793 that the first land grab took place when the Dutch annexed **Walvis Bay**. Two years later, the British took the Cape Colony off the Dutch and the following year claimed Walvis Bay for themselves. Africans along Namibia's coastline had engaged in trade with European shipping for some time, but the advent of whaling off Namibia – which started in the late seventeenth century but peaked between 1790 and 1810 – led to a significant increase in the volume of trade, centred on Walvis Bay.

The arrival of the Oorlam

From the 1790s, the Oorlam began to emerge, migrating north in ever-greater numbers. The Oorlam were of mixed-heritage, predominantly of Khoikhoi, European and slave descent, who through acculturation in the Cape now dressed as Europeans, and spoke Afrikaans as well as Khoisan. They had ceased to be exclusively pastoralists, possessed guns, oxen and wagons and engaged in cattle-raiding. Their influence on indigenous peoples in the area was far greater at that time than that of any European missionaries or traders. The oldest systematically designed and built structure in Namibia is at ||Khauxa!nas and was erected around 1795 by the leader of the Oorlam, **Klaas Afrikaner**, who had fled the Cape Colony, accused of murder. The Oorlam inhabited the settlement until the 1820s before moving further northwards.

Meanwhile, in 1806 two missionaries from the London Missionary Society built the first **church** in Namibia, in Warmbad (|Aixa-aibes). This didn't initially go down well with the local Oorlam, and the missionaries had to flee after an attack by Jager Afrikaner (Klaas's son) in 1811. After numerous setbacks, it was the German Protestant **Rhenish Missionary Society** (RMS) that emerged as the dominant mission society in the region, having established their first mission in Bethanien (|Ui‡gandes) in 1814. Relations between the RMS and the Oorlam proved difficult, and conversion rates remained very slow, yet the missionaries nevertheless became an important part of Namibian society, creating mission stations, providing food and shelter to the impoverished, and acting as power brokers between groups. The mission stations in turn attracted traders – predominantly Afrikaners – who set up trading posts. The

1600s–1700s	1793	1790s	1814
Bantu-speaking peoples such as the Owambo, then the Herero, migrate down from East Africa	The Dutch make the first European land grab, founding Walvis Bay, which is soon annexed by the British	The cattle-raiding Oorlam arrive from the Cape in increasing numbers	The first Rhenish Missionary Society mission is established in Bethanien

RMS and other missionaries were also instrumental in promoting European and Christian values: rigid sexual mores, literacy, square houses and Victorian-style clothes – inspiration for the "traditional" Herero, Damara and Nama dresses today. In the same period, mining, trade in ivory and ostrich feathers, arms and cattle all increased, and the frequently cash-strapped missionaries played a pivotal role in this commerce.

Nama-Herero conflicts

The northward migration of the Oorlam caused conflict with the other Nama groupings in southern Namibia, such as the **Bondelswarts**, who were defeated by the Oorlam in 1823, and in 1830 became the first local grouping to sign a protection treaty with the Cape government. By the 1840s, the greatest of the Nama-Oorlam clan leaders, **Jonker Afrikaner** (grandson of Klaas), had established a de facto state in southern and central Namibia, centred on Windhoek, and had two thousand armed men at his disposal. Jonker enriched his own followers by raiding cattle and people and trading in them, simultaneously impoverishing the local Herero and San groups.

When Jonker died in 1861, the Herero under **Maharero** (also known as Kamaharero) rebelled, with the encouragement of the local white traders and missionaries, and began the bloodiest conflict so far on Namibian soil, which aimed to break the dominance of the Nama-Oorlam, now under Christian Afrikaner (Jonker's son). At the **Battle of Otjimbingwe**, in 1863, Christian Afrikaner died along with two hundred Nama-Oorlam, against around sixty Herero. This battle heralded a series of further violent clashes and cattle raids, in which the balance of power began to tip away from the Nama-Oorlam. A period of Herero dominance followed in central Namibia, formally marked by the signing of the **Okahandja peace accords** in 1870, brokered by German missionaries, between Jan Jonker Afrikaner (Christian's brother) and Maharero. The peace accords also permitted the Basters (see p.344) to settle in Rehoboth, but the threat of more Boer trekkers migrating from the Transvaal prompted Maharero and other Herero leaders to formally request British protection in 1874. The Cape government were quite interested in extending their control over Namibia, and set up the **Palgrave Commission** to canvas opinion in Namibia, but the British government were not keen to increase their responsibilities, and in the end only annexed Walvis Bay and the offshore islands in 1878.

German rule 1884–1915

With the British reluctant to venture further inland from Walvis Bay, the Germans took the initiative. In 1883, the Bremen tobacco merchant **Adolf Lüderitz** bought the anchorage and land around Angra Pequeña for £100 in gold and two hundred rifles, thus founding the first permanent colonial settlement in Namibia. Three months later he bought another 140 kilometres of coastline for £500 and sixty rifles, hoodwinking the local Nama-Oorlam group, the Bethanie people, into including the 80 kilometres inland, too. Thus, **Lüderitzland** was founded, and in 1884 Lüderitz asked Germany for protection (against the British). The German Chancellor, Otto von Bismarck, hesitated until he was sure the British had no colonial ambitions in the area, and then, on August 7, 1884, the crews of two naval vessels raised the German flag at Angra Peqeña, Swakopmund, Cape Cross and Cape Frio, thus laying claim to the entire coast

1840s	1862–70	1870	1884
Nama-Orlaam Jonker Afrikaner secures control of central and southern Namibia	The Nama-Herero wars are waged; the Herero under Maharero, the Nama-Oorlam under Christian then Jan Jonker Afrikaner	The Okahandja peace accords are signed between the Nama and Herero	Adolf Lüderitz establishes the first permanent German settlement

from the Orange to the Kunene rivers, and establishing the German protectorate of **Deutsch-Südwestafrika** or German South-West Africa (SWA). Lüderitz then bought up the rest of the coastline north to Angola, bankrupted himself and in 1885 sold the lot to the Deutsche Kolonial-Gesellschaft für Südwest-Afrika (that he himself had set up), and then, the following year, drowned in a boating accident in the Orange River.

Raising the flags was the easy bit; asserting German authority over the interior would take over twenty years. The incredibly tiny cadre of German officials started out by offering "protection" treaties with African elites in southern and central Namibia in exchange for land and the right to trade and mine, though the military who would have had to afford such protection did not arrive until 1888 and the German state did not actually agree to pay for the running of the state until 1992.

The first group to sign a "Treaty of Friendship and Protection", on October 11, 1884, were the Basters – a group of mostly (and proudly) mixed descent (the word is a corruption of "bastard") – who had set up the **Free Republic of Rehoboth** in 1872 in southern Namibia, after trekking northwards from the Cape Colony. The first imperial commissioner, **Dr Heinrich Göring** (father of the Nazi air chief), secured the biggest coup, getting Maharero to sign up, so that by 1885 most of the people of central and southern Namibia had entered into formal relations with the Germans.

Early resistance to German authority

The first notable resistance to German rule came from the new Nama leader, **Hendrik Witbooi**, a charismatic, religious visionary who refused to negotiate with the Germans. Through armed conflict and by persuasion, Witbooi slowly became the dominant leader in the south for the next two decades. It was to protect themselves against Witbooi that many of the clans of central and southern Namibia (including Maharero) had signed treaties with the Germans. Meanwhile, in the north of the country, tensions erupted over the arrival of Boer trekkers from the Transvaal who attempted to settle in Owamboland, buying 50,000 square kilometres from the Owambo chief Kambonde. The **Republic of Upingtonia** was declared on October 20, 1885, named after the leader of the Cape Colony, Thomas Upington (whose protection they hoped, but failed, to secure). Having withstood more or less daily attacks from other disgruntled groups, including the local San, their leader William Jordan was murdered in 1887, and the republic was dissolved and placed under German protection.

In 1888, Maharero pulled out of the protection treaty with Germany, forcing Dr Göring to retreat from Otjimbingwe to Walvis Bay. The German government sent out **Curt von François** and twenty Schutztruppen (protectorate troops) to try and restore colonial authority; when the force was increased to fifty, Maharero was persuaded to re-sign the protection treaty.

German consolidation

The biggest obstacle to German rule now was the great southern leader, Hendrik Witbooi, whose status was given a boost with the death of his great Herero rival, Maharero, in 1890. In April 1893, emboldened by the arrival of extra Schutztruppen, von François launched a surprise attack on Witbooi's headquarters at **Hoornkrans**, killing many of his followers (including women and children). Witbooi himself escaped with around two hundred fighters, and it took over a year of guerrilla warfare before he

1884	1884–88	1888	1894
Germany claims German South-West Africa as a colony	Local groups are forced into signing treaties of "friendship and protection" with the Germans	The first Schutztruppen arrive in Namibia to ensure compliance	Nama leader Hendrik Witbooi finally surrenders by signing the Treaty of Gurus

finally agreed to sign the Treaty of Gurus in 1894, granting him a degree of independence in return for supplying troops to fight on the side of the Germans. This agreement was just one of a number of diplomatic (and military) victories ruthlessly achieved by the new head of German colonial administration, **Theodor Leutwein**, whose stated goal was "colonialism without bloodshed". The conditions were finally right for German settlers to arrive in SWA in some numbers, and an infrastructure of roads, railways and harbours began to take shape on the back of cheap African labour throughout the 1890s. This necessitated the start of large numbers of contract workers being brought down from the north, and stricter controls over the movement of the black populace, including the introduction of the pass system in certain areas, which anticipated its more widespread institution after the Namibian War. However, with the arrival of **rinderpest** (cattle disease) in 1897, the whole country was catapulted into a major crisis. The epidemic caused untold suffering among African pastoralists, while settler cattle losses were much lower, as they were given priority (and were more receptive) when it came to vaccinating cattle.

The Namibian war of resistance and genocide 1903–09
Small-scale armed resistance to German rule continued to flare periodically after the *rinderpest* crisis, as the Germans bought up land for newly arriving German colonists from the devastated farming communities of the **Herero**. By 1904, the Herero had reached breaking point, and in January of that year, taking advantage of an uprising in the south by the Bondelswarts, they staged a full-scale rebellion. Under the leadership of **Samuel Maharero** (son of Maherero), Herero fighters attacked remote German farms across central SWA and killed as many as 150 Germans, sparing the women and children, and the missionaries. The Germans were taken by surprise, and for the next few months, Leutwein struggled to try and defeat the Herero, who now controlled most of central SWA (apart from the garrisons and towns). In June, Leutwein was relieved of his post and the Kaiser sent **Lothar von Trotha** out to SWA to put down the uprising "with rivers of blood and money", with as many as twenty thousand Schutztruppen sent to the country to make sure of it.

The colony thrives and falls
Following the war, the Germans set about trying to create a disciplined labour force to supply the country's mines, recruiting from the defeated and displaced African population. They colonized the lands now free of the Herero and Nama, increasing the number of German farms threefold and the German settler population from five thousand to fifteen thousand, with some 21 percent of the country now allocated to commercial farms. For the first time, the Germans began the process of bringing **Owambo Kings**, in the north, under their control, by obtaining declarations of obedience. On the Kaiser's birthday in 1912, on the site of the concentration camp in Windhoek, the victors erected the **Reiterdenkmal**, an equestrian monument of a Schutztruppe, to commemorate the soldiers and settlers who had died in the conflict (see box, p.84). In the same year, exports exceeded imports for the first time and SWA became the only German colony ever to make a profit, helped in part by the discovery of diamonds near Lüderitz in 1908 (see p.132).

1897	1904–09	1904	1905
The *rinderpest* wipes out almost all cattle, causing major suffering among African populations	The Herero and Nama rise up against the German colonists	Over 10,000 Herero die of starvation after being forced into the desert following defeat at the Battle of Omakari	Hendrik Witbooi dies in battle fighting the Germans

THE GENOCIDE

The collective punishment against the Herero and Nama peoples that took place between 1904 and 1907 was one of the first genocides of the twentieth century, in which tens of thousands perished.

German military commander **Lothar von Trotha** spent several months building up supplies and troops in order to surround the Herero in the Waterberg Plateau. Then, on August 11 1904, at the **Battle of Omahakari** (also known as the Battle of Waterberg), four thousand heavily armed Schutztruppen attacked around six thousand Herero fighters who were defending some forty thousand women and children. Hopelessly outgunned, the Herero managed to retreat into the desert to the east, where ten thousand died of starvation and thirst. The Germans denied the Herero access to the waterholes on the edge of the desert, and on October 2, Trotha issued his infamous **Extermination Order** stating that "within the German boundaries, every Herero, whether found armed or unarmed, with or without cattle, will be shot" – though this order was belatedly revoked in Berlin. Samuel Maharero and a small number of followers made it to Botswana and were granted asylum by the British; the rest were rounded up in concentration camps, including the so-called "death camp" on Shark Island off Lüderitz (see box, p.128), and used as slave labour building the railways. More than half of those imprisoned died, and altogether it's estimated around 65,000 Herero (eighty percent of the population) perished in the conflict.

Just as the Herero were being exterminated in the east, an alliance of several groups of **Nama** rose up in the south, under leaders such as the veteran Hendrik Witbooi, who died in the fighting in October 1905, and **Jacob Morenga**, nicknamed the "Black Napoleon" by the Germans, who was eventually killed by combined German-British forces in 1907. The struggle against the Nama continued until 1909 because after every German victory, the Nama dispersed and employed guerrilla tactics to continue the fight. As the war dragged on, von Trotha was relieved of his post, but sailed back to Germany to a hero's welcome.

Trotha's replacement was the first civilian governor, **Friedrich von Lindequist**, who successfully completed the ethnic cleansing of the Herero, persuaded the Nama to surrender and then sent them to concentration camps to be used as slave labour – again, the unspoken policy was to exterminate them as a people, and, by the end of the war, an estimated ten thousand Nama (fifty percent of the population) had been killed. Those who survived were forced into "native territories" in a policy which both anticipated the ghettoes of the Nazi Holocaust and the "bantustans" of apartheid.

In 2004, on the hundredth anniversary of the war, a visiting German minister acknowledged the act as genocide and offered an apology, but ruled out any compensation being paid to the victims' descendants, offering development aid instead; Germany is now Namibia's biggest aid donor. The German government has now agreed to a full official admission and apology, though Herero and Nama activists continue to demand reparations.

With the outbreak of **World War I**, the dream came to an abrupt end. The border between German SWA and South Africa became a flash point, and there were several border skirmishes (and even a Boer uprising in support of Germany). Between September and December 1914, Louis Botha (the South African prime minister at the time) and Jan Smuts – who was later to become South Africa's prime minister – led over thirty thousand troops of the South African Army into Namibia. Heavily outnumbered, the Germans retreated and eventually agreed to an unconditional surrender at **Khorab** on July 9, 1915 – so, without much of a struggle, 31 years of German colonial rule came to an inglorious end.

By 1909	1908	1915	1915
In total almost 80 percent of the Herero and 50 percent of Nama populations are killed in battle or die later in concentration camps	Diamonds are discovered in Lüderitz	Following the outbreak of WWI, Jan Smuts leads 30,000 South African troops into German South-West Africa	The Germans surrender several months later

South African rule 1915–90

The first five years of South African rule were relatively liberal in the Police Zone (central and southern SWA), despite being exercised by a military government based in Windhoek. Yet it was ruthless in the north, though much of the work had been done for the regime by the appalling famine of 1914–1915, which caused thousands to die of starvation, and those who survived were considerably weakened. Thus, the South Africans were able to establish a base in Ondonga without bloodshed. However, King Mandume Ya Mandemufayo in neighbouring Oukwanyama resisted South African control and paid for it with his life.

After the war, all Germany's colonies were forfeited, and in 1920 South-West Africa became a **League of Nations Mandate**, a "trust territory" assigned to South Africa to look after on behalf of the British. The country was never officially annexed, but was administered initially as a de facto province of South Africa, its white minority having representation in the whites-only parliament of South Africa, its administrative buildings flying the South African flag, though it was granted greater autonomy much later. The South African economic priority in Namibia was to recruit cheap African labour for the region's mines and to subsidize poor Afrikaaner settlements in the Police Zone.

Racial segregation and resistance

The interwar South African state also sought to systematically impose racial segregation on Namibia; building on earlier restrictions introduced by the Germans, they created **"native reserves"** (precursors of apartheid's bantustans) in the early 1920s – these reserves were mostly on marginal, arid land, and became places of extreme poverty. At the same time, white settlers were invited in from South Africa, and given large farming concessions and plenty of support to kick-start their enterprises. Over the next twenty years, African populations within the Police Zone in particular were further oppressed through greater restrictions on movement through the pass system and curfews, unfair taxes, and restricted trading rights. In the far north, the large population was squeezed into the small strip of land above the newly instituted Red Line, ostensibly a veterinary fence, marking the official northern border of the Police Zone. Overpopulation, droughts and food shortages drove larger numbers of men to migrate south as labourers on white farms, in mines or on infrastructure developments.

South African rule met with sporadic resistance, with the **Bondelswarts** being the first to take up arms in 1922. The South Africans were taking no chances, however, and the SWA Administrator himself led the attack, with two planes from Pretoria bombing the Bondelswarts into submission, killing one hundred and wounding more than 450 (out of a population of one thousand). The **Rehoboth Basters'** rebellion in 1924 was also put down by the South African armed forces, who marched into the town, backed by warplanes, and arrested six hundred people.

World War II and apartheid

During **World War II**, South Africa extended its control over the country, interning around a thousand German males, incorporating the police into the South African Police, and switching the local currency to the South African Rand. With the League of Nations superseded by the **United Nations (UN)** in 1945, South African Prime Minister Jan Smuts asked for permission to officially rule SWA as a fifth province, using the

1920	Early 1920s	1939–45
Under a League of Nations mandate, South-West Africa is officially placed under South African control, on behalf of the British	South Africa establishes "native reserves" for the black population, dispossessing them of land and violently crushing rebellions	Many black Namibians fight with the South African army against Nazi Germany

results of a dubious referendum held among Africans in Namibia to support his argument. When the UN refused, South Africa went ahead anyway, formally **annexing** the country in 1947. In 1948, the National Party came to power in South Africa and began to establish **apartheid**, or racial segregation, both in South Africa and Namibia.

Early independence movements and the formation of SWAPO

In 1957, migrant Owambo labourers in Cape Town – among them Andimba Toivo Ya Toivo, a pivotal figure in the independence movement before being incarcerated on Robben Island – formed the opposition **Owamboland People's Congress (OPC)**. This was followed, in 1959, by the establishment of a group within Namibia itself, the Ovamboland People's Organisation (OPO), founded in Windhoek by **Sam Nujoma**. At the same time, the Herero-dominated South-West Africa National Union (SWANU) became the first political party to be formed in Namibia, co-founded by **Chief Hosea Komombumbi Kutako**. Throughout the 1950s, the South African authorities had been passing further apartheid legislation, but had implemented only a limited number of forced removals. But the protests that followed the attempted relocation of Windhoek's black population to Katutura – and their violent aftermath (see box, p.88) – proved to be a watershed moment, prompting Nujoma and other OPO leaders to go into exile and establish a broader nationalist movement. The **South-West Africa People's Organization (SWAPO)**, formed in 1960, became the dominant force in the liberation movement and the only one recognized by the Organization of African Unity (OAU).

Negotiations with the UN

Because of Namibia's history as a League of Nations mandate, and the fact that much of the political opposition was now in exile, the **United Nations (UN)** and the **International Court of Justice (ICJ)** became an important focus in the campaign for self-determination for Namibia and remained so until independence. In 1960 Ethiopia and Liberia – free African nations that had been League of Nations members – brought a case against South Africa to the ICJ to try and get their occupation of Namibia ruled illegal. When the ICJ finally made a judgement in 1966, the case was controversially kicked out, so the UN itself took up the baton and revoked South Africa's mandate.

In 1963, to deflect international criticism, South Africa set up the **Odendaal Commission** into SWA, which recommended that the best way forward was an intensification of apartheid and the creation of new "bantustans" or homelands for particular non-white ethnic groups, such as Owamboland and Damaraland. These were established in Namibia from 1968 onwards, though more than half the country was reserved for the white minority on the most agriculturally profitable land, and in areas that included most of the territory's mineral wealth.

South Africa's intransigence led directly to the beginning of the armed struggle by SWAPO's military wing, the **People's Liberation Army of Namibia (PLAN)**, which had been founded in 1962. On August 26, 1966, eight helicopters of the South African Defence Force (SADF) attacked a PLAN guerrilla base in Omugulugwombashe, northern Namibia – an event now commemorated by a public holiday in Namibia known as **Heroes' Day**.

In 1971, the ICJ finally ruled South Africa's occupation of Namibia to be unlawful, prompting the two main Lutheran Church leaders to write an open letter to the South

1947	1948	1960
South Africa formally annexes South-West Africa, having rejected the UN demand to hand back control of the land	The National Party comes to power in South Africa and begins apartheid policies there, exerting greater control over Namibia	SWAPO is formed by Andimba Toivo Ya Toivo and Sam Nujoma. Nujoma is forced into exile in Angola

African prime minister supporting Namibian independence. This was followed by a prolonged **general strike** of contract workers and campaigns against the "bantustan" police by SWAPO's Youth League.

The independence struggle intensifies

The successful campaign for **Angolan independence** from Portugal in 1975 increased pressure on South Africa to withdraw from Namibia – but their response was to step up their military campaign against SWAPO, attacking their bases in southern Angola. Along with the USA and Zaire, South Africa became heavily involved in supporting **Jonas Savimbi's UNITA** (National Union for the Total Independence of Angola), whose armed wing were engaged in a civil war against the new Soviet/Cuban-backed MPLA government in Luanda, the capital of Angola. Whenever Namibian independence came up, the Americans would always link it to the withdrawal of Cuban troops from Angola. This "Linkage", as it became known, was the biggest stumbling block to Namibian independence – the country was effectively at the mercy of the ongoing Cold War between the USA and the Soviet Bloc.

The message that the fight was against communism was also a key propaganda strategy in ensuring the continuous enlistment of recruits – both white and non-white – for both the SADF and later the **South-West Africa Territorial Force** (SWATF). While white males were automatically conscripted into the army, with stiff jail penalties if they refused, non-whites "volunteered". By the late 1970s the SADF had sixty thousand combat troops engaged in SWA; SWATF had a ten-thousand-strong force, which swelled to 22,000 by 1987. Ironically, Namibia's high-quality road network is due to the SADF's need to facilitate troop movement, just as some of the other infrastructural development in the north came about because of the SADF's presence. Although sometimes portrayed simplistically as a black liberation struggle against the white colonial oppressors, in reality the war was much more complex. The SADF's successful recruitment of black Namibians into various battalions – mostly organized according to bantustan – was attributable to a number of factors: their ability to exploit long-standing ethnic animosity and the widespread fear of communism; and their winning of "hearts and minds" by establishing hospitals, providing school teachers and giving agricultural support. Moreover, the only way for many non-white men to escape crippling poverty and support their family – especially in years of drought – was to sign up for the army. Arguably the South-West Africa government's most successful combat force was the notorious Koevoet, which consisted predominantly of Owambo members, who eventually led counter-insurgency operations into Angola against SWAPO.

UN Resolution 385

In 1976, the UN passed **Resolution 385**, calling for South Africa to withdraw from Namibia and allow UN-organized elections. Later that year, they also formally adopted the name Namibia to replace SWA, and recognized SWAPO as the legitimate representative of the Namibian people. The following year, the UN's **Western Contact Group (WSG)** of five Western powers, dominated by the USA and keen to install a pro-Western government in Namibia, negotiated with South Africa and in 1978 came up with **Resolution 435**, which didn't require South Africa to withdraw before the elections and let them keep Walvis Bay.

1966	1968	1976
The UN formally revokes South Africa's mandate to rule South-West Africa. SWAPO begins military campaign against South African occupation	South Africa begins implementing apartheid "bantustan" or homeland policies in Namibia	The UN calls for South African withdrawal and UN-run elections, which are rejected by South Africa

Despite agreeing to Resolution 435, on April 4, 1978, South Africa went ahead with **Operation Reindeer**, attacking a SWAPO base at Cassinga in southern Angola, and killing six hundred people – an event commemorated by the national holiday of **Cassinga Day**. South Africa also unilaterally held elections, without UN supervision, which were inevitably boycotted by SWAPO and other parties. The elections were won by the multiracial but white-dominated **Democratic Turnhalle Alliance** (DTA), whose support came from a very narrow demographic. However, South Africa was looking to create the widest possible anti-SWAPO front, so with that in mind, the DTA government was dissolved in 1983 and the Multi-Party Conference formed. Two years later, a **Transitional Government of National Unity** (TGNU) was put into office, with the South African Administrator-General, Louis Pienaar, given a veto over all legislation. There was no election for the TGNU, but censorship was relaxed a little, and, with the release and return of much of its imprisoned leadership, SWAPO began to stage mass rallies and help establish the first black trade unions.

Independence

By the late 1980s, the financial costs of the Namibian/Angolan conflict were crippling South Africa – in addition, some 2500 South African soldiers had lost their lives. In 1988, South Africa invaded Angola again, to try and destroy SWAPO and PLAN bases there, but were defeated, and finally signed the **New York Accords** with Angola and Cuba, agreeing to comply with Resolution 435 and to withdraw its troops from southern Angola, in exchange for the withdrawal of Cuban troops. The first-ever UN-supervised elections took place in 1989, with SWAPO winning 57 percent of the vote (and 41 out of 72 seats), and DTA winning just 29 percent of the vote. The new assembly unanimously elected **Sam Nujoma**, president of SWAPO since its foundation in 1960, as the first president of Namibia.

Namibia's independence officially began on March 21, 1990, with twenty heads of state from around the world (and a recently freed Nelson Mandela) attending celebrations in the National Stadium in Windhoek. Despite fears that far-right elements might try to destabilize the new order, the remarkable feature of Namibia since independence has been its relative **political stability**. South Africa had always insisted that Namibia must be a multi-party democracy and a capitalist state, and it held onto Walvis Bay until 1994, when it felt sure SWAPO did not intend to install a one-party state (which had always been their stated aim during apartheid). The same year, Nelson Mandela became president of South Africa and offered to wipe off Namibia's apartheid-era debts.

Nujoma's stated policy of **national reconciliation** assuaged the white minority, but there was no Truth and Reconciliation Commission in Namibia, just a de facto amnesty for all pre-independence acts of violence – including SWAPO human rights abuses in Angola and Zambia, attested to by former detainees and greeted with hysterical denials by the SWAPO leadership. However, this failure to allow different populations to air their grievances and attempt a mutual understanding of the very different historical narratives of the period leading up to independence has resulted in simmering tensions that persist today.

1989	1990	1994
The first Namibian elections are held; SWAPO wins 57 percent of the vote, installing Sam Nujoma as president	Independence formally begins on March 21	Walvis Bay is finally handed over to Namibia and Sam Nujoma is elected for a second term

Like much of southern and central Africa, Namibia quickly had to face up to the threat of **HIV and AIDS**, which had infected over twenty percent of the adult population by 2000 – rates have since reduced slightly – and created around 100,000 orphans. The most serious threat to Namibian stability has come from the dispute over the then Caprivi Strip – now the Zambezi Region – where the **Caprivi Liberation Army** (CLA), under their ex-DTA leader Mishake Muyongo, began campaigning for self-rule in 1994. Following the government discovery of a military training camp in 1998, and a rebel attack on the Caprivi capital Katima Mulilo, a state of emergency was declared in the eastern Caprivi. The eventual government crackdown a year later silenced the CLA, and development money is being poured into the region to help ensure national unity. Nevertheless, the region remains a potential source of further conflict, especially since the recent convictions of those accused of plotting the uprising – following a 12-year-long trial – are being contested, while the government, in turn, is seeking to overturn the acquittals (see box, p.271).

Post-independence

Ten years after independence, the subject of **land reform** remained high on the political agenda, partly due to events in nearby Zimbabwe, where black farmworkers were invading white farms, with the encouragement of the ZANU government of Robert Mugabe, a close ally of Sam Nujoma. In 2002, the new prime minister **Theo-Ben Gurirab** announced that land reform was a priority, but said that the government would not condone plans to invade white-owned farms. Nevertheless, Sam Nujoma made a famously vicious attack on Tony Blair at the Earth Summit in 2002, backing Mugabe and blaming the British for the problems in Zimbabwe. That said, so far only around twelve percent of the commercial farmland has been taken from white farmers and given to black citizens, and an estimated 35 percent of Namibia's rural population live below the poverty line.

There was (and remains) a widespread feeling among many Namibians that President Nujoma's fifteen-year rule – the constitution was changed so he could serve three terms – produced a huge rise in corruption. Nujoma's nominee, **Hifikepunye Pohamba**, won the 2004 presidential elections, promising to root out corruption, setting up an Anti-Corruption Commission and restricting the number of foreign trips made by his cabinet. Pohamba stepped down for the 2014 elections – the first in Africa to use electronic voting – and was replaced by **Hage Geingob**, with SWAPO winning eighty percent of the popular vote (and 77 out of 96 seats). In 2015 President Pohamba was awarded the prestigious (and lucrative) **Mo Ibrahim Award** for outstanding African leaders who rule well, raise living standards and then leave office. Like his predecessor, Pohamba failed to make many inroads into land reform, leaving President Geingob to tackle Namibia's three biggest problems for the last 25 years: corruption, social inequality and unemployment.

1999	2004	2014
The Caprivi secessionist conflict is finally ended by government military intervention and the imprisonment of the rebel leaders	Hifikepunje Pohamba becomes Namibia's second president and a visiting German minister offers an apology for the Herero-Nama genocide	Former prime minister Hage Geingob is elected Namibia's third president as SWAPO wins 80 percent of the vote

Peoples

Wading into the political minefield of "ethnicity" and "race" is always a tricky affair in Namibia, as in other post-colonial states, since these socially constructed categories have predominantly come into being over the last two centuries, inevitably shaped and manipulated by decades of pernicious racial and ethnic differentiation, segregation and social stratification during successive colonial and apartheid eras. Up until then, social affiliations and lifestyles would seem to have been much more contingent than colonial historical accounts make out. At the same time, the arbitrary carving up of Africa by the colonial powers to demarcate particular nations cut across peoples, and, over time, has played its part in eroding or hybridizing cultural practices and weakening social ties.

The Namibian government's need to promote a unified, national identity for its estimated 2.3 million population has been an understandable post-independence response to all this. Indeed, a favourite metaphor of Namibia's current president, Hage Geingob, is that of "one Namibian house" in which the "bricks" of ethnicity and race will gradually be indistinguishable as they are glued together by new legislation, then plastered and painted over. It is also true that intermarriage and co-settlement over many generations, both voluntary and coerced, have also helped to blur racial and ethnic boundaries, as has increasing urbanization. What's more, census data no longer collects figures on ethnicity; rather, numbers are imputed from information on first language use in the home. That said, however, many Namibians still identify with one or more ethnicities – historically, culturally, linguistically – at particular times, to differing degrees and for a variety of reasons. The ongoing simmering disputes about land rights, for example, are replete with claims to ethnicity and specific cultural identities.

Therefore terms denoting race and ethnicity should be understood as being looser, more indistinct and more fluid than language permits in the necessarily oversimplified sketch of Namibia's main populations given below. And it's important to acknowledge that race and ethnicity, however constructed, are central to the fault lines of inequality that persist today.

The main social groups

The earliest inhabitants of the land that is now Namibia were those that belong to the **Khoisan** language group (see box, p.369), who arrived many thousands of years ago: **San** groupings, joined later by **Nama** and then, much later, by **Damara** populations (see p.354). Moving down from East Africa, so colonial history relates, came Bantu-speaking peoples: the **Owambo**, in around the fourteenth century, followed a couple of centuries later by **Otjiherero**-speakers including the **Himba** (see p.356). Other **Bantu**-speaking peoples include the main groups that now primarily reside in the Kavango and Zambezi regions. Speakers of Indo-European languages arrived in the late nineteenth and twentieth centuries: the Germans, ancestors of present-day German Namibians, and various Afrikaans-speaking people (see p.358). Those claiming Afrikaans as a first language include white **Afrikaners**, who came from South Africa, and are of Dutch descent, and those with a mixed African-European heritage, including the **Nama-Oorlams** and the **Basters** (see box, p.142).

San (Bushmen)

Renowned for their ancient rock art, tracking and hunting skills, the hunter-gatherer ancestors of the 30,000 plus **San** or **Bushmen** living in Namibia are considered to be the original inhabitants of southern Africa. The controversial terms "San" and "Bushmen" have been both preferred and discarded as **derogatory** by different groups on account of their original meanings; though some groups will choose one word over the other, most want to be known by their individual nations since a collective term does not exist in their own languages. Dispersed across various countries in the region, the Namibian populations are currently spread around northern and eastern areas of the country. The **Ju|'hoan**, **Naro**, **‡Aullen** and **!Xoo** who have not become totally westernized and are living in urban areas predominantly inhabit the Kalahari area of eastern Namibia; the **!Kung** and **Khoe** are found in the Kavango and Zambezi regions, and the **Hai||om** live near the Grootfontein area.

In pre-colonial times, dispersed San groups lived in small family groupings of between fifteen and fifty, congregating in larger groups around a permanent water source during the dry winter months. Rather than owning land, the San believed themselves to be the custodians of **!nores**, their traditional hunting grounds where men would hunt or trap animals while the women would usually forage for roots, nuts and berries, which were the mainstay of the San diet. While different groups' religious beliefs varied, belief in a supreme being among other deities and a focus on healing were common, as well as the importance of ancestral spirits and communication with the spirit world through the shaman. This would often happen during the famous "trance dances", which still persist in some rural communities, though to a very limited extent.

Throughout history, San groups have been denigrated and persecuted by both Bantu-speaking and white settlers, being gradually forced off their lands, enslaved and even hunted down. Hai||om communities were famously forced off their land in Etosha National Park (see p.241) during the 1950s. Similarly the Khoe were displaced in favour of a nature reserve on the Kavango River. During the apartheid era the demarcation of the Bushman homeland resulted in a 90 percent reduction of the Ju|'hoan's traditional hunting grounds. What's more, unlike in other homelands, the San had no say in its administration. In the 1970s, San lifestyles suffered a further blow when SADF bases were established in or near their areas, and the South Africans recruited San to work as trackers and soldiers in counter-insurgency operations against SWAPO. An estimated quarter of all San became dependent on army wages and services and abandoned any reliance on the land. When the conflict ended and independence beckoned, around half took up the offer to relocate to South Africa, afraid of how they might be treated by the Namibian government for having been on the wrong side of the struggle.

Since independence, San groups continue to be among the most **marginalized**, lacking land, food security and adequate representation, with many suffering from poor health, and struggling with social ills such as alcohol abuse and violence both within San groups and against non-San. Though traditional San lifestyles have all but vanished and many communities are disintegrating, there are glimmers of hope: hunting restrictions have been lifted in some areas, and some rural communities, with the help of government and NGOs, are managing to survive with a mixed economy involving foraging, crop cultivation and livestock grazing.

Nama

The **Nama**, who call themselves the **|Awakhoen** (meaning the Red Nation), like the San, are descended from ancient peoples who have lived in southern Africa for several thousand years. Like the San, they also speak a Khoisan click language, **Khoekhoegowab** – more easily referred to as Nama, though many also speak Afrikaans, especially those of **Nama-Orlaam** descent. While the indigenous Nama were predominantly semi-nomadic pastoralists, herding cattle, goats and sheep, they also lived as hunter-gathers when the situation demanded. By the 1830s they were also engaging in long-distance trade, having been influenced heavily by the arrival of Nama-Orlaam, with their ox carts, guns and adoption of Christianity.

Although there was initially a lot of **conflict** among and between Nama and Orlaam groups, by the end of the century their differences had more or less dissolved through co-settlement and intermarriage and the need to come together to confront common threats, such as the Herero, and then later the Germans.

In the nineteenth century there were fourteen identifiable groups living north of the Orange River – nine Nama, five as Oorlam; these days the fourteen groups all think of themselves as Nama, generally named after a former Orlaam leader, such as **|Khopesen** (Witboois), or the place where they have settled, such as **!Amain** (Bethanie people). Nearly all live in settled communities located in the more arid south of Namibia, around Keetmanshoop, where many Nama work on commercial farms; others struggle with subsistence farming, though communal agricultural projects have been initiated in some places. Exceptions include the **‡Aonin** and **!Gommen** (Topnaars), who live in the Namib's Kuiseb River area (see box, p.234) and further north in Sesfontein, respectively. These groups also differ from other Nama groups in not owning communal land, but inheriting it through particular lineages. Only in the Richtersveld Transfrontier Park, which straddles the border with South Africa (see p.154), do some Nama still practise a semi-nomadic way of life. Like the Herero, the Nama lost much of their land, cattle and people in uprisings against the Germans. Today they number around 60,000, or five percent of the Namibian population.

After independence, the **Nama Traditional Leaders Council** was set up in an attempt to sustain common elements of Nama culture without losing the distinctiveness of individual groups. In particular, Namas are renowned for a strong tradition of praise poetry, music and storytelling.

Damara-speaking peoples

The **Damara** peoples of Namibia share a language with the Nama, now referred to as **Nama-Damara**. They refer to themselves as **‡nūkhoen**, meaning "black people", and, along with other Khoisan groups (the San and Nama), are considered to be some of the country's earliest inhabitants. The Damara migration into present-day Namibia is more of a mystery, though recent thinking suggests that, like the San, they migrated from the central Kalahari area, though at a later time, well over a century later. According to early European accounts, they were the most widespread of the indigenous communities with no common group identity, found in pockets all over central and northern Namibia. Colonial historians labelled them as hunter-gatherers, but evidence suggests great versatility depending on where they were living. The relatively dispersed populations variously practised livestock farming, agriculture, horticulture, cultivating pumpkins and tobacco, and some were known to be skilled blacksmiths. Their extensive yet dispersed spread of communities led to contact with various other groups, which resulted in different cultural practices and no centralized social structure. Damara tended to live in extended family groups, and only in the second half of the nineteenth century were they forced into a more developed group identity through the appointment of a chief, or "king", **Cornelius Goreseb**.

As with the San, the dispersed nature of Damara society also made it easy for them to be squeezed out by the more numerous and better armed Herero and the Nama in the latter half of the nineteenth century. Some Damara fled to the mountains, gaining them the name "Berg-Damara"; others were gradually incorporated into a labour economy – sometimes forcibly, working for the Herero, in particular, as servants or herders. From 1879, the Damara were also the first group to be shipped as indentured labourers to the Cape, often under duress.

The first Damara "reserve" was created in Okombahe in 1906 – after the RMS persuaded the Herero chief to give up some land in exchange for rent. During the apartheid era Damaraland was extended northwest, as far as Sesfontein, though only around a quarter of the Damara population now live in this area. As many live in Windhoek, where they are variously employed in government – the current president is Damara – and private enterprise; the rest are predominantly in central-northern urbanized areas. However, Okombahe's importance has been revived as the seat of the Damara's royal household, where the current 33 Damara groups converge on the first weekend every November for the annual **Damara Cultural Festival**, during which they pay homage to their ancestors, share oral histories, sing and dance. This jamboree only started in the 1970s in an attempt to re-affirm a collective Damara identity.

Oshiwambo-speaking groups

Namibians who might identify themselves as **Owambo** (also Ovambo, previously Aawambo) are a loose association of eight currently recognized social groups, who collectively form the country's majority population (around 50 percent). The shared language is **Oshiwambo**, though **Oshindongo** and **Oshikwanyama** are the mutually intelligible standardized dialects that are taught at school. The Owambo originally migrated down from the Great Lakes area of East Africa, settling both sides of the Kavango River in what is now southern Angola and northern Namibia, in around the fourteenth century. Over time, populations grew, spread and separated into the different Owambo groups that exist today in Namibia: the most numerous are the **Kwanyama**, followed by **Ndongo** and much smaller populations of **Kwambi, Mbalantu, Kwaluudhi, Kolonkhadi** and **Ngandjera** and, more recently, the **Owambandja**. Forty-five percent of Owambos currently populate the northern administrative regions of Oshikoto, Oshana, Ohangwena and Omusati – collectively referred to as the Four 'O's – which are Namibia's most densely populated regions outside the Windhoek area (Khomas), and suffer from high unemployment.

The Owambo traditionally are crop and stock farmers, who also fish when seasonally inundated depressions – **oshanas** – flood. Their main agricultural produce are mahangu (pearl millet), sorghum and beans, with cattle the primary livestock. Owambos also have a long history of trading. These days, due both to their numerical superiority and the political dominance of SWAPO, Owambos occupy the majority of **senior government positions** and are involved at senior levels in all Namibia's major industries: mining, fishing and tourism.

Pre-colonial Owambo society was organized in kingdoms, with headmen underneath the king. It was both polygamous and matrilineal, though the colonial and post-colonial systems of government have weakened these structures. These days, only the Ndonga, Ngandjera and Kwaluudhi still recognize their kings, though they are now aided by councillors, as well as headmen, and in some groups females are now allowed to occupy senior traditional leadership roles. The spread of Christianity in the north via Finnish missionaries in the late eighteenth century (see p.342) severely eroded traditional belief systems and customs, though they persist, often in hybrid form. In many rural areas, for example, Owambos still recognize **Kalunga** as the supreme being, even as they may also espouse Christianity and indeed use the term to refer to the Christian conception of God; the **onganga** (traditional spiritual healer) too is still seen by some as an important medium for communicating with ancestral spirits.

The traditional Owambo **homestead** (ehumbo) comprises a distinctive high wooden palisade with rondavels enclosed by yet more fences and labyrinthine passages demarcating activity-specific areas. These are gradually altering; deforestation and pressure on natural resources has led to greater use of mud, cement block and aluminium, while urban migration has led to further housing and lifestyle changes. However, a visit to the Uukwaluudhi Royal Homestead at Tsandi (see p.254), or the

Nakambale Museum and Restcamp in Olukonda (see p.250), provides fascinating insights into Owambo histories, traditions and changing cultures.

Otjiherero-speaking groups

The **Herero** (or OvaHerero), like the Owambos, are Bantu language-speakers, who migrated down from East Africa, and are estimated to have arrived in the northwest of present-day Namibia in the mid-sixteenth century. Four groups live in Namibia: **Herero**, **Mbanderu**, **Himba** and **Tjimba**. The Himba (see below) and Tjimba remained in the northwest, whereas the Herero and Mbanderu migrated in a southerly direction and were well established around central Namibia when the first Europeans landed. The fact that an estimated 80 percent of Herero and Mbanderu lost their lives in attempted genocide by the Germans – by way of reprisal for their failed uprising against the colonists – at the beginning of the twentieth century (see p.346) has left a profound scar on Herero and Mbanderu communities, who are still seeking reparations from the German government. Those who died are commemorated annually in the various **flag days** (see box, p.70), notably in Okahandja, when the men parade in paramilitary uniforms and the women wear their modern "traditional" attire. This consists of billowing petticoat-laden dresses culturally appropriated from Rhenish missionaries, topped with an anvil-shaped cloth headpiece turned up at the ends, representing the horns of cattle.

Cattle became central to traditional Herero culture – at least from the latter part of the nineteenth century, since although many arrived in Namibia primarily as semi-nomadic cattle herders, some had no cattle, and besides, they also traded and practised agriculture and horticulture when necessary. Above all, cattle denoted social status and had religious significance, playing a symbolic role in Herero communications with their ancestors. Ancestors, in turn, acted as mediators, with the Herero supreme being, **Ndjambi Karunga**, venerated at the **okuruwo** (sacred shrine and hearth), in each **onganda** (homestead). In pre-colonial times there was no centralized political structure, which was attributed to the Herero's system of dual descent: religious or sacred property, status within the family and place of abode were taken from the father's line (oruzo), whereas the inheritance of wealth and secular possessions was passed on matrilineally (eanda). However, the spread of Christianity and Western capitalism has caused the matriclans to all but disappear.

These days, Herero-speakers form Namibia's third-largest ethnic group in Namibia. However, having lost many beasts to Nama cattle raiders in the mid-nineteenth century, and their traditional grazing lands to the Germans, with further losses occurring through the apartheid homeland system, Herero no longer regard cattle with the same cultural significance. Many Herero now live in urban areas engaged in a range of jobs and professions, though others are employed on commercial cattle farms in central Namibia and some still keep herds on communal lands north of the Red Line.

Himba

The **Himba** (or OvaHimba) share a common ancestry and language with the Herero – **OtjiHimba** being a dialect of Otjiherero. Different historical trajectories, however, as well as living in some of the country's most remote, inaccessible mountainous areas, have allowed them to maintain many of the traditions they shared with the Herero, and to remain more culturally distinct. However, more recent contact with the media, formal schooling, and an increase in tourism is causing rapid change, particularly among the younger generation. A population of around 50,000 Himba lives in the northwestern reaches of the Kunene Region and southwestern Angola, both sides of the Kunene River. As with the Herero in former times, cattle are central to Himba identity, now a marker of social status rather than as a provider of meat, though occasionally one is slaughtered for a special occasion. Goats and sheep, supplemented by cows' milk, chicken eggs as well as cultivated millet and maize, constitute their main diet. Recent droughts have resulted in huge losses of cattle, which has further threatened their traditional way of life.

Though a few communities still practise a semi-nomadic lifestyle, more and more are becoming settled. Most rural Himba settlements, however, still live in an extended family **homestead** (onganda) in a collection of dome-shaped homes constructed with mopane wood covered with goatskin, and arranged in a circle surrounding the **sacred fire** (okuruwo), which is always kept burning, as a means of communicating with the ancestors, and through them to the supreme being, **Mukuru**. The kraal for the sacred livestock rarely features these days, as few Himba can now afford to keep cattle purely for ritual purposes.

Polygamy is still widely practised, as are arranged marriages, and the dual heritage structure (now abandoned by the Herero; see opposite) that allows for differentiated inheritance down both the female and male lines still persists.

In recent years, the Himba and related Zemba and Hakaona have made various national and international **protests** against the Government of Namibia regarding human rights violations, such as the lack of recognition of their traditional authorities, and ongoing plans to build a dam on the Kunene River (see box, p.260).

Kavango

Named after the region's life source, the **Kavango** peoples are primarily concentrated along the riverbanks and fertile floodplains of the 400km stretch of the Kavango (or Okavango) River that forms the northern border between Namibia and Angola. They are Bantu-speaking riverine people who had originally come from East Africa and settled in the Upper Zambezi, before migrating further south at various stages between the sixteenth and eighteenth centuries. Inevitably, fishing was central to their diet, and was practised by both women and men, but they also used to hunt water-loving antelope and grow sorghum, mahangu and maize on the floodplain terraces. Though the antelope are no more, fishing and crop cultivation continue, and from the latter half of the nineteenth century cattle farming became a feature of Kavango life. Equally important was trade with the eastern Owambo groups, especially among the more westerly Kwangali, who arguably had more interaction with their Owambo neighbours than with the groups that were later classified as Kavango. In more recent times, **woodcarving** has also grown as an industry, while many young Kavangans now work as labourers in mines, on farms or in urban areas.

The 200,000 Kavango broadly comprise five Bantu-speaking groups: the **Kwangali**, **Mbunza**, **Shambyu**, **Gciriku** and **Mbukushi**, with the more numerous Kwangali and the Mbunza sharing the same language of **RuKwangali**, which is one of Namibia's national languages, and the other groups speaking other dialects. Each group is ruled by a **king**. Just as crucial to the structure of Kavango societies is clan membership, passed down through the maternal line, though people of the same clan do not necessarily live together. Despite the success of Christian missionaries – both Catholic and Finnish Lutheran – traditional cosmology is still important, such as belief in the supreme being, **Karunga**, and the power of the ancestors to ward off evil spirits and protect the family.

Initially, the biggest threat to the Kavango groups – beyond power struggles and land disputes – came from the Tawana in present-day Botswana, supported by the British; the Gciriku in particular incurred major loss of life and goods; the Shambyu and Mbukushu also suffered. By the end of the nineteenth century many of the Kavango were impoverished and were reportedly even reduced to selling their own kin to slave traders, though slaves were also snatched in raids. German colonial influence was minimal, since the lack of mineral wealth made the area unappealing to settlers, and very few Kavango were forced to become migrant labourers. Of greater impact was the arrival in 1909 of the Portuguese, who established forts along the northern bank of the Kavango, where most of the population were living at the time. After failed armed resistance, the Shambyu fled further into Angola, only returning several years later. Once the other polities had been raided regularly, they fled across the river. The South African era, however, was a different matter; following forced removal from the river, Kavangans resisted, resulting in harsh retaliation by the paramilitary Koevoet (see p.349). Following Namibian independence, and the end of the civil war in Angola, cross-border trade has increased, and migrating Angolans – many of whom are Kavangans – have caused the population to double in size in recent years.

The Zambezi Region (formerly Caprivi)

The thin 450km sliver of land known as the **Zambezi Region** has been a melting pot of cultures over many centuries. These days five main Bantu-speaking groups constitute the 90,000-plus population (four percent of the national total): the **Masubia** and the **Mafwe** are by far the largest groups, with smaller numbers of **Mbalangwe**, **Totela** and **Mayeyi**. Even smaller groups of **Khwe** (San/Bushmen) and **Mbukushu** live in the drier, western part of the region. Unsurprisingly, given the fact that the Zambezi Region shares borders with both Angola and Zambia and is a short hop from Zimbabwe, it has attracted a lot of migrants from these countries in recent years, especially in the regional capital, Katima Mulilo.

Available pre-colonial history in the Zambezi Region is particularly hazy about the earliest people there; besides, group affiliations, names and identities have shifted substantially over time. Among various small, decentralized groups, including some San, two powerful kingdoms sought variously to impose themselves, both of which have laid claim to being the original settlers. The Masubia, riverine people based round the area of the Linyanti-Chobe confluence in eastern Zambezi (see p.361) who are thought to have arrived around the mid-fifteenth century, named the area Itenge, and the **Lozi**, the dominant kingdom-cum-empire of the time, based in Barotseland (southern Zambia), pushed them out as they expanded their kingdom. The Lozi Kingdom, apart from being overrun by the northward migrating Makololo for a twenty-year period in the mid-nineteenth century, was the dominant force in the area, until the Germans instituted direct rule in 1909. Based in the floodplains of the Zambezi, the Lozi Kingdom was highly organized, and as well as bringing many disparate groups under its rule, it predominantly ruled indirectly, exacting tribute and making the occasional raid to secure slaves. Today **SiLozi** is still the lingua franca of eastern Zambezi, and is taught in schools – a legacy of colonialism, which has been reinforced in post-independence language policy even though the actual number of Lozi in the region is very small.

With four perennial rivers in the region and fertile **floodplains**, fishing and agriculture have inevitably been important to the people's predominantly subsistence livelihoods. In addition to mixed livestock farming, mahangu and maize are cultivated alongside green vegetables such as spinach and cabbage, supplemented by seasonal fruits. **Commercial fishing** has also become more common, although recent overfishing has led to a depletion of stocks. Craft work in **basketry** and **pottery** also have a rich history in the region, and the main urban area of Katima Mulilo has long been an important trading centre.

Afrikaans-speaking groups

Just over ten percent of the population speak **Afrikaans** as a first language. These are a mix of white Afrikaners, of predominantly Dutch descent, who migrated north from present-day South Africa to escape the British colonizers at the end of the nineteenth century, and whose numbers swelled once South Africa took over the custodianship of present-day Namibia in the wake of World War I. The majority of Afrikaans-speakers, however, comprise people of mixed heritage, generally African and European, who were labelled "coloured" during the apartheid years, but who self-identify in varying ways. These include the **Basters** (see box, p.142), who consider themselves as culturally distinct from other people of mixed heritage, in part because of their particular history, having secured the right to landownership in 1870 and a degree of self-determination for an extended period.

German-speakers

German-speaking Namibians are almost exclusively the descendants of ethnic **German colonists** who arrived in the country at the end of the nineteenth century (see p.343), predominantly as traders, troops and government officials, with numbers swelling further during the diamond boom (see box, p.132) to around 13,000 settlers and fluctuating numbers of Schutztruppen. Immediately after World War I around half the German settlers were deported, though later the remainder were granted British citizenship, which was later revoked at the outbreak of World War II. Today, the current German–Namibian population is around 30,000, living mainly in the urban areas of Windhoek, Swakopmund, Lüderitz and Otjiwarongo, where they run many of the major businesses and tourism enterprises, and hold positions in government. More controversially, some still own large farms acquired during the colonial era, which are the subject of ongoing land disputes.

Many German–Namibians are church-going Lutherans, though over half the Namibian population belong to one of the country's three evangelical Lutheran churches. German food and drink are also important to community identity, the greatest manifestation of which is the annual Windhoek Oktoberfest (Ⓦoktoberfestnamibia.com), where traditional activities such as log-sawing, beer-lifting and strongman competitions are held, aided by copious beer and Bavarian specialities such as *obatzda* (a spicy, cheesy concoction) and roast pork knuckle.

Landscapes

The Namib Desert

Although Namibia can arguably be divided into five distinct geographical areas, it is the spectacular dune fields of the **Namib Desert** – now a UNESCO World Heritage Site – that outsiders most readily associate with the country. Probably in existence for about eighty million years, the constantly evolving landscape of the Namib stretches around 2000km from the Olifants River in the Cape Province of South Africa, along the Skeleton Coast, to San Nicolau in southern Angola, a 200km-wide swathe of land bounded on the west by the Atlantic Ocean's Benguela Current, which is pivotal in maintaining the desert environment as its icy waters prevent the formation of rain clouds over the sea. On average, the Namib receives around 15mm of rainfall annually on the coast – though much of the moisture for plant and animal life is gained from fog (see box, p.211) – and around 100mm on the higher eastern areas inland, though some years it gets no rain at all. In addition to the famous dune seas, the Namib comprises vast tracts of flat gravel plain from which protrude a number of striking **inselbergs** – isolated hills or mountains that have remained after the surrounding rocks have been eroded – such as the Spitzkoppe and Brandberg.

The Great Escarpment

At the same time as marking the eastern limit of the Namib, these inselbergs constitute part of another of the country's main geographical areas: the **Great Escarpment**. Probably formed around eighty million years ago by the uplifting of the Earth's crust after the break-up of the supercontinent Gondwana, it is not a continuous ridge, as large tracts have been eroded over time, and some areas, such as the Spitzkoppe, Brandberg and the Erongos, have also been shaped by subsequent volcanic activity. The escarpment is at its most dramatic in the Naukluft Mountains, but also includes the impressive ranges in the northwest – the Baynes, Stellrand and Hartmanns mountains – and the inaccessible Huns Mountains west of the Fish River Canyon in the south. When soaking up the breathtaking views from one of Namibia's loftier highland passes, such as the Gamsberg and the Spreetshoogte, this imposing geological phenomenon is much easier to appreciate. Namibia's mountain ranges are cleft by steep ravines, which run westwards towards the coast, and were eroded by flowing rivers in former times. Now the country's main rivers are mostly dry sandy beds – except in times of exceptional rain – such as the Swakop, Omaruru and Ugab, whose underground waterflow nevertheless supports large trees and shrub vegetation, which are vital to the survival of Namibia's desert-dwelling creatures.

The Central Highland Plateau and the Kalahari

The escarpment, in turn, forms the western edge of the undulating **Central Highland Plateau**, which extends roughly from north of Otjiwarongo to close to the border with South Africa, maintaining an altitude of around 1000m. Here the climate is less harsh and the vegetation cover more pronounced, as it receives slightly more rain. The plateau's eastern limit is less defined as it slopes gently downwards, melting into the flat, acacia-studded sand sheet that is the **Kalahari**, which continues across the border into Botswana and northern South Africa. This southern part also contains a burnished, rippling dunescape. For purists, the Kalahari is not a true desert, being classified as semi-arid since much of it receives over 100mm a year, though few lay people would quibble, given its abundance of sand, extreme temperatures and absence of surface water.

The Zambezi Region

In the far northeast of Namibia, and along the panhandle, in the **Zambezi** (formerly Caprivi) **Region**, the climate changes dramatically. Though the area remains flat and often sandy, the **perennial rivers** of the Kavango (Okavango), Zambezi and the Kwando – which morphs into the Linyanti, and then the Chobe – plus the higher annual rainfall (roughly 400–600mm and above) nourish relatively luxuriant **subtropical** vegetation and **wetlands**.

Vegetation

Almost three quarters of Namibia is classified as **savannah** land. In central regions **thornbush savannah** predominates, comprising prickly, thin-leafed acacia shrubs and grasslands. In the northern areas, which receive greater rainfall, denser, more broad-leafed **woodland savannah** is in evidence. Acacia trees punctuated by huge **baobabs** and clumps of **makalani palms** thrive here, while the even wetter parts of the Kavango and the Zambezi regions support the larger, riverine forests and deciduous broad-leaved trees that characterize **mopane woodlands**. However, the flat land is covered in thick deposits of Kalahari sand.

Along the entire length of the Namib Desert and in the arid southern region trees and grass are scarce, although ephemeral **stipagrostis grasses** survive by having hardy seeds that can withstand the desert heat and lack of water, lying dormant for decades after the plant itself has withered, ready to germinate in the rare times of favourable rainfall. In such years, Namaqualand, a region just north of the Orange River that spans the |Ai–|Ais/Richtersveld Transfrontier Park and the Tsau ||Khaeb (Sperrgebiet) National Park and stretches over the border into South Africa, is famed for its kaleidoscopic carpet of **spring flowers**, which bloom in August and September.

Succulents too, such as the striking **quiver tree**, which adorns many a sunset shot of southern Namibia (see box, p.149), have various desert survival strategies, notably a waxy coating on their leaves to reduce transpiration and leaves and stems that can swell to store water. Other plant adaptations to the arid environment include slow growth, as epitomized by the scraggly **welwitschia** (see box, p.218); thin or spiny leaves that reduce water loss and help prevent them being eaten by animals – as exemplified by the **!nara melon** (see box, p.233); and hollow, large or expandable trunks or stems that can store water, as exhibited by the giant pot-bellied baobab and the slightly skinner **moringa** tree, whose silvery bark reflects the sun. **Lithops** – a type of succulent, whose name means "stonelike" – disguise themselves as beach pebbles, to avoid being eaten, their low-lying or absent stem providing another means of preserving moisture.

On the desert gravel plains, **lichens** – ancient organisms that are a mix of algae and fungi – abound, clinging to patches of exposed rock or the gypsum soil crust. Colours and shapes vary, from yellow to green, purple or pink, especially when exposed to moisture, usually in the form of fog. In contrast, some appear like withered dead plants once the sun is beating down on them as they shrivel to avoid losing moisture.

Wildlife

The chance to spot large mammals in their natural habitat is what lures many visitors to Africa, and although Namibia can't compete with the vast animal-filled plains of Tanzania and Kenya, numbers are increasing, especially in the north, due to the success of the government's conservancy-based conservation strategy (see box, p.364), the removal of many fences allowing the animals greater freedom to roam, and the higher rainfall, which therefore provides more vegetation for them to eat. Yet, even in the drier desert and semi-desert areas, there is plenty of animal life to engage your attention, especially in terms of reptiles and invertebrates.

Our Namibia field guide (see p.22) has further detailed information on the main mammals and some of the birds you're likely to see across the country.

Mammals

There are 217 identified mammal species in Namibia, 26 of which are endemic (or near endemic). In the Zambezi Region, where the protected areas have been incorporated into the five-country Kavango–Zambezi Transfrontier Conservation Area, or KAZA (see box, p.285), numbers of free-roaming **elephant**, **buffalo** and **lions** have shown a significant increase in recent years. It is here too – along the perennial rivers – that the majority of Namibia's **hippo** population resides.

However, the easiest and most accessible place for watching large mammals in Namibia is **Etosha National Park**, which harbours four of the Big Five – only buffalo are absent – and a host of other smaller mammals. Namibia possesses the world's largest numbers of free-roaming **cheetah** and **black rhino**; again, though, if you want to improve your chance of a sighting, head for Etosha, or one of the private game reserves (see p.243). **Desert-adapted black rhino** and **elephant** frequent the remote dry riverbed valleys in northwest Namibia and provide a major attraction for visitors to lodges in that area. The endangered **wild dog** is most numerous in Khaudum National Park in the northern Kalahari, although a handful have also been sighted in the Zambezi Region.

Twenty species of **antelope** graze the savannah lands of Namibia, ranging from the large 500kg **eland** to the diminutive **Damara dik-dik**, which weighs a mere 5kg. Most emblematic is the desert-dwelling **gemsbok** – a large oryx, which features on the national coat of arms. Rarer species of antelope in Namibia include the swamp-living **sitatunga**, **puku** and **oribi**, found only in the wetlands in the Zambezi Region, as well as the **black-faced impala**, a near-endemic that is only resident in the northwest, but whose numbers are swelling, thanks to conservation efforts.

Other safari favourites to look out for in your travels include **giraffe**, **zebra** – Burchell's and Hartmann's mountain zebra – **blue wildebeest**, **spotted** and **brown hyena**, **black-backed jackal** and **warthog**, alongside less well-known, smaller nocturnal mammals such as the **honey badger**, **aardvark** and the **bat-eared fox**.

Reptiles and amphibians

Even the seemingly lifeless desert areas of western Namibia contain a fascinating array of smaller creatures, including numerous **reptiles** and invertebrates – many unique to the Namib – which have evolved extraordinary ways to survive in the harsh arid environment (see box below). With the help of a good guide, you can seek them out in the sand by going on one of the many informative desert **tours** into the desert from either Sossusvlei or Swakopmund (see p.112 and p.213). Observing the swivelling eyes and colour-changing coats of **chameleons** and the seemingly adhesive feet of **geckos** in action can be just as compelling as watching a herd of elephant taking a bath.

Unsurprisingly, given Namibia's arid, rocky landscape, reptiles outnumber mammals in terms of species diversity, with around 250 at the last count, half of which are **lizards**. In fact, the country has more varieties of lizard than anywhere else in Africa. Examples include the extremely dapper, multicoloured **Attenborough's flat lizard** (*Platysaurus attenboroughi*) – named after the renowned naturalist and TV wildlife presenter – which is endemic to the Richtersveld area. A more common sight, scarpering across rocky outcrops and boulders in the Erongo and Kunene regions, and bobbing its head, is the brilliant blue-and-orange **Namib rock agama** (*Agama planiceps*), another endemic. Of course, the largest reptile, whose hulking armoured frame is a spine-chilling fixture along the banks of Namibia's perennial northern rivers, especially in the Zambezi Region, is the **Nile crocodile**. Over a thousand are estimated to be in that region alone, with some adult males weighing in at over 500kg – the equivalent of two quad bikes – and over 4m long; they are increasingly coming into conflict with the region's growing human population.

Snakes too are another feature of Namibian fauna – 11 of the 80 plus present are potentially deadly, including several spitting cobras and the black mamba, though very few people actually die of snake bites; moreover, snakes tend to scarper at the slightest detection of human presence.

In contrast to reptiles, Namibia's amphibians are fairly thin on the ground outside the Zambezi Region, due to the absence of water, though there are nevertheless fifty species of **frog**, seven of which are endemic. Outside the wetland areas, many of these frogs

---

THE NAMIB'S EXTRAORDINARY ENDEMICS

The Namib Desert – after which Namibia is named – has existed for over 55 million years, and harbours an extraordinary selection of resourceful, **desert-adapted creatures**, many of which are **endemic to the region**. These include the **sidewinder snake**, whose lateral shuffle facilitates its movement on the steep dune slope, while enabling it to keep most of its body off the hot sand at any one time. The eyes, located on the top of its head rather than the side, allow it to spot its prey while remaining submerged in sand. Another desert inhabitant that makes good use of the dunes' steep slopes is the **cartwheeling spider** (dancing white lady spider), which bundles itself into a ball and rolls downhill at speed to escape predators.

Other Namib curiosities include the various **Tenebrionid beetles**, or **tok tokkies**, as they are known locally, on account of the tapping noise made by the males to attract a mate. This acrobatic beetle stands on its head on the tops of dunes, facing west, to allow the incoming coastal fog to condense and form droplets on its body, which then trickle down into its mouth.

The bizarre **Grant's golden mole**, another Namib endemic, is unlike most moles: rather than living in permanent burrows, it "swims" through sand, covering up to 6km a night. This extraordinary-looking creature has eyes that have been long buried under a layer of skin and fur, almost non-existent ears, a leathery snout and fine, dense fur to help it push through the sand.

Another favourite of wildlife documentaries is the **Namib dune gecko**, the world's only fully web-footed gecko, whose feet are adapted to help the reptile walk across the sand at night and burrow into it during the hottest part of the day to escape the extreme temperatures. Its enormous eyes help it to spot prey in the dark, while during the early morning when fog is present, the gecko licks the condensation off its eyes and face with its long tongue. The **shovel-snouted lizard** also possesses feet designed to help it bury itself in sand when necessary, but when on the dune surface, it balances on two legs at a time, holding the other two aloft, before switching legs, to minimize heat transfer from the sand, earning it the nickname the "thermal dancing lizard".

NAMIBIA'S CONSERVANCIES

A landmark policy enacted in 1996 paved the way for rural communities to form **conservancies**; in essence, government was promoting sustainable natural resource management, including protection of wildlife, by granting **communities** rights to wildlife management and training. The thinking behind this is that by involving communities more, and ensuring they derive greater benefits, conservation efforts are likely to be more successful. While only four conservancies registered when the programme started in 1998, now 82 are operational. In addition, 32 **community forests** have been established, where villagers manage natural vegetation sustainably, for example by earning income from harvesting fruits and resin, running plant nurseries, or granting permits for timber extraction.

By and large the conservancy programme has succeeded in increasing income for communities to spend on **development projects** for education, health care, and so on, as well as providing **extra earnings** for individual households, both in periodic cash handouts and in the employment opportunities generated. Where conservancies are working well, indirect benefits have included greater community cohesion and a sense of ownership, plus skills acquisition through training, while the conservation returns have included improved community awareness and attitudes towards conservation, more sustainable land use and increases in wildlife.

Most conservancies derive income through **trophy hunting** or tourist-related activities. Controversially, trophy hunting has reaped the greatest financial rewards, providing more immediate return at both the community and household level, including families getting meat handouts after the kill. Moreover, profits from hunting in many cases are helping to pay for conservation work. **Eco-tourism initiatives** have had more mixed fortunes; although 25 community campgrounds are now registered, they receive fewer visitors than commercially run campgrounds, perhaps because nobody knows of their existence, or on account of their more basic facilities – they rarely have electricity – or because contact with the community in advance is difficult, especially in remote villages out of mobile phone coverage.

More generally, although some conservancies have been very successful, especially in Kunene (see box, p.259), others have struggled. Continuing **challenges** include the lack of capacity in some communities to plan and manage resources, in part due to the shortage of capacity and/or resources at the national level to provide adequate support and training. The long-standing Namibian-based NGO Integrated Rural Development and Nature Conservation (⬤irdnc.org.na) has been instrumental in this regard with conservancies in Kunene, and more recently in the Kavango and Zambezi regions. However, the national organization that had earlier been supporting community-based tourism (CBT) across the country has recently closed down, with the newly formed government department now tasked to assume supervision of such activities is yet to get going.

Without the necessary support, however, community ventures are struggling to compete with the well-marketed private lodges in Namibia. It is no surprise then, that, increasingly, conservancies are joining forces with **private investors** who have experience in the tourism sector, to establish and run a lodge in exchange for a share of the profits, guarantees of employment and training, plus a say in the management. There are now thirty such joint ventures.

More general concerns have also been raised about community-based natural resource management, for example the fact that relating conservation to tourism might not help address **loss of biodiversity**, as focus is likely to be on protecting animals that tourists want to see – or hunt – at the expense of other, less obviously appealing, wildlife. The issue of **human-wildlife conflict** is also an ongoing challenge, especially as predator numbers – due to conservation success – are increasing. Although conservancies often use some of their profits to compensate farmers for loss of livestock to predators, or help improve livestock protection and repair installations damaged by elephants, there has been an increase in predator killings in some areas.

aestivate in the mud round pans and oshanas until these briefly fill with water, at which time the frogs emerge to mate and breed at speed before the water dries up once more. If you're in or around Oshakati at the time, you'll find many of the hefty **African bullfrogs** being sold by the roadside or at the market in Oshakati.

Birds

Namibia's diverse **birdlife** should not be overlooked, boasting over 730 species. Of these, only one – the dune lark – is a true endemic, but there are fourteen near-endemic species to keep twitchers busy, such as the bare-cheeked babbler and the Damara tern. Casual birdwatchers are more likely to be excited by the vast pink carpet of **flamingos** covering Walvis Bay Lagoon – and Etosha Pan during the breeding season – and the many smaller, more colourful birds: dazzling **kingfishers**, iridescent **sunbirds** (distant relatives of hummingbirds), kaleidoscopic **bee-eaters** and **rollers**. Size matters too: elegant **cranes** and stately **ostriches** and **storks** (even the ugly, hairy marabou) are impressive, as are the countless large raptors – the black-and-white **bateleur** with its distinctive red beak, the rare **Cape vulture**, with its bald neck and head, and the splendid **African fish eagle**, which crowns the Namibian coat of arms, and whose evocative call is often dubbed the "voice of Africa". The most accessible and the best **birdwatching locations** include the Walvis Bay Lagoon (see p.223), Etosha (see p.241) and the Zambezi Region (see p.268), where two-thirds of the country's species can be found around the perennial rivers and wetlands. The prime birdwatching season is between September/October and April, when European migrants arrive, and many birds are sporting their colourful breeding plumage.

Marine life

Namibia's **marine life** is often neglected by tourists, in the rush to spot large mammals, yet the cold-water upwelling of the Benguela Current, which brings abundant nutrients to the surface, provides rich pickings for the many fish that constitute Namibia's buoyant fishing and game fishing industries and may end up on your plate. The current also serves **dolphins** and migrating **whales** (July–Nov, peaking Aug–Oct), most easily spotted on a boat trip from Walvis Bay (see p.223). The small Heaviside's dolphin is the most commonly sighted cetacean, with bottlenose and dusky dolphins much rarer visitors, while humpbacks are more frequently sighted than southern right or Bryde's whales.

Conservation

As the first African country to enshrine protection of the environment in its constitution, and with around forty percent of its land protected in some way, Namibia is widely acknowledged as being a world leader in innovative **conservation efforts**. Notably, poaching has decreased in recent years, while numbers of rare or high-value large mammals have increased. Namibia is the only country in the world with an expanding population of free-roaming lions; desert-adapted elephant numbers have more than doubled since 1995; and locally extinct species in the Zambezi Region, such as eland, roan and sable antelope, giraffe and blue wildebeest, have been reintroduced and are thriving. Critical to the successful recovery of wildlife has been the establishment of **conservancies**, a government initiative, launched in the late 1990s, to make community development integral to conservation strategies (see box opposite).

Books

Though Namibia has a strong oral tradition, literature – beyond a few historical and autobiographical accounts – is still in its infancy. This is hardly surprising, given black Namibians' lack of access to decent formal schooling for many years, compounded by the lengthy independence struggle, during which time energies were focused elsewhere. Thus, contemporary literature written in English by Namibian authors is thin on the ground, though more is available in indigenous languages, as well as in German and in Afrikaans. What's more, the emphasis is often more on content than on style. Nor is fiction set in Namibia but penned by non-Namibians exactly plentiful. The little that exists to date has tended to be autobiographical, with much focusing on the country's colonial experiences and the independence struggle. What follows is a brief selection of books in English that are mainly still in print, but are sometimes only available secondhand or as an eBook. Books marked with a ★ are particularly recommended.

HISTORY

Tessa Cleaver and Marion Wallace (eds) *Namibia: Women in War*. A collection of oral histories mainly collected in 1989 that "give voice" to women and illustrate the multiple oppressions they faced.

Colin Leys and Susan Brown (eds) *Histories of Namibia: Living Through the Liberation Struggle*. Life histories told to the authors by eleven Namibians who grew up during the 23 years of war, which give insight not only into their experiences of anti-colonial resistance, but also into the oppressive, authoritarian structures of the liberation movement itself.

★ **Henning Melber** *Understanding Namibia: The Trials of Independence*. This important critique of post-independence Namibia chronicles SWAPO's uneasy transition from liberation movement to governing party, and raises important questions about the country's future. Though a little heavy on detail for the casual reader, the

views of this German-born Namibian academic, who was a member of SWAPO in exile and former Director of the Namibian Economic Policy Research Unit in Windhoek, are well worth digesting.

David Olusoga and Casper Erichsen *The Kaiser's Holocaust: Germany's Forgotten Genocide and the Colonial Roots of Nazism*. Compelling though controversial work which argues that the Herero genocide in German South-West Africa by the Kaiser's troops set the pattern for Hitler's Nazism.

★ **Marion Wallace, with John Kinahan** *History of Namibia: from the Beginning to 1990*. The most comprehensive history of the country to date; scholarly, and overly dense in patches, it traces the country's development from the earliest human settlements to independence, drawing on multiple sources and attempting a refreshingly Afro-centric take on Namibian history.

NATURAL HISTORY

Favourite field guides are very much a matter of personal choice, depending on whether you prefer photos or illustrations, or you want a weighty authoritative tome rather than a more selective pocket guide, though both are usually available in electronic form these days. There are also several good apps to help with bird and mammal identification: Sasol's *eBirds of Southern Africa* (on iOS and Android) is recommended, and consider *iTrack Africa* (available on iOS), to help you differentiate one paw print from another.

Louis Liebenberg *First Field Guide to Animal Tracks of Southern Africa*. Pioneering field guide to tracking wildlife. Contains sketches, distribution maps and paw print illustrations to help decipher common tracks that are found in Namibia and the rest of southern Africa.

Kenneth Newman *Newman's Birds of Southern Africa*. Probably the most comprehensive field guide to the area, with excellent illustrations. This most recent tenth edition has been updated by the author's daughter, Vanessa. Note that it's a weighty volume – even the paperback version.

Mary Seely *The Namib: Natural History of an Ancient Desert*. Though some years old now, this scholarly, yet accessible, handy-sized paperback still serves as an excellent introduction to the wonders of the Namib. Written by an expert who has spent countless years living and working in this desert, it is illustrated with drawings and rather faded photos.

★**Ian Sinclair** *Pocket Guide: Birds of Southern Africa*. Pretty comprehensive for a pocket guide, covering over half the region's birds – the ones you're most likely to see – and ideal for the casual or novice birdwatcher, with distribution maps, timelines indicating when species are present, and behavioural notes to aid identification. The photos are excellent, even if harder to use for identification than illustrations.

Chris and Mathilde Stuart *Pocket Guide: Mammals of Southern Africa*. Covering just over a third of the region's land and marine species, with an emphasis on the larger, more visible characters, this easily accessible guide is ideal for the novice safari-goer or backpacker concerned about weight, though there is an ebook version. Their authoritative *Mammals of Southern Africa* encompasses the region's 337 mammals, with even their skulls illustrated.

Martin Withers and David Hosking *Wildlife in Southern Africa*. Nicely photo-illustrated portable guide with a bit of everything – mammals, birds and a few reptiles and smaller critters – which is good for most safari mammals and handy if you want an all-in-one book, but dissatisfying if you're particularly keen on birds or reptiles.

FICTION AND MEMOIRS

André Brink *The Other Side of Silence*. Superbly written, but you'll need a strong stomach for this unrelentingly bleak tale of an abused young German girl from an orphanage who is shipped out to service the Schutztruppen in German South-West Africa, where things only get worse.

Margaret Daymond et al (eds) *Women Writing Africa Vol.1: the Southern Region*. Fascinating, eclectic collection of oral and written narratives by women from all over southern Africa – including many from Namibia – from the mid-nineteenth century onwards. Entries include praise poems, historical documents, letters, short stories and even legal documents, which aim to make women's voices heard, since they are so often absent from historical accounts.

Joseph Diescho *Born of the Sun*. A Namibian classic by the country's best-known indigenous author, this moving autobiographical tale follows a young man from a northern village under pressure from missionaries and the bullying colonial administration, to the harsh realities of South African mines, and his resistance to the inhumanity of apartheid.

★**Martin Henno** *The Sheltering Desert*. An engaging memoir of Robinson Crusoe-style desert survival as two German geologists and their lovable dog Otto take refuge in the Namib's Kuiseb Canyon for several years to avoid entanglement in World War II.

★**Kaleni Hiyalwa** *Meekulu's Children*. Pioneering and thoughtful fictional tale set in an Owambo village in northern Namibia during the liberation struggle – all the more remarkable because the author, who spent years in exile, writes from the perspective of those who stayed.

★**Lauri Kubutsile** *The Scattering*. Unflinching yet intimate tale of two women caught up in the horrors of war: one a Herero woman whose husband disappears fighting the Germans in South-West Africa, the other a farmer's daughter in the Transvaal, forcibly married to a neighbour who goes off to fight in the second Anglo-Boer

War and ends up in a British concentration camp. Both women endure appalling suffering but somehow survive the madness made by men.

Henning Mankell *Daniel*. A bleak exploration of cultural dislocation and colonial attitudes by the author of the *Wallander* series. An unloveable Swedish entomologist misguidedly rescues an orphan boy in the Kalahari and takes him back to Sweden with tragic results. Set in the 1870s.

Ellen Namhila *The Price of Freedom*. Autobiographical account of nineteen years in exile, which follows the writer's seismic cultural shifts as she travels from SWAPO camps in Angola, via the Gambia to Finland and back home. It's a valiant attempt at interweaving how she recalls experiencing events at the time with a more reflective assessment borne of experience and maturity.

Andreas Neshani *The Purple Violet of Oshaantu*. Set in an Owambo village, this first novel is an ambitious and occasionally muddled tale of the friendship between two women with contrasting family situations, which explores issues of culture, patriarchy and women's oppression.

Margie Orford *Blood Rose*. The writer, who grew up in Namibia, deftly depicts the seedy underbelly of Walvis Bay, which provides the backdrop for this highly readable thriller featuring serial killer profiler-cum-investigative journalist Clare Hart. Better than it sounds.

Garth Owen-Smith *An Arid Eden: A Personal Account of Conservation in the Kaokoveld*. International award-winning conservationist draws on a lifetime's commitment to the cause in Namibia's northwest, providing a must-read text for all serious conservationists. One of the instigators of community-based natural resource management in southern Africa, and co-founder of Conservancy Safaris Namibia (see p.56), leaves the reader with plenty to ponder.

Fran Sandham *Traversa: A Solo Walk Across Africa from the Skeleton Coast to the Indian Ocean*. Although obviously

not exclusively about Namibia, this entertaining and witty tale of wanderlust – written by an ex-Rough Guides editor – is a seriously good read.
Mari Serebrov *Mama Namibia.* A well-researched

fictional tale set against the very real Herero genocide, narrated from the dual, and occasionally intertwining, perspectives of a young Herero girl, and a Jewish doctor in the German army.

PHOTOGRAPHY

Gerald and Marc Hobermann *Namibia.* The ultimate coffee-table book, brimming with page after page of jaw-dropping photos of the country's wonderful scenery, which is matched only by its equally jaw-dropping price tag.
Jim Naughton and Lutz Marten *Conflict and Costume: The Herero Tribe of Namibia.* The stunning photographs of Herero "traditional" attire take centre stage, but the well-researched text on the Herero's appropriation and subversion of German colonists' clothing provides the necessary historical context.
Amy Schoemann *The Skeleton Coast.* Superb photographs

accompanied by informed text on the Skeleton Coast from someone whose entire family has been associated with exploring and protecting this inaccessible environment for many years.
Sandra Shields *Where Fire Speaks: A Visit with the Himba.* Award-winning black-and-white photo-narrative interwoven with thought-provoking text as the author, who spent several months among the Himba, looks at changes brought about by modern developments, including tourism, which threaten their traditional way of life.

Language

There are up to thirty languages spoken in Namibia (depending on how you define a language, as opposed to a dialect); fourteen of these have full orthographies. Thirteen have been recognized as national languages (ten of which are indigenous); these include eight Bantu languages, predominantly dialects of Oshiwambo, but also Otjiherero, Setswana and SiLozi; two Khoisan click languages, plus the three Indo-European languages of Afrikaans, English and German. After Oshiwambo, which is spoken by around half the population, Nama and Damara are the most widespread, spoken by around eleven percent, followed by Afrikaans (ten percent), Otjiherero (nine percent) and Zambezi Region languages, such as SiLozi (five percent).

Prior to independence, Afrikaans and English were both **official languages**, though Afrikaans was the dominant means of communication in government, the medium of instruction in schools, and the general lingua franca. German enjoyed "semi-official" status. At independence, **English** – the first language of less than one percent of the population – was chosen to be the sole official language, as it was seen as the language of liberation and national unity, and one which would provide economic opportunity and social mobility. The reality, as in many other post-colonial states, is that, despite government's best efforts, many pupils and teachers in state schools struggle to learn and teach in English, especially in rural areas, and **Afrikaans** still persists as the lingua franca, particularly among the older population and in the more rural areas. When you hear English being spoken, it is often **Namlish** – a local variety with many phrases and grammatical usages similar to those used in other southern African countries; phrases such as "now now", meaning "right now", or "I am coming", rather than "I'll be back", are in common usage. That said, in lodges, campgrounds and in tourist areas you'll find most people are fluent in English, though they will appreciate any effort to manage at least a greeting in their language (see box, p.370).

THE KHOISAN CLICK LANGUAGES

Khoisan languages such as Khoekhoegowab (Khoekhoe for short) or Nama-Damara spoken by the Nama and Damara, and Jul'hoan, spoken by the majority of San communities in Namibia, are **click languages**, and while you are unlikely to grasp how to pronounce the click consonants properly, unless you spend a long time with communities that speak these languages, you will hear them regularly and come across the written forms on road signs, at the very least. Although Jul'hoan actually possesses 48 click consonants – plus four tones to further complicate matters – there are essentially four types of click to get to grips with in any click language, which all only feature at the beginning of a word:

| A dental click that makes a high-pitched "tut tut!" sound at the back of your teeth.
! An alveolar click that sounds like popping a cork, made by putting your tongue just behind the ridge at the back of your mouth.
|| A lateral click sound is made by sucking on the molars and is often described as the sound made when urging on a horse, which may not leave you any the wiser.
‡ A palatal click that sounds like a sharper pop, or like someone snapping their fingers, made by drawing the tongue down quickly off the roof of the mouth.
  There are plenty of online videos on the subject to help you get some practice in before you arrive in Namibia.

NAMIBIAN GREETINGS

ENGLISH	OSHIWAMBO	OTJIHERERO
Good morning	(s) Wa lele po? (pl) Mwa lele po?	(s) Wa penduka nawa? (pl) Mwa penduka nawa?
Good afternoon	(s) Wa uhala po (pl) Mwa uhala po	(s) Wa uhara nawa? (pl) Mwa uhara nawa?
How are you?	Ongiini?	Peri vi?
I'm fine	Ondi li nawa	Mbi ri nawa
Thank you	Iyaloo	Okuhepa
You're welcome	Oshi li nawa	Okuhepa
Goodbye	(s) Kala po nawa (pl) Kalei po nawa	Kara nawa (to someone leaving) Karee nawa (to someone staying)

Glossary

biltong dried cured meat, often chewed as a snack

boerewors long spicy beef sausage comprising ninety percent meat, but with some pork, lamb or a combination of both added

boma originally a word for a protected livestock enclosure; in modern tourism usage, an open-sided thatched area, often with a fire-pit at the centre, and used for entertainment purposes

bottle store off licence or liquor store

braai Afrikaans word for barbecue

brötchen German word for bread rolls

circle roundabout

CLA Caprivi Liberation Army

conservancy community registered with the Ministry of the Environment to protect the wildlife and habitats in exchange for rights over tourist operations in the area

cuca shop small, unlicensed bar/shop in northern Namibia that sells alcohol and sometimes other goods, named after a popular Angolan beer

dankie widely used Afrikaans word for "thank you"

donkey wood-fired water heater/geyser, commonly used in campgrounds

droëwors dried spicy sausage, often from pork or game meat

guestfarm a working farm (usually) that also accommodates a small number of guests, and often offers farm-related activities and family-style dining round a single table

inselberg isolated mountain rising out of a flat plain

kopjie (or koppie) Afrikaans word denoting a small rocky hill in a generally flat area

kloof Afrikaans word for a ravine

kraal Afrikaans word for a fence or thornbush enclosure for cattle or other livestock, or enclosure for traditional huts in Owambo culture, for example

lapa large, open-sided thatched area supported on poles

location apartheid-era word – still in common usage and synonymous with township – which denoted an underdeveloped urban residential area set aside for non-whites on the periphery of the main town/city

mahangu pearl millet, a staple Owambo crop

mealie-pap South African word for porridge made from ground maize (mealie-meal)

MET Ministry of Environment and Tourism

mokoro traditional dugout canoe

NWR Namibia Wildlife Resorts

!nara melon a desert fruit

OAU Organization of African Unity

OPO Owamboland Peoples' Organization

Omuramba Otjiherero word for an ancient (dry) riverbed in the Kalahari that only fills occasionally after very heavy rain

oshana shallow seasonally flooded depression in northern Namibia

oshifima Oshiwambo word for porridge made from ground maize

pan a salt and/or clay pan – a large, very slight depression covered in a crust of salt and

NAMA-DAMARA	RUKWANGALI	SILOZI
!Gâi‖goas	(s) Moroka (pl) Morokeni	Mu zuhile
!Gâi tses	(s) Muna	Mu tozi
Matisa?	Nyove yilye? Or Ngapi?	U pila cwang?
! !Gâia gangans	Ame nawa one	Eni ni iketile hande
Kai-gangans	Mpandu	Ni itumezi
Aios	Name ngocikwawo	Mwa amuhelwa
!Gâise !gû re (to someone leaving) !Gâise hâ re (to someone staying)	Tomugendipo nawa	Mu siale hande

other minerals where water has collected, then evaporated; theoretically a more degraded vlei, the term is often used interchangeably with vlei (from the Afrikaans)

PLAN People's Liberation Army of Namibia

potjie Afrikaans word for a three-legged cast-iron pot used directly over an open fire, to make a slow-cooked stew (potjiekos)

restcamp Simple, inexpensive accommodation – almost always including camping, self-catering and B&B options – where travellers stay overnight, rather than a destination in itself

RMS Rhenish Missionary Society

robot traffic light

rock shandy popular soft drink, half lemonade and half soda water, with a dash of Angostura Bitters

rondavel corrupted Afrikaans word for a traditional round African hut with conical thatched roof, or a westernized version made of stone, often used as a chalet

SADC Southern African Development Community

SADF South African Defence Force

sangoma IsiZulu word in common parlance for traditional African healer

Schutztruppen German colonial troops – literally "protection troops"

spätzle German soft egg noodles

shebeen formerly an unlicensed bar during the apartheid era but which now often refers to any local, informal bar

sosatie kebab

sundowner alcoholic drink enjoyed at sunset

SWA South-West Africa, the name for Namibia when ruled by the German colonists and later South Africa

SWANU South-West Africa National Union – the first political party to be formed in Namibia

SWAPO South-West Africa People's Organization – the former national liberation movement and now the ruling party in Namibia

SWATF South-West Africa Territorial Force – an auxiliary arm of the SADF

township see "location"

veld from the Afrikaans word for "field", which usually refers to a wild/uncultivated open expanse of land

vlei the Afrikaans word for shallow marshy depression that fills with water during the rains, often referred to as a pan, though vleis in less arid parts of South Africa, for example, tend to support more vegetation

Small print and index

A ROUGH GUIDE TO ROUGH GUIDES

Published in 1982, the first Rough Guide – to Greece – was a student scheme that became a publishing phenomenon. Mark Ellingham, a recent graduate in English from Bristol University, had been travelling in Greece the previous summer and couldn't find the right guidebook. With a small group of friends he wrote his own guide, combining a contemporary, journalistic style with a thoroughly practical approach to travellers' needs.

The immediate success of the book spawned a series that rapidly covered dozens of destinations. And, in addition to impecunious backpackers, Rough Guides soon acquired a much broader readership that relished the guides' wit and inquisitiveness as much as their enthusiastic, critical approach and value-for-money ethos. These days, Rough Guides include recommendations from budget to luxury and cover more than 120 destinations around the globe, from Amsterdam to Zanzibar, all regularly updated by our team of roaming writers.

Browse all our latest guides, read inspirational features and book your trip at **roughguides.com**.

Rough Guide credits

Editors: Greg Dickinson, Olivia Rawes
Layout: Anita Singh
Cartography: Rajesh Chhibber, Richard Marchi
Picture editor: Aude Vauconsant
Proofreader: Jan McCann
Managing editor: Keith Drew
Assistant editors: Payal Sharotri, Divya Grace Mathew

Production: Jimmy Lao
Cover photo research: Nicole Newman
Editorial assistant: Aimee White
Senior DTP coordinator: Dan May
Programme manager: Gareth Lowe
Publishing director: Georgina Dee

Publishing information

This first edition published July 2017 by
Rough Guides Ltd,
80 Strand, London WC2R 0RL
11, Community Centre, Panchsheel Park,
New Delhi 110017, India
Distributed by Penguin Random House
Penguin Books Ltd, 80 Strand, London WC2R 0RL
Penguin Group (USA), 345 Hudson Street, NY 10014, USA
Penguin Group (Australia), 250 Camberwell Road,
Camberwell, Victoria 3124, Australia
Penguin Group (NZ), 67 Apollo Drive, Mairangi Bay,
Auckland 1310, New Zealand
Penguin Group (South Africa), Block D, Rosebank Office
Park, 181 Jan Smuts Avenue, Parktown North, Gauteng,
South Africa 2193
Rough Guides is represented in Canada by DK Canada, 320
Front Street West, Suite 1400, Toronto, Ontario M5V 3B6
Printed in Singapore
© Rough Guides, 2017
Animal tracks © Louis Liebenberg
Maps © Rough Guides

392pp includes index
A catalogue record for this book is available from the
British Library
ISBN: 978-0-24127-401-9

Help us update

We've gone to a lot of effort to ensure that the first edition
of **The Rough Guide to Namibia** is accurate and up-to-
date. However, things change – places get "discovered",
opening hours are notoriously fickle, restaurants and
rooms raise prices or lower standards. If you feel we've got
it wrong or left something out, we'd like to know, and if
you can remember the address, the price, the hours, the
phone number, so much the better.

Please send your comments with the subject line
"**Rough Guide Namibia Update**" to mail@uk.roughguides.
com. We'll credit all contributions and send a copy of the
next edition (or any other Rough Guide if you prefer) for
the very best emails.

Acknowledgements

Sara Humphreys Appreciation is due to the Namibia
Tourism Board for providing information and photos,
and to many Namibians encountered while travelling
round the country. In the Rough Guides office, I'm
grateful to Keith Drew for entrusting me with the job
and to Ed Aves for his energy and contributions to the
synopsis. Credit is also due to Aude for finding some
fabulous photos. On the editorial front, thanks go to
Olivia Rawes for her suggestions for the Vic Falls chapter,
while eternal gratitude – and some Bajan rum – is owed
to the unflappable Greg Dickinson, whose support and
conscientious input far exceeded his editorial duties, as
the deadlines loomed ever larger. I am also grateful to Val
Humphreys for trawling booklists, to Máiréad Dunne for
camping company stretching from Sossusvlei to Katima
Mulilo, and to Adrian – as ever – for his insights on Namibia
and chauffeuring duties round the northwest, as well as
tolerating more late nights and weekends of writing up.

ABOUT THE AUTHOR

Sara Humphreys A freelance researcher, writer and educator, Sara has toiled, travelled and tarried in various countries in sub-Saharan Africa, Latin America and Europe, including a year living in Opuwo, northwest Namibia, helping untangle post-independence curriculum changes. When not travelling, she can be found swinging in a hammock in Barbados.

Photo credits

All photos © Rough Guides, except the following:
(Key: a-above; t-top; b-bottom/below; l-left; c-centre; r-right)

1 AWL Images: Danita Delimont
2 Alamy Stock Photo: Hemis / Colin Matthieu
4 Getty Images: imageBROKER / Christian Heinrich
7 Alamy Stock Photo: imageBROKER / Thomas Dressler
8 Alamy Stock Photo: John Dambik
9 Alamy Stock Photo: LOOK Die Bildagentur der Fotografen GmbH / Andreas Strauss (b). **SuperStock:** Kristian Cabanis (t); Andy Nixon (c)
10 Dreamstime.com: Znm
12 Dreamstime.com: Znm
13 Alamy Stock Photo: Ben McRae (b). Robert Harding Picture Library: Mint Images / Frans Lanting (c). SuperStock: imageBROKER / Michael Nitzschke (t)
14 Alamy Stock Photo: Panther Media GmbH / Willy64331 (b). **Getty Images:** EyeEm / Natalie Bundi (t)
15 Alamy Stock Photo: AfriPics.com (br); Chad Case (t). **Dreamstime.com:** Bernhard Richter (bl)
16 4Corners: Cornelia Dörr (t); SIME / Onlyworld / Antoine Lorgnier (br). **Getty Images:** Theo Allofs (bl)
17 Alamy Stock Photo: imageBROKER / Martin Moxter (b). **Getty Images:** Andreas Suchert (t)
18 Alamy Stock Photo: imageBROKER / Stefan Espenhahn (b). **Getty Images:** Moment RM / Maria Swärd (t)
19 Alamy Stock Photo: M.Sobreira (t); vario images GmbH & Co.KG / McPHOTO (c). **Robert Harding Picture Library:** Karen Deakin (b)
20 123RF.com: atosan
23 123RF.com: Artush (t, bl). **Alamy Stock Photo:** Brendon Boyes (br)
25 123RF.com: Jens Hülsmeier (cr). **Dreamstime.com:** Pasojo (tr); Znm (bl). **FLPA:** Minden Pictures / Anup Shah (br). **Namibia Tourism Board:** (tl)
27 123RF.com: hecke (cr); Nico Smit (tl); Oleg Znamenskiy (tr, br). **Dreamstime.com:** Cathywithers (bl). **FLPA:** Mark Sisson (cl)
29 123RF.com: Sam D Cruz (bl); Gleb Ivanov (br); wrangel (c). **Alamy Stock Photo:** Chris Wildblood (tl). **Getty Images:** Nigel Dennis (tr)
31 123RF.com: Gerrit David De Vries (cr); friedemeier (tl); Nico Smit (tr). **Dreamstime.com:** Andries Alberts (bl); James Buys (c); Smellme (cl, bc); Znm (br)
33 123RF.com: dirkr (bl); Andrea Marzorati (tr, cr); perseomedusa (tl). **Dreamstime.com:** Ricardo Ferreira (cl); Steffen Foerster (br)
35 123RF.com: dirkr (br). **Dreamstime.com:** Jezbennett (tr); Johan Lamprecht (bl); Outdoorsman (tl)
37 123RF.com: Maurizio Giovanni Bersanelli (bl). **Dreamstime.com:** Volodymyr Byrdyak (br). **Namibia Tourism Board:** (tl, tr)

39 Dreamstime.com: Steve Allen (bl); Ecophoto (br); Vladislav Jirousek (tr). **iStockphoto.com:** 2630ben (c). **Robert Harding Picture Library:** Mint Images / Frans Lanting (tl)
41 Dreamstime.com: Ecophoto (cl); Hamish Mitchell (tl); Carlos Neto (cr); Pytyczech (bl). **Getty Images:** Minden Pictures / BIA / Ralph Martin (br). **SuperStock:** Westend61 (tr)
42 Getty Images: George Steinmetz
74–75 SuperStock: imageBROKER / Fabian von Poser
77 Alamy Stock Photo: TravelCollection / Lengler, Gregor
93 AWL Images: Danita Delimont Stock (t). **Getty Images:** Tom Cockrem (bl). **Namibia Tourism Board:** (br)
104–105 Getty Images: Photographer's Choice / Siegfried Layda
107 Dreamstime.com: Mirko Vitali
115 Namibia Tourism Board: (t, b)
136–137 Getty Images: Moment RF / Hannes Thirion
139 Alamy Stock Photo: Top-Pics TBK
147 Dreamstime.com: 3000ad (b). **SuperStock:** Andy Nixon (t)
166–167 Robert Harding Picture Library: Nico Tondini
179 Alamy Stock Photo: hemis.fr / MATTES RenΘ (b); imageBROKER / Christian Handl (t)
205–206 Getty Images: Moment Open / JLR
207 Getty Images: Gallo Images / Heinrich van den Berg
221 Getty Images: Mark Hannaford (b). **SuperStock:** Martin Moxter (t)
236–237 Getty Images: Theo Allofs
239 4Corners: SIME / Onlyworld / Antoine Lorgnier
251 Alamy Stock Photo: Danita Delimont (tr). **Getty Images:** Heinrich van den Berg (b). **iStockphoto.com:** GroblerduPreez (tl)
266–267 Namibia Tourism Board
269 Alamy Stock Photo: imageBROKER / Oliver Gerhard
281 Alamy Stock Photo: ERIC LAFFORGUE (b). **Getty Images:** Aldo Pavan (t)
296–297 Getty Images: Ignacio Palacios
298 Alamy Stock Photo: imageBROKER / Guenter Fischer
309 SuperStock: Roger de la Harpe
323 Alamy Stock Photo: Mark Eveleigh (b). **Getty Images:** travelgame (t)
340 Robert Harding Picture Library: Oliver Gerhard

Cover: Camelthorn tree in front of Sossuslvei dune **AWL Images:** Nature in Stock

Index

Maps are marked in grey

Map symbols

The symbols below are used on maps throughout the book

International boundary	(i) Information centre	Lighthouse	Beach
State/province boundary	@ Internet café	($) Bank	Park/forest
Chapter-division boundary	Post office	Winery	Swamp fill
Motorway	Hospital/medical centre	Point of interest	Pan fill
Main road	Swimming pool	Viewpoint/lookout	Campground
Minor road	Building	Mining	Swamp/marshland
Pedestrianized road	Museum	Golf course	Mountain range
Path	Church	Immigration post	Mountain peak
Unpaved road/4WD track	Christian cemetery	National park	Gorge
Railway	Cemetery	Gate/park entrance	Cave
Coastline	Castle	Transport stop	Cave painting
Dry river	Fortress	Parking	Fuel station
Pass	Tower	International airport	Waterfall
Bridge	Stadium	Domestic airport/airfield	Spring

Listings key

- Accommodation
- Eating
- Drinking & Nightlife
- Shopping

ROUGH
GUIDES

ESCAPE THE EVERYDAY

ADVENTURE BECKONS

YOU JUST NEED TO KNOW WHERE TO LOOK

roughguides.com

Long bus journey?
Phone run out of juice?

1 Denim, the pencil, the stethoscope and the hot-air balloon were all invented in which country?

a. Italy
b. France
c. Germany
d. Switzerland

2 What is the currency of Vietnam?

a. Dong
b. Yuan
c. Baht
d. Kip

3 In which city would you find the Majorelle Garden?

a. Marseille
b. Marrakesh
c. Tunis
d. Malaga

4 What is the busiest airport in the world?

a. London Heathrow
b. Tokyo International
c. Chicago O'Hare
d. Hartsfield-Jackson Atlanta International

5 Which of these countries does not have the equator running through it?

a. Brazil
b. Tanzania
c. Indonesia
d. Colombia

6 Which country has the most UNESCO World Heritage Sites?

a. Mexico
b. France
c. Italy
d. India

7 What is the principal religion of Japan?

a. Confucianism
b. Buddhism
c. Jainism
d. Shinto

8 Every July in Sonkajärvi, central Finland, contestants gather for the World Championships of which sport?

a. Zorbing
b. Wife-carrying
c. Chess-boxing
d. Extreme ironing

9 What colour are post boxes in Germany?

a. Red
b. Green
c. Blue
d. Yellow

10 For three days each April during Songkran festival in Thailand, people take to the streets to throw what at each other?

a. Water
b. Oranges
c. Tomatoes
d. Underwear

flysaa.com

FLY SAA.
START YOUR ADVENTURE.

Southern Africa is ready. Are you?
With direct flights to Johannesburg
and daily connections to the new
Victoria Falls airport, your journey
to breathtaking views begins with us.
Visit flysaa.com or call 0844 375 9680.

Victoria Falls
Victoria Falls, Zimbabwe

SOUTH AFRICAN AIRWAYS
A STAR ALLIANCE MEMBER

★★★★
4 STAR AIRLINE
SKYTRAX

PLACES YOU'D LOVE TO BE
STORIES YOU'D LOVE TO TELL

Our journeys change lives

Reservations